The Road
to Guilford Courthouse

The Road
to
Guilford Courthouse

The American Revolution
in the Carolinas

John Buchanan

John Wiley & Sons, Inc.

New York • Chichester • Weinheim • Brisbane • Singapore • Toronto

The illustration on the title page is *A View of Charles Town* by Thomas Leitch, c. 1773–1774. From the collection of the Museum of Early Southern Decorative Arts, Winston-Salem, North Carolina. Used with permission.

This book is printed on acid-free paper. ♾

This publication is designed to provide accurate and authoritative information in regard to the subject matter covered. It is sold with the understanding that the publisher is not engaged in rendering professional services. If professional advice or other expert assistance is required, the services of a competent professional person should be sought.

Library of Congress Cataloging-in-Publication Data
Buchanan, John
    The road to Guilford Courthouse : the American revolution in
  the Carolinas / John Buchanan.
      p. cm.
    Includes bibliographical references and index.
    ISBN 0-471-32716-6 (paper)
    1. North Carolina—History—Revolution, 1775–1783—Campaigns.
    2. South Carolina—History—Revolution, 1775–1783—Campaigns.
    3. United States—History—Revolution, 1775–1783—Campaigns.
    I. Title.
    E263.N8B83   1997
    973.393—dc20   96-9575

Printed in the United States of America

10 9 8

To my wife, Susi,
and my brother, Charles

Contents

Preface   *ix*

Prologue: Charleston   *1*

1 The Battle of Sullivan's Island   *3*

2 The Rice Kings   *17*

3 Southern Strategy   *25*

4 The Approach March   *34*

5 Charleston Besieged   *44*

6 The Rise of Banastre Tarleton   *58*

7 Into the Back Country   *73*

8 Hearts and Minds   *90*

9 Trouble in the Back Country   *104*

10 More Trouble in the Back Country   *122*

11 A Hero Takes Charge   *142*

12 The Battle of Camden   *157*

13 The Partisans Fight On   *173*

14 The Rise of Patrick Ferguson   *194*

15 To Catch Ferguson   *208*

16 King's Mountain   *225*

Contents

17 Retreat and Turmoil   242

18 A General from Rhode Island   260

19 The Stage is Set   276

20 Tarleton Pursues Morgan   296

21 Cowpens   319

22 Bayonets and Zeal   334

23 Patience and Finesse   359

24 Guilford Courthouse: "Long, Obstinate, and Bloody"   372

The Major Characters in Order of Appearance
and What Happened to Them   384

Notes   402

A Select and Annotated Bibliography   429

Index   437

Preface

This book is about the British campaign of 1780–1781 to regain the Carolinas from the American Rebels. On learning of my subject, a friend of mine, well educated, well read, intellectually curious, looked surprised and admitted, "I really don't know what happened south of Philadelphia." He is not alone. Despite copious writings and intense study beginning in the decade it occurred and continuing to this day, it remains for the reading public an historical terra incognita. Yet the tactical masterpiece of the War of the Revolution occurred in the South, and a battle "long, bloody, and obstinate" that went far in deciding the great issue at stake. We will also witness in the southern Back Country a little known but savage civil war far exceeding anything in the North.

Now to turn to a few technical matters. Eighteenth-century spelling, although somewhat imaginative, is not a challenge to comprehension, and I have transcribed words as spelled by the writers without the intrusion of the annoying (sic). I have also retained the erratic but delightful eighteenth-century manner of captalization. Punctuation is a different matter. Ours is a vast improvement over eighteenth-century practice, in which overuse of commas and semicolons is exasperating when reading and transcribing. I have been occasionally ruthless in eliminating the many marks so dear to those pesky punctuators, but not, I emphasize, at the risk of creating ambiguities or changing meanings.

I use the term English and British interchangeably, although British rightly referred then as now to English, Scots, Welsh, Anglo-Irish, and the Protestant inhabitants of the province of Ulster in Northern Ireland—and those Americans who stayed loyal to the Crown and became known to their enemies and forevermore as Tories. The latter called themselves Loyalists and sometimes in battle to identify themselves, King's Friends. It is currently fashionable to use their terminology, but I prefer Tory because it is short, descriptive, and sanctified by two centuries of popular usage: there can be no mistake to whom one is referring.

For the same reasons I use the word Rebel to refer to the American revolutionaries. They never used the word. They called themselves Whigs or Patriots. It will be quite clear in the text that when I refer to the American army, or American militia, I am referring to the Rebels. The Tories were also Americans, of course, but one has to draw the line somewhere.

In the eighteenth century the word partisan in the military sense had two meanings. It was used to describe light troops trained for skirmishing at the van or on the flanks of an army on the move, as rear guards for a retreating army, and also for scouting, sentry duty, raids, foraging, and so on. Ideally, light troops were fast moving and did not require the cumbersome, slow-moving wagon trains that marked eighteenth-century armies. Daniel Morgan, who obviously had given the matter considerable thought, believed it was "incompatible with the nature of light troops to be encumbered with baggage," and ordered 100 packsaddles so that supplies and provisions could be carried by pack horses. Light troops were chosen for speed afoot, agility, marksmanship, and other physical and mental attributes that would serve them well on special missions. But it should be clearly understood that these men were regulars in every sense of the word. The German Jägers were light troops, and one source quoted often in this book, the Jäger Captain Johann Ewald, regular soldier to the core, referred to himself as a partisan captain.

The second meaning of partisan in the eighteenth century referred to irregular fighters, or, as we more commonly say today, guerrillas, a word that first appeared in English early in the nineteenth century in connection with the Spanish uprising against Napoleon's armies. During World War II, partisan was the word used to refer to irregulars in Russia and Eastern Europe, especially Marshal Tito's forces in Yugoslavia; but since then guerrilla has become the common description of such fighting men. I raise this point because of Captain Ewald's use of the word, and also because I have followed tradition and use partisan (and occasionally guerrilla) in the text to refer to the Back Country militia of the Carolinas led by such men as Francis Marion, Thomas Sumter, Andrew Pickens, and several less well-known but formidable characters whom we will meet along the way.

Until 1783, Charleston was spelled Charlestown and Charles-Town, but unless within a quotation I use the modern spelling throughout.

It is customary to thank one's spouse last, but Susi's support, advice, and cheerful willingness to tramp more battlefields than she cares to remember deserve top billing. I can never express how much I owe her, for so long and in so many ways.

At John Wiley & Sons I am deeply grateful to my good friend Charles Ellis, who asked to read the manuscript, found it deserving of serious consideration, then stepped back and let the system work. I could not have asked for a more skilled and sympathetic editor than Hana Umlauf Lane. And I must not fail to also thank her husband, John Lane, who represents the kind of reader for whom the book is meant. The same may be said for Joanne Palmer, whose interest in the book and careful work on its production are very much appreciated.

A friend and former colleague at The Metropolitan Museum of Art, Bradford Kelleher, counseled me on the publishing world he knows so well and offered encouragement as well as good food, fine wine, and engaging conversation.

I owe much to Dr. Dennis M. Conrad, who read most of the manuscript and saved me from errors that were if not compromising at least embarrassing, and led me to a few sources I had neglected as well as helped me with the maps. I am very grateful for his assistance and trenchant critique. Although he will continue to disagree with some of my assertions and assessments, his input made it a better book. I hasten to add that all the contents are my responsibiity, not his.

Ranger Virginia Fowler at the Cowpens National Battlefield Park was helpful with place names then and now. Joe Anderson, Superintendent, Landsford Canal State Park, South Carolina, kindly directed me to the fording place. Christopher C. Revels of the King's Mountain National Military Park tracked down an image of the elusive Patrick Ferguson. I am most grateul to all these dedicated public servants.

Professors John Mack Faragher and Don Higginbotham were prompt, courteous, and informative in reply to my queries.

In the Department of Arms & Armor, The Metropolitan Museum of Art, Donald LaRocca, Associate Curator, and Robert Carroll, Armorer, were unstinting of their time and expertise on technical matters relating to eighteenth-century muskets and rifles. If I did not get it right, the fault is mine. The head of the Department, Stuart Phyrr, kindly allowed me to use the departmental library.

My good fortune in living near the New York Public Library and its vast holdings and knowledgeable librarians was never more appreciated. I also did much of my reading in that venerable gem among New York City cultural institutions, the New York Society Library, and for the professional skills and many kindnesses of its staff, including a most efficient interlibrary loan service, my heartfelt thanks. For interlibrary loan service I must also also thank Carol Briggs, Librarian of the Hillsdale Public Library, Hillsdale, New York.

Andrew Pickens Miller kindly allowed me to reproduce the portrait of his famous ancestor. Lowell Kenyon retrieved the negative from his photographic archives and produced the print; and Brandon Fortune of the National Portrait Gallery, Washington, D.C., set me straight on the painting's attribution.

To the kindness of the children of William B. Willcox—Ellen W. Ham, Faith M. Willcox, and Alan F. Willcox—I owe permission to reproduce the map of "The Operations against Charleston, 1780," from their father's book.

Several people were involved in allowing me to use the maps from Volume VII of *The Papers of General Nathanael Greene*: Dr. Dennis M. Conrad, as noted above; Ron Maner, Managing Editor, Vicky Wells, Rights and Contracts Manager, and others at the University of North Carolina Press; Lyn Malone, who adapted and expanded the maps for the Greene papers; and Diane Nourse and

Renee Holly of Thomson-Shore, Inc., who supplied the duplicate negatives. To all, heartfelt thanks.

Historical editors past and present, known and unknown, must not be forgotten. As one who many years ago worked daily with official records and historical manuscripts as an archivist, I fully appreciate the nature of their labors, and my appreciation is deeply felt.

I am very thankful to the following people for their help and the many courtesies extended: Angela Mack and Marianne Clare, Gibbes Museum of Art, Charleston; Edward Schultz, Historic Brattonsville; Shirley Mays, Independence National Historical Park, Philadelphia; Micheal A. Hudson, Kentucky Historical Society; Jennifer A. Bryan and Kimberly S. Martin, Maryland Historical Society; James Kilvington, National Portrait Gallery, London; Liza Kavellas, National Portrait Gallery, Washington; Mette Bligaard, Det Nationalhistoriski Museum på Frederiksborg, Hillerød, Denmark; John C. Powell, The Newberry Library; Margaret Heilbrun and Wendy Haynes, The New-York Historical Society; Wayne Furman, The New York Public Library; Earl Ijames and Stephen E. Massengill, North Carolina Division of Archives & History; Beth Bilderback, South Caroliniana Library, University of South Carolina; Arlene P. Shy, William L. Clements Library; Georgianna Watson and Wendy Swik, U.S. Military Academy Library, West Point; Tory Gillett, University of North Carolina Press; Donna T. Anstey, Yale University Press; Ellen Cohn, Franklin Papers, Yale University.

And finally to my brother Charles, for his interest and yeoman service as chauffeur on my second field trip through the Carolinas, many thanks, Pete. Let's do it again.

J. B.

New York
July 1996

Prologue: Charleston

The story of the road to Guilford Courthouse begins in Charleston, where the most intriguing view of the city is still from the deck of a boat far out in the harbor, looking directly at East Bay Street. The scene is remarkably similar to Thomas Leitch's oil painting of 1774: a low, huddled harborscape, famous church spires piercing the sky beyond, the long row of houses extending along the waterfront, and rising above them from occasional vantage points the cupola of the Old Exchange Building, once at water's edge. There in 1791 the Rice Kings of the Low Country greeted President George Washington. The view reminded the Charleston writer and historian Beatrice St. Julien Ravenel of the Cadiz waterfront, but it is not the Cadiz I recall. Nor does Charleston have the "Mediterranean flavor" she attributed to it in *Architects of Charleston*. Perhaps the city she knew did, before gentrification, but no longer. It is too pretty, too neat, too clean, and, old as Charleston is by American standards, it lacks the requisite centuries to merit such comparison. The patina of antiquity demands patience.

As if frozen in time, the view nevertheless offers a most pleasing aspect, quite unlike any other American city. New York and San Francisco immediately present to the visitor entering their harbors sights dramatic and breathtaking, bespeaking money and power. Subtlety awaits the traveler to Charleston. The city does not reveal itself as easily, either from the harbor or in the somnolent streets of the Historic District. It rests quietly under a subtropical sun, ever aware of past glories yet always conscious that the ancestor worship for which it is famous can be combined in this tourist-driven town with the business of making money, a practice in which the earliest of those revered ancestors were quite expert.

The restrained harborscape also gives no indication of the high dramas that have occurred here in full view of the city's inhabitants. By far the best known is the bombardment of Fort Sumter in 1861, the official beginning of the Civil

1

War. But that tragedy is of far less interest than the American Revolution. The Revolution was the most important event in American history. The Civil War was unfinished business. The armies of the Revolutionary War were small but the stage global, the characters larger than life. The American Revolution was the first of the great modern revolutions, arguably the most important, and certainly the only one that did not end in tyranny or one-party rule.

It was, of course, messy. All revolutions are. Lenin, wrong about the important things, was right that to make an omelette one must break eggs. But as revolutions go, it was far less terrifying than the French, Russian, and Chinese revolutions. I write this, I must admit, with the gifts of hindsight and two centuries' remove from danger. Had I, or you, lived at that time and fallen into the wrong hands or chosen the losing side, life would have been terrifying indeed. And often tragic. We will come across conspicuous examples on our meandering journey from Charleston to Guilford Courthouse, as we follow the fortunes of Lieutenant General Charles, Earl Cornwallis, his dreaded lieutenants, and his faithful, enduring troops in the British campaign of 1780–1781 to reconquer the Carolinas for the crown.

1

The Battle of Sullivan's Island

*"When those ships . . . lay along side of your fort,
they will knock it down in half an hour"*

The War of the Revolution was a little over a year old when the Battle of Sullivan's Island took place in Charleston Harbor. The action occurred four years before the serious British effort in the South, but it is a rousing tale and serves to introduce a major theme of British strategy as well as some of the key players. In the year before Sullivan's Island the British had been bloodied by Yankee militia during their retreat from Lexington and Concord in April 1775, and the following month at Bunker Hill had suffered appalling casualties before prevailing. The American attempt to take Canada in the winter of 1775–1776 had failed, but in the lower Thirteen Colonies the Rebels had wrested control from royal governors. In South Carolina itself Low Country planters and merchants had secured the coastal plain and then, despite a series of tense standoffs that we will cover later, rolled over the King's Friends in the dangerous Back Country by the end of 1775. In March 1776 the British army evacuated Boston and sailed to Halifax, Nova Scotia. By now London realized that it had a real war on its hands, and British eyes increasingly focused on New York City, the Hudson River, and the classic Lake Champlain/Lake George invasion route from Canada. But while generals in Halifax and ministers in London schemed and gathered forces, it seemed plausible to London that a quick expedition southward would reap great benefits by encouraging the King's Friends in those parts, and even putting them on such a footing that they would be able to maintain themselves against the Rebels.[1]

It was therefore in the summer of 1776 that Commodore (later Admiral) Sir Peter Parker, in command of a naval squadron, and that strange, troubled man Major General Sir Henry Clinton, commanding 2,200 British regulars, attacked Sullivan's Island, where Fort Sullivan guarded the entrance to Charleston Harbor. Lord Cornwallis, making his first appearance in the American war, was Clinton's second in command, but he played a minor role. Among the lowliest of junior officers serving under His Lordship was a twenty-two-year-old cornet of cavalry whose anonymity on his first tour of duty in South Carolina would be matched by infamy on the road to Guilford Courthouse. His name was Banastre Tarleton.

Acting on instructions from London, Sir William Howe, the Commander in Chief North America, had ordered Sir Henry Clinton to sail south from Boston with a small force and rendezvous off the Cape Fear River in North Carolina with Lord Cornwallis, who would sail with seven regiments under the protection of Commodore Sir Peter Parker's squadron from Cork, Ireland. Clinton had been given command of the southern district and ordered, as he described it in his memoir of the war, *American Rebellion*, "to support the Loyalists and restore the authority of the King's government in the four southern provinces."[2] After accomplishing that, he was to sail north and rendezvous with Sir William Howe for the summer campaign against George Washington and his ragtag American army.

Clinton's primary objective was Charleston, the most important southern port and then the richest city in North America. But the Royal governor of North Carolina, Josiah Martin, had convinced British authorities that on the way North Carolina could also be reclaimed for the King. Clinton's mission seemed to the King and his ministers rather simple. As Sir Henry Clinton described it, "For it seems that the governors of those provinces had sent home such sanguine and favorable accounts of the loyal disposition of numbers of their inhabitants, especially in the back country, that the administration was induced to believe 'that nothing was wanting but the appearance of a respectable force there to encourage the King's friends to show themselves, when it was expected they would soon be able to prevail over'" the Rebels.[3]

At Cape Fear the British intended to link up with Tory forces from the interior, especially the Scottish Highlanders settled in the vicinity of Cross Creek, about 100 miles from the coast.[4] Much was expected of these legendary fighters, who set out for the sea on 20 February 1776 following a stirring speech by their commander, Brigadier General Donald MacDonald. By 26 February, in the middle of a swampy landscape, they learned that six miles in front of them about 1,000 Rebels were entrenched in front of Moore's Creek Bridge, well armed with muskets and the two cannon they had named "Old Mother Covington and her daughter." By then General MacDonald, reputed to be almost seventy, was too ill to continue in active command. At a council of war MacDonald argued for caution, but the young bloods among his officers prevailed over the opinions of an old, sick man. The decision was made to attack at dawn. General MacDonald's impetuous deputy, Lieutenant Colonel Donald McLeod, took command. Although the Tories numbered about 1,600, only 500 had firearms.

They marched at 1 o'clock on the morning of 27 February. At the bridge they found empty entrenchments. The Rebels had withdrawn and formed on the other side of Moore's Creek, which was about fifty feet wide. An advance party discovered that about half of the bridge's planks had been removed and the two stringers greased with soap and tallow. That made no difference to Donald McLeod. Elan would carry the day. About eighty men armed with broadswords were formed in the center to act as an assault force under Captain John Campbell. "King George and Broad Swords" was the rallying cry. As they had done so often in the old country, to the beat of drums, to the keening of the great war pipes, the Highlanders charged into disaster. Following McLeod on one stringer and Campbell on the other the broadswordsmen made their precarious way across the bridge. The Rebels let McLeod and Campbell reach their side of the creek. Then, at close range, Old Mother Covington and her daughter boomed and muskets roared. Not a Highlander was left standing on the bridge. Some fell between the stringers into Moore's Creek and drowned. McLeod and Campbell were killed immediately, although it was said that Donald McLeod half rose and pointed his sword at the Rebel works only a few feet away before he was hit again and fell forever. Thirty dead were later counted but there were probably more at the creek bottom and in the swamps. Their fate convinced their comrades to run far and fast, but for most it was neither far enough nor fast enough. The pursuing Rebels, who had two men wounded, one of whom later died, took about 850 prisoners, including the ailing General Donald MacDonald.

That short fight should have been a warning to the British, but it was not heeded in London among those who made important decisions. The Highlanders, however, did pay heed. Not only soundly defeated, they were so hounded by Rebel neighbors that many men spent the next four years hiding in woods and swamps. London, however, maintained the hope that they would rise again once a British army appeared among them, and the threat of another rising could not be ignored by the Rebels.

Meanwhile, Sir Henry Clinton, who had left Boston on 20 January, arrived off Cape Fear on 12 March to find that he had no Tories to link up with and no sign of Lord Cornwallis. His Lordship, scheduled to leave Cork in December 1775 but hindered by bureaucracy, had finally sailed on 13 February, but terrible storms delayed and dispersed the fleet and even drove some ships back to Cork. The first sails appeared off Cape Fear on 18 April, and most of the others did not drop anchor until 3 May. A final straggler limped in on 31 May. Such were the perils and uncertainties of eighteenth-century seaborne troop movements and communications.[5]

Foiled in North Carolina, the invasion fleet of some fifty ships anchored off Cape Fear while Clinton and Parker decided what to do. Should they go to the Chesapeake, as the deposed Royal Governor of Virginia urged, or to Charleston, as the deposed Royal Governor of South Carolina insisted? Clinton had authority to act at his discretion, and given the lateness of the season and the oppressive heat and humidity, he preferred acting in the Chesapeake before rejoining Sir William Howe in the North. But when two British officers sent by Parker to reconnoiter the approaches to Charleston returned with news that the fortifications on Sullivan's Island were unfinished and quite vulnerable, Sir Peter opted for Charleston and Sir Henry, strangely passive, went along.[6]

General William Moultrie (1730–1805) by Rembrandt Peale.
Oil on canvas. (Gibbs Museum of Art/Carolina Art Association.)

The operation was really a reconnaissance in force, and Sir Henry would have been pleased to capture Sullivan's Island and hold it for a decisive effort against Charleston at a later date. But as Clinton's biographer, William B. Willcox, pointed out over thirty years ago, the operation was a ridiculous misuse of resources based on a flawed concept. If the British took Sullivan's Island, the occupiers would be as cut off and isolated in 1776 as the Union defenders of Fort Sumter would be in 1861.[7]

Nevertheless, the attack should have been successful. The American commander at Fort Sullivan, Colonel William Moultrie (1730–1805), was as dilatory in ensuring that all was ready for battle as he was brave and inspiring once the shooting began. As his contemporary William Henry Drayton described him, "He was an officer of very easy manners, leaving to others many things to perform, which his own personal attentions would have much quickened."[8]

Born in Charleston, the son of Dr. John Moultrie, a native of Scotland, and Lucretia Cooper, Moultrie was a veteran of the Cherokee War on the far frontier. He lived on a plantation in St. John's Berkeley, which he acquired through a combination of purchase and marriage in 1749 to Elizabeth Damaris de St.

Julien. After her death he married another woman with famous Low Country names, Hannah Motte Lynch, daughter of Jacob Motte, widow of Thomas Lynch. Moultrie was a political moderate, but when decision-time came he chose rebellion and was appointed Colonel of the 2nd South Carolina Regiment. After the war he would be twice governor of South Carolina, and his presence in that high office was a blessing for a state wracked by the violence of its political factions, for he was a highly respected figure of good sense and experienced in the ways of men. His postwar political success did not extend to his private fortunes. During the Revolution he suffered heavy financial losses and they continued after the war. William Moultrie's brother John, a physician and Lieutenant Governor of East Florida, was an ardent Tory. After the Revolution John moved his family to England where he spent the rest of his life. The split in the Moultrie family is the first of several in families both well known and obscure that we will observe in what became a vicious civil war.

Moultrie was a simple, straightforward man, blunt, convivial, well liked. But he had serious faults. Lack of promptness and diligence is objectionable in anyone; in a soldier it can be fatal. Carelessness and failure to exercise proper supervision are inexcusable when lives and the fates of nations are at stake. We must plead William Moultrie guilty to all these sins. But what a fighter he was. What confidence he exuded. His coolness under fire was precisely what his unblooded recruits needed. His was a strong character and it was never shown to better advantage than on the ramparts of Fort Sullivan: calm, collected, in shirt sleeves, smoking his pipe, directing a fire well aimed and decisive.

But his failure during the several months he had to place the fort in a state of readiness put the garrison at grave peril. As the British knew from their reconnaissance, Fort Sullivan was half finished, defensible only on the southern wall, facing the ship channel, and the western wall. The other two walls, including the rear, were only seven feet high. If the British ships sailed past the southern wall and worked around to the cove behind the fort, enfilading fire would drive the Americans from their guns. In the meantime, if infantry put ashore by Clinton on Long Island (now Isle of Palms), just north of Sullivan's Island, crossed the Breach, the narrow inlet separating the two islands, the Americans would be caught between the navy's devastating bombardment and the merciless bayonets of Clinton's regulars.

The Americans thought this was a major effort and Charleston in grave danger of bombardment and assault. Assistance was sought far and wide, in the Low Country, from the Back Country of the two Carolinas, as far as the young settlements on the Watauga River deep in the Appalachians in what is now eastern Tennessee. The Rice Kings—the planters of the Low Country who had grown quickly and incredibly rich on the grain called Carolina Gold—held the inhabitants of the rude lands beyond their narrow strip of coast in contempt. To Governor John Rutledge they were a "pack of beggars." But with their safety and property at stake the Rice Kings were pleased to have at their sides uncouth Back Country settlers and wilderness riflemen capable of savagery equal to their Indian foes.[9]

From throughout the South their pleas were answered. Lieutenant Colonel William Thompson, the redoubtable Scotch Irish Indian fighter from the South Carolina Back Country, brought with him his veteran 3rd Regiment of Rangers, 300 strong. "Old Danger," as his Rangers called him, would command at a key spot. Destined to reinforce "Danger" Thompson with a Virginia Continental regiment was the gallant warrior-preacher from Virginia's Shenandoah Valley, John Peter Muhlenberg. Stiff-necked Lieutenant Colonel Thomas Sumter, flawed by ego, consumed by ambition, haunted by low birth, was in command of the 2nd South Carolina Rifle Regiment. He and his men would be onlookers at this fight, but many a bloody field awaited Sumter, and as the partisan leader known as the Gamecock he would become famous throughout the land. Serving directly under Moultrie in the thick of the fight, like Sumter his wider mark yet to be made, was Major Francis Marion, the man who would become an American legend as the Swamp Fox. And from the North there rode into town a few days after 4 June a general sent by the Continental Congress to lead them. He was accompanied, as always, by two dogs, one of them once described by the New Englander Jeremy Belknap as a "native of Pomerania, which I should have taken for a bear had I seen him in the woods."[10]

Major General Charles Lee was an Englishman, an ex-British army officer of radical opinions who had declared for the American cause and offered his services to Congress. He was brave, eccentric, energetic, and obnoxious. His opinions, freely expressed, could be brutal. He also suffered from a not uncommon human malady: delusions of grandeur, a state undoubtedly further encouraged by John Adams's hyperbolic statement, "We want you at N. York—We want you at Cambridge—We want you in Virginia." If not afflicted with brief periods of madness, his violent temperament and language made him unfit to be commander in chief and should have precluded him from theatre command. But, despite his serious faults of character, Charles Lee was an intelligent and experienced soldier who had served in America during the French and Indian War and distinguished himself in action in Portugal in 1762. As a soldier of fortune, he had observed the Russian Army fighting the Turks. The best-known impression of him is a caricature, but Abigail Adams confirmed that "The elegance of his pen far exceeds that of his person," and all who knew him in England thought it the "only successful delineation of either his countenance or person." We know that he was a small, thin man with a big nose, a sarcastic manner, and dogmatic opinions. Private Simeon Alexander of the Hadley, Massachusetts, militia, who saw Lee at the siege of Boston, recalled many years later that "the soldiers used to laugh at his great nose."[11]

But Charles Lee was not a comic figure. Widely read in literature and political philosophy, he emulated his hero, Jean Jacques Rousseau, in seeking the perfect society. He was an early and ardent proponent of American independence, although he later changed his mind, and was accused by some of treasonous activities. He came to a sad end, largely of his own making. At the Battle of Monmouth in 1778, George Washington hotly criticized him on the battlefield, in front of other officers, and took over personal command of the army

Caricature of Charles Lee, A.H. Ritchie
after Rushbrooke.
*Engraving, 1813. (Portrait File, Miriam
and Ira D. Wallach Division of Art, Prints
and Photographs, The New York Public Library,
Astor, Lenox and Tilden Foundation.)*

for the rest of the action. Lee responded with a letter quite characteristic of him that prompted Washington to order a court martial. Lee was found guilty, and after Congress ratified the finding he demanded that it retract his conviction, whereupon Congress dismissed him from the army. In retirement he continued to attack Washington in letters and print. His death in Philadelphia in 1782 was hardly noticed.

William Moultrie, who came to know Charles Lee better than he probably wished, was nevertheless fair in his estimate of the man: "His presence gave us great spirits, as he was known to be an able, brave and experienced officer, though hasty and rough in his manners, which the officers could not reconcile themselves to at first: it was thought by many that his coming among us was equal to a reinforcement of 1,000 men, and I believe it was, because he taught us to think lightly of the enemy, and gave a spur to all our actions." Lee's rough manners and brutal candor were clearly shown the day he inspected a battery that had been planned by the rich and powerful Chief Justice of South Carolina, William Henry Drayton, a man who had played a key role in South Carolina's rebellion and whom we will examine in some detail later in our story. "What damned fool planned this battery?" asked Lee. Told it was Drayton, he said, "He might be a very good chief justice, but he is a damned bad engineer." He paid dearly for those slashing remarks. Drayton neither forgot nor forgave. When Lee's conviction by court martial was before Congress for approval, Congressman William Henry Drayton led the charge that resulted in confirmation of his conviction.[12]

Lee's behavior would have infuriated anyone on the receiving end of his terrible tongue. To the Rice Kings it was intolerable, but their incipient rebellion against Lee was quelled by the wartime governor of South Carolina, John Rutledge, known as the "Dictator." Rutledge issued general orders that put Lee in command of all state troops and militia and made it clear to one and all that General Lee's orders "are to be obeyed."

Once he had authority, Lee lent a much-needed sense of urgency to the impending crisis. He organized men and materials and got things moving on the defenses of the city proper and on the islands. He was appalled when he inspected Fort Sullivan and in his "hasty and rough" manner let Moultrie know exactly how he felt. It was, he said, a "slaughter pen," and he strongly recommended that the garrison should be withdrawn and the fort abandoned. Lee reckoned without the "Dictator." Governor Rutledge insisted that Fort Sullivan be defended, and Moultrie seconded the Governor. At one point Rutledge sent Moultrie a confidential order consisting of three short sentences not susceptible to misinterpretation. "General Lee wishes you to evacuate the fort. You will not without an order from me. I will sooner cut off my hand than write one. John Rutledge." Lee had no choice but to accept and threw himself into the task of strengthening the fort, sending an engineer and an army of slaves and spending much time himself on the island. There was time only for improvement of the rear wall, but not enough to withstand a serious bombardment. "General Lee's whole thoughts," Moultrie wrote, "were taken up with the post on Sullivan's Island; all his letters to me shew how anxious he was at not having a bridge for a retreat; for my part I never was uneasy on not having a retreat because I never imagined that the enemy could force me to that necessity; I always considered myself as able to defend that post against the enemy."[13]

But Lee persisted, as Moultrie recalled: "General Lee one day on a visit to the fort, took me aside and said, 'Col. Moultrie, do you think you can maintain this post?' I answered him, 'Yes I think I can,' that was all that passed on the subject between us." But Lee did remove from the island over half of Moultrie's supply of 10,000 pounds of powder.[14]

There were those who agreed with Lee. Captain Lamperer, an experienced seaman who had been master of both a man-of-war and a privateer, visited Fort Sullivan on the day of the battle and told Moultrie, "Sir, when those ships . . . come to lay along side of your fort, they will knock it down in half an hour," to which Moultrie replied, "We will lay behind the ruins and prevent their men from landing."[15]

The inadequacy of the fort and his unhappiness with Moultrie continued to gnaw at Lee, as Moultrie describes in this passage from his *Memoirs*. "Gen. Lee, I was informed, did not like my having command of that important post, he did not doubt my courage, but said, 'I was too easy in command,' as his letters shew." Lee bombarded Moultrie with written observations and instructions. On 21 June he wrote tartly of his concern with improper construction of the traverse, an earthen breastwork he had ordered built to protect the rear of the fort, and of his fear of gunners firing at too great a range. On the same day he wrote again. "I hope you will excuse the style of my last letter, I must once more repeat that, it did not arise from any diffidence in your judgement, zeal, or spirit, but merely from an appreciation that your good nature, or easy temper, might, in some measure counteract those good qualities which you are universally known to possess. As you seem sensible that it is necessary to exert your powers, I do not, I cannot wish this important post in better hands than yours." But the very next day he wrote again in his badgering style: "Every body is well persuaded of your spirit and zeal, but they accuse you of being too easy in command; that is, I suppose, too relaxed in discipline ... which, in your situation, give me leave to say, there is not a greater vice. Let your orders be as few as possible but let them be punctually obeyed. I would not recommend teasing your men and officers with superfluous duties or labor; but I expect that you enforce the execution of whatever is necessary for the honor and safety of your garrison." Lee then asked Moultrie to excuse the "prolixity and didactic style of this letter, as it arises ... in some measure for my concern for the reputation of a gentleman of so respectable a character as Col. Moultrie." Then in the next sentence he continued to nag Moultrie on details.[16]

Poor Moultrie. As if it were not enough that he suffered from gout before and during the battle, he felt the full weight of Lee's passion for detail. Charles Lee wallowed in a morass of eighteenth-century micromanagement, and those of us who have suffered the twentieth-century version can only sympathize with Moultrie. Granted his shortcomings, which did indeed place the garrison in jeopardy, with action impending the last thing Moultrie needed was the incessant waspish nagging and nitpicking of his commanding officer. The time had passed for peevish scoldings, yet up to the day of the battle Lee considered sacking Moultrie. On 28 June he informed Governor Rutledge that unless Moultrie obeyed his orders he would replace him with Colonel Francis Nash of the North Carolina Continental Line. But it was too late. The wind and the sea intervened.[17]

The British fleet had arrived off Charleston bar on 4 June. It was no simple matter to get large sailing ships inside a harbor when a bar, or sandbank, blocked passage at low tide and allowed entry at high tide only by way of a channel. Charleston Harbor was "surrounded" by such a sandbank. Four years later Captain Johann Hinrichs of the Jäger Corps, a Hessian mercenary unit that was part of the second British expedition against Charleston, described the obstacle in his diary. "There are five channels through the Bar. The deepest, the Ship Channel, has twelve feet of water at low tide and twenty-one and one-half at high tide and does not permit the passage of ships heavier than an English 40-gun ship without their being lightened. At some places the Bar is covered with only three to four feet of water."[18] Finding and navigating the proper channel demanded careful preparation. Soundings had to be taken in small boats, and the ship channel found and marked. On 7 June the smaller warships and Clinton's troop transports passed the bar to a safe anchorage in Five Fathom Hole, which was thirty feet deep and beyond the range of Fort Sullivan's guns. (See the map on page 50.)

Although Sullivan's Island was the goal, Sir Henry Clinton thought the surf on that island too dangerous for a landing, and between 9 and 15 June he put his troops ashore on Long Island, immediately north of Sullivan's Island. It was a fateful decision. There remained the two large ships, *Bristol*, Parker's flagship, and *Experiment*, each mounting fifty guns, to get over the bar, for as Hinrich's diary entry makes clear, even at high tide their draughts were too deep for them to pass through the channel. Each had to be lightened by removing their guns, which were then taken over the bar by small craft. After *Bristol* and *Experiment* crossed the bar at high tide, guns and ships were reunited at Five Fathom Hole. It was not until 26 June that the British were ready for action. Even allowing for customary British dawdling, this relatively small operation is a signal lesson in the hard labor that attends war before the firing even begins.

And for naval forces weather could mean the difference between victory, defeat, or even being able to come to grips with the enemy. Sailing ships require a southerly wind to come abreast of Fort Sullivan. At 10:00 A.M. on 27 June Parker's flotilla weighed anchor and got underway with a southeast breeze behind it. But the ships had sailed only about a mile when the wind shifted to the northwest, and Parker was forced to drop anchor and await a favorable wind.[19]

The following morning, Charles Lee boarded a small craft to go out to Sullivan's Island for his showdown with Moultrie. But a crossing that today takes a few minutes by automobile via the Cooper River Bridge was hostage to wind and wave in 1776. Lee was forced back to the mainland by rough water. Conditions were much improved by the time the British made their move, but then it was too late for Lee to act. At 10:30 A.M., the wind favoring him, Parker signaled his captains to weigh anchor. Moultrie meanwhile had ridden three miles from the fort that morning on his way to inspect Colonel William Thomson's position at the Breach when he saw "men-of-war loose their topsails. I hurried back to the fort as fast as possible; when I got there the ships were already under sail. I immediately ordered the long roll to beat and the officers and men to their posts." It was a very sultry day. The sun burned overhead. The light wind hardly ruffled the waters.[20]

"This will not be believed when it is first reported in England"

Bearing down the channel were eight British men-of-war mounting 260 guns and one bomb ship, *Thunder*, equipped with two heavy, wide-mouthed mortars to lob explosive shells into the fort. Its deck was laid with reinforced spar plank-ing to absorb the terrible recoil. The armed transport, *Friendship*, accompanied *Thunder*. In stately line of battle *Active, Bristol, Experiment, Solebay* arrived about 11:15 A.M. and anchored some 350 yards offshore. Laying farther out and not immediately engaged were the frigates *Actaeon* and *Syren* and the corvette *Sphynx*. Moultrie in his half-finished fort had thirty-one guns and the 4,600 pounds of powder Lee had left him. With Moultrie were about 400 men of his own infantry regiment, the 2nd South Carolina, and a twenty-man detachment from the 4th South Carolina Artillery. Of the 6,500 men gathered to defend the city, these few would bear the overwhelming brunt of the action, and most of them had never been to war.[21]

"They were soon abreast of the fort," Moultrie wrote, "let go of their an-chors with springs upon their cables and begun their attack most furiously." Im-mediately things began to go wrong for the British. *Thunder* was anchored too far from the fort to deliver effective fire. To gain distance more powder was added to the mortars, whereupon the reinforced planking eventually broke down. *Thunder*, without voice, was out of the fight after wounding one Rebel and killing "three ducks, two geese, and one turkey."[22]

The flanking movement by land was no more successful. The Breach, the inlet between Long Island and Sullivan's Island and still known by the same name, is today about seventy-five yards wide and spanned by a bridge. There was no bridge in 1776, but its width was probably about the same. The Amer-icans under Colonel William "Danger" Thompson were entrenched on the Sullivan's Island side. Sir Henry Clinton had accepted intelligence reports that the Breach could be easily forded by his troops. It was, he was told, eighteen inches at low tide. The reports were wrong. And, uncharacteristically, Sir Henry had not done his own advance reconnaissance. Once ashore, and under cover of night, Sir Henry himself led his officers in fruitless searches for a shallow channel, but even at low tide they waded into water shoulder deep and getting deeper. The shallowest channel, it turned out, was seven feet. Captain James Murray, who was there with the 57th Foot, thought that had the army moved quickly after the mistake was discovered the troops could have been reembarked and landed on Sullivan's Island under covering fire by the fleet.

But Clinton was stubborn. Murray wrote, "So much was the General pre-possessed with the idea of this infernal ford, that several days and nights were spent in search of it." Clinton had 2,200 regulars to Colonel William "Danger" Thompson's 780 mixed bag of regulars and militia. But when the British at-tempted to force their way across in shallow draught boats they could make no headway against American riflemen and gunners firing from behind palmetto and earthen breastworks. A Charleston Tory who had joined the British expe-dition and served aboard one of the boats said that "it was impossible for any set of men to sustain so destructive a fire as the Americans poured in . . . on this occasion." Until nightfall, when Clinton withdrew his force from the inlet, the two sides sporadically popped away at each other across the Breach while Commodore Sir Peter Parker played out his role in the British fiasco.[23]

About an hour after the naval bombardment began, the British attempted an ominous move. *Actaeon*, *Syren*, and *Sphynx* weighed anchor and headed for the western end of Sullivan's Island, where they intended to initiate the dreaded enfilading fire that so worried Charles Lee. Even Moultrie admitted that had they succeeded "they would have driven us from our guns." But the maneuver clearly revealed bad planning on the part of the Admiralty. Although Charleston Harbor was well known to many British naval officers, not one of these men had been assigned to Parker's squadron, and Sir Peter had failed to avail himself of the services of one who was close by, Lieutenant John Fergusson, who sat out the action just down the coast at Savannah. Parker used instead dragooned black pilots, who may not have been local men. The ships stood out too far and all three were soon stuck fast on a shoal called the Middle Ground, where Fort Sumter was later built. *Actaeon* and *Sphynx* even collided and *Sphynx* lost her bowsprit. Legendary British seamanship was not in evidence that day, although Charlestonians had another answer: "Almighty Providence confounded the plan."[24]

Syren and *Sphynx* were finally refloated and after repairs rejoined the fight, but *Actaeon* was stuck fast and did not again figure in the battle. All thoughts of another such maneuver were given up. But Parker's ships kept pounding away at Fort Sullivan. An observer in Clinton's ground force described the fleet as an "eternal sheet of fire and smoke." British overconfidence evaporated. James Murray of the 57th wrote, "After the first hour we began to be impatient and a good deal surprized at the resistance of the battery. But when for 4 hours the fire grew every moment hotter and hotter we were lost in wonder and astonishment." As the guns roared, small craft passed back and forth between warships and transports to remove the wounded and deliver replacements to man the guns. General Lee, who had seen many battlefields, observed during a visit to the fort that it was "one of the most furious and incessant fires I ever saw or heard." Moultrie's preoccupation with incessant cannonading, however, did not stop Charles Lee from continuing to micromanage from a distance. While the battle raged he sent a letter to Moultrie by an aide, Major Otway Byrd. "If you should unfortunately expend your ammunition without beating off the enemy or driving them on the ground, spike your guns and retreat with all order possible; but I know you will be careful not to throw away your ammunition." Moultrie instead asked for more powder.[25]

One would think that this simple, half-finished fort would have been demolished. That it was not is the reason the palmetto tree is the centerpiece of the South Carolina state flag. Fort Sullivan was made of the basic materials at hand: four double walls of palmetto logs placed sixteen feet apart, dovetailed and bolted, with the space between exterior and interior walls filled with sand and marsh clay. Had the walls been made of pine or hardwoods they would have been destroyed and the flying splinters turned into lethal weapons against the defenders. But palmetto wood does not splinter. It is soft, spongy, and the British cannonballs sank into the porous wood as they did into the sand. At least 7,000 cannonballs were fired into the fort and the logs and sand simply absorbed them. It was computed that the British expended slightly over 34,000 pounds of powder, while the Americans, short of powder because of Charles Lee's belief that the fort could not be held, used about 4,766 pounds. Thus their rate of fire was necessarily low. Moultrie ordered that each gun be fired every ten minutes, and then only when openings appeared in the smoke enveloping Parker's ships. And at 3 P.M. he had to temporarily suspend firing because the garrison was running dangerously low on powder. About 800 pounds of powder were procured from the mainland and a schooner anchored in the cove behind the island; around 5 P.M. Moultrie ordered his guns back into action.[26]

The accuracy of the American fire astounded all. A British surgeon with the fleet had nothing but praise for American gunnery: "Their artillery was surprisingly well served . . . it was slow, but decisive indeed; they were very cool, and took great care not to fire except their guns were exceedingly well directed." General Lee concluded on his visit to the fort during the battle, "Colonel, I see you are doing very well here. You have no occasion for me. I will go up to town again." There were anxious moments when Fort Sullivan received simultaneous broadsides from more than one ship, which caused the entire superstructure to shake. But it held. William Moultrie, who had never doubted, described a particularly satisfying moment at the height of the battle. "It being a very hot day, we were served along the platform with grog in firebuckets, which we partook of very heartily. I never had a more agreeable draught than that which I took out of one of those buckets. . . . It may be very easily conceived what heat and thirst a man must feel in this climate . . . upon a platform on the twenty-eighth of June, amidst twenty or thirty heavy pieces of cannon in one continual blaze and roar and clouds of smoke curling over his head for hours together. It was a very honorable situation, but a very unpleasant one."[27]

But ultimately very satisfying. Moultrie's well-served guns wreaked havoc on the British. *Bristol's* cable was cut by gunfire and she swung end to end to Fort Sullivan. All the guns were pointed at her, and the word was passed along the firing platform: "Mind the Commodore—mind the two fifty-gun ships." *Bristol* was raked from stem to stern by fire so devastating that the rear of Commodore Sir Peter Parker's breeches were literally blown away, leaving "his posteriors quite bare." At one point Parker was the only man left on the quarterdeck. Despite entreaties, bloody with wounds, unable to walk without the help of two men, he refused to leave his post, intrepid behavior hardly remarked on in British accounts of the battle because it was expected of British naval officers. If the waters of the channel had not been smooth and the Americans short of powder, *Bristol* probably would have gone down. As it was, she suffered so much damage that carpenters had to be sent to her while the battle raged to make emergency repairs. Between *Bristol* and *Experiment* alone sixty-three men were killed and 127 wounded, and their captains each lost an arm. Captain John Morris of *Bristol* underwent amputation on board, then insisted on being carried to the quarterdeck where he resumed command until struck down again. He died several days later and lies in a lost grave on Isle of Palms.[28]

Firing slackened with the setting sun. All firing ceased at 9:30 P.M. At 11:30 P.M., silently, without the usual piping of bos'uns' whistles, the ships slipped their cables, and on the tail end of the ebb tide withdrew to Five Fathom Hole. In the morning *Actaeon* was set afire by her crew and abandoned. It was all over.

Two Englishmen were astounded by the results. General Charles Lee admitted that "The behavior of the Garrison, both men and officers, with Colonel Moultrie at their head, I confess astonished me." Lee's contribution to the victory was psychological in lending confidence to the city's defenders, and although he was right that Fort Sullivan was a potential slaughter pen, it did not turn out that way. It was the leadership in battle of the careless but gallant Moultrie backed by the superb gunnery and cool determination of his officers and men that were key to victory. The British surgeon wrote, "This will not be believed when it is first reported in England. I can scarcely believe what I myself saw that day—a day to me one of the most distressing of my life."[29] A Yankee balladeer later celebrated the Rebel victory with A *New War Song*, by Sir Peter Parker.

> Bold Clinton by land
> Did quietly stand
> While I made a thundering clatter;
> But the channel was deep,
> So he could only peep
> And not venture over the water.
>
> De'il tak 'em; their shot
> Came so swift and so hot,
> And the cowardly dogs stood so stiff, sirs,
> That I put ship about
> And was glad to get out
> Or they would not have left me a skiff, sirs!
>
> Now bold as a Turk
> I proceed to New York
> Where with Clinton and Howe you may find me.
> I've the wind in my tail,
> And am hoisting my sail,
> To leave Sullivan's Island behind me.[30]

It was truly a glorious victory, as stubbornly fought as the better-known action at Bunker Hill, and unlike the northern fight a real as well as moral victory. The American troops had behaved well and, in the language of the time, "Almighty Providence" on that occasion looked over them. But there would be a next time, and the British would learn from their defeat. When they returned they would come in strength and their methods would be near faultless.

2

The Rice Kings

Pioneers

Old Charleston has been described as a city-state because of its domination over that narrow, humid, fever-ridden strip of wetlands and pine barrens paralleling the Atlantic Ocean that we call the Low Country. Charleston was the Low Country and the Low Country was Charleston, and to refer to either means both.

The pioneers who settled the Low Country in the final quarter of the seventeenth century were mythologized by twentieth-century descendants as aristocrats who created the "gentlest, the most humane, the most chivalric civilization that America has ever known," which was destroyed in the Civil War by the "sword of misunderstanding" and succeeded by a sordid industrial civilization reeking of materialism.[1] In truth, they were hard men on the make, as grasping and ruthless as any flinty-eyed Yankee merchant, parvenus to the core, and by the evidence parvenus they and their descendants remained through the period with which we are concerned. Like most pioneers, they perched for a while on the edge of a frontier, in their case the littoral.

The littoral, that strip of earth forming the edge of the continent, where land meets sea, if not manicured is a place of beauty, whether sand or saltmarsh or rocks. The beauty of the untouched parts of the coastal strip extends inland to the lower reaches of the rivers with the American names that run eastward to the great ocean and whose wetlands extend far beyond their banks: Little Pee Dee, Big Pee Dee, Waccamaw, Sampit, Santee, Edisto, Ashepoo, Combahee, Coosawhatchie, and like alien presences among them Black and Cooper and Ashley. It was to the untouched littoral and the salt marshes and swamps of the coastal plain in the spring of 1670, relatively late in the settling of the coast of British North America, that three ships brought 148 men and women, overwhelmingly English, among them names that would become famous in the history of South Carolina. Most of them were from the mother country, but some were English from, significantly, the densely populated sugar island of Barbados, settled since 1624. Its occupants, both white and black, were highly experienced in the plantation system of agriculture, and the English from Barbados would wield an influence on the mainland far beyond their numbers.[2]

For a decade they and other arrivals occupied a site not on the familiar peninsula shaped like a serpent's head, but on the west bank of the Ashley River almost directly across from where the Citadel now stands. In 1680, with a population of about 1,200, perhaps one-third black slaves, the settlement was removed to the present site of Charleston. The city then and throughout the glory years of the eighteenth century was a working city, impressive for its time but busy, noisy, and dirty, a tough, brawling seaport town where in one month, November 1718, the city fathers hanged forty-nine pirates on the Battery at harborside.[3]

Rice was king by the 1730s. But before that came to pass the colonists had to survive the Spanish enemy in Florida and Indian tribes in the vicinity. Spain had explored the land long before the coming of the English, and their legal claims were probably better, but demography soon overcame legalities. By 1700 the 1,500 Spaniards in Florida were faced by some 3,800 whites in South Carolina, and a half century later the English were ten times as strong. Spain's hegemony in the region had passed. Indians posed a greater threat. Between 1715 and 1718 a now forgotten tribe, the Yamasee, waged a now-forgotten war that was carried almost to the walls of Charleston and came very close to destroying the colony. It is of interest to us because armed black slaves served in militia units. But fear of rebellion prompted a request to the Assembly that slaves in the army be disarmed and disbanded. The Yamasee War was the high watermark in colonial days for black militia and soldiers. Fifty-six years later General Nathanael Greene, his manpower resources terribly strained, asked the Rice Kings to draft blacks for his army of reconquest. They reacted with horror and disbelief and rejected his request out of hand.[4]

The Yamasee War inflicted real grief and hardship on three races, but it is not an exaggeration to state that the debilitating effects of climate and disease brought over the long run far more grievous suffering to all the races of the Low Country. The heat and humidity that last the better part of the year are "so intense as to be almost unendurable" wrote a young Frenchman in 1687. As if heat and humidity were not enough, white men, women, and children died of disease like flies. Smallpox among all and diphtheria among children were common European diseases that had quickly spread to the New World. But the Low Country was also afflicted with two scourges that were dreaded and not understood. It was not known then or for some two centuries that yellow fever and malaria were carried by mosquitoes within the marshes and swamps that made the Low Country, in the words of a seventeenth-century writer, "a great charnel-house." A connection was eventually made between fever and residing on plantations in the summer months, and many planters moved to their Charleston townhouses during the worst time. Even safer for those rich enough was to spend summers in Newport, Rhode Island, which became known as the "Carolina hospital." What these fortunates left behind from roughly June through October was a white man's graveyard. This is not to claim immunity for the Indians, who were devastated by alien diseases, some tribes to the point of extinction; or for blacks, African born or natives, who succumbed in such numbers to disease and brutally hard labor that they could not sustain themselves by natural increase during the middle decades of the eighteenth century. Smallpox was no respecter of race, and blacks were apparently far more susceptible to respiratory diseases than whites and on more than one occasion were decimated by epidemics. But to whites was reserved, if not uniquely certainly to a far greater degree, the twin terrors of the Low Country: yellow fever and malaria. Why this was so has to do with their presence in West Africa, from which most of the slaves came and where they had gained a degree of immunity. Black immunity to these two scourges was not total, but their resistance was much higher than that of whites. This did not go unnoticed in the eighteenth century. Lord Montagu was only one of many European observers who claimed that rice and other products "cannot be raised and extended but by the labour of Slaves provided by the African trade."[5]

Thus were blacks and their progeny for that and other reasons going well beyond the scope of this book doomed to unremitting hard labor in the beautiful but fetid wetlands of the Carolina Low Country.

"It far surpasses all I ever saw, or ever expected to see in America"

On the twin foundations of rice and slave labor the Rice Kings quickly built a brilliant if brittle society. Progress from a rough, crude frontier environment was quite phenomenal. By 1740, only seventy years after the colony was founded, the English evangelist George Whitefield noted in Charleston "an affected finery and gaiety of dress and deportment which I question if the Court end of London could exceed." This despite the various disasters that nature seemed to delight in inflicting on the Low Country. Pestilence and disease had been with them from the beginning, and in the year 1700 they suffered their first disastrous hurricane, which was followed by others, all of fierce proportion, all killers—1713, 1728, 1752. "In such a case," wrote the colonial historian David Ramsay, "between the dread of pestilence in the city, of common fever in the country, and of an expected hurricane on the island, the inhabitants ... are at the close of every warm season in a painful state of anxiety, not knowing what course to pursue, nor what is best to be done." Perhaps it was the monumental vicissitudes of life in the Low Country that helped persuade many merchants who made their fortunes early to return to England to enjoy their riches and pursue more. Most persevered, however, and from various parts of the world immigrants arrived. Most were Englishmen from the home island or the British West Indies. But there was a sizeable group of Scottish merchants, and by 1750 enough Sephardic Jews to form a congregation. French Huguenots, from both the Continent or England, began arriving in the 1680s, and many of them assimilated quickly and became Rice Kings. There were also in the 1740s and 1750s and beyond shiploads of poor immigrants destined for the Back Country: Germans, Swiss, and from Northern Ireland restive, pugnacious Scotch Irish Protestants.[6]

The government of South Carolina was quite candid in its reasons for encouraging settlement of the hinterlands. These people were to provide a shield for the Low Country against the western Indians, primarily the Cherokee and Creeks, and a manpower reserve in case the Rice Kings needed assistance in quelling slave uprisings. The Germans and Swiss struck west and settled in what was sometimes called the middle country, from the Savannah River on the south to the Santee on the north. Some Germans went on farther to the Dutch Fork, an area between the Saluda and Broad Rivers just beyond modern Columbia, while English settlers pushed on even farther into the upper part of the Fork. Many of the Scotch Irish entering through Charleston port went northwest into the Williamsburgh District, centered around the village of Kingstree. Beyond the Scotch Irish, from Pennsylvania trekked Welsh settlers who took up lands called the Welsh Tract on the Big Pee Dee River in the vicinity of Cheraw, just below the North Carolina line. Beginning in the 1750s, another migration began overland from Pennsylvania that had a tremendous impact on our story. This was the eruption of the Scotch Irish southward. But that fascinating tale will fall into its own place in the narrative.

The South Carolina Assembly, dominated by the Rice Kings, supplied the new immigrants with generous amounts of food, livestock, and farm implements, with, as we know, very specific ulterior motives. What the Rice Kings did not do was allow people they considered lesser breeds representation in the governing body, or provide them with courts where they could file land claims and seek justice. For that they had to journey a hundred miles or more to Charleston, which meant that most of the time they had no justice and no place to register land, wills, and other legal documents. The Rice Kings would pay dearly for their snobbery and lack of political wisdom. David Duncan Wallace, a native son who became one of the state's leading historians, wrote that by this policy "The unhappy sectional antagonism that was for so long to blight South Carolina was already deeply planted."[7] But for the time being the Rice Kings were safe behind their barrier of Back Country farmers and frontiersmen, and from the 1730s forward Charleston grew and prospered and both amazed and troubled strangers who came to call.

During the British occupation Sergeant Roger Lamb of the Royal Welsh Fusiliers, although he took a dim view of a city in which black slaves were far more numerous than whites "in this boasted land of liberty," and called the water "putrid" and the "climate unhealthy," noted "splendid equipages" and inhabitants who "are very extravagant in their living." The Hessian Jäger Captain Johann Hinrichs, who was in the city in 1780, wrote in his diary that "No other American city can compare with Charleston in the beauty of its houses and the splendor and taste displayed therein. The rapid ascendancy of families which in less than ten years have risen from the lowest rank, have acquired upwards of £100,000, and have, moreover, gained their wealth in a simple and easy manner, probably contribute a good deal toward the grandiose display of splendor, debauchery, luxury and extravagance in so short a time. Furthermore, the sense of equality which all possessed during this time of increasing incomes induced the people to bid strangers to enjoy their abundance with them and earned the renown of hospitality for this city, which she owes, perhaps, more to vanity and pride than to true generosity of spirit."[8]

On the eve of the Revolution, a young, well-connected New Englander, Josiah Quincy, Jr., arrived in Charleston following a voyage from Boston through storms that left him prostrate: "exhausted to the last degree, I was too weak to rise, and in too exquisite pain to lie in bed." But in a reference that many observers made to the sickly pallor of fever-ridden Carolinians, he wrote his wife in March 1773 that "There are such a multitude of ghosts and shadows here, that I make not so bad a figure on comparison." On the splendor and prosperity of the town he had no reservations. "The number of shipping far surpasses all I had ever seen in Boston. I was told there were then not as many as common at this season, tho' about 350 sail lay off the town." In an oft-quoted passage Quincy wrote that "This town makes a most beautiful appearance as you come up to it, and in many respects a magnificent one. Although I have not been here twenty hours, I have traversed the most popular parts of it. I can only say in general, that in grandeur, splendour of buildings, decorations, equipages, numbers, commerce, shipping, and indeed in almost every thing, it far surpasses all I ever saw, or ever expected to see in America. Of their manners, literature, understanding, spirit of true liberty, policy and government, I can form no adequate judgement. All seems at present to be trade, riches, magnificence, and great state in everything: much gaiety, and dissipation." Quincy's final remarks have been linked to his Puritan heritage, but as we have seen the European soldier Captain Hinrichs presented in even stronger terms the same picture of a nouveau riche society greatly enjoying itself.[9]

In Charleston and on his return journey Josiah Quincy moved in the best company, but reserved his special attention for a memorable dinner at Miles Brewton's "most superb house," which many think still the finest house in Charleston, and for a plantation north of Georgetown, where he "spent the night at Mr. J[oseph] Allston's, a gentleman of immense income, all of his own acquisition. He is a person between thirty-nine and forty, and a few years ago begun the world with only five Negroes—now has five plantations with an hundred slaves on each." This was the family that spawned South Carolina's only world-class artist, the nineteenth-century romantic painter, Washington Allston. Allston was a contemporary and close friend of the Charleston miniaturist Charles Fraser, who is the best visual guide to the old Low Country beyond Charleston. Forty of his lovely, dreamlike watercolors, done between 1796 and 1806, go far beyond words in depicting the lives led by the Rice Kings.[10]

"Internal enemies"

Charleston past and present is an easy target for critics. The society that at-tained its brilliant apogee in the late eighteenth century was built on a bed of quicksand that was known and frequently acknowledged: black slavery so closely intertwined with single-crop agriculture that the two were inseparable. A black majority was building by about 1710, when the term "internal enemies" came into vogue among Low Country whites. Lieutenant Governor Broughton warned in 1737, "Our negroes are very numerous and more dreadful to our safety than any Spanish invaders." He was echoed in 1768 by Lieutenant Gov-ernor William Bull, who wrote to Lord Hillsborough that the whites have a "nu-merous domestic Enemy . . . thick sown in our plantations, and require our utmost attention to keep them in order." The following year *Timothy's Gazette* warned with regard to the slave trade, "This scarcely needs comment; every-man's own mind must suggest the consequences of such enormous importa-tions." To put it into figures, in 1770, five years before the Revolution began, the estimated population of the Low Country was 88,244, of which 19,066 were white and 69,178 black.[11] The Low Country establishment clearly saw the peril then and for the future, but lacked the will to do what needed to be done. Po-litically, socially, economically above all, the fruits of slavery were too enjoyable. How sweet it could be was described by Richard Lathers, a northern Democrat who knew the Low Country well and was very sympathetic to the Rice Kings. In his *Reminiscences* Lathers drew a clear picture of the average planter's way of life in the 1830s; with a possible change in the cash figures, this standard of liv-ing had been set well before the American Revolution, at least by 1750, when the South Carolina Low Country had become the richest society in America.

"A rice plantation and two hundred negroes worth about $150,000 to $200,000 furnished an income sufficient to support a family of five to ten per-sons in comparative luxury, since this enabled them to have carriages and houses, a town house, and a villa in some retreat, in addition to the homestead. The natural increase of the negroes in twenty or thirty years was sufficient to educate the children in high-grade seminaries at home or abroad and to pro-vide marriage portions for the daughters."[12]

For those people and for their ancestors who built the system, there was no acceptable solution, and in this way they were no different from societies before or since.

"We none of us can expect the honours of state"

This is our vision of the city-state created in the late seventeenth and eigh-teenth centuries by men and women who for the most part came to America seeking opportunity. They quite frankly wanted to get rich, and some did and very quickly, which puts them squarely in the American mainstream—but with a peculiar twist. Within the lifetimes of the Revolutionary War generation, those who got rich because of brains, ability, drive, luck, the accident of birth, canny marriages, or combinations thereof came to be called aristocrats, and historians and writers of every political persuasion have commonly referred to the Low Country aristocracy. Let us, however, put this myth to rest. America has never had an aristocracy, only pretenders and strivers.[13]

The Low Country establishment, however, believed the fiction, and this led to a wrenching crisis between them and the mother country they loved and whose aristocracy they aped. For them rebellion made no economic sense. Their incredible prosperity was closely tied to the British mercantile system, and those ties went beyond the snug economic link. Many sons were sent to England at an early age for their education. Arthur Middleton (1742–1787), heir to a great Low Country fortune, spent nine years away attending Westminster School, Cambridge, and for his law studies Middle Temple. His friend William Henry Drayton—Charles Lee's "damned bad engineer"—his background interchangeable with Arthur Middleton's, his ancestry impeccable, his fortune assured, went to England when he was eleven to be educated at Westminster School and Balliol College, Oxford. While there he was looked after by another Rice King, Charles Pinckney and his wife Eliza Lucas Pinckney, who were living in Surrey supervising the English education of their own sons, Charles Cotesworth Pinckney and his brother Thomas. The brothers spent over sixteen years in England, yet returned home to serve steadfastly the cause of independence from Great Britain.[14]

After ten years in England, William Henry Drayton returned home and in March 1764 he married an heiress, Dorothy Golightly, who was even richer. In his political career he was more vocal than his friend Arthur Middleton. His views, over time, ran the gamut from a staunch defense of the rights of the Crown to flaming revolutionary ideology, and at no time was there doubt about where he stood. As a King's Friend he became so unpopular that he left again for England, where he was presented at court as a defender of British rights. As a Rice King, William Henry Drayton was at the top of the heap in South Carolina and accustomed to deference. In England he was just another colonial, and it has been suggested that he returned home in 1772 with the bitter taste reserved by the British aristocracy for colonials whatever their status at home.[15]

Back in South Carolina William Henry Drayton was appointed an assistant judge by his uncle, Lieutenant Governor William Bull. But he was enraged when he discovered that he was subject to being replaced by an Englishman. The same thing had happened to Charles Pinckney, who in the 1750s had been replaced as Chief Justice by an English appointee of the Crown. Such men were called placemen, English political hacks receiving patronage from English sponsors, a practice that was just one more nail in the coffin of the first British Empire. More than one Rice King spoke with bitterness of such appointments to the New Englander Josiah Quincy, Jr. "The council, judges, and other great officers are all appointed by mandamus from Great Britain," Quincy recorded in his journal entry of 25 March 1773. "Nay, even the clerk of the board, and assembly! Who are, and have been thus appointed. Persons disconnected with the people and obnoxious to them. I heard several planters say, 'We none of us can expect the honours of state; they are all given away, to worthless, poor sycophants.'"[16]

The men who in less than a century had achieved great wealth and most of its trappings seethed over such treatment and hankered after power in their own right. The causes of the American Revolution are beyond the scope of this book, but of the Rice Kings some explanation is required. Although various factors influence historical events of great consequence, a taproot usually exists, and we would not be led astray if we consider the observation made as early as 1681 by French planters on Guadalupe and Martinique. They asked permission of Colbert, Louis XIV's Minister for Finance, to trade with the English colonies: West Indian rum and molasses for New England provisions. In their plea to Colbert, they maintained that "the English who dwell near Boston will not worry themselves about the prohibition which the King of England may issue, because they hardly recognize his authority." (A good mercantilist, Colbert refused permission.)[17]

This growing apart, which eventually led to American insistence on self-government within the empire while the British were bent on tightening the screws of empire, was exacerbated in South Carolina by men who, presumably aside from their maker, came to recognize no authority but their own. Ten years before the Civil War, a writer in the *Constitutional Union* of Georgia found in them "an overweening pride of ancestry; a haughty defiance of all restraints not self-imposed; an innate hankering after power, and self opinionated assumption of supremecy." The speculation that William Henry Drayton bitterly resented his treatment in England and by placemen comes to mind when considering a conclusion by Frederick P. Bowes in his excellent study, *The Culture of Early Charleston* (1942): "Theirs was an intellectual decision, founded on their concepts of right and honor and the best interests of their class. Proud, cultivated, sensitive, they could not tolerate interference to accept the inferior status imposed on them by the British government. Rather than submit to this indignity they resolved to take up arms, fortified in their minds with the conviction that they were defending the inestimable Rights of Life, Liberty, and property."[18]

They may well have rationalized their deep attraction to the principles of liberty, their unswerving devotion to John Locke's words. Yet well before 1776 they had indeed attained that "overweening pride," that arrogance, that sense that they, having created the best of all possible worlds, were more capable than any other earthly power of managing their affairs.

But more than pride and arrogance are required to confront naked power unsheathed. The victory at Sullivan's Island in 1776 and the failure of the British in the intervening four years to challenge their control had left the Rice Kings complacent. But 3,000 miles away in London chancelleries, and far to the north at British headquarters in New York, plans were being made to humble these proud men. Beginning early in February 1780 and for the next three years they would be tested to their cores. For now we turn to the events leading to the siege of Charleston and the subsequent adventures of British and German soldiers in a land more forbidding than they had ever encountered.

3

Southern Strategy

A Logical Plan

On 11 February 1780 a powerful British fleet began landing troops on Simmons Island (now Seabrook Island), thirty miles south of Charleston. Two of the men who led them we met briefly four years before during the British debacle at Sullivan's Island. Lieutenant General Sir Henry Clinton, quarrelsome, neurotic, indecisive, commanded the combined naval and ground force. His second once again was the aggressive Lieutenant General Charles, Earl Cornwallis, thirsting for independent command, for fame and glory. The naval commander, Admiral Marriott Arbuthnot, was a sixty-eight-year-old curmudgeon who long before should have been put out to pasture. The grand campaign to subdue the South had begun in earnest.

Almost five years had elapsed since the "Shot heard Round the World" on Lexington Common. In the South an Indian war incited by British agents ravaged the frontier beginning in July 1776, but ended almost a year later with the proud Cherokee nation suing for peace, their towns burned, their food supplies destroyed, over 2,000 killed, most of their lands east of the Appalachians gone forever. Prominent in the campaign was a South Carolina militia commander of uncommon ability, Andrew Pickens of Long Cane Creek. He will become familiar to us as our story unfolds. But during the four years following Sullivan's Island the greater part of the South had been left relatively untouched. The North had seen the heavy fighting. Between the late summer and fall of 1776 the American army was decisively defeated at the Battle of Long Island, driven north from Manhattan, forced west of the Hudson, swept from New Jersey. George Washington's brilliant victories at Trenton and Princeton in the Christmas campaign of 1776 kept the Revolution alive and put the British on the defensive in New Jersey. But the American defeat in early September 1777 at the Battle of Brandywine opened the Rebel capital of Philadelphia to British occupation, and less than a month later, at Germantown, the Americans again engaged the army of Sir William Howe and again the British proved their superiority to the Rebel army in formal eighteenth-century combat. Yet during the few short weeks following Germantown an event occurred in northern New York that changed the nature of the war. At Saratoga in October 1777 General John Burgoyne surrendered a proud army of British and Hessian regulars. France, ever poised to exact revenge for the loss of Canada to the British, saw its chance and by January 1778 decided to ally itself with the American Rebels. For both sides it was a new war, for the Rebels a world in which they were no longer alone, for the British a world turned suddenly very hostile and in which more than thirteen rebellious colonies were at stake.

The Battle of Monmouth on 18 June 1778 had been the last major engagement in the North. Although minor engagements and a major campaign in New York against the Iroquois took place, the war had essentially stalemated there. But elsewhere for England it became ominous. War with France (June 1778), then Spain (June 1779), followed by Holland (January 1781) gradually stretched British resources: Gibraltar, Minorca, the Cape of Good Hope, India— enemies eventually beset England everywhere. It even feared invasion. France and Spain planned for it and readied an invasion fleet. The threat eventually came to naught but was yet another grave concern in London. Also engaging more than the casual attention of the King and his ministers were the fabulously rich sugar islands of the West Indies, then considered more valuable than the mainland colonies. Once France with its large navy entered the war cries for protection from the Sugar Kings and English merchants engaged in the sugar trade were heard clearly in London. There was also the possibility of picking off some of the French sugar islands. These were excellent reasons for looking south. Another was the conviction that became an obsession of the British government that the southern colonies contained vast numbers of loyal subjects who would rise once a powerful British army arrived. Had not Tory refugees thronging London bent ears far and wide at every opportunity with that message, delivered with a fervor only the dispossessed command? The ministers and their royal master were convinced. The archaic machinery of eighteenth-century government once more creaked into action. Operations were moved to the South. There, the script read, the British and their faithful American subjects would roll northward. One by one, South Carolina, North Carolina, Virginia would fall. The North, isolated, blockaded, besieged on all sides, would not be able to hold out.[1]

The British strategy had in common with other well-laid plans a cold, clear logic unencumbered by evidence.

A Fearful Voyage

The stage had been set for the Carolina campaign by the British capture of Savannah in 1778. The following year they successfully defended the city against a combined French and American force whose unexpected failure led to mutual recriminations between the allies. A little over two months later, on the day after Christmas 1779, ninety British troopships escorted by fourteen warships sailed past Sandy Hook out of New York Harbor, bound for Charleston and conquest. All the way the potential for disaster loomed over the 8,500 soldiers and 5,000 sailors. "It may be safely said," recorded Captain Johann Hinrichs of the Jäger Corps, in his diary, "that the most strenuous campaign cannot be as trying as such a voyage."[2]

The first storm struck on 27 December and ended on 30 December. On New Year's Day 1780 the wind turned northeast and became "stronger hour by hour," Hinrichs's fellow officer, Captain Johann Ewald, wrote in his journal. The ensuing storm lasted six days. Ewald described it. "On January 1 we saw several ships in the fleet which had lost some of their masts in the storm and appeared to be in distressed circumstances. Toward evening the second storm came up, combined with rain, hail, and snow, which continued in the most terrible manner until the forenoon of the 6th. The fleet had become separated in such a way that one could count only twenty sail in the farthest distance. Since the storm came out of the southeast and drove us toward land, the sailors were greatly worried about shipwrecks on the Great Bank of Cape Hatteras, which extends over thirty nautical miles into the ocean."[3]

On 7 January there was a small storm, and then on the 9th and 10th, off St. Augustine, where they had been driven by the winds, a tempest attended by a dreadful occurrence: all the cavalry and artillery horses, many suffering from broken legs, had to be thrown overboard. It must have been a scene out of Hades: men struggling on pitching decks to heave over the sides panicked, kicking horses, the screams of animals with broken legs.[4]

The storm dismasted ships. Some went down. One vessel packed with Hessian soldiers was driven all the way across the Atlantic to landfall in England. On 17 and 18 January four transports raised distress signals and the troops were taken off and distributed among other vessels. And just in time, for another storm arose on the 18th and raged for two days. It was during this storm that Captain Ewald saw a "ship with Hessian grenadiers . . . so close to ours that had not a big wave flung us a great distance away both ships would have collided and sunk, for no ship could help itself, since all sails were lowered with rudders tied down."[5]

By 24 January two-thirds of the fleet had reassembled. But they were in the Gulf Stream off Florida, well south of their goal. Sir Henry Clinton later wrote that the fleet was "almost beyond hope of being able to regain the American coast," and he blamed Admiral Marriott Arbuthnot: "Who can say I am not liberal with the old Admiral, when 'tis known that owing to his obstinacy that we got into the Gulf Stream, and our voyage was delayed, and we met with great losses."[6]

On 29 January, however, at 2:00 P.M., Captain Ewald was moved to recall Xenophon when a "sailor cried out from the mast, 'Land!' I do not believe that the Ten Thousand Greeks, when they beheld the Black Sea after their difficult retreat through Asia, could have been more joyful over the sight of the sea than we were over the word 'Land!' Every face brightened."[7]

There were a few more anxious days, especially during a dense fog on 31 January, but on 1 February 1780, "about four o'clock in the afternoon," wrote Ewald, "we caught sight with true joy the lighthouse of Tybee on the coast of Georgia. Toward six o'clock in the evening a large part of the fleet anchored safely in the mouth of the Savannah River, where to our joy we found over eighteen sail of the fleet which we had given up for lost. On the 3d I visited several of my good friends on board their ships to hear some news."[8]

But the fleet and the army still had to get to Charleston. Sir Henry Clinton was not enthusiastic about once more risking his army at sea, which "excited in me no small dread of being again driven from the land." He preferred proceeding by inland waterways. But at a council of war his second in command, Lord Cornwallis, as well as a majority of the other officers present, spoke strongly against Clinton's proposal, and Clinton bowed to their advice. The dismounted cavalry, whose horses had become shark food, and 1,400 infantry under Brigadier General James Paterson were put ashore to mount a diversion via Augusta, a little over 100 miles northwest of Savannah, before rejoining the main force. With Paterson were the boy cavalry commander, Lieutenant Colonel Banastre Tarleton; and a favorite of Clinton's, Major Patrick Ferguson, an officer of Fraser's Highlanders (71st Foot) detached to command northern Tory regulars, the American Volunteers. The fleet would sail up the coast. Arbuthnot proposed a landing at a point closer to Charleston than Clinton and a naval officer, Captain George Elphinstone, who knew the coastal waters, thought wise, as Arbuthnot's destination would have kept the fleet at sea longer. Clinton yearned to get his army on dry land. Arbuthnot was either persuaded or overruled in favor of a landing on Simmons Island.[9]

The fleet left Savannah on 9 February and that night anchored off Trench Island (today Hilton Head). The next night it anchored off Hunting Island. On the 11th the delicate part of the operation began, and it was out of the hands of Arbuthnot, Clinton, Cornwallis, and all the other senior officers. They were dependent on a thirty-four-year-old naval officer whose professional skills were exceeded only by his coolness under pressure.[10]

Captain George Keith Elphinstone (1746–1823) was born at Elphinstone Tower near Stirling, Scotland, fifth son of the 10th Lord Elphinstone. He had a long career, beginning at age fifteen when he entered the navy, encompassing the American Revolution, the wars of the French Revolution, and the Napoleonic Wars. He became an admiral famous in his time, in 1801 was made Baron Keith of Stonehaven Marischal, and in 1814 a Viscount. The judgment on Keith is that he was a good commander, solid, but not great. Yet he had an attribute that rests with the gods, and raises very competent people like Keith well above the herd: as captain and admiral he had the reputation of being lucky. A military man can ask for little more, for all who follow Mars know that without it brilliance means nothing. And Keith made few serious errors of judgment in a series of momentous enterprises carried out over several years, including the capture of the Cape of Good Hope from the Dutch.

Both Clinton and Captain Ewald left good descriptions of Elphinstone's feat in navigating the very tricky North Edisto inlet to a safe anchorage off Simmons Island. "The transports," wrote Clinton, "having got into North Edisto harbor without accident . . . very fortunately escaped a violent tempest that succeeding night, whereby the expedition might have been defeated had we been again entangled with the Gulf Stream, which would have been certainly the case had the admiral persisted in his first design. For this piece of good fortune we were indebted to Captain Elphinstone's zealous and animated exertions, as also to his perfect acquaintance with all the island navigation of the Carolina coast, which enabled him to run the ships boldly up that difficult channel, which a person of less knowledge and decision of those matters would probably not have hazarded." The job took Elphinstone from noon until almost evening. Captain Ewald wrote that "Although the mouth of this harbor is so narrow that only two ships at a time can wind through the sandbars, Captain Elphinstone guided the entire fleet through safely."[11]

Lieutenant General Sir Henry Clinton had arrived on the threshold of his great opportunity: the fleet safely at anchorage, unopposed landings on 11 and 12 February, thirty miles north the richest city in America.

Sir Henry Clinton

We met Sir Henry briefly during the Battle of Sullivan's Island, where his role, largely passive, and his mistake in not carrying out proper reconnaissance prior to landing his troops, were both uncharacteristic of him. Now, four years later, no longer deputy but commander in chief, also on this occasion commanding in the field, he launched a ground campaign that began with gradual envelopment and the formal tactics of eighteenth-century siege warfare and ended in a savage civil war echoed in the cries and lamentations of widows and orphans on both sides and the despair of the dispossessed. Given the critical nature of the campaign and the intriguing personality of Sir Henry Clinton, we should take a closer look at the man.[12]

He was of ancient lineage. One branch of his family was ennobled in the thirteenth century. He was the grandson of the 6th Earl of Lincoln and the son of Admiral George Clinton, who became a Royal Governor of New York. His first cousin and patron was the 2nd Duke of Newcastle. Not rich but well born and able, and very well connected, for young Henry Clinton the world was a far friendlier and more promising place than for the great majority of his compatriots. The emphasis placed on Clinton's aristocratic ancestry is as deliberate as the system that was his birthright. The British officer corps of that day, and continuing until the debacle of the Crimean War (1854–1856) forced gradual reform, comprised almost exclusively a very small minority of aristocrats and gentry. The admission of men of common origin was rare. Pay was minimal, a mere "honorarium," hardly changing from the establishment of the purchase

Sir Henry Clinton by A.H. Ritchie, 1777.
Engraving. (Collection of The New-York Historical Society.)

system in 1683 until its abolishment in 1870. An officer purchased his initial commission and all subsequent ranks through full colonel. Prices were steep and increased as he went upward. Seniority and ability were not factors. It was a system that effectively kept out men without means and reserved the corps, especially its upper ranks, for the tiny class that ruled Britain. On the face of it the system was iniquitous and has been held up to ridicule, especially when connected with blunders by men whose ignorance was exceeded only by their arrogance. In the course of our story we will meet American commanders superior to their counterparts in the British Army, but the rank of sergeant was the most they could have expected in that army. Yet defenders observe that the purchase system produced England's two greatest captains, Marlborough and Wellington. Under it the British expelled France from North America, and after losing the real jewel in the crown to the Americans went on to conquer an even wider empire as well as to play a decisive role in the downfall of Napoleon.[13]

This was the privileged world into which Henry Clinton was born on 16 April 1730. We know nothing of his childhood. When his father was appointed Governor of New York, the entire family went with him to the New World, where the boy was commissioned in one of the Independent Companies that were detached from British regiments to serve in the colonies. He served briefly at the fortress of Louisburg in Nova Scotia, and nearby had a narrow escape

when his party was ambushed by French and Indians. For a lad with military ambitions, however, prospects were far more certain at the center, not the periph-
ery, of empire. Two years after his return to England he was commissioned in the
Coldstream Guards. Seven years later he became a Lieutenant Colonel in the 1st
Foot Guards (later the Grenadier Guards). In 1760 he went with his regiment to
Germany to fight in the Seven Years War. He served with gallantry and distinction, was chosen aide-de-camp to Prince Charles of Brunswick, and was severely
wounded at Johannesburg. In the same year he became a full colonel.

In 1772 Sir Henry Clinton was promoted to Major General and also elected
to Parliament. His life and career seemed ever upward. Then, after five years
and five children, eight days after the birth of their daughter Harriet, Clinton's
twenty-six-year-old wife, Harriet Carter Clinton, passed to her reward. He was
devastated. He retreated into a shell from which his friends tried in vain to free
him. He even risked offending his patron, the Duke of Newcastle, by not taking his seat in Parliament. His best friend, Major General William Phillips, believed there was more to Clinton's behavior than mourning a dead wife, and he
wrote to Sir Henry with the candor of a man who cared deeply for the welfare
of a close friend. "Whenever you wish to turn the course of your affliction into
any other channel, you deviate, in my opinion from that very nice and delicate
affection that you had for Mrs. Clinton, and to the natural and praiseworthy
sorrow for her loss. To lose the melancholy soothings of sighs and tears in re-
searches after things of no concern or consequence to her dead or you living is
to lose the tribute due her virtues in an inexprimable maze of error; and I must
think that you injure her memory whenever you have other reflections but such
as arise from having lost her."[14]

Phillips concluded: "Quit all vain notions, and be the man of sense and resolution. I mean of sense and resolution to throw off every unseemly way of
thinking. I do not desire you to cease grieving. It would be inhuman in me to
desire it, and it would be unfeeling and unjust in you not to have grief of the
most serious and poignant kind. All I seek is to draw your sorrows to the only
real point, that sensible and full concern you must necessarily feel at the death
of your wife."

For two years Clinton ignored his responsibilities and the entreaties of
friends. In April 1774 he left England for the Balkans in the company of four
men, including his old if improbable friend, a man well known in his time,
Henry Humphrey Evans Lloyd, historian, soldier of fortune, and quite possibly
a British spy. Lloyd was then a general in the Russian army and traveled with
four Russian servants. Clinton, whose well-developed sense of humor appeared
when he was not burdened with responsibility, thought his friend resembled a
sergeant major in charge of a Russian recruiting party. He left a journal of the
trip, and in it revealed his strong attraction to both man-made and natural landscapes, the "old castles, small farms, villages, hermitages, mills; shrubbery, woods
all in bloom; all sorts of birds in high song, nightingales in every bush—a most
enchanting scene."

The party reached Vienna on 14 May, and by June was making its way through the wild lands of Transylvania and Wallachia, where Clinton found the mountaineers "much more savage than my friends the Indians." On 19 June they reached their destination, the main Russian army camp in Bulgaria. In his splendid biography of Clinton, William Willcox describes the hazardous 2,500-mile journey, ostensibly undertaken to observe the Russian army in action against the Turks, as "bizarre," its real reason to find release from the troubles at home. I agree with the latter opinion, but instead of "bizarre" I find the very idea of the journey exhilarating as well as reasonable. It is not an uncommon human trait to seek relief from despondency, whatever its cause, by going far away, even if the journey promises to be perilous. Indeed, peril can be the magnet. Professor Willcox also places great emphasis on Phillips's letters to Clinton, indicating that something other than the death of his wife was gnawing at the man, something dark, "unseemly." But we lack any clue as to what it might have been. Certainly, Phillips's opinions cannot be ignored, for he was close to Clinton and an eyewitness to his behavior. But does Willcox place too little emphasis on Clinton's grief for his dead wife? He would not be the first surviving spouse to sink into a deep and prolonged period of inability to cope with normal everyday activity. And was Clinton's behavior "more intense than the mores of his time and class condoned," as Willcox maintains?[15] Lord Cornwallis, a fellow aristocrat not burdened with Clinton's introspective nature, was so shattered by the death of his wife that he fled England to fight in a war he did not believe in.

If Clinton took the trip to recover from his malaise, it worked. He returned to England in September 1774 and plunged into political and military affairs. Two years later he sailed for Boston. His traveling companions, like Clinton better known today in America than in their homeland, were Major General Sir William Howe and Major General John Burgoyne. Howe and Burgoyne, especially the latter, are better known than Clinton, yet he was superior to both in intelligence and as a tactician, and proved to be the only British general in America to have a strategic grasp of the conflict.

At two famous actions prior to launching the southern campaign in 1780, Clinton revealed his preference for flanking movements and for cutting off the enemy's possibility of retreat by fixing the foe between two strong forces. He recommended the latter at the Battle of Bunker Hill, proposing to land a detachment behind the American fortifications to support the main force commanded by Sir William Howe. Had General Thomas Gage, then Commander in Chief, accepted the advice the British probably would have been spared their appalling casualties before prevailing. As Sir William Howe's deputy during the British attack on New York, Clinton planned the flank march that fooled Washington and ended with the American army trapped on Brooklyn Heights. Clinton's performance at Sullivan's Island was an aberration. His second appearance at Charleston looked to be vintage Clinton, thus the indirect approach of landing the army unopposed thirty miles south of Charleston. But he still faced a long approach march through difficult terrain, and at the end of it he would have to engage in one of the most perilous military maneuvers—moving his army across a body of water in hostile territory where a sizeable enemy force lurked. A look at the map on page 50 reveals the difficulties Clinton faced, and the opportunities presented to the American commander, General Benjamin Lincoln, who surely would take advantage of them. The city he defended was at the end of a narrow peninsula, which could be cut by siege fortifications while the tricky sea approach was blockaded by the enemy fleet. Thus it defied common sense to allow an enemy army to make its approach march relatively unmolested and gradually seal all avenues of escape. Surely the American general would not permit that to happen?

4

The Approach March

A *"famous Jäger Captain"*

"What a land to wage war in!" The reaction of Captain Johann Hinrichs to the terrain on Simmons Island was understandable, and he spoke for his comrades, German and British. ("What a land to plunder!" Hinrichs might say if he could return today, for Simmons, renamed Seabrook, has gone the way of Hilton Head and Kiawah: sanitized, anesthetized, manicured, it slumbers in such splendid seclusion that if in our time Sir Henry Clinton appeared with his army he would have to apply to a property owner for a pass in order to disembark his troops.) These were men who had for the most part campaigned on the well-tended plains of northern Europe, where agriculture had been practiced for centuries and the groomed landscape even today makes many long-settled parts of North America seem raw and wild.

Grenadiers, English and Hessian, and the 33rd Foot were put ashore on the evening of 11 February, the first day of the landings. Clinton and Cornwallis went with them. Captain Peter Russell wrote in his journal that "a Gale of Wind came on this Evening from the North East accompanied with Rain so that it was lucky we got in as we did." He also revealed that "some of the troops lost their way in the woods and the Genl lay under a Tree in the rain." The following day Hinrichs described "a column making its way through a wilderness of deep sand, marshland, and inpenetrable woods where human feet had never trod! Even Elphinstone, our guide, led us two miles out of our way. Sometimes we had to struggle, singly or two abreast, through marsh and woodland for half a mile." Where impeccably clad joggers now frown suspiciously at strangers, Captain Ewald described a seven-hour march "through a pathless and marshy wood, which continued with the greatest difficulty until five o'clock in the evening. A path often had to be cut through the bushes with axes and bayonets in water up to the waist." At midnight Ewald and his men had to move again, over a mile, where "We had nothing but stinking water." Even at that time of year his comrade Hinrichs had complained earlier in Georgia, "a German, accustomed to a colder climate, finds the heat nearly intolerable." And to European eyes a gloom pervaded the landscape that Ewald ascribed to Spanish moss, which fascinated them. "The trees are covered with a sort of moss which hangs down from the highest point over all branches like horses' tails. This phenomenon absorbed our complete attention because of its rarity, giving a very melancholy appearance to a forest." But Captain Ewald strongly approved of Clinton's choice of that wild, forbidding island on which to land his army. "By this maneuver . . . the enemy had been deceived in such a manner that we did not find a single man of the American army in this area. For no one, either in the countryside or in the army, had believed that any person would think of landing in this area and marching toward Charleston from this side." The question remained: how quickly would the Americans react?[1]

On the British side, the best account of the siege of Charleston, including the approach march, is the diary kept by Captain Johann Ewald (1744–1813) of the Field Jäger Corps from the German principality of Hesse-Hanau. Jägers (Jäger is German word for hunter), were elite light troops who could move quickly in open formations over broken country, much in the manner of modern infantry. They were mostly, and ideally, raised from men who earned their living in the outdoors: hunters, game wardens, and foresters who were experienced in fieldcraft and weapons before recruitment. They were armed with short German rifles instead of muskets, and as marksmen many were equal to the famed American riflemen. The Jägers' overall numbers in America never exceeded 700. They usually operated in detachments assigned to reconnaissance missions, patrols, headquarter guards, and foraging parties. In large battles and on the march they maneuvered as skirmishers ahead of the main body or on the flanks and as the rear guard covering retreats. During sieges they occupied the forward trenches.

The "famous Jäger Captain" and diarist, Johann Ewald, was an excellent troop leader and an interesting man. Born in Cassel of a bookkeeper and a merchant's daughter, he entered the Hessian service as a cadet at the age of sixteen and remained on active duty for fifty-six years. He saw hard service against the French in the Seven Years War. The following fourteen years were spent in garrison duties, studying military science, and publishing his first military treatise. At the age of twenty-six he almost died because he was young and hot-blooded. "Merry and glad, I went with a few good friends to one of the best inns in Cassel, called the 'Hof von England.' We greatly enjoyed supper—but alas!—the excellent wine made us fly into a passion; we started arguing, and I immediately fought a duel with one of my friends outside the inn in the darkness. I was severely wounded—I lost my left eye. No sooner was I hit than we all came to our senses. I swam in blood, while my friends shed tears." He endured "three extremely painful operations," and over a year passed before he could leave his room with one good eye and one of glass. Many years later his son wrote, "The saber cut by which he lost his left eye and the black ribbon he always wore after the American War suited him well, augmenting his soldier-like appearance." In 1774 Ewald was promoted to Captain in the Life Jäger Corps. This "amazed the nobles," his son noted, for Ewald was a commoner, and although there were more openings for talent in continental armies than in Britain's, the accident of birth also made a big difference there, especially for appointments to elite units. Two years later he sailed for America and went into action almost immediately and thereafter participated in several hot engagements. In larger actions Ewald led the van of Cornwallis's column that enveloped Washington's right wing at Brandywine, and served with equal distinction at Monmouth. Everywhere he went he entered in his diary clear, detailed, candid, and reliable accounts of what he did and what he saw. What a pity that he was ordered back to New York in May 1780, and therefore did not accompany Cornwallis on His Lordship's grand adventure.

After the war Ewald returned to Hesse-Cassel and was twice denied promotion because he was not of noble birth. In 1788, a forty-four-year-old captain, despairing of promotion in his homeland, he entered Danish service, was appointed lieutenant colonel, and in 1790 was ennobled and became Johann von Ewald. He served his adopted country well during the Napoleonic Wars and became a national hero. A student of war as well as a most able practitioner, Ewald wrote eight books and became one of the most important military writers of his time. *Treatise on Partisan Warfare* (1785) was praised by Frederick the Great; and *Treatise on the Service of Light Troops* (1790) was translated into English and used by Major General Sir John Moore, who is credited as the originator of modern light infantry training, to help train British troops for the Peninsula War. The "famous Jäger Captain" ended a Royal Danish Lieutenant General and Commanding General of the Duchy of Holstein. His son left the best measure of him. "Though his military talents were excellent, he himself did not think much of them. He ventured only to think of himself as an experienced officer of light troops, an able detachment commander, and, at the utmost, a general capable of commanding the vanguard of an army." What refreshing candor. It will be even more appreciated as we observe the careers of men who combined lesser talents with swollen egos.[2]

Captain Johann Ewald served in the vanguard as the British army in South Carolina began its circuitous approach to Charleston. Unless otherwise noted, the quotations that follow are from his diary.

Early on the morning of 14 February, the Jägers and the 33rd Foot, Lieutenant Colonel James Webster commanding, set out in search of Stono Ferry, the crossing point on the Stono River from Johns Island to James Island. We will meet on several occasions the 33rd Regiment of Foot (today the Duke of Wellington's West Riding Regiment) and its very able and gallant commander. The colonel of the 33rd under the purchase system was Lord Cornwallis himself, but the field commander was Webster, regarded by Ewald as a "very meritorious man." Sergeant Roger Lamb, who saw wide service in the American War and left excellent accounts, praised the 33rd Foot as "exceedingly well disci-

Lieutenant General Johann von Ewald. Painting by
C.A. Jensen, after a drawing by H.J. Aldenrath.
(Det Nationalhistoriske Museum
på Frederiksborg, Hillerød.)

plined, by that able disciplinarian, Colonel Webster. . . . I never witnessed any regiment that excelled it in discipline and military experience." Webster's force did not have a map and the inhabitants, especially the men, had left and "spies and guides were very scarce," Ewald reported. They found a black boy of eleven or twelve who knew the way, but he "spoke such a poor dialect that he was extremely hard to understand." The boy undoubtedly spoke the gullah dialect of the Low Country blacks. Webster's force made its way across the island until about noon it reached a "stone and log causeway that ran zigzag through an inpenetrable morass without its end being visible." Ewald took their young guide whom they barely understood and led an advance guard of a corporal and eight Jägers and marched down the causeway. When will we reach the Stono River? they asked the boy. "Soon, soon." A half hour later they saw ahead of them "high ground and several houses. We asked . . . whether the elevated land and the houses lay on this side of the river or on the other, but no one could understand his gibberish." They soon found to their discomfort that what they saw was on the other side of the river, that the "houses were fortified and occupied with men and guns, and that a line of troops, foot and horse, had deployed be-hind them at some distance." They were suddenly, and unexpectedly, within rifle shot of the Americans.

Captain Ewald admitted that "Each of us silently wished to get out of this affair with honor, but we were in column on a narrow causeway between im-passable morasses that formed the right bank of the Stono River, which sepa-rated us from the enemy. In this situation it depended upon the enemy to shoot us to pieces." Colonel Webster reacted quickly. He ordered the column to about face and march out of range. The Americans simply watched, not firing a shot, and "we certainly didn't want to fire any!" When the Jägers and the British were safe, they "laughed heartily, and were astonished over the strange behavior of the enemy. In such circumstances, I have usually found that good luck does not desert the bold, but generally punishes the fainthearted or those who lose their heads."

Captain Ewald's next move may have been encouraged by the failure of the Americans to take advantage of the perilous situation of Webster's command. Some Jägers told him they had seen vessels on the river, which Ewald thought might be galleys propelled by oars, placed there for defense since the Americans knew the British would have to cross in that area. He decided to reconnoiter, hoping to "render a service to the Commander in Chief." Taking Lieutenant Jo-hann Ernst von Wintzingerode with him, he rode back to within rifle shot and waved a handkerchief at the Americans. Several American officers "took off their hats and caps and gave us a countersignal, which I accepted in good faith." The two Germans rode to the riverbank and engaged the Americans in con-versation across the river. Ewald's pretext was that he had noticed the uniform of the Pulaski Corps and wondered whether a man named Leopold, whom he had known in Saxony, was with them. All the time his eyes took in everything. The Jägers had been mistaken. The only vessel was a half-burned galley. "Jok-ingly, we wished to see each other soon, and I bid them adieu. They politely warned us to be careful, because this river was full of alligators, some of which were twelve to sixteen feet long."

Clinton and Cornwallis arrived early the next morning. "I took pleasure in telling them about my discovery of yesterday, and my daring little enterprise was amply rewarded by the approbation of the Commander in Chief." That night the Americans silently abandoned their position. Ewald reported that "Clinton ordered the 1st Battalion of the Light Infantry to cross at Waite's plantation with the aid of several small boats that had been dragged with great effort over-land to Stono River from Bohicket Creek, for we still had no contact with the fleet." The boats were then rowed to Stono Ferry and the Jägers and the 33rd Foot crossed. The British were across the Stono, on James Island, and not a shot had been fired by the defenders of Charleston.

Now that he was across one river, Clinton needed intelligence, a labor force to build fortifications, and food for the army. Three days after the crossing the Jägers were dispatched in three parties for these purposes. Each had black guides, but German-accented English on one side and gullah on the other did not afford much intelligible communication. Captain Ewald led one party and was again introduced to the pleasures of traversing Low Country terrain. "On my way I was obliged to cross three creeks with marshy banks where the inhabitants had removed all the bridges, and I was compelled to wade through water over my navel. I had one hundred jägers and left a few behind at each creek to secure my withdrawal. A short distance behind the last creek I found a plantation from which all the people had fled except an aged woman, who trembled and begged forbearance for her life." Nearby a house servant was captured who "agreed quite sensibly" to tell what he knew of the whereabouts of the American forces. What he told them, through either design or ignorance, was largely wrong. He said that "General Lincoln had an encampment with five thousand men behind Cox Swamp, and that General Moultrie, with two thousand men, had occupied the works of Charlestown and Sullivan's Island; secondly, that another corps was stationed at a fortification which had been thrown up at Ashley Ferry on the left bank [the Charleston side] of the Ashley River." Lincoln was actually at his headquarters in Charleston with about 2,500 men; and on that very day Moultrie had been ordered to Bacon's Bridge, twenty-two miles north of Charleston on the British side of the river where, four days later, he reported a total strength of 606 men, horse, and foot: the French volunteer Chevalier Pierre-François Vernier commanding the cavalry, Colonel Francis Marion the infantry. What was true, and would prove of special interest to Sir Henry Clinton, was the presence of Americans behind fortifications at Ashley Ferry, on the Charleston side of the Ashley River. Ewald took the black house servant back to camp with him to relate what he knew to the general officers.[3]

While the British plodded forward, the Americans watched them. Moultrie optimistically reported to Lincoln that "The rains have filled our rivers and swamps so much, that it is almost impossible for the enemy to drag their cannon and artillery stores along. I think they cannot pass this way." On 25 February he related information to Lincoln that revealed British plans in general. "I was informed by several persons, that 90 flat-bottomed boats and canoes went down Stono, towards the Cut a few days ago." The question remained. When and where would the boats reappear for the assault on the peninsula?[4]

Clinton left nothing to chance on this, his second try at Charleston. Several days were spent building fortifications at Stono Ferry in order to control the entire Stono River and support the next leapfrog, from James Island to the mainland, and also repel the expected attack by General Lincoln. The fortifications were finished on 24 February, and the next day Lord Cornwallis brought his corps across the Stono onto James Island. On the 26th, "several officers of the 7th and 23rd regiments of the Clarke Brigade begged General Leslie to allow them to go out on patrol to share the glory of the service with the light troops." Early that day fifty men under three officers went out to "collect Negroes and livestock, if any were still left."

Captain Ewald described the reaction of the Americans. "The Chevalier Vernier was informed at once by the country people, who were devoted to him, while they hated us from the bottom of their hearts because we carried off their

Negroes and livestock. After he had observed these people for a long time, marching like a changing of the guard, Vernier followed alongside them on their return march until they were inside the narrow approaches between the ponds. Since they had not seen or heard anything of the enemy on their way out, they marched back in all tranquillity and without formation. Suddenly Vernier attacked them on all sides and killed or wounded nearly half of these people, who had their impertinent and unskilled officers to thank for their misfortune."

The Jägers rushed to the rescue of their British comrades. They got there just in time, a hot fire fight developed, and Vernier withdrew. British carelessness had cost ten dead and nine wounded. Ewald claimed that "we surely killed and wounded just as many of the enemy," but he had no bodies to prove it, although seven prisoners were taken. The Americans had finally drawn blood, and probably taught the British a valuable lesson about warfare in the Low Country marshes and swamps. It was a small but nasty fight of the kind that would characterize the southern campaign, the only difference being that it was fought by regulars on both sides. It is also an interesting fight because it lends credence to the myth that the British army spent the war blundering through the North American wilderness as if on parade. There is just enough truth to it to feed the myth and keep it alive, but, when necessary, British and German infantry regiments of the line could and did adapt to forest fighting, as we will see in the bloody finale to our story.[5]

By 1 March the British had become "masters of James Island," and two days later the 1st Battalion of Light Infantry crossed the Wappoo Cut and established itself on the mainland. The bridge across the cut was repaired. The bloody skirmishing with Major Pierre-François Vernier's 1st Cavalry of the Pulaski Legion continued. But slowly, steadily, Sir Henry Clinton brought his army forward in well-planned stages. He has been criticized for the slowness of his approach, but the Sullivan's Island debacle must have been constantly in mind. The second attempt at Charleston was completely his show, and he was obviously determined not to fail.

He also had on his hands an admiral he disliked and distrusted, who had not yet brought the fleet across the bar to complete the naval blockade of the city. And any day might bring a major challenge from General Benjamin Lincoln and his Continentals. On 10 March Lord Cornwallis led his strong corps onto the mainland. The Hessian Grenadiers secured the bridge over the Wappoo Cut and the other units were dispersed to various stations to establish strongpoints. On the 11th a welcome sight appeared, especially for the light troops, who had been campaigning for a month in terrain more severe than most of them had ever experienced. "A number of ordnance, supply, and transport ships entered the Stono River and anchored in the bay where the Wappoo Canal joins the Stono River, whereupon it was made known to the army that it was to fill all its needs from there. It was high time, too, for we Jaegers had almost nothing left on our bodies and on our feet." This reminds us that the importance of logistics to regular armies cannot be overestimated. Food, clothing, ammunition: without replacement the army would eventually just stop, unable to proceed. And forage for horses that carried men and pulled artillery and wagons was as important then as gas and oil and spare parts are in our time. Supply was a continual, often serious, problem for both armies wherever they campaigned in America, and in the Carolinas in the years 1780 to 1781 it eventually became critical.[6]

Meanwhile, the skirmishing continued. On 12 March, Ewald wrote, Colonel "Abercromby . . . ordered me to march on ahead with forty jagers and lie in ambuscade along the road. But the enemy did not follow further than rifle-shot range of the ambuscade. I waited all night without having had a drink of water the whole day in the oppressive heat, and withdrew to the camp in complete silence." That final sentence in its spare simplicity speaks volumes for soldiers throughout the ages. Tired, thirsty, frustrated troops, after a night of tension lying in silent ambush, returning as silently to surroundings they no doubt cursed. "We do not have the most pleasant area for our post. The wood which surrounds us is full of wolves, snakes, and various poisonous insects, but they keep away from us because of our large night fire. During my strolls I discovered alligators from ten to twelve feet long in a deep, marshy pond which connects with the Wappoo and thus with the Ashley River." As the season progressed mosquitoes would become a constant plague, especially near water. Anyone who has encountered Low Country mosquitoes will testify that they are without exaggeration bigger, faster, and meaner than northern mosquitoes: in the words of a British officer, "a greater plague than there can be in hell itself."[7]

Middleton Place and Drayton Hall

At the point where Wappoo Creek flows into the Ashley, the British used black labor gangs, as was the custom of both armies, to build a triangular fortification opposite the southern fortifications of Charleston. There ten artillery pieces were mounted to shell American ships and the fortifications on the opposite shore. Just north of the site the old Ashley River Road still follows the right bank. Two years before the British took it the Massachusetts Rebel Elkanah Watson wrote: "The road to Ashley River is delightful. We passed many elegant seats, with fine gardens and grounds. The road, in some places, is shaded with lofty trees, from which we were sweetly serenaded with the music of beautiful birds. . . .

"On this river are situated the choicest plantations, and the most elegant and numerous country-seats in the State. The extensive marshes, bordering upon this and adjacent streams, had recently been converted into highly productive rice plantations, for which they are well adapted." Of the "choicest plantations" and "most elegant" seats passed by Elkanah Watson only two, Middleton Place and Drayton Hall, remain in their original magnificence, but they rank among the finest historical sites in America. Both knew the solid tread of our "famous Jäger Captain," both have much to tell us about the Rice Kings, and one figured prominently in British plans for the march to Charleston.[8]

On 22 March General Alexander Leslie led the van consisting of the Jägers, the 33rd Foot, and the light infantry on the road toward Drayton Hall and Middleton Place. When the column arrived at the bridge crossing St. Andrew's Creek American artillery fire greeted them. Leslie decided against a frontal assault and asked the intrepid Jäger Captain "whether I would not attempt to cross a little further up the creek, which would force the enemy to leave his post." Captain Ewald answered for professional soldiers of all armies in all wars. "Who would say 'No' if he thinks of distinguishing himself? I accepted the offer. I was permitted to select fifty jägers, supported by the worthy Captain [Charles] Boyd, my close friend, with three companies of light infantry. We took a detour through the woods and about seven o'clock in the evening reached and crossed the creek, which was no deeper than three feet. But we found a swamp on the other side a good half hour wide, which was so muddy and deep that many of our men sank in up to their chests. Meanwhile Fortuna and Bellona did not let us sink. The enemy, who could have destroyed us here because we were dispersed and every man was compelled to work his way through the swamp, abandoned his post to us. We had only a small skirmish with his rear guard and two wounded."9

The next morning "Captain Boyd and I received orders to try to get to Drayton's house." The reference was to Drayton Hall, a Georgian mansion on the British side of the Ashley. They had no cavalry to scout and act as a buffer against a superior enemy force or an ambush, but they met only a small party of horsemen that kept its distance. "Toward noon we reached the zoological garden of Drayton's plantation, where we took post and were now out of danger." They had reached not Drayton Hall but the present site of Magnolia Gardens. In 1780 it was a plantation that had been owned by the Draytons since 1671. There they met Dorothy Drayton and asked her "to refresh our hungry souls with bread and wine, which she gladly did, and in return for which she received a *savvegarde*," a safeguard, or safe conduct, to protect her from being molested. Dorothy Drayton was more than the mistress of Drayton Plantation. She was the wife of William Henry Drayton, the notorious Rebel whom Charles Lee had called a "damned bad engineer."10

The Jägers were joined at dawn the next day by General Leslie and the light infantry, and again Ewald and his men were sent out in advance of the main party. Leslie "ordered us to shoulder arms and advance to Middleton's plantation to reconnoiter the area and the banks of the Ashley River, and to collect Negroes, forage, and cattle." Their immediate object, Middleton Place, was the site of a garden that is the only original eighteenth-century landscape garden left in the United States. It was begun in 1741 by Henry Middleton, of the third generation of Middletons to live in America. He was assisted by an unknown English gardener. Others were also involved. One hundred slaves labored ten years to create the vision. If the Jägers had approached the garden on the main axis of the triangle that enclosed it, they would have walked across the greensward, flanked by pollarded crepe myrtles, around the great house (burned in 1865) to a bluff a quarter of a mile above the river. From the bluff the land gently descended over six terraces of lawns to delicate twin butterfly lakes divided by a grass walkway. Just beyond, the Ashley River flowed in a line that pointed directly at the house, the canal so vital to a garden inspired by the principles of the French master and creator of Versailles, André Le Nôtre, but this one natural and lifegiving. From his vantage point Captain Ewald would have been able to look for signs of Rebel presence on the broad brown savannahs that stretched out on either side of the Ashley. But given his responsibilities in the van of the army, for which he and his men acted as eyes and ears, he probably did not dwell on the importance of Middleton Place in documenting the rise of the society of the Rice Kings in eight short decades from raw frontier to a magnificent formal French garden.[11]

The heir to this splendid estate was the radical revolutionary Arthur Middleton, friend and neighbor of a fellow radical, William Henry Drayton, whose father owned a few miles downriver a country seat called Drayton Hall, begun in 1738 and finished in 1742. Then surrounded by outbuildings, including a solar-heated orangerie to protect citrus trees during cold snaps, the great brick house, noble in its classical severity, is thought by some to be the country's best early Georgian house. It most certainly was another triumph of a new class aspiring to unrivalled position and power.[12]

In late March 1780, however, aspirations were no substitute for big battalions, and like Johann Ewald the man with the big battalions had more immediate concerns than with what these pseudo baronies represented. Sir Henry Clinton had decided that Drayton Hall was the key place for the next step in the British army's slow but inexorable march on the citadel of the Rice Kings.

5

Charleston Besieged

The Noose Tightens

Fog shrouded the Ashley on the morning of 29 March 1780. The wind was from the southeast. In the darkness of the early hours, on flat dark waters where eyes could not see, twenty-two flatboats escorted by armed galleys glided silently upstream. The oars were muffled. The Americans waiting at Ashley Ferry with artillery behind triple breastworks to challenge a British crossing heard nothing. The flatboats passed by, steadily, silently, to a secret rendezvous, the landing at Drayton Hall five miles upstream. The troops had been gathered the previous afternoon at Drayton's plantation. They were the elite of the army. Light infantry and Jägers, English and Hessian Grenadiers, Clarke's English Brigade, Webster's crack 33rd Foot, Fraser's Highlanders, a troop of 17th Light Dragoons, and the field artillery. The Jägers and the light infantry made up the assault party, and the resourceful Elphinstone was there to direct the landings. Lord Cornwallis commanded.[1]

"One hour before daylight the army set out to Drayton's landing place, where several armed ships and a number of flatboats were lying in line along the right bank to transport the troops to the left bank," wrote Captain Ewald. At first light the troops boarded. Captain Peter Russell recorded that "This important event was effected without giving the least alarm with the Boats, or suffering the least opposition in our landings."[2] By 8 o'clock, Captain Ewald wrote, the "light infantry and the jägers climbed up the left bank of the Ashley River at Benjamin Fuller's plantation, opposite Drayton's house. The river here forms a full bend, and this plantation was situated on elevated ground. Some distance away several groups of horsemen and a number of riflemen appeared, who honored us with a few rifle shots; without any damage, however. They seemed to be observing rather than hindering us.

"The light infantry spread out beyond the plantation in the shape of a crescent, which became larger as the troops increased. The three jäger divisions, under their captains, had to advance to the center and select their positions at both ends of the crescent, and as the crescent expanded they had to try to gain ground. I took possession of a pleasure grove to the left of the crescent, on this side of a bushy ravine. On the other side lay a very imposing plantation, behind which at a distance of three to four hundred paces the enemy cavalry and infantry appeared, which had divided into three groups just like the jägers."

The Americans then disappeared, and Ewald called for volunteers to scout ahead. Several Jägers "crawled under cover to the plantation to see if one of the inhabitants could be found or caught there." On their return they reported that the Americans were on the other side of the plantation house, "where they could not be observed from here, and that they could not get into the house without being captured.

"I then took twenty men and went cautiously through the ravine with four men deployed one after the other; as soon as they were through, I let four more men go, and gradually all twenty men." The manuevering of the light infantry and the Jägers, and the description of the volunteers crawling through the underbrush, could depict movements by twentieth-century infantry. It is further evidence that European armies were aware of the need under North American conditions for light troops trained to take maximum advantage of cover and concealment. But being aware of what is needed and acting on it are often two different things. The British never had enough light troops, and their light infantry was too often used as regular line infantry.

Ewald continued: "I reached the opposite height safely, and had a dozen shots fired into the windows and doors of the dwelling. The occupant of the house appeared at once. I beckoned to him with my hat, but he went back into the house. I immediately ordered several more shots fired at the house, whereupon he appeared with his better half and approached me. But since I did not consider myself safe here, I ordered the good man, whose neatly dressed spouse clung firmly to his arm and would not leave, to go back with me through the very muddy ravine. Both good people trembled like an aspen leaf. I spoke kindly to them, assuring them that no harm would come to them if they would tell me the truth of what I wanted to know, and what they themselves knew."

The plantation was the Horry place, in the present area of the Charleston Air Force Base, and the couple probably Elias Horry II, then seventy-three years old, and his wife Margaret Lynch Horry. Their son, Peter, was engaged in overseeing work on Charleston's fortifications. They told Ewald that the Americans behind the house were under Colonel William Washington and Ewald's skirmishing foe, the Chevalier Vernier. General Lincoln, they said, had 7,000 men in the city. They were either lying for the cause or ignorant of Lincoln's true situation. At that time Lincoln had about 2,200 men, although after reinforcements arrived his force exceeded 5,000. They said that the "garrison would defend itself to the utmost . . . and that they had placed their entire hope on the works [Fort Moultrie] on Sullivan's Island. The fort was mounted with forty-two heavy guns which would defend the entire channel in the vicinity if the fleet should try to pass it to bombard the city from the water side. They considered such an undertaking to be impossible." Ewald "had a mind to send this good man to Lord Cornwallis, but since his spouse begged me with tears in her eyes not to do so, I let it go and made a verbal report of his statement personally."

In return for Ewald's humanity, Elias Horry "offered us breakfast, which offer I accepted with thanks, since we were all hungry and very thirsty because of the extraordinary heat of the sun. At once a basket with Madeira wine and bread was served, which I consumed with my regular gang. The Negro had hardly returned with his basket when a number of riflemen appeared, with whom we skirmished until nearly afternoon, during which two jägers were wounded. It seemed as if these gentlemen had agreed with our host to let us breakfast first in peace."

Between mid and late afternoon the other units and the artillery were brought over and the army began its march to Charleston. There was constant skirmishing with American units that withdrew before the Jägers and light infantry and, in Ewald's language, hung on the "queue of the army . . . so that we now marched between two fires. About nine o'clock in the evening the army moved into camp near the Quarter House [a tavern], six English miles from Charlestown. Since the right flank was protected by the Ashley River, the army formed a front facing three sides. The entire army, with the troops General Paterson had assembled at Savannah, may well now consist of ten thousand men. This piece of land we now occupy lies between the Cooper and Ashley rivers and is called the Charlestown Neck [as it still is]. At the Quarter House it is well over a good hour wide [walking], but in front of the city the width is scarcely a half an hour. Hence this terrain was easy to occupy, since we were protected on both sides by navigable rivers. But on the left side, that is, the front facing the city on the side of the Cooper River, we were not secure against a landing, since the enemy was still master of this side through his fleet."[3]

Sir Henry Clinton was jubilant. River crossings are among the riskiest military operations, and his had gone off without a hitch. Furthermore, finding themselves outflanked and the British behind them—a favored Clinton tactic—the Americans immediately abandoned their breastworks at Ashley Ferry. As Clinton wrote after the war, another "uninterrupted, commodious passage was opened thereby for the transportation of the stores and remaining troops. The following day the army moved toward Charleston without any other resistance from the enemy than an ineffectual scattering fire on the head of the column. And in the night of the 1st of April we broke ground within 800 yards of the rebel works."[4]

Although it is true that American resistance was relatively feeble, what is labeled "ineffectual scattering fire" by generals kills troops on the front line. Captain Ewald's description of the events of 30 March remain vivid over two centuries. The skirmishing was almost continual. "Meanwhile, the enemy was forced back from one ditch to another up to an advanced fleche [an outwork, part of a system of fortifications, angled like an arrow with two faces and a rear entrance] which lay almost under the cannon range of the fortifications, where severe firing occurred. Captain Bodungen, who led the vanguard, went around the fleche, whereupon it was abandoned by the enemy. But we had scarcely mastered it and had scarcely reformed a little, when we were attacked again with considerable violence and driven back, whereby three jägers were stabbed with bayonets. The light infantry came hurrying to our support, and the enemy was driven back beyond the fleche for a second time. At that moment the Commanding General appeared and ordered us not to advance one step further, since it was presumed that the enemy merely intended to provoke us by his maneuver and lure us under the fortifications into a violent cannonade.

"The enemy, perceiving that his maneuver was not successful, attacked the jägers and light infantry once more with a complete brigade supported by six guns. At this time the English artillery arrived and opened fire on the enemy, who withdrew to the city but was not pursued beyond the fleche. The jägers were relieved by the light infantry. The Commanding General had the jägers assembled and personally extended his warmest thanks to them, while everyone in the army, under whose eyes the action had occurred, expressed thanks and delight to us. We had nine killed, five missing, and eleven wounded, and the light infantry had probably lost just as many. We counted over thirty dead of the enemy, among whom was a staff officer."

Night fell, "an extraordinarily dark and silent night. I could hear the barking of dogs, the calls of 'Who's there?' on the ramparts of the city, and the mournful cries of the wounded who had remained on the field, crying for help. They surely were from the enemy, and I felt sorry that I could not help them." Captain Ewald was able to ascertain that he was in a garden at Gibbes's plantation, where the Jägers had been posted. For an hour he searched the area on his hands and knees, as the Jägers dared no lights so close to an enemy that might sally forth. "I luckily found an old Negro. The jägers had heard his cough, which the poor fellow could probably no longer hold back. He told me that the marshy Black's Creek, which fell into the Ashley River, lay in front of me a thousand paces away. While crawling around I had fallen more than once into water and swamp over my knees, but how could I have guessed that this wet area was not passable. Meanwhile, I remained under arms without a fire and relieved my sentries often to keep them awake. In the middle of this unpleasant night I remembered that this day had been my birthday, which I had thought of celebrating fully since I had kept all of my bones intact." He was thirty-six.

The following morning, "To my pleasure, daylight dispelled the dark night and I discovered with delight that I had spent the night in a very lovely and well-laid out pleasure garden." It was a famous garden made by the late owner, John Gibbes, whose plantation was called The Grove. The gardens were extensive and had contained greenhouses and a pinery. The terraces and all but one of the greenhouses had been destroyed in May 1779 by General Prevost's British army from Georgia during its advance on Charleston. It is said that John Gibbes

was so distressed at this needless act of vandalism that he died shortly thereafter. The Jägers took a few more, gentler, liberties with the property. After he
had inspected and rearranged his sentries, Ewald returned to the garden to find
that his soldiers had removed from the fully furnished house a "few beautiful tables of mahogany and several dozen chairs, on which my jägers rested their
weary bones. One of them had even hung up a large mirror on a tree, a novelty which amused everyone so much that all hardship was forgotten."

That afternoon a patrol of light infantry found the five missing Jägers, all
dead, all killed with bayonets. The eyes of one had been cut out. Captain Ewald
thought that this meant the Americans had lost heavily in the previous day's
action and that it had made them angry.[5]

An "active, spirited, sensible Man"

Major General Benjamin Lincoln (1733–1810) of Massachusetts, commanding
general of the American troops who had clashed with Ewald's men and the light
infantry before withdrawing behind Charleston's fortifications, would have been
appalled to hear of the Jäger with his eyes cut out.[6] General Lincoln possessed
many good qualities. He was a man of some ability who seemed to be in general aware of his limitations and was liked and respected by almost all who came
into contact with him: his soldiers, the Rice Kings, Washington himself, who described him to Congress as an "active, spirited, sensible Man." Lincoln had a
deep integrity recognizable to those who dealt with him. The Rice Kings, despite different backgrounds, despite military disasters, asked Lincoln after the
War to look after the sons they sent to Harvard. When Daniel Shays led a rebellion of western Massachusetts debtors in 1786, Lincoln was put in command
of the troops sent to quell the insurgency; he did it with humanity and a "del-
icately Cautious" policy that prevented the trouble from escalating and spreading to other states. His advice, unheeded, to the Supreme Judicial Court of
Massachusetts before the trial of the captured rebels is a good measure of the
man: "I hope they will [be merciful] and do it with a grace, and that she may
evidence a disposition to forgive and embrace cordially those who are forgiven
to regain the affections of the deluded and to bring them to order and to esteem government."

He was born of a yeoman family in Hingham, Massachusetts. His father,
also Benjamin, was a farmer and maltmaker and active in local politics and the
militia. When he was twenty-three the younger Lincoln married Mary Cushing
of Pembroke, Massachusetts. He was elected to the same town clerk's office that
had been held by his father and grandfather and eventually succeeded his father as Colonel Benjamin Lincoln, commanding officer of the Third Suffolk
militia regiment. Lincoln became an active revolutionary. In the early years of
the war he saw service in New England and New York and commanded the
right wing at the Battle of White Plains. Washington liked the man almost on
sight, and it was on his recommendation that Congress in February 1777 appointed Lincoln a major general of the Continental Line. Washington sent him

to assist Schuyler against Burgoyne, with the specific task of raising and organizing the New England militia. Lincoln performed admirably; it was he who sent out the militia columns that cut Burgoyne's communications with Canada. He fought under Gates at Saratoga, where he received a ball that shattered his right ankle, a wound that bothered him for years and made one leg two inches shorter than the other.

This was the general Congress put in command of the Southern Department in 1778 to succeed its first failed appointee, General Robert Howe, a North Carolina rice planter who had led an unsuccessful expedition against St. Augustine and lost Savannah to the British. Lincoln rode south to take up as difficult an assignment as given to any American general during the war. He was a man "about five feet nine inches in stature, and of so uncommonly broad person, as to seem to be of less stature than he was," for he weighed 224 pounds "and it sagged." Fat, dumpy, lame to boot, yet with a "countenance exceedingly kind and amiable," he also had an unfortunate affliction. "In the midst of a conversation, at table, and when driving himself in a chaise, he would fall into a sound sleep. While he commanded troops against the Massachusetts insurgents, he dictated dispatches, and slept between the sentences. His sleep did not appear to disturb his perception of circumstances that were passing around him. He considered this an infirmity, and his friends never ventured to speak to him of it." Lincoln undoubtedly suffered from narcolepsy, in which periods of sleep are brief but deep.

In a perceptive essay on Lincoln's character, the late Clifford K. Shipton maintained that Congress gave him the Southern Department because "what was needed was not a brilliant soldier but a man who could gather and control the militia; any pitched battle was sure to be a disaster." Events would reveal that this premise was wrong. A brilliant soldier who could control militia as well as regulars was precisely what was needed, and under the right commanders pitched battles need not be disasters, although Benjamin Lincoln was not one of the right commanders. He attempted to invade Georgia, failed, and lost a good part of his army. He almost lost Charleston as the result of a daring invasion of South Carolina by General Augustine Prevost, a Swiss mercenary in British service, and scandalous behavior by South Carolina authorities, who were ready to negotiate an agreement with Prevost that would have spared Charleston in return for South Carolina neutrality. The arrival of Lincoln's forces, back from the abortive Georgia campaign, and William Moultrie's stand against neutrality, put an end to that malodorous business. But the fighting that followed was botched by the Americans and Prevost's smaller force got away.

In October 1779, three months before Sir Henry Clinton's expedition sailed from New York into the teeth of winter storms, the joint Franco-American assault of Savannah was repulsed. Lincoln led his defeated army back to Charleston. It is true that he was ill served by subordinates. The best of them, Moultrie, was a fighter anywhere, anytime, but by his record only effective behind fortifications. He simply lacked the ability to maneuver forces in the field. But commanding generals cannot be excused because of the faults and failures

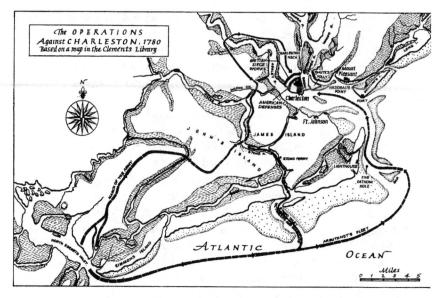

The Operations Against Charleston, 1780.
Reproduced from William B. Willcox, Portrait of a General: Sir Henry Clinton in the War of Independence *(New York: Alfred A. Knopf, 1964). Courtesy of the heirs of William B. Willcox: Alan F. Willcox, Ellen W. Ham, and Faith M. Willcox.*

of subordinates. The famous sign on Harry Truman's desk, "The Buck Stops Here," too often honored in the breach, is a sound criterion on which to judge leadership. The campaign was not over, however, and with the city's walls and the treacherous sandbars at the mouth of the harbor protecting them, the Americans, as they had proved at Sullivan's Island, could be formidable.

"Joy to you, Sir"

George Washington believed, and most observers contemporary and since agree, that the key to Charleston's defense was control of its harbor. And all contemporaries were aware that it was only a matter of time before a French fleet appeared again on the North American coast. Control of the sea was critical in the American Revolution, and in the end seapower decided the military issue.

Even before the British invasion fleet had left New York, Congress had taken steps to help defend Charleston Harbor. An American naval squadron consisting of the frigates *Providence, Boston, Queen of France,* and *Ranger* had arrived in Charleston on 23 December 1779, together mounting 112 guns. The small force was commanded by the experienced, if undistinguished, Rhode Island seaman, Commodore Abraham Whipple. South Carolina added four ships with a total of 106 guns. Two French ships mounted forty-two guns between them. That gave the Americans a total of 260 guns afloat, and forty-odd guns at Fort Moultrie on Sullivan's Island, where Sir Peter Parker had been humiliated in 1776. The American flotilla was outnumbered and outgunned by the British, but it seemed a formidable force, with the advantage of being able to pick its anchorage and await the approach of a foe at the mercy of wind and tide.

It was hoped that the British could be met at the bar and stopped. But at the end of January Lincoln was informed that the American ships could not anchor just inside the bar. When he asked why, Whipple replied that the enemy would choose an easterly wind to cross the bar, but then the swell would be too great to allow the American ships to anchor in a position that would enable them to deliver broadsides at the British. Lincoln was disturbed enough to belabor the point. He wrote again, asking that Whipple anchor close enough to the bar to command the entrance. Whipple then replied that the water was not deep enough. Now Lincoln got upset. He rejected Whipple's reply and reminded him that he had been sent to Charleston with his squadron in the first place to protect the bar and deny the British the harbor. He also requested from Whipple a report on the depth of the channel, the distance from the bar to the anchorage at Five Fathom Hole, and if there were any place in the channel where the American ships could anchor. A board of three naval captains and five pilots was convened to study the matter and report. In the meantime Lincoln himself spent two days in a boat making his own inspection of the waters.

On 27 February the board reported that there was no anchorage within three miles of the bar. "In the place where the ships can be anchored, the bar cannot be covered or annoyed. . . . Our opinion is that the ships can do most effectual service for the defense and security of the town, to act in conjunction with Fort Moultrie, which we think will best answer the purpose of the ships being sent here. . . . Our reasons are that the channel is so narrow between the fort and the middle ground, that they may be moored so as to rake the channel and prevent the enemy's troops being landed to annoy the fort."[7]

Admiral Marriott Arbuthnot, meanwhile, was not happy with his situation. He had the devilishly tricky sandbanks of Charleston to navigate and the knowledge that awaiting him was an American flotilla and a fort named Moultrie that, as Fort Sullivan in 1776, had more than embarrassed the British. He decided to cross the bar with only his four frigates and two forty-four-gun ships and one fifty-gun ship. British sailors then went through the same laborious process of lightening the three big ships that Parker's men had done in 1776, raising their draughts high enough to pass through the ship channel. The Americans had destroyed the lighthouse and the beacon that marked the channel, but the lighthouse ruins gave the pilots a target. The job was completed in a few days, but the weather turned, and for sixteen days the ships were tossed about, Arbuthnot wrote, "on the open coast, in the winter season of the year, exposed to the insults of the enemy."

By 20 March all was ready. Arbuthnot's flagship, *Roebuck*, took the lead. Small boats preceded her, taking soundings. *Roebuck*, slowly, ever so slowly, "her sailing master carefully keeping her compass needle pointed at west-by-north and her bowsprit at the ruins of the lighthouse, crawled throught the Ship

Channel and into the sanctuary of Five Fathom Hole." She was followed by *Romulus* and *Renown*, the frigates *Richmond*, *Raleigh*, *Blonde*, and *Virginia*, and the armed vessel *Sandwich*. The operation was over before dark. Clinton had watched it from James Island. His relief was expressed in raptures uncharacteristic of him, as he wrote that same day with obvious sincerity, not to Arbuthnot whom he loathed, but to his favorite naval officer in the expedition, Captain George Elphinstone: "Joy to you, Sir, to myself, and to us all upon your Passage of that infernal Bar. Your anxieties have been great, and I assure you I have not been without mine on your account."[8]

The helplessness of the British ships as they inched their way through that perilous passage is obvious. When we also realize that the three big ships were without their guns, their exposure is even more striking. What a pity that the waters between the bar and Five Fathom Hole precluded an American anchorage. And how shocking that it was not until 27 February that the general commanding the southern department, with direct responsibility for the defense of Charleston, discovered that the bar was undefendable. But the British still had to run the gauntlet guarded by Fort Moultrie and the American fleet.

Whipple had moored his ships in the channel between the middle ground and Fort Moultrie, following the recommendation of the board. An attempt was apparently made to obstruct the channel, but it failed: waters too deep, channel too wide, tide too rapid. But had not the board of naval officers studied the channel and pronounced it defensible? Whatever the validity of the excuses, Commodore Whipple, on second thought, decided that the British force was so superior there was no hope of stopping them from forcing the channel, breaking through the American squadron, and cutting off its line of retreat. The decision was made to withdraw the ships to the inner harbor. Most of their guns were removed and placed in the harbor fortifications protecting the entrance to the Cooper River. The ships, along with some merchant vessels, were sunk at the entrance to the river, and a boom was strung across and secured to their sunken masts. Three of Whipple's Continental frigates stood by to offer support fire. Edward McCrady, an historian of South Carolina early in this century, wrote: "Such was the ignominious end of the fleet sent by Congress to assist South Carolina in her dire necessity. Had Moultrie been in command, somebody would have been hurt before the harbor was abandoned."[9]

Far to the north, George Washington reacted with gloom to the developments in a private letter of 26 April. "I sincerely lament that your prospects are not better than they are.... This brings your affairs to a dangerous crisis and increases my apprehensions."[10]

The remaining naval activity was anticlimactic, although it was a splendid show, with great expenditure of shot and powder, and a flood of exuberant prose. Arbuthnot made his move on 8 April to force passage "under the most violent gunfire from Fort Moultrie," reported Captain Johann Ewald, who thought "it the most majestic and beautiful spectacle that one can imagine. The fort was veiled in fire and smoke, and the roar of forty-three heavy guns resembled a terrible thunderstorm. Despite all dangers threatening the fleet, it sailed quite slowly past the fort with colors flying proudly, one ship behind the other, without firing a shot. As soon as it had passed the enemy fort, each ship made a sudden turn, fired a broadside, and sailed to its designated anchoring place." Captain Ewald believed that "only an English fleet can execute such a masterpiece. It appeared, too, as if all the heavens wished to enhance their brilliant performance, for it was the most beautiful weather in the world, with hardly any wind; the maneuver was carried out only with the aid of the flood tide." British losses were minimal: twenty-seven men killed and wounded, some damage to masts and rigging but none to hulls, a transport ship with naval stores run aground and lost. Fourteen vessels were safely in the harbor to add their guns to those mounted in the British siegeworks. American gunnery that day made a mockery of the word.[11]

Could Moultrie have stopped Arbuthnot? Speculation would be fruitless. We can say, however, that Abraham Whipple's historical invisibility is deserved. A fighting sailor would have met Arbuthnot in the narrow channel off Fort Moultrie and fought it out to the bitter end. He may have gone down with colors flying, but the British would have known that they had been in a fight, and at least as much good and probably more would have been done as by the fleet's "ignominious end" in providing an anchor for a boom across the Cooper. Benjamin Lincoln, good man though he was, must bear the responsibility for allowing it to happen.

The Siege

There was nothing "majestic or beautiful" about the landward approach, no sights with the "noble appearance" of warships under sail. It was dirty work, and dangerous day after bloody day, with nights full of tension for the besiegers as they waited for sallies by the besieged that could end in melees in dark, narrow trenches where weapons were bayonets, picks, shovels, knives, knees, and fists. Yet there was a mathematical preciseness about an eighteenth-century siege that was impressive in its own right. Sieges were conducted, as we would say today, by the book, and that particular "book" was written in the seventeenth century by Sebastien le Prestre de Vauban (1633–1707), an exceptional Frenchman who was one of the rarest of our species: an innovative soldier. Vauban's genius and good fortune led to his becoming history's most celebrated military engineer and a marshal of France. (What a pity that we cannot linger over his other accomplishments, among them applied science and economics, as well as his plea well in advance of his time for religious freedom.) Sieges before Vauban were conducted without system and led to heavy casualties among the attackers. Although he may not have invented some of its constituent parts, Vauban's method, perfected by him over several years in forty-eight sieges, forty of which he directed as chief engineer and none of which failed, was followed almost without variation by European armies in the eighteenth century.[12]

The observation that simplicity is the hallmark of a master is readily apparent in Vauban's work. One can imagine an eighteenth-century European officer scratching his head and musing, "Why didn't I think of that?" The main problem was to emplace enough artillery to silence or reduce the enemy's guns and then to bring the artillery close enough to breach the walls, thus opening the way to an infantry assault. But how to get the artillery and supporting infantry gradually close enough without taking heavy losses stymied Western soldiers for two centuries. The obvious answer was by digging trenches toward the defensive works, but before Vauban the trench systems used were haphazard at best, chaotic at worst. He brought order to siegecraft, and under normal conditions his methods guaranteed success.

The first step was to gather men and materials out of range of gunfire and observation. Approach trenches were dug to within 600 to 800 yards of the defenses, which was the effective range of cannon fire. At that point a trench twelve to fifteen feet wide and three feet deep was dug at right angles to the approach trenches. Excavated earth was used to make a parapet three to four feet high in front of the trench. This trench, facing the defenses, paralleled the point of attack, and was called the first parallel. It was dug not in a straight line but in a rough sort of crescent shape so that it would face the point of attack from the front and the sides. Sometimes it was used as a *place d'armes*, where men and supplies would be gathered. Redoubts (small, enclosed temporary works) were built at intervals in front of the first parallel for the emplacement of artillery. One or more approach trenches would then be dug from the first parallel toward the enemy's works, but in zigzag lines to prevent the enemy from sweeping these approach trenches with enfilading fire. At a second predetermined point, usually halfway toward the defenses, a second parallel trench was dug. Then the approach trenches would be pushed out again in zigzags to the third, and final, parallel trench, near the foot of the defensive outworks. Between the second and third parallels, demi-parallels—short parallel trenches—were dug on the flanks of the approach trenches. In all the parallels, regular or small, infantry was gathered to protect against sorties from the garrison aimed at destroying work parties, trenches, and artillery batteries. At the first alarm they would rush from the parallels to the approach trenches to engage the enemy. As the besiegers closed in, artillery would be pushed forward to begin the work of blasting an opening in the defenses.

The closer the working parties and the infantry guards got to the defenses the more dangerous it became. Specially trained men, called sappers, then took over the digging. At the head of a regular approach trench, a squad of sappers would begin digging a narrow, shallow trench called a sap. The lead sapper would excavate only a foot and one-half wide and deep. He would push ahead of him a two-wheeled contraption called a mantalet, or sap shield, to protect him from enemy fire. As he went along he would place gabions one after another; these hollow cylinders of wickerwork or strap iron were filled with earth to strengthen the trench. His fellow sappers behind him widened and deepened the sap and put fascines—bundles of sticks tied together—on the parapets. If necessary, working parties from infantry units later dug the sap to regular size. If the defenders of the garrison made a fast, determined sortie, the sappers were in great danger of being bayoneted before their infantry could reach them. Recognizing the danger, Vauban paid his sappers in advance at piecework rates, which increased with the danger.

This was all very formal, and barring interruption by relief forces it was most likely to result in eventual surrender by the besieged. In the hands of a master of his craft, a siege could be ended in a very short time. At the siege of Maestricht in 1673, where Vauban first used parallels, the city surrendered thirteen days after the trenches were opened. At Charleston, according to Johann Ewald, the British lacked a master. But whether sieges were short or long, all concerned were anxious to avoid the awful alternative of a fortified place being carried by assault, with its attendant butchery, especially if attacking troops who had taken heavy casualties got out of control. It was common practice, therefore, and Vauban's royal master Louis XIV so decreed, that once the citadel was breached and one assault repulsed, a commander might surrender without losing honor.

The main defenses of Charleston crossed the peninsula parallel to the present Marion Square—within easy walking distance of the tip of the peninsula—about 800 yards from the point where the British broke ground to begin their laborious advance on the city. The defense works stretched from near the Cooper across the peninsula to the wetlands bordering the Ashley. The center work was called a hornwork. According to Captain Ewald, the inner wall facing the city was made of "bricks to the strongest thickness." The mixture of lime and oyster shells was two feet thick on the outer slope facing the enemy. There were eighteen cannon mounted on the hornwork. Two ditches were in front of the defenses. The ditch just under the works was twelve feet wide and six feet deep with double palisades. It was filled with groundwater and dams were built at each end to retain the water. The ditch was protected by an abatis of pointed trees dug into the ground and sticking outward on a slant. The outer ditch, "forty to sixty paces in front of the works," was eighteen feet wide and eight feet deep and also protected by an abatis. At both rivers the Rebels built "sluices to control the water passing from the rivers into the ditch." On each plank was a detached bastion protected by ditches 12 by 6 feet with double-palisades. In all, ninety-three cannon were mounted along the works. When he examined the defenses after the siege, Captain Ewald thought the British attack should have been made on either bastion, "for it was impossible to blast a breach in this hornwork. This work was too solidly built for us to reach our objective here," and exposed the attacking troops to "flanking fire from both sides, as indeed we experienced."[13]

On 30 March the British began moving artillery, ammunition, tools, siege materials, and provisions across the Ashley to the peninsula. At sunset on 2 April, protected by infantry, 500 workers opened the trenches without opposition. A few nights later the Americans fired solid shot and thirty explosive shells, which killed four English grenadiers. On the 4th more artillery fire killed three men of the 33rd Foot and severely wounded two Hessian grenadiers. On that day the British covered the flanks of their position by beginning work on redoubts near the Ashley and the Cooper rivers. This work drew the immediate attention of the Americans. Captain Ewald and 100 Jägers were posted at the Cooper River redoubt. Again on 4 April, as Ewald described it, "About ten o'clock in the morning the two frigates *Boston* and *Providence*, both 32 guns . . . set sail and got in position such that they could fire on the flank and the rear of the work in which I was posted. For over an hour we had to endure heavy cannon fire. These vessels surely would have succeeded in destroying the work if the diligent and indefatigable Moncrief [British engineer officer in charge of the siege] had not brought up two 12-pounders and a howitzer to a promontory on Cooper River, whose first shots damaged the *Boston*, whereupon the frigates fired several more sharp salvos and withdrew to their station. Toward evening an enemy brigantine whose deck was crowded with people of both sexes attempted the same pastime. It fired twenty-three shots at us and sailed back."

That night and throughout the next day American fire was violent, and toward evening "the enemy redoubled his fire." The battery emplaced by Moncrief thereupon used random fire onto the Cooper to prevent the frigates from gaining the flanks of the redoubts. At 9 P.M. Sir Henry Clinton ordered batteries across the Ashley from Charleston to, in Ewald's words, "play upon the city, which quieted the enemy fire somewhat. A terrible clamor arose among the inhabitants of the city, since the firing came entirely unexpectedly. During this time I had approached quite close to the city to discover the effect of these batteries, and in the short intervals between shooting I could often hear the loud wailing of female voices, which took all the pleasure out of my curiosity and moved me to tears." The next day the Americans were quieter, and the British placed a battery of guns manned by sailors in the first parallel.[14]

On the 6th of April "the energetic Captain Elphinstone hauled a large boat on rollers overland from the Ashley River into the Cooper River. It is being armed with two 6-pounders to intercept the boats of the besieged, which are still passing unhindered from the city across the Cooper River to the mainland, or at least to make this crossing unsafe." Further pressure was put on the following night, but not without more of the backbreaking labor attending war. Not only did sailors have to move big guns from ships to boats and back again to get across Charleston bar, they were also drafted for an even more difficult task, hauling the cast-iron monsters through muck and mire. On the 7th, "as soon as night fell, we began moving the heavy pieces to the left-wing redoubt. But since the swamp lying between the highway and the redoubt was not covered sufficiently with heavy boards, everything except for one 24-pounder mired in the swamp, and we had great difficulty in moving even this one piece to its position. All the pieces and ammunition, and practically everything required for the siege, must be brought from the landing place up to the destination points by the sailors and Negroes, all of which takes up considerable time."

Despite the presence of Elphinstone's gunboat, dragged across the peninsula with such great effort, at 1 o'clock on the afternoon of 8 April "eleven American schooners and sloops loaded with troops sailed down the Cooper River to the city right before our eyes." The reinforcements were 750 Virginia

Continentals under Brigadier General William Woodford; they had marched 500 miles in twenty-eight days to reach their beleaguered comrades. The inhabitants and the garrison were esctatic, "shouted for joy three times from their works, which mingled with an hourly pealing of bells and a continuous cannon and mortar fire at our parallels and redoubts, during which our batteries on Fenwick's point were completely silenced."

The British continued to dig and haul cannon forward and take a few casualties almost every day, which was expected and bearable. They were determined, however, to seal off the city and allow no more reinforcements to enter. That meant they had to control the countryside on the opposite bank of the Cooper River, where American horse and foot were stationed to prevent that from happening. The clash that resulted was as battles go if not minor certainly not a major action, but when it came it was swift and brutal and brought to the instant attention of the Americans a twenty-five-year-old English cavalry officer whose name in a few short months would become anathema in the South.

6

The Rise of Banastre Tarleton

"An attack in the night was judged most advisable"

Gallery 38 in the National Gallery, London, contains a striking full-length portrait of an English officer in unusual uniform and pose. Instead of the ubiquitous red coat he wears the close fitting, waist-length green jacket of the British Legion. It is trimmed with gold and has gold buttons and dark velvet collar and cuffs. His is not the usual eighteenth-century tri-cornered hat but a dragoon's helmet with plume, worn at a jaunty angle. Tight white breeches and calf-high boots complete his dress. A broad leather sword belt crosses his chest, and behind one leg can be seen the hilt of a saber and its scabbard. Usually described as a stocky man with a powerful frame and coarse features, here he is portrayed as slim and boyish, which reminds us of the admonition never to accept a portrait at face value. He has a bold nose, full, sensuous lips, and a haughty expression. On close examination it is obvious that from his right hand two fingers are missing: lost "For King and Country!" he was known to cry out at political rallies, as he thrust the mangled stumps in the air. Behind him rise the smoke of battle and two wild-eyed chargers whose reins are tightly held by a trooper while the young officer, a foot resting on a cannon barrel laying on the ground, bends forward slightly from the waist and reaches behind his knee to adjust his breeches. The pose is believed to have been inspired by the fourth-century B.C. statue of *Hermes*, a version of which had recently been imported into England and become a sensation when put on view at Landsdowne House.[1]

Booted, spurred, and resplendent, thus was Lieutenant Colonel Banastre Tarleton immortalized on his return to England in the year 1782 by Sir Joshua Reynolds. And it is well that artist and subject took advantage of the opportunity, for the most famous British cavalryman of his day, the toast of London that year, confidante of the Prince of Wales, lover of a famous actress, is practically unknown to twentieth-century Britons.

General Sir Banastre Tarleton by Sir Joshua
Reynolds, 1782.
(Reproduced by courtesy of the trustees,
The National Gallery, London.)

Banastre Tarleton (1754–1833) was born to a wealthy merchant family of
Liverpool whose money came from sugar and slaves, and all his life he was faithful to his heritage. He attended Oxford for a while, then briefly studied law at
Middle Temple, where Richard Brinsley Sheridan knew him and formed a low
opinion of his character. Tarleton's true calling awaited him, and had it not been
for war his life no doubt would have ranged somewhere between obscurity and
anonymity. In April 1775 he purchased a commission as a cornet, the lowest
commissioned officer rank, in one of the army's most distinguished cavalry regiments of the line, the 1st Dragoon Guards (King's). Early the following year he
took leave of his regiment and sailed for America with Lord Cornwallis's force
that joined Sir Henry Clinton off Cape Fear and subsequently took part in the
Clinton/Parker fiasco at Sullivan's Island. On the expedition's return to New
York in August 1776, Tarleton volunteered for duty with the 16th Light Dragoons. His rise thereafter was rapid. He was one of four officers and twenty-five
troopers who on 13 December 1776 raided White's Tavern in Basking Ridge,

New Jersey, and captured William Moultrie's tormentor, General Charles Lee. In a letter to his mother he claimed most of the credit, and to give him his due John Graves Simcoe, a very able officer who served throughout the American war and saw Tarleton in action, described him as "full of enterprise and spirit, and anxious of every opportunity of distinguishing himself." His superiors thought well enough of him to promote him in January 1778 to Captain of the 1st Company of Liverpool Royal Volunteers, skipping the rank of lieutenant. That same month he was part of a force of 200 dragoons under Sir William Erskine, commander of British cavalry in America, which attempted to capture another well-known American officer. They had intelligence that Henry Lee, who became the famous cavalry leader better known as Light Horse Harry and the father of the even more famous Robert E. Lee, was at Spread Eagle Tavern near Valley Forge. But Lee and his men barricaded themselves inside and successfully fought it out. Tarleton and a squadron charged to run off the horses, but a volley killed five troopers and the rest drew off. Tarleton's horse was hit three times, he was dusted with buckshot, and his helmet was shot off his head. Thus Banastre Tarleton and Light Horse Harry Lee introduced themselves to each other. When they met again the stakes would be much higher.[2]

In August 1778 Sir Henry Clinton promoted Tarleton to Lieutenant Colonel of the British Legion, a regiment of horse and foot recruited from among New York Tories. He had gone from cornet to lieutenant colonel in four years, and he was not quite twenty-four years old.[3]

During the southern campaign Tarleton was commander of British cavalry, which consisted of the troopers of the British Legion and a company from the 17th Dragoons. The reader will recall that the British horses had been lost during the terrible voyage from New York. Tarleton and his dismounted cavalry had been left with General Patterson at Savannah to make their way to South Carolina by land and to confiscate what horses could be found. They managed to mount themselves, but poorly, having to make do with swamp ponies and farm horses. Twice on the march Tarleton had clashed in very minor skirmishes with George Washington's kinsman, the Virginia cavalryman Colonel William Washington, and each had scored a victory of sorts. Tarleton was known to his foes, but he was not yet a household name to Rebel and Tory alike. That would soon change.

Elphinstone's gunboats on the Cooper River could not by themselves stop reinforcements and supplies from reaching Charleston. The British had to take and occupy the countryside along the Cooper in order to seal off hope of succor or escape. Thirty-two miles north of Charleston is Monck's Corner. On the night of 13–14 April, 1780, Monck's Corner was a country crossroads occupied by 500 Rebels under General Isaac Huger (pronounced you-gee). The cavalry was commanded by Lieutenant Colonel William Washington. Just north of the junction was Biggins Bridge, which crossed the Santee River. Huger's job was to keep open Charleston's line of communications. Sir Henry Clinton decided to deal with him and draw the noose tighter.

On 12 April Lieutenant Colonel Banastre Tarleton and his British Legion left Quarter House and proceeded north to Goose Creek, on the road to Monck's Corner. Tarleton's infantry was commanded by Major Charles Cochrane; some eighteen months later, while he stood next to Cornwallis on a rampart at Yorktown, an American cannonball would tear Cochrane's head from his body. Reinforcing the Legion were the American Volunteers, a northern Tory unit under Major Patrick Ferguson, who along with Tarleton would play a critical role in the southern campaign. The next day the force was joined by the commander of the expedition, Lieutenant Colonel James Webster, with his own 33rd Foot and the 64th Foot. The British numbered 1,400. The plan was simple: the British Legion and American Volunteers, Tarleton in command, would proceed swiftly and silently at night and attempt to take the Americans by surprise. Webster and the main body would follow to provide any necessary support. As we will see, Tarleton's postwar *History* must be used with care, but there is no need for strictures with regard to his description of the action. "An attack in the night was judged most advisable," he wrote, and the small advance detachment of horse and foot set out, with "Profound silence . . . observed on the march." It was 10:00 P.M., according to the diary of Lieutenant Anthony Allaire, a Tory from the Huguenot community of New Rochelle, New York, who served in Ferguson's command.[4]

Living as we do in a world in which our waking hours are spent in almost constant light, to capture the full flavor of that eventful night and other nights two centuries ago we must try to imagine darkness we never know, a world whose nights were filled with almost constant dark, not the half dark to which we are accustomed but a deep, Stygian gloom that existed between sundown and sunup, relieved, if the weather was right, only by the moon and the stars. The difference between that night in 1780 and our time can be measured in silence as well as light. People made noises, and so did animals and the wind and the rain and other sounds of nature, but there were no motors, no constant hum of traffic in the distance. There was a stillness both day and night that are rare today, found only in the great empty places.

That is what it was like at 10 o'clock on the night of 13 April 1780 when Banastre Tarleton and the vanguard took the road to Monck's Corner with the aim of letting loose Milton's "brazen throat of war." It was very dark and the only sounds were of marching feet and horse hooves on the dirt road and the creak of saddles. Scouts captured a black man who tried too late to move off the road to avoid them, which indicates how quietly the British were marching. The man was carrying a letter from General Huger to Charleston. He was taken to a nearby farmhouse and given a few dollars, questioned, and the letter read, and thus Tarleton learned how Huger had deployed his troops. In "Profound silence" the march continued. Lieutenant Allaire recorded in his diary that the Americans, "Luckily for them . . . were under marching orders, which made them more alert, when the alarm was given, than usual, which alone prevented their being taken completely by surprise." But the Americans were surprised, for which there can be no excuse. The British ran into no scouts, encountered no patrols. Tarleton told well and without embellishment what happened when he reached his goal.[5]

"At three o'clock in the morning the advanced guard of dragoons and mounted infantry, supported by the remainder of the legion and Ferguson's corps approached the American post: a watch word was immediately comunicated to the officers and soldiers, which was closely followed by an order to charge the enemy's grand guard on the main road, there being no other avenue open, owing to the swamps upon the flanks. . . . The order was executed with the greatest promptitude and success. The Amercans were completely surprised. General Huger, Colonels Washington and Jamieson, with many officers and men, fled on foot to the swamps . . . where, being completely concealed in darkness, they effected their escape. . . . Without loss of time Major Cochrane was ordered to force the bridge and meeting house with the infantry of the British legion: he charged the milita with fixed bayonets, got possession of the pass, and dispersed everything that opposed him."[6]

Huger and his colonels had committed errors grievous enough to warrant a court martial. They had placed the cavalry in front of the bridge and the infantry behind, instead of the other way around; their failure to send out patrols was neglect bordering on if not actually criminal. Although the Americans may have been in marching order, Tarleton was right in claiming surprise, "which prevented the Americans recovering from the confusion attending an unexpected attack." They paid dearly for their lack of security. Huger lost fourteen men killed, nineteen wounded, and sixty-four captured, and, according to Tarleton, "fifty wagons, loaded with arms, clothing, and ammunition." The rest of the Americans, Lieutenant Allaire wrote, "made off with great expedition." A critical gain for the poorly mounted British was the capture of the horses belonging to the American officers and cavalry, such "a valuable acquisition for the British cavalry" that a Tory newspaper announced, "Colonel Tarleton took so great a number of exceeding fine horses as enabled him to produce four hundred as well mounted and well appointed cavalry as would do him credit *en revue* at Wimbleton."[7]

Monck's Corner was Banastre Tarleton's first notable victory in the South, and it established a pattern he would maintain to the end: swift approach, sudden appearance, immediate assault with British officers' weapons of choice—sabers and bayonets. He used it time after time, and it is not unreasonable to suggest that American commanders, learning of his tactics firsthand or from embarrassed comrades, also would have learned early in the campaign to be ever alert when there was the slightest suspicion that Tarleton was afield. He was a very able cavalry commander: brave, vigorous, bold, swift of movement, alert for opportunities, on the march a driver of men and horses, relentless in pursuit of his prey. That he had grave defects of character cannot take from him his brilliant exploits on behalf of King and Country—and Banastre Tarleton.

Two incidents following the action at Monck's Corner also established another pattern for fights involving Tarleton and the British Legion. One was the fate of Johann Ewald's skirmishing opponent during the British advance up the right bank of the Ashley, Chevalier Pierre-Francois Vernier, who commanded the remnants of Pulaski's Horse. Seeing the game was up, Vernier asked quarter from the Legion and instead was slashed and hacked with sabers, "mangled in the most shocking manner," according to Charles Stedman, a Philadelphia Tory who served with the British and wrote a valuable history of the war. Stedman was there and had Vernier taken into a tavern, laid on a table, and covered with a blanket. The Chevalier lingered in agony for hours, cursing the Americans as cowards for fleeing, his killers as barbarians for refusing him quarter. In his final moments, Stedman wrote, he was "frequently insulted by privates of the Legion."[8]

The other incident was described by Stedman and Lieutenant Allaire. Near Monck's Corner was a plantation owned by a prominent Tory, Sir John Colleton. Tory women, including Lady Colleton, were gathered there. Some Legion dragoons, for whom women of either side were fair game, entered the house and "most shockingly abused" Lady Colleton (who received a bad cut on her hand from a broadsword), Miss Betsy Giles, Miss Jean Russell, and Mrs. Fayssoux, an "amiable lady in the greatest distress imaginable," who had to be bled by the British surgeon before she regained her composure. All the women apparently emerged with virtue intact, as Stedman refers to the dragoons having "attempted to ravish several ladies at the house." Lieutenant Allaire's commanding officer, Major Patrick Ferguson, who had a chivalrous reputation, was so enraged that he wanted to line the dragoons up and shoot them. But the expedition commander, Lieutenant Colonel James Webster, ordered them sent to Charleston, where Stedman believed they were "afterwards tried and whipped."[9]

This was not the only time the British Legion was criticized by its own side for brutal behavior, and the incidents would be surpassed in brutality. Monck's Corner revealed Tarleton's darker side, which was never distant. His march discipline was rigid, and in attack the Legion was almost always faithful to his commands, but in the aftermath of battle he was on more than one occasion indifferent to the behavior of his troops. That the southern campaign especially was in large degree a civil war made it all the more important to keep troops under control. The Tories, like the Rebels, were fighting for their homeland, and they could be as vicious as their enemies. The fight at Monck's Corner foreshadowed many a fight to come, all American affairs with only a few British officers present. Feelings of mercy for the other side were rare, and it was up to the officers, British or American, to do their duty and maintain discipline as firmly after combat as before. There were few complaints on that score about the record of Patrick Ferguson, who led both Tory regulars and militia. Of Banastre Tarleton, however, it is not unfair to state that in time and with reason he became the most hated man in the South.

Immediately after Monck's Corner the British fanned out over the countryside. Webster's command, including Tarleton's and Ferguson's Tory regulars, blocked access to Charleston by way of the Cooper River. Lieutenant Colonel Francis, Lord Rawdon, arrived from New York on 18 April with 2,500 reinforcements and deployed the 42nd Royal Highlanders (Black Watch), the Hessian von Ditfurth Regiment, and three first-rate Tory regular units, the Queen's Rangers, Prince of Wales American Volunteers, and Rawdon's own Volunteers of Ireland. Charleston was invested. Lincoln and his army were trapped.[10]

"Absurd, impolitic, and inhuman to burn a town you mean to occupy"

While the war of movement swirled to the north, the besieging British army moved inexorably toward the American defenses, spadeful by spadeful, yard by yard, trench by trench.

On 13 April, while Tarleton was positioning himself for "an attack in the night," a grenadier was killed and two infantrymen wounded in the trenches, and toward midday an incident occurred that infuriated Clinton. The British batteries on Charleston Neck and James Island bombarded the city with carcasses—iron shells pierced with holes and filled with ignited combustibles, for use against buildings and ships. They had the desired effect; several houses were set on fire, "a deplorable sight," wrote Ewald, "since it served no purpose." Arbuthnot and his flag captain, Captain Sir Andrew Snape Hammond, disagreed, and the next day sent the following message ashore to Elphinstone: "The Admiral and Sir A.S.H. begs their compliments to you and begs you will burn the Town as soon as possible and send 24 pound shot into the stomacks of the women to see how they will deliver them."[11]

Fortunately for Charleston and posterity the brutes on the quarterdeck were not in command. "Absurd, impolitic, and inhuman to burn a town you mean to occupy," Clinton stated, and ordered his artillery commandant, Major Peter Traille, to stop such bombardments.[12]

Throughout the siege Clinton did not view the carnage of war from afar. Captain Ewald was a witness. On 14 April, "At sunset the Commander in Chief came into the trenches and took the firing in very good part." Another eyewitness wrote to a friend in England that "The General, from the first moment to the hour of surrender, was the most indefatigable officer in the lines, where at all hours, and in perilous ones, he exposed his health and his life." Clinton acted completely in character. General William Keppel criticized him after the Battle of Long Island for exposing himself in a reckless manner, advising the Duke of Newcastle to "give your cousin a dressing for sporting away a life which does not belong to him but to his King and country." And at Monmouth, an observer wrote, Sir Henry "showed himself the soldier but not the wise general on this occasion, exposing himself and charging at the head of a few dragoons." Certainly, Clinton did not have to go where he did and do what he did and as often, and the criticism is in part well taken. But for sharing dirt and mud and peril with his troops he must also be applauded. After all, of what good is a general in any age who never gets shot at? The sad irony is that it did not endear him to the troops, who loved the equally courageous Cornwallis.[13]

The digging and killing continued. Not many men were lost on either side, but to troops on the line one is too many, for who knows whose number will be up next. From their cannon the Americans fired scrap iron and broken glass, which Captain Ewald considered "not very dangerous," but "my men lost their composure and thought of nothing else than to conceal themselves," and to reassure them Ewald had five protective traverses dug. By late April the lines were so close that Ewald wondered why the Americans had not sallied to kill sappers, take prisoners, and wreak havoc. The reason usually given was that they had too few men, which is not convincing, especially given their minimal losses when they finally did venture forth. In the wee hours of 24 April, 200 Virginians and South Carolinians rushed into the British trenches "with bayonet in hand and without firing a shot," Ewald wrote. In the melee they killed two Jägers, badly wounded four, and took two Germans and eight Englishmen prisoners. The Rebels had two wounded and one killed, but the single death brought deep sorrow to the hero of Sullivan's Island. William Moultrie wrote to a friend that "my poor brother Tom was killed on his return into our lines."[14]

The situation in the city was becoming critical, but on the world stage we should not overestimate the siege of Charleston. As sieges go it was not the stuff of legend. Constantinople (1453), Malta (1565), Leningrad (1941–1943): those were sieges. But although material damage and personal suffering cannot be compared with those epics, as Clinton's noose tightened and the possibility of an assault loomed, the psychological stress heightened, and not just on civilians. Of deepening concern to Benjamin Lincoln and his officers was the fate of the Continental regiments, the only American army in the South. For some, however desperate the attempt might appear, the only possible decision was somehow to get the troops across the Cooper and strike out for open country. What good this might have done, especially after the American debacle at Monck's Corner and the arrival of Lord Rawdon with reinforcements, is highly questionable; from our perspective we can only watch with raised eyebrows Benjamin Lincoln or any of his lieutenants meeting Sir Henry Clinton and the British army in formal battle. And had the fleeing regiments in mind not battle but flight, the picture of Tarleton descending on their rear and flanks like a hound from Hell and the swiftly moving Lord Cornwallis right behind to administer the coup de grace could easily have become reality. Nevertheless, to sit in Charleston and await the inevitable was more than some men could bear and we can only sympathize with their spirit. One way or another, the army was doomed, and how many of them must have cursed the lost opportunities as they wasted away in disease-ridden prison hulks rocking on the waters of Charleston Harbor. For some, British bayonets might have been preferable to death from yellow fever and dysentery. But the matter was decided among a very few men, military and civilian, and the latter were out of control.

Sir Henry Clinton, strictly following custom, had on 10 April called on Lincoln to surrender the city. General Lincoln replied that he felt it his duty to continue to resist. But he also urged Governor John Rutledge to leave. On 13

April Rutledge crossed the Cooper. He took with him the conservative members of his council. The young radicals were left behind, and the firebrand Christopher Gadsden was appointed Lieutenant Governor. On 21 April the drums beat on the American defenses. A parley was requested. Lincoln sent a proposal to Clinton, offering to surrender in return for the honors of war, another time-honored custom by which the defenders would be allowed to leave the city with colors flying, bands playing, bayonets fixed, in possession of arms and equipment. Clinton was too sure of his position and the outcome to even contemplate accepting the offer. Captain Ewald informs us that "negotiations were broken off at nine o'clock in the evening, and a severe cannonade from both sides followed." On the night of 23 April, Lord Cornwallis crossed the Cooper with a northern Tory regiment, the Volunteers of Ireland, and Tory militia from both Carolinas. He joined the forces under Lieutenant Colonel Webster, and assumed overall command of the troops blocking any escape by land. His forces, in conjunction with marines and sailors landed by Arbuthnot, easily took two American positions on the left bank of the Cooper, actions that definitely sealed off Lincoln's army.[15]

General Lincoln had contemplated evacuating the city. After the British bombardment on the night of 13 April, when several houses were set afire, he held a council of war for the first time, informed his officers of his thoughts, and asked for advice. General Lachlan McIntosh was blunt: get the army across the Cooper immediately. But Lincoln would not act on either his own misgivings or McIntosh's urgent advice. He sent his officers away, asked them to think about it, and said he would gather them again to discuss it further. He knew the situation was desperate, but he was almost certainly correct in believing that Congress wanted the city defended, and he was not the man to defy his civilian masters. And he made the mistake of allowing the Lieutenant Governor, Christopher Gadsden, to sit in on the next council, which he called on 25 April. His officers were adamant that the city could not be held but an attempt had to be made to save the Continental regiments. Gadsden was absolutely opposed to such a course. Lincoln held another meeting of his officers the following day at which an incredible scene took place. Gadsden attended with the Governor's Council, all of whom supported him. William Moultrie recorded in his *Memoirs* that "when the citizens were informed upon what the council were deliberating, some of them came into the council, and expressed themselves very warmly, and declared to General Lincoln that if he attempted to withdraw the troops and leave the citizens: that they would cut up his boats, and open the gates to the enemy. This put a stop to all thoughts of evacuation of the troops, and nothing was left for us but to make the best terms we could."[16] The civilians deserved to be put in irons and imprisoned, but Lincoln was not up to that. And by that time it probably would not have done any good. A besieged city needs a hard man in charge. But a hard man needs a hard citizenry behind him.

Digging and dying went on amid the difficulties and inconveniences of life in the field, which seem of little note on a printed page but are of obsessive importance to soldiers who experience them. "For the dangers and difficult work," Captain Ewald noted, "were the least of the annoyance: the intolerable heat, the lack of good water, and the billions of sandflies and mosquitoes made up the worst nuisance. Moreover, since all our approaches were built in white, sandy soil, one could hardly open his eyes during the south wind because of the thick dust, and could not put a bite of bread into his mouth which was not covered with sand. The few wells we had dug in the trenches for water were mixed with sand and as white as milk." Ewald and his men preferred to end it by the awful alternative of assault with bayonets: "The enemy kept three pitch fires burning in front of their works, since they expected to be taken with sword in hand, which was really the unanimous wish of the besieger, so that the disagreeable task might come to an end."[17]

But Clinton was not ready for an assault. The water-filled trench in front of the American defenses first had to be drained, which meant that the British sappers had to dig to that point, and the infantry had to stand by to protect them in case the enemy sallied. On the 29th "we advanced from the left head of the sap toward the dam to destroy the lock and let the water out of the canal which protected the front of the enemy's fortifications on the right. Cannon and small arms fire continued against this work the entire night, during which six English grenadiers were killed and fourteen English and Hessian grenadiers wounded, mostly slightly." By the next night the water began to drain off. The Americans, knowing what danger they would be in if the canal drained, resisted fiercely. On the first of May, while the British worked at cutting through the dam, "The cannon and small arms fire remained constant, and four English and three Hessian grenadiers were killed and just as many wounded." Later that day a Jäger and a light infantryman "were killed and a jäger had his arm shot off." The next day American fire was so effective that it "destroyed the lodgment at the advanced ditch and held up the work opposite the dam so much that little was accomplished." On 4 May the "fire of the besieged was violent" but the "water ran off noticeably." This spurred the front-line American troops. "The 5th. In the evening at ten o'clock the cannon and musketry fire of the besieged was so violent and directed with such good effect that the workers could do little. I occupied the advanced approaches today. Last night the besieged started a counterapproach from their bastion on the right opposite the sap to the dam, which greatly hindered our work. I tried to protect the workers as much as possible, but there were at least one hundred sharpshooters in the hole, whose fire was so superior to mine that the jägers no longer dared to fire a shot." But the British and their German allies kept doggedly at it and by the night of 6 May "The sap leading to the dam had progressed so far that all the water drained out of the canal, which the enemy could not prevent by his incessant grapeshot and musketry fire."[18]

There was no glory in this kind of warfare. It demanded that men keep their nerves intact day and night for long stretches while under continual fire, which is no mean task but goes largely unheralded. Glory lay elsewhere. On 6

May, when the canal was drained and preparations for an assault could finally begin, Banastre Tarleton, riding hard, again humiliated the Rebels.

"Resistance and slaughter soon ceased"

Unaware of what plans the Americans might be hatching to the north to relieve Charleston, Sir Henry Clinton ordered Lord Cornwallis to see to the safety of the British rear and prevent the escape of the garrison. Cornwallis committed the wide country from the Cooper northward to his cavalry commander. He ordered Tarleton to inform him immediately of any "material movement of the enemy in that quarter; I must likewise recommend it to you to take every opportunity to procuring intelligence, either from the town, or the Santee River and back country." He did not keep the young commander on a short rein but gave him freedom to move where he would and base himself as he pleased, but in those days without radio and aircraft he insisted that Tarleton report to him "whenever you move, that I may know where to find you." Since he knew Tarleton would always be on the move, he gave him permission to destroy captured stores if there was danger that the enemy might retake them. Cornwallis concluded his letter of 25 April with a clear and firm admonition: "I must recommend it to you in the strongest manner to use your utmost endeavors to prevent the troops under your command from committing irregularities, and I am convinced that my recommendation will have weight, when I assure you that such conduct will be highly agreeable to the commander in chief."[19]

American cavalry, some newly arrived from the north, others survivors of Monck's Corner, were gathered at several places along the Santee River. On 5 May Colonel Anthony White crossed to the south bank of the Santee. The following day he and his troopers captured an officer and seventeen infantrymen of Tarleton's command. White then headed for a place called Lenud's Ferry on the Santee, where wetlands covered by a canopy of trees rising high out of the black waters stretch on either side far beyond the main channel.

Gathered on the north bank of the river were Colonel Abraham Buford and 350 men of the Virginia Continental Line, on their way to reinforce Charleston. Two survivors of Monck's Corner, Colonel William Washington and Colonel Jamieson, were on the south bank with some dragoons. Tarleton, also moving toward the Santee, met a Tory who had witnessed the capture of his men and gave him accurate intelligence. He had only 150 troopers of the British Legion with him and was in a sort of no man's land, but he never hesitated. A forced march brought him to the south bank of the Santee by 3:00 P.M.

All the Americans—Colonels White, Washington, Jamieson, and their men—were surprised by the sudden appearance of the British. Buford, on the other side of the river, could offer no support. Once again there were no patrols out, no scouts to sound the alarm in time for men to deploy. They were further surprised by Tarleton's tactic. On sighting the Americans he immediately formed and ordered a charge. As with his account of Monck's Corner, Tarleton's description of the action at Lenud's Ferry in his *History* is accurate and to the point. The Americans "being totally surprised, resistance and slaughter soon ceased. Five officers and thirty-six men were killed and wounded. . . . All the horses, arms, and accoutrements of the Americans were captured. Colonels White, Washington, and Jamieson, with some officers and men, availed themselves of their swimming, to take their escape, while many who wished to follow their example perished in the river. The British dragoons lost two men and four horses in the action; but returning to Lord Cornwallis's camp the same evening, upwards of twenty horses expired with fatigue."[20]

How must William Washington have felt? In the space of about three weeks he had twice been taken by surprise, and only the proximity of swamps and a river had saved him from death or capture. Another brilliant exploit by Banastre Tarleton, and this time no report of "irregularities" by the British Legion. Perhaps Cornwallis's letter had convinced him that his job had not ended once the fighting was done.

"The most ragged rabble I ever beheld"

The day after the action at Lenud's Ferry, Fort Moultrie, scene of the valiant American defense in 1776 when it was known as Fort Sullivan, surrendered to British sailors and marines without putting up a fight. Major Patrick Ferguson was among the British officers who went ashore with the assault party. The end for Charleston was near. On 8 May Clinton called for unconditional surrender, but Lincoln still thought he could negotiate and gain the honors of war. Clinton, who was losing patience and actively preparing for an assault, refused. The defenders would surrender their arms and go into captivity or face the storming of the city and whatever horrors that might bring. Negotiations were broken off at 9 P.M. The following evening, beginning at 8 o'clock, the final cannonade began. William Moultrie described it. "At length we fired the first gun, and immediately a tremendous cannonade—about one hundred and eighty, or two hundred pieces of heavy cannon were discharged at the same moment. The mortars from both sides threw out an enormous number of shells. It was a glorious sight to see them, like meteors, crossing each other, and bursting in the sky. It appeared as if the stars were tumbling down. The fire was incessant almost the whole night, cannonballs whizzing, and shells hissing, continually among us, ammunition chests and temporary magazines blowing up, great guns bursting, and wounded men groaning along the lines. It was a dreadful night! It was our last great effort, but it availed us nothing. After it, our military ardor was much abated."[21]

On the morning of 11 May, at 2:00 A.M., the firebrand Christopher Gadsden and the Governor's Council, accompanied by some leading citizens, came to General Benjamin Lincoln and asked him to surrender the city under the best terms he could get. It was a meeting one would have liked to attend, if only to study the expressions of Christopher Gadsden and his fellow supplicants. The physician and historian David Ramsay was in the city at the time and stated that on the same day "petitions were presented from a great majority of the inhabitants, and of the country militia, praying general Lincoln to accede to the terms offered by Sir Henry Clinton." All of this while the troops on the fortifications, made of sterner stuff, were still fighting. According to Johann Ewald, who was in a lodgment about thirty paces from the main Rebel fortifications, American "cannon and musketry fire were horrible, and, certainly, almost every minute cost the lives of several men. Without noticing it, due to the frightful musketry fire, the besieged were lucky enough to demolish all our dismantling and breach batteries."[22]

"Toward eight or nine o'clock in the morning," Ewald continued, "orders were given to fire on the city with red-hot shot, which set fire to several houses and made the sight still more terrible and melancholy, whereupon the enemy fire weakened somewhat. The Commander in Chief, who pitied the city being reduced to ashes, issued orders about ten o'clock to stop the firing of red-hot shot, and granted the besieged time to reconsider. But since the enemy fire increased with scrap iron and stone missiles, our firing continued until two o'clock in the afternoon.

"During this murdering and burning I heard the sound of a drum. Just then I was in the lodgment, which had been built through the advanced ditch. I heard that it was a parley, shouted we should cease fire, and sent jagers in all directions. At that moment, [a] Lieutenant Colonel . . . of the light infantry appeared and handed me a letter from General Lincoln, addressed to General Clinton. We both sat down in the lodgment. I sent for wine, and we both comforted our souls after such difficult business."[23]

There remained details to haggle over. There would be no honors of war. Benjamin Lincoln, his officers, and his men would march off as prisoners, Lincoln and the senior officers to relatively comfortable quarters and with the hope of exchange for Britons in American hands. Prison hulks awaited the other ranks and junior officers. The militia, and civilians who had taken up arms and manned the fortifications, were released on parole. This was a military term long before it became associated with criminals. It comes from the French *parole d'honneur* (word of honor), and it meant that if you were taken prisoner and offered and accepted parole you gave your word of honor that you would not take up arms against your captor unless you were exchanged. Parole was not a concept taken lightly but a most serious matter. To break parole was to risk execution if retaken, and there were examples of this during the Revolution, sometimes formally, at other times summarily on the battlefield when a known parolee was captured bearing arms. It is important to add, however, that the victor, granting parole, had certain responsibilities too, and this would soon become a matter of heated dispute between the Rebels and the British.

By the standards of many ages, including our own, losses at the siege of Charleston were light. The Americans lost eighty-nine killed and 138 wounded. Far more serious to the cause were the 3,371 men captured, of whom 2,571 were Continentals. This meant that there was no American army in the South. The British had seventy-six killed and 189 wounded. The actual surrender came on the 12th of May, the day after the drum Captain Ewald heard beat for parley. An observer saw "tears coursing down the cheeks of General Moultrie." Benjamin Lincoln, a good man promoted beyond his abilities, limped out of the city "at the head of the most ragged rabble I ever beheld," wrote a British onlooker.[24] Lord Cornwallis was not there. He was across the Cooper with his command and did not participate in the ceremonies, such as they were. Which was just as well. The noble Earl's opportunity was nigh. It was the greatest British victory of the war, and it belonged to Sir Henry Clinton, who was at the peak of his career as he watched the Americans lay down their arms.[25]

We indicated previously that Sir Henry, not a great general but quite competent and the most able of the four British commanders in chief during the American Revolution, had a seriously flawed personality. In the end, his flaws outweighed his intelligence and ability and helped to render hollow his great victory at Charleston. "He was driven by an urge to quarrel," his biographer William Willcox wrote, and this judgment cannot be faulted. The British generals who served in America were as a lot quarrelsome, but Clinton was in a class by himself. He could not get along with his peers or his superiors. He had one of the most irritating traits in the collection of human failings: a total lack of tact. "I have accustomed myself, wherever I go, to hear all [and] see all I can, and form my own sometimes mistaken opinions in consequence." All very well had he kept those opinions, mistaken or otherwise, to himself, or had he been able, in the manner of a skilled courtier, to pass them on to his superiors without angering them. A "shy bitch," as he called himself, he never exhibited that part of his personality when laying out to his superiors their failings as commanders. Yet as commander in chief he could not bring himself to be equally blunt in face-to-face confrontations with subordinates who challenged his authority. As subordinate himself he failed to take into account the feelings and pride of superiors; in command he failed to exert his authority over subordinates. He planned so very well, but with the exception of the Charleston campaign lacked the strength of character to carry out those plans. He was indeed a most neurotic man, and the reasons for his condition elude us.[26]

In the final chapter of his biography of Clinton, Professor Willcox teamed with a fellow professor, the psychotherapist Frederick Wyatt, in an attempt to understand why Clinton behaved as he did. Their conclusion was that Sir Henry had a deep-rooted authority conflict that went back to his childhood. The problem is that all we know about Clinton's childhood is that he had one. Willcox admitted ignorance of Clinton's early years. The theory was presented as conjecture, and in Willcox's responsible hands conjecture did not descend to psychobabble. "It seems to be sound," Willcox wrote, "and is presented as perhaps true" [emphasis Willcox's].[27]

It is enough for us to know that Sir Henry Clinton could not measure up to the job of commander in chief, and that his character flaws also jeopardized his actions in subordinate capacities. Had he been born a century or so later and filled the post of a modern chief of staff, under a wise and sympathetic commander who saw his very real gifts and was able to capitalize on them, Sir Henry might have gone down in history revered and honored by his countrymen. But that too is mere conjecture.

Sir Henry did two things before turning over command in the field to Lord Cornwallis and leaving for his headquarters in New York. He gave the Earl specific instructions that his primary responsibility was to safeguard Charleston and South Carolina. Cornwallis was not to take the army into North Carolina if such a move would jeopardize his main task. Sir Henry's second decision was a rare, and very serious, error of judgment, one of those mistakes so clear to posterity but eminently reasonable at the time to those who commit them. On 3 June 1780 he issued a proclamation declaring that all men who had been given parole were released from that state, required to swear allegiance to the crown, and henceforth expected to serve when called on to maintain His Majesty's government in South Carolina. Consternation followed by anger swept the ranks of the recently vanquished. It was one thing to give up the fight against seemingly hopeless odds, quite another to pledge active support to the victor against brethren still in the field. Some men fled to the Patriot ranks. Others took the pledge but had no intention of honoring it. Quite unaware of the mischief he had created, the conqueror of Charleston took ship to New York.[28]

7

Into the Back Country

*"I love that army, and flatter myself that I am not
quite indifferent to them"*

They were opposites, Clinton and Cornwallis, but in one important respect very much alike. Each man had been devoted to his wife, and the early deaths of those women profoundly affected the husbands they left behind. For each life lost its meaning, and for each England palled. As we have seen, Sir Henry finally fled to the wild lands of Eastern Europe. Cornwallis, opposed to the American War, on record as a Member of Parliament as voting against coercive measures, nevertheless joined King and Country to return once more to a harsh and unforgiving land and find solace in the army he also loved.

Charles Cornwallis was born to privilege and position in a house on Grosvenor Square in London on New Year's Eve, 1738.[1] His father, also Charles, descended from a landed family that had established itself in Suffolk by the late fourteenth century; in 1661 it was rewarded by Charles II with a barony for the faithful and valiant service of Sir Frederick Cornwallis in the Stuart cause during the civil wars and exile on the continent. The infant's father, the fifth Baron Cornwallis, served the Hanoverians as faithfully if not excitingly in various positions and received his reward as Viscount Brome and the first Earl Cornwallis. (Viscount Brome—the name comes from Brome Hall, then the family seat in Suffolk—thereafter became a courtesy title for heirs to the earldom before they inherited.) His mother, Elizabeth Madan, was also well connected, and Cornwallis's biographers believe that the marriage helped his father obtain the earldom. She was the daughter of Lord Townshend—not the one familiar to Americans for the Townshend Acts—and the niece of one of the great men of English history, Sir Robert Walpole. To round off his heritage rather nicely, his father's brother, Frederick Cornwallis, also married a Townshend woman and became Archbishop of Canterbury. The family did not have great wealth, but

Charles, 1st Marquess Cornwallis, by Thomas
Gainsborough, 1783.
(By courtesy of the National Portrait Gallery, London.)

there was enough money as well as a birthright of interlocking social and political connections whose value was immeasurable, especially for an ambitious lad
attuned to the nuances of preferment. We need not feel sorry for the young Viscount Brome.

His first stop after home was Eton, where he spent one or two years that
apparently influenced him greatly, and where he also received a blow in one eye
from a hockey stick that disfigured him for life. A "very military" boy, according to his father, he was commissioned as an ensign in the 1st Foot (Grenadier)
Guards in 1756, about one month before his eighteenth birthday. Then, however, he did something out of the ordinary. There was no Sandhurst in those
days. British officers did not go to school to learn how to become soldiers. If
they thirsted for military glory, they went to war and learned on the job. There
was a military academy at Woolwich, but it was for training engineer and artillery officers. Men of Cornwallis's class did not build fortifications and siegeworks or manage heavy guns. His type stood straight and firm as an example to
the other ranks and took infantry within range of enemy musketry to trade volleys at 100 or fifty paces before placing reliance on their favorite weapon, the

bayonet, delivered with a vigor and enthusiasm that would do credit to the playing fields of Eton. Or they became cavalrymen, for they had ridden from boyhood over hill and dale and hedgerows, and to those experiences they had only to add brilliant uniforms and heavy sabers and their natural dash.

But Charles Cornwallis, Viscount Brome, chose to go to school, and in 1757 he crossed the Channel with a Prussian veteran, Captain de Roguin, as his tutor and traveling companion. The military academy in Turin was highly rated, and Cornwallis enrolled there. He stayed only a few months, and it is really quite impossible to state that he benefited very much from his studies, which included German, mathematics, and fortifications, as well as ballroom dancing twice a day five days a week, for an officer and gentleman was then expected to be able to deport himself with grace and dignity on formal occasions. I expect that, in addition to his dancing lessons, he learned more from whatever Captain de Roguin imparted from his experiences, and also from dining at midday during the school week with men de Roguin knew from the war: the governor and lieutenant governor of the academy. His education was broadened every Thursday and Sunday, when he attended the King of Sardinia's court.

It must have been a fascinating experience for the boy, for he was still a boy, and a pleasant interlude, but the real thing soon beckoned. The Seven Years' War (called the French and Indian War in America) had begun in 1756, and two years later Cornwallis's regiment was ordered to Europe to join England's German allies. He was in Geneva when he heard of his orders, but Switzerland then did not boast today's transportation network, and the young man never caught up with his regiment. In Germany, however, after six weeks as a volunteer with the forces of the Prussian soldier, Ferdinand, Duke of Brunswick, he became aide-de-camp to the Marquis of Granby, who eventually became commanding general of the British forces on the continent. He served three years in the field as a staff officer, an invaluable experience. But Charles Cornwallis in America was at his best as a battlefield commander, and it was against the French in Europe that he earned his spurs in this role. In May 1761 he became Lieutenant Colonel of the 12th Foot, and over the next year he led the regiment into several hot fights.

Then, in July 1762, a letter arrived from England informing Cornwallis that his father had died. The boy who had left England as Viscount Brome returned a seasoned veteran and battle captain, and also as the 2nd Earl Cornwallis. As a peer of the realm, that autumn he took his father's seat in the House of Lords. He was not quite twenty-four.

The young earl also fell in love. There were obviously deep fires within that stolid, burgher-like exterior revealed equally when he rode onto a battlefield and in his marriage. Jemima Tullekin Jones, daughter of Colonel James Jones of the 3rd Foot Guards, brought little if any money to the marriage in an age when the size of a dowry could make or break a proposed match. But she was a most attractive young woman, tall, willowy, with fine features and the lovely white neck of a swan. It was a love match, and in the year of their marriage, 1768, Cornwallis set politics aside and for the next few years the couple were rarely apart. Two children were born to them, a girl, Mary, and a son, Charles. They apparently led an idyllic existence in the Suffolk countryside, content with each other and their children and rural pursuits. But the outside world never waits, and it has a way of pulling back to it men like Charles, 2nd Earl Cornwallis.

He remained, of course, a member of the House of Lords, and in 1766 he purchased the colonelcy of the 33rd Foot. News from America was growing grimmer each year, and Cornwallis was opposed to the government's policy. In 1765 he voted against the Stamp Act. The next year he joined four other peers to vote against the Declaratory Act, legislation stating that Britain had the right to pass laws for the colonies on any matter. There was no doubt where Lord Cornwallis stood. Yet George III liked him. He was made aide-de-camp to the King in 1765, a member of the Privy Council in 1770, and Constable of the Tower of London in 1771. We do not know why the King held in such high esteem this man who opposed his American policy. His biographers believe it may have been their similarities: sobriety, dignity, devotion to family, and also to principles in which each believed. Perhaps, too, the King recognized that in Cornwallis he possessed a servant who in extremity would faithfully serve King and Country despite his sympathy for the Americans.

Cornwallis volunteered for service in the colonies and on 1 January 1776 was appointed Lieutenant General in the British army in North America. He served as Clinton's deputy, although the blame for the fiasco at Sullivan's Island was Parker's and Clinton's. He saw much action in the middle colonies prior to the siege of Charleston and his own grand adventure in the South. At the Battle of Long Island, where he led the reserve of the column commanded by Clinton that outflanked the Americans, Cornwallis saw hard fighting against foes who would become even more familiar—the Maryland and Delaware regiments. Washington fooled and embarrassed him at Trenton by stealing away while the earl and his soldiers slept and defeating Cornwallis's rear guard at Princeton. But the earl's rapid pursuit and steely resolve, unique among British generals in America, were made evident that day, and in the Carolinas the Americans would learn to respect those qualities.[2]

Cornwallis was with Howe at Brandywine, and at Monmouth, with the elite of the army, tried repeatedly to drive Nathanael Greene's regiments from their position but finally had to withdraw and leave the field to the Americans. His personal courage was beyond doubt and would be proven again in the Carolinas, and he could drive an army in hot pursuit faster than any other British general in America. But he had not displayed special gifts for either tactics or strategy. The successful flanking movements at Long Island and Brandywine were conceived by others. The only time he had been alone with a command in a major tactical situation, in the sense that he was quite out of touch with headquarters, was at Trenton, and he botched it. His only contribution to strategic thinking had been to support Howe's move to Philadelphia instead of assisting Burgoyne's army coming down from Canada, and that had led to disaster. By the time he took command of the southern army he had shown neither brilliant flair nor uncommon abilities, but there was no doubt that he was a very solid performer when the guns began to roar. To be fair, he was third in line of command under Howe, second under Clinton. To prove his mettle, perhaps he was the kind of man who needed an independent command, his own theatre of operations, without superiors close by looking over his shoulder.[3]

Cornwallis did something after the Battle of White Plains that does not sit well and has never seemed characteristic of the man. But there is no doubt that he did it, and the memory of it ate like a cancer inside Sir Henry Clinton. During the battle Clinton, who was then Howe's deputy, commanded the rear guard. Howe had assigned him a definite route of march, but as the tactical situation developed Clinton decided to change it and so informed Howe. Sir William jerked him back with a sharp order to proceed as ordered. Clinton exploded in front of Cornwallis. "I cannot bear to serve under him," he said, and swore he would "prefer the heading of three companies at a distance from him to serving in any capacity immediately under him." Cornwallis repeated the outburst to Howe, who stored it away and bided his time.

A little less than a year later, when Howe was about to depart on his Philadelphia expedition and leave Clinton in charge in New York, he dropped his little bomb. Sir Henry left a record of the exchange in the third person, which was not uncommon then. "When the Commander in Chief informed Sir Henry Clinton that he proposed leaving him in the command at New York, he also said he had no doubt he would be much pleased with such an arrangement, as he understood from Lord Cornwallis *Sir Henry Clinton would gladly prefer the heading of three companies at a distance from him to serving in any capacity immediately under him.* Though Sir Henry Clinton was struck with astonishment by this unexpected speech, he candidly acknowledged that it immediately brought to his recollection some words of that tendency which he had once uttered in a peevish mood in the presence of Lord Cornwallis, at a moment when he happened to be a little ruffled by a message from His Excellency; but that he had long since totally forgot the circumstance. Nor could he conceive what could be His Lordship's motive for troubling His Excellency with the repetition of a private conversation, which he must have known was not meant to go farther."

Although Clinton usually avoided confrontations, in this case he did not suffer in silence. He faced Cornwallis and told him what he thought of his conduct and recorded that His Lordship "made a very awkward apology, and so the affair ended." But it did not, of course, with a man like Clinton who locked within himself for future use all slights, wrongs, abuses, and acts of betrayal, actual or imagined. Strictly speaking, it was not treachery on Cornwallis's part, but it was a dishonorable act by a normally honorable man, which can only lead us, I believe, to the reasonable speculation that the noble Earl's ambition got in the way of his sense of honor.[4]

Cornwallis arrived in England on leave in January 1778, and stayed about six months. While he was there a fateful decision was taken by the King and his ministers on the command in America. Sir William Howe had offered his resignation because he did not agree with the government's strategy and had been refused the reinforcements he wanted. Who to replace him? The post was offered to Lord Jeffrey Amherst, who wisely declined. There was Cornwallis, of course, but his failure to crush Washington at Trenton and his embarrassment there at the hands of the "Fox" was fresh in London's memory. For various reasons, there was no other general quite suitable; it came down to the King's either refusing to accept Howe's resignation or agreeing to replace him with Sir Henry Clinton. Lord North at first thought Sir Henry's appointment would be a mistake, and wrote to George III, "It is certainly not desirable, if it can be avoided, to employ any general who declares himself unwilling to continue in his command and complains of slights and ill treatment." But the cabinet was unable to come up with an alternative, and in early February 1778 Howe's resignation was accepted and the supreme command in America offered to Clinton. He accepted it with the uncertainty that was such a deep part of his character.[5]

Cornwallis returned to America that June as Clinton's second in command. He almost immediately tried to resign, but the King refused his request. Primadonnish characteristics are not unknown among generals of any nation, but was a country ever cursed as Britain in the late eighteenth century with such a collection of temperamental, argumentative soldiers? And not one of them was a truly first-rate general. Yet in all fairness to them, they were matched in overall ineptness by the cabinet and their monarch.

For the second time in 1778, Cornwallis returned on leave to England, departing in November and arriving about a week before Christmas, this time, however, with a critical assignment from Sir Henry to convince the government of the need for reinforcements and, if successful, to return with them. The biographers of both men agree that at the time they seemed to be on amicable terms, and Cornwallis did indeed deliver the message. But his attention was diverted to a crisis at the very heart of his being. Jemima, Countess Cornwallis, was desperately ill. Friends thought that she was wasting away because of her husband's prolonged absences, but she may have had hepatitis. Cornwallis resigned his position in the British army in America, and the King accepted it. In late January Cornwallis wrote to Clinton, "The very ill state of her health in which I found Lady Cornwallis has render'd me incapable of any attention but to her, and the thoughts of her danger is forever present in my mind." Three weeks later she died.[6]

Cornwallis was desolate, solitude his only desire. Later in the year he wrote to his brother that Jemima's death "effectually destroyed all my hopes of happiness in this world." He decided that he must leave England. In April he wrote to Clinton that he did not wish to command in America but if offensive operations were planned he would "with great pleasure come out and meet you; This country has now no charms for me, & I am perfectly indifferent as to what part of the world I may go." But not five days later he wrote Clinton again that he was ready to return to America. He offered his services once more to his monarch and George III accepted. In early May he informed his brother William, "I am now returning to America, not with views of conquest and ambition, nothing brilliant can be expected in that quarter; but I find this country quite unsupportable to me. I must shift the scene; I have many friends in the American army; I love that army, and flatter myself that I am not quite indifferent to them."[7] This was part of the problem between Cornwallis and Clinton. Sir Henry might share danger with his troops and lead them to victory as he did at Charleston, but he was just not the kind of man to win over the rank and file. Nor were the officers for the most part his men. He was a loner, Sir Henry, and the army must have sensed it. There is an inborn subtlety to leadership that those who do not possess it never understand. People will do their jobs for whoever is in charge because they must, but they only do it willingly and beyond the call of duty for those to whom they give their hearts.

When Cornwallis returned to New York in July 1779, he was not accompanied by Clinton's requested reinforcements, whereupon Clinton offered his resignation to London. He expected it to be accepted and that Cornwallis would succeed him, but because of the usual dithering in London and the months that it took for communications between Britain and America he could not hope for an early answer. In fact, he still had not heard by the end of the year when the great expedition left New York for Charleston.

Cornwallis's protestations to the contrary, he must have wanted the command. He was an ambitious man and confident of his abilities, and the army preferred him. It was a delicate situation awaiting a spark to set off an explosion: a commander in chief who had submitted his resignation, his probable successor waiting in the wings, to say the least an uneasy relationship between them, and the army engaged in a major operation. Clinton regarded with suspicion his deputy and the officers close to him, especially His Lordship's close friend and aide-de-camp, Captain Alexander Ross. But as Cornwallis might succeed him, Clinton had consulted with him and requested his advice every step of the way, and Cornwallis had cooperated. On 19 March 1780 the answer both were awaiting finally arrived. Clinton had submitted his resignation the previous summer, the government had finally made a decision in November, and it was not until operations around Charleston were well advanced that he received word from Lord Germain, who informed him that the King was "too well satisfied with your conduct to wish to see the command of his forces in any other hands." After the war Clinton wrote that the decision was "perhaps not a little mortifying to the noble Earl whom I had taken the liberty of recommending to succeed me."[8]

A few days after the arrival of the letter from London Cornwallis told Clinton that he no longer wished to be consulted, for if he was not to succeed, he no longer wished to share responsibility for decisions. Thereafter, according to Clinton, "His Lordship's carriage toward me immediately changed. And from this period he was pleased to withdraw his counsels and to confine himself to his routine of duty in the line, without honoring headquarters with his presence oftener than required." Cornwallis had no right to do that, and Clinton could have demanded that he provide counsel and advice to his commander in chief. But that was not Sir Henry's way. Instead, he accused Cornwallis of previously spreading rumors of his resignation and alienating his officers. Cornwallis denied the charge and accused Clinton of disobeying the King's order with regard to British officers holding both regular and provincial ranks. This infuriated Clinton. He reached back into his long memory and confided to his journal: "I ought to have seen through him when he betrayed my private conversation with him to Sir William Howe in '76. All since is of a piece." He wrote further, "'Tis not time for altercation, but I can never be cordial with such a man." Cornwallis sought relief by asking for a command detached from the main army, and on 23 April he was given Webster's corps on the left bank of the Cooper. But Clinton was uneasy at his being out of sight and described his feelings in Shakespearian rhetoric: "He will play me false, I fear; at least Ross will."9

But the campaign was not over. There was, after all, still a war to fight, and off to the west a Back Country to pacify. That seemed to go quite well. Before Clinton's departure for New York on 5 June, British forces marched into the interior and occupied five key towns, from Georgetown in the Low Country, sixty miles north of Charleston, and continuing in a great semicircle through South Carolina to Augusta just across the Savannah River in Georgia. In between crown forces took control of two very important positions: Camden, a busy settlement 124 miles northwest of Charleston, on the direct road to a village in North Carolina called Charlotte; and Ninety Six, a trading post about 175 miles west of Charleston. The hamlet of Cheraw at the head of navigation on the Big Pee Dee, just below the North Carolina line, and the strongpoints of Rocky Mount and Hanging Rock north of Camden completed the defense line. Stunned by the fall of Charleston, Back Country rebels, in control since 1775, offered no resistance. Even Andrew Pickens, one of the toughest and most effective militia leaders, accepted British parole. On 22 May Clinton gave the job of organizing Tory forces in the Back Country to Major Patrick Ferguson, whom he appointed Inspector of Militia under Cornwallis, but without consulting the Earl. The reader will recall that it was Ferguson who wanted to shoot out of hand the troopers of Tarleton's British Legion who had assaulted Tory women after the action at Monck's Corner. Objections to his appointment were raised by Lieutenant Colonel Nisbet Balfour, who told Clinton that Ferguson had a hot temper and was harsh with troops. Clinton rejected Balfour's advice; he said that he had never received such reports about Ferguson and that he too had been victimized by false charges. It was a fateful decision.10

Another critical event with far-reaching consequences occurred six days later at a place remote from Charleston called the Waxhaws. With it began a continuous bloodletting in the Back Country, and Banastre Tarleton and the British Legion set the tone.

"Slaughter was commenced"

Colonel Abraham Buford, who had watched helplessly from the opposite bank of the Santee at Lenud's Ferry while Banastre Tarleton and his British Legion dragoons scattered the commands of Colonels Anthony White and William Washington, stayed where he was on hearing the news of the fall of Charleston.

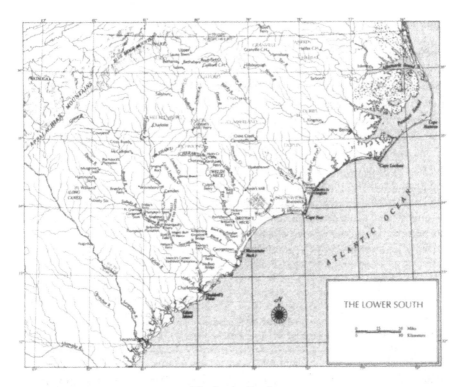

The Lower South.
From the Papers of General Nathanael Greene, Volume VII, *edited by Richard K.*
Showman. Maps adapted and expanded by Lyn Malone. Copyright© 1994 by the University
of North Carolina Press. Used by permission of the publisher.

General Isaac Huger, victim of Tarleton at Monck's Corner, then ordered Buford to fall back all the way to Hillsborough, North Carolina, in the northern part of that state, about forty miles from the Virginia line. Buford had a long way to go. With him were Governor John Rutledge and a few members of his council.

On the 18th of May Lord Cornwallis broke camp and marched with 2,500 men to Lenud's Ferry and crossed the Santee. Sir Henry Clinton had given him the task of pacifying the rest of the state and setting up strongpoints. Cornwallis's goal was Camden, on the same road taken by Buford. The earl had learned that Governor Rutledge was with Buford and wanted to capture him as well as attack Buford's force. But Buford had a ten-day lead, too much for the British infantry to catch him. As he would on many occasions, Cornwallis turned to Tarleton and his fast-moving light troops.

On 27 May Tarleton left Nelson's Ferry on the Santee with 270 men: forty British regulars of the 17th Dragoons, 130 Legion cavalry, and 100 mounted Legion infantry. He also took one small artillery piece, a three-pounder. Because of Buford's long head start, Cornwallis was not certain that Tarleton could catch him, and he gave his young cavalry commander discretion to continue, turn back, or attack if he could catch Buford. It is doubtful that Tarleton, ruthless driver of men and horses, ever considered turning back. The heat was oppressive, but Tarleton pushed horses until they died beneath their riders, commandeered mounts wherever he could find them, doubled up when necessary, and never let up. The small column arrived in Camden the next day and stopped to rest. But not for long. At 2:00 A.M. on the 29th Tarleton and the Legion marched. By dawn they reached Rugeley's Mill, about eleven miles north of Camden on the road to Charlotte. Governor Rutledge and his party had been there, entertained and given lodging by a prominent local Tory, Colonel Henry Rugeley, who was not alone in the Carolinas in hedging his bets. Learning that the British had reached Camden, Rugeley awakened his distinguished guests at midnight and urged them to flee. If the Rebel Governor of South Carolina was to be taken, it would not be in Henry Rugeley's house. Nor was Tarleton told that he had been there. He did learn that Buford was only twenty miles ahead, wrote out a summons to Buford to surrender, and sent it on by Captain David Kinlock. The Captain's mission was meant to either trick Buford into surrendering by greatly exaggerating British numbers or at the very least delay him. The letter read in part: "You are now almost encompassed by a corps of seven hundred light troops on horseback, half of that number are light infantry with cannon, the rest cavalry: Earl Cornwallis is likewise within a short march with nine British battalions." Delaying Kinlock so his infantry could reach a clearing, Buford then sent a one-sentence reply to Tarleton: "Sir, I reject your proposals, and shall defend myself to the last extremity."[11]

"By this time," Tarleton wrote, "many of the British cavalry and mounted infantry were totally worn out, and dropped successively into the rear; the horses of the three pounder were likewise unable to proceed." At that point, with a column strung out for miles, many commanders would have stopped. Not Tarleton. When in hot pursuit he was like a man possessed. At three o'clock in the afternoon, a few miles south of the North Carolina line in a district then called the Waxhaws, first contact was made. In appalling heat Tarleton had come 105 miles in fifty-four hours, an exceptional march rate. Within view of both commanders, without ceremony or preliminaries, Tarleton's advance guard immediately attacked Buford's rear guard. They captured an American sergeant and four dragoons. Lieutenant Pearson, commanding the rear guard, was sabered and unhorsed, and as he lay on the ground was sabered in the face, slantwise, and his nose, lips, tongue, and jaw split. Pearson survived in an age before plastic surgery, unable to "articulate distinctly after his wounds were healed."[12]

Buford formed for battle. He had detached his supply wagons and sent them on. He could have used his artillery, but it also continued the march, and a Rebel source later accused its commander, Captain Carter, of dishonorable conduct. Buford had his 350 Virginia Continentals and a detachment of William Washington's dragoons, although Washington was not present. He deployed the

Continentals into a single line. We have no information on what he did with the dragoons. Tarleton assigned fifty cavalry and about fifty dismounted infantry to harry the American left flank. Captains Corbet and Kinlock were to charge the center with the forty men of the 17th Dragoons and part of the Legion cavalry, while Tarleton with "thirty chosen horse and some infantry assaulted their right flank and reserve." Some British stragglers on their jaded horses were beginning to arrive and were ordered to form a reserve in the event of a repulse.[13]

Tarleton's small force formed on a low hill opposite Buford's center and in full view of the Americans. As Tarleton intended, the high ground was a good spot to regroup in case the attack failed, and also "made no inconsiderable impression" on the minds of his enemy. The forty troopers of the 17th Light Dragoons were a spot of red amid the green-jacketed British Legion. At 300 yards, Tarleton wrote, the "cavalry advanced to the charge. On their arrival within fifty paces, the continental infantry presented," but as he thundered across the clearing toward the American lines Tarleton could hear the American officers shouting to their men to hold their fire until the British were closer. It was an appalling error of judgment by Buford. The order to fire did not come until the charging horsemen were in the faces of the long line of Continentals—a mere ten yards away, time for only one volley. Tarleton's horse was killed under him, and a few other "officers, men, and horses suffered by their fire, but the battalion was completely broken, and slaughter was commenced." The Americans were literally ridden down. "Thus in a few minutes," Tarleton wrote, "ended an affair which might have had a very different termination."[14]

It was a superb performance, Tarleton at his best. Outnumbered, bone weary from the brutal forced march in the awful Carolina heat, he never looked back. His postwar description of the affair was clear and accurate, for when he won his *History* can be trusted. "The complete success of this attack may, in great measure, be attributed to the mistakes committed by the American commander." Tarleton felt that if Buford had formed his wagons "into a kind of redoubt to protect artillery and infantry against a cavalry charge" the British either would not have attacked or would have been repulsed. "Colonel Buford also committed a material error, in ordering the infantry to retain their fire . . . which when given, had little effect either upon the minds or bodies of the assailants, in comparison with the execution that might be expected from a successive fire of platoons . . . commenced at the distance of three or four hundred paces." But the Americans had not even raised their muskets to prepare to fire until the British cavalry was only fifty paces away. Abraham Buford and his officers had doomed the Continentals: 113 were killed and 203 captured, of whom 150 were wounded, some grievously. Abraham Buford did not share his command's fate, escaping "by a precipitate flight on horseback." Tarleton lost five killed and twelve wounded.[15]

Tarleton dashed off a brief report to Cornwallis that very day, and on the following morning a more complete recounting. Cornwallis forwarded both to Clinton on 2 June with his own letter of praise for Tarleton, and on 5 June Clinton sent them to Lord Germain in London. Exactly one month later all the letters were printed in a *London Gazette Extraordinary*, and then reprinted in newspapers throughout England. Finally, in this most frustrating war, Britain had a hero. And America a villain.[16]

For the fighting that took only minutes was followed by a massacre that lasted longer. The British Legion, Americans all, began butchering their vanquished countrymen. Some writers consider the American charges typical wartime propaganda. One points out that cavalry charges followed up by infantry bayonet attacks are messy, and there is no doubt that in hand-to-hand fighting the line between massacre and a wild instinct for survival is shadowy. The most complete statement charging a massacre did not appear until 1821, in a letter from Dr. Robert Brownfield to William Dobein James.[17] Brownfield was a surgeon with Buford. Very early in the fight, apparently almost as soon as his line was broken, Buford decided to surrender and sent forth Ensign Cruit with a white flag. Brownfield charged that Cruit was "instantly cut down" by the British, and that "the demand for quarters, seldom refused a vanquished foe, was at once found to be in vain; not a man was spared, and it was the concurrent testimony of all the survivors that for fifteen minutes after every man was prostrate they went over the ground plunging their bayonets into every one that exhibited any signs of life, and in some instances, where several had fallen over the other, these monsters were seen to throw off on the point of the bayonet the uppermost, to come at those beneath."

Dr. Brownfield also described the terrible ordeal of Captain John Stokes, who "received twenty-three wounds, and as he never for a moment lost his recollection, he often repeated to me the manner and order in which they were inflicted." Stokes was engaged in swordplay with a dragoon when another dragoon with a single blow "cut off his right hand through the metacarpal bones." Both dragoons continued their attack on Stokes, cutting off his left forefinger and hacking his left arm in "eight or ten places from the wrist to the shoulder. His head was then laid open almost the whole length of the crown to the eye brows. After he fell he received several cuts on the face and shoulders. A soldier, passing on in the work of death, asked if he expected quarters. Stokes answered, 'I have not, nor do I mean to ask quarters. Finish me as soon as possible.' He then transfixed him twice with his bayonet. Another asked the same question and received the same answer, and he also thrust his bayonet twice through his body." A British sergeant offered him protection, and Stokes asked to be laid down beside a British officer who was having his wounds attended, "that I may die in his presence." The sergeant carried out his wish, but while engaged had to "lay him down and stand over him to defend him against the fury of his comrades." Doctor Stapleton, Tarleton's surgeon, was dressing the wounds of the British officer, and Stokes, "who lay bleeding in every pore, asked him to do something for his wounds, which he scornfully and inhumanely refused until peremptorily ordered by the more humane officer, and even then only filled the wounds with rough tow, the particles of which could not be separated from the brain for several days." (Tow is rough cloth—flax, hemp, or jute—broken up for spinning.) Captain John Stokes had an iron constitution and a strong will to live. He survived the war, became a federal judge in North Carolina, married and had children, and died in his eighties. Stokes County, due north of Winston-Salem, is his memorial.

If we had only Brownfield's account, the charge of wartime propaganda would ring truer than it does. The brutalities of the British Legion at Monck's Corner were never denied; and Cornwallis's strong letter of 25 April to Tarleton (quoted in Chapter 6) on preventing his troops from "committing irregularities" tells us that both Cornwallis and Clinton were aware of the Legion's behavior after that earlier fight. There is further evidence, also from British sources. Charles Stedman, the Philadelphia Tory who became Cornwallis's commissary general, had seen the British Legion in action at Monck's Corner and described the travail and fate of Chevalier Vernier. He was also with Cornwallis's main force marching to Camden, but he most certainly spoke to British troops who had been present at the Buford fight. In his history of the war he wrote that "the king's troops were entitled to great commendation for their activity and ardour on this occasion, but the virtue of humanity was totally forgotten." The other British source was Tarleton himself, and his words leave no doubt that terrible things happened after the Americans tried to surrender. Keep in mind that he went down when his horse was killed during the charge. "The loss of officers and men was great on the part of the Americans, owing to the dragoons effectually breaking the infantry, and to a report amongst the cavalry that they had lost their commanding officer, which stimulated the soldiers to a vindictive asperity not easily restrained."[18]

Tarleton's reputation in America never recovered. He became immediately Bloody Tarleton and Bloody Ban. The American cry of "Tarleton's Quarter" and "Buford's Quarter" would be heard again and again on southern battlefields. It would be an exaggeration to state that the fight in the Waxhaws began the savagery that marked the war in the South, for it had started as early as 1775, Rebels savaging Tories, Tories savaging Rebels. But Tarleton and his Legion stoked embers that became a fire nearly raging out of control, for it roused a people whose heritage was border fighting in all of its barbaric excesses.

"Strangers to our laws and customs"

Banastre Tarleton could not have known that the people who dominated the Waxhaws, where he had caught up with Buford, would become his mortal foes. And in truth, supremely self-confident as he was, foreknowledge probably would have made no difference to the dashing young cavalryman. He would have regarded them, to use John Rutledge's phrase, as a "pack of beggars." Precisely the opinion held of them by many in colonial America.

They were belligerent, loyal, bigoted, valiant, crude, and tough. The men drank hard, fought hard, and moved often. Their young women shocked sensibilities with public displays of bosoms and legs rarely seen in eighteenth-century America. In South Carolina, wrote a preacher, "the Young Women have a most uncommon Practice, which I cannot break them off. They draw their Shift as Tight as possible to the Body, and pin it close, to shew the roundness of their Breasts, and slender Waists (for they are generally finely shaped) and draw their Petticoats close to their Hips to shew the fineness of their Limbs—so that they might as well be in Puri Naturalibus." An Anglican clergyman watching a boat-load of them embark in a Northern Ireland port called them "the scum of the universe." Wrote James Logan, Provincial Secretary of Pennsylvania and an Ulsterman himself, "a settlement of five families from the North of Ireland gives me more trouble than fifty of any other people." Charles Woodmason, the Anglican missionary in the South Carolina Back Country who failed to stop the young women from showing off their shapes, described these people as "Ignorant, mean, worthless, beggarly Irish Presbyterians, the Scum of the Earth, and Refuse of Mankind." Another epithet was "white savages." The rejection and vilification they experienced were equal to and in some cases surpassed that met by all other immigrant groups down to the present day. But those original immigrants and their descendants have always had two priceless advantages: they were white, and their ancestry was British. In the long run, that has made all the difference. Revenge would eventually be theirs and sweet, for by the late eighteenth century and with gathering force in the nineteenth, they stepped onto the national stage and became part of the American establishment in politics, business, religion, law—all aspects of American life.[19]

They were, of course, the Scotch Irish. It is an American term that was current in the eighteenth century and perhaps more common then than the records indicate. It apparently did not come into widespread use until the middle of the nineteenth century when it differentiated them from a different people, the Celtic Irish Catholics, then fleeing to America in vast numbers to escape starvation. After the English, the Scotch Irish became the second largest ethnic group in British North America in the eighteenth century, and their influence on the American character is beyond measure. During the Revolution the great majority were Rebels, and their contribution to victory was critical. Given their importance to our story, who were they, where did they come from, and why do we call them Scotch Irish?

There are Celtic myth enthusiasts who believe that the Scotch Irish were Celts, have peopled with Highlanders whole American landscapes where there were none, imagined bagpipes on American battlefields that never echoed to their wails, conjured a Celtic culture for an entire American region where it never existed. But the Scotch Irish were not Celts by either blood or culture. Their ancestors were Lowland Scots, inhabitants of a poor, backward, violent land. The difference between the Lowland Scots and the more famous Highland Scots should be established immediately. All that Lowlanders and Highlanders had in common, besides wretched poverty, was a political line on the map separating Scotland and England, and their incompatibility survived the Act of Union (1707) of the two kingdoms well into the nineteenth century. They might have lived in different countries, for they were very dissimilar people and they hated each other.

The hardening split between Highlanders and Lowlanders had developed at least by the late fourteenth century and was rendered the more intransigent by deep ethnic and cultural differences. The original inhabitants of the Lowlands were Celts, but by the seventh century A.D. and lasting for centuries the original Celtic stock that survived conquest was thoroughly diluted by waves of alien invaders and immigrants of Germanic stock—Germans and Norwegians and Normans and English and Flemings and Dutch who conquered and stayed—until the Lowlanders by the late fourteenth century were an English-speaking people of a mixed ethnic background that was overwhelmingly Germanic. The Highlanders were Gaelic-speaking Celts, "wild wykked helend-men," who were not brought under English control until after their final defeat in 1746 at Culloden Moor. Tartans and kilts, bagpipes and bonnets, and all the other Highland paraphernalia, real and fake, popularized in the nineteenth century by Sir Walter Scott and the British royal family, were alien to the Lowlanders. To these differences was added after the Protestant Reformation the profound distinction between Protestant Lowlanders and largely Catholic Highlanders in an age of fierce religious conflicts.[20]

In the early seventeenth century, in a continuation of an effort England had begun five centuries before to subdue Ireland, James I of England, who was also James VI of Scotland, confiscated the Ulster lands of the Irish aristocracy and created the Plantation of Ulster. On it were settled Scottish Lowlanders and English farmers and Londoners, Protestants all. Earlier settlements under private initiative were also composed of Scottish and English Protestants. James also hoped that flooding the land with Lowland Scots and English would prevent joint actions by Irish Celts and Scottish Highland Celts. Thus were the seeds planted for the terrible "troubles" we have witnessed on our television sets for the past decades.[21]

Many of the Lowland Scots who went to Ulster in large numbers to escape poverty had exchanged one border for another. In Scotland they had fought with their fellow borderers the English in a barbarous manner for 400 years. Raid and counter-raid and butchery had succeeded each other in dreary procession. Yet, ironically, if the Lowlanders bore a cultural resemblance to any people, it was to their enemies the English of the border counties, and in America they would mix easily with them, fight shoulder to shoulder, even follow and lead them into battle.[22] In the borderlands of Ulster incessant and savage war was waged with the "wild Irish," as the Celtic Irish were then commonly called. The Lowlanders who became Ulster Scots mingled and intermarried with the English and with French Huguenots, but so rarely with the Celtic Irish Catholics that the two distinctive communities remained bitter enemies.[23] At the same time the settlers prospered as farmers, weavers, and in the woolen and linen trades. Their prosperity, however, caused English protests, and late-seventeenth-century laws restricting their trade brought them economic distress. Anti-Presbyterian laws, taxation to support the Church of England, rapacious and absentee English landlords, and throughout the eighteenth century a series of severe economic depressions led to massive discontent. Poverty, often desperate, once more became their lot. Beginning about 1715 and ending in 1775 when the Revolution temporarily blocked immigration, about a quarter of a million Scotch Irish fled Ulster for America. The Celtic Irish Catholics were not part of this movement. There were few of them in colonial America.

They were "strangers to our laws and customs," complained the Philadelphia Quaker James Dickinson of the Scotch Irish, and this has a ring of familiarity to twentieth-century ears. But the strangers' descendants became lawmakers themselves in their new land, and for good and ill their customs and characteristics would become deeply woven into the American fabric. Once here, they never looked back. They had arrived in the promised land. They never cared to see Ulster again.[24] Among them were a sprinkling of yeoman farmers and a thin upper stratum of provincial gentry known as the Ascendancy. The latter included such families as Polk, Calhoun, and Jackson: to the young Republic they would supply national leaders.[25]

As a group, however, the Scotch Irish were overwhelmingly poor. Some early arrivals went to Massachusetts, but they and the Puritans were incompatible, and they pushed on to western Massachusetts and north to Maine and New Hampshire. Although there were more Scotch Irish in the colonies north of Pennsylvania than generally supposed, they made their greatest colonial impact in central and western Pennsylvania and the southern Back Country. They poured in largely through the ports of Philadelphia and New Castle, Delaware, and from there struck out for the Back Country. From Lancaster County west, Pennsylvania became their American homeland, and they treated it as they did every place they went, as theirs to take and keep. They introduced to America the tradition of squatting on unused property and daring anyone to put them off. They handled Indians roughly and were little less gentle with white authorities. Once when officials including a sheriff and surveyor tried to intimidate some Scotch Irish, "A body of some seventy joined circlewise around Mr. Parsons' instrument, and began narrowing in upon it, the front ones on foot, the rear ones on horseback." The official party left. Their attitude toward land as reported by the Provincial Secretary of Pennsylvania was simple: they "alleged that it was against the laws of God and nature, that so much land should be idle, while so many Christians wanted it to labor on, and to raise their bread."[26]

Their numbers increased dramatically by immigration and a lively fertility. From Pennsylvania the Scotch Irish spread southward by means of the Great Philadelphia Wagon Road, across the Potomac and through Maryland to the Great Valley of Virginia, the beautiful Shenandoah. German settlers dominated the Valley's northern reaches, but many Scotch Irish stopped in the central and southern parts, some for good, others until the urge to seek something better prodded them onward. The irrepressible Charles Lee lived in the Shenandoah before the war, and is reported to have said that Virginia was neither a democracy nor an aristocracy but a macocracy. Those who went into the far southwestern mountains of Virginia we will meet again during one of the most dramatic episodes of the war. Nor are we finished with the people who chose to continue south to Wachovia in North Carolina, from whence they followed the Catawba Trading Path to Waxhaw Creek, where the first handful of white settlers arrived in May 1751.[27] They and their progeny and kindred folk spread out over the fertile, well-watered, rolling uplands in that large swath of land between Charlotte and Camden called the Waxhaws and claimed it as their own.

These were the people who buried Buford's dead soldiers where they died, nursed the wounded at the Waxhaws Presbyterian Church, and plotted dark deeds of revenge. These were the people who in the blackest time for the cause would bend but never break. They were hard men and women, accustomed to privation, travail their normal lot, mercy to an enemy never uppermost in their thoughts.

8

Hearts and Minds

Rice Kings as Revolutionaries

The war had now left Charleston behind. We will visit the city again but only in passing. The action moved to the Back Country. Dedication by the Rice Kings to the proposition that all men are not created equal would lead to big trouble in the Back Country, a very large and dangerous area as central to our story as the Low Country that, following the fall of Charleston, takes precedence in the bitter and bloody struggle for the Carolinas. To better understand what is about to occur, we must go back to 1775 and the coming of the Revolution to South Carolina, and the adventures of William Henry Drayton in his attempt to forge an alliance between the radical Rice Kings and the "pack of beggars" they loathed.[1]

We met Drayton and his friend, neighbor, and fellow Rebel Arthur Middleton in Chapter 2, and subsequently we took a brief look at the magnificent estates their fathers had built on the Ashley River. In a portrait of Arthur Middleton and his family, Benjamin West portrayed Arthur as a slim, elegant young man. But Arthur Middleton's politics turned out to be far from refined. His father Henry had openly opposed British policies since 1770, and in 1774 he became the first President of the Continental Congress. Henry was at heart a moderate who deeply desired reconciliation with Great Britain; following the fall of Charleston he took British protection. His son Arthur was a radical who succeeded to his father's seat in the Continental Congress, was the Middleton who signed the Declaration of Independence, and after the surrender of Charleston was imprisoned at St. Augustine for the rest of the war. We must keep firmly in mind, however, that in their society the word radical meant one who favored independence. It had nothing to do with democracy or social equality. Rice Kings, from staunch Tories to radical Rebels, abhorred both. Rice Kings believed in self-government by the rich and the well born, that is, by themselves.

We must also understand that the rebellion in South Carolina began not among Back Country farmers and hardscrabble frontiersmen, but in the Low Country—of, by, and for the Rice Kings. Yet, as we have noted with Henry Middleton, we must not think of the men who established the Provincial Congress in 1775 as being of one political mind. Basic dissatisfaction with critical aspects of British rule was a common factor, but after that opinions and goals varied widely. For some, separation from Britain was unthinkable, and they fought to prevent the radicals among them from taking the colony to the point of no return. Gradually, however, and not without stubborn opposition, men imbued with a passion for radical change gained ascendency. A Secret Committee of five was established for the specific purpose of seizing public stores of arms and powder. The committee chairman, that once staunch defender of the Crown turned revolutionary, was William Henry Drayton, who could not at that early date announce his true goal, independence from Great Britain, but could and did strain every measure of his being to achieve it. Another member was his fellow revolutionary, Arthur Middleton. Although they could not immediately take measures as drastic as they wished, events occurring elsewhere played into their hands.

On 3 May 1775 information was received from London that the British government was considering the use of Indians and slaves against the colonists. The twin spectres of an Indian war and a black insurrection were enough to make their blood curdle, for the vast majority of the 80,000 to 100,000 blacks lived in the Low Country cheek to jowl with some 20,000 whites. That it was probably false information was unknown to the multitude and irrelevant to the radicals. Five days later came hard news from Massachusetts that undermined the go-slow policy of moderates and conservatives: Minutemen and British regulars had skirmished at Lexington. First blood had been spilled. On 1 June the Provincial Congress met and began taking measures that widened the fissure between Englishmen, but without Charles Pinckney, who resigned its presidency in favor of Henry Laurens. Pinckney was reluctant to go further in defiance of his King, and though he never became an active Tory he accepted British protection after the fall of Charleston. Other members of the family became distinguished revolutionaries.

The Provincial Congress raised three regiments and elected officers. "The military ardor was so great," wrote William Moultrie, "that many more candidates presented themselves, from the first families in the Province, as officers ... than were wanted."[2] A Council of Safety was appointed and given broad executive authority, including supreme power over military affairs. Familiar Low Country names made up its membership, and we should not be surprised to find among them William Henry Drayton and Arthur Middleton. But the most divisive measure taken by the Congress before it adjourned had been debated since the previous year and put off because of strong opposition by those who deeply feared the consequences. Events would prove their fears justified, but they could no longer stem the tide. The Provincial Congress resolved that an Association of all citizens of the colony was necessary in order to resist "force by force," and to that end a brief statement of purpose was provided that citizens would be required to sign.

The Association, as the document was known, solemnly engaged on behalf of South Carolina that "whenever our Continental or Provincial Councils shall decree it necessary, we will go forth, and be ready to sacrifice our lives and fortunes to secure her feedom and safety." The ruling body as a whole, however, was not ready to cross the Rubicon. They offered their lives and fortunes "until a reconciliation shall take place between Great-Britain and America, upon constitutional principles—an Event which we most ardently desire." But this offering of an olive branch was followed by a final sentence that guaranteed civil war: "And we will hold all those persons inimical to the liberty of the colonies, who shall refuse to subscribe this association." The choice was clear and stark: you are with us or against us, and your signature or lack of it will tell the tale. In the Low Country, where the Rebels were in control, retaliation against resistance, even speech, was swift and harsh. In June Laughlin Martin and James Dealy were charged with being in favor of distributing arms to blacks, Indians, and Roman Catholics, and Martin specifically charged with calling for a toast: "Damnation to the Committee and their proceedings." The charge was turned over to the Secret Committee. At the end of the charge, in disguised handwriting thought to be William Henry Drayton's, is the sentence: "SECRET, tar and feather him." The Committee ordered the sentence to be executed, and Laughlin and Dealy underwent the terrible ordeal of being stripped naked, tarred with hot oil, feathered, and paraded through the streets of Charleston.[3]

Although there was a similar, even more chilling, incident in the Georgia Back Country that bears directly on our tale and is described later, such tactics were almost impossible in South Carolina once the Low Country was left behind. The long decades when the Rice Kings had ignored the needs of the Back Country and their continued contempt for the great majority of its inhabitants made the "gentlemen" of the establishment most unwelcome in many backwoods cabins and rude communities. But now the settlers were needed, and the need was great, for about three-quarters of South Carolina's white population of 60,000 to 70,000 lived in the Back Country. If the "pack of beggars" went Tory, the Rice Kings would be in deep trouble.

William Henry Drayton:
A Rice King in the Back Country

About twenty miles west of Charleston the lovely but fever-ridden marshes and swamps of the coastal plain gave way to a featureless pine belt. Beyond this tedious land, in the central and western reaches of South Carolina, was country that actually had hills and vistas and air that was fresh instead of fetid. It was still hot, very hot. Tarleton and the Legion had found how hot it could be on their relentless march to the Waxhaws, about 165 miles from the coast. In the eighteenth century this was the Back Country, from roughly fifty miles outside Charleston westward another 150 miles to Ninety Six, and there were settlers beyond, angering the Cherokee by encroaching on treaty land.

William Henry Drayton
*Engraving. (South Caroliniana Library,
University of South Carolina.)*

Ninety Six was a fortified village more important then than hundreds of far larger American towns today, second only to Camden as a Back Country outpost. It got its name because it was thought to be ninety-six miles from the Cherokee town of Keowee in the southwestern corner of South Carolina. It was described a few years later in the diary of the northern Tory, Lieutenant Anthony Allaire, as containing "about twelve dwelling houses, a courthouse, and a jail . . . situated on an eminence, the land cleared for a mile around it, in a flourishing part of the country, suppled with good water, enjoys a free, open air, and is esteemed a healthy place."[4] Ninety Six began in the 1730s as an Indian trading post on the Charleston Path, the route from Indian country to the coast, along which moved furs and millions of deerskins. When the Rice Kings, aroused by actual and threatened force, finally deigned in the late 1760s to provide the Back Country with judicial districts, the first courthouse was established at Ninety Six.

In the late summer of 1775 the Rice Kings moved to ensure the support of the Back Country. Yet William Henry Drayton, the leader of the delegation sent to convince the *"profanus vulgus"* to heed the call of their betters, had in 1769 written in the *South-Carolina Gazette* of the mechanics of Charleston that no one who could "boast of having received a liberal education" could consider consulting on public affairs with men who could only advise on "how to cut up a beast in the market to the best advantage, cobble an old shoe in the neatest manner, or to build a necessary house," and concluded that "nature never intended that such men should be profound politicians, or able statesmen."[5] All this was no doubt a minor inconsistency to a politician with a cause. But whatever one may think of Drayton's beliefs, given who he was and where he came from, to undertake such a mission in the dangerous Back Country took courage.

Drayton was accompanied by the Reverend William Tennent and three other men. Their mission was "to explain to the people the causes of the present disputes between Great Britain and the American colonies" and to "quiet their minds," the eighteenth-century version of winning hearts and minds. Drayton also carried with him a confidential letter signed by Henry Laurens, President of the Council of Safety, that authorized him "to call upon all and every officer of the militia and rangers for assistance, support, and protection; and they and each of them are hereby ordered to furnish such assistance, support, and protection as you shall deem necessary." To give teeth to the letter, the entire South Carolina militia was organized into three divisions and ordered "to hold themselves ready by turns to march at twelve hours notice."[6] To a man like William Henry Drayton, this was a blank check to take forceful action if talk proved useless.

The Reverend William Tennent was a native of Northern Ireland, a noted Presbyterian preacher whose father was one of the founders of the College of New Jersey, later Princeton, from which William graduated. It was thought by the Council of Safety that he was best equipped to address the concerns of the Scotch Irish, many of whom were still Presbyterian but in 1775 rarely Princetonians. Tennant had helped draft the Association. Because the Baptists had made dramatic inroads in the Back Country's religious mosaic, South Carolina's leading Baptist preacher, the Reverend Oliver Hart, accompanied Drayton and Tennent. The need to include Hart is a clue to what was going on beyond the genteel Anglican spirituality of the Low Country. In the Back Country were Germans Lutheran and Reformed, Scotch Irish Presbyterians, French Huguenots, Independents, Baptists, Seventh-Day Baptists, New Light Baptists, and "an hundred other sects," wrote the Reverend Charles Woodmason. In a splendid sentence Lieutenant Governor William Bull described the denominations to Lord Hillsborough in 1770 as "subdivided ad infinitum in the back parts, as illiterate enthusiasm or wild imagination can misinterpret the scripture," while "every circle of Christian knowledge grows fainter as more removed from the center."[7] Drayton and the preachers were joined by Colonel Richard Richardson, who had migrated from Virginia and established himself in the Back Country of the upper Santee as a successful planter, militia officer, and man of affairs; and Joseph Kershaw, an important merchant from Camden who along with Richardson had been elected to the First Provincial Congress. But the fiery William Henry Drayton was the key member of the mission.

Drayton and Tennent left Charleston on 2 August 1775. They found neither the journey nor the mission easy going. Travel then was an endurance contest. The Reverend Charles Woodmason once described a journey to baptize several children as "A Shocking Passage. Obliged to cut the Way thro' the Swamp for 4 miles, thro' Canes, and impenetrable Woods—had my Cloaths torn to Pieces." The country Woodmason described lay on their path. To add to their discomfort, the arrogance of the Rice Kings left many settlers ill disposed to even listen to the message. William Tennent recorded in his diary that the people believed "that no man from Charleston can speak the truth, and that all the papers are full of lies." To the Council of Safety in Charleston he described the "unchangeable malignity of their minds and . . . bitterness against the gentlemen as they are called." A large, important ethnic group, the Germans, were afraid of losing their land, which had been given to them by the King. They wanted no part of rebellion. After a week spent in the German settlements near modern Columbia, during which Tennent recorded, "Mr. Drayton harangued them and was followed by myself," Drayton had to report that "the Dutch are not with us."[8] But the Germans were not dangerous to the cause, because their deepest desire was for both sides to leave them alone so they could cultivate their farms.

The Scotch Irish and English settlers presented the real danger. The former, traditionally considered as totally for rebellion, had among them a sizeable minority who favored the crown, especially those who had immigrated recently through the port of Charleston. At King's Creek on the Enoree River in the upper reaches of the Dutch Fork, that large area between the Broad and Saluda Rivers, William Henry Drayton met in debate the two ablest supporters of the King, Robert Cunningham and Thomas Brown. Cunningham was a Scotch Irishman who had migrated south from Pennsylvania to the Saluda River valley. He was a man widely respected and of great influence among many of the Back Country settlers. He may have come down on the side of the Tories out of personal resentment. Cunningham, Moses Kirkland, and James Mayson were candidates for colonel of a Back Country regiment authorized by the Council of Safety. Mayson got the command, and years later the prominent Rebel militia commander, Andrew Pickens, who spoke seldom but never arrived at a judgment idly, said that this "so exasperated the others that they immediately took the other Side of the Question." Pickens felt that Cunningham would have been the best choice, and if he "had been appointed Colonel at that time, we would not have had so violent an opposition to our cause in this Country."[9]

Thomas Brown was a man of some means who had immigrated to Georgia from Yorkshire in 1774. On the same day that Drayton left Charleston for the Back Country, Brown had faced alone about 100 Sons of Liberty at a friend's house near Augusta, about forty-five miles southeast of Ninety Six. He described what happened in a letter to his father of 10 November 1775. When he refused to declare for the cause the mob rushed him. Brown shot "their Ringleader," Chesley Bostick, through the foot, and when they took his pistols he drew his sword and "kept them at bay for some time," but a "cowardly miscreant" hit him in the back of the head with a rifle butt and fractured his skull. The blow would leave Thomas Brown with headaches for life, and exposed him to immediate indignities that aroused the passions of Tories and gave him the nickname of "Burntfoot" Brown to Rebels, who recalled it for many years after the Revolution. The Rebels ransacked his house. They tarred his legs and held his feet over burning wood. They used knives to cut off his hair and then scalped him. He lost two toes, and it was many months before he could walk normally. The Georgia Council of Safety thought the affair highly amusing: "The said Thomas Brown is now a little remarkable, wears his hair very short and a handkerchief around his head in order that his intellect . . . may not be affected."[10]

Thomas Brown, however, was made of stern stuff. His travail occurred on 2 August, yet on 15 August he was in South Carolina debating William Henry Drayton, who referred to him as Robert Cunningham's "worthy companion of tar and feather memory." Thomas Brown would lose all in the end and start life anew in the Bahamas, but before the war was over many a Rebel would pay dearly for Brown's pain and humiliation. He and Robert Cunningham were intelligent leaders, and Brown was tough to boot. They had many followers, and also working for them was the desire of many others to be left alone by both parties, and the feeling that would live for a century or more after the Revolution that Charleston and the "gentlemen below" could not be trusted. At the debate at King's Creek, Brown read to the crowd Sir John Dalrymple's *Address of the People of Great Britain to the Inhabitants of America*. Dalrymple, a lawyer in Lord North's cabinet, pointed out the great dangers of revolt: the power of the British military, the possibility of a slave revolt, the economic consequences. He argued that the differences between England and the colonies could be settled without difficulty. He also included a sentence that would have instant meaning to the settlers. "It is hard that the charge of our intending to enslave you should come oftenest from the mouths of those lawyers who in your southern provinces at least, have long made you slaves to themselves." At meeting after meeting Drayton harangued the people, but he could not "quiet their minds."[11]

From King's Creek the antagonists proceeded to the home of one of the most influential men in the Back Country, described by the Reverend Tennent as "the great and mighty nabob, Fletchall." He was Colonel Thomas Fletchall, a "very corpulent man" at 280 pounds, who owned 1,665 acres and about fourteen slaves on Fair Forest Creek, a few miles from the present Union, South Carolina. Fletchall was a colonel of militia, a magistrate, and a coroner. His brother-in-law was Ambrose Mills, the leading Tory of western North Carolina, whose tragic and undeserved fate we will later observe. If Drayton and his companions could have swung Fletchall to the cause, they might well have succeeded by persuasion. But after three hours of discussion Fletchall would not budge. Drayton was forced to report to the Council of Safety that "We endeavored to explain everything to him. . . . We endeavored to show him that we had confidence in him. We humoured him. We laughed with him. Then we recurred to argument . . . to join his countrymen and all America. All that we could get from him was this. He would never take up arms against the King, or his countrymen; and that the proceedings of the Congress at Philadelphia were impolitic, disrespectful, and irritating to the King."

However George III may have felt, William Henry Drayton was irritated beyond measure. It shows in his descriptions of Robert Cunningham and Thomas Brown, with whom he argued at Fletchall's place. Of Cunningham, "the man's looks are utterly against him; much venom appears in Cunningham's countenance and conversation." Brown was "the spokesman ... his bitterness and violence is intolerable." The atmosphere between Drayton and Brown became so heated that they would have come to blows had not Fletchall intervened and sent Brown to bed. Drayton did discover, however, that although Thomas Fletchall was steadfast against rebellion, he was also indecisive and preferred a reasonable compromise, especially when Cunningham and Brown were not around. It was their turn to be irritated when Fletchall was persuaded to muster his regiment on 23 August at John's Ford on the Enoree River for another stump meeting and debate.[12]

From Fletchall's Colonel Richard Richardson and Joseph Kershaw left the party and went home. Richardson undoubtedly departed to get the militia regiments ready for action. The Reverend Tennent made a circuit, to the Camden District where he failed to get anyone to sign the Association, then back west to what was called the New Acquisition (modern York County). There and in the Thicketty area between modern Spartanburg and Gaffney he finally met friendly settlers in a Scotch Irish stronghold who did not hesitate to sign. The Baptist preacher, Oliver Hart, traveled west from Fletchall's a short distance to the Lawson's Fork area (modern Spartanburg). William Henry Drayton joined him there at the home of Captain Joseph Wofford, and on the 21st, wrote Hart, "A beef was barbecued, on which we all dined." They also found a new militia regiment being organized by Colonel John Thomas, Sr., in support of the Provincial Congress and the Association.[13]

Despite this good news, Drayton was under no illusions. He and his fellow commissioners had so far little to show for their efforts, and Drayton wrote to the Council of Safety of the upcoming meeting at John's Ford, "I do not expect any success; I apprehend some insults." He was right. When he and Tennent and Hart converged at John's Ford where they had hoped to harangue some 1,000 militiamen they found only 250. But the Tory leaders were there in strength. Fletchall, of course, Cunningham, Brown, and Moses Kirkland. Kirkland had just returned from Charleston, where he met with the Royal Governor. Matters were coming to a head, a terrible tension was in the air. Some of the Tory leaders were armed with swords and pistols, and Drayton carried a dirk and two pistols. The Reverend Tennent recorded in his diary that Drayton harangued the militia "and was answered in a most scurrilous manner by Kirkland ... and a terrible riot seemed on the point of happening." Others cooled down passions and violence was averted. But there was no doubt now that in the spreading country beyond the forks of the Broad and the Saluda the King's Friends had the advantage. Tory leaders were convinced that the Provincial

Congress desired independence from Great Britain. That was not quite right, for as we know the Congress was badly divided on the issue. But when Thomas Brown accused William Henry Drayton of fomenting rebellion he was right, although Drayton could not yet admit his true goal to either King's Friends or his fellow legislators in Charleston. The following day he and Tennent wrote to the Council describing the harangues by Kirkland and Brown: "Imagine every indecency of language, every misrepresentation, every ungenerous, and unjust charge against the American politics, that could alarm the people, and give them an evil impression of our designs."[14]

William Henry Drayton now showed his mettle. The majority of the Council of Safety in Charleston was appalled at the thought of civil war. Drayton, however, was a true revolutionary, a man prepared to take the struggle to the bitter end. If he could not persuade, he would force compliance, and one way would be to deprive the Tories of their leaders. Thomas Fletchall, Robert Cunningham and his brothers, Thomas Brown, Moses Kirkland, and others had to go. He had known it for some time. Two days before the final, tumultuous meeting at John's Ford, Drayton wrote to the Council that "vigorous measures are absolutely necessary." He admitted that if Tory leaders were seized "some commotion in all probability will follow; but, I am so well acquainted with the situation of the disaffected parts of the country, and with such parts, as may be brought against them, that I am under no apprehensions for the consequences: provided prompt and vigorous measures attend every appearance of insurrection."[15]

Moving away from Fletchall's territory, Drayton and Tennent went to the Ninety Six District, from where Tennent eventually traveled to Georgia and returned to Charleston by way of the Savannah River. Drayton stayed on. He was alone now. Since he had decided it was time for action he probably preferred it that way. He alerted Major Andrew Williamson of the Ninety Six militia regiment and posted Colonel Richard Richardson and Colonel William "Danger" Thompson with their men close enough to act quickly if necessary. In addition to the letter he had from Henry Laurens, previously quoted, he also took as authority to act a letter from the Council of 11 August that referred to a reported threat by Moses Kirkland against Augusta. It stated that "they were perfectly satisfied he [Drayton] would leave nothing undone that should appear to be necessary." But there were sharply contending forces on the Council. The next letter to Drayton, dated 31 August, "viewed with horror the spectacle of civil war." The Council admitted that the Tory leaders might be easily seized, "but may not our enemy prove a hydra, and start twice as many heads to bring on their four thousand adherents with fury to rescue their first leaders, or to revenge their cause?" Nevertheless, the Council reaffirmed his original power and authority, and went even further: "He is thereby required and empowered, to take every decisive step, and to use every vigorous measure, which he may, or shall, deem proper to promote the public service."[16]

Bold in one sentence, timid in another, practically urging Drayton to use force in his discretion, yet cautioning him on the danger of provoking civil war, the Council's correspondence might well have confused another man. But

William Henry Drayton knew precisely what was going on in Charleston at the Council's meetings. His informant, of course, was his old friend and neighbor, fellow radical and Council member, Arthur Middleton, who in separate communications kept him regularly apprised of the Council's divisions and reported some of the language used during the tense debate that preceded the writing of the Council's letter of 31 August. Opponents of stern action had fulminated on the "Danger of creating civil war—young man—hot—rash—decisive step and vigorous measures meant too much." With only seven of the thirteen members of the Council present and voting, the decision to increase Drayton's powers had carried by only a four-to-three vote, and Arthur Middleton further reported that "two of the affirmatives were on the point of retracting." Middleton advised, for Drayton's own sake, a judicious mixture of vigor and caution.[17]

Drayton easily handled Moses Kirkland in early September. Kirkland lost his nerve when Drayton mustered militia and issued a Declaration warning people against Kirkland. Moses Kirkland fled to Charleston, where the Royal Governor, Sir William Campbell, gave him asylum on a British ship in the harbor. Drayton then moved against Colonel Thomas Fletchall, Thomas Brown, and Robert Cunningham. A combination of factors led him to negotiations instead of battle. He had raised not quite 1,000 militiamen to confront the Tories, but Thomas Fletchall had about 1,200 men; the odds were not in Drayton's favor, and, especially given the situation in the Council, he could not afford a defeat. He resorted to the classic technique of sowing discord among his enemies. He knew that Fletchall was a weak link. He invited the Tory leaders to Ninety Six to discuss the situation. Thomas Brown and the Cunninghams did not trust Drayton and refused to attend. But Thomas Fletchall went and was bamboozled by Drayton.[18]

What emerged on 16 September 1775 was the Treaty of Ninety Six, in which the Tories promised not to assist British troops in any way, and the Rebels agreed to punish any of their people who molested or harmed a Tory. The Treaty ended with an ominous sentence: "All persons who shall not consider themselves as bound by this treaty must abide by the consequences." Without giving away anything, and without shedding blood, William Henry Drayton had under the terms of the treaty neutralized the Back Country. But once again he did not delude himself. He knew that perilous times remained, and in his letter of 17 September transmitting the Treaty to Charleston he reminded the Council of Safety that "our situation is utterly precarious while the Governor is at liberty. He animates these men, he tempts them, and although they are now recovered, yet their fidelity is precarious if he is at liberty to jogg them again. . . . Gentlemen, allow me in the strongest terms to recommend that you make hostages of the Governor and the officers. To do this is not more dangerous than what we have done." Arthur Middleton introduced a motion to take Governor Campbell into custody, but strong conservative opposition, yearning for reconciliation with the mother country and fearing to go beyond forgiveness by London, voted it down.[19]

On the other side enraged opposition greeted Thomas Fletchall when he arrived at the Tory camp beyond the Saluda River and circulated the Treaty.

Thomas Brown wrote to Governor Campbell that at Ninety Six Fletchall "had such frequent Recourse to the Bottle as to soon render himself *non compos*." Robert Cunningham rejected the treaty out of hand, whereupon William Henry Drayton wrote to him and specifically asked if he felt himself included under the treaty. Cunningham said he did not, setting himself up for a charge of sedition and subsequent arrest. Thomas Brown went to Charleston to see the Governor, was arrested, interrogated, and ordered by the Council of Safety to leave South Carolina. He eventually reached St. Augustine. William Henry Drayton's tactic of separating leaders and followers was working well. Moses Kirkland and Thomas Brown were out of the province, Robert Cunningham was a fugitive, and Thomas Fletchall was not the man to lead a counterrevolution. Drayton had not wholly succeeded in winning hearts and minds, and he knew that simmering emotions could quickly come to a boil. But Arthur Middleton had been urging him for some time to "hurry down" to Charleston to lend his fervor for the cause to combating the reluctance of the conservatives to take the vigorous steps necessary to prepare the city for a possible British attack. But before leaving the Back Country he had one more job to do. In late September he headed for the Congarees, the site of a trading post just below modern Columbia. At Congarees Store he sat down with Good Warrior and other Cherokee chiefs with whom the Rebels wanted good relations and engaged in a familiar ritual.

There had been a particularly brutal Indian war in the South Carolina Back Country in 1760–1761. It had occurred for the usual reasons: white desire for Indian land and the quite reasonable desire of the Cherokee to defend what was theirs. It was, of course, accompanied by the usual mind-numbing brutalities committed by each side whenever whites and Indians went at each other. Dark rumors had been circulating for some time that Thomas Brown and Robert Cunningham were trying to raise the Cherokee against the Rebels, and that John Stuart, Superintendent of Indian Affairs for the Southern Department, and his deputy, Alexander Cameron, were also attempting to incite the Indians. The rumors may have been untrue, but truth is irrelevant at such times. In a "Friends and Brother Warriors, I take you by the hand" speech, Drayton gave the Rebel version of the dispute with Great Britain, solicited Cherokee friendship and good will, and promised them arms and powder, which they badly needed. Presents were distributed to the chiefs before they went home. Drayton then headed for Charleston.[20]

The Tories "are much terrified and come in with fear and trembling"

On 1 October 1775 William Henry Drayton was chosen President of the Provincial Congress. On the same day it was learned that Robert Cunningham had been captured by Rangers in Ninety Six District. He was brought to Charleston to appear before the Congress, where his words were read to him and he was questioned by Drayton. Robert Cunningham admitted to his words and stoutly continued to maintain that he was not bound by the Treaty of

Ninety Six. He was thereupon taken to Charleston jail and denied permission "to converse or correspond with any person whatsoever, or to have the use of pen, ink, or paper."[21]

The capture and jailing of Robert Cunningham led to the Tory insurrection in the Back Country so feared by the conservative faction in Charleston. On 3 November Robert's brother, Patrick Cunningham, and sixty men captured the wagon carrying the promised arms and powder to the Cherokee. The Tories also used this occasion to spread their own rumor: the Rebels, they said, were conspiring to bring the Cherokee into the struggle on their side. If there was anything that all people—Rebel, Tory, and neutral—could agree on it was the horror of an Indian war. The Rebels hotly denied the Tory rumor, as Tories had denied the same tales about them. The influential Rebel militia officer in the Ninety Six District, Major Andrew Williamson, gathered his militia to recover the arms and powder and arrest Patrick Cunningham and his men. The Provincial Congress, after a contentious debate followed by a 51–49 vote in favor, ordered Colonel Richard Richardson to assemble several militia units. William Henry Drayton gave Richardson instructions to seize Patrick Cunningham and several other men, whom he named. And Congress, ever prudent, instructed Drayton to invoke the Treaty of Ninety Six and demand that the insurgents deliver the men named before Richardson's force was mustered, in which case the expedition would be cancelled. Among those volunteering to serve with Richardson was a man who five years later would become a household name. But Thomas Sumter was under some suspicion because earlier the Tory Moses Kirkland had recommended Sumter as his successor to command a company of rangers. Colonel Richardson, who was related to Sumter by marriage, vouched for him and he was accepted; however, William Henry Drayton noted that "The Colonel, nevertheless, from his seeming connection with Kirkland, proposes to keep a sharp eye upon Mr. Sumter's conduct."[22]

Major Williamson meanwhile had erected a temporary stockade fort at Ninety Six. He had 562 men. On the late morning of 19 November, drums beating, colors flying, Patrick Cunningham and his Tory insurgents marched into Ninety Six, took possession of the courthouse and the jail, and invested the stockade. They were almost 2,000 strong. The two forces fired away at each other for three days, inflicting minimum casualties. It was the first bloodshed of the Revolution in South Carolina. Negotiations then began that eventually resulted in a treaty on 22 November. The treaty stipulated that the Rebels would give up the stockade, level it, and fill up the well they had dug. Public differences between the two parties would be submitted by the Tories to Governor William Campbell, and by the Rebels to the Council of Safety. Persons of both parties were not to be molested on returning home. Then came a key provision in the eyes of the Tories: if reinforcements arrived, they would be bound by the treaty.

This was the high point of Tory resistance in the Back Country in 1775. The treaty was not worth the paper it was written on, because the Rebels refused to recognize it. On 30 November Colonel Richardson held a council of war at which it was decided that the army was not bound by the treaty Major Williamson had signed. On 8 December Richardson issued a proclamation stating that Patrick Cunningham and others had violated the Drayton and Fletchall Treaty of Ninety Six, and demanded they surrender the captured arms and powder and the arms and ammunition of their followers. Richardson gave them five days to comply. Otherwise, "I shall be under a necessity of taking such steps as will be found disagreeable but which I shall certainly put in execution for the public good." Patrick Cunningham spurned the proclamation. Richardson, true to his word, marched on the insurgents.

It was a walkover. Richardson had built up an army of between 4,000 and 5,000 militiamen and state troops from the Low Country, the Back Country, and North Carolina. This was a very large force for the time and place, and it had the intended effect, both military and psychological. Meeting little resistance, Richardson's army swept through Tory strongholds. He reported to the Council of Safety that the army "proved to them what government can do in putting down opposition. That . . . they are much terrified and come in with fear and trembling—giving up their arms, with contrition for their late conduct." The "great and mighty nabob," Thomas Fletchall, was found hiding inside a hollow sycamore tree, all 280 pounds of him, and sent under arrest to Charleston. Only Patrick Cunningham and some two hundred diehards held out. They fled westward, just inside Cherokee country, and camped "at a place called the Great Cane Break on Reedy River." Colonel Richardson had no intention of allowing what William Henry Drayton called "this nest of sedition and of turbulent spirits" to go free. On the afternoon of 21 December he detached from the army 1,300 cavalry and infantry under the command of Colonel William Thompson. Readers will remember "Old Danger" from the Battle of Sullivan's Island. After a twenty-three-mile march, in the wee hours of the following day they could see Cunningham's campfires about two miles away. Just before daybreak they moved out and attempted to surround the camp. They had almost succeeded when they were discovered. Some Tories fled through the gap in Rebel lines. Of the 200 about seventy got away, including Patrick Cunningham, who had not even time to saddle a horse but galloped off bareback. According to Rebel sources, he called out for every man "to shift for himself." The rest were taken prisoner, along with all the baggage, arms, and ammunition. The Tories lost five or six killed; the Rebels had one wounded.

For four long years, the Tories in the Back Country would scarcely raise their heads until British troops and Tory regulars from the north took up positions at the strongpoints after the fall of Charleston. How had this happened in a region reputed to be a Tory stronghold? Although there was certainly strong Tory sentiment among the settlers, there were never as many Tories as the British thought. And this brief survey of Tory strength and resistance has for the most part neglected Rebel sentiment in the Back Country. Obviously, it too was considerable. But Drayton and his colleagues tended to concentrate on areas where Tories were numerous in order to win converts and eliminate threats to the cause. As we have seen, they made little headway. Yet from the end of August, when William Henry Drayton resorted to force and ordered militia commanders to deploy, it took only four months to end Tory resistance. Drayton's tactic of separating the followers from their best leaders played a key role, as did his decision to take off the gloves and move from the stump to the battlefield. When insurrection finally came, the Rebels raised an overwhelming force, led by two first-rate militia commanders. During the campaign the American commanders adopted a policy of firmness combined with forebearance and leniency that Colonel Richardson believed "have had a good effect." As he wrote on 2 January 1776 to Henry Laurens, "had I burnt, plundered and destroyed and laid waste, seizing on private property, then thousands of women and children must have been left to perish—a thought shocking to humanity." Drayton reported that had not Colonel Thompson intervened at the rout of Patrick Cunningham's diehards, "great slaughter would have ensued," because "The troops were so enraged against this party of insurgents, or King's men, as they call themselves." At the same time, Richardson continued to be firm against insurgency. Drayton reported that although Richardson had been humane, "he nevertheless deemed it prudent to hold some check over their future conduct, for which purpose he caused many of the insurgents to sign an instrument of writing by which they imposed upon themselves the penalties of forfeiting their estates real and personal should they ever take up arms again against, or disturb the peace and tranquillity of, the Colony."[23]

Revolutionaries—true revolutionaries—are aggressive, ruthless, and generally seize the main chance, as William Henry Drayton did when he saw that stump-speaking was getting him nowhere. But defenders of the status quo tend toward caution and legalisms and inaction until it is too late. Thomas Brown later proved himself an able and vigorous leader of King's Rangers, but that was later, after South Carolina had been lost. Perhaps if he had rolled the dice he would have lost in 1775, but when men had gathered and were ready and willing to fight he and Robert Cunningham decided that only the Royal Governor of South Carolina, Lord Campbell, could make that decision and sent the men home. Brown later wrote to Campbell that without British regulars "we are of Opinion twould be an Experiment rather too hazardous."[24] Men who make such decisions may be estimable in many respects, but they neither win nor defeat revolutions.

We now return to the late spring of 1780. Charleston has fallen. The Rice Kings are cowed, imprisoned, or in exile. British and Tory regiments are moving westward into the Back Country. Crown commissioners are spreading the word that the King's rule has been restored. Uncertainty and suspicion reign. A spirit of revenge is in the air. On both sides passions begin to boil over.

9

Trouble in the Back Country

The Making of a Rebel: I

"I was born in Lawrence [Laurens] District, S. C., on the seventeenth of January 1764. My father, Thomas Young, soon removed to Union District, where I have lived to this day." So begins the *Memoir* of Thomas Young, son of Thomas Young, whose thirst for vengeance would equal Thomas Brown's. He described his introduction to civil war at the age of fifteen simply and with candor.

"In the Spring of 1780, I think in April, Col. Brandon was encamped with a party of seventy or eighty whigs, about five miles below Union court-house, where Christopher Young now lives. Their object was to collect forces for the approaching campaign, and to keep a check upon the tories. They had taken a prisoner one Adam Steedham, as vile a tory as ever lived. By some means, Steedham escaped during the night, and notified the tories of Brandon's position. The whigs were attacked by a large body of the enemy before day and completely routed. On that occasion, my brother, John Young, was murdered. I shall never forget my feelings when told of his death. I do not believe I had ever used an oath before that day, but then I tore open my bosom, and swore that I would never rest until I had avenged his death. Subsequently, a hundred tories felt the weight of my arm for the deed, and around Steedham's neck I fastened the rope as a reward for his cruelties. On the next day I left home in my shirt sleeves and joined Brandon's party. Christopher Brandon and I joined at the same time, and the first engagement we were in was at Stallions', in York County."

Young's commander, Colonel Thomas Brandon (1741–1802), was born in Pennsylvania of Scotch Irish descent, and had come down the Great Wagon Road and Catawba Trading Path with his parents and siblings to South Carolina. An inveterate enemy of Tories, Brandon had the reputation of showing little mercy. He had received information about a party of Tories stationed at a house owned by a family named Stallions and with about fifty militiamen moved to attack them. Just before arriving at the house, Brandon divided his force. He took the larger party and circled to the rear in order to intercept any Tories trying to escape. Captain Love took sixteen men, including Thomas Young, to the front of the house to mount an attack. Thomas Young told what happened.

"Mrs. Stallions was a sister of Captain Love, and on the approach of her brother she ran out, and begged him not to fire upon the house. He told her it was too late now, and that their only chance for safety was to surrender. She ran back to the house and sprang upon the door step, which was pretty high. At this moment the house was attacked in the rear by Col. Brandon's party, and Mrs. Stallions was killed by a ball shot through the opposite door." The tragedy did not stop the attack. After several rounds were fired, the Tories, Young continued, "ran up a flag, first upon the end of a gun, but as that did not look exactly peaceful, a ball was put through the fellow's arm, and in a few minutes it was raised on a ramrod, and we ceased firing." The only Rebel casualty was shot through the wrist and thigh while next to Thomas Young. The Tories had two killed, not counting the unfortunate Mrs. Stallions, four wounded, and twenty-eight taken prisoner. "After the fight Love and Stallions met and shed bitter tears. Stallions was dismissed on parole to bury his wife and arrange his affairs."[1]

Before his sixteenth year was out Thomas Young had fought at King's Mountain, Hammond's Store, and Cowpens, was captured by the British, met Banastre Tarleton, and escaped to fight again. He saw the war end in his twentieth year. He will later tell us a macabre tale that more than indicates how he quickly became hardened to the horrors of war.

The fight at Stallions was not unique, although the dramatic death of Mrs. Stallions probably was not a common occurrence. The latest conservative count of Revolutionary War actions in South Carolina alone is 213,[2] and most were small, unheralded encounters like this one, which probably would have escaped notice if Thomas Young had not been there and described it in his memoir. Casualties often were few but psychological damage deep. When small numbers are involved, a few deaths have as much impact as hundreds or thousands when armies clash, and the significance is magnified when those involved are friends and neighbors and kin, some on one side, some on the other. This kind of fighting would go on for almost two years, and not all were small fights—some backwoods encounters would involve hundreds of men on each side.

In London, however, Lord George Germain, quite out of touch with reality, pictured a Southern landscape teeming with King's men, and believed that the application of "fire and sword" would suppress the "American peasants."[3] Nor was Lieutenant General Charles, Earl Cornwallis, then aware that beyond humbled Charleston dark passions simmered. On 30 June he wrote to Clinton that the capitulation of Ninety Six and the "dispersion of a party of rebels who had assembled at an iron-work on the northwest border of the province . . . put an end to all resistance in South Carolina." So sanguine was Cornwallis that in the same letter he expressed confidence "that with the forces at present under my command (except there should be a considerable foreign interference) I can leave South Carolina in security and march the beginning of September with a body of troops into the back part of North Carolina, with the greatest probability of reducing that province to its duty."[4] Yet he knew that on 20 June 1780, ten days before he wrote Clinton, this rosy picture had suffered its first major crack.

Big Fight at Ramsour's Mill

Ramsour's Mill (modern Lincolnton, North Carolina) was about twenty miles north of the South Carolina line, thirty-four miles northwest of Charlotte. To call the fight there a battle would lend it a formality it did not possess. It was a clash of two armed mobs. Toward the end the fighting resembled an old-fashioned Pier 6 brawl between longshoremen and strikebreakers, and not an Englishman within sight or sound. But it was deadly nonetheless, and this encounter at which professional soldiers might sneer had a significant impact on the British campaign in the Carolinas.

By various emissaries Cornwallis specifically instructed the North Carolina Tories to remain quiet until he was in a position to support them with the British army in his planned invasion of the province in early September. One of them was Lieutenant Colonel John Moore of the North Carolina Loyalist Volunteers, whose home was about six miles west of Ramsour's Mill. Moore had served with the British in South Carolina, and had left Cornwallis's column while it marched to Camden to deliver His Lordship's message to the Tories. He arrived in tattered regimentals, a sword swinging at his side. According to a contemporary of Moore's, the Rebel captain Joseph Graham, Moore spoke to forty Tories assembled "in the woods on Indian Creek, seven miles from Ramsour's."[5] He told them that Lord Cornwallis did not want them to rise but to ready themselves and gather the harvest, for the British army would need provisions; as soon as the harvest was in the army would enter North Carolina to support them. At the same time, the North Carolina Rebel militia leader, Brigadier General Griffith Rutherford, was in the Charlotte area with 700 men keeping an eye on British forces under Lord Rawdon to the south of him in the Waxhaws. Serving with Rutherford were our two main sources for the ensuing events: the Scotch Irishman Captain Joseph Graham and the Yorkshire-born Major William Richardson Davie, a militia officer of sterling qualities who will come to our attention on other occasions. Both wrote their accounts many years later, but their narratives have not been seriously disputed.

Learning of Tory gatherings to the west, Rutherford ordered Colonel Francis Lock to raise men and disperse the Tories. Lock began gathering men from the militia of Rowan, Burke, and Lincoln Counties. As Rutherford had reacted to Moore's return and activities, Moore now reacted to Rutherford and Lock. He directed Tories to join him on 13 June at Ramsour's Mill, and 200 men arrived that day. It has been said that John Moore did not intend to begin an insurrection. Whatever he intended, matters got out of hand. Among the Tories who appeared at Ramsour's Mill was Major Nicholas Welch of Moore's regiment. Welch, too, was from the area. He had just come from Cornwallis's army, and to the Tories gathered at Ramsour's Mill he related the details of Buford's defeat. Graham described Welch's impact on his fellow Tories: "He wore a rich suit of regimentals, and exhibited a considerable number of guineas, by which he sought to allure some, while he endeavored to intimidate others by an account of the success of the British army in all operations of the South and the total inability of the Whigs to make further opposition. His conduct had the desired effect, and much more confidence was placed in him than in Colonel Moore."[6] By 20 June 1,300 Tories had assembled, although one-quarter were without arms. They held a low ridge. The slope in front of them was largely open, providing a clear field of fire for over 200 yards.

Colonel Francis Lock had sent riders to various parts with a message for militiamen to gather at a place called Mountain Creek, sixteen miles from Ramsour's Mill, closer than Rutherford's men. Some of Lock's men were mounted, among them South Carolina partisans under Thomas Young's commander, Colonel Thomas Brandon. By Monday the 19th Rebel bands totaling 270 men under Major Joseph McDowell and other militia leaders had converged on Colonel Lock's camp. Lock now had 400 fighters.

There had been further communication between General Rutherford and Colonel Lock, and according to Major William Richardson Davie they "agreed to attack Moores camp at Ramsours . . . for this purpose Col Lock marched to cross the [Catawba] River at Sherrills & Beatie's fords while General Rutherford also moved to cross below. . . . These divisions were to have met in the night near the enemy and to have attacked them at the break of day, but the march of both parties was too circuitous, and the point of rendezvous too distant to insure punctuality."[7] That the two forces missed their rendezvous at the appointed time is an occurrence common in war, even with highly trained regulars using the latest in twentieth-century communications equipment. And to have joined up at night was asking the near impossible. It was the decision to go ahead and risk Lock's small force, outnumbered more than three to one with the Tories holding the high ground, that tells the tale of militia officers.

No matter what a militia officer's rank, he could not give an order to other officers, especially from other regiments and counties, and expect unquestioned obedience. They were citizen soldiers, and they brought to war their civilian ways of doing things. Consultation, persuasion, and agreement were absolutely necessary. Lock called a council of war. The officers assembled believed that to stay where they were invited attack by the Tories. The prudent thought that they should either retreat and recross the Catawba and wait for reinforcements, or withdraw to General Rutherford's main force. The bold—or the foolhardy—insisted, wrote Joseph Graham, that "they should march during the night and attack the Tories in their camp early the next morning." Sharp words may have passed, for Captain Graham related that "The more prudent members of the council could not brook the insinuation of cowardice, and, trusting to that fortune which sometimes crowns even rashness with success, it was unanimously resolved immediately to march and at daybreak to attack the Tories."[8] That General Rutherford might not approve was irrelevant. He was not there, and they would do as they pleased. Their men were largely unorganized, undisciplined, and inexperienced. When the fighting started, they did largely as they pleased, too. The same description fits the Tory horde on top of the ridge. Rebel and Tory alike were mostly small farmers. Few if any had ever been in battle. Neither side was in uniform and were dressed in the common clothes of the time and the place. To prevent casualties from what we now call "friendly fire," the Tories had green twigs on their hats, and the Rebels put pieces of white paper on theirs.

The Rebels marched immediately, 400 against about 1,000 armed Tories. When they got close to Ramsour's Mill, they halted for an hour while the officers met to plan the attack. "It was determined that the companies commanded by Captains Falls, McDowell and Brandon should act on horseback and march in front. No other arrangements were made and it was left to the officers to be governed by circumstances after they should reach enemy."[9] The march continued, and at daybreak the Rebels arrived within a mile of the Tory positions.

To guard against surprise, the Tories had placed twelve men as pickets along a road on the flat ground. Colonel Lock's force lined up with the mounted men in front and the footmen two deep behind them. "Without order or system," they began to walk toward the enemy. The Tory picket guards, placed to prevent surprise, were apparently surprised. They fired and fled. The mounted Rebels pursued, across the flat and up the slope to within thirty paces of the Tory line. That line had not been completely formed, and some panic ensued. When the Tories saw that the Rebel horsemen were few in number they recovered and delivered a fire so hot that the Rebel horse had to retire behind their foot soldiers, several of whom chose to believe that the issue had been decided, joined the mounted men in the rear, and never saw action. Some horsemen kept the malingerers company, but the others rallied and returned to the fight. The brunt of the action, however, fell on the Rebel foot, which kept advancing, although strung out in small, patchy groups for over 400 yards. There were no hard-eyed sergeants to keep these men in line, and in truth it was well that they advanced as they did, because there were riflemen on the Tory side capable of blasting big gaps in solid lines of advancing troops, and it is most unlikely that the militia would have withstood such heavy losses in one fell swoop.

The Tories, emboldened by the flight of the mounted men, came some distance down the slope, but like the Rebels without order. As groups of Rebels arrived, filled the gaps, and formed more or less a straight line, firing by both sides became heavy. The Tories returned to their position on the ridge and were able to pour a heavy fire on the exposed Rebels on the slope, who fell back toward the bottom, pursued halfway by the Tories. There was apparently no officer coordinating Rebel movements. Captain Graham wrote that "after the actions commenced, scarcely any orders were given by the officers. They fought like common soldiers, and animated their men by their example, and they suffered severely. Captains Falls, Dobson, Smith, Bowman and Armstrong were killed; and Captains Houston and McKissick wounded."[10]

Small parties of Rebels, anxious to continue the fight but seeking better cover from the galling fire, worked their way to opposite ends of the slope and began turning both Tory flanks. This is an age-old tactic, and they probably acted instinctively. That they turned the Tory flanks simultaneously was certainly fortuitous. The Rebel center at the same time held firm. The Tories began retreating up the ridge to their left and ran into advancing Rebels. Now the fighting came to close quarters and became ugly. It was hand to hand. Rebels and Tories, Americans all, began bashing in skulls with clubbed muskets. Screams, shouts, and curses rent the air. The Rebels began to get the better of it. Some Tories discarded their green twigs and mingled with the Rebels to escape death or capture. Others started to flee across the ridge and down its back toward Ramsour's Mill. The Rebels pursued until they possessed the entire ridge. Incredibly, Lock's small band, minus the faint of heart whose number we do not know, had driven almost 1,000 armed Tories off the high ground.

But it did not appear to be over. Beyond the mill and across the creek, a large body of Tories had assembled. The Rebels assumed that a counterattack was in the offing and frantically tried to organize a defense of the newly taken ground. They could only collect eighty-six men. Men were dragooned wherever they could be found, but the total came to only 110. An estimated 170 dead and wounded Rebels were strewn about the slope and ridge. Where had the rest gone? Captain Graham reported that some were tending their wounded friends and others "scattered during the action,"[11] which implies early departures. But given their almost complete lack of training and discipline, their inexperience, and the particularly savage nature of the fighting, the overall performance of Colonel Lock's command was valiant.

The situation was regarded as perilous, and Major Wilson and Captain William Alexander were dispatched to ride hard to General Rutherford and urge him to come quickly. The two met Rutherford's column about seven miles from Ramsour's Mill. Rutherford immediately ordered Major William Richardson Davie and his sixty-five dragoons, by his account, to start "at full gallop" and the infantry to "hasten on with all possible speed." Two miles down the road Davie met men coming from the battle who told him that the Tories had retreated, but he pressed on. As it turned out he and his men were not needed, although Rutherford did send Davie and his dragoons "in pursuit of the fugitives with orders to clear that part of the country of all stragling parties."[12]

Lieutenant Colonel John Moore, who had come home from fighting with the British around Charleston, proud in his worn regimentals, had led the King's Friends to disaster. After the loss of the ridge he and other Tory officers proved themselves unable to salvage the situation. Of Major Nicholas Welch there is no further mention. Gathered on the other side of the creek, even with their losses the Tories numbered well in excess of the gallant little Rebel band holding the ridge. And they had with them 200 fresh, well-armed men from Burke

County. A determined assault probably would have retaken the ridge. But the Tories decided that they had been beaten and worked out a trick to allow an unmolested retreat. They sent an emissary under a flag of truce to ask for suspension of hostilities so they could bury the dead and care for the wounded. Major James Rutherford and another Rebel officer met the emissary forward of the line so he could not see how few their numbers were. Rutherford boldly rejected the request and gave the Tories ten minutes to surrender. While this was going on John Moore told his men to scatter. When the officer with the flag returned only fifty remained, and they left almost immediately. Moore, with thirty men, returned to the main British army at Camden. The British were furious with him for having risen prematurely and seriously considered a court martial, but decided against it as politically unwise. Cornwallis wrote to Lord Rawdon, whom he had left in command at Camden, "The affair of Tryon County has given me great concern. Although I had my apprehensions that the flame would break out somewhere, the folly and imprudence of our friends are unpardonable."[13]

There were no official returns after militia clashes. We are dependent on participants whose reports often conflict with each other. The best estimate for Ramsour's Mill is that the Tory losses equaled the Rebels', which gives us a total of 140 killed and 200 wounded. Three hundred and forty men scattered about. That was serious fighting, and the scene on the ridge and its surrounding slopes must have made a deep impression on the survivors. Fifty-six dead alone lay on the front side of the ridge where the hottest action occurred. The slips of white paper in the hats of the Rebels had made good targets, and some excellent riflemen among the Tories had scored several head shots. Limbs and skulls had broken under clubbed muskets. A few men had been hit so hard that gunlocks were imbedded into their heads. Under a tree two brothers lay dead. But the most melancholy scenes were reserved for the evening of the mayhem and the following day, when families of the dead and wounded, Rebel and Tory, came to search, to collect corpses and broken bodies. These scenes would repeat themselves again and again on Carolina fields. Tradition has it that seventy unclaimed bodies were buried in a common grave on the ridge, but the grave has never been found.

It was a humiliating defeat for the Tories. Twice the King's men in North Carolina had risen prematurely, and twice they had been crushed by Rebel militia. Chapter 1 briefly described the first clash, in 1776 at Moore's Creek Bridge near the coast, when Highland Scots trying to rendezvous with the British at Cape Fear had been knocked out of the war. Now Ramsour's Mill, and "in a few days," wrote William Richardson Davie, "that district of country lying between the [Catawba] River, the mountains" and the South Carolina line "was entirely cleared of the enemy."[14] It would seem that Lord Germain's theory of overwhelming Tory strength in the Carolina Back Country might be in question. Of course, it was early on, and North Carolina had not yet felt the tread of British regulars, and matters seemed to be going very well in South Carolina, where the strongpoints had been established and according to official reports resistance ended.

Action at Cedar Springs

But embers of resistance were alive in South Carolina, despite the consternation caused by the fall of Charleston. They were minor affairs, mere pinpricks in contrast to the great British victory and the westward march of their victorious columns. But they indicated that the Scotch Irish, especially those between the Broad and Catawba Rivers, had yet to be reckoned with. Sometime in June, at a Baptist meetinghouse a few miles southwest of Winnsboro, Rebel militia riding behind Colonel William Bratton, Major Richard Winn, and Captain John McClure dispersed a gathering of Tories. Forty miles to the north at Alexander Old Field about a mile from modern Great Falls, on 7 June, Captain McClure and the Scotch Irish preacher Reverend John Simpson led thirty-two Rebel horsemen in a surprise attack against 200 Tories and routed them. Again, it was a small affair, with few casualties.[15]

At about that time or a little later Lord Rawdon, in command at Camden, sent a commissioner west of the Catawba to meet with the people and read them a proclamation. The meeting was held at William Hill's Iron Works on Allison Creek not far from the Catawba. According to the *Memoirs* of William Hill, who was present, the Commissioner stated that "he was empowered to take their submissions & give paroles and protections to all that choose to become British Subjects." He then began reading from Lord Rawdon's Proclamation, which maintained that the Continental Congress had abandoned both Carolinas and that George Washington and the Continental Army had "fled to the mountains." William Hill could stand no more. He interrupted the Commissioner and "took the stand himself." He told the people that these were lies meant to "intimidate and deceive" and reminded them that "we had all taken an oath to defend and maintain the independence of the State . . . and that if we could not raise a force to meet the foe . . . we cd. keep in a body, go into No. Ca., meet our friends, and return with them to recover our State." Hill reported "visible animation in the countenance of the citizens and their former state of despondency visibly reversed, and the poor Commissr. was obliged to disappear with his proclamation & protections for fear of the resentment of the audience." Now that he had the audience with him and they seemed eager to organize, William Hill advised them to elect two colonels, which they did, choosing Andrew Neel and William Hill. The men then chose "all other of their officers to form into companies etc. We then formed into a camp and erected the American Standard. And as soon as this was known there were men both of the states of Georgia and South Carolina adding daily to our numbers that we soon became a respectable body."[16]

These actions and activities could not be tolerated by the British. The King's Friends had to be protected, Rebel bands dispersed and disarmed, the disaffected forced to recognize that the rebellion had failed. By July British forces in the interior were fully deployed and actively searching for Rebel bands. But two bloody encounters that month proved the Rebel cause to be if not well at least definitely alive.

On the southern edge of modern Spartanburg, South Carolina, there is a place once called Cedar Springs. In early July 1780, Colonel John Thomas, Jr., who had succeeded his imprisoned father as commander of the Rebel's Spartan Regiment, camped there with about sixty men. The reader will recall that the raising of this regiment was one of the few bright spots in William Henry Drayton's mission in the Dutch Fork. Thomas was trying to collect the regiment and march to join the forces gathering under Thomas Sumter. He had to be cautious, for as we know from Drayton's foray to the home of Thomas Fletchall this was strong Tory country. Unknown to Colonel Thomas, Major Patrick Ferguson, traveling the Back Country to raise Tory militia, had learned of his presence and ordered a detachment to proceed to Cedar Springs and attack. Colonel Thomas's father was a British prisoner in the jail at Ninety Six, and while visiting him there the senior Thomas's wife, Jane Thomas, overheard some Tory women talking about a surprise attack on the Rebel camp at Cedar Springs the following night. Early the next morning Jane Thomas saddled her horse and pushed hard for Cedar Springs. Sixty miles and many hours later she rode out of the darkness into the Rebel camp and warned her son and his comrades. She then went home. Colonel Thomas and his sixty men kept their campfires going and retired a distance into the woods, concealed themselves, and waited. Sometime during the early hours of 12 July 150 Tories charged the camp expecting to catch the Rebels wrapped in their blankets. They were met by a blaze of fire from the woods that left many of them dead on the field and scattered the survivors in panic. It was a short affair, an overwhelming Rebel victory, and further evidence that the loss of Charleston and the deployment of British troops throughout the state had not completely killed enthusiasm for the cause. On the same day, some fifty miles east of Cedar Springs, the issue was joined again.[17]

"My Lord Hook was shot off his horse"

On 11 July 1780, roughly fifty miles due south of Ramsour's Mill, in what is now York County, South Carolina, young James McClure and his brother-in-law Edward Martin were in Captain John McClure's house melting pewter dishes to make bullets for Rebel partisans. James's mother and his sister Mary were also at home. Without warning, British raiders swooped in and captured them all. It was their bad luck to be taken by the brutal Philadelphia Tory, Captain Christian Huck of Banastre Tarleton's British Legion. Tarleton was in Charleston, but the Legion was in the field. Huck had been detached on 16 June by Colonel George Turnbull, a New York Tory commanding the British strongpoint at nearby Rocky Mount, on the Catawba River just south of Great Falls. When he rode out Huck had thirty-five British Legion dragoons, twenty mounted infantry of De Lancey's New York Volunteers, and sixty Tory militiamen. Turnbull wrote Cornwallis the same day, "I have taken the liberty to order Captain Huck to destroy the Iron Works. They are the property of Mr. Hill, a great Rebell." On his way to the Iron Works, Huck was also bent on seizing the Rebel Presbyterian preacher, John Simpson. Near Simpson's house his soldiers shot and killed a harmless boy, William Strong, as he walked along the road carrying his Bible. Simpson had already left home with Captain John McClure to join Thomas Sumter. His wife, hearing the gunfire that killed young Strong, rushed her four children from their home, hid in an orchard, and watched Huck's men loot and then burn the house. Huck then moved on to William Hill's place. As Hill and other Rebel officers and their men had withdrawn and joined Thomas Sumter east of the Catawba, Captain Huck burned the Iron Works without opposition. This enraged the Rebels, but it was a legitimate military target where cannon and other ordnance were cast. Whether it was a wise target was quite another matter, for Hill also made farm tools for Rebels and Tories alike within a radius of some fifty miles, and ground their grains in his grist mill, and cut their logs in his saw mill. Huck burned everything he could not carry off. When Cornwallis was informed he wrote to Sir Henry Clinton, "The submission of General Williamson at Ninety-Six . . . and the dispersion of a party of rebels, who had assembled at an iron-work, on the north west border of the province . . . put an end to all resistance in South Carolina."[18]

Colonel Turnbull next ordered Captain Huck to march through the New Acquisition (modern York County) to the Indian line, gather Tory militia, and harry the Rebels. Huck's force is said to have reached 400 by the time he reached Captain McClure's house on 11 July, but by the next morning he appears to have had with him only his original force of approximately 115 men. The house was looted and young McClure and Martin tied up to await execution in the morning, for Huck swore that he would hang them. When James McClure's mother protested, Huck struck her with the flat of his sword. Huck and his men then rode to the home of Colonel William Bratton, who was also with Sumter. Three old men were taken prisoner there, and Mrs. Bratton was ordered to prepare a meal. Huck also demanded the location of her husband's camp. She refused, and it is said that a trooper threatened to cut her throat with a reaping hook. But Captain John Adamson, a Tory from Camden, stopped him. Taking James McClure, Edward Martin, and the other prisoners with him, Huck moved his force about a quarter of a mile north to camp for the night at the plantation of James Williamson. The prisoners were dumped in a corn crib to await hanging in the morning. For one of the better known and more important irregular actions of the war in the Back Country, there is little agreement on details of how many were on each side and which Rebel leaders were present. But what happened after the arrival of Rebel militia is not a mystery, and it is the significance of this fight, not the variance in details, that matters. From either arrogance or carelessness, Huck failed to keep note of the whereabouts of the people he had plundered and terrorized that day. There are two versions of who rode to get help.[19]

McClure family tradition maintains that it was James McClure's sister, Mary McClure, who saddled a horse, rode thirty miles, and found her father John in Sumter's camp. Bratton family tradition, supported by Historic Brattonsville, claims that Martha Bratton sent Watt, a family slave, who found Colonel Bratton west of the Catawba. Wherever McClure and Bratton were somebody found them. William Bratton and John McClure immediately got 150 men into their saddles and rode hard for home. They were joined by another 350 riders, including a unit commanded by Captain Edward Lacey, Jr. As at Ramsour's Mill, organization was practically nonexistent, each militia unit following the time-honored custom of taking orders only from its own commander, which was undoubtedly the reason why a force originally numbering 500 men arrived near Williamson's Plantation with only about 250 present and ready to fight. Captain Lacey had another problem: his father, a rigid Tory, lived two miles from Huck's camp and would not hesitate to betray his son for the King. Father and son had never seen eye to eye. As a thirteen-year-old in Pennsylvania Lacey, Jr., had run away and joined Braddock's expedition against the French. Eventually recovered by his father, the boy had run off a second time and traveled with the exodus of emigrants moving south along the Great Wagon Road. This time, instead of searching out his son to bring him home again, Edward Lacey joined him and also settled in South Carolina. But his political views did not change with geography, and his son took the precaution of posting a guard around his father's house. The old man escaped but was recaptured. Captain Lacey then took no chances and ordered his father tied to his bed.[20]

The Rebels headed for the Tory camp. They learned that Huck's men were camped at Williamson's in tents between rail fences that lined the road leading to the house. Huck was sleeping in Williamson's house. He had made a bad choice of ground, and was as careless as the Rebels at Monck's Corner. He had no patrols out, no pickets posted. There were sentries on the road in front of the house, but they failed to hear the Rebels creeping up on them in the early hours before first light. The Rebels split into two parties and approached from both sides. At dawn, at seventy-five paces, they opened fire from behind the fences. Surprise was complete. The Tories attempted to resist but were broken by intense fire. Huck ran outside and mounted his horse. Lieutenant Hunt of the British Legion, who escaped and whose account was recorded in Lieutenant Anthony Allaire's diary, said Huck tried to get away but was shot in the neck and killed, but another eyewitness offered a different version of the behavior and fate of "my Lord Hook."[21]

Sixteen-year-old James Collins, whose adventures we will follow on several occasions in this narrative, said in his *Autobiography* that he had dismounted and was advancing through a peach orchard behind a log house with Moffitt's band when the British "troops were soon mounted and paraded. This, I confess, was a very imposing sight, at least to me, for I had never seen a troop of British horse before, and thought they differed vastly from us—poor hunting-shirt fellows. The leader drew his sword, mounted his horse, and began to storm and rave, and advanced on us; but we kept close to the peach orchard. When they had got pretty near to the peach trees, their leader called out, 'disperse you damned rebels, or we will put every man of you to the sword.' Our rifle balls began to whistle among them, and in a few minutes my Lord Hook was shot off his horse and fell at full length; his sword flew out of his hand as he fell and lay at some distance." Including Huck, an estimated thirty-five Tories were killed and twenty-nine wounded and many captured. Tarleton wrote after the war that only twelve Legion dragoons and twelve Tory militiamen escaped. The Americans had one killed and one wounded. After it was over James McClure, Edward Martin, and the other prisoners were rescued from the corn crib where they were awaiting execution. The Tory John Adamson, wounded, taken prisoner, and threatened with death, was not only spared, but taken into the Bratton home and nursed when Martha Bratton told of how he had saved her.[22]

Huck's defeat was very important for its psychological effect. Militia had soundly defeated Tory regulars, including dragoons of the hated and feared British Legion. Even Lord Cornwallis admitted that the state of affairs in South Carolina might not be as he had recently reported. "Lieutenant Colonel Turnbull's letter gave me very serious concern," he wrote to Nisbet Balfour, commandant at Ninety Six. "The unlucky affair that happened to the detachment under Captain Huck of the Legion has given me great uneasiness."[23] Had he known the full story his feeling would have gone beyond uneasiness. Many men in that part of South Carolina who had Rebel sympathies, but were unsure whether it was wise to challenge British might after Charleston and Tarleton's coup in the Waxhaws, began to flock to the standard raised by Brigadier General Thomas Sumter, who came to be known as the Gamecock.

A Blue Hen's Chicken

Thomas Sumter (1734–1832) is not a sympathetic character.[24] Wearing his ego on his shoulder, he had few peers as a prima donna and could spot a slight, intended or not, around a corner. He was careless with security and lives. His penchant for bloody and repeated frontal assaults was unnecessarily costly and finally led one officer to swear to Sumter's face and before others that never again would he serve under the Gamecock. But of all his partisan foes, Lord Cornwallis considered Sumter the most troublesome and obstinate. Thomas Sumter was a fighter who kept alive the flame of resistance and acted as a beacon for like-minded men at a time when others believed all was lost and entered British lines to accept parole. Generals are like artists—one does not have to like them, only to respect what they do when they do it well. His contemporaries recognized the steel within him, and the Gillespie brothers, Back Country gunsmiths and breeders of fighting cocks, best put it into words. At a time when resistance to British arms appeared suicidal, Sumter came to them seeking arms. He wore his old Continental blues with scarlet facings and a cock's feather in his hat. Cockfighting was then a widely popular sport among Americans, and it was held that "no cock could be truly game whose mother was not a blue hen." Sumter in his sartorial splendor, with his iron resolve, reminded the Gillespie brothers of Old Tuck, a chick of the blue hen who had never lost a fight. He was a "Blue Hen's Chicken" the brothers proclaimed, and he became known then and forever more as the Gamecock. In the Back Country, there could be no higher accolade.[25]

Thomas Sumter, by Rembrandt Peale.
(Independence National Historical Park Collection.)

Thomas Sumter was born of poor English immigrant parents on the Virginia frontier, raised in humble circumstances, and spent the better part of a long life trying to hide his origins while striving for position and fortune. William Martin, who knew Sumter in Virginia, said that "it seems as if he felt mortified at the idea of his low birth . . . and that he wished everything connected with his early life to be forgotten."[26] During the French and Indian War he served with the Virginia militia in western Pennsylvania and the Ohio country and was promoted to sergeant. He was also with the Virginia militia when it cooperated with South Carolina forces during the Cherokee War of 1760–1761. Although he did not see action, his presence was a turning point in his life, for he was in the right place at the right time. With the conclusion of peace, one of the chiefs asked that the peace treaty with Virginia be carried by a Virginian deep into the Cherokee country. It was a perilous mission. Anyone who has hazarded wilderness journeys is aware that chance or momentary carelessness can bring disaster, and whoever carried out the mission to the Cherokees faced possible human foes as well. No one was ordered to go, but Captain Henry Timberlake volunteered, as did Sergeant Thomas Sumter, who may have served in Timberlake's company. They were accompanied by an interpreter, John McCormack. The government of Virginia did not provide them with funds, so Sumter borrowed sixty pounds from Alexander McDonald to buy a canoe, provisions to last ten days, and trade goods should they need to secure horses. It was a loan that would later bedevil him.

Whatever experience any of them may have had in the wilderness, all three behaved like greenhorns and were lucky to survive. Bad weather and their blunders stretched a normal six-day journey to nineteen. Their return trek was eased by a guard of 100 Cherokee warriors. In the colonial capital of Williamsburg one of the chiefs expressed a desire to meet King George III. Three Cherokee chiefs were chosen to make the journey to London, and to escort them who but Captain Henry Timberlake and Sergeant Thomas Sumter. William Shorey, an interpreter, completed the group. Thomas Jefferson was in Williamsburg then and attended the farewell ceremony. Their ship *Epreuve* arrived in Plymouth harbor on 16 June 1762, minus William Shorey, who had died in mid-Atlantic.

The Cherokee chiefs were a sensation in London. They dined with the Lord Mayor, their portraits were painted by Sir Joshua Reynolds, and Oliver Goldsmith visited them in their lodgings. Wherever they went great crowds formed—10,000 people when they dined at Vauxhall Gardens. Timberlake and Sumter seized the opportunity and passed as British army officers, resplendent in newly purchased scarlet coats. At their audience with the King, Thomas Sumter from Preddy's Creek, Virginia, translated the speeches. How accurate he was is quite another matter, but who was to know? When it came time for them to return, Sumter agreed to escort the chiefs for fifty pounds in advance and another 100 on arrival in Charleston.

They reached Charleston on 28 October and immediately Sumter took the chiefs to the Royal Governor, Thomas Boone. The Cherokees praised Sumter's treatment of them to the Governor, who then implored the sergeant to escort the Indians to Tomotley. On 10 November they set off, with horses and wagons supplied by Governor Boone. About sixty miles northwest of Charleston Sergeant Thomas Sumter looked around him very carefully at a place called Eutaw Springs before proceeding on the journey to Indian country.

He spent the winter with the Cherokee in the village of Tomotley. Then came another incident in which Sumter was at the right place at the right time. A lieutenant of Canadian militia, Baron des Jonnes, appeared in the Cherokee towns and told the Indians that the French would conquer in their struggle with the English. Sumter requested permission from the Cherokee chiefs to arrest the Canadian. After some hesitation they agreed, provided he accomplish it without assistance. Sumter went to the town where des Jonnes was then exhorting the Cherokee. A wrestler from youth, and with recent experience wrestling with the Indians, Sumter without preliminaries seized des Jonnes and threw him to the ground, where the two men struggled until blood flowed. Thomas Sumter prevailed. He then tied des Jonnes onto his horse, mounted behind him, brought him to Fort Prince George, near modern Clemson, and turned him over to the commandant. Des Jonnes was immediately sent on to Charleston and from there to England. Sumter followed at a more leisurely pace, looking over the land as he went, and again stopped at Eutaw Springs. Even then he probably had an idea for a store on that site. In Charleston he was given a hero's treatment and related to the Governor's Council his adventures among the Cherokee. *The South-Carolina Gazette* told the tale of des Jonnes's capture, and Governor Boone wrote to Lord Egremont and requested that he indemnify Sergeant Sumter for his efforts.

In that late winter of 1763, Thomas Sumter decided to return to his birthplace. On the way he paused for another look at Eutaw Springs. At Preddy's Creek he had many tales to tell, but someone else had a more urgent story for the law. Alexander McDonald, who in 1761 had lent Thomas Sumter the sixty pounds that had enabled him to begin his adventures, had not been repaid. The toast of Charleston, veteran of a hazardous wilderness journey, temporary translator of Cherokee for George III, and captor of a French spy, soon found himself jailed for debt. Friends helped him make bond that November, but it appeared that he also owed money to Samuel Cowden and Company, and he was jailed at Staunton, Virginia, unable to post bail. With a friend's help he escaped, and three weeks later Thomas Sumter was at Long Cane Creek, the boundary between South Carolina and Cherokee country. Had Sumter taken the classic American solution to problems financial, criminal, and marital, immortalized in a ditty from a later frontier: "Hey! What was your name in the States? Was it Thompson or Johnson or Bates? Did you murder your wife and flee for your life? Hey! What was your name in the States?"

There were desperate men on the South Carolina frontier. It was infamous for bandits and cutthroats. On many an American border men in Sumter's position, wanted at home, took the outlaw route and never looked back. We have no indication that he even considered that option. With his Cherokee ties he could have prospered as an Indian trader. But Thomas Sumter had another road open. Unlike his future foe, Lord Cornwallis, he had neither position nor privilege, but there were men of rank and influence in Charleston who considered him a hero and an enterprising fellow. He saddled his horse and for the second time in his life followed the Cherokee Path from Ninety Six to Charleston. On the way, of course, he observed what had become a ritual, a stop at Eutaw Springs, but this time he looked at a particular piece of land that pleased him. He reached Charleston in July 1764 and asked the provincial government for 400 pounds for providing escort for the Cherokee chiefs, only to be informed that South Carolina had not hired him. It proved a temporary setback. In London Lord Egremont was more than generous, and from the British government he received 700 pounds.

Thomas Sumter immediately headed for Eutaw Springs, bought his land, and established a very well situated store stocked with all of the things a thriving farm and plantation economy demanded. Thomas Sumter, merchant, had realized a dream. But there were other dreams. He had important neighbors. Francis Marion lived four miles away. On the other side of the Santee River was Colonel Richard Richardson, whom we met when he led the Snow campaign against the Tories. He was another adventurer from Virginia, and had done very well for himself. He became Sumter's in-law and later vouched for him when William Henry Drayton questioned Sumter's loyalty. Nearby were the Canteys, descendants of Tiege Cantey, a Scotch Irishman on the make who had arrived with nothing and started a dynasty. Richardson had married a Cantey woman. Another Cantey woman, Mary, was a widow wealthy and available. Mary Jameson was eleven years older than Thomas Sumter. Her left side, including her arm and leg, were crippled from childhood infantile paralysis. They were married in the summer of 1767 and settled on her plantation at Great Savannah across the Santee River from Eutaw Springs. In August 1768 Mary Sumter was delivered of an heir, Thomas, Jr. Thomas Sumter had done very well for himself and looked forward to doing even better.

Sumter spent the ensuing years expanding his business interests and participating in the great American game of land speculation. He participated little in politics, but years later, according to one biographer, listening to a speech by the Charleston radical Christopher Gadsden turned him toward resistance to British policies. That may well be, but we cannot be accused of idle speculation in attaching more importance to family ties: his in-laws, the powerful Cantey family, were Whigs.

Matters were coming to a head between those who were challenging Great Britain and those who were loyal, and on 11 January 1775 the first Provincial Congress met in Charleston. It was made up of familiar names: Laurens, Rutledge, Pinckney, Drayton, Gadsden, Richardson, Moultrie, Marion—and representing his district, where the Canteys were powerful, Thomas Sumter, who had indeed come a long way. But not as far as he wished. When it was time to form regiments and appoint officers, positions of great prestige as well as power, Sumter was left out in the cold. He returned to his business affairs, stayed in touch politically, kept very close to his in-law, the highly influential Colonel Richard Richardson, and bided his time. One thing held against him was his friendship with Moses Kirkland. When Kirkland resigned his commission as a captain of rangers and went over to the Tories, he recommended Sumter as his successor. If, as one of Sumter's biographers claim, Sumter did not realize that this would place him under suspicion, it was naive of him. Perhaps his obsession for status clouded his judgment. Whatever the case, Sumter applied to the Council of Safety for Kirkland's commission. His application was tabled. It was then that William Henry Drayton reported his conversation with Richard Richardson, who strongly vouched for Sumter but agreed to monitor his conduct. Not even that satisfied the Council, and Sumter's application was dismissed.

Richardson then advised Sumter to raise a company of local militia, which he did, and not surprisingly the men elected him their captain. Shortly thereafter, Captain Thomas Sumter was also chosen by friends, neighbors, militiamen, and his in-laws to represent them at the second South Carolina Provincial Congress. And in November 1775, when Richard Richardson led his army into the far reaches of the Back Country to crush Tory resistance in the Snow Campaign, Captain Sumter accompanied him as adjutant general. After Richardson disbanded the army, he wrote to the Council of Safety: "The prisoners I send in a boat from this place to Nelson's Ferry under the command and guard of Capt. Thomas Sumter, who on this expedition I constituted Adjutant-General, who has behaved very well and has been to me and the cause, of extra service."[27]

Richardson's patronage and Sumter's faithful service paid off in February 1776, when the Provincial Congress authorized new regiments and appointed officers. Thomas Sumter was unanimously elected Lieutenant Colonel and commanding officer of the 2nd Regiment of Riflemen. With 3,000 pounds from the state treasury, Sumter immediately rode to the Back Country, to the Waxhaws and other places where hard men accustomed to the use of arms were to be found, and recruited among them and the Catawba Indians. But for long years glory eluded him. He and his regiment watched while Moultrie and Marion traded shot and shell with the British at the Battle of Sullivan's Island. During the 1776 campaign against the Cherokee, the Riflemen acted as the reserve and never saw combat; their most active duty was to join the rest of the army in burning Cherokee villages and cornfields. During this period the state regiments were taken into Continental service, and Sumter became an officer of the Continental Line. But he continued to be frustrated in his desire to lead his men into battle. Throughout General Robert Howe's error-ridden campaigns in the South Carolina and Georgia coastal areas the 2nd Regiment marched and countermarched and suffered dysentery and malaria and insects and bad food without ever firing their weapons in action. In September 1778, with South Carolina no longer in immediate danger from either the British or the Cherokee, Thomas Sumter resigned his commission and turned to his private affairs. He remained at Great Savannah with his family during the fighting between Benjamin Lincoln and Prevost around Charleston, the Franco-American debacle at Savannah, even the siege of Charleston and the surrender of the city to the British. Then Sumter removed with his family to their summer home farther up country in the High Hills of Santee. But the war caught up with him there too, and along with thousands of other men in the Carolinas he was faced with a critical decision.

On 28 May 1780 his son Tom was out riding when a neighbor galloped up with news that Banastre Tarleton and the British Legion were heading their way. It was Tarleton's famous dash to the Waxhaws in pursuit of Buford. Young Tom Sumter rode home to warn his father. From his immediate reaction, it appears that Thomas Sumter had known for some time precisely what he would do at such a time. While Soldier Tom, his African body servant, saddled their horses, Sumter donned his old regimentals. He kissed his wife and son goodbye, and then he and Soldier Tom rode off to war. He had no rank, no men, no prospects. Thomas Sumter, Jr., wrote to his own son many years later: "He left us on the 28th of May, 1780, only a few hours before Tarleton's Legion passed us in pursuit of Buford."[28]

It was well that he left quickly. The British knew of him, and Tarleton sent Captain Charles Campbell to bring him in. Mary Sumter was sitting in a chair inside her home. The dragoons of the Legion picked up the chair and carried her in it outside and set it on the lawn. Then they looted the house and the smokehouse. Then they set the house on fire. Gathered in a small group on the lawn, Mary Sumter, and her son Tom, and the house servants watched the house burn. The story is told that a Legion dragoon with a guilty conscience slipped a smoked ham under her chair.

Sumter rode north with Soldier Tom through the Waxhaws to American headquarters at Salisbury, North Carolina. He proposed to raise militia and fight a guerrilla war against the British; the proposal was approved and he was given $19,000 in treasury certificates. With veterans from his old 6th Regiment and some 200 Catawba Indians, Sumter found other South Carolinians on Hagler's Branch near the present town of Fort Mill, South Carolina. Governor John Rutledge and what remained of the government of the State of South Carolina were in exile. There was no one available to pass laws, issue decrees, raise troops, or appoint officers. But there were men in camp capable of making tough decisions and they were burning to continue the fight—Colonel William Bratton, Colonel William Hill, Colonel Richard Winn, Captain Edward Lacey, and others. All of the men present met in convention and elected Richard Winn president. The first order of business was to elect a commander in chief. William Hill and William Bratton were nominated, but Richard Winn, who had served with Sumter in the Snow Campaign, suggested his old comrade. Sumter was asked if he would accept if chosen. He replied, "With me as with you it is liberty or death."[29] On 15 June 1780 Thomas Sumter was elected commander in chief of the South Carolina militia and appointed Brigadier General. Although this was all done in a semi-wild backwoods setting, it was carried out as though the members of the convention were in knee breeches and lace in a grand legislative chamber. President Winn was directed to make out Sumter's commission and sign it. All present agreed to serve under Sumter until the end of the war. Each man was his own commissary, agreeing to provide horse and weapons, food and clothing. Acting as a "convention of the whole," as recalled by Colonel Hill, they solemnly promised "they would oppose the British and Tories by force of arms, which arms was never to be laid down until the British troops was drove from the State of South Carolina and the independence of the United States acknowledged."[30]

Lord Germain, Sir Henry Clinton, and Lord Cornwallis were not aware that South Carolina was back in the war, and that facing them was a man of whom Light Horse Harry Lee wrote, "Enchanted with the splendor of victory, he would wade in torrents of blood to attain it."[31]

10

More Trouble
in the Back Country

The Making of a Rebel: II

Deep in the Carolina Back Country, in late November 1763, toward the end of a long and arduous journey from Pennsylvania, Elizabeth Heland Collins went into labor. The family was four miles short of its destination. In a cabin lent by a man named Jourdan, Elizabeth Collins delivered her fourth child. "Thus I was born by the way and have been a wayfaring man ever since," admitted James Potter Collins in *Autobiography of a Revolutionary Soldier,* written in Louisiana in his seventy-fourth year, before he moved on to Texas.[1]

Collins's father Daniel was an Anglo-Irishman from Waterford, his grandfather Charles "a man of considerable wealth; my grandmother Susannah was of a noted family of the Radcliffes." After Daniel's father died, the boy objected to his family's intention to educate him for the Anglican ministry, but he was still a minor and his mother insisted, so Daniel ran away to America. There he became a schoolteacher in Pennsylvania, served in the French and Indian War, and married Elizabeth Heland, whose parents had immigrated from Ireland some time after Daniel. Following James's birth in the borrowed cabin, the family settled in what is now York County, South Carolina, in the area served by William Hill's Iron Works. Daniel became clerk of the first court held in the county. James's mother died when he was three giving birth to her seventh child, who also died a few days later. His father married a widow who already had one child and with Daniel she had thirteen more, making a total of twenty children in the family. As James recalled in his memoir, "I recollect to have eaten at my father's table, when fifteen of his children, all grown, and mostly all heads of families, sat at the same table." Daniel Collins taught school in the winter and worked his farm the rest of the year. James attended school every winter until he was about twelve, and worked on the farm at such a young age that he was ploughing "before I could turn the plough at the end of the land." His father was a disciplinarian and insisted that the Sabbath be strictly obeyed. James's middle name, Potter, was the name of the minister who had baptized him.[2]

Daniel, who as a boy had run away to America to escape his mother's dominance, began planning his son's life, and ironically proposed sending him away to college to become a preacher. James declined. Daniel then suggested a mechanical occupation for the boy, but James wanted to be a woodworker. Instead, Daniel bound him to the tailor McMavey for five years, but McMavey moved away and returned James to his home. Apparently Daniel then overrode his son's objections and sent him to Charlotte to study for the ministry. But the war interrupted his studies and once again he had to return home. His father then decided that James would become a cobbler, but James complained so much that Daniel put him under the tutelege of a weaver. "I was not averse to the weaving business and made considerable proficiency in the trade." The Revolution, however, ended the plans of both father and son, and James's *Autobiography* describes for us the terrible tensions that began to appear in the Back Country and led to civil war.[3]

"I began to grow up—times began to be troublesome, and people began to divide into parties. Those that had been good friends in times past became enemies; they began to watch each other with jealous eyes, and were designated by the name of Whigs and tory. Recruiting officers were out in all directions, to enlist soldiers." James wanted to follow his older brother into the army. Daniel was strongly opposed, but James was equally stubborn. A compromise was worked out. James became a teenage Rebel spy. "There was a Mr. Moffitt in the neighborhood who was then captain of the militia, was pretty shrewd and an active partizan. I had often been sent on business by my father in various directions through the country, and was frequently employed by others to hunt stray horses, etc.; consequently I became acquainted with all the by-paths for twenty or thirty miles around. Moffitt consulted my father and it was agreed that I should be made use of merely as a collecter of news. In order to prepare me for business, I had to receive several lectures. I was furnished with documents—sometimes a list of stray horses with marks and brands, sometimes with papers and other business. I was to attend public places, make no inquiry, only about the business I was sent on, and pay strict attention to all that was passing in conversation and otherwise. I succeeded for some time without incurring the least suspicion, by which means the Tories were several times disappointed in their plans without being able to account for the cause."[4]

Eventually he was exposed and accepted his father's advice to stop, but his earlier urge to join the regular army returned. Daniel Collins then reached back to his own experience in the French and Indian War and convinced James that he would be better off in the militia. He told his son that "the time was at hand when volunteers would be called for, and by joining them I would be equally safe; if I went into battle I stood as fair a chance; besides I would be less exposed, less fatigued, and if there should be any time of resting, I could come home and enjoy it; he said he had had some experience and learned a lesson from that."[5]

The time of which Daniel Collins spoke soon came, and as it turned out for father as well as son. After Captain Christian Huck burned William Hill's Iron Works, Daniel rode there to view the ruins. James described his return: "My step-mother asked him thus: 'Well Daniel, what news?' My father replied, 'Nothing very pleasant. I have come home determined to take my gun and when I lay it down, I lay down my life with it;' then turning to me said, 'my son you may prepare for the worst; the thing is fairly at issue. We must submit or become slaves, or fight. For my part I am determined—tomorrow I will go to join Moffitt.' "[6]

Why Daniel Collins and other Back Country settlers became Rebels is a more complex question than the motivation of the radical Rice Kings and is not conducive to definitive answers. The Tory officer Colonel Robert Gray observed, "The whole province resembled a piece of patch work, the inhabitants of every settlement when united in sentiment being in arms for the side they liked best and making continual inroads into one another's settlements."[7] Family and religious ties were important, although as we have already seen and will see again some families split on the issue. Preferment promised and delivered by each side bought the allegiance of some. Men of influence and substance drew to them people within their sphere. We have seen the influence wielded for the Tories in the upper Dutch Fork by Colonel Thomas Fletchall, whereas along the Catawba the Rebel William Hill was a magnet for men like Daniel Collins and others who lived within roughly a fifty-mile radius of Hill's Iron Works. It has also been suggested that many Back Country Rebels fought to acquire slaves from defeated Tories.[8] There is some evidence of such plundering later in the war, when the Rebel tide was riding higher in South Carolina. But it is simply unsustainable to argue that at the darkest hour for the cause, with a victorious British army spreading throughout the land, that Back Country settlers who became Rebels put their lives and the well-being of their families on the line, subjecting themselves to hunger and privation and dire peril, in order to steal slaves. It also ignores a significant factor behind the rebellion. The origin of the settlers played a key role in choosing sides. Generally, the native born as well as foreign born who had been in America long enough to have migrated down the Great Wagon Road from Pennsylvania became Rebels. Recent arrivals from Ulster and other areas of North Britain tended to become King's Friends. This certainly indicates that the Scotch Irish and and their cultural allies who had spent some decades in Back Country America were well along the road to their personal vision of liberty, which did not translate into an orderly imperial society. Independence was their goal, and it was unencumbered by economic motives.

But as in all causes different degrees of fervor could be found. There were, claimed James Collins, three kinds of patriots: "those who were determined to fight it out to the last let the consequences be what it might . . . those who would fight a little when the wind was favorable but so soon as it shifted to an unfavorable point would draw back and give up all for lost ... those who were favorable for the cause, provided it prospered and they could enjoy the benefit but would not risk one hair of their heads to attain it." There was no question in which rank Daniel and James Collins stood.[9]

The "next day we shouldered our guns and went to Moffitt," James recalled. When they arrived, Moffitt said, " 'Well, Daniel, I suppose you intend to fight.' My father said he had come to that conclusion." Captain Moffitt turned to James, who carried an old shotgun. " 'Well, James,' he said to me, 'we shall have plenty for you to do. ... We will try to take care of you and not let the Tories catch you.' "[10] Thus 16-year-old James Collins rode off to war, to the peach orchard at Williamson's and the death of "my Lord Hook," to the life of a guerrilla fighter on the run, on to the bloody fields of King's Mountain and Cowpens. Unlike our other teenage warrior, Thomas Young, he admitted doubts, fears, second thoughts, yearnings to be away from it all. He also left us a valuable description of the outfitting of a militia guerrilla band.

Captain Moffitt's band was composed, as James described it, of a "set of men acting entirely on our own footing, without the promise or expectation of any pay. There was nothing furnished us from the public; we furnished our own clothes, composed of coarse materials, and all home spun; our over dress was a hunting shirt of what we called linsey woolsey [coarse linen and wool, or cotton and wool] well belted around us. We furnished our own horses, saddles, bridles, guns, swords, butcher knives, and our own spurs; we got our powder and lead as we could, and often had to apply to the women of the country, for their old pewter dishes and spoons, to supply the place of lead; and if we had lead sufficient to make balls, half lead and half pewter, we felt well supplied. Swords, at first were scarce, but we had several good blacksmiths among us; besides, there were several in the country. If we got hold of a piece of good steel, we would keep it; and likewise ... take all the old whip saws we could find, set three or four smiths to work in one shop, and take the steel we had to another. In this way we soon had a pretty good supply of swords and butcher knives. Mostly all of our spurs, bridle bits and horsemen's caps were manufactured by us." They made their caps of leather greased with tallow, with two steel straps crossed to reinforce it, " a small brim attached to the front, resembling the caps now worn, a piece of bear skin lined with strong cloth, padded with wool passed over from the front to the back of the head; then a large bunch of hair was taken from the tail of a horse, generally white, was attached to the back part and hung down the back; then a bunch of white feathers, or deer's tail, was attached to the sides, which completed the cap." Unlike British and Tory regulars, they traveled light. "We carried no camp equipage, no cooking utensils, nor any thing to encumber us; we depended on what chance or kind providence might cast in our way, and were always ready to decamp in a short time."[11]

These were the formidable partisan fighters of the Back Country Lord Cornwallis would learn he had to reckon with. But at the time he had other concerns. One was a column of Continentals that had entered North Carolina. Another was the crush of administrative details that would not go away.

The Continentals

While throughout the Back Country men and boys were choosing sides and gathering into bands, to the north an American army dispatched by George Washington "to give further succor to the southern states"[12] was slowly making its way to the Carolinas. It was small even by the standards of this war, about 1,400 strong, and worn by years of hard marching and fierce battles, by hunger and privation. But the Continental Army was no longer the ill-trained, ill-disciplined force that had taken the field in 1775. The main reason it had fared so poorly against the British in most battles was lack of training and experience on the part of officers and men, including George Washington. They gained experience and could be valiant fighters, as the Maryland and Delaware Continentals proved at the Battle of Long Island early in the war. But when it came to maneuvering in formal battle against the superbly drilled British and Hessians the American regulars almost always came up short. If Charles Lee had prevailed, the war would have been fought by militia units operating as guerrillas, which would have visited on all of the states the horrors that wracked the Carolinas. Washington and others realized this and were adamant that the new nation required the dignity of regular forces that fought in the European manner. This, ironically, presents the familiar picture from school days of rigid, shoulder-to-shoulder formations of scarlet masses marching with blind obedience against Lee's vision of shadowy, hawk-eyed Americans in buckskin behind fences and trees, picking off the redcoats one by one. That is the myth, and if it were true, how did the British win most of the battles? And why did many battles end with Americans fleeing in disarray? The reason why European armies and eventually the young American Army fought as they did will be covered in more detail when we discuss the British Army, but for now it is enough to know that the state of weapons technology at the time demanded that in formal battle armies move in close-order formations and wheel and turn, fire and advance and withdraw as solid units on command. Armies marched in columns and fought in extended lines two and three deep, and they had to know how to quickly and efficiently move from one formation to the other. That was the crux of the American problem: the troops did not know how and their officers did not know enough to teach them how. That began to change gradually on 23 February 1778, when there rode into the army's camp at Valley Forge a man too often presented as a comic figure but who in reality was a master of his trade, an inspired drillmaster, and a shrewd judge of the American character.

He called himself Friedrich Wilhelm Augustus Heinrich Ferdinand, Baron von Steuben (1730–1794), and he was introduced to America as a former lieutenant general in the Prussian army of Frederick the Great.[13] It has been said that he was none of those. But the "von" added by his grandfather was unquestioned two generations later, and the Prince of Hohenzollern-Hechingen had created him a *Freiherr*, or baron. Captain, however, was the highest rank he had attained in the Prussian army. Von Steuben left the Prussian army in 1763 for unknown reasons, although later in life he claimed to have been the victim of a personal enemy. Fourteen years later financial necessity led him eventually to Paris and the good offices of Benjamin Franklin and Beaumarchais. The latter paid his travel expenses, and the crafty Franklin, knowing that Lieutenant General Baron von Steuben, formerly "in the King of Prussia's service," would open more doors than Captain von Steuben, wrote him a glowing letter of recommendation and sent him off, another in a long line of European adventurers seeking fame and fortune in the New World.

The story is a familiar one. The stocky Prussian, furious with troops who understandably failed to comprehend orders from a man whose English was so limited to be nearly nonexistent, swearing at them in German and French and frustrated in knowing only "Goddam!" in English, with the troops laughing at him. His comic reputation was thus established for posterity. But he was never a ridiculous figure. Picturesque, perhaps, but also a hard-bitten professional soldier who knew what he was about. Captain Benjamin Walker, who spoke French, offered to translate, swearing and all, and slowly, awkwardly, a transformation began. The men he drilled that winter and spring of 1778 were not rabble; many had seen as much action as von Steuben. And it was a tough, dedicated army. Von Steuben felt that a European army faced with the incredible privations that were the lot of the Continental Army would have disintegrated. But the army was not well trained and could rarely meet British regulars in a stand-up fight or even enter or leave battlefields in an efficient manner. Marching was often in single file, and there had been cases where battles had been decided before the rear of the column caught up with the head. Every day, day after day, week after week, in fair weather and foul, von Steuben, Walker, and the troops practiced close-order drill and all the maneuvers that an eighteenth-century Western army needed to know. Von Steuben did not insist on transferring the Prussian drill and manual of arms wholesale. He adapted them to the conditions he found. Nor did he attempt to instill fear as a motivating factor for either drill or fighting, for he had quickly learned to gauge the American temper. He wrote to a European friend, "The genius of this nation is not in the least to be compared with that of the Prussians, Austrians or French. You say to your soldier, 'Do this' and he doeth it; but I am obliged to say 'This is the reason why you ought to do that'; and then he does it."[14] This American characteristic, still alive, is a precious thing and should be nurtured.

The army that emerged in the summer of 1778 still had a way to go to reach the same level of professionalism as British and Hessian regulars. But it seemed to many observers that a miracle had been wrought. The first test came that summer at Monmouth, where some of the best regiments of the British army, led personally by both Lord Cornwallis and Sir Henry Clinton, dashed in vain against Continentals who stood like rocks under a broiling Jersey sun.

The regiments that Washington sent southward were the cream of the Continental Army before the arrival of Baron von Steuben, and his training gave them the necessary techniques and sharpened their edge. The infantry of the Maryland Line and the Delaware Line were as good as any the British army could offer, which made them very good indeed. They were divided into two brigades: the 1st Maryland commanded by Brigadier General William Small-wood, and the 2nd Maryland and the Delaware Regiment commanded by Brigadier General Mordecai Gist. Both were supported by uncommonly able subordinates, especially Lieutenant Colonel John Eager Howard of the 1st Maryland and Captain Robert Kirkwood of the Delaware Regiment. In overall command of the little force was another European soldier who was one of the most gallant of the foreign volunteers: Major General Jean, Baron de Kalb, who was neither a Baron nor a "de," having begun life in 1721 as Johann Kalb, son of Bavarian peasants.[15]

In all societies there are people far from their birthplaces who attempt to embellish their backgrounds, and claiming spurious titles is a game still going on in Europe. De Kalb can be excused his lie, for his fighting heart could be the envy of many an aristocrat. Had he not done it he would have remained in the ranks, a sergeant at best. He left his birthplace of Huettendorf when he was sixteen and as far as we know never looked back. The next seven years are a blank in his biography, and when he emerges in 1743 we are confronted with Lieutenant Jean de Kalb of the French army. Getting away with it was all the more remarkable because the Regiment Loewendal was officered almost exclusively by German noblemen whom one assumes were familiar with the noble pedigrees of their homelands. It would be fascinating to know how he did it, and the identity of his patron. His physical presence was surely an important factor in his rise. He was over six feet, with strong features and a robust frame. His aquiline nose lent credence to his bogus genealogy. De Kalb's physical endurance was legendary. He was in his mid-fifties during the American war but could march thirty miles a day on foot and often did, for he preferred walking to riding. His personal habits were spartan, and he bore cheerfully with his troops the hardships and inconveniences of war.

De Kalb crowned his achievement in 1764 by marrying an heiress. Anne van Rabais was the great-granddaughter of a Dutch cloth manufacturer who settled in France in the seventeenth century at the inducement of Colbert, Louis XIV's chief minister, as part of an attempt to improve French manufactures. His success brought van Rabais a patent of nobility, which de Kalb lacked. That did not stop him from describing himself and his father on the marriage certificate as *Jean de Kalb, chevalier, fils du feu Jean Leonard de Kalb, Seigneur de Huettendorf* (Jean de Kalb, knight, son of the late John Leonard de Kalb, Lord of Huettendorf). It is all very amusing. De Kalb married up and into money to boot, while with good reason we may speculate that van Rabais preened as he married his daughter into the old aristocracy.

In 1767, the year his wife's parents died and she inherited the fortune and the family seat, the French government sent him to America to ascertain whether the colonists were resolute in their opposition to English policies and whether France might gain revenge for their loss of Canada. He returned with his report but it was pigeonholed. In 1776, aged fifty-five, still seeking glory, perhaps bored with the comforts and daily pursuits of domestic life, he kissed wife and children goodbye and went to America with Lafayette. After some delay he was commissioned a Major General by Congress. De Kalb was one of its happier choices.

The march south was not easy. The column left Morristown, New Jersey, on 16 April 1780. It reached Hillsborough in the northern reaches of North Carolina on 22 June. It was slow going because the men had to forage for food along the way, and there was little of it, as the corn crop was not yet harvested. They had only enough wagons to hold their tents; the rest of the baggage was carried on the soldiers' backs. De Kalb expected reinforcements from the state militias along the way. He received none. After resting a week at Hillsborough, he decided to press on. One of the soldiers wrote: "We marched from Hillsborough about the first of July, without an ounce of provision being laid up at any one point, often fasting for several days together, and subsisting frequently upon green apples and peaches; sometimes by detaching parties we thought ourselves feasted, when by violence we seized a little fresh beef and cut and threshed out a little wheat; yet, under all these difficulties, we had to go forward."[16] At Buffalo Ford on Deep River, approximately thirty miles south of modern Greensboro, North Carolina, they had to stop. There was no more food, a not uncommon condition with the Continental Army, but that was of little consolation to hungry troops, many of whom were ill. At Deep River they remained, scrounging for food and awaiting a new commanding general.

De Kalb was now the senior American officer in the Southern Department. Given his experience and proven ability, had he not been a foreigner and had he friends with influence, he might have been given command. He never received serious consideration, and there is evidence that he did not wish it. Washington wanted Nathanael Greene. Congress, which had first chosen Robert Howe, and then Benjamin Lincoln, both of whom were promoted beyond their abilities, decided this time to go with a hero with whom it was smitten, the conqueror of Burgoyne, Major General Horatio Gates.

Governing a Conquered Province

While the little American army on the Deep River in North Carolina desperately scoured a barren countryside for food, and Thomas Sumter planned and carried out violent deeds, Lord Cornwallis busied himself in Charleston with the burdens of administering a conquered province.[17] For a warrior, and that is precisely what Cornwallis was, it must have been an excruciating bore. But with high command come responsibilities beyond rallying troops and facing enemy fire with unflinching demeanor. Leaving Lord Rawdon in charge at Camden and the surrounding area, Cornwallis returned to Charleston in late June, intending to spend the rest of the summer organizing and seeing to the civilian administration of South Carolina. Of crucial importance were supplies for his army: food, clothing, arms, ammunition, wagons, horses. And he had to get them to his posts scattered along the great arc from Cheraws to Ninety Six. The roads were terrible, and in the Back Country during the rainy season the red clay of the southern piedmont became nearly impassable. And it rained hard that summer of 1780. Wagons were scarce, because Clinton had taken the army's back to New York, and he had also taken all of the cavalry except Tarleton's British Legion and the forty troopers of the 17th Light Dragoons. These units were usually well mounted. To add to the fine horses taken from the Americans at Monck's Corner, Tarleton without ceremony confiscated what he needed. Plenty of horses were required because the Legion in detachments was constantly on the move. Cornwallis and his outposts had to communicate, the only way was by courier, and the British soon found that to send out one man as a messenger was almost surely to sign his death warrant. South Carolina, it seems, was not quite pacified. Couriers, therefore, required escorts. Tarleton complained that "this service injured them infinitely more than all the preceding moves and actions of the campaign, and though hitherto successful against their enemies in the field, they were nearly destroyed in detail by patrols and detachments required of them during the intense heat of the season."[18]

There was plenty of food at first; not until the final stage of his campaign did Cornwallis's army experience a condition common to the Continentals, and then it was only temporary. But he had to establish a system for feeding the army, as he could not rely on supplies from either New York or England. The army had to live off the country. One of the men Cornwallis appointed to provide the army with supplies, Charles Stedman of Philadelphia, traveled with the army. He paid Tories for food and other supplies but confiscated them from Rebels. Stedman was a good choice for Cornwallis and an excellent choice for us, for in exile in England he wrote a valuable history of the war that is especially useful when he was either an eyewitness or close to actions in which he received information while it was fresh in participants' minds.

Beyond his supply needs, critical as they were, Cornwallis as military governor and representative of the Crown in the Carolinas faced a problem more serious in the long run. It was a matter of allegiance, of hearts and minds, of who was loyal and who was disloyal and how you recognized the difference and motivated the King's Friends to make the stern sacrifices necessary for victory. In this matter his Lordship found himself deeply frustrated. Even occupied Charleston was not free of Rebel activity. Cornwallis wrote to Clinton that the diehards held "constant meetings in town & carried on correspondence with the country to keep up the flame of rebellion" and spread "false reports throughout the whole province to encourage the disaffected & intimidate others."[19]

But it remained for Cornwallis's commander at Camden, the Anglo-Irish aristocrat Francis, Lord Rawdon, product of Harrow and Oxford, to provide the most vivid description of what the British faced, in his case among the Scotch Irish of the Waxhaws, and the frustration it engendered. In 1778 Sir Henry Clinton had raised a Tory regiment in Philadelphia. It was called the Volunteers of Ireland, and it was commanded by Lord Rawdon. In a letter of 5 December 1780 to Cornwallis, Rawdon recalled that "soon after your Lordship had first taken possession of Camden, you detached me to Waxhaw with my own regiment, thinking that as it was an Irish corps it would be received with the better temper by the settlers of that district, who were universally Irish and universally disaffected. My conduct towards the inhabitants, and the extraordinary regularity of the troops under my command, I must assert to have been such as ought to have conciliated their firmest attachment; yet I had the firmest proofs that the people who daily visited my camp, not only held constant correspondence with the Rebel militia then assembling at Charlotteburgh, and with those who were harrassing Lieut.-Colonel Turnbull's detachment, but also used every artifice to debauch the minds of my soldiers and persuade them to desert from their colours. The encouragement they gave to the men, and the certain means of escape with which they furnished them, succeeded to a very alarming degree, and the rage of desertion was not stopped by our return to Camden." Rawdon added that "I soon found . . . that I was betrayed on every side by the inhabitants. Several small detachments from me were attacked by persons who had the hour before been with them as friends in their camp," and deserters were "actually furnished horses . . . and forwarded . . . from house to house till they were beyond the reach of pursuit."[20] What Lord Rawdon experienced is the nightmare that professional soldiers face when guerrillas wage unrelenting war in pursuit of a cause the professionals do not understand. And it is clear that Rawdon did not understand. He thought that proper conduct by him and his troops would lead to conciliation. That this did not occur amounted to betrayal in his eyes.

The American Rebels provided a hard school for young Lord Rawdon (1754–1826), and if he never comprehended what made them in their darkest hours fight and die he certainly learned his trade. As a soldier he performed admirably, from his first action at Bunker Hill in 1775 to his relief of Ninety Six in 1781, and he went home a seasoned and skillful officer, rated the "ablest of all" by the historian of the British army Sir John Fortescue.[21] Rawdon was one of the few who emerged from Britain's trauma with an untarnished reputation. He was a general in the Napoleonic Wars and served with his usual skill. But the crowning achievement of his life came after his appointment as Governor General of India in 1813. He defeated those most formidable warriors, the Gurkhas, and his skillful campaign of 1817–1818 against the Mahratta and Pindari sealed British domination of the subcontinent. He was rewarded by being made the Marquess of Hastings. He left India in 1824, exhausted and impoverished, and was given the post of Governor General of Malta. He died there and was buried on the ramparts, but not before the execution of his request that following his death his right hand be severed, preserved, and interred in his widow's coffin after she died.

The Gamecock Afield:
Rocky Mount and Hanging Rock

Rebel successes against the Tories west of the Catawba, culminating in the defeat and death of Captain Christian Huck, had swelled Thomas Sumter's force to several hundred men. Aware that their enthusiasm would wane without action, in late July Sumter made his first move against Lord Rawdon's outposts.

North of Camden there were British strongpoints at Hanging Rock, which was about 15 miles south of where Tarleton had cut Buford to pieces; and at Rocky Mount, just south of modern Great Falls on the west bank of the Catawba River and almost twenty miles west of Hanging Rock. While Major William Richardson Davie, with forty dragoons and 40 mounted infantry, created a diversion at Hanging Rock, Sumter took 600 men to deal with the Rocky Mount strongpoint.[22] Only 150 of De Lancey's New York Volunteers held the post, but their position was well chosen and fortified. On the crest of a high hill surrounded by open woods and overlooking the Catawba River were three log buildings in which firing loopholes had been cut. The position was surrounded by a ditch and abatis (felled trees imbedded side by side in the ground with their sharpened ends facing the enemy).

On 30 July 1780 Sumter attempted to surprise the garrison, but he was detected. The Tory commander was Lieutenant Colonel George Turnbull, the officer who sent "my Lord Hook" on his final raid. Sumter dispatched a note to Turnbull demanding surrender. Turnbull replied by inviting Sumter to take it if he could. Since Sumter had no artillery, he had few choices. The fight lasted eight hours, yet the Rebels lost only six killed and eight wounded, and the Tory losses were roughly the same, which suggests a day largely spent sniping. Most of the American casualties occurred when Sumter ordered a frontal assault. Some men got close but Colonel Andrew Neel and six men died needlessly in an assault bound to fail and the others withdrew. Sumter called for volunteers to attempt to set the roofs of the log houses on fire. There followed what must have been a long, embarrassing silence, until Colonel William Hill agreed provided another would join him. Sergeant James Johnson volunteered, and the two men dashed across open ground under covering fire from their comrades. It took two perilous forays and a severe arm wound suffered by Colonel Hill before the flames took. Divine Providence on that occasion, however, was looking over the Tories. A rainstorm put out the fire. Stymied, Sumter and his men retreated and bivouacked six miles away on Rocky Creek, which they were unable to ford because it was in flood stage from the storm.

There was a grim aftermath to the fight for two Rebels captured by the Tories. According to Lieutenant Anthony Allaire's diary, they had previously served with Colonel Turnbull, had drawn ammunition, and then gone over to the Rebels. During the fight, they had been heard to call out, "take back your ammunition again." They had, of course, signed their own death warrants, and it is highly unlikely that the niceties of military justice were observed. Turnbull ordered their execution, and Allaire recorded that "They were both hanged as a reward for their treachery."[23] It was a scene often repeated on both sides.

The next day Sumter returned to his camp at Land's Ford on the Catawba, then an important fording place for columns of armed men from both sides that crossed and recrossed the Catawba at this point. Sumter's first foray against the British had not been auspicious. But William Richardson Davie, sent to Hanging Rock to divert attention from the main effort, had scored a coup.

Davie arrived at Hanging Rock, which had a British garrison of 500 men, at 1:00 P.M. and reconnoitered before deciding where to attack. While engaged in reconnaissance, he was told that three companies of mounted infantry from Colonel Morgan Bryan's North Carolina Tory militia had just ridden in and halted at a farmer's house that was in full view of the British garrison. They probably numbered about sixty or seventy riders. Davie immediately formed a daring plan to envelop the Tories. But it had to be done quickly and by surprise, before the garrison could intervene. The farmer's house was beside a lane that ran from woods past the house to the British encampment. Rebel and Tory militia, the reader will recall, dressed alike in the common clothes of the country. Taking advantage of that, in a particularly bold move Davie sent his forty mounted riflemen, probably under Captain David Flenniken of Mecklenburg County, North Carolina, on a march past the camp sentries to a point on the lane above the house. Half of the dragoons entered the lane below the house; the remaining twenty rode slowly into the field.

Davie described clearly and succinctly the ensuing confusion, terror, and slaughter visited on the Tories. "This disposition was made with such promptitude that the attention or suspicion of the enemy was never excited. The rifle company under Capt. Flenniken passed the camp sentries without being challenged, dismounted in the lane and gave the enemy a well directed fire. The astonished Loyalists fled instantly the other way, and were immediately charged by the dragoons in full gallop and driven back in great confusion; on meeting again the fire of the infantry they all rushed impetuously against the angle of the fence where in a moment they were surrounded by the dragoons who had entered the field and literally cut to pieces: as this was done under the eye of the whole British camp no prisoners could safely be taken, which may apologize for the slaughter that took place on this occasion. They took sixty valuable Horses with their furniture and one hundred muskets and rifles; the whole camp beat to arms but the business was done and the Detachment out of their reach before they recovered from their consternation."[24] Banastre Tarleton could have done no better. The feat of Davie and his eighty men, who suffered no losses, was a textbook model of a partisan operation.

On the 5th of August Davie's little band rejoined Sumter at his camp at Land's Ford. They were determined to drive the British from their posts at Rocky Mount and Hanging Rock and believed that if one fell the other would be evacuated. They numbered in all about 800 riders: 500 from just across the line in the Rebel stronghold of Mecklenburg County, North Carolina, and 300 South Carolinians. A council of war was held by the officers and they decided to attack Hanging Rock because it was an open camp, with no fortifications beyond simple earthworks. Davie recalled that "in those times [it] was absolutely necessary" for the officers to explain to their men what was intended and obtain their approval, and in this case the militia "entered into the project with great spirit and cheerfulness." A night march brought them by midnight to within two miles of the British camp. Riding in Davie's command was a thirteen-year-old boy who grew up to become an American folk hero and seventh President of the United States. Andrew Jackson, Waxhaws born and bred, had joined his older relatives in serving the cause. William Richardson Davie by all accounts became Jackson's ideal as officer and gentleman. He gave the boy a pistol and made him "a mounted orderly or messenger, for which I was well fitted, being a good rider and knowing all the roads."[25]

Hanging Rock was held by 500 Tory regulars and militia under Major John Carden. Although they were outnumbered by the Americans and had no fortifications to fight behind, their position was strong. The site today is completely overgrown by thick woods and underbrush, but it bears examination because of what it tells us about Sumter the tactician. In 1780 there was much open farmland, room for cavalry to maneuver, and clear fields of fire. Protecting the British front was a deep ravine with very steep sides and a creek running through it.[26]

The Tory force was composed for the most part of well-trained provincial units. There were 160 infantry from Tarleton's British Legion; a detachment from the Prince of Wales Loyal American Volunteers, another northern Tory unit; the North Carolina Loyalist Volunteers; part of Colonel Thomas "Burntfoot" Brown's Rangers—Brown was not present; and the rest of Colonel Morgan Bryan's North Carolina Tory militia, already roughly handled by Davie. They suffered from a weakness chronic to British arms. They did not know Sumter's whereabouts or intentions, whereas he knew not only where they were but how their units were deployed.

Sumter was aware that the Prince of Wales detachment was on the right; the British Legion infantry and North Carolina Loyalist Volunteers under Lieutenant Colonel John Hamilton in the center, joined presumably by Brown's Rangers; and Morgan Bryan's North Carolina militia "some distance on the left, and separated from the centre-camp by a skirt of wood," William Richardson Davie wrote. He also stated that "the position of the regular troops could not be approached without an entire exposure of the assailants, and a Creek with a deep ravine covered the whole front of the Tory camp." Sumter proposed to divide his force into three columns, march to the center, dismount, and attack. Davie argued that the horses should be left where they were and the approach made on foot. He feared the "confusion always consequent on dismounting under a fire and the certainty of losing the effect of a sudden and vigorous attack." Davie was overruled. The columns were divided: Major Davie commanded the right with his men, Major Richard Winn's band,[27] and detached companies of South Carolinians; Colonel William Hill led the left with South Carolina units; and Colonel Irwin commanded the center column with his Mecklenburg County militia. Sumter commanded the whole. The operation highlights Thomas Sumter's strengths and weaknesses. As a historian of South Carolina observed, he had the power to animate men, and he knew that with militia a spirit of enterprise must be constantly in the air. On this occasion his intelligence was accurate, and the rapid night march, always a risky maneuver, a success. His tactics, however, reveal an utter lack of imagination. He proposed to lead all his troops to the center, dismount in view of the British, and launch a frontal assault across a creek and ravine against an enemy who had the advantage of a clear field of fire. He might well have received a bloody repulse had not the fortunes of war intervened.

The columns set out, led by local Rebel guides. But all three turned off the road to the left to avoid British pickets and a patrol. They meant to "return to it under the cover of a defile near the camp, but the guides through ignorance or timidity led them so far to the left that the right and center divisions fell together with the left upon the Tory encampment." Whether by error or, as Davie remarked, fear on the part of the guides, it was fortuitous. The Tories were completely surprised, as all three columns attacked Morgan Bryan's North Carolinians simultaneously from two sides. The British flank had not just been turned, as military historians are fond of saying, it was rolled up and sent flying toward the center, "routed with great slaughter." The Rebels chased them and soon ran up against the Legion Infantry and some of Hamilton's North Carolina volunteers, who delivered fire from behind a fence.

But the Rebels were in full cry, as recounted by Davie: "Their impetuosity was not checked a moment by this unexpected discharge." Sumter's men broke the Legion and the volunteers who joined the wild flight of Bryan's men, "yielding their camp without another struggle to the Militia." In this fighting the Prince of Wales detachment was destroyed as a fighting unit, losing all its officers and but a handful of men. Fortunes were almost reversed when the Rangers from Brown's regiment "passed by a bold and skilful manuevre into the wood between the centre and Tory encampment, drew up unperceived, and poured a Heavy fire on the militia forming from the disorder of the pursuit." Sumter's men were not to be denied. With a coolness under fire usually attributed only to regulars, and with tactics that twentieth-century infantry could not improve upon, "these brave men took instinctively to the trees and bush heaps and returned the fire with deadly effect. In a few minutes there was not a British officer standing, one half of the regiment had fallen, and the others on being offered quarters threw down their arms." The remaining British prepared for a last stand. They "drew up in the center of the cleared grounds in the form of a Hollow Square" and fixed bayonets. The Rebels were on the verge of a crushing victory and the destruction of a British strongpoint.

Then the men who had attacked with elan and displayed intrepid behavior under fire fell apart. The lure of loot overwhelmed them. Hundreds of partisans began plundering the British camp, found the liquor supplies, and started getting roaring drunk. Sumter and his officers implored them in vain to return to their duty. Only Davie's dragoons and about 200 infantry could be formed at the edge of the woods, and the fire they directed at the British proved ineffectual. Then the Legion infantry, Hamilton's volunteers, and Tory militia were observed rallying at the edge of the woods on the other side of the British camp. Fearing a flank attack, Davie led his little band of horsemen around the camp under cover of trees and charged the British. Although Davie was outnumbered, the British, still reeling from their previous reverses, "were routed and dispersed." Sumter and his officers by then agreed that there was no hope of further action by the hundreds of men busily plundering the British camp. Unofficial action by the other ranks became officially approved. The camp would be stripped before retiring. At that point a new threat developed. Cavalry of the British Legion suddenly appeared on the Camden road. Davie and his faithful riders immediately charged and the British, as Davie recorded, "all took the woods in flight & only one was cut down." The Legion without Tarleton, both foot and horse, had not lived up to its reputation.

The affair now took on a comic-opera appearance. An hour was spent plundering the camp and drinking its liquid supplies, "taking the paroles of British officers, and preparing litters for the wounded. All this was transacted in full view of the British troops, who in the mean time consoled themselves with some military music & an interlude of 3 cheers for King George, which was immediately answered by 3 cheers" from the Rebels. Finally, loaded with plunder, reeling from strong drink, the Rebels marched off, if march is the proper word. Major Davie had a good view of their progression from his post as commander of the rear guard. "It is easy to conceive that this retreat could not be performed according to the rules of the most approved tacticks. However under all these disadvantages they filed off unmolested along the front of the Enemy about 1 O'clock."

They left behind 200 Tory casualties while suffering only twelve killed and forty-one wounded. They had not fulfilled their main purpose of destroying the strongpoint, but it was a clear-cut victory nonetheless over the kind of trained, disciplined Tory regulars the British expected to be a key factor in retaking the Carolinas. Sumter's tactics would remain primitive, but his ability to rally men and lead them on grand enterprises was vital to the cause. And young William Richardson Davie had again shown himself a leader of uncommon ability and judgment. Lord Rawdon must have been furious, frustrated, and mortified, not least because the action had taken place practically on his doorstep, his headquarters at Camden some twenty miles south.

Nine days later a detachment sent by Sumter again embarrassed the British within a short ride of Camden. At Wateree Ferry south of Camden the British had built a redoubt and garrisoned it with thirty troops under the command of Colonel Matthew Carey. Moving toward Fort Carey was a British supply convoy from Charleston. Sumter knew about it, of course, and resolved to capture it. He sent Colonel Thomas Taylor with a strong force on the mission. On 15 August Taylor surprised and captured Colonel Carey and his men, and thirty-six wagons loaded with supplies, including rum, which surely gladdened militia hearts. He learned from the prisoners the location of the convoy, and rode out and took another prize: fifty wagons with supplies, six wagons with baggage, 300 head of cattle, and some sheep. He then rejoined Sumter, who slowly began moving north. But the affair had not ended. The British wanted their goods and people back, and encumbered as he was with plunder and prisoners, Sumter's column could not move with its accustomed speed. Taylor's coup is also connected with the American army that had marched south under de Kalb and was then given by Congress to Horatio Gates. It will all fall into place, but at this point we should turn to the adventures of other active Rebel guerrilla bands that were operating farther to the west, and the Tory regulars and militia commanded by Major Patrick Ferguson, Inspector of Militia.

Chasing Rebels

Ferguson and his forces were constantly on the move in the Ninety Six District and northward. In addition to the local Tory militia, who were his special concern, he had his own command, the American Volunteers, about 100 redcoated Tory Regular infantry he had brought with him from New York and New Jersey on Sir Henry Clinton's expedition to capture Charleston. Lieutenant Anthony Allaire, whom we first met at Monck's Corner and have caught glimpses of since, left a diary of his service with the Volunteers. It is not as informative as Johann Ewald's diary, and often repeats erroneous second- and third-hand information; but Allaire presents a clear picture, probably without meaning to, of constant Rebel activity in a state officially pacified. His daily entries of marching and countermarching, the frustrations inherent in attempting to engage well-mounted, elusive guerrillas, and the daily drudgery of soldiering common to all armies in all ages give life to events of 200 years ago that were critical to the eventual triumph of the cause.

Lieutenant Allaire had arrived at Ninety Six on 22 June 1780. On 9 July, he wrote, "The American Volunteers moved from Ninety Six at seven o'clock in the evening, under the command of Captain [Abraham] DePeyster, and marched seven miles to Island Ford, of Saluda River, on our way to meet a party of Rebels that were making approaches towards our lines." Allaire and the surgeon, however, missed the departure and did not catch up until 1:00 A.M., and being without baggage went to a house to sleep. "We found two women, and spent the night, though not to our satisfaction. It afforded some merry scenes with those two modest country women." Had it been Tarleton's British Legion instead of Ferguson's American Volunteers at that place, the women might well have been raped, but Ferguson's reputation among Americans of all persuasions was unblemished with regard to the personal behavior of his regulars. But there must have been little sleep for our young lieutenant, despite the innocent sleeping arrangements, because the Volunteers were on the road at 5:00 A.M. and marched nine miles to the plantation of Colonel James Williams. "Mrs. Williams and the children were at home, and were treated with the utmost civility. Col. Williams is with the Rebels, and is a very violent, persecuting scoundrel."[28]

The American Volunteers "got in motion" at 5:00 A.M. the next day, marched eight miles, and "halted during the heat of the day," then "got in motion at six o'clock in the evening and marched eleven miles to Duncan's creek, where we halted at a Widow Brown's." On the 12th they forded the creek and the Enoree River, made an eight-mile night march, and met a courier who gave them the "disagreeable news" of Captain's Huck's defeat and death that day at Williamson's Plantation. On the 13th the Volunteers forded the Tyger River, made a twelve-mile night march to Sugar Creek, and found 200 Tory militia encamped. They were in the general vicinity of Cedar Springs, where Jane Thomas had warned her son of the approach of the British. Allaire wrote that "the Rebels, we hear, are collecting in force at the Catawba Nation and Broad River." He also heard "every hour news from different parts of the country of Rebel parties doing mischief."[29]

On the 18th of July Major Patrick Ferguson rode into camp with news of reinforcements, and probably impending action. Three days later Lieutenant Colonel Nisbet Balfour arrived from Ninety Six with the British light infantry. The son of an Edinburgh bookseller, Balfour would have a long and distinguished career in the British army. Cornwallis had put him in command at Ninety Six. According to William Moultrie, Balfour was "a proud, haughty Scot, carried his authority with a very high hand; he had a tyrannical, insolent disposition, treated people as the most abject slaves."[30] With due allowance for a moderate measure of exaggeration, this is an accurate overall description of the British officer class in its imperial role, and in America it was a not unimportant factor in the estrangment between the mother country and the colonies. (Balfour, by the way, had a low opinion of the abilities of his fellow Scot, Patrick Ferguson.) In three succinct diary entries, Lieutenant Allaire described the ensuing operation.

"*Saturday, 22d.* The Light Infantry, American Volunteers, and three hundred militia got in motion at seven o'clock in the evening; made a forced march of twenty-five miles to Lawson's Fork to surprise a party of Rebels, who, we were informed, lay there. We arrived at James Wood's plantation at six o'clock in the morning; greatly disappointed at finding no Rebels here. We were informed they were at Green River—twenty-five miles farther.

"*Sunday, 23d.* Got in motion at one o'clock in the morning and countermarched to our old ground, Fair Forest Ford.

"*Monday, 24th.* Very much fatigued; slept all day."[31]

The following day at 2:00 A.M. Balfour left with the light infantry to return to Ninety Six. The American Volunteers remained in the field and three days later continued their routine of marches and countermarches, tension and tedium relieved by the killing of a "Continental rattle-snake, with thirteen rattles on," and the arrival of a courier, "a Capt. Cook, aged sixty years, who has buried four wives, and now has his fifth on her last legs." The month of July ended when they "got in motion at six o'clock in the morning and marched ten miles to Mitchell's Creek, Fair Forest; a very wet, disagreeable day; got thoroughly soaked." Thus the glory and romance of a soldier's life.[32]

About a week later information was received that Rebels were gathering at Ford's Mills. Allaire and the Volunteers once more "got in motion" and made another forced night march, this one of sixteen miles: "got to our ground at Jemmie's creek at six o'clock in the morning of the 7th, where we heard the Rebels had moved seven miles to Phillip's Ford." Determined to bring the Rebel band to bay, the Volunteers made another forced night march on the 7th, "fording Jemmie's creek and the South and North branches of the Tyger river." But on arriving at 4:00 A.M. on 8 August they found the Rebels had left thirty minutes before, having "intelligence of our move, and were likewise alarmed by the firing of a gun in our ranks." But the British would not give up, and Major Patrick Ferguson himself was at hand to direct the chase.[33]

The Rebel band was led by Colonel Elijah Clarke of Georgia and Colonel Isaac Shelby of the Holston settlements across the mountains. They probably had about 600 mounted men with them.[34] The combined British force numbered somewhere between 400 and 600, but not all the units had arrived in time to join the fight. Allaire and his fellow American Volunteers, being on foot, did not participate but afterwards took part in the pursuit, and Allaire, who was only about three miles away, certainly got fresh information of what took place from comrades who were at the initial engagement.

Allaire states that the action occurred on 8 August at Cedar Springs, where about a month before Mrs. Jane Thomas had warned her son of the approch of the British. Other sources, however, put the location not at the springs but a mile or so away, perhaps in a peach orchard. But this is of small moment. The Rebels knew that Ferguson's men were close and when they chose their ground remained alert and deployed for battle. According to Allaire, three Rebels reconnoitering the British camp were spotted and chased and two caught while the other galloped toward the Rebel position with British horsemen in hot pursuit. Shelby and Clarke, alert as a matter of course in this dangerous country, were warned of the British approach and impending attack.

They did not have long to wait. The British advance force, numbering by Anthony Allaire's count 144 dragoons and mounted militia, were led by Captain James Dunlap. Ferguson with the main force, including Allaire and the American Volunteers, followed only a few miles behind. Lieutenant Allaire wrote that "Dunlap and his party rushed into the centre of the Rebel camp, where they lay in ambush, before he was aware of their presence." The fight was short and savage, hand to hand. Both American sources and Allaire agree that Elijah Clarke was in the thick of it and was wounded, by saber strokes to the head and neck according to the American participants; but he stayed on his feet and fought on. Captain Dunlap, according to Allaire, "got slightly wounded and had between twenty and thirty killed and wounded—Ensign McFarland and one private taken prisoner. The Rebel loss is uncertain." Dunlap's horsemen were driven from the field. But the Rebels could neither tarry nor risk a full-scale engagement with Ferguson's entire force. Leaving four dead on the field, Clark and Shelby retreated toward North Carolina, with about fifty prisoners when the British, according to Isaac Shelby, "made great effort to regain . . . and continued their pursuit for several miles . . . on one of the warmest days ever felt." Draper relates that when Ferguson and his troops gave up the chase but were still in view, Clarke and Shelby formed their men on a ridge and "bantered and ridiculed them to their hearts' content."[35]

Writing after the war, Banastre Tarleton's deputy, Major George Hanger, put his finger on the tactical problem faced by the British: "The crackers and militia in those parts of America are all mounted on horseback, which renders it totally impossible to force them to an engagement with infantry *only*. When they chuse to fight, they dismount and fasten their horses to fences and rails; but if not very confident in the superiority of their numbers, they remain on horseback, give their fire, and retreat, which renders it useless to attack them without cavalry: for though you repulse them and drive them from the field, you can never improve the advantage, or do them material detriment."[36] Sir Henry Clinton had left Cornwallis with only about 240 regular cavalry: Tarleton's British Legion, and the forty troopers of the 17th Light Dragoons. They were quite simply not enough to fight the type of war chosen by the partisans, especially as the Tory mounted militia were inferior to the Rebel horsemen.

Frustration was the lot of Ferguson's command. It was tireless in its pursuit of the Rebels, but the Rebels were just as tireless in maintaining a presence and engaging in the classic guerrilla tactic of avoiding battle unless it suited them. And on the one occasion during a month of pursuit when Ferguson's force closed with the main Rebel band, the partisans were waiting for the British and mauled them before departing for the safety of North Carolina where they could rest and refit. In hindsight, the outcome of that month of maneuver and pursuit is not surprising. Ferguson was facing uncommon men who were natural leaders and firm in their devotion to the cause. Many of them, Clarke and Shelby especially, had been schooled in Indian wars. They were gifted partisan leaders, and riding behind them were formidable men accustomed to weapons, horses, and rough life in the field. Even General Nathanael Greene, whose highly critical views of militia were well known and often justified, in a letter to Alexander Hamilton nevertheless admitted that "there is a great spirit of enterprise among the back people; and those that come out as Volunteers are not a little formidable to the enemy. There are also some particular Corps under Sumpter, Marion and Clarke that are bold and daring."[37]

Elijah Clarke: Partisan Leader

The Clarke that Greene referred to was Colonel Elijah Clarke (1733–1799).[38] He is an obscure figure today, but he was a fierce and relentless warrior for the cause in Georgia and South Carolina. He was born in Edgefield County, South Carolina, probably of Scotch Irish descent. He was unschooled, but that has never been a barrier to successful leadership in irregular warfare. He was wounded in battle on more than one occasion, once almost to the point of death, but always recovered and persevered. Elijah Clarke's life after the war was one of repeated dubious ventures in quest of status and wealth. He took service with the French as a major general at $10,000 per year and acted in support of the notorious French minister to the United States, Citizen Genet, in his aborted scheme to oust the Spanish from West Florida. He then raised troops and established his short-lived "Trans-Oconee State" in Creek Indian territory. Militia sent by the Governor of Georgia ended that scheme. He may also have been involved in later plots against the Spanish as well as the Yazoo Land Fraud. But his checkered postwar history did him no harm in the popular mind. Through it all Elijah Clarke remained a hero of the Revolution, and he was still a hero when he went to his grave in 1799.

During the first part of August 1780, while Sumter and Davie were operating on the Catawba and the Wateree against Lord Rawdon's forces, and the small American army under Horatio Gates was approaching South Carolina, Elijah Clarke and Colonel Isaac Shelby, following the second encounter at Cedar Springs, arrived at the Broad River camp of the North Carolina militia general, Charles McDowell. We will treat Shelby in some detail later, but for now it will suffice to know that he led 200 riders from the outer reaches of the southern frontier westward across the mountains in what is now East Tennessee but then belonged to North Carolina. In the context of the Revolution, Shelby's riders are known as the Over Mountain men, although the British also called them backwater men. The British knew little about them or their settlements, and at this time they may not have realized that Shelby's force was east of the mountains. The men carried what came to be known as Kentucky Rifles and they were reputed to be crack shots. As with all militia, their enlistments were for short periods, often only three months.

General McDowell's scouts had reported a force of about 200 Tories at Musgrove's Mill on the Enoree River, about thirty miles north of Ninety Six. There was a ford at that site, and the Tory mission was to guard it. McDowell also knew that the main British force, led by Major Patrick Ferguson, was somewhere in the general area, but this threat was not deemed serious enough to prevent a strike at Musgrove's Mill. The Rebels would not concede the upper Piedmont to Ferguson. He was an energetic soldier who had the reputation of being one of the few British officers who gave time and effort to sitting down and discussing issues and listening to the problems of the Back Country people instead of treating them as inferior colonials. A man like that had the potential of being a far more dangerous foe than Tarleton. It was imperative, therefore, that the partisans continue to strike into the territory where Ferguson recruited and patrolled and show the local Tories that the British could not protect them. Clarke and Shelby, along with militia officers from South Carolina, decided to hit Musgrove's Mill.

The British now faced fierce, tenacious opposition in the mid-Piedmont from Thomas Sumter, and in its western reaches into the foothills of the Blue Ridge from Elijah Clarke, Isaac Shelby, and others. And drawing nigh was to British eyes a threat even more ominous: the Continentals under the command of the Hero of Saratoga, Major General Horatio Gates.

11

🪖

A Hero Takes Charge

The Hero of Saratoga

In 1928 the distinguished military historian Hoffman Nickerson described Major General Horatio Gates as a "snob of the first water," with an "unctuously pious way with him, not entirely unlike Dickens's immortal Uriah Heep," and such a "repellent personality" that "he still awaits his biographer." Nickerson then administered the cruelest cut of all, maintaining that by the time of the Saratoga campaign Gates was "so empty of fighting spirit as to lay him open to suspicion of personal cowardice." In 1952 the distinguished military historian Lynn Montross strongly defended Gates, maintaining that in 1778 there began "a campaign of character assassination that has few parallels in American history. From that time onward, Gates would be attacked at every opportunity, by fair means or foul, until few rags remained of his military reputation." Gates's character and career invite such extremes of opinion, and a valiant attempt at even-handed treatment, Paul David Nelson's scholarly work of 1976, is less than convincing. For Horatio Gates does not lend himself to efforts to be eminently fair. He was, above all, a man of modest abilities, but he thought otherwise. That, I believe, and his origins, governed his actions throughout a long and tumultuous career.[1]

Horatio Gates (1727–1806) was born in England to a servant couple, and that beginning without doubt burdened his psyche to the grave.[2] Ordinarily, this accident of birth would have precluded his admission to the British officer class, but his mother was housekeeper to the mistress of the Duke of Bolton, who used his influence to get Horatio's father a job in the customs service. When Horatio was fourteen the Duke again intervened on behalf of the family, and his father became surveyor of customs at Greenwich. In 1745, following the rising of the Scottish Highlanders for Bonnie Prince Charlie, the Duke, to ingratiate himself with the royal family, raised a regiment of infantry for service against the

Horatio Gates, by Charles Willson **Peale, 1782.**
(Independence National Historical Park Collection.)

Stuarts. Since it was a new regiment, officers could be appointed without recourse to the purchase system. There is apparently no documented proof that
the Duke of Bolton interceded, but how else would eighteen-year-old Lieutenant Horatio Gates, son of a housekeeper, have become an officer and a gentleman? He could not, of course, expect a career similar to either Sir Henry
Clinton or Lord Cornwallis. There would be no commission in a Household
Guards regiment for the likes of him. Although he had entered the service outside the purchase system, it would apply thereafter, and for most of his life
money was in short supply. Life in the army would be a struggle for patronage
and preferment and lead to eventual frustration, and Gates would have been
less than human had it not embittered him against his country and the class
that ran it.

In the beginning, however, it appeared that he might prevail despite his
handicaps. Instead of fighting wild Highland Scots, he was sent to Germany and
served in the War of the Austrian Succession. There is no indication that he
saw combat. He specialized in staff work, and on the death of the regimental
adjutant Gates succeeded to the post. At the end of the war his regiment was

disbanded and Gates discharged. His brightest prospect seemed to be the offer of land in Nova Scotia for thousands of discharged officers and men, and his application came to the attention of the commander of this semimilitary expedition, Colonel Edward Cornwallis, uncle of our Lord Cornwallis. Edward Cornwallis required an aide-de-camp, and Gates with his staff experience seemed the right man. The job paid a not insignificant 200 pounds per year, and Gates was unemployed. He took it and arrived in Halifax in June 1749. Gates was a convivial, gregarious man and got along well with his fellow officers, one of whom was the well-connected Robert Monckton, but he needed a permanent appointment in the army. Cornwallis appointed him acting captain in the 45th Regiment of Foot, which did not require a cash outlay; but it was not permanent, and when a captaincy became available in the 45th Gates could not raise the 400 pounds to buy it, even though it was a paltry sum as such purchases went.

Edward Cornwallis returned to England in 1752, and Gates thereafter served as aide-de-camp to two successors and met his future wife, Elizabeth Phillips. Her father was a major and the nephew of Colonel Richard Phillips, former Governor of Nova Scotia. On her maternal side she was related to the Earl of Thanet. She was a formidable person, and we are indebted to the irrepressible Charles Lee who about thirty years later described her as "Medusa who governs with a rod of scorpions." But the prospective bridegroom of a young woman well above him in the social scale required better prospects. Like young Sir Henry Clinton he decided that London was the place to seek them, and by January 1754 Gates had taken lodgings in the great city. The situation was not encouraging. The Duke of Bolton had withdrawn from politics. Edward Cornwallis was out of favor. By June he had given up and booked return passage to Halifax.

Then came great news. In the American wilderness the French had clashed with a British provincial force under the command of Lieutenant Colonel George Washington. The hawks of eighteenth-century Britain clamored for war. A captain of the 4th Independent Company of Foot, then based in Maryland, was ill and wished to sell his commission, and Edward Cornwallis recommended Gates. The officer had an agent, who offered it to Gates for 1,400 pounds. Gates, of course, did not have that kind of money. He and the agent negotiated and a deal was struck for a down payment and the balance on credit. The new captain rushed back to Halifax as fast as the winds would carry him and on 20 October 1754 married his Medusa. In late March 1755 Captain Horatio Gates joined his new company in Frederick, Maryland. It was part of the army that Major General Edward Braddock was about to lead into the wilderness against the French and Indians. Here, for the first time, Gates met George Washington. He may also have met Charles Lee, a young lieutenant in the 44th Foot, but probably he did not come across a big, brawling wagoner with the supply column named Daniel Morgan.

The story of Braddock's defeat is a familiar one. It fostered the legend of British ineptitude for forest warfare and colored subsequent accounts of the battles of the American Revolution. It is not surprising. Although Braddock did not, as often alleged, blunder into an ambush, bad tactics and the panic that swept the ranks of British regulars led to disaster. Horatio Gates was lucky to survive. On the day of the battle, his company was in the van, along with the elite grenadier companies of the 44th Foot. The commander of the van was Lieutenant Colonel Thomas Gage, who twenty years later would order the assault on Bunker Hill. With Gates was Captain Robert Cholmley, who was along because this was Gates's first troop command; it is also evidence that Gates had not experienced battle in Germany, for Cholmley's assignment was to make all combat decisions. Horatio Gates's first taste of battle was brief. He was shot in the left side of his chest in the first few minutes. Had he been abandoned on the field during the blind panic that soon overtook the regulars, no doubt the scalping knife would have been his fate. But Private Francis Penfold, wounded himself, picked up his stricken captain and carried him to the rear and safety. To his credit, Gates never forgot his savior, and years later took Penfold into his household and supported him.

Although it cannot be proven, given Gates's subsequent history, I believe that this terrifying wilderness experience seared his soul. He had three more opportunities to fight Indians during his career, and managed on each occasion to avoid his duty.

After his recovery Gates served at forts in New York's Mohawk Valley, while his wife remained in New York City. A son, Robert, was born to them in 1758. But Gates was still a captain serving in dreary frontier posts. Then his old patron Edward Cornwallis secured for him an appointment as brigade major to Brigadier General John Stanwix at Fort Pitt. Even better, Stanwix was soon succeeded by an old friend of Gates's Halifax bachelor days, Brigadier General Robert Monckton, who had been second in command to James Wolfe on the Quebec expedition. Monckton's father was Viscount Galway, his mother daughter of the Duke of Rutland—a good man to serve under and stick close to.

Although the war on the North American continent had ended, there was still fighting against the French and Spanish in the West Indies. Monckton was given command of an expedition, and in December 1761 the fleet passed Sandy Hook on its way to Martinique. After it merged with another British fleet off Barbados, it consisted of 173 ships and 11,000 men. Gates did not serve as a troop commander, but in his old role as a staff officer he gained priceless experience in military administration as General Monckton and Admiral Rodney swept over the French opposition. And his reward was handsome. Gates was chosen by General Monckton to take the news to England, where by tradition the messenger received a promotion. Monckton recommended him to the King "as a very deserving Officer, and who has now served upwards to twelve years in America, with much Credit." In April 1762, a little over a month after he arrived in England, Gates was appointed a major in the 45th Foot and given 1,000 pounds to help him purchase a lieutenant colonelcy when one became vacant. This seemed to be his big break, and he sent for his wife and son.

But not only did his new commission mean a cut in pay, there were no vacancies for a lieutenant colonel. Perhaps, however, things could be fixed. He had good friends. Edward Cornwallis had married Charles Townshend's sister, and Townshend, who was Secretary of War, agreed to write to the Commander in Chief of North America, Sir Jeffrey Amherst, requesting a post calling for a lieutenant colonel's rank for Gates; Lord Ligonier, who was now Commander in Chief of the Army, sent a similar letter. It would appear that with such powerful patrons Major Horatio Gates, his wife, and his son were well advised to sail for New York in August 1762. But the family arrived to find that the position for which Major Gates had been recommended had been filled, and he had now lost his assignment to the 45th Foot, although his pay continued for a while. Robert Monckton was then Royal Governor of New York, and he took Gates on as political aide. But the following year Monckton returned to England and Gates was out of a job. There was also the danger that he might be retired at half pay. Again, the best place to seek preferment was London, and one year after their arrival in New York the family set sail again.

Gates now experienced nothing but frustration and failure, and the strain on a less than sterling character proved at times too much. Convivial he might be, but he was also a quarrelsome man when affairs did not go his way. He had a vicious argument with Edward Cornwallis's wife, so he could expect no more help from that quarter. His wife's father died without a farthing. His mother and his wife had a falling out. Majors' commissions for regiments stationed in America were available but he wanted a colonelcy. None came his way. In 1769 he sold his commission, resigned from the army, and set his eye on India. Robert Monckton was angling for command of the East India Company's army; if he got it, he promised that Gates would be his deputy. Both men waited four years while Parliament dawdled, and the command finally went to another. But even before that Gates's impatience had led him to push Monckton for news; Monckton, no doubt frustrated himself, replied sharply, which displeased Gates, and another friendship ended. It was also the end of the line for him in England. Bitter at a system that he felt had failed him, never driven by ideology but by social and economic frustration, Horatio Gates decided to seek better days by emigrating to America. He and his family sailed for Virginia in August 1772.

Near Shepherdstown, in what is now West Virginia, he bought 659 acres on the Potomac River and built a large limestone house that he called Traveller's Rest. He became a slaveholder, a local justice, and a lieutenant colonel in the militia. "I was such a Fool to stay so long in England, Vainly hoping for what I never obtained." he wrote to Robert Monckton's brother-in-law less than a year after his arrival.[3] When Lord Dunmore's War broke out, however, he decided that he did not want to fight Indians, professing to find the war nothing but a land grab, thus morally repugnant. Lord Dunmore refused to accept his reasoning, whereupon Gates claimed to be too ill to join the expedition and got away with it. It would not be the last time that he claimed to be too ill to fight Indians. And his sense of morality on this occasion did not extend to refusing his veteran's bonus: 5,000 acres of Indian land.[4]

Gates consorted with radical patriots and was in contact with that other ex-British officer and fiery republican Charles Lee, who also was living in Virginia.

On 29 May 1775 he heard of the clash at Lexington, Massachusetts. He wasted no time. By 2 June he was at Mount Vernon to offer his services to George Washington. In a country where few had served as professional soldiers or had experience in handling large bodies of men, such an offer could not be taken lightly. After Washington became commander in chief, he specifically urged Congress to commission Charles Lee and Horatio Gates. At last, in a fledgling army to be sure, but an army nonetheless, Horatio Gates realized one of his fiercest ambitions. He was now Brigadier General Horatio Gates of the Continental Army, and Adjutant General to the Commander in Chief. The experienced staff officer was given the task of organizing the army, and on 21 June he received orders from George Washington to proceed immediately to Boston. First, however, he took care of some business that revealed an ever-present side of his character. Always the political general, on his way to Boston he stopped at Philadelphia to make himself known to Congress, and there began ingratiating himself with the New England delegation. He next stopped in New York City to visit old friends and study the lay of that political landscape. When he finally got to the American army's camp in Cambridge, he engaged in what he did best as a soldier, the organization and administration of an army.[5]

During the early months of the war he rendered valuable service to George Washington, and had he been content to continue in that capacity the cause would have benefited and he would have come down to us fondly remembered and honored. But Horatio Gates had ambitions that went beyond military administration. His easy manners and homely style appealed to New Englanders, and he returned their admiration, treating Yankee militia as a politician would handle constituents. He "never desired to see better soldiers than the New-England men made," he told some New England politicians. This was utter nonsense. If Gates believed what he said he was a fool; if not, he was engaging in political pandering. John Adams and he became friends when the future President of the United States visited the camp. Normally the most sensible of men, Adams waxed silly over Gates, as he did over most matters military, probably because he was a frustrated warrior who longed for martial glory but knew that he was not cut out for it. Gates stroked Adams and encouraged his belief that the talents of the ex-British officer were being wasted. Adams returned the flattery. "I wish you was a Major General," Adams wrote in April 1776, "what say you to it?" Gates certainly did not decline, and probably preened. Robert Troup, who was one of his aides during the Saratoga campaign, maintained that Gates was "more subject to the fascinating, and corrupting influence, of flattery than any man I have ever been acquainted with."[6]

The following month Congress promoted Gates to Major General and put him in charge of the militia at Boston. As events worked out, he went instead to northern New York, where he began his long campaign of intrigue against the commander of the Northern Department, Major General Philip Schuyler, in order to supplant him. But he also worked hard at Fort Ticonderoga to reorganize and outfit the badly demoralized force that had retreated from Canada, again doing what he did best. Ignorant of boat construction, he showed good sense in putting Benedict Arnold in charge of building a fleet to contest the British on Lake Champlain. Although Arnold lost his naval battle, the British were delayed long enough so that their commander, Sir Guy Carleton, thought it too late in the season to continue the campaign and returned to Canada. George Washington then recalled Gates and his troops to Pennsylvania.

Gates arrived in Washington's camp on 22 December 1776. The date is significant. On Christmas day and into the night Washington and the ragged Continentals crossed the Delaware during a fierce storm and the next morning surprised and overran the Hessians at Trenton. But Gates was not with them. He had left a few days earlier for Baltimore, where Congess was then in session. His biographer kindly speculates that illness led him to the legislative battlefield at Baltimore instead of the field of honor at Trenton—too ill to fight, but not too ill to lobby—although even he finds Gates's choice "odd."[7]

His time in Baltimore was well spent. He turned down another appointment as Washington's adjutant general. He preferred direct appointment by Congress to an independent command, and on 25 March 1777 Congress gave him command of the army in the Northern Department at Fort Ticonderoga. There he continued his campaign to oust General Philip Schuyler as commander of the Northern Department.

We cannot allow ourselves to get bogged down in the machinations that went on between the Gates and Schuyler factions and their various ups and downs, but a word about Schuyler is in order. In one sense he resembled Gates: uncharismatic, certainly not a battlefield commander, but a competent administrator capable of managing an army. There the resemblance ends sharply, and there Schuyler's troubles began. For he was a Hudson Valley counterpart of the Low Country Rice Kings, sharing their disdain for social inferiors, which meant most of mankind. Schuyler reserved his special contempt for New Englanders, who returned the feeling with equal heat. Wealthy, the fourth generation of his family in America, related to other equally proud Hudson Valley families—Van Rensselaers, Van Cortlandts, Van Schaicks, Livingstons—married to Catherine Van Rensselaer, he was an imperious man who did not suffer rabble in arms gladly. But the Yankees would not tug forelocks to anyone, especially a Dutchman from New York. It was a most difficult political problem, and a potentially perilous situation, for the New England militia were vital to the defense of the Northern Department.

Encouraged by the New England faction, Gates lobbied Congress incessantly, even to the point of leaving his command and hurrying southward to the halls of Congress where he eventually engaged in a shouting match in the chamber when he was allowed to take the floor. It was an incredible scene, and one would think such behavior would have finished him. But his seduction of the New England politicians and militia, and the latter's reluctance bordering on refusal to serve under Schuyler, as well as Schuyler's frequently expressed pessimism regarding the military situation, finally carried the day. On 4 August 1777, Congress made Horatio Gates commander of the Northern Department, replacing Schuyler. Taking his time, as was his way, Gates did not reach Albany until 19 August. The full story of the Saratoga campaign lies outside our tale and is important at this point in the narrative only because of the reputation it gave Gates, which led to his being given command of the Southern Department after the fall of Charleston. Also outside our scope is the raging argument at Saratoga between Gates and Benedict Arnold and the break between the two men. As for his victory over Burgoyne, Gates must receive full credit for his role. Even Hoffman Nickerson, who obviously despised the man, admitted that "events were to prove that he had thoroughly gauged the character of Burgoyne."[8] But Gates must share the credit; he was only one of many important factors in the victory. The stage had been set on his arrival. Schuyler's scorched earth tactics had slowed Burgoyne's advance to a crawl and taken a severe physical toll on the British army. Barry St. Leger had been stopped in the Mohawk Valley by Continentals and New York militia, and sent fleeing to Canada by Arnold, who had been dispatched by Schuyler. General Benjamin Lincoln, sent by Washington to help Schuyler handle the New England militia, had used those forces to raid Burgoyne's line of communications at Ticonderoga. At Bennington the Germans had been overrun by John Stark and his New England men.

If ever a man landed in the right place at the right time to enhance his career, it was Horatio Gates. Time and numbers, a mediocre opponent, and the two best American battle commanders of the war were on his side and he made the most of them by being cautious and not committing any major mistakes. It is well that he remained in camp while the fighting raged, because leading troops into battle was not his forte, and by his record not to his liking. He sat in a good defensive position and waited for Burgoyne to come to him, and when the Englishman obliged he followed sound advice and sent against the British his peerless field commanders, Daniel Morgan and Benedict Arnold. Those were Gates's contributions to victory, and they were not inconsiderable, although he was by no means the indispensable man in the mix.

But the high point of Gates's life was also his ruin, for victory swelled to the bursting point his delusion that he was indeed a great captain, and the delusions of others down to this day that he was uniquely qualified to handle militia and the only American general who knew how to use militia in concert with regulars. It also led some of his contemporaries to the erroneous conclusion that the Hero of Saratoga was more qualified than Washington to lead the revolutionary armies. Horatio Gates cannot be accused of conspiring to supplant Washington, although I would maintain, given his delusions, that he at least had daydreams about becoming commander in chief. But in the context of the times whether a conspiracy existed is irrelevant. Washington believed that it did and thereafter never trusted Gates, and to the Great Virginian's faithful followers Horatio Gates became an object of loathing and scorn.

After Saratoga and his appointment by Congress as President of the new Board of War, Gates decided that he would organize a Franco-American expedition to take Canada and began planning. He had been obsessed with this idea since the winter of 1775 and never abandoned it, for he always believed what his spies along the border and disaffected Canadians told him—that the Canadians were ripe for revolt and required only the appearance of an American army to declare for union with the rebellious states to the south. In truth, the French Canadians were not going to rise for anyone. But Gates was a very credulous man. Major General Alexander McDougall, not a Gates fan by any means, nevertheless gauged him accurately in a letter to Governor George Clinton of New York: "I could hardly believe he was so extremely credulous as I found him to be. He is the most so in his profession of any man I ever knew who had seen so much service." This sober judgment lends weight to the stinging pen of his friend Charles Lee, who accused Gates of the same weakness but in the unmatchable Lee style: "If you were to tell him that a French army was ascending the Potowmack, mounted on the backs of alligators, he would believe it." George Washington, appalled at this "child of folly," opposed it publicly on military grounds and privately for reasons of state, for he clearly saw the peril of potential French control to the north and west of the rebellious colonies and, in alliance with Spain, New Orleans.

Out of his depth yet unaware of it, Gates persisted in his dream of northern conquest. In 1778, while all this was going on, he was once again put in command of the Northern Department, but this time under Washington's overall command. Congress gave him explicit instructions to organize a punitive expedition against the Iroquois in New York State. He delayed, vacillated, dissimulated, and meanwhile dreamt of Canada and kept planning his grand campaign. Congress asked Washington to find out what was happening, but he too ran up against Gates's stubborn refusal to fight Indians.

Finally, in January 1779, Congress put an end to the Canadian folly. Thwarted, Gates once again lost control of himself and wrote an ill-advised letter to John Jay, President of Congress, in which he hinted that Washington was planning another invasion of Canada by a route that would benefit, in Gates's words, "individuals and not the public." The letter was ignored. That March Washington asked Gates to take command of an expedition against the Iroquois. If he declined, the command would go to General John Sullivan and Gates would assume Sullivan's post at Providence. Gates chose Providence. He felt that at fifty-seven he was too old and weak for such an arduous command and complained that "your Exly. should offer me the only command to which I am entirely unequal." This is a most interesting excuse, given his acceptance the following year of the far more arduous Southern command.[9]

In November 1779 Gates requested and received permission from Washington for leave to spend the winter at Traveller's Rest. There his correspondence with Congress kept him busy. Canada received much of his attention, but he was also interested in the South and began lobbying southern congressmen. Following the fall of Charleston the Southern Department required a new commander. Congress knew that Washington preferred Nathanael Greene. But Gates still had strong friends, and the record of his great victory at Saratoga could not be ignored. On 13 June 1780 Horatio Gates was given independent command of the Southern Department, and that summer the Hero of Saratoga began his journey southward. His sardonic colleague Charles Lee advised him to beware of exchanging his Northern laurels for Southern willows. Gates's subsequent actions offer no evidence that he gave heed to the warning.

Francis Marion Meets the Continentals

We left Major General de Kalb and his hungry Continentals at Deep River in North Carolina, awaiting their new commander. Although the troops were unhappy with their condition, which was not desperate but certainly severe, their morale remained steady. In "A Narrative of the Southern Campaign of 1780," de Kalb's adjutant, Colonel Otho Holland Williams, described their mood. "Inaction, bad fare, and the difficulty of preserving discipline when there is no apprehension of danger, have often proved fatal to Troops and ruined whole armies. But here the activity of the officers and the persevering patience of the privates preserved order, harmony, and even a passion for service."[10]

Into this miserable camp one day rode a Rice King who at first glance did not engender confidence. Colonel Francis Marion (1732–1795) was a small, dark-visaged man with thick, misshapen knees and ankles who had within him a touch of genius.[11] He was a South Carolina Continental officer without a command. A descendant on both sides of French Huguenots, Marion was a seasoned veteran by the time he met Jean de Kalb and Otho Holland Williams. During the Cherokee War of 1760–1761, Lieutenant Francis Marion of Captain William Moultrie's company had led thirty men in advance of 1,200 British regulars and the rest of the provincial regiment into a pass where they knew Cherokee warriors lay in ambush. In a fierce forest fight Marion and his men cleared the pass for the British regulars, but only Lieutenant Marion and eight men were standing when it was over. His exploit did not go unnoticed. "He was an ac-tive, brave and hardy solider, and an excellent partisan officer," wrote William Moultrie.[12]

Between then and the crisis with the mother country, Marion lived quietly on the Santee, by 1773 prosperous enough to buy a plantation, which he named Pond's Bluff, on the banks of the river, four miles from Eutaw Springs and the store of his fellow planter Thomas Sumter. Two of his passions, hunting and fishing, would stand him in good stead, for he came to know well the swamps and fields, the paths and byways of the land drained by the Santee.

Marion served in the Snow Campaign of 1775 against the Tories, and stood with William Moultrie on the ramparts of Fort Sullivan; he personally aimed the cannons that delivered the accurate fire that sent Sir Peter Parker hieing for home. He was present at the ill-fated Franco-American siege of Savannah in 1779, and was afield during Sir Henry Clinton's approach march against Charleston. Then occurred one of those chance events that can change a person's life and exert an impact on a larger world. During the siege of Charleston Marion, who drank spirits sparingly if at all, was attending an all-male dinner party at the house at the corner of Orange and Tradd (perhaps 106 Tradd), hosted by William Moultrie's adjutant general, Captain Alexander McQueen. Following the custom of the day, McQueen locked all the doors and first-floor

Francis Marion (not a true likeness, but the landscape
is where he rode).
(South Caroliniana Library, University of South Carolina.)

windows so his guests could not escape the heavy drinking that was going on. Marion's solution was to go to the second floor and jump out the window, but he badly fractured an ankle on landing, which put him in the category of an officer unfit for duty and required to leave the city in April 1780 under a general order issued by General Benjamin Lincoln.

"Fortunately for Carolina," William Moultrie wrote, "he went out, and when he went he was so lame that he was obliged to sculk about from house to house among his friends, and sometimes hide in bushes until he grew better; he then crept out by degrees and began to collect a few friends; and when he got ten or twelve together he ventured out."[13] A foolish affair had spared the man who became an American legend, but there was no reason for de Kalb and his soldiers to know that one of history's great guerrilla leaders had ridden into their camp, for Marion had not yet earned the name of Swamp Fox. De Kalb sent Marion and his band to the Pee Dee country to scout for intelligence and supplies, so they missed the arrival in camp on 25 July 1780 of the Hero of Saratoga.

The Hero Arrives and Takes Charge

Gates "was received," wrote Otho Holland Williams, "with respectful ceremony; the baron ordered a continental salute from the little pack of artillery." Outwardly, and probably inwardly, too, General Gates was a most assured commander. He almost immediately "ordered the troops to hold themselves in readiness *to march at a moment's warning,*" to the "great astonishment of those who knew the real situation of the troops." Otho Holland Williams, who became deputy adjutant with Gates's arrival, was one of the astonished officers. When some officers tried to explain the army's condition to Gates, he assured them, Williams wrote, "that plentiful supplies of *rum* and *rations* were on the route and would overtake them in a day or two—assurances that were certainly too fallacious and that were never verified."[14]

On the 27th, two days after Gates's arrival, the army took the direct road to Camden. It had been de Kalb's intention to strike west, where there was a better possibility of securing supplies among a friendly population, and to approach Camden in a rough semicircle and operate in the general vicinity of the strongly Rebel Mecklenburg County, in North Carolina. The army would be close enough to strike at Camden if the opportunity arose, but also close to friendly territory in the rear to which it could retreat if necessary. Williams got the job of presenting these views to General Gates: "presuming on the friendship of the general," he tried to dissuade him from the direct approach. The countryside, explained Williams, "was by nature barren, abounding with sandy plains, intersected by swamps, and very thinly inhabited," the people mostly hostile to the cause, and the country already stripped of what little provisions and forage had existed. Otho Williams urged Gates to take the route to the northwest, about where the Yadkin River becomes the Pee Dee, to the "little town of Salisbury, in the midst of a fertile country and inhabited by a people zealous in the cause of America." He pointed out that the "most active and intelligent officers" agreed with this route, for it not only promised a "plentiful supply of provisions, but because the sick, the women and children, and the wounded in case of disaster, might have an asylum." In that area the army would have a place to repair arms, protect supply convoys coming from the north, and could approach Camden "with the river Wateree on our right and our friends on our backs."[15]

Williams prepared a short written statement of these views, including the names of officers who agreed, and gave it to Gates, who told him, as Williams recalled it, that "he would confer with the *general officers* when the troops should halt at noon. Whether any conference took place or not the writer don't know. After a short halt at noon . . . the march was resumed."[16]

Gates was probably influenced by a letter from Thomas Sumter to de Kalb, which de Kalb had given him. It was an optimistic report of "shoals of militia"[17] awaiting him and the weakness of the British position at Camden, where, Sumter reported, Rawdon had only 700 men. The information was outdated by the time Gates read it. Spurning the advice of his senior officers, anxious to join up with General Richard Caswell and his "shoals" of North Carolina militia, Gates continued the march through the inhospitable pine barrens.

The countryside, according to Williams, was desolate, exceeding the "representations that had been made of it." The few rude dwellings were "abandoned by the owners and plundered by the neighbors." Everyone was "flying from his home and joining in parties under adventurers . . . until the British army should appear, which they seemed confidently to expect." Yet the army marched on, and "the distresses of the soldiery daily increased." The first corn crop was gone, the second was not ready to eat, yet the soldiers picked green corn anyway and boiled it with lean beef of cattle found in woods and swamps, "not unpalatable to be sure, which was attended with painful effects. Green peaches . . . substituted for bread . . . and had similar consequences." The straits in which the army found itself are best seen in the ingredient used by the officers to thicken their soup: the powder usually reserved for their wigs. Not to fear, however, according to Horatio Gates, and the troops were again "amused with promises" of rum and rations.[18]

Food was expected at a place called May's Mill, but there was none there. Although "mutiny was ready to manifest itself" and Williams admitted there was cause for it, the regimental officers, by mingling with the men and talking to them, and "appealling to their own empty canteens and mess cases, satisfied the privates that all suffered alike." Another eyewitness to conditions that required extraordinary efforts by the officers was Sergeant Major William Seymour of the Delaware Line: "We were fourteen days and drew but one half pound of flour. Sometimes we drew half a pound of beef per man, and that so miserably poor that scarce any mortal could make use of it"—a striking comment in an age when people were far less finicky about what they ate. They lived "chiefly on green apples and peaches" Seymour's *Journal* continues, "which rendered our situation truly miserable, being in a weak and sickly condition."[19]

General Gates was kept well informed of events and the temperament of the troops, and "perhaps conceiving himself in some degree accountable to the army for the steps he had taken," he told Otho Williams that General Caswell of the North Carolina militia was at fault for not cooperating and probably contemplating a risky venture from which he would have to be extricated; and that the North Carolina government had promised him provisions that had not arrived. But now it was too late for the other route, as "retrograde movement would dispirit the troops and civilians alike."[20] Gates has been defended for his decision to take the direct approach to Camden because of his desire to link up with the North Carolina militia, thus reinforcing his army.[21] But this reveals only his inordinate faith in militia. On the 7th of August, General Richard Caswell and 2,100 North Carolina militiamen joined Gates's "Grand Army," as he liked to term it. The Continentals and their officers were amazed at the furnishings the militia officers brought with them to ease life in the field. Tables, chairs, and bedsteads were strewn about. Camp security was totally absent, and one militia officer thought Otho Williams's evening inspection "an unseasonable hour for *gentlemen to call*."[22]

It was about this time that Gates made a decision further clouding his generalship. He had with him Armand's Legion, comprising sixty horse and sixty foot, led by Colonel Charles Armand, a French volunteer. He also had about seventy mounted South Carolina volunteers. Colonel William Washington, who had sought refuge in North Carolina after his twin disasters at Monck's Corner and Lenud's Ferry, rode into camp with his surviving cavalry. But Gates sent him packing. In the middle of some of the world's finest cavalry country, where Banastre Tarleton and his Legion had ridden rampant, he told Colonel Washington that he did not think cavalry would be of use in the South. That incredible decision left him at the most with some 130 horsemen to collect intelligence, provide shock tactics in a critical combat situation, or cover a retreat.[23] He then pushed his Grand Army on, through the barren countryside, past the melancholy site of Buford's Massacre, to Rugeley's Mill, about fifteen miles north of Camden. There 700 Virginia militia under General Edward Stevens joined him. They had been issued bayonets for their muskets, but unlike the men they would soon meet in battle they had not been taught how to use them.

Sometime after 27 July Francis Marion and his little band rejoined the army, and their appearance temporarily lightened the mood of the soldiers. It was at this point in his "Narrative" that Otho Williams described Marion's horsemen as "distinguished by small black leather caps and the wretchedness of their attire; their number did not exceed twenty men and boys, some white, some black, but most of them miserably equipped; their appearance was in fact so burlesque that it was with much difficulty the diversion of the regular soldiery was restrained by the officers." Horatio Gates's opinion of Marion and his volunteers mirrored the soldiery. Otho Williams recorded that the "general himself was glad of an opportunity of detaching Colonel Marion at his own instance towards the interior of South Carolina, with orders to watch the motions of the enemy and furnish intelligence." The little horseman was not displeased. The exploits of Sumter had inspired him to similar ambitions, and the militia of the Williamsburg District north of Charleston had asked that a Continental officer be sent to lead them. He rode off at the head of his men and boys, white and black, a legend in the making.[24]

Meanwhile, Gates made another foolish decision. Thomas Sumter, who also had self-delusions, wrote Gates a letter setting out his version of grand strategy and requesting a detachment be sent to him to assist in taking the British supply convoy making its way to Camden, an action described earlier. Gates was faced with the probability of a major battle, although one wonders from his actions before and after whether he gave it serious thought. Whatever his state of mind, whatever his powers of concentration on what really mattered, he acceded to Sumter's request. With an enemy army of unknown strength somewhere before him, he weakened his own by sending 100 Maryland Continentals, 300 North Carolina militia, and two artillery pieces to Sumter.

Gates's decisions to this point have been explained as understandable if not excusable by his acceptance of Sumter's optimistic but faulty intelligence, pressure from North Carolina officers to assume the offensive, and the General's intention to take the strategic but not the tactical offensive. Gates in this view never meant to engage the British in pitched battle. His purpose was to throw up and occupy defensive works a few miles north of Camden and from there sever British supply lines and force them to abandon Camden by bringing Sumter from the west and Marion from the east to positions behind Camden. The evidence for this is strong, especially the statement made by one of Gates's aides, Thomas Pinckney, who said he asked Gates point blank if he meant to attack the British and Gates said that he did not because most of the army was composed of militia. On 14 August Gates sent on ahead an engineer, Colonel John Christian Senf, and Lieutenant Colonel Charles Porterfield to choose a site for defensive works.[25]

To his biographer the fatal flaw in the plan was Gates's expectation that the British would behave as he foresaw: Rawdon, cut off from aid, quitting Camden; Cornwallis remaining in Charleston. But there are flaws as basic that reveal defects of mind and character in the American general. It is not surprising that he did not resist the urgings of North Carolina authorities, for he had always courted popularity. He furthermore undertook a complicated campaign in country he did not know based to a considerable extent on the grand design of Thomas Sumter, a man he had never met and knew little of. And one of the important characters in the design, Francis Marion, was a man of whom Gates knew so little that he was pleased to get rid of him.

Although overall one can accept the explanation for Gates's actions, belief is strained by the contention that this also explains his neglect of cavalry, because he would not need them if he intended to settle down behind defensive works. Who then, may we ask, would scout the countryside for intelligence, provisions, and forage, and be there for contingencies if Gates was forced to abandon his works? Sumter and Marion? But if they were to be the eyes and ears of the army, they had already failed.

For Horatio Gates, his forte the minutiae of administration, although with the southern army his performance in even that capacity had not lived up to advance billings, did not know that some fifteen miles to the south the British had concentrated their force under the personal command of Lieutenant General Charles, Earl Cornwallis, who was at his best in the middle of a fight: hard, cool, decisive. And it would soon be time to fight.

12

The Battle of Camden

The British Infantryman

On 9 August 1780 Lord Cornwallis received a dispatch from Lord Rawdon that Horatio Gates was advancing on Camden with an army reported to be 5,000 strong. His Lordship needed no further stimulus to leave behind administrative cares that bored him and political problems that defied solutions and proceed to that activity to which men like him were born. He left Charleston the next day and rode up the right bank of the Ashley to Drayton Hall. He then rode day and night for Camden and arrived on the evening of 13 August. He later wrote to Clinton and Lord Germain that he "saw no difficulty in making good my retreat to Charles Town with the troops that were able to march, but in taking that resolution I must have not only left near 800 sick and a great quantity of stores at this place, but I clearly saw the loss of the whole province except Charlestown, and of all Georgia except Savannah, as immediate consequences, besides forfeiting all pretensions of future confidence from our friends in this part of America."[1] They seem only words in an expected and formal report to his superiors outlining his choices. His very nature and the disastrous effect a withdrawal would have on the Tories made it inevitable that he would seek battle. I believe he knew that as soon as he read Rawdon's dispatch in Charleston.

He had a good army. It was small but very professional. Under Lord Rawdon were solid Tory regulars: Tarleton's British Legion of horse and foot, with the master himself leading the cavalry; and Rawdon's own Volunteers of Ireland. There were also a Royal North Carolina Regiment and North Carolina militia. The British regulars were first rate: Cornwallis's own 33rd Regiment of Foot (West Ridings), three companies of the 23rd Regiment of Foot (Royal Welsh Fusiliers), four companies of light infantry brought in from Ninety Six, and five companies of Fraser's Highlanders (71st Foot). The Royal artillery rounded out the regulars. The total muster was 2,239 men. Although Cornwallis thought

Gates had 5,000, he never hesitated to plan for battle. That again can be attributed to his warrior nature and self-confidence, but also no doubt to his knowledge of the splendid instrument he had at hand: the British infantryman.

The traditional picture of the composition of this British army is that they were the dregs of society. "Scum of the earth," Wellington is reputed to have called them a generation later. That judgment was challenged by Sylvia Frey in *The British Soldier in America* (1981), who claims that at the very least a large number of the rank and file were honest urban workers and rural laborers for whom there was no work and who were left with two choices: begging or taking the King's shilling. Frey presents a good case, and support is offered by the Anglo-Irish schoolteacher Sergeant Roger Lamb, who saw extensive service in America and had a good opinion of his fellow soldiers. Or perhaps that eighteenth-century British army best fits one not entirely facetious description of the present British army: football fans disciplined by sergeants and led by aristocrats. Whatever they were, only the deeply prejudiced would disagree that those soldiers were a tough, tenacious breed and their performance in America magnificent. Saddled with as mediocre a lot of generals as ever ill served a nation, they deserved far better, for it was the rank and file, not their leaders, military or civilian, who kept England in the war for eight long years.

They were savagely disciplined. The common punishment was flogging with a cat-o'-nine tails, giving rise to one of their nicknames—"bloody backs."[2] Three hundred, 500, 1,000 lashes were not uncommon. For receiving stolen goods Thomas MacMahan, a private in the 43rd Foot, received 1,000 lashes "on his bare back" and his wife, Isabella, "100 lashes on her bare back, at the Cart's Tail, in Different portions and the most Conspicuous Parts of the Town, and to be imprisoned three months." Men died under the lash. We are, of course, repelled by such measures, especially in a society in which the mere spanking of schoolchildren is not only unacceptable but in some states illegal. But the eighteenth-century was a brutal age, and the European method of warfare demanded unquestioning obedience.

The common weapon of the eighteenth-century European and American foot soldier was the single-shot, smoothbore, flintlock musket.[3] It was loaded from the muzzle by pouring powder down the barrel followed by a lead ball, and ramming powder and ball down into the breech with a ramrod that fastened under the outside of the barrel when it was not in use. The soldier also poured a little powder into the pan, a small, scooped-out recess in the metal on top of the musket at the breech. This was the priming powder. The flint was held in the jaws of the cock (called a hammer on modern guns) and protruded so it could strike the frizzen, a piece of steel that also acted as the pan cover. When the soldier was ready to fire he drew back the cock to half cock, then raised the frizzen to the vertical, revealing the priming powder in the pan. He then drew back the cock to full cock. When the trigger was pulled the cock snapped forward and down and the protruding flint struck the frizzen. This sent a small shower of sparks into the pan, igniting the priming powder and creating a flash of flame that set off the charge inside the barrel. Those are the essential steps for preparing a musket for action and firing it. Misfiring could result from the priming powder blowing away in a strong wind or becoming drenched by rain. Faulty flints, common in the British army, also affected the performance of the flintlock musket, while common to the American army was an insufficient number of waterproof cartridge boxes.

The musket was a long, heavy, cumbersome weapon, running four and one half to five feet long and weighing eight to fourteen pounds, depending on the model. But we must keep two things uppermost in mind. First, although more sophisticated muskets existed, the flintlock musket was state of the art in the sense that it was the infantry weapon of choice for distribution to the troops. Second, it was very inaccurate. One reason for its inaccuracy was because the inside of the barrel was smooth instead of rifled and thus failed to give the ball the spinning motion required for accuracy as it was launched into flight. In addition, the black powder fouled the barrel quickly, but an infantryman in battle did not have time to clean his barrel and consequently the ball had a very loose fit. This also sacrificed accuracy but made for fast loading and firing.

A noted marksman and shooting authority of the day, Major George Hanger, who was Banastre Tarleton's deputy commander of the British Legion in the southern campaign, wrote that "A soldier's musket, if not exceedingly ill-bored (as many of them are), will strike the figure of a man at eighty yards; it may even at 100; but a soldier must be very unfortunate indeed who shall be wounded by a common musket at 150 yards, provided his antagonist aims at him; and as firing at a man at 200 yards with a common musket, you may just as well fire at the moon and have the same hopes of hitting your object. I do maintain and will prove, whenever called on, that no man was ever killed at 200 yards by a common soldier's musket, by the person who aimed at him."[4]

This meant that to do real damage infantry had to get close to the opposing line—at least within seventy-five to eighty yards for any chance of hitting anyone—and aggressive officers attempted to close within thirty to fifty yards of an enemy line before firing by volleys. Soldiers were not allowed to fire at will, although in the real world as a battle raged on and death and confusion reigned, officers and sergeants were often unable to enforce this prohibition. The point is, these men were not marksmen. They were not trained to aim at enemy soldiers but to point their weapons in the direction of the enemy line and pull the trigger on command. Speed in reloading and firing, not individual accuracy, was the aim. If the distance was right and not too many weapons misfired, terrible damage could be done to an enemy line. The British soldier's musket required twelve separate motions for loading. Sergeants taught these motions by rote until they became automatic, and in action loading and firing was by command, provided the system did not break down in the heat of battle. Standing shoulder to shoulder in long lines three deep (gradually changed to double lines), infantry was trained to deliver volleys in a single explosion of flame and smoke, the eighteenth-century version of massive firepower. The average soldier could reload and fire, in theory always on command, two to three times per minute.

The lead balls were big, weighing about an ounce, and they could do frightful damage. They knocked men to the ground and tore up flesh and bone and muscle. Chest and stomach wounds almost invariably meant death, arm and leg wounds amputation in an age without anesthetics, which also often meant death following hours, even days, of agony. As lines of opposing infantry traded volleys, the shrieks and screams of the wounded and the shouted commands of officers and sergeants filled the air around the living as they reloaded and fired, reloaded and fired. File closers, men marching behind the lines, stepped over the dead and dying to take their places, and if there were not enough file closers the sergeants dressed the lines and men closed ranks. Battles were often decided by which side could take the most punishment. Advancing infantry hoped that a waiting foe would begin firing at too long a distance. If they could close fast, absorbing losses with stoicism, then deliver a volley or two at thirty or fifty yards, the issue might be decided. France lost Canada on the Plains of Abraham when James Wolfe's thin red line took its losses and delivered close quarter volleys that shattered and routed the French regulars.

But this is only part of the story, for the eighteenth-century foot soldier also had at his command a fearful but most simple weapon that in the Revolutionary War British officers came to rely on even more than firing by volleys. The British bayonet was sixteen to nineteen inches long.[5] It added a foot and a half to a five-foot musket. It had a socket rising from the base; the socket had a right-angled slot that fit over the muzzle and with a half turn locked into place. It was called the socket bayonet. The very simplicity of the bayonet and its rare use in our age of automatic infantry rifles belies its importance and effectiveness in earlier times. The sight of a line of disciplined British infantry, advancing at a trot and shouting huzzas, muskets leveled and protruding from them some eighteen inches of cold steel at charge bayonet, was known to turn American militia bowels to jelly and heels to quicksilver. British officers were well aware of this. General John Burgoyne instructed his officers "to inculcate in the men's minds a Reliance upon the Bayonet. Men of half their bodily strength, and even Cowards, may be their match in firing; but the onset of the Bayonet in the hands of the valiant is irresistible."[6]

The socket bayonet was not even a century old by the time of the American Revolution. Simple in concept, terrible in application, by the early eighteenth century it had revolutionized infantry tactics. European armies disbanded units of pikemen, who were no longer needed to protect musketeers from cavalry charges or while they reloaded or changed formation. In essence, the infantryman now had two weapons in one: it could kill either at a distance or at close quarters. The bayonet was technologically the more dependable of the two, and its use was a tactic that required little imagination, an attribute neither widely distributed among British officers nor desirable for those delivering or receiving such an attack. Holding a deep contempt for their American foes, British officers were quick to call on the bayonet when faced with opposition, and the splendid other ranks were just as quick to respond. Invariably, militia would panic and flee. And invariably, American generals, including George

Washington, ignored painful lessons and repeatedly lined up militia in formal ranks in open fields to await the onslaughts of highly trained, rigidly disciplined British and German regulars, and raged when those precisely placed lines crumbled into stampeding herds. The proper use of militia in formal battle awaited one of the rare generals of the war who can truly be called brilliant. That man was not Horatio Gates.

"Gentlemen, What is Best to be Done?" asked the Hero of Saratoga

In the meantime, Horatio Gates remained unaware that a force largely composed of the formidable fighting men we have just described, under a fighting general, was fifteen miles to his south. On 15 August Gates issued a General Order for a night approach march, apparently to the position about five and one-half miles north of Camden where he intended to prepare defensive works. The army would march at 10:00 P.M. Colonel Armand's sixty horsemen would provide the van. It was another error in judgment. As we remarked of the approach march to Ramsour's Mill, night movements are fraught with danger and prone to error even when conducted by well-trained regulars or high-quality partisan militia. Otho Williams described the consternation of the officers: "Others could not imagine how it could be conceived that any army consisting of more than two-thirds militia, and which had never been once exercised in arms together, could form columns and perform other manoeuvres in the night, and in the face of an enemy." On the eve of battle this move was yet further evidence of Gates's inexperience in handling an army on the march. He also had trouble counting troops, estimating his "Grand Army" to number "upwards of seven thousand." Otho Williams was astonished, went to the separate units to get real returns, and reported to Gates that the actual number was 3,052. Gates said, "There are enough for our purpose."[7]

The final touch was a hasty meal for the troops, described by Otho Williams as "quick baked bread and fresh beef with a dessert of molasses mixed with mush." Sergeant Major Seymour of the Delaware Line described its effect: "Instead of rum we had a gill of molasses per man served out to us, which instead of livening our spirits served to purge us as well as if we had taken a jallap, for the men all the way as we went along were every moment obliged to fall out of the ranks to evacuate." Thus marched the Grand Army of Major General Horatio Gates toward its destiny.[8]

By sheer coincidence, Lord Cornwallis that same night also decided on a night march, also beginning at 10:00 P.M., with a view to an early morning attack on the Americans at Rugeley's Mill. He proceeded north from Camden, then northwest on the old Waxhaws road. Tarleton's dragoons were in the lead. They knew the road well, for it was the way they had pounded in pursuit of Buford. The night was hot, humid, and moonless. Stars provided the only light. The British crossed Saunders Creek and began climbing the moderate grade that is still there. At 2:00 A.M., before Tarleton's dragoons reached the rise, the

cavalry screens of the two armies literally bumped into each other. For about fifteen minutes wild confusion ensued. Cavalry pistols cracked, sabers clanged,
muskets roared. Armand's horse, driven back by Tarleton's dragoons and, as
Williams described, "recoiling suddenly on the front column of the infantry, dis-
ordered the First Maryland Brigade and occasioned a general consternation
through the whole line of the army." But 100 Virginia state troops, under the
command of the brave and experienced Lieutenant Colonel Charles Porterfield,
moved immediately in support of Armand. They "executed their orders gallantly," wrote Otho Williams, "and the enemy, no less astonished than ourselves,
seemed to acquiesce in a sudden suspension of hostilities." Neither side wanted
a pitched battle at night. Before that suspension, however, the Americans suffered a grievous loss when Charles Porterfield received a mortal wound.[9]

The two sides separated and waited under arms for the dawn. A few prisoners had been taken by each side, and from a British soldier Otho Williams
learned that "Lord Cornwallis commanded in person about three thousand regular British troops, which were in line of march about five or six hundred yards
in front." Otho Williams told de Kalb what he had learned, then took the news
to Gates, who reacted with visible shock. "The general's astonishment could not
be concealed," Williams wrote, and an immediate council of war was called.
The "unwelcome news was communicated" to the general officers. General
Gates then said, "Gentlemen, What is best to be done?" No one spoke for a few
moments. De Kalb had made it clear to Williams before the officers met that
he thought Gates should order a retreat. But on this occasion he said nothing.
Then Brigadier General Edward Stevens, in command of the 700 Virginia militiamen, "exclaimed, 'Gentlemen, is it not too late *now* to do anything but
fight?'" No one tempered Stevens's rashness with prudence. Otho Williams described the end of the council of war: "No other advice was offered, and the
general desired the gentlemen would repair to their respective commands."[10]

The Americans formed for battle before first light. To the right of the Waxhaws road was the cream of the army: General Mordecai Gist's 2nd Maryland
brigade, comprising three regiments of the Maryland Line and the Delaware
Regiment. Hungry, in a weakened condition from constant diarrhea, they were
nevertheless well trained, well disciplined, hardbitten veterans. Gist was a brave
and experienced officer, and Lieutenant Colonel John Eager Howard one of the
finest regimental commanders in American history. With his company was the
incomparable Captain Robert Kirkwood of Delaware, "whose heroick valour
and uncommon and undaunted bravery must needs be recorded in history till
after ages," wrote Sergeant Major William Seymour of the Delaware Line. Baron
de Kalb was in overall command of the right wing. Together with General
William Smallwood's three regiments of the 1st Maryland brigade, which was
held in reserve astride the sandy road, the Continental troops numbered 900
men on the field and fit for duty. To the left of the road Gates placed General
Richard Caswell's 1,800 North Carolina militiamen. Caswell, a successful politician, was without distinction as a military leader. To their left was General Edward Stevens and his 700 Virginians. Stevens was an experienced officer and a

brave man, but most of his men had never been in battle. They had been given bayonets, but they had not been taught how to use them. Armand's 120 horse and foot were behind the Virginians, ostensibly in support, but they apparently did not participate in the battle. About seventy mounted South Carolina volunteers were present, but seem to have done nothing. Seven pieces of artillery manned by about 100 men were placed at various points along the line.[11]

Otho Holland Williams informs us that General Gates stationed himself and his staff behind Smallwood's reserve, which was about 200 yards behind his battle line, too far to observe events or intervene quickly in a crisis. One of the general's aides, Thomas Pinckney, who remained strongly pro-Gates, confirmed that Gates was with the reserve when the battle began, although he did not mention the distance. There is no indication that Gates had a plan or had put his mind seriously to work. This is especially revealed in the disposition of his army. In placing his weakest troops on the American left, facing the British right, Gates revealed either blind faith in militia or failure to think. Thomas Pinckney was adamant in a letter written forty-two years after the battle that Gates had no intention of attacking the British during his march on Camden, "assigning as his reason the number of Militia who formed the bulk of his Army." Yet when he was forced to battle, Gates by his dispositions practically guaranteed that his militia would face harrowing duty.

For it was not by chance that the Rebel militia ended up facing seasoned British regulars. The British army, following well-established European military tradition, almost always placed its senior brigade or regiment on the right, a position that took precedence in assigning the "posts of honor" for battle and a tradition that Gates followed by placing a continental brigade on the American right. But his placement of the militia on the left meant that in all probability they would face the flower of Cornwallis's army. As an ex-British officer of twenty-four years of service, as an American officer who had seen five years of war, did Gates not realize this? Or was he so overwhelmed by a situation that by the record he had never faced—combat command—that he simply forgot a concept then basic to his profession?[12]

Far in advance of Gates Otho Williams was astride his charger in front of the waiting lines of Americans. As the first streaks of light appeared in the sky, Williams peered southward for any sign of movement. The Americans held the high ground, although the slope was not steep. There were widely spaced pine trees and little undergrowth. Both flanks were anchored by wide swamps, which meant that they could not be turned if units on the flanks stood firm. There was about a mile of ground between the two swamps. The British situation was similar, except that they had to attack uphill. About a mile to their rear was Saunders Creek, reported by Senf and Porterfield as deep and only passable at the ford. But it was a threat to the British only in the event of a crushing defeat and hot American pursuit.

Lord Rawdon commanded the British left wing facing de Kalb's regulars. His forces included his own regiment, the Volunteers of Ireland, and Tarleton's British Legion Infantry. The men were high-quality Tory regulars. Rounding out

Otho Holland Williams, by Charles Willson Peale
(Independence National Historical Park Collection.)

Rawdon's left wing were Lieutenant Colonel John Hamilton's Royal North Carolina Regiment and Colonel Morgan Bryan's North Carolina Volunteers. Cornwallis thought Hamilton a "blockhead," and Bryan's men had been twice cut to
pieces at Hanging Rock, first by Davie, then by Sumter. But it was the regulars
who would bear the brunt of the fighting. The right wing, the primary post of
honor, was assigned to seasoned British regulars of famous regiments: 33rd Foot,
Royal Welsh Fusiliers, and the five companies of light infantry. These formidable
units would face the Virginia and North Carolina militia.

In command of the right wing was the officer Johann Ewald described as
that "very meritorious man," one of the finest regimental commanders of the
war, Lieutenant Colonel James Webster. He had steely courage and the added
virtue of being able to think on his feet, and on the 16th day of August 1780
he would prove it. Webster, the son of an eminent minister of Edinburgh, was
a soldier's soldier. Three contrary characters in our story—Cornwallis, Clinton,
and Tarleton—ended their American adventures agreeing on little, but for
James Webster each had only praise. He was Cornwallis's premier regimental

commander, a right hand the Earl could hardly imagine himself without. Clinton in his postwar apologia recalled the light infantry getting into serious trouble at the Battle of Monmouth, and "as I was looking about me in search of other troops to call their support ... I perceived the Thirty-third Regiment, with that gallant officer, Colonel Webster, at their head, unexpectedly clearing the wood and marching in column toward the enemy," and in concert with the First Grenadiers extricating the light infantry. Webster, wrote Clinton, "was an officer of great experience and on whom I reposed the most implicit confidence." Tarleton in his memoirs paid Webster a handsome tribute as a man who "united all the virtues of civil life to the gallantry and professional knowledge of a soldier." This was the man along with his splendid regiments facing Generals Stevens and Caswell and their raw Virginians and North Carolinians.[13]

Stationed in the center of the British line were four guns of the Royal Artillery. Should things go wrong or if an extra punch was needed, Cornwallis had in reserve two battalions of the intrepid kilted infantry of Fraser's Highlanders, and in column behind the Scots, astride their chargers, Banastre Tarleton and his British Legion cavalry. Two artillery pieces were on either side of the road with the Highlanders. Answering fit for duty that day were 2,239 British soldiers, a little over 800 fewer than the Americans but outnumbering them by almost 1,700 in the critical category of high-quality regulars. Given the swamps on the flanks of both armies, there was no room for maneuver. Terrain on this occasion dictated tactics. This would be head-on stuff. It is not recorded where Cornwallis stationed himself, but it was most certainly not 200 yards behind his troops. He was somewhere up close, probably in the center between his main battle line and the reserve, but we can be confident that he was where he belonged, and in control. For His Lordship knew, in the words of a twentieth century fighting general, that "There can be no question that the place for the general in battle is where he can see the battle and get the odor of it in his nostrils." Cornwallis probably appeared as a young American had seen him three years before at the Battle of Brandywine: "He was on horseback, appeared tall and sat very erect. His rich scarlet clothing loaded with gold lace, epaulets, etc., occasioned him to make a brilliant and martial appearance."[14]

The British advanced by column at dawn. It was already hot, the air still, the humidity oppressive, a typical Carolina August day. Gates did not, as some contend, misinterpret the British movement and for that reason order an attack by the militia, for the simple reason that he was too far behind his troops to see what the British were doing. From his forward post Otho Holland Williams saw the British "displaying." When he wrote, display in the military sense meant to deploy, and one meaning of deploy was to spread out troops into two or three extended lines known as the line of battle. The British were coming on in column preparatory to "displaying" the regiments into line of battle. Williams, an experienced officer, recognized this. He ordered the artillery to open fire and then galloped 200 yards or more to Gates's position behind Smallwood's reserve to report what was happening. Thomas Pinckney confirmed Williams's arrival but admitted he did not hear all that was said. Williams told Gates that the "enemy seemed to be displaying their columns by the right." Gates listened and said nothing. An observer said that he "had on a pale blue coat with epaulettes, with velvet breeches, and was riding a bay horse." The horse proved to be a splendid beast. Although Pinckney denied that Gates hesitated, Williams wrote that the General "seemed disposed to wait events—he gave no orders." Otho Williams then "observed, that if the enemy, in the act of displaying, were briskly attacked by General Stevens brigade, which was already in line of battle, the effect might be fortunate, and first impressions were important."[15] If the Virginians had been reliable regulars, the suggestion might have made sense, but in making it Otho Williams, in other matters a fine officer and destined under another general to render critical service to the cause, showed that he, too, did not know how to use militia on an open field against regular forces. But Horatio Gates did not question his subordinate's judgment.

Said Gates, "Sir, that's right—let it be done."[16]

He then sent Pinckney to tell de Kalb to attack on the left.[17]

Otho Williams "hastened to General Stevens, who instantly advanced with his brigade, apparently in fine spirits," Williams thought. By that time, however, the British right wing had "displayed" into line of battle. In an attempt to draw the British fire at too long a range, Williams asked for volunteers among the Virginians to run forward with him and take to trees Indian fashion and provoke the British into premature volleys. Forty or fifty men joined him. But Williams's spur-of-the-moment tactic did not work.[18]

Cornwallis, who stayed close to the action and did not need an adjutant to brief him on the situation, saw the movement of the Virginians. He wrote in his report of 21 August to Lord Germain, "I directed Lieutenant-Colonel Webster to begin the attack, which was done with great vigour." The right wing advanced, he wrote, "in good order and with the cool intrepidity of experienced British soldiers."[19] On they came, 33rd, Fusiliers, light infantry, about 800 strong, shouting, a solid line of red with bayonets fixed closing the gap on some 2,500 Virginia and North Carolina militia. General Edward Stevens ordered his Virginians to prepare to use the bayonets they had never before used. They declined. Instead they stared briefly at the terrible sight confronting them, closing on them, and the effect was electric.

The American left wing collapsed. The Virginians went first, the North Carolinians on their heels. Before the British could even reach them almost 2,500 men dropped their weapons and fled.

Otho Williams, who had been forced back to the line of Virginians, watched helplessly and later described the British charge and the American flight: "the impetuosity with which they advanced, firing and huzzaing, threw the whole body of militia into such a panic that they generally threw down their *loaded* arms and fled in the utmost consternation. The unworthy example of the Virginians was almost instantly followed by the North Carolinians." As Williams observed, the scene is difficult to picture. "The writer avers it of his own knowledge, having seen and observed every part of the army, from left to right, during the action. He who has never seen the effect of panic upon a multitude can have but an imperfect idea of such a thing." He continued, "Like electricity, it operates simultaneously—like sympathy, it is irresistible where it touches."[20]

The 1st Maryland, standing in well-ordered ranks in reserve, was directly in the path of the fleeing militia. Their steadiness proved to be no example as they were thrown into disorder "created by the militia breaking pell-mell" through them. The Virginians, unfamiliar with the country, fled the way they had come, finally stopping at Hillsborough, North Carolina, 180 miles northward. The North Carolinians, wrote Williams, "fled different ways, as their hopes led, as their fears drove them."[21]

Four days after the battle General Edward Stevens, mortified at the behavior of his Virginians, wrote to his governor, Thomas Jefferson, that once they began to run "it was out of the power of man to rally them." He asked Jefferson to "picture it as bad as you possibly can and it will not be as bad as it really is."[22]

Fifty-four years later Garret Watts of the North Carolina militia confessed in his pension application to joining the stampede.

"I well remember everything that occurred the next morning. I remember that I was among the nearest to the enemy; that a man named John Summers was my file leader; that we had orders to wait for the word to commence firing; that the militia were in front and in a feeble condition at that time. They were fatigued. The weather was warm excessively. They had been fed a short time previously on molasses entirely. I can state on oath that I believe my gun was the first gun fired, notwithstanding the orders, for we were close to the enemy, who appeared to maneuver in contempt of us, and I fired without thinking except that I might prevent the man opposite me from killing me. The discharge and loud roar soon became general from one end of the lines to the other. Amongst other things, I confess I was amongst the first that fled. The cause of that I cannot tell, except that everyone I saw was about to do the same. It was instantaneous. There was no effort to rally, no encouragement to fight. Officers and men joined in the flight. I threw away my gun, and, reflecting I might be punished for being found without arms, I picked up a drum, which gave forth such sounds when touched by the twigs I cast it away. When we had gone, we heard the roar of guns still, but we knew not why. Had we known, we might have returned. It was that portion of the army commanded by de Kalb fighting still."[23]

For de Kalb and his faithful Continentals paid no heed to the flight of the militia. "The regular troops," wrote Otho Williams, "who had the keen edge of sensibility rubbed off by strict discipline and hard service, saw the confusion with but little emotion." They also may not have realized the extent of the disaster on their left, for as Cornwallis later reported to Germain, there was "at this time a dead calm, with a little haziness in the air, which preventing the smoke from rising occasioned so thick a darkness that it was difficult to see the effect of a very heavy and well supported fire on both sides." Besides, the Continentals were winning their fight. Twice they repulsed the Volunteers of Ireland and the Legion infantry, then counterattacked with the bayonet, drove the British before them, and took prisoners. The Volunteers of Ireland were so roughly handled they nearly broke and might have had it not been for a general who had the smell of battle "in his nostrils." Cornwallis saw the crisis on his left and rode boldly to meet it. A captain of the Volunteers of Ireland described the earl "with great coolness, in the midst of a heavier fire than the oldest soldier remembers," rallying the troops by words and example. The danger to his left was stemmed, and on the right James Webster sealed the fate of the Continentals. Instead of allowing his infantry to pursue militia who were well out of the fight he swung his entire wing to the left and continued its charge.[24]

One North Carolina militia regiment and its officers stood fast. They were stationed next to the Delaware Line, and perhaps the stoic example of those splendid troops steadied them. Whatever the reason for their faithfulness, they were the first to catch the brunt of Webster's flank attack. Led principally by General Gregory, who had lost the rest of his brigade to panic, and Lieutenant Colonel Henry Dixon, whose regiment it was, this unit met the British regulars like veterans. One of their opponents, Sergeant Roger Lamb of the Royal Welsh Fusiliers, wrote that they "acquited themselves well" and "kept the field while they had a cartridge to fire; Gregory himself was twice wounded by a bayonet," and many "who were made prisoners had no wound except from bayonets."[25]

Baron de Kalb, already wounded and fighting desperately, apparently unaware that he had been abandoned by his commander in chief and most of the army, called for General Smallwood's 1st Maryland Brigade in reserve to move up and support the 2nd Brigade. Otho Williams reported that the 1st Maryland, where order had been restored after the militia had stampeded through their ranks, gave Webster's regiments a "severe check which abated the fury of their assault and obliged them to assume a more deliberate manner of acting." But the troops "being greatly outflanked and charged by superior numbers were obliged to give ground. At this critical moment the regimental officers . . . reluctant to leave the field without orders, inquired for their commanding officer, Brigadier General Smallwood, who . . . was not to be found; notwithstanding . . . a number of other brave officers . . . rallied the brigade and renewed the contest." Smallwood had left the field. But his command fought on, trying in vain to link up with 2nd Brigade, only several hundred feet away, and "Again they were obliged to give way and were again rallied." The British closed in on three sides. The situation was growing increasingly desperate. Otho Williams, who had gone to 1st Brigade to assist its officers, now returned through fire and smoke to 2nd Brigade, "which he found precisely in the same circumstances." Baron de Kalb had been unhorsed and was fighting on foot, bleeding now from several wounds. Williams "called upon his own regiment (the 6th Maryland) not to fly and was answered" by Lieutenant Colonel Benjamin Ford: "They have done all that can be expected of them. We are outnumbered and outflanked. See the enemy charge with bayonets."[26]

The battle had lasted about one hour when Cornwallis delivered the coup de grace. He sent Tarleton and his Legion cavalry around to the rear of the Continentals. As the British infantry closed in with bayonets on the front and flanks, Tarleton and the Legion horse in full charge crashed down on the American rear. The ranks were broken, the soldiers who could fled for their lives to the dense swamps. Most ran as individuals or in small groups. Tarleton reported that "Brigadier General Gist moved off with one hundred Continentals in a body by wading through a swamp on the right of the American position, where the British cavalry could not follow; this was the only party that retreated in a compact state from the field of battle." But Otho Williams stated that Major Archibald Anderson of the Maryland Line "rallied as he retreated a few men of different companies," and that "fifty or sixty men formed a junction on the rout and proceeded together." With them were a few officers, two of whom would on another day and another field turn the tables on the British in full: Lieutenant Colonel John Eager Howard of Maryland and Captain Robert Kirkwood of Delaware.[27]

Otho Williams got away, and later lamented that "many fine fellows lay on the field," and of them all none was finer than the old lion who began life as a peasant boy in Bavaria and ended it in a distant land a true aristocrat to his core. Jean, Baron de Kalb stopped fighting when he had been wounded eleven times and could no longer stand. Bullets, bayonets, and sabers had felled him. It is reported that some British troops stripped him of his resplendent uniform coat, but that behavior was quickly stopped. Cornwallis rode to where de Kalb had been carried, and said, "I am sorry, sir, to see you, not sorry that you are vanquished, but sorry to see you so badly wounded." If de Kalb replied, the record has not survived. Perhaps he could not speak, for he was in agony. Cornwallis had him carried to Camden in a litter and given medical attention.[28]

The action was not quite over. Pursuit and mopping up awaited, or, as Banastre Tarleton the master of pursuit put it in his delicate way, "rout and slaughter ensued in every direction." It continued for twenty-two miles, until, he admitted, "fatigue overpowered the exertions of the British." The noncombatants who could got away as fast they could. Otho Williams described how "the cries of the women and the wounded in the rear, and the consternation of the flying troops, so alarmed some of the waggoners, that they cut out their teams and taking each a horse" fled. The heavy baggage and the camp followers had been ordered to the Waxhaws the night before, but the order had been ignored and all the baggage was taken by Tarleton except for that belonging to Gates and de Kalb, and poor de Kalb would never need his. Some writers claim that Armand's cavalry tried to protect the baggage train, but according to Williams, who was there, they plundered it, and Sergeant Major Seymour agreed: "As for Col. Armand's horse, they thought upon nothing else but plundering our waggons as they retreated off." Otho Williams also described another horror to the rout when some of the fleeing militia met other militia "advancing to join the American army; but learning of its fate from the refugees they acted ... in concert with the victors ... captivating some, plundering others, and maltreating all the fugitives they met." Traveling that road of terror, Otho Williams came across General Caswell's baggage, which contained a "pipe of good Madeira, broached, and surrounded by a number of soldiers. . . . He acknowledges that in this instance he shared in the booty and took a draught of wine, which was the only refreshment he had received that day."[29]

Another American traveled the sandy road that same day, on a mission of confiscation. Charles Stedman, Cornwallis's commissary general, described what he saw in his *History* of the war. "The road for some miles was strewed with the wounded and killed who had been overtaken by the legion in their pursuit. The numbers of dead horses, broken waggons, and baggage scattered on the road formed a perfect scene of horror and confusion: Arms, knapsacks, and ac-coutrements found were innumerable; such was the terror and dismay of the Americans."[30]

American losses have never been estimated with accuracy because of the overwhelming nature of the defeat and the shambles that followed. The Conti-nentals took the heaviest losses, then the North Carolina militia, presumably because of the stout fight put up by Dixon's regiment. If the historian Christo-pher Ward is correct, the Virginia militia left the field so quickly their total ca-sualties were three wounded. The best total estimate seems to be 250 Americans killed and 800 wounded, and all of those captured. Often overlooked because of their great victory are the 324 British casualties: sixty-eight killed and 256 wounded. Many fewer than the Americans, of course, but in a small army not to be taken lightly.

The Hero Rides Hard to Regroup

And what of Horatio Gates? What role did he play in the debacle once it began? None, sad to say, which is why he is not mentioned in the preceding narrative after stating emphatically to Otho Williams, "Sir, that's right—let it be done." Thomas Pinckney, after delivering Gates's order to de Kalb, rejoined Smallwood's reserve, "near which I had left the General, & made the inquiry I could for him, but without success." Pinckney stayed at his post, was wounded, and taken prisoner.[31] On 20 August 1780, about 180 miles from the awful field of Camden, in Hillsborough, North Carolina, his missing general wrote a report to Congress.

"At daylight the enemy attacked and drove in our light party in front, when I ordered the left to advance and attack the enemy; but to my astonishment the left wing and North-Carolina militia gave way. General Caswell and myself, as-sisted by a number of officers, did all in our power to rally the broken troops, but to no purpose, for the enemy coming around the flank of the Maryland di-vision completed the rout of the whole militia, who left the continentals to op-pose the enemy's whole force. I endeavored with General Caswell to rally the militia at some distance . . . but the enemy's cavalry continuing to harass their rear, they ran like a torrent and bore all before them. Hoping yet that a few miles in the rear they might recover from their panic and again be brought into order, I continued my endeavor . . . in vain.

"The militia having taken the woods in all directions, I counseled with General Caswell to retire towards Charlotte. I got here late in the night; but reflecting there was no prospect of collecting a force at that place adequate to the defense of the country, I proceeded with all possible dispatch hither, to endeavor to fall upon some plan of defense."[32]

If one were cruel, one might suggest that Major General Horatio Gates should instead have fallen on his sword. It must be added, of course, that for public consumption far better generals than he, such as Nathanael Greene and Daniel Morgan, defended his behavior, questioning only his decision to fight at all. But generals are very much like doctors and lawyers: when one of theirs gets into trouble they close ranks against the outside world and deny that anything untoward has occurred, for who knows what fortune may bring. Junior officers, on the other hand, despite the trite charge that they lack knowledge of the "big picture," in private at least unleash their bitterness at superiors who fail them. There is a rarely quoted comment in Otho Williams's "Narrative" bearing precisely on the reaction of officers who had been in the battle. From Salisbury, Williams wrote, "many officers wrote to their friends . . . and being chagrined and mortified at not overtaking their commanding general in so long a retreat, expressed themselves with great disgust and freedom." Otho Williams's own criticism was indirect. "The only apology that General Gates condescended to make to the army for the loss of the battle was, 'a man *may* pit a cock, but he *can't* make him fight'—'the fate of battle is uncontrolable'—and such other common maxims as admit of no contradiction."[33]

Gates's excuse that he was trying to rally the militia grows stale as we watch him ride farther and farther from the scene of combat. He had to have heard the heavy firing behind him and realized that the Continentals were still fighting. But on that 16th day of August 1780 he kept riding to the rear, to Rugeley's Mill five miles up the road, by that night to Charlotte sixty miles away, by the 19th 180 miles to Hillsborough. He had no trouble outdistancing Tarleton's cavalry, for he was mounted on the fastest horse in the American army, a famous racer sired by the famous stud Fearnaught. On his ride he met William Richardson Davie and his horsemen advancing toward Camden. Without stopping he called out that Davie should retire to Charlotte or the British dragoons would be upon him. Davie replied that "his men were accustomed to Tarleton and did not fear him," but Gates was pressing hard for Charlotte and probably did not hear him. General Isaac Huger then appeared, also riding to the rear, and Davie asked him how far he should go in obeying the orders of General Gates, and Huger replied, "Just as far as you please, for you will never see him again." Davie then sent an officer in pursuit of Gates with the message that if the General so desired Davie would go on and bury the dead, to which Gates replied, "I say retreat! Let the dead bury their dead."[34]

Can we possibly imagine Lord Cornwallis behaving in such a manner? Or

George Washington? One hesitates to call any man a coward, and the history of war is full of tales of men who ran one day and performed acts of gallantry the next. But we are entitled to expect of officers that they never shirk, never run. In an age when generals commonly exposed themselves to inspire their troops and often paid with their lives, Major General Horatio Gates was conspicuously absent from the battles at Saratoga and rode far and fast from Camden's terrible field.

It took Gates three days to reach Hillsborough. It took de Kalb three days to die.

13

🏃

The Partisans Fight On

Fishing Creek:
"a perfect rout, and an indiscriminate slaughter"

Banastre Tarleton rode out of Rugeley's Mill the day after Camden and headed west toward the Catawba River. Behind him was the British Legion, horse and foot, and the light infantry, in all about 350 strong. Fierce, pounding, relentless, "Bloody Ban" was once again in pursuit. His prey, Thomas Sumter and his column, burdened by loot and British prisoners, was on the other side of the river. Cornwallis had not forgotten the loss of the supply convoy and his people, and when he received information of Sumter's general whereabouts he gave Tarleton his marching orders. Sumter had been moving slowly until the night of the 16th, when three riders dispatched by William Richardson Davie an hour after Gates had passed Davie on his flight to Charlotte caught up and informed the Gamecock of the disaster that had befallen the Grand Army.[1] Sumter quickened his pace, but on the night of the 17th he camped at Rocky Mount and did not leave until daylight. Tarleton pushed men and horses as only he could and reached the Catawba the same day. From his cold camp on the east bank he could observe Sumter's campfires. The British ate cold food and waited to see if Sumter would choose to cross the river at Rocky Mount. If he did, they would have him. According to William Richardson Davie, Sumter had been warned that Tarleton was parallel with him across the river, and in the morning he continued his line of march up the west bank. As soon as Tarleton's scouts brought him word of Sumter's route, he crossed the river on boats he had secured the day before and set out on a grueling forced march to catch Sumter and bring him to battle.

Both columns passed through country visited by Benson Lossing in 1849, when there had been little if any change to the river. Lossing drew a delightful sketch of the Great Falls of the Catawba, and wrote that "Almost the whole volume of the river is here compressed by a rugged island into a narrow channel, between steep shores, fissured and fragmented, as if by some powerful convulsion. There are no perpendicular falls; but down a rocky bed the river tumbles in mingled rapids and cascades, roaring and foaming, and then subsides into comparative calmness in a basin below."[2]

Through Lossing's "wild and romantic" countryside the two forces marched northward under a blazing Carolina sun. Sumter thought he was safe. He proceeded only eight miles upriver to where Fishing Creek, a considerable body of water, empties into the Catawba, two miles north of the Great Falls, and there at high noon halted in line of march. The march conditions had been punishing. On that day two centuries ago the weather was very hot and humid, enervating for men and beasts, and the road was on a series of steep, roller coaster hills, long and heart pounding. But it was the same weather and terrain for both sides, and when Tarleton's infantry told him they were "overpowered by fatigue" and could not keep up, he did the same thing as when he pursued Buford. Choosing 100 dragoons of the Legion and sixty men of the light infantry, he doubled up so the foot soldiers could ride and pushed on. His pace was as torrid as the weather, his resolve as fierce as ever. That his 160 faced 800 did not deter him.[3]

At Fishing Creek relaxation was the order of the day. Thomas Sumter partially undressed and lay down in the shade of a wagon. The Continentals stacked their arms in proper military fashion. William Richardson Davie wrote that the men were allowed to "indulge themselves as they pleased in rest and refreshment, some strolled off to a neighboring plantation, some went to the river to bathe, and numbers sought in sleep some respite from their fatigue. In this unguarded and critical moment, Col. Tarleton approached the American camp." Davie, who was not there, is supported by an eyewitness.[4]

Colonel Moffitt's band, in which sixteen-year-old James Collins served, had looked for Sumter immediately after hearing the terrible news of Camden, but, as Collins admitted, "jumped out of the frying pan into the fire; we met Sumpter retreating rapidly; we joined in the retreat until we came to Fishing Creek, a place where it was thought we could halt in safety and rest, but not so. Sumpter encamped on the main road, near the creek; we were encamped a short distance above, on his left, where another road crossed the creek; there was a guard or picket posted at a short distance in the rear; the men were all fatigued; some had kindled fires and were cooking and eating; others tumbled down and were fast alseep, and all scattered in every direction. We had drawn some provisions, and forage for our horses. . . . Our horses were mostly close at hand, and but few saddles off."[5]

Tarleton states that before napping Sumter had sent out patrols to scout the road south to Rocky Mount but that they did not go far enough. The two pickets mentioned by James Collins were over the crest of the hill and could not be seen by their comrades. Five miles from where he had mounted the sixty foot soldiers behind his horsemen, Tarleton's advance guard came on the sentries, who fired and killed a Legion dragoon. His comrades, incensed, rode down both pickets and sabered them to death. This annoyed Tarleton, because he wanted a prisoner to interrogate. Four dragoons and a sergeant continued in advance of the main column and came to the crest of the hill overlooking Sumter's camp, "where, instantly halting, they crouched upon their horses and made a signal to their commanding officer. Tarleton rode forward . . . and plainly discovered over the crest of the hill the front of the American camp, perfectly quiet, and not the least alarmed by the fire of the vedettes." Tarleton learned afterward that the firing had awakened Sumter, who "demanded the cause of the two shots, and that an officer just returned from the advanced sentries had reported that the militia were firing at cattle: A common practice in the American camp." Sumter accepted the explanation.[6]

Tarleton wasted no time. As at Monck's Corner, as at Lenud's Ferry, as at Buford's Massacre, he acted immediately and described the ensuing action clearly and concisely. "The cavalry and infantry were formed into one line, and, giving a general shout, advanced to the charge. The arms and the artillery of the continentals were secured before the men could be assembled. Universal consternation immediately ensued throughout the camp; some opposition was . . . made from behind the wagons, in front of the militia. The numbers and extensive encampment of the enemy occasioned several conflicts before the action was decided." James Collins gave essentially the same account. "Before Sumpter could wake up his men and form the enemy were among them cutting down everything in their way. It was a perfect rout, and an indiscriminate slaughter. No quarter was given; we were preparing in all haste to secure our own safety. The greater part of our number dashed through the creek, at the fording place, and pushing on with all possible speed, reached the highland. There they waited for friends, but none appeared until a few blasts from the bugle directed some stragglers to them."[7]

It was another superb coup for Tarleton, overwhelming and quite incredible. Outnumbered five to one, up against seasoned partisans and 100 first-rate Continentals, his audacity and aggressiveness, his refusal to bow to adversity, had once again humiliated the Rebels. For the price of a mere sixteen men killed and wounded the British killed and wounded 150 Rebels and captured about 310, including all the Continentals. They released all of the British prisoners, took two artillery pieces, 1,000 stand of arms, two ammunition wagons, and recovered "forty-four carriages loaded with baggage, rum, and other stores." But the great prize eluded them. "Colonel Sumpter," Tarleton wrote, "who had taken off part of his clothes on account of the heat of the weather . . . amidst the general confusion, made his escape." Sumter had leaped onto an unsaddled horse and galloped away. Two days later he rode alone into Davie's camp at Charlotte.[8]

That night young James Collins and his comrades slept in the woods, and the boy had very serious second thoughts about the adventure he had undertaken, for never before had he been forced to ride for his life. "After I laid down I began to reflect. Well, thought I, if this be the fate of war, I would willingly be excused. I devised several plans to get out of the scrape, but none appeared

likely to have the desired effect, and there was no safety in retreating." The following day Moffitt's band returned to the battleground to search for five missing men. Some of Sumter's men also appeared. "The dead and wounded lay
scattered in every direction over the field; numbers lay stretched out cold and
lifeless; some were yet struggling in the agonies of death, while here and there
lay others, faint with the loss of blood, almost famished for water, and begging
for assistance. The scene before me I could not reconcile to my feelings, and I
began to repent that I had ever taken part in the matter; however, by custom,
such things become familiar."[9]

And out of the fight at Fishing Creek came a prize that could turn the head
of a boy. They found on the field a "good looking rifle, with a shot-bag and all
the apparatus." Colonel Moffitt gave the rifle to James Collins: "you have been
wanting a rifle for some time; here is one I think will suit you; she is light, and
I think a good one . . . I think you can do better with her than with your little
shotgun." Captain Chambers agreed: "he seems to be a lucky boy, and it is well
to encourage him." The approbation of the two officers and the gift of the rifle
steadied James Collins. "I confess it had the effect of a stimulant, and in some
measure reconciled me to my lot." The boy was more than reconciled, and like
many he became a man before his time. We will have further occasions to observe him as he served faithfully and well in engagments that became part of
the American legend.[10]

Big Fight at Musgrove's Mill

Immediately prior to the dramatic events we have just witnessed, we left Elijah
Clarke and Isaac Shelby in Joseph McDowell's camp in North Carolina, where
they were plotting a strike at Musgrove's Mill in country patrolled vigorously by
British partisan forces under the command of Major Patrick Ferguson.

Ferguson himself with most of his force was camped only a few miles from
their route of march. Their approach had to be swift and silent, and so they decided to ride the forty-odd miles under cover of darkness. This would also mean
cooler hours for horses that would be pushed hard in order to arrive at the
Enoree by dawn. Colonel William Brandon and Colonel James Williams knew
the country and acted as guides.

Two hundred "picked men well mounted" rode out of McDowell's camp "one
hour before sundown" on 17 August 1780, the day after Camden, an event of
which they knew nothing. They kept to the woods until night fell, then followed
a track all night. The pace was mostly at a canter, and according to Isaac Shelby
they "never stopped to even let their horses drink." They forded many streams
and rivers large and small: Thicketty and Gilky and Pacelot and Tyger and Fair
Forest. Their march discipline was the equal of regulars. They "arrived within
half a mile of the enemy camp just at break of day," in position and undetected.
Half a dozen scouts were sent out to reconnoiter. Crossing the Enoree by a circuitous route, the scouts cautiously approached the Tory camp, observed what

they could, then began their return. On top of a ridge they ran into a five-man enemy patrol returning to camp. Shots were exchanged, one Tory fell dead, another two were wounded, and the surviving pair galloped for their camp. The six Rebels, two slightly wounded, fled to their comrades, who were waiting on a wooded ridge a half mile north of the ford.[11]

At about the same time a man who lived nearby appeared at the Rebel position with very unsettling news. During the previous evening Colonel Alexander Innes had arrived from Ninety Six with 200 Tory regulars from the New Jersey Volunteers and De Lancey's New York Battalion and 100 mounted South Carolina Royalists, all on their way to join Major Patrick Ferguson. Instead of dealing with 200 Tory militia, the 200 Rebels were faced with 500 Tories, 200 of whom were regulars. If not desperate, their situation was tenuous, for one thing was certain. They had to fight—the horses could go no farther.[12]

But to attack, as they had planned, was out of the question. This decision was made immediately and just as quickly they set about preparing their defense. There was no overall commander, an arrangement frowned on in official military circles, and admittedly it carries the potential for turmoil, but it was often the case when militia took the field and was quite workable when men of reason were involved. The horses were sent to the rear and placed under guard. The partisans then formed a semicircular defense line some 300 yards long and crossing the road that led to Musgrove's Ford. In about half an hour they had raised breast-high works constructed of brush and downed logs. Shelby commanded the right, Williams the center, Clarke the left. Behind him, Clarke placed a reserve of forty men. On each flank, hidden from view, were twenty horsemen.

The Rebel commanders now approved a tactic that has to be as old as war itself. Captain Shadrach Inman, a veteran of partisan fighting in Georgia, suggested it and was given twenty-five men to carry it out. He would cross the Enoree, engage the enemy, feign confusion and retreat but maintain contact, drawing the foe across the river and into the defensive semicircle where the main Rebel force waited with orders not to fire until the British were almost on top of them. Shelby would fire first to give the signal. Inman and his men performed to perfection. The British came on in three wings. Inman and his riders engaged the center, then withdrew, attacked again and withdrew, repeating the pattern to the Enoree and across its dark waters toward Rebel lines that bristled with rifles and muskets loaded and primed. At about 150 yards the British began firing, but they largely overshot the Rebels (as we know, at that range muskets were inaccurate under ideal conditions). The Rebel lines remained quiet, waiting for Shelby's signal. The Tory regular infantry, elated at driving before their fixed bayonets Rebels who would not stand, shouting "Huzza for King George!," swept up the side of the ridge to the ringing of their own shouts and their drums and bugles sounding the charge.[13]

At about seventy yards Shelby's rifle barked. The Rebel lines erupted in an explosion of fire and smoke that staggered the British and momentarily stopped their advance. But they were men well trained and disciplined. They would not be stopped by one volley. The Tory regulars, led personally by Colonel Alexander Innes, who was mounted on a charger, drove at Shelby' right flank in a bayonet charge. The frontier riflemen, whose weapons were slow loading and without bayonets, were always at a disadvantage in such situations. Shelby's flank, in danger of being overwhelmed by sheer numbers, slowly began to bend, like a sapling under pressure. The rest of Shelby's line as well as the center under Williams and the left wing under Clarke held firm, largely against Tory militia.

Clarke's foresight in maintaining a reserve now paid off. He ordered the forty men to go to Shelby's aid. Their response was immediate, their support critical. At just about the same time the British suffered a grievous loss when a Watauga rifleman, William Smith it was said, shot Colonel Alexander Innes off his horse. Badly wounded, Innes was carried to the rear. "I've killed their commander!," Smith shouted.[14] The riflemen rallied. There now rose above the din wild sounds that chilled the blood, sounds Captain Abraham DePeyster of De Lancey's New York Battalion would remember well. The "yelling boys" he called them. Shelby's Over Mountain men, whose usual foes were Cherokee and Creeks, paid those warriors the ultimate tribute. With shrill Indian war cries, they followed Shelby in a furious charge on the regulars. As slowly as the Rebel line first bent, the British were forced back, and now the twenty horsemen stationed on Shelby's flank under the command of Josiah Culbertson of South Carolina burst out of their hiding place and charged in support of the riflemen.

The Tory regulars did not yield ground easily. The fighting was desperate and at close quarters. The British took a heavy loss in officers. Besides Innes being out of action, a rifleman named William Beebe shot Major Fraser from his saddle, Captain Peter Campbell of New Jersey was killed, and of the regulars' seven surviving officers five were wounded. Shelby said a stalwart Tory militia captain, William Hawsey, "was shot down near our lines while making the greatest efforts to annimate his men." Elijah Clarke, whose wing had remained steady throughout the fighting, then led his men over their breastworks in a wild, screaming charge. Isaac Shelby was in awe watching Elijah Clarke in battle. "It was in the severest part of the action," a friend of Shelby's later recalled, "that Colonel Shelby's attention was arrested by the heroic conduct of Colonel Clarke. He often mentioned the circumstances of ceasing in the midst of battle to look with astonishment and admiration at Clarke fighting." The charge of Clarke and his men ended in a melee so confused that the Tory militia commander Colonel Daniel Clary, the bridle of his horse grabbed and held by two Rebels on either side, retained his composure, shouted, "Damn you, don't you know your own officers!," was released, and galloped off to safety.[15]

The survivors of the proud force that had surged up the ridge followed. Through smoke "so thick as to hide a man at twenty yards," recalled Isaac Shelby, the Tories "broke in great confusion . . . dead men lay thick on the Ground over which our men pursued the enemy." It was during this pursuit that the man who had played such a key role in planning and executing the fight was killed in action. Captain Shadrach Inman was shot seven times, once in the forehead, and fell dead under an oak tree.[16]

The entire action probably lasted about one hour, with the fierce struggle on Shelby's flank taking some fifteen minutes. The British defeat was complete, and this did not bode well for the Tory cause. In the middle of strong Tory country a small band of daring Rebel guerrillas had badly hurt and sent flying in disarray regulars and militia more than double their number. The British loss was sixty-three killed, ninety wounded, seventy taken prisoner, a total of 223 out of Innes's combined force of 500. The Rebels lost four killed and seven wounded. They were elated. Different emotions swept through the inhabitants of the countryside as anxious relatives of Tory militiamen arrived to peer at dead faces, hoping they would not find those they were looking for.

The Rebels, however, had no time for the dead. Their elation was understandable, and in the swell of victory they fixed their eyes on that always tantalizing prize, the fort at Ninety Six, twenty-five miles to the south. It was reported to be in weak condition. Clarke, Shelby, and Williams decided to move out immediately and take it, although their optimism may have been misplaced. Lieutenant Colonel John Harris Cruger of New York was the commander at Ninety Six, and he was tough and very able. But the issue was never joined. The Rebels were remounted and ready to ride when Francis Jones, a courier from General Charles McDowell in North Carolina, rode into their midst and handed over a letter from General Richard Caswell to General McDowell informing him of the disaster at Camden. All Rebel detachments were urgently advised to flee to safer parts. McDowell himself was no longer at the camp from which Clarke and Shelby had left, having moved to Gilbert Town (modern Rutherfordton), deeper into North Carolina.

Turning their tired horses to the northwest, with seventy prisoners in tow, the victors of Musgrove's Mill traveled all that day and night, sometimes dismounting and trotting to spare their horses. One of Ferguson's detachments, learning of their presence, pursued them and at one point on the evening of the battle was only thirty minutes behind, but according to Isaac Shelby "their horses broke down and could follow no further." During the retreat, as on the advance, Shelby recalled, "the Americans never stopped to eat, but made use of peaches and green corn for their support." On the 19th of August, sixty miles from Musgrove's Mill, they finally halted. In forty-eight hours they had completed two forced marches, had neither slept nor rested, and had fought and won against a superior force an action renowned for its ferocity, "one of the hardest ever fought in the United States with small arms," Isaac Shelby claimed. Shelby also recalled that "the excessive fateague ... effectually broke down every officer on our side that their faces and eyes swelled and became bloated in appearance as scarcely able to see."[17]

On top of their exhaustion was news of Gates's debacle, but the Rebels were determined not to yield. Isaac Shelby proposed that all concerned consider raising an army from the Over Mountain men and the Back Country militia to deal with Ferguson. A courier service was established to keep everyone informed of Ferguson's movements—Captain David Vance of the North Carolina militia called them "news-bearers." James Jack and Archibald Nail were assigned to bear news "over the Yellow Mountain to Shelby," Joseph Dobson and James McKay to Cleveland and Herndon, Robert Cleveland and Gideon Lewis from Benjamin Cleveland to Shelby. "Thus the news went the rounds as fast as horses could carry their riders."[18]

Gates may have lost most of his army, but they had won their fight, and they were not prepared to surrender the Back Country to the King's Inspector of Militia, Major Patrick Ferguson.

"Contemptible remains"

Far to the east, however, there occurred a loss of resolve after Camden among some of the Rice Kings. They obviously agreed with Lord Cornwallis, who wrote to Lord Germain on 21 August, four days after his great victory over Horatio Gates: "The Rebel forces being at present dispersed, the internal communications and insurrections in the province will now subside." On 16 September His Lordship issued a proclamation sequestering the estates of all Rebels. This was a step short of outright confiscation, and to save their estates some men of rank and fortune who had previously served the cause were among the 164 who signed a notice published on 21 September in the *Royal South-Carolina Gazette*. The notice congratulated the noble earl on his victory and referred to Rebels in the field, or imprisoned because they refused to yield, as "the contemptible remains of that expiring faction" opposing "that government under which they formerly enjoyed the highest degree of civil and political liberty." Among the distinguished Low Country signatories were Daniel Huger, Colonel Francis Pinckney, and Gabriel Manigault.[19]

Many of their fellow Rice Kings were made of sterner stuff. One of the "contemptible remains" was William Moultrie, who was imprisoned at Hadrell's point across the Cooper River from Charleston. Moultrie had always been a political moderate, and his brother was a Tory. The British thought that he might be ripe for conversion. What a coup if they could turn the victor of the Battle of Sullivan's Island! He was told that if he would abandon the Rebel cause he might absent himself from South Carolina for a while. "Thus you would avoid any disagreeable conversations, and might return at leisure to take possession of your estates for yourself and your family." He was also offered a military command in the British army outside the mainland colonies. "Good God!" Moultrie replied on 12 March 1781. "Is it possible that such an idea could arise in the breast of a man of honor? . . . You say by quitting the country for a short time I might avoid disagreeable conversations, and might return at my own leisure and take possession of my estates for myself and family; but you have forgot to tell me how I am to get rid of the feelings of an injured honest heart, and where to hide myself from myself; could I be guilty of so much baseness I should hate myself and shun mankind. This would be a fatal exchange from my present situation, with any easy and approved conscience of having done my duty and conducted myself as a man of honor." Moultrie, who placed honor above assets, never recovered financially from his devotion to the cause—but he never had to hide from himself.[20]

Nor did his former lieutenant and fellow planter Francis Marion. Less than two weeks after Cornwallis's crushing victory at Camden, Marion made his first strike.

Francis Marion: Fights at Great Savannah and Blue Savannah

Colonel Henry Middleton Rutledge told his son Archibald, "Do you know, that when he was born he was so small that he was put in a quart measure to be weighed, and that he almost got lost in it."[21] The Colonel, born in the house where the Swamp Fox once took refuge, was repeating Low Country lore about Francis Marion.

Francis Marion was indeed a very small man. He was also a man of contradictions. He had a reputation for humaneness, even kindness, yet he was a disciplinarian so strict that during his tenure as commander of the 2nd South Carolina Regiment an officer characterized him as "an ugly, cross, knock kneed, hook-nosed son of a bitch."[22] His personal habits were spartan. His favorite drink was said to be a mixture of vinegar and water. Within him combined a judicious mixture of caution and daring, so that he rarely slept in the same camp two nights running yet did not hesitate to attack when he was outnumbered.

Marion understood perfectly the function of a guerrilla leader. When his faithful subordinate Peter Horry (pronounced oo-ree) suggested building a redoubt to control an area, Marion explained: "The open field was our play, that the enemy knew better how to defend forts and entrenched places than we did, and that if we attempted it, we should fall into their hands." He understood, too, the critical importance of mobility, which is why he took special pains to mount his men well and balked whenever General Nathanael Greene issued instructions to deliver horses to the Continental army. Superior mobility was one of the primary secrets of his success, which Lord Rawdon admitted as the reason why "we have never been able to force them to a decisive action." Another reason was his finely tuned sense of military security. Sumter, as we have seen, could be cavalier about security. Marion never was; his caution was legendary. Obviously there was, too, in Francis Marion that quality of inspired leadership that men and women find hard to define but always recognize when they see it.[23]

But even under such a gifted leader the militia's manner of service could drive passions to the boiling point. Regulars might enlist for a period of years or even the duration—not militia. This has led to more heated controversy from the days of the Revolution to the present than even militia's propensity to run when faced by regulars in orthodox battle. Militia enlisted for short periods, often limited to three months, and when their time was up they went home, even if it was on the eve of battle, as Horatio Gates, who thought he knew militia, would discover just before the second battle of Saratoga. They often went home even before their period of service was up because without the prospect of action they grew bored with the "dull routine of camp duty," Captain Joseph Graham recalled.[24]

This practice drove the officers of the Continental Army wild with fury and frustration, emotions to which Francis Marion, Continental officer turned guerrilla, was not immune. For "his little party," Moultrie wrote, "would sometimes be reduced to five and twenty men—as is common with the militia, they grow tired, and have a pretence to go home, or sometimes without any pretence at all."[25] More than most Continental officers, Marion was aware of the personal and economic needs of the militia, but on at least one occasion he fell into such deep despair that he seriously considered quitting the field because of the failure of the men to heed his call to the colors. His close friend and comrade Hugh Horry, brother of Peter, begged him to relent, he did, eventually the militia straggled in, and they all went to war again. But most militiamen, unlike the Continentals who were overwhelmingly young and unmarried, had families to worry about. Spring planting had to be done by a certain time or there would be no crops, and crops planted but unharvested did no one any good. There were cows to milk, hogs to slop, butchering to be done, fences to repair, and as farmers and serious country gardeners know if just one season passes with no one tending to the borders the result will be an invasion of the weeds, bramble, and bush that were driven back and kept at bay through years of unrelenting, backbreaking labor. The women were often as tough as their men, and women and children could do much, but farming is a partnership; one person cannot do it all, and boys old enough to do the work of their fathers were, like sixteen-year-old James Collins, probably serving under arms with them.

After one action Marion wrote to General Gates, "So many of my men were desirous of seeing their wives and families which have been burnt out, that I found it necessary to retreat the next morning."[26] Yet despite their volatile ways and the real needs that tore them from their duty, the Patriot militia was a key ingredient to victory throughout the states. The role of these part-time citizen soldiers was so decisive that it is a theme we will return to often.

Soon after leaving Gates's camp, Marion set out to destroy all craft on the Santee River and guard the crossing places. On 17 August he met the Williamsburg militia at Witherspoon's Ferry on Lynches River. He did not know that Gates had been defeated the previous day. Splitting his force, he sent Peter Horry to the lower reaches of the Santee with orders to work his way up river to Lenud's Ferry, destroying river craft as he marched. Marion marched about sixty miles to the Santee toward Lenud's Ferry, and from there trudged upriver on the same task. By 19 August he had reached Nelson's Ferry, then an important landmark and crossing point on the Santee River, now submerged under the waters of Lake Marion. There he received a private report that he did not immediately share with his men, fearing that information of Gates's debacle might discourage them almost before he had begun campaigning. That same night he learned from a young ensign who had deserted from the Tory militia that six miles away, on the site of Thomas Sumter's abandoned plantation at Great Savannah (today also submerged beneath Lake Marion), over a hundred American prisoners from Camden were encamped with a thirty-six-man escort, which included regulars of the 63rd Regiment of Foot. Marion, with fifty-two mounted partisans available, wasted no time. He would attack at dawn, 20 August 1780.

At Sumter's empty house Captain Jonathan Roberts of the 63rd had never heard of Francis Marion and had no inkling that a Rebel band was nearby and bent on his destruction. Although sentries were posted, the escorts' arms were stacked outside the plantation house, in the manner of the Continentals who had been with Sumter at Fishing Creek. Marion arrived before first light. He sent Hugh Horry and sixteen men as a blocking force to the ford at Horse Creek. Marion would attack from the rear with the rest of the men. But Horry's party met a sentry who fired at them, whereupon Hugh Horry immediately did exactly the right thing. He led his sixteen riders on a mad charge down the lane leading to the house and got to the stacked weapons before the British troops could retrieve them. At the same time Marion charged from the rear. It was over in minutes. While suffering only two wounded, Marion's band killed or took prisoner twenty-six of the enemy and freed 147 Continentals.

The action at Great Savannah was a small affair, but it would be the first of many, and it stung enough for Cornwallis to order an investigation by Major James Wemyss, who concluded, accurately, "I am afraid negligence will mark the whole of it."[27]

No one ever accused Francis Marion of negligence. A sixty-mile march to the northeast soon removed his little band from any possible pursuit. He stopped in a watery land at a place called Port's Ferry, somewhere on the Great Pee Dee River just north of Snow's Island.

The area in which Marion now found himself was also a Scotch Irish stronghold, and most of them, as elsewhere, were strongly Rebel or at the very least partial to the cause. But Loyalists were also present among them, and Major Micajah Ganey was able to muster about 250 men into a Tory militia regiment. Ganey's deputy, Captain Jesse Barefield, was a farmer and ex-Rebel who had gone over to the Tories after experiencing what he felt was contemptuous treatment by South Carolina Continental officers of the Low Country gentry class. (In this respect, the Rice Kings with few exceptions were no different than their counterparts in the British army.) When Ganey learned of Marion's presence, he mustered his men and marched on 4 September. But Marion, whose scouts ranged widely and constantly, received a report of their gathering the day before and though he had at hand only fifty-three men he decided to take Ganey by surprise. Ever cautious, he told no one of his intentions.

On the morning of the 4th, Marion's little band set out, all mounted, with the veteran officer Major John James leading the way with picked horsemen. They rode north, along the course of the Little Pee Dee River. They all wore white cockades in their hats to distinguish them in the heat of battle. Scouts ranged in front of the column. Some two hours after they had started a scout galloped up to Major James to report a large group of mounted men on the road just ahead. They were forty-five in all, the Tory advance guard led personally by Micajah Ganey. James shouted, charged, and his men followed. James knew Ganey. He aimed his great charger, Thunder, directly at him. Ganey and his horsemen, surprised and intimidated by the sudden appearance of the Rebels, scattered and fled. James chased Ganey. They had galloped about half a mile when Ganey met some of his men who had dismounted and were preparing to put up a fight from a thicket. It was only then that Major John James realized that he was quite alone—whereupon he pulled the oldest trick in the book. Spurring Thunder on, he shouted, "Come on, boys! Come on! Here they are! Here they are!"[28] The now thoroughly demoralized Tories leaped onto their horses and fled again, their leader joining them.

The Rebels had one man wounded. Of Micajah Ganey's forty-five Tory horsemen, thirty were killed or wounded. Only fifteen got away, and they departed so fast that no one warned Captain Jesse Barefield with the infantry of what had happened. From prisoners Marion learned that Barefield and his men were three miles ahead of him. The Rebels continued their advance. When he learned that Marion was near, the veteran Barefield deployed his men into line and waited for the attack. But Frances Marion was neither a Tarleton nor a Sumter. Although as we have seen he would not hesitate to take on a superior force, his tactics depended on situation and terrain, and in this particular situation he declined to charge with his fifty-three riders some two hundred foot with loaded muskets. Instead, he also chose an old, instinctive tactic. He retreated in a manner suggesting confusion and fear, and at a place called Blue Savannah he set up an ambush amid tangled thickets. (Blue Savannah, whose exact location remains in doubt, was a swampy area on the Little Pee Dee.)

Captain Jesse Barefield and his column pursued, but their march discipline—if it ever existed—broke down. The men were apparently strung out and in disorder as they came opposite Marion's ambush site. The Rebels had not dismounted, and when they came it was at full charge with pistols at close range and heavy sabers slashing. Tory astonishment turned to terror. Their scattered, ineffectual fire managed to wound three men and kill two horses. They then took to their heels and disappeared into "an Impassable Swamp to all but Toreys."[29] Marion would not allow pursuit into the swamp. He often used swamps himself, and he knew that they could be deadly traps as well as secure hiding places. For a while, the Rebels shouted insults at their foes, cursed them, dared them to come out and fight. Then they rode back to Port's Ferry, about twenty miles south.

In the short space of two weeks, at widely separated points, Francis Marion had first defeated British and provincial regulars, then routed a Tory force that had a five to one superiority. Following that coup, sixty new men rode into his camp and volunteered to follow him. From a man unknown to the British and ignored by Continental officers, he had almost overnight become a real threat on Cornwallis's right flank. The dispersal of Ganey's force had ended before it could spark a Tory uprising in the wide expanse of country north of Georgetown. And Marion's presence and aggressiveness threatened Georgetown itself, an important port and British strongpoint.

Lord Cornwallis, anxious to move into North Carolina, wanted the disturbances to the east of him cleared up before he marched. He gave the job to Major James Wemyss of the 63rd Regiment. Cornwallis sent him out with explicit instructions to organize the Tory militia so that it could successfully combat Marion's guerrillas and march through "the country from Kingstree Bridge to Peedee, and returning by the Cheraws." He was to disarm anyone untrustworthy, "punish the Concealment of Arms and Ammunition with a total Demolition of the Plantation," and hang without trial any person who had broken parole by a hostile act.[30] Wemyss carried out his orders with a vengeance, but his two major accomplishments were quite unintended. Major James Wemyss became the second most hated man in the Carolinas (no one could displace Tarleton), and Francis Marion's most successful recruiting officer.

His first act was to steal the horses of all Rebel sympathizers among the planters of the High Hills of Santee and the Santee River in order to mount his infantry from the 63rd Foot. Then he began burning and hanging, with special attention given to the homes of Marion's followers. Marion had hoped to oppose Wemyss, but it soon became apparent that Wemyss's force of 200, augmented by 400 regulars and Tories at Kingstree and Georgetown, would overpower his band. Many of Marion's men quite naturally wanted desperately to see to their families. Marion dismissed those men who needed to go home, left behind Captain John James and ten men to gather intelligence, and with the sixty remaining with him did what all wise guerrillas do when faced with overwhelming force: he got out of the way, in his case retreating northward all the way across the North Carolina line to wait out this time of misfortune.

Wemyss in the meantime cut a wide swath from Kingstree to Cheraw. He left behind him desolation. For seventy miles and in some places fifteen miles wide he burned and hanged. He reported to Cornwallis that he had burned over fifty homes and hanged several men. He burned the Presbyterian church at Indian Town because, he said, all such places were "sedition shops." In addition to homes he burned gristmills, blacksmith shops, and loom houses. Sheep and cattle not taken for food were slaughtered with bayonets and their carcasses left to rot. The Tory militia, unable to hold the country on its own, was allowed to plunder. Among the men Wemyss hanged was Adam Cusack, who denied that he had ever taken parole, but Wemyss had a gibbet erected beside the road. Cusack's wife and children stood before Major Wemyss's horse, begging for the life of husband and father. To no avail. Adam Cusack swung before their eyes. Dr. James Wilson, who lived nearby, also attempted to intercede, and for his pains lost his home to Wemyss's torches. Sending his wife to safety in North Carolina, Wilson joined Marion.

James Wemyss also reported to Cornwallis that "I have done everything in my power to get at Mr. Merrion, who . . . commanded about 150 men on my arrival in this Part of the Country. Altho' I never could come up with them, yet I push'd them so hard as in a great Measure to break them up; the few that still continue together have retreated over Little Peedee." But he also knew that he had left behind him seething anger and that the Tory militia could not on its own deal with the Rebel militia. Cornwallis replied, "Your account is not so agreeable."[31]

"The bravery and importance
of the American Militia"

Nor was the situation directly in front of His Lordship any more agreeable. He had begun his march northward on 8 September, moving from Camden to the Waxhaws, where he encamped on the North Carolina line. Once a rich area of prosperous farms, several months of war had reduced its value to any army for food and forage. There was sickness in the army. Tarleton himself was danger-ously ill with yellow fever. For two weeks Cornwallis waited in his camp along Waxhaws Creek while the sick recovered, and also for news of James Wemyss's expedition against Francis Marion. In the meantime, young Andrew Jackson's ideal officer, the exceptional William Richardson Davie, newly promoted to Colonel, had no intention of allowing the twin disasters of Camden and Fish-ing Creek to stop his harassment of Cornwallis's army.

During Tarleton's illness, the British Legion was commanded by his deputy, the rakish, eccentric Major George Hanger, who was an excellent shot and an authority on firearms but little else. His autobiography, published in 1801, is short on his American experience and long on philosophical nonsense, although it does contain his prediction of eventual civil war between the northern and southern states. The Legion, according to William Richardson Davie, began to "spread havoc and destruction," and he resolved to attack it under Cornwallis's very nose. He had eighty mounted partisans, and seventy riflemen under Major George Davidson. He marched on 20 September with the intention of launch-ing a night attack "to check if not entirely disperse these lawless Marauders," and "after taking a considerable circuit to avoid the Patroles of the enemy about 2 o'clock in the morning . . . turned Lord Cornwallis right flank and approached a plantation where the Tories were said to be encamped." But the Legion had changed position a few days before. In the wee hours of the morning of 21 Sep-tember Davie had to seek out "terrified or disaffected people" for information as to the Legion's whereabouts. He finally learned that the Legion had "retired within the flanks of the British Army to the plantation of . . . Capt. Wahab, which was overlooked by the camp of the 71st regiment, and that they might amount to three or four hundred mounted infantry." Davie was unwilling to back off and marched his 150 men without being observed; they reached Wahab's Plantation about sunrise. Captain James Wahab, whose property it was, served with Davie that day, which probably accounts for the perfectly executed approach march.[32]

When the Rebels arrived the British were getting ready for an early foray. They had called in their sentries, and sixty men with some of the British Legion were mounted near the house. As he had at Hanging Rock, Davie broke up his

William Richardson Davie, by Charles Xavier Harris, after the
lost original by John VanderLyn, 1800
(Courtesy of the North Carolina Department of Archives & History.)

force into three units and attacked by surprise from different directions. He gave
a clear account of the action. The house "stood about the middle of a Lane,
covered on the same side by a corn field cultivated to the very door. A company of infantry were detached thro' the corn with orders to take possession of
the Houses and immediately fire on the enemy. The Cavalry were sent around
the corn field with directions to gain the other end of the lane & charge the
foe as soon as the fire commenced at the Houses." Davie himself took forty riflemen to the other end of the lane. The "Houses were briskly attacked, and
the Cavalry charged at the same moment. The enemy being completely surprised had no time to form and crowded in great disorder to the other end of
the lane when a well reserved fire from the rifle men drove them back upon the
cavalry and Infantry who were now drawn up at the Houses, & by whom they
were instantly attacked; thus pushed vigorously on all sides they fluctuated some
moments under the impressions of terror and dismay and then bore down the
fences and fled in full speed."

Given the proximity of the British army, especially Fraser's Highlanders, which had beat to arms soon after the firing began, Davie could neither pursue nor tarry. British horses and arms were immediately collected, Davie's infantry mounted, and the surplus horses secured to take along. By then, as Davie recounted, the Highlanders were moving "briskly to attack the detachment, but as they entered one end of the lane the Americans were marching out of the other in good order." James Wahab, whose wife and children had suddenly found themselves in the middle of the war, "had been exiled for some time from his family. . . . They gathered round him in tears of joy and distraction, the enemy advanced, and he could only embrace them, and in a few minutes afterwards turning his eyes back towards his all, as the detachment moved off, he had the mortification to see their only hope of subsistence wrapt in flames. This barbarous practice was uniformly enacted by the British officers in the Southern States. However casual the encounter might be, when it happened at a plantation their remaining in possession of the ground was always marked by committing the Houses to flames."

There was another barbarous practice committed that day, and Davie admitted it. The Rebels took no prisoners. He explained it by stating that he had given the order because it was to have been a night attack, and "these orders in the hurry of the morning were not revoked. This circumstance, the vicinity of the British quarters, and the danger of pursuit satisfactorily account for no prisoners being taken." Davie said the British lost fifteen or twenty dead and forty wounded, although a contemporary source claimed that there were sixty British dead. The Rebels had one man wounded from friendly fire when he was mistaken for an enemy. The loot was significant: ninety-six horses with their furniture and 120 stand of arms. That same afternoon Davie and his men arrived safely at their camp. Before the week was out they would again embarrass the British and Cornwallis would be sorely vexed at the incident.

Cornwallis decided to break camp and march on Charlotte, forty miles away. He had 2,200 men, 1,500 of whom were British regulars. Banastre Tarleton was still in his sickbed. The incompetent Major George Hanger led the British Legion, which provided the van for the army. On the 24th of September William Richardson Davie's "patroles gave information that the enemy were in motion on the Steele-Creek road leading to Charlotte." Davie had 150 men: his own dragoons, the mounted infantry of Major George Davidson who had been with him at Wahab's Plantation, and Captain Joseph Graham and his Mecklenburg County militia. Davie wrote that his men skirmished with the van and "hovered round the British army and on the . . . night of the 25th captured a number of Prisoners, and about midnight took post at Charlotte, seven miles from the place where Cornwallis was encamped." Davie described Charlotte on the day of the action, 26 September 1780: "The Town situated on rising ground contains about twenty houses built on two streets which cross each other at right angles, in the intersection of which stands the Court-House. The left of the town as the enemy came up was an open common, the right was covered with underwood up to the gardens." The Yorkshire-born Davie, "relying on the firmness of the militia was determined to give his Lordship some earnest of what he might expect in No Carolina." Davie dismounted twenty dragoons and "posted them under the Court-House where they were covered breast-high by a stone wall, the two other companies were advanced about eighty yards and posted behind some houses and gardens on each side of the street."

The Rebels watched as the British Legion cavalry supported on each flank by the Legion infantry and Lieutenant Colonel James Webster's light infantry advanced on the town. Behind them, also in view, were Lord Cornwallis and the rest of the British army. Faced by armed men behind a stone wall, Major Hanger should have used his infantry to roll up the American flanks and force them into the open. Then a cavalry charge could have been devastating. But Hanger decided to play hell-for-leather cavalryman. Hadn't it worked before, at Monck's Corner, Lenud's Ferry, Buford's Massacre, Fishing Creek? In addition to his basic incompetence, he probably had the usual British officer's disdain for American militia—Rebel or Tory. At a distance of three hundred yards from the stone wall Hanger formed "with a front to fill the street." The bugle sounded the charge and the "cavalry advanced in full gallop." But Davie was not Buford. He did not wait until the Legion horse was on top of him before acting. At sixty yards he gave the order to fire. The crashing volley broke the Legion's charge. The horsemen fled.

The light infantry pressed its attack on the right. There were not enough men to stop them, and Davie withdrew the two companies to the stone wall. The men remaining on the flanks were "hotly engaged" with the British infantry, but Davie instructed the men behind the stone wall to hold their fire for the cavalry, which was forming again, and when they came, stated Davie, "They were again well received by the militia and galloped off in the outmost confusion in the presence of the whole British army." Since his flanks were beginning to be turned under pressure from the light infantry, Davie drew off his infantry companies in "good order, successively covering each other, and formed in a single line at the end of the street about one hundred yards from the Court-House under a galling fire from the British light infantry who advanced under cover of the Houses and gardens. The British cavalry soon appeared again, charging in columns by the Court-house, but on receiving a fire reserved for them by part of the militia they wheeled off behind the houses."

One of those charges, probably the third, was prompted by Cornwallis. He had ridden to the van and was agitated by what he found: Webster's infantry doing the fighting and the fabled British Legion horse in disarray. He ordered them to advance once more. They did not move. He probably grew red in the face, for his Commissary General, Charles Stedman, who was present, reported that he shouted, "Legion, remember you have everything to lose, but nothing to gain."[33]

When he saw that he could hold no longer, Davie ordered a retreat by the Salisbury road. He stated that the British pursuit was carried out with "great caution and respect for some miles," until the Legion cavalry charged the rear guard, which was forced to flee, but on reaching the main body and "receiving a fire from a single company the Cavalry again retreated." American losses have been put at thirty killed, but Davie listed only five dead and six wounded. One of the wounded, Captain Joseph Graham, who thought Davie's decision to fight a mistake, claimed that during the Rebel retreat the British "manoeuvered with great skill," and believed "the small damage sustained in proportion to the risk appeared providential." Perhaps Graham's judgment at least partially stemmed from the severity of his wounds: shot three times, sabered six times, he "was left on the ground as dead."[34]

George Hanger, who had botched what should have been a smooth, methodical clearing of a pesky enemy, dismissed the action as a "trifling, insignificant skirmish." Tarleton, whose cavalry Hanger had mishandled, wrote that "a charge of cavalry under Major Hanger . . . totally dispersed the militia," but when Tarleton or his command lost or performed poorly he either lied or offered specious excuses. British observers of the action were more candid. Stedman wrote of the entire army being held up by a handful of militia, and Lieutenant Roderick Mackenzie of Fraser's Highlanders wrote after the war that no "entreaties" or "exertions" could "induce the legion cavalry to approach the American militia. They retreated without fulfilling the intentions of the General. He, therefore, much dissatisfied ordered the light and legion infantry to dislodge the enemy, which they immediately effected."[35]

Davie admitted that seeking the action "carries a charge of temerity" on his part, but he excused it because of the results and "that zeal which we are always ready to applaud." He had once again shown that he was highly skilled at deploying troops in the field and handling them in battle. It is also a measure of his leadership that in all the actions in which we have observed him his militia performed like seasoned regulars. He was very proud of them. Davie was an elegant, refined, well-educated man of good family who could never be described as a man of the people, and in the long years after the war he came to loath democracy and its leveling tendencies. But he maintained that the behavior of the Rebels at Charlotte "furnishes a very striking instance of the bravery and importance of the American Militia; few examples can be shewn of any troops who in one action changed their position twice in good order although pressed by a much superior body of Infantry and charged three times by thrice their number of Cavalry, unsupported & in the presence of the enemys whole army and finally retreating in good order."[36]

Davie and his men were not through. In conjunction with General William Davidson of the North Carolina militia, they would effectively control the countryside of Mecklenburg County. British foraging parties could count on being harried and ambushed every time they rode out from Cornwallis's lines, and British couriers probably had the most dangerous job in the army. A lone courier was a dead man. The reader will recall Tarleton's complaint that his cavalry was worn down by the constant escort duty they were required to provide. Lord Cornwallis had an uncertain line of communication with his commanders at Charleston and the strongpoints throughout South Carolina. This state of affairs became even more ominous when he decided to deal with the Back Country warriors on his western flank. In the meantime, from his eastern flank other disquieting news came to Cornwallis. Francis Marion was in the field again.

Francis Marion: Fight at Black Mingo

Two days after William Richardson Davie and his militia trounced the British Legion horse at Charlotte, Marion, returning to his haunts after the passage of Major James Wemyss, struck at a place called Black Mingo.[37]

Wemyss's terror tactics had not worked. In the Williamsburg District hatred seethed amid the stink of burned buildings and slaughtered animals. Major John James reported all of this to Marion where he was camped in the malarial fastness of the Great White Marsh across the line in North Carolina. On 24 September 1780 the little guerrilla captain led his small band out of the marsh and headed south. They camped that night on the banks of the Waccamaw. The next day, guided by the brothers Britton and Samuel Jenkins, they rode through Little Pee Dee Swamp to the river, swam their horses across it, continued on to the Great Pee Dee at Port's Ferry, and crossed on boats. They did not stop there. At dusk, at Witherspoon's Ferry, the place where Marion had first met the Williamsburg Militia, they crossed Lynche's River. On the opposite bank were Captain John James and ten men. Others soon appeared. Marion received reports of enemy troop dispositions. He had sixty riders and wondered if he should risk battle. But the men were eager, and so on they rode, another dozen miles through the night toward Shepherd's Ferry on the Black Mingo.

Black Mingo Creek was quite broad, with wetlands disappearing into mysterious swamps. It had some importance in the eighteenth century, as schooners were able to navigate it and carry local products to market. The Willtown Bridge, about a mile above Shepherd's Ferry, spanned Black Mingo. Near the ferry was the Red House, a tavern owned by Patrick Dollard. Here Colonel John Coming Ball, a Tory Rice King, and his forty-six King's Friends were camped. Ball's mission was to control the road and be ready to ride to counter Rebel activity.

Marion and his men arrived about midnight and made for Willtown Bridge. A Tory sentry heard horse hooves on the wooden planking of the bridge and fired an alarm shot. Marion continued his advance and once across the Black Mingo galloped toward the tavern. When he reached the road he stopped and ordered most of his men to dismount and fight on foot, for he had to assume that the British had made Dollard's tavern into a strongpoint. But Ball had deployed his men in a field to the west of the tavern, in the path of the approaching Rebels.

Marion's plan was somewhat complicated for a night assault. While one group under Captain Thomas Waites maneuvered in front of the tavern, Hugh Horry led the main attack on foot. The horsemen were then to strike the British left flank, while Marion and a handful of men remained in reserve. The attack started badly. The Tory militia had strict orders to fire only on command, and Ball let the shadow figures of Horry's men come within thirty yards before he gave the order to fire. At that range only darkness could have saved the Rebels from heavier losses. The blaze of fire killed Captain George Logan and severely wounded and knocked Captain Henry Mouzon and Lieutenant John Scott to the ground. The men fell back, shocked by the sudden blast of fire in the night. But Captain John James stopped them, turned them around, and sent them forward again, this time more cautiously, seeking cover as they moved. At the same time Captain Thomas Waites and his command attacked the Tory right flank. In minutes it was over. The Tory militia delivered one more fire, scattered, ineffective, then fled for the swamp that can be seen today. According to Peter Horry, they ran twenty miles to Georgetown and then beyond, not stopping until they had gained the other side of the Santee River.

The Tories lost three killed, one wounded, and thirteen captured, and several bodies were later found in the swamp; Marion had two dead and eight wounded, and two of the latter, Captain Mouzon and Lieutenant Scott, were so badly hurt they never again took the field. Marion had also learned a lesson. In the future when he had to make clandestine movements across bridges, he covered the planks with blankets. Loot was plentiful, including abandoned weapons, ammunition, and baggage, and several horses that their Tory owners had no time to retrieve in their mad dash for safety. One was John Coming Ball's mount, and Frances Marion claimed it, revealed a sense of humor by renaming it Ball, and rode the animal for the rest of the war.

The fight at Black Mingo engaged only 107 men and lasted but fifteen minutes. That, however, is often the nature of guerrilla war. And in the case of South Carolina it proved once again that overall the Tory militia of which the British on their drawing boards had expected much was no match for the Rebel militia. Among the reasons none was more important than the caliber of leadership on both sides. It is true that the victors wrote the histories, as they always do, but that astute Tory observer Colonel Robert Gray also believed that Sumter and Marion "established a decided superiority in the militia line," whereas Tory militia officers were unable to "inspire their followers with the confidence necessary for soldiers."[38] The Rebels had a host of outstanding militia leaders, beyond the triumvirate of Sumter, Marion, and Pickens, but the Tories in the South had only two men who could claim to be militia leaders of the first rank: Thomas "Burntfoot" Brown and David Fanning. Brown remains controversial, despite the effort of his recent biographer to rehabilitate him. Cornwallis banished him from South Carolina because of his brutal recruiting methods, and he was thereafter relegated to the military backwater of Georgia, where he gallantly defended Augusta against Elijah Clarke but forever blackened his name by hanging thirteen Rebel prisoners and turning others over to the Indians for torture. David Fanning's notable exploits in North Carolina came too late to have any bearing on the outcome of the war, and Fanning never fought the best of the Rebel leaders.

The irony of the Revolution in South Carolina is that it was started by the Rice Kings and saved by the Back Country militia, which was overwhelmingly composed of men the Rice Kings held in contempt. From the Williamsburg District to the Piedmont to the foothills of the Blue Ridge, mounted militiamen scorned by Rice Kings and Continental generals alike maintained their allegiance to the cause through one disaster after another to Continental armies. They demoralized the Tory militia and held their own against British and provincial regulars in classic guerrilla style in actions large and small, some lost to memory in the mists of time. The most famous of these actions became an enduring legend of the Revolution, and we now turn to the events that led to that memorable battle and the characters involved.

14

The Rise of Patrick Ferguson

A Scottish Soldier

Before the Battle of Camden we left Lieutenant Anthony Allaire of the American Volunteers deep in the western reaches of the South Carolina Back Country engaged in the frustrating endeavor of trying to catch will-o-the-wisp Rebel bands. The Volunteers were camped near Winnsboro, where they witnessed the hanging of a man named Smith for deserting from the Tory militia to the Rebels. Word came to them on 19 August of Cornwallis's great victory, and also orders to join the pursuit of Sumter. At 7 P.M. the Volunteers marched. But at that very moment another courier arrived from Colonel Alexander Innes with news of the Rebel victory the previous day at Musgrove's Mill and Innes's urgent request for support. "This," wrote Anthony Allaire, "to our great mortification, altered the course of our march. At eleven at night we got in motion; marched all night; forded Broad River at sun-rising." The Volunteers and the militia accompanying them continued for the rest of that month to traipse the semi-wild Back Country in search of elusive Rebels. On the 23rd Major Patrick Ferguson left them and proceeded to Camden, where he had been summoned by Lord Cornwallis. On 1 September "Major Ferguson joined us again from Camden with the disagreeable news that we were to be separated from the army, and act on the frontier with the militia."[1] Anthony Allaire had not an inkling of just how disagreeable the experience would be. Nor did his commander, Major Patrick Ferguson, who was elated at the mission given to him by Cornwallis.

Ferguson's critical task was to protect Cornwallis's left flank, to move northward in the far Back Country, parallel with the main army as it thrust into North Carolina. Ferguson and his American Volunteers and South Carolina Tory militia would deal with the Rebel partisans, preventing them from harassing the British army, crushing them if possible. He was also to organize the North Carolina militia in Tryon County.

Patrick Ferguson
(Courtesy of the National Park Service—Kings Mountain National Military Park.)

Yet Cornwallis did not really trust Ferguson's ability to carry his assignment off. As early as June Ferguson's fellow Scot, Nisbet Balfour, then commandant of Ninety Six, wrote to Cornwallis that Ferguson had "great matters in view, and I find it impossible to trust him out of my sight. He seems to me to want to carry the war into North Carolina himself at once." On 3 July Cornwallis replied, "Entre nous, I am afraid of his getting to the frontier of N. Carolina and playing us some cussed trick." Even after he had given Ferguson specific orders to move into North Carolina Cornwallis wrote to Sir Henry Clinton on 29 August, "Ferguson is to move into Tryon County with some militia whom he says he is sure he can depend upon for doing their duty and fighting well; but I am sorry to say that his own experience as well as that of every other officer is totally against him."[2]

Who was this man in whom Cornwallis lacked confidence but gave awesome responsibility? We have met him on occasion since the action at Monck's Corner, but we have not subjected him to close inspection. He is a key player in our story, however, and it is time to place Major Patrick Ferguson, Inspector of Militia, under somewhat more intense scrutiny.

The problem with Patrick Ferguson is the haze of romance that surrounds him, the man, and the Scottish soldier, a figure over which the Anglo-American world can become somewhat silly. It is true that the Scots are a martial race, and Scottish regiments have won more than their share of accolades around the world, but mention the name and there are immediately conjured images of pipes and kilts and claymores and Bonnie Prince Charlie and lost causes that tend to fog minds. It has been claimed that Ferguson was a brilliant soldier. It is true that he had a very good mind, especially for technical subjects, and his career certainly did not follow the norm. But a brilliant soldier? Let us follow his adventures in the Carolina Back Country and decide for ourselves.

Although of delicate constitution as boy and young man, he otherwise began life under favorable conditions.[3] He was born in 1744 to an Aberdeenshire laird, James Ferguson of Pitfour, and Anne Murray, daughter of the fourth Lord Elibank. His father, a lawyer, defended the defeated followers of Bonnie Prince Charlie at Carlisle in 1745, and became Lord Pitfour in 1764. Patrick Ferguson's elder brother was a supporter and personal friend of Pitt the Younger and served in Parliament for thirty years. His mother's brother was Major General James Murray, who was one of the three brigadiers under James Wolfe on the famous expedition against Quebec, where he commanded the left wing on the Plains of Abraham.

Patrick Ferguson was destined for the army from an early age. His uncle, James Murray, wrote to his mother, "You must no longer look upon him as your son. He is the son of Mars and will be unworthy of his father if he does not give proof of contempt of pain and danger."[4] He was sent to a military academy in London where he studied gunnery, fortifications, and other military subjects. At age fifteen he was commissioned in the Royal North British Dragoons, a storied unit that became famous in later years as the Scots Greys. He saw extensive combat in Germany and exhibited the courage expected of an officer and some dash beyond that. But he became ill and was invalided home, where he spent most of the years from 1762 to 1768. His family then purchased him a commission in the 70th Regiment in Tobago, where his younger brother George was governor. He saw considerable combat there during a formidable slave insurrection and again distinguished himself in action. But he was eventually stricken with the constant companion of western armies in the tropics, debilitating fever, and had to return home in 1774. From then until 1776 there occurred the first recorded instance of his keen technical mind at work. It has been suggested that he began tinkering with the loading mechanism of a particular rifle because of the fearsome reputation of American riflemen. The result, the so-called Ferguson Rifle, became as shrouded in romance and myth as the man who gave it his name.

Unlike the smoothbore musket, spiral grooves, or riflings, were cut inside the barrel of a rifle. Their function was to make the ball spin as it traveled the length of the barrel. The spinning motion continued throughout the flight of the ball, which meant that part of the ball that first appeared as it came out of the barrel remained foremost throughout its flight. This was in direct contrast to the ball coming out of a smoothbore musket and tumbling over and over in flight. Although the musket had a greater range than the rifle, for it to hit anything past about eighty yards was pure luck. The eighteenth-century rifle, however, shot accurately at medium range, about 200 yards, and it was not unknown for experts to score hits at up to 400 yards. That is the essence of the difference between the two weapons, and I have only gone into the subject in this detail for two reasons: a good part of Patrick Ferguson's reputation rests on his alleged "invention" of the Ferguson Rifle; and the fog of romance and myth that surround another famous weapon, the American, or Kentucky, Rifle, which will concern us generally and in connection with Patrick Ferguson.

Ferguson is often credited, erroneously, with the invention of a breechloading rifle. A breechloader, whether handgun, long gun, or artillery piece, is loaded at the rear end of the barrel, the way we load weapons today, whereas a muzzleloader, as described earlier, is loaded at the front end. Breechloading weapons appeared very early in the history of firearms. There are fourteenth-century references to breechloading artillery, and by the second quarter of the sixteenth century the first breechloading rifles had been made in Germany. In the opening years of the eighteenth century, a Huguenot gunmaker in Paris, Isaac de la Chaumette, invented a new system of breechloading; in 1721 he patented his invention in England, where he had emigrated, and his gun was made there by a fellow French gunmaker, Georges Bidet. Prior to Chaumette, a plug was unscrewed from the barrel and the ball loaded through the hole; but the soldier had to either put the plug in his pocket or somehow hold on to it while he also held the gun, loaded it, and screwed the plug back in, all the while keeping one eye cocked at the enemy line. Chaumette's screwed plug passed from the top of the weapon through the breech and was attached to the trigger guard, which was moveable. The soldier gave the trigger guard a complete turn. This drew the plug back far enough to reveal a hole into which the ball was dropped, followed by a charge of powder. The trigger guard was turned back to its original position. The pan was then primed, and the rifle was ready to fire. Chaumette's new system is obvious: no longer did the soldier have to fumble with a loose plug while loading his weapon and then face the potential difficulty, especially while under fire, of engaging the threads while trying to screw the plug back into the barrel.

But Chaumette's rifle fouled easily, and Patrick Ferguson contributed to its technology by modifying the threads to prevent fouling. In 1776, Ferguson patented his version of the Chaumette rifle. His modification was not fundamental; the breechloading design was Chaumette's, and it is highly questionable whether a separate patent should have been allowed.[5] But it was, and Chaumette's invention became the Ferguson Rifle to historians and fiction writers alike. The all-time best-selling author of westerns, the late Louis L'Amour, published a tale entitled The Ferguson Rifle, in which the hero as a lad is given a rifle for his very own by none other than Major Patrick Ferguson.

All of this is meant to give Isaac de la Chaumette the credit due him and to observe that there was nothing unique about breechloaders by the time Patrick Ferguson modified the male threads on a breechloading system that had been invented almost half a century before his birth. Ferguson's technical achievement was certainly laudable but has been blown out of proportion. More impressive than his technical advance was his ability to get the weapon adopted, at least temporarily, as the British Army's first breechloader. He gave two demonstrations, one before George III at Windsor Castle, the other in the summer of 1776 at Army ordnance headquarters at Woolwich before the top brass.

Ferguson gave a stellar performance in heavy rain and high winds, firing up to six shots per minute and exhibiting a flair for showmanship by hitting the "bull's eye at 100 yards, lying with his back on the ground," according to the *Annual Register* of 1 June.[6] The weapon was also fitted to accept a bayonet. His audience was so impressed that 100 rifles were authorized for manufacture, and Ferguson was instructed to organize recruits into a company of riflemen for service in America. The reader should keep in mind as the story of Patrick Ferguson and his rifle unfold that he was what most men, including soldiers, are not: a firearms expert and a skilled marksman.

Ferguson led his new command into action for the first time on 11 September 1777 at the Battle of Brandywine. In a letter to a kinsman, Adam Ferguson, he claimed considerable success and implied cowardice on the part of the American light troops, who "have learnt to rely upon their heels," an observation supported by several American officers.[7] But some Americans were obviously putting up effective resistance, because of the eighty riflemen Ferguson took into the battle forty were killed or wounded, and Ferguson's right elbow was shattered by a rifle ball. He never regained the use of his right arm.

During the skirmishing an incident occurred that added to the romance surrounding this Scottish soldier. He and his men were laying on the ground at the edge of the woods "when a Rebell officer remarkable by a huzzar dress passed towards our army within 100 yards of my right flank, not perceiving us. He was followed by another dressed in dark green or blue mounted on a very good bay horse with a remarkable large high cock'd hat." Ferguson could have killed the second officer, for he was at a range at which he had "seldom missed a Sheet of paper and could have lodged half a dozen balls in or about him before he was out of my reach . . . but it was not pleasant for me to fire at the back of an unoffending individual who was acquiting himself very cooly of his duty so I let him alone." The following day Ferguson was informed by a British surgeon that wounded Rebel officers whom he had attended told him that "Gen'l Washington was all the morning with the Light Troops, generally in their front and only attended by a French officer in a huzzar Dress, he himself mounted and dressed as above directed. The oddness of their dress had puzzled me and made me take notice of it. I am not sorry that I did not know all the time who it was."[8] On the face of it, Ferguson had an opportunity given to few, to change the course of history by killing the indispensable man.

But Ferguson's second in command that day, and present during the incident, was the prominent New York Tory, John P. de Lancey, who always insisted on a different version. De Lancey's daughter married James Fenimore Cooper, who many years later wrote a letter to the New York *Mirror* specifically to refute Ferguson's version. Ferguson had never seen Washington, but de Lancey had conversed and dined with him in Philadelphia in 1774 when Washington visited de Lancey's regimental mess. De Lancey, Cooper wrote, "to whom the person of Washington was so necessarily well known, constantly affirmed that his commander was mistaken. I have often heard Mr. De Lancey relate these circumstances, and though he never pretended to be sure of the person of the unknown horseman, it was his opinion from some particulars of dress and stature that it was the Count Pulaski."[9] But Patrick Ferguson went to his grave believing that he had spared the great Virginian, and the tale lives on.

Ferguson lost his rifles and his command. During his long recuperation and while he taught himself to write and fence and shoot with his left hand, the Commander in Chief in America, Sir William Howe, ordered the rifles put in storage and the men scattered throughout various light infantry units. Enthusiasts believe that Howe's act saved the Revolution. Stabler minds reject that fantasy. But almost all writers allege that Howe acted as he did because he resented the unit's being organized and assigned to him without his knowledge or approval, a fait accompli by the home authorities. If true, it would be neither the first nor last example of brass-hat pique combined with obtuse bureaucracy. But was Howe also unsettled by the unit's heavy casualties? And was he also aware that the rifle to which Ferguson gave his name had certain technical deficiences that made it unsuitable as a standard firearm for infantry battalions?

The English firearms expert J. N. George had actual personal experience in loading a Ferguson rifle. He stated that the "whole process of loading could be performed with surprising ease and speed when the rifle was in the hands of an expert." He believed that "the rifle was by reason of its greater accuracy, the ideal weapon for light troops moving in open order, and firing at long ranges, whilst the musket, with its greater stopping power, and its higher rate of fire, was of more use in close engagement between infantry battalions, or in repelling a charge of cavalry. Therefore, the most effective armament would consist of a combination of the two weapons, with the musket predominating, but with a sufficiency of rifles and (what was more important) of skilled riflemen, to eke out the smooth-bores when accurate shooting was called for." Note in both instances George's emphasis on the skill necessary to operate the rifle, and then consider the opinion of another English authority, Howard L. Blackmore: "The reader may well ask why, if the Ferguson rifle performed so well in its trials and in battle, no more were made or that the issue was not extended to other units. There were two main reasons. First there was an inherent weakness in the stock, which had to be cut away to take the plug housing at the very place where it was already narrow and liable to fracture; the result can be seen in some of the existing specimens which are cracked across the stock between the lock and the trigger guard. Secondly, the operation of the rifle required some skill and the standard cartridge could not be used."[10]

Thus the evidence is strong that the Ferguson rifles manufactured in 1777 lacked two vital requisites for a standard infantry weapon. Such a weapon must be rugged enough to withstand the misuse and abuse that in practice all such weapons undergo in the hands of average soldiers in the field. It also must be simple in operation, for as I have stated previously, few men, including soldiers, are firearms experts or skilled marksmen. I do not mean to imply by this discussion that armies never turn blind eyes to superior weapons or keep in service far too long weapons that have become obsolete. Of course they do. But such matters are often not as clear-cut as they appear.

In the months following Brandywine Ferguson found a sponsor. He gained the respect and confidence of Sir Henry Clinton, Howe's successor as commander in chief. Neither man was cut from the usual mold, both marched to their own drummers. Perhaps the older man recognized in the Scottish soldier a kindred spirit. Clinton, a highly intelligent man, would have appreciated another keen mind. Until Ferguson was fit for action, Sir Henry used him in intelligence work. But on 4 October 1778 Captain Patrick Ferguson again took the field, at Little Egg Harbor in New Jersey. With 300 men of the 70th Foot and the 3rd New Jersey Volunteers, the man with one good arm struck swiftly and burned ten large prize vessels, salt works, storehouses, and homes on a twenty-mile sweep along the Mullica River. When he returned to the mouth of the river he learned that the same Count Pulaski whom he may have mistaken for Washington at Brandywine was camped ten miles away with his legion of horse and foot. This unit was ill disciplined, and Pulaski, whose gallant death at Savannah a year later blinded posterity to his grievous faults as a soldier, on this occasion at least did not include camp security among the military virtues. Silently in the wee hours of 14 October Patrick Ferguson and 250 men rowed ten miles to Mincock Island and at 4 A.M. burst into the three houses in which the American infantrymen were sleeping, fell on them with bayonets, and killed at least fifty, including their commander, Lieutenant Colonel, Baron de Boze. Ferguson reported to Clinton that "It being a night attack little quarter could, of course, be given, so that there are only five prisoners." Sir Henry was delighted. Another Scottish officer took the long view: "These sort of things will never put an end to the war." Clinton continued to favor Ferguson. He had confidence in the Scot's "partisan abilities," and in 1779 sent him to supervise the rebuilding of the fortifications at Stony Point. Noted one observer, "Capt. Ferguson, a strange adventurer tho' a man of some genius—had undertaken to make that Post formidable in a short time."[11]

The relationship between Ferguson and Clinton became close enough for the younger man to write a series of letters to Sir Henry between August 1778 and March 1780 in which he went into considerable detail on operations, the Rebel army, and the British army, and recommended how the war could be won. He was right, especially given American conditions, on the virtues of light infantry fighting in open formation instead of the rigid close formations of the regiments of the line, and recommended that light troops make up half of the army. But his underestimation of the Continental Army—indeed, his contempt for it—led him to present the augmentation and increased use of light troops as a measure that the Rebels would be unable to counter, for "What could the rebels possibly oppose to this body of Chosen Soldiers." In common with his fellow officers, he placed great reliance on the bayonet, "the favorite arm of our soldiers," and claimed that the Continentals "have not as yet attain'd confidence enough to use Bayonets," which was no longer true. But his comment on the bayonet, and his conviction that the British had "gain'd that superiority in the woods over the Rebels which they once claimed," should be kept in mind by the reader as the story of Patrick Ferguson develops. Finally, he seriously advocated wholesale destruction of Rebel strongholds, beginning with New England. Then operations by "numerous Loyalists to the Southward" and "Indians from the Back settlements Added to the Terrors of the Example of New England, & of the fear of their own Slaves would probably bring about a thorough settlement in that feeble Province." Given his reputation among historians as a humane soldier, who is reported to have stated, "We came not to make war on women and children, but to relieve their distress," it is worth quoting him at some length on the subject.[12]

"Suppose the Army was to proceed through the Sound, destroy New Haven & the other nests of privateers on its way, then land in Connecticut, march 50 miles up the west Side of the river, endeavour to demolish Springfield 20 miles further up where there is a Magazine, etc., and destroy all the houses, grains & fodder throughout that fertile & populous tract—excepting the houses (but not the Crop or moveables) of known Loyalists. As the houses are of wood & the harvest now in, a lighted Straw would be sufficient at each settlement, & the Indian corn still being on the Ground might be consumed by the horses of the Army. After this . . . the Army might Cross the River, proceed in the same manner down the East side & thus in a fortnight ruin the Granary of New England."

Ferguson also suggested that while the Connecticut Valley was being burned "a part of the Strong Garrison at Rhode Island might in conjunction with the Navy endeavour to destroy New London" and thereafter the main army would enter Rhode Island and "burn Providence," then march north for the purpose of "demolishing the Town wharffs & Docks of Boston (whilst a Part of the reinforced garrison of Halifax with some Ships of War should create a Diversion by endeavouring to destroy the privateering Towns of New Salem, Marblehead & Cape Ann." Finally, the "Army might march back to Rhode Island . . . & lay waste a new Tract." He proposed to do all of this in autumn, "before the End of November," when the "consequences must prove very decisive, for the consumption and waste of both Armys, added to the burning of their Grains and depriving the Cattle of all means of Subsistance during the hard Winter of that Country, together the interruption of their Indian Corn harvest, must reduce to great want a people who have always found difficulty in subsisting without foreign supplys."[13]

Ferguson predicted no serious opposition, a dubious proposition given past British experience in the hinterlands. And his almost cavalier recommendation to burn and destroy on a wide scale and leave the populace to cope with a New England winter without food or shelter ran directly counter to the policy of the British government. Later in the war another British officer, Brigadier General Charles O'Hara, wrote to the Duke of Grafton that England had two choices: give up the fight or wage a "war of desolation, as every part of the Continent is exposed to invasion, where the object is only to Ruin and Devastate and not make Establishments—this idea is shocking to Humanity, but however dreadful it must be undertaken on the Principle that I am persuaded either this Country or England must be sacrificed." Ferguson was of the same mind: "It is by our

Exertions in America alone that the West Indies can be secured; & it is by our operations in the middle colonys only that we can continue in possession of Florida, Nova Scotia & Canada." O'Hara and Ferguson were referring to the view held by many Englishmen, including the king, that the loss of America would mean England's demise as a great nation. We know from our twentieth-century vantage point that they were wrong. And what Marlborough did to Bavaria in the early eighteenth century would not be countenanced in America by the king and his ministers. Scorched earth was simply not in the cards. The British government's long-run aim was reconciliation with a then overwhelmingly kindred people. The officer corps, especially the higher officers, felt the attachment, despite their haughtiness and disdain for colonials. Sir Henry Clinton's friend General William Phillips expressed a commonly held view when he wrote, "Here pity interposes, and we cannot forget that when we strike we wound a brother." Patrick Ferguson's grand plan of wholesale destruction for the reconquest of America was a pipe dream.[14]

In October 1779 Ferguson was promoted to major in the 2nd Battalion of Fraser's Highlanders, and he sailed with Clinton when the great British armada left New York harbor for the conquest of the Carolinas. He was in command of 300 of the best men of the New York and New Jersey Tory units. His command was among those ordered to march under General Patterson from Savannah to the approaches of Charleston. During the march Ferguson fell victim to "friendly fire." Tarleton's Legion infantry mistakenly attacked Ferguson's Volunteers in the night and he was stabbed with a bayonet in his good arm. He recovered without permanent damage to the left arm, but for a time was reduced to riding with the reins in his teeth. Major George Hanger wrote that the "Whole army felt for the gallant Ferguson."[15]

Ferguson was appointed Inspector of Militia by Clinton on 22 May 1780. This was the most difficult assignment of his career, and in fairness to Ferguson it should be emphasized that such an assignment to any officer in any age would be fraught with difficulties and peril. His job was to raise, equip, and train militia units from among men who had not performed well against the Rebels in 1775, and with them fight a partisan war in the semi-wild, inhospitable Carolina Back Country against guerrilla fighters who were cunning, tough, fast moving, sometimes savage, and often brilliantly led. In addition to the operational vicissitudes he faced, Ferguson's political situation was most awkward. Although there is in his behavior not a hint of disloyalty to Cornwallis, he was Clinton's protégé and not of the earl's inner circle. Cornwallis's attitude toward Ferguson's assignment was clearly unenthusiastic, and the commandant of Ninety Six, Nisbet Balfour, reinforced his doubts in a letter to the earl. "As to Ferguson, his ideas are so wild and sanguine . . . it would be dangerous to trust him with the conduct of any plan." But Ferguson's nickname was not Bulldog for nothing. His position was not enviable, but he persevered, determined to succeed.[16]

An ambitious man possessed of great energy and fervor, anxious to put his ideas to the test, Ferguson spent many hours recruiting and training Tory militia. He wore about his neck a silver whistle that he blew in various ways to in-dicate commands—bringing to mind the training of gun dogs. His provincial regulars, the American Volunteers, had socket bayonets for their muskets and were well trained in their use. But socket bayonets were of no use to those mili-tiamen armed with rifles. Ferguson therefore had them whittle down the han-dles of their knives in order that they might be stuck into the barrels of their rifles, just as seventeenth-century musketeers had done with their plug bayonets before the invention and adoption of the socket bayonet.

He immediately ran into serious problems. On 20 July 1780, he wrote to Cornwallis from his camp at Fair Forest Ford, known as a Tory stronghold: "There is great difficulty in bringing the militia under any kind of regularity. I am exerting myself to effect it without disgusting them, and, on the whole, not with effect." But he was overly optimistic. These men were of the same society as those who made up the Rebel militia; indeed, some had campaigned in South Carolina militia units against the Cherokee, and in one regiment were men who had served under the paroled Rebel leader Andrew Pickens. Their complaints against Ferguson's regimen have the same ring as those by Rebel militia the country over. Sometime at the end of the summer of 1780 Major Zachariah Gibbs of Ferguson's militia wrote his own letter to Cornwallis. "Since I received your Lordship's orders for that purpose, the summer has been little else but marching and countermarching, never two days calm space to mind our farms or any domestic comfort."[17]

Ferguson, sounding very much like a Continental officer, lamented such attitudes and the militia's lack of discipline. They were, he wrote to Lord Rawdon, "unaccustomed to military restraints & became so homesick" they would simply go home and leave him with much smaller units than he expected. Thinking that disgrace before their comrades would straighten them out, he had men who took French leave drummed out of camp with their heads shaved and without arms. It didn't work. He admitted that his regiments "would soon be-come very thin" if such punishment were taken against "every lad who left camp when the whim struck him." He then drew up a statement that he had six reg-iments sign declaring that a man who did not answer a call to arms "abandons the royal cause, & acts a treacherous part to the society in which he lives." It went on to denounce any man who was absent without leave "a worse traitor & enemy to his King and Country" than Rebels who violated parole.[18]

It is unlikely that this measure solved the problem. Tory or Rebel, militia would be militia, and despite his reputation as the one British officer who took the time to discuss the issues with the people of the Back Country, and despite his obvious dedication to his mission, Patrick Ferguson had yet to prove that he understood how to handle militia. They were not regulars and never would be, and attempts to train and discipline them in the manner of regulars were fruit-less. In a previous chapter we quoted William Richardson Davie on the Rebel militia attack on Hanging Rock: "in those times [it] was absolutely necessary" for the officers to explain to their men what was intended and obtain their approval, and in this case the partisans "entered into the project with great spirit and cheerfulness." It is impossible to envision any British officer, Ferguson not excepted, commanding in such a manner.

Ferguson did describe his men's better qualities, which "render them, when under a certain degree of discipline with a few real officers very fit for rough & irregular war, being all excellent woodsmen, unerring shots, careful to a degree to prevent waste or damage to their ammunition, patient of hunger & hardship & almost regardless of blankets, cloathing, rum & other indulgences"[19] so dear to the hearts of regulars. There is no reason to doubt this description of the Tory rank and file. They came of the same people as the Rebels, had endured the same daily Back Country hardships as their fellow Americans on the other side, had learned the same skills of survival. Yet in general they had not performed well in battle against the Rebels. I have already discussed superior Rebel leadership and their superb use of classic guerrilla tactics. Just as important was the zeal that animated the men who rode behind the Rebel chiefs. Physically tough the Tories might be, as inured to hardship in the field as their foes and as skillful with their weapons, yet from the beginning they had not shown in a consistent manner the moral qualities critical to a cause. Their counterrevolutionary fervor, shall we say, fell far short of the revolutionary fervor of their foes. There were exceptions, to be sure, but not enough to make an appreciable difference. And did the man who led them, Patrick Ferguson, truly understand irregular war? He claimed to, but up to the time that Cornwallis detached him to cover the army's left flank the conspicuous military successes in the country patrolled by his forces belonged to the Rebels.

Yet despite this lack of success, despite Cornwallis's misgivings, on 2 September 1780 Major Patrick Ferguson, some seventy of the American Volunteers, and several hundred Tory militiamen set out for western North Carolina and the foothills of the mighty Appalachians. Lieutenant Anthony Allaire maintained his diary of marches and countermarches and "getting in motion," and provided a graphic report of what kind of medical attention awaited the wounded of either side in the Back Country. At Wofford's iron works they met a "Rebel militia-man that got wounded in the right arm at the skirmish at Cedar Springs, the eighth of August. The bone was very much shattered. It was taken off by one Frost, a blacksmith, with a shoemaker's knife and carpenter's saw. He stopped the blood with the fungus of the oak, without taking up a blood vessel."[20] We can only assume that the Rebel's anesthetic was a liberal supply of whiskey. But given the state of surgery then and the resemblance of military field hospitals to slaughterhouses, the Rebel could have been in worse hands than Frost the blacksmith.

On 7 September Ferguson and his men crossed into North Carolina and marched to Gilbert Town, about 55 miles west of Charlotte, where Ferguson set up his base of operations. Lieutenant Allaire described it as containing "one dwelling house, one barn, a blacksmith's shop, and some out-houses."[21] Here, as our story proceeds, in the dark of night would occur a bloody deed in the savage Carolina conflict that in English we call civil war but is best expressed in the telling German word *Bruderkrieg* (brother's war).

Lieutenant Allaire presents a positive picture of the situation in that part of North Carolina. He describes a skirmish with Colonel Charles McDowell's band on Cane Creek, about twenty-two miles north of Gilbert Town, when forty American Volunteers and 100 militia finally came into contact with Rebels: "We totally routed ... those congress heroes. Our loss was two wounded and one killed."[22] Rebel accounts collected years after the skirmish claim that McDowell initiated the action and that several Tories were killed before the Rebels retreated; but Allaire's account was written immediately after, so let us give this one to the good Lieutenant in return for his months of fruitless tramping through the Carolina Back Country in search of "congress heroes." And it is a fact that after this action Charles McDowell and his men crossed the mountains and took refuge with the Over Mountain Men at the Watauga Settlements.

But though Allaire can be trusted as an eyewitness to a fight, his political acumen was not acute. Two days later he wrote that "the poor, deluded people of this Province begin to be sensible of their error, and come in very fast." What Lieutenant Allaire, and at least for a while Patrick Ferguson, did not know was that many if not most of the people coming in to take British protection and even to swear oaths of allegiance to George III were doing so as part of a deliberate Rebel policy to save the region's cattle herds. According to written statements made in 1797 by two prominent North Carolina militia officers, General Joseph McDowell and Colonel David Vance, both of whom participated in the campaign, Colonel McDowell, who was then in charge, suggested this trick to the leading men of the country. Some absolutely refused and instead drove all the cattle they could find to the heads of deep mountain coves. Others were prevailed on to follow McDowell's suggestion. In doing so they risked and often bore the brunt of public obloquy for their actions, for obviously this deliberate policy to deceive the British and save Rebel herds could not be shared with the populace lest leaks occur.

But Patrick Ferguson did begin to suspect that he was the victim of a ruse. His men were in need of meat, and so he took a force into the field to search for Rebel cattle. Accompanying him was the noted Indian fighter Captain—later Colonel—John Carson, one of the men who had agreed to Charles McDowell's policy. They found a large herd roaming in the cane-breaks. Ferguson's men assumed that the cattle belonged to Rebels and began slaughtering them. John Carson, who knew who owned the cattle, watched without comment until over 100 head had been slaughtered. Then he observed that it was possible that they belonged to three Tories who had joined Ferguson's force. The upshot of this incident was that the owners of the cattle, loyal Tories all, were incensed, the Rebels made sure that the story was spread abroad, and Patrick Ferguson realized that he had been outwitted. But John Carson's good name, temporarily sacrificed for the cause, was not easily recovered. Many years after the Revolution a man charged that John Carson had been a Tory. John

Carson's son, Samuel, a member of Congress, thereupon challenged the slanderer to a duel and killed him.[23]

Lieutenant Anthony Allaire also became aware that the countryside harbored people not "sensible of their error." On the 15th of September, with forty American Volunteers and a few hundred militia, he "got in motion" again, in one four-mile stretch found Cane Creek "so amazingly crooked that we were obliged to cross it nineteen times," and on the following day encountered a "very handsome place," still known as Pleasant Gardens, a settlement "composed of the most violent Rebels I ever saw, particularly the young ladies."[24] For despite the ability of Ferguson and his command to move at will through the countryside, despite numbers of people coming into Gilbert Town for protection, implacable enemies were everywhere in the Back Country, including militia bands to the north that had not yet even entered the main contest. They were located in Wilkes and Surry Counties on the upper reaches of the Yadkin River, under strong leaders, Colonel Benjamin Cleveland and Major Joseph Winston. And far to the northwest, deep in the Appalachians, 100 miles or so over the steep, tortuous trails of the Blue Ridge, were small bands of pioneers who had moved beyond where the British government had forbade them to go as early as 1763. They were the cutting edge of an irresistible flood of humanity driven by the twin hungers of land and opportunity. They were part of a vast folk movement to America that began prior to their coming and is still going on. One of their leaders, John Robertson, described their purpose with a candor rare and unfashionable in our times: "We are the Advanced Guard of Civilization; Our way is across the Continent." The British called them, among other things, Backwater men. They are known to history as the Over Mountain Men.

The Over Mountain Men

The men and women who were the Over Mountain People have been portrayed by uncritical patriotic writers as without exception stainless heroes and heroines, and by the hypercritical in our time as unprincipled aggressors and little better than savages whose sole legacies to the future were violence, bigotry, and ignorance. Both portrayals widely miss the mark.

Pioneering is a messy business; combined with conquest it is an ugly business and has been since human beings began coveting the property of others. We pay little attention today to the moral questions involved in similar folk movements that began before recorded time and have continued since. Like their predecessors throughout the world, eighteenth-century Over Mountain Americans were people living under vastly different assumptions than exist in America in the late twentieth century. The British novelist L. P. Hartley put it well: "The past is a foreign country; they do things differently there."[25] To which we may add that the further removed we are from want and danger, the more generous our consciences.

The Over Mountain People were largely Scotch Irish, but the mixing had already begun, for among them were sizeable numbers of English and some Germans and Welsh. At the time of which we write they lived in the extreme northeastern corner of what is now Tennessee, along the Watauga, Nolachucky, and Holston Rivers, where Tennessee, Virginia, and North Carolina meet. They were squatters on Cherokee land, for it was the official policy of the British government to keep white settlers east of the mountains, and to that end the Proclamation Line of 1763 was established. The line followed the watershed of the Appalachian Mountains. The country west of the line was Indian territory under the charge of the commander in chief of the British Army in America. That did not prevent sixteen families from North Carolina, led by James Robertson and his deputy John Sevier, from crossing the mountains and stopping their wagons on the banks of the Watauga River, at a beautiful spot called Sycamore Shoals (modern Elizabethton, Tennessee). There they established the Watauga settlements and leased two large tracts of land from the Cherokee.

It was all quite illegal. The Royal Governor of Virginia, Lord Dunmore, called it a "dangerous example,"[26] and from the British point of view, and the Cherokee, he was right. But who was going to do anything about it? Three years later the Watauga Association purchased their leased lands from the Indians, but other Cherokee, including young Dragging Canoe, vehemently objected. The subject of Indian land tenure, wellspring of historical and modern controversies, is not our concern. All we need know is that Dragging Canoe and several hundred warriors were back in July 1776, this time in war paint. But the besieged settlements, outnumbered and on their own, held; and from one fort Over Mountain riflemen sallied and in a hard fight on the South Fork of the Holston defeated the Cherokee.

The Indian threat would not end for several years. The bitter struggle in the Appalachians was a phase in a war that began in the early 1600s and lasted for almost three centuries: undeclared, unrelenting, unforgiving. The Over Mountain Man, hardened by the toil of pioneering, was further hardened by Indian fighting. His life could indeed be short, nasty, and brutal. But if he survived falling trees, fever, snake bites, drowning, disease, backbreaking labor, blood poisoning, and the scalping knife, he rode into a fight a warrior for the ages.

15

To Catch Ferguson

"The Sword of the Lord and of Gideon!"

On or about 10 September 1780 a lone rider headed west from Ferguson's camp at Gilbert Town and began the long climb from the foothills up one of the steep trails that climbed the great mountains to where the waters no longer ran east. He was probably in haste, and probably pushed his horse as fast as he could without its foundering. His name was Samuel Phillips. He was a Rebel who had been a British prisoner, but Patrick Ferguson had paroled him, for Samuel Phillips was a distant kinsman of Colonel Isaac Shelby, and he carried a message for Shelby and all the Over Mountain Men. Deadly in intent and import, the message had been given verbally to Phillips by Ferguson: "If they did not desist from their opposition to the British arms, he would march over the mountains, hang their leaders, and lay their country waste with fire and sword."[1]

Samuel Phillips made a beeline for Shelby's place, where he found his kinsman and delivered Ferguson's message. We described in an earlier chapter Shelby's proposition after the victory at Musgrove's Mill and the retreat of the Rebel band into North Carolina that a volunteer army from both sides of the mountains be raised to deal with Ferguson. We will never know whether this would have happened in a timely manner without Ferguson's threat. We do know that Isaac Shelby needed no further goad. A few days later he was about forty miles away, interrupting Colonel John Sevier at a horse race. It would have been hard to find two better men to command their respective militias than Isaac Shelby (1750–1826) and John Sevier (1745–1815).[2]

Shelby's father, Evan, was born in Wales in 1720 and was brought to America in about 1735 by his parents, who settled in western Maryland. Evan Shelby became a well-known pioneer and Indian fighter and eventually a general of militia. Isaac Shelby was second in command of his father's company at the famous battle of Point Pleasant (1774) against the Shawnee, and if he gained his

Isaac Shelby, by Matthew Harris Jouett, c. 1820
(Photo Courtesy Kentucky Historical Society.)

rank and position because of his father this was a case where nepotism was a positive factor. Isaac Shelby was an exceptional leader, and by the end of his life became one of the country's most admired men.

After the Revolution Shelby settled in Kentucky. He married Susannah Hart, daughter of Kentucky pioneers in April 1783; they had eleven children and lived together near Stanford, about forty miles south of Lexington, for forty-three years. In May 1792 Isaac Shelby became the first governor of Kentucky, and in that position the warrior showed himself an adept politician and wise statesman, as he kept the state on a true course at a time of conspiracies and shifting political currents and opportunism. During the War of 1812 he again served as governor and at the age of sixty-three once more went to war, personally leading the Kentucky militia to Detroit and the defeat of the British and Indians in the Old Northwest at the decisive Battle of the Thames. A few years later President

James Monroe wanted him as Secretary of War, but he declined because of his age. Isaac Shelby was partially paralyzed by a stroke in 1820, but his mental faculties remained unimpaired until, six years later, with only Susannah Shelby at his side, as he wished, another stroke killed him. All this, though, was in the future. Our story finds him returning home from Kentucky, where he was prominent in exploration and settlement, on hearing that Charleston had fallen. Arriving at his home on the Holston in July 1780, he found a message from Colonel Charles McDowell imploring him to bring men to the aid of the beleaguered Rebels on the eastern side of the mountains. Within a few days the twenty-nine-year-old Isaac Shelby was in the saddle again, with 200 mounted riflemen behind him. They were the men who followed him at Cedar Springs, they were the "yelling boys" Captain Abraham DePeyster heard at Musgrove's Mill.

John Sevier's grandfather was a French Huguenot who fled to London from Paris in the late seventeenth century. He married an Englishwoman named Smith and they had two sons, both of whom ran away to America when very young. One of them, Valentine, was John Sevier's father. After landing at Baltimore Valentine Sevier headed west and settled in Virginia's Shenandoah Valley not far from the present town of New Market. He married a Valley woman, Joanna Goade. Their son John Sevier was born in 1745, and in 1761 John married Sarah Hawkins. The precocious couple had at least six, perhaps seven, children by 1773, when John Sevier decided to seek fame and fortune over the mountains in the Holston country.

Sevier first settled six miles from Isaac Shelby, but later moved to the Watauga and Nolachucky settlements. He was at the siege of Fort Watauga in July 1776, and there according to legend met his second wife, Catherine Sherrill, who is said to have landed in his arms while running from Indians. Only a grump would bother questioning the tale, or other versions of it, and we do know that four years later, following Sarah's death, John Sevier married the woman known as Bonny Kate. John Sevier loved life's pleasures, but to his contemporaries he also seemed fearless in the face of danger. He was one of the Appalachian frontier's most effective Indian fighters, meeting the warriors in battle more than thirty times. His political life after the Revolution was equally turbulent, but much too complicted to detain us, as were his speculations in land, which was one of the forces that drove him. After his political fortunes sank as low as they could possibly go, they were rapidly repaired when he came to the support of the new Constitution. He was elected the first governor of Tennessee, 1796–1801, and served again as governor, 1803–1809, and was in Congress from 1811 to 1815. During this time he and Andrew Jackson became bitter political enemies. The end came for the old campaigner, I think fittingly, on 24 September 1815, in a tent on the banks of the Tallapoosa River in Alabama, where at age seventy he was a Commissioner appointed by President James Madison to fix the boundary between the Americans and his old enemies, the Creek Indians, and still engaged in the land game.

When Isaac Shelby arrived at the race and repeated Ferguson's message, John Sevier immediately agreed to raise his militia and, acting in concert with

Shelby, cross the mountains and attempt to take Ferguson by surprise. Both men also conferred with North Carolina militia officers under the command of Colonel Charles McDowell, who were among those who had taken refuge on the Watauga. Sevier and Shelby set the tone of the expedition by displaying a harmony of intent and action that was a model for independent military commanders engaged in a joint endeavor. They were both proud and ambitious men, but at this time of mutual peril to themselves and their followers the egocentric behavior that marred the career of Thomas Sumter was conspicuous by its absence. In addition to raising his own men, Sevier agreed to contact other officers from North Carolina and gain their participation. Shelby would do the same with Colonel William Campbell, the militia commander in Washington County, Virginia, who lived forty miles from him. All involved had to act quickly; before parting to carry out their respective tasks Shelby and Sevier set the date and place of rendezvous: 25 September 1780 at Sycamore Shoals. This left little time to prepare, at the most two weeks, probably somewhat less.

The participation of William Campbell and his militia was critical. Both Isaac Shelby and John Sevier had to leave enough fighting men behind to defend the settlements against an expected attack by the Cherokee, whose nearest towns were only eighty to 100 miles from the Holston and closer to the Watauga. Shelby wrote Campbell, explaining the mission and why the Virginians were needed. He sent his brother Moses with the message.

Like most men of the southern frontier and Back Country, William Campbell (c. 1745–1781) was descended from Ulster Protestants, who in 1726 emigrated to Lancaster County, Pennsylvania, and later followed the Great Wagon Road to the Shenandoah Valley.[3] His father Charles, who may have been born in Ulster, married the daughter of John Buchanan, Sr. Charles Campbell served as a militiaman in the company of Captain John Buchanan, and in 1752 became a captain himself. A prosperous farmer, he also engaged in exploration and the neverending American game of land speculation. His prosperity enabled him to give William a good education for the time and place: English, history, mathematics. But late in life Charles Campbell took to excessive drinking, which led to his death in 1767. William Campbell, his mother, and his three sisters then moved to the Holston country in the far mountains of Virginia.

Campbell as a young man was described by Lyman Draper as being about six feet two inches, muscular, with light colored hair, perhaps reddish, and bright blue eyes. He became a captain of militia and served in Lord Dunmore's War against the Shawnee, but his regiment was a day too late to participate in the Battle of Point Pleasant. In September 1775 he took his company of riflemen to Williamsburg, where it became a unit of the First Virginia Regiment commanded by Patrick Henry. There he met, courted, and married Patrick Henry's sister, Elizabeth. Between the end of 1775 and the summer of 1779 he was engaged in his private affairs and government activity not involving military action. Beginning that summer, however, he was active with his militia against uprisings by Virginia Tories. In April 1780 he succeeded Isaac Shelby's father, Evan, as Colonel of militia, and almost immediately took the field once again against

Tory bands, this time in North Carolina as well as Virginia. Later in the war, while serving as a Brigadier General of militia during the Virginia campaign, William Campbell was suddenly, as Draper recorded, "taken with a complaint in his breast" and died a few days later, 22 August 1781. He was thirty-six.

Isaac Shelby's letter arrived about the same time that Campbell returned from campaigning against Tories. Campbell declined to join Shelby and Sevier. He agreed that the British army had to be opposed, but replied that he would take his men to the Virginia–North Carolina line and meet Cornwallis there, a proposal that leaves one with little if any confidence in William Campbell's sense of strategy. Shelby immediately wrote again and sent his brother Moses off once more. He went into more detail and explained that two things had to be accomplished: a force strong enough to protect the settlements from Indian attacks had to be left behind, and a force strong enough to meet Ferguson in battle had to march east. Without Campbell's Virginians they could accomplish one mission but not both. Shelby also wrote to William Campbell's cousin and brother-in-law, Colonel Arthur Campbell, who was actually the top military officer of Washington County, and pleaded with him for aid. We do not know what passed between the two Campbells, but after consultation it was agreed on 22 September that the Washington County militia would march with the Over Mountain Men. On the same day the Campbells sent a courier with a message to that inveterate hater of Tories, Colonel Benjamin Cleveland, commander of the militia of Wilkes County, North Carolina, with whom the Campbells had cooperated in their campaign against the King's men. Cleveland was asked to gather his men and rendezvous in North Carolina at Quaker Meadows.

The deadline of 25 September was met. On that day a multitude gathered where the Watauga River at Sycamore Shoals ran swiftly over the rocks. John Sevier rode in from the Nolachucky with 240 riflemen, and Isaac Shelby from the Holston with another 240, and from just over the line in Virginia's Blue Ridge William Campbell with 200 men. Technically the Virginians were not Over Mountain Men, but only a pedant would insist on this. They were the same breed.

Their numbers were increased by Charles McDowell's 160 refugee militiamen from Burke County, North Carolina, already camped at Sycamore Shoals. McDowell was not there. He had ridden back over the mountains to spread the word that the Over Mountain Men were coming and that all good men should gather. Captain David Vance of the North Carolina militia dictated in 1795 a narrative of the campaign that gives the flavor as well as some details of the storm generated by Ferguson's march into the Back Country. Vance was a seasoned soldier. He had fought with the North Carolina Continentals at Brandywine, Germantown, and Monmouth. He had survived the terrible winter at Valley Forge, and as a militia officer had fought in two particularly vicious Back Country actions: Ramsour's Mill and Musgrove's Mill. David Vance recalled that "the orders given to the volunteers were to equip themselves as quickly as possible and have nothing to provide when they were called on to march, but to saddle their horses and march on the shortest notice. Those who could not go supplied those who could. . . . It was also announced to volunteers by the officers that a battle with Ferguson was determined upon, and that they might rely on a battle before they returned home."[4] On both sides of the mountains hard men were gathering.

At Sycamore Shoals Arthur Campbell arrived unexpectedly with another 200 Virginia riflemen, for on reflection he feared the force might be too small. He then returned to Virginia to guard a frontier braced for Indian attacks. Mingling on the broad flats by the singing river with the men chosen to ride against Ferguson were riflemen who would remain to man Fort Watauga, as well as many others come to spend a final night by the campfires: women, children, and men too old for the rigors of campaigning, there to see the riders off, praying they would see all of them again but knowing when they returned there would be empty saddles among the files of horsemen.

No time was wasted. They left the next day, Tuesday, 26 September 1780. But first, befitting a time and a community in which religion played a major role, with leaders of the expedition being Presbyterian Elders, a stern preacher, thirty-one-year-old Reverend Samuel Doak, of Ulster descent, Virginia born, Princeton graduate, sent the men on their way with a sermon taken from Gideon and the Midianites, ending it with a rousing cry, "The sword of the Lord and of Gideon!" To which the Over Mountain Men responded with a ringing shout, "The sword of the Lord and of our Gideons!"[5] Then, 1,040 strong, they rode out to catch Major Patrick Ferguson.

In common with the Back Country militia who joined them on the other side of the mountains, these frontier fighters neither had nor needed an administrative structure. The position of commissary so vital to regular armies was unnecessary, for each man was his own commissary. Each had a rolled blanket in which to sleep, a cup with which to drink, and a wallet or saddle bags filled with food, mainly parched corn meal mixed with maple sugar that could be eaten cold or warmed up with a bit of water. The horses were expected to find their own forage when hobbled during stops and at night. The Over Mountain Men were armed with tomahawks, and large knives for cutting, eating, fighting, and scalping. Across the pommels of their saddles rested their principal weapon, for which they were famous on two continents—the American rifle.

Long, slim, elegant, the American rifle at its best was a masterpiece of the gunsmith's craft. Deadly at 200 yards, in the hands of an expert marksman it was dangerous at 300 to 400 yards, although enemies were rarely taken under fire at those extreme ranges. Known since the early nineteenth century as the Kentucky rifle, very few were ever made in Kentucky. Most were crafted by Pennsylvania gunsmiths of German birth or descent. Those carried by the Over Mountain Men are often described as Deckhard rifles, but Deckhard is probably a corruption of the last name of Jacob Dickert of Lancaster, one of the most famous Pennsylvania German gunsmiths and renowned for the accuracy of his barrels. How many of the rifles carried by the Over Mountain Men actually had Dickert barrels we do not know. Since Lyman Draper used the term and had talked to survivors, the word Deckhard may have been current at the time and used generically to indicate the highest quality. In any case, the American rifle within very restricted circumstances was a fearsome weapon, and especially early in the war at the siege of Boston and the battles at Saratoga terrified British troops, who were unaccustomed to being shot from such great distances. The rifle was also very effective in several Back Country engagements.

But the American rifle had serious drawbacks as a weapon of war and played a minor role in the War of the Revolution. It was a hunter's weapon, perfectly adapted to its purpose, with a smaller caliber that enabled the rifleman to carry more ammunition on a long hunt. In contrast to the musket it was more fragile and it could not be used as effectively in extremity as a club. There was no way to attach a socket bayonet to defend oneself when the rifle was empty. It took a minute to reload, and in one minute on open ground a charging English or Hessian soldier armed with a bayoneted musket could cover a lot of ground. In skirmish lines on broken ground and from behind cover the rifle was a superb weapon, but out in the open riflemen unsupported by regular infantry trained to fire by volleys and fight with bayonets ran the risk of being run through once they had fired. Such seasoned and able American officers as Anthony Wayne and John Peter Muhlenberg preferred musketmen to riflemen for orthodox warfare. But the most authoritative word on the subject was given to Captain Joseph Graham in 1780 by the most famous rifleman of his time— Daniel Morgan. Referring to the Battle of Saratoga, Morgan told Graham that "my Riflemen would have been of little service if we had not always had a line of Musquet and Bayonette men to support us, it is this that gives them confidence. They know if the enemy charges them they have a place to retreat to and are not beat clear off."[6]

The Over Mountain Men, therefore, had to hope that they could catch Major Patrick Ferguson on ground suited to their style of warfare and the American rifle. But how likely was it that an officer of his experience would allow himself to be caught in such a situation?

The column climbed Yellow Mountain, following Gap Creek, crossed the Little Doe River, and camped that night at Shelving Rock on the Big Doe River. They covered about twenty miles that first day through snow "shoe-mouth deep."[7] Near their camp several horses were shod by a blacksmith named Miller, but many remained unshod; it was a problem that would plague them during the expedition. Ensign Robert Campbell, who kept a memorandum book of the march, wrote that "on the top of the mountain there was about one hundred acres of beautiful table land, in which a spring issued, ran through it, and over into the Watauga." Here the waters began running east, and at this place James Crawford and Samuel Chambers of Sevier's command deserted. It was immediately suspected that they were on their way to warn Patrick Ferguson, for Tories, though few, were not unknown on the frontier. The original plan to take the southern trail was, therefore, immediately changed, and the long column struck out on a northerly route. It was hard riding down very steep, often dangerous ravines through some of the continent's finest mountain scenery. From vantage points they could see ahead of them range after range of forested mountains shimmering in a slight haze. Many of the men from Shelby's and Sevier's regiments had returned the month before suffering from malnutrition. But once again they had answered the summons to action. Down those dark slopes with the nearly constant sound of rushing mountain streams on first one flank and then the other the long file of horsemen rode, tenacious in their resolve to catch Ferguson, through Gillespie's Gap from which they could see the valleys of the Catawba, down through the foothills into gentler country, and on to the rendezvous on 30 September at Quaker Meadows, the Back Country farm of the McDowells.

They received a warm welcome, and Charles McDowell's brother, Major Joseph McDowell, told them to use the rail fences for building cooking fires and for warmth at night. On the same day they were joined by the militia from Wilkes and Surry Counties, situated to the north in country drained by the Yadkin River. Three hundred and fifty strong, they were under the command of Colonel Benjamin Cleveland, all three hundred pounds of him, and Major Joseph Winston. Both were experienced and able men.[8]

Unlike many of his fellow commanders, Benjamin Cleveland (1738–1806) was uneducated, gross, and brutal. He and his men terrorized Tories in the Yadkin country by a simple expedient: the hangman's noose, used summarily and frequently. A little under six feet, he was in his prime, according to Draper, "finely proportioned," but as he grew older he became nearly as broad as tall. The Cleveland family, including Benjamin's father, John, emigrated from the district of that name in the North Riding of Yorkshire. His father was a house joiner who settled on Bull Run in Prince William County, Virginia, and married Martha Coffee. Benjamin Cleveland was born there.

When he was a child his parents and grandparents moved west near the Albermarle County line, and Benjamin grew up in a crude border environment. He married Mary Graves, who came from a well-established, somewhat affluent family. We can assume that she did not have an easy time of it, for Benjamin Cleveland remained primarily interested in gambling, horse racing, and running with the friends of his bachelor days. About 1769, however, he and his wife joined the Graves family in a move to the headwaters of the Yadkin in North Carolina, where his father-in-law's servants helped Benjamin establish a farm. But Cleveland also remained a hunter and Indian fighter, and with the coming of the Revolution his commanding presence and natural leadership abilities eventually projected him to command of the Wilkes County Militia.

During the ensuing years, the reputation he earned for cruelty and summary executions was not a myth. The most horrifying tale related by Draper concerns two Tories taken from a jailhouse, one of "whose crimes rendered him particularly obnoxious to the people." His end was quick and simple. They stood him on a log, put the noose around his neck, threw the end of the rope over a tree limb, fastened it, and kicked the log out from under him. Cleveland then fetched the other Tory and pointed to his dangling comrade, who may still have been kicking. Said Cleveland, "You have your choice, either to take your place beside him, or cut your own ears off and leave the country forever." The second Tory knew his man and called for a knife, "which he whetted for a moment on a brick, then gritting his teeth, he slashed off his own ears and left with the blood streaming down his cheeks, and was never heard of afterwards."

After the war Benjamin Cleveland lost his farm due to a defective title and moved to Oconee County, South Carolina, the very western tip of the state, where he squatted on land that was still Indian territory. His hanging days were not finished. When he captured the former Tory Henry Dinkins, a notorious white horse thief and plunderer who lived among the Cherokee, he hanged him on the spot, which made Benjamin Cleveland quite popular in the district. He served for many years as a judge, and a contemporary who knew him said that he spent most of his time on the bench snoozing while lawyers argued. He grew so large that he could no longer mount his horse, and the daughter of General Andrew Pickens, Mrs. Jane Miller, related, "We were always afraid when Colonel Cleveland came to stay overnight with us, lest the bedstead should prove unequal to his ponderous weight." He reached 450 pounds at his greatest, and although his weight decreased considerably in his last year, he was at the breakfast table when he died. Benjamin Cleveland, however, was not a comic character. He was a most effective guerrilla leader and a fearful man to have as an enemy.

His neighbor from Surry County, Joseph Winston (1746–1815), also had Yorkshire ancestors, although the family had first migrated to Wales before crossing the Atlantic and settling in Virginia. Aside from commanding presences and courage in battle, however, there was little similarity between the two men. Winston was a man of some education and formal manners. But this did not prevent him at the age of seventeen from joining a company of rangers during the French and Indian War. In a fight with Indians in 1763, in which several of his comrades were killed, Winston had his horse shot out from under him and was himself shot in the body and thigh. The rangers by then had scattered, so he hid until rescued by a faithful comrade who put young Winston on his back and carried him for three days until they reached safety. He carried the ball in his body for the rest of his life, and on occasion suffered from it. He settled in North Carolina in 1769, joined the militia, served in 1776 in the expedition that crushed the Tory Highlanders, and was with General Rutherford on an expedition against the Cherokee. He was active against the Tories in the North Carolina Back Country. After the war Joseph Winston became a successful politician; he was elected to three terms in Congress and eight times to the North Carolina Senate.

The Search Is Complicated by Politics

While the Over Mountain Men enjoyed at Quaker Meadows what was probably their most comfortable camp on the march to date, well to the east of them, in dense woods on the banks of the Catawba, a high-stakes drama was unfolding, whose outcome would be critical to their goal of catching Major Patrick

Ferguson. Colonel James Williams, who had fought at Musgrove's Mill, had taken the seventy prisoners from that fight to Hillsborough, North Carolina, where Governor John Rutledge of South Carolina had established his government in exile. According to Colonel William Hill of Thomas Sumter's command, Williams claimed all credit for the victory, whereupon Governor Rutledge promoted him to brigadier general of militia. Williams and Sumter did not get along and had previously clashed over supplies that Sumter and his officers claimed Williams had misappropriated for his own use. James Williams had his own band, but neither he nor any of his followers left records of this event or those that followed, so we must rely on the memoirs of William Hill, a loyal follower of Thomas Sumter to his final breath.

In September Colonel Williams rode into Sumter's camp on the Catawba, had his new commission read to the militia, and ordered them to form "under his immediate command." William Hill wrote that "much to his well deserved mortification they all to a man knowing his recent conduct in deserting his post and embezzling the public property as before mentioned refused to have anything to do with him or his commission and if he had not immediately left the camp he would have been stoned out of it." But a commission issued by Governor Rutledge could not be lightly dismissed, and the host assembled in the woods as a convention, as they had done when Sumter was chosen their leader, and voted to send a delegation to Governor Rutledge with a very simple message: they would serve only under Thomas Sumter. That canny politician made sure that the officers who constituted the delegation were his most loyal followers, and to further ensure his continued command he went with them to Hillsborough and gained a private meeting with the governor. Until the matter was settled, Colonel William Hill and Colonel Edward Lacey, both staunch Sumter men, were left in command.[9]

The delegation left the Catawba on or about 30 September, the day the Over Mountain Men and the North Carolina militia rendezvoused at Quaker Meadows; they arrived at Hillsborough on 4 October. Two days later Governor Rutledge commissioned Sumter a brigadier general and gave him command of all militia in South Carolina. Thomas Sumter had won the political battle, but the time taken to resolve it, and his decision to go to Hillsborough, meant that he missed one of the key battles of the War of the Revolution. Williams had not given up, however, and further mischief-making by him threatened to lead the operation astray.

As the political battle of which they were unaware was being waged, the combined force of 1,390 mountaineers and Back Country militia left Quaker Meadows on 1 October and marched eighteen miles south to a gap in South Mountain near the head of Cane Creek, where they camped that night and the next. There were now five colonels in camp but no commanding officer, for which the colonels felt a need. Most of the men might be seasoned fighters, but they were also militiamen, who were prey, noted Shelby, to "the little disorders and irregularities which began to prevail among our undisciplined troops," which is a sensitive understatement to describe some of the unruliest men in

America. This "created much uneasiness in the commanding officers—the Colonels commanding the regiments."[10]

They met that evening to discuss the situation. It was decided to send a messenger to General Gates at Hillsborough to ask for an officer to lead them. Their first choice was the celebrated Daniel Morgan, whom we have yet to meet. In the meantime, Shelby recalled, "we should meet in council every day to determine on the measures to be pursued, and appoint one of our own body to put them in execution." This presented two major problems: who was to be, as Shelby termed him, permanent officer of the day; and how much time could they afford to lose while they waited for a commanding officer to arrive? Isaac Shelby stated many years later that he was opposed to delay, "when expedition and dispatch were all important to us." He and the others were also opposed to the appointment as officer of the day the senior colonel among them, Charles McDowell, who was judged to lack the energy to lead the expedition. Although Shelby's recollections put him in a good light, they have not been challenged. The diplomacy, firmness, and good judgment he displayed years later as Governor of Kentucky during perilous times were already apparent in the thirty-year-old militia leader.[11]

Addressing the assembled colonels, Shelby argued that delay was fatal, especially if Ferguson was only some eighteen miles away in Gilbert Town, where they thought him to be. Since, he said, "we were all North Carolinians except Colonel Campbell, who was from Virginia; that I knew him to be a man of good sense and warmly attached to the cause of his country; that he commanded the largest regiment; and that if they concurred with me, we would, until a general officer should arrive from Head-Quarters, appoint him to command us and march immediately against the enemy. To this proposition one or two said, 'agreed,' No written minute or record was made of it. I made the proposition to silence the expectations of Col. McDowell to command us."

The ploy worked. Charles McDowell accepted the decision, but since he was not to command, he told the colonels, he would carry the message to General Gates and leave his brother Joseph in command of his regiment. Shelby, who was the best qualified to command, had maneuvered McDowell out of the job by handing it to Campbell, the least experienced of them all. It was, however, a nominal command, for Campbell, Shelby specifically noted, was "to be regulated and directed by the determinations of the Colonels, who were to meet in council every day." Shelby had also convinced his comrades that they could tarry no longer. They headed south toward Gilbert Town in search of Ferguson. William Campbell was commander in name, but Isaac Shelby was the driving force.

The man they sought was not at Gilbert Town. On 27 September, the day after the Over Mountain Men left Sycamore Shoals, Ferguson had begun withdrawing in a southerly direction. Word had come to him of the Rebel force moving over the mountains, although he did not yet have details. He had also received a message from John Harris Cruger that Elijah Clarke on his withdrawal after the siege of Augusta was heading in his direction. Ferguson hoped to waylay Clarke, and on the 30th, wrote Anthony Allaire, Ferguson's force "lay at James Step's with an expectation of intercepting Col. Clarke on his return to the mountains; but he was prudent enough to take another route."[12] On the same day the deserters from Sevier's regiment, James Crawford and Samuel Chambers, reached Ferguson and reported the rapid approach of the Over Mountain Men, their numbers, and their intent.

Ferguson then realized the seriousness of his situation, but he waited three days to send a message to Lord Cornwallis informing him that he was moving "toward any reinforcement that your Lordship may send."[13] He entrusted his dispatch to Abram Collins and Peter Quinn, inhabitants of the region, and told them to make haste. But Rebels at a house at which the couriers ate became suspicious of their desire to eat and run and followed them, and Collins and Quinn were forced to take evasive action that led to considerable delay in their journey. By the time they reached Cornwallis the issue had been decided. In the meantime, on Sunday, 1 October, Ferguson and his column "got in motion at five o'clock in the morning and marched twelve miles to Denard's Ford of Broad River."[14] From there, on that day, Patrick Ferguson issued his famous appeal to the men of North Carolina:

Gentlemen: Unless you wish to be eat up by an inundation of barbarians, who have begun by murdering an unarmed son before his aged father, and afterwards lopped off his arms, and who by their shocking cruelties and irregularities, give the best proof of their cowardice and want of discipline; I say, if you wish to be pinioned, robbed, and murdered, and see your wives and daughters, in four days, abused by the dregs of mankind—in short, if you wish or deserve to live, and bear the name of men, grasp your arms in a moment and run to camp.

The Back Water Men have crossed the mountains; McDowell, Hampton, Shelby, and Cleveland are at their head, so that you know what you have to depend upon. If you choose to be pissed upon by a set of mongrels, say so at once, and let your women turn their backs upon you, and look out for real men to protect them.

Pat. Ferguson, Major 71st Regiment[15]

The results were much less than he hoped for, and one wonders if the tone and language of his dramatic appeal frightened more than steeled men. Did they really wish to confront barbarians running around the countryside lopping off people's arms? Which was more important, their limbs or their womens' virtue? Perhaps the best policy was to lay low and see which way the wind blew. The allegiance of many was lukewarm regardless of the side they professed to be on, and there were others throughout the Back Country who fit the description of a man who lived near King's Mountain, one Solomon Beason, "half-Whig, half-Loyalist, as the occasion required." Ferguson turned east and marched down the left bank of the Broad, toward Charlotte and Cornwallis's encampment. On Monday, 2 October, he marched only four miles, but the next day the column "got in motion at four o'clock in the morning" and covered twenty miles to a place near Tate's Plantation, where Ferguson camped for two days.[16]

The Over Mountain Men and their Back Country comrades were not far behind but unsure of either Ferguson's exact location or his destination. On Wednesday, 4 October, they camped near Gilbert Town. A reinforcement of thirty mounted Georgian partisans from Elijah Clarke's band rode into camp to join whatever action was contemplated against Ferguson. But first the elusive Scot had to be found. Various sources in the area reported that Ferguson was fifty to sixty miles south and on his way to Ninety Six. South they kept going then, following Ferguson's route, and on the way they were joined by Major William Chronicle from the South Fork of the Catawba; behind this "young man of great promise" rode twenty South Fork Boys. At some point, perhaps with Chronicle's band, James Collins and his comrades joined the Over Mountain Men's column. Young James gave a clear explanation of their motivation: "Our danger began to increase. Ferguson was coming on with his boasted marksmen, and seemed to threaten the destruction of the whole country. The Tories were flocking to his standard from every quarter, and there appeared very little safety for us; but as God would have it a patriotic party sprang up. . . . As they advanced their numbers kept augmenting: our chance at safety was to join, if possible, the advancing patriots. We fell in their rear, took their trail, and pushed on till we overtook them without being intercepted."[17]

At Denard's Ford on the Broad, where Ferguson had turned east, the Rebel column lost the trail and continued south. They still thought that Ferguson was headed for Ninety Six. Their belief was fortified on 5 October when General James Williams and Colonel Thomas Brandon of South Carolina intercepted the column between Gilbert Town and Alexander's Ford on the Green River. Williams and Brandon had ridden in from Thomas Sumter's camp, and they introduced a brand of military politics that made the question of who would command the Colonels' regiments appear simple.

Thomas Sumter's command of 400 men was then camped at a place called Flint Hill, several miles northeast of Gilbert Town. Sumter's men knew that the Over Mountain Men were on the march. We had left Patrick Ferguson on the 3rd and 4th of October some twenty miles to the east, camped at Tate's Plantation. There was a Rebel spy in Ferguson's camp, an old man who learned that Ferguson intended to fight and had sent a message to Cornwallis asking for reinforcements. On the night of 4 October the old man set out for Sumter's camp, arrived the next morning, and told Colonels Hill and Lacey what he had learned. Privy to the same information, that day James Williams and Thomas Brandon slipped out of camp. Brandon, the reader will recall, was that tough Tory-hater with whom sixteen-year-old Thomas Young had gone to war in the spring of the year.

Their absence was noted, and Colonel Hill was told they were seen taking a trail toward the mountains. They returned after sunset and were immediately interrogated—not too strong a term—by Colonel Hill. He learned that they had met the column of Over Mountain Men and North Carolina militia and had arranged a rendezvous with Sumter's South Carolinians at the old iron works well to the south on the Pacolet River in South Carolina, on the way to Ninety Six. According to Colonel Hill, a heated exchange took place. He wrote that "I then used the freedom to tell him [Williams] that I plainly saw through his design, which was to get the army into his own settlement, secure his remaining property, and plunder the Tories." Williams retorted that it was up to the North Carolinians to worry about Ferguson; South Carolina must look out for itself. Hill was having none of that parochial attitude and immediately set out to correct Williams's mischief. As he was still suffering from the severe arm wound he had received at the fight at Hanging Rock, he asked Colonel Edward Lacey to make the dangerous night ride, find the other column, and inform them of Ferguson's true whereabouts.[18]

Lacey was the man who had ordered his Tory father tied to his bed before the successful attack on Captain Christian Huck, and he now showed the same decisiveness and resolve. Taking a guide who knew the country, he set out at 8:00 o'clock that evening. Twice on the way, when they got temporarily lost, Edward Lacey thought the guide might betray him and pulled his pistol, cocked it, and threatened to kill the man; but the guide convinced Lacey of his innocence and after some eighteen to twenty miles on the trail they arrived at the campsite on the Green River in the wee hours of Friday, 6 October. Now it was Colonel Lacey's turn to come under suspicion. He was blindfolded and led to the colonels. He introduced himself but they had no knowledge of him. As his guide had convinced him, Lacey finally convinced the colonels that James Williams had lied to them, Ferguson was to the east headed in the direction of Charlotte, and speed was of the essence before Ferguson could be reinforced by Cornwallis. The colonels were won over by Lacey. It was agreed that the combined forces would meet that evening at a place well known to all, the Cowpens, just over the South Carolina line. It was still dark when Edward Lacey swung back into the saddle to retrace his route to the South Carolinians' camp at Flint Hill.

The Scent Grows Warm

As circumstances would have it, the Over Mountain Men and their Back Country allies were ready for a forced march. Thursday, 5 October, had been a low day. Horses were beginning to give out, men on foot were lagging, discouragement appeared among some. Undoubtedly there was grumbling. Ferguson was said to be some fifty miles ahead, and Ninety Six was at least another fifty miles beyond. Despite their individual fighting prowess, we must always keep in mind that these were militiamen, often creatures of the moment. In common with their militia comrades the country over they felt free to express their displeasure and ask aloud whether the game was worth the candle. The Over Mountain Men among them carried the burden of wondering about the well-being of their families beyond the mountains. How long could they afford to stay away from home? Would ashes and corpses instead of cabins and loved ones greet them on their return? The colonels knew their men well and moved quickly to maintain a sense of purpose. They spent the night at Alexander's Ford selecting the fittest men and horses and chose about 700 riders for a forced march. Captain David Vance of the North Carolina militia said that orders were given to those unable to undertake a "severe march" for any reason to "fall back into the foot troops and give their horses to footmen . . . a number of exchanges were made." The colonels were probably still engaged in selecting the fittest when Edward Lacey rode into their camp, for "there was mighty little sleep that night," an old soldier named Continental Jack reminisced sixty-four years later. The officers left in charge of the men on foot and riders with the weaker horses were urged to come on with their men as fast as possible. Then, as first light revealed the dark shapes of the hills around them, the 700 picked riders rode off with their colonels to rendezvous with the South Carolinians at Cowpens twenty-one miles away.[19]

While the 400 South Carolina horsemen camped at Flint Hill waited for Colonel Lacey's return, James Williams continued his efforts to lead the force to Ninety Six. On the morning of 6 October he circulated throughout the camp and ordered men and officers to prepare to march to the old iron works on the Pacolet. Right behind him walked Colonel William Hill, countermanding his order. Colonel Hill instructed those who agreed with him to form to the right, and those, in Lyman Draper's words, "who preferred to plunder rather than courageously to meet the enemy to form a line on the left." An overwhelming majority formed to the right. On Colonel Lacey's return at ten o'clock that morning the South Carolinians marched for Cowpens. James Williams and his few followers brought up the rear, although Colonel Hill had told him to "absent himself and not attempt to march with us or the North Carolinians, as the consequences would be serious." Sumter's men, however, merely expressed their animosity toward the outcasts by shouting insults and throwing stones at them during the march.[20]

With Williams and Brandon was 16-year-old Thomas Young, already a veteran. He continued to serve with distinction and left us his account of the upcoming battle but not, unfortunately, his viewpoint of the struggle for control of the command. Another youngster we have already met who provided memoirs of the campaign was that other seasoned fighter of sixteen, James Collins. He served under Major William Chronicle, and tells us that "The pursuing army had not a single baggage wagon or any kind of camp equipage; everyone ate what he could get, and slept in his own blanket, sometimes eating raw turnips, and often resorting to a little parched corn, which by the by, I have often thought, if a man would eat a mess of parched corn and swallow two or three spoonfuls of honey, then take a draught of cold water, he could pass longer without suffering than with any other diet he could use."[21] And we will meet another teenage soldier, Robert Henry, one of Billy Chronicle's South Fork Boys. He too was sixteen, and he left us a bloody tale of hand-to-hand combat.

The colonels' column arrived at Cowpens after sunset on 6 October. The South Carolinians under Hill and Lacey arrived either just before or just after them. Cowpens, as the name implies, was a place where cattle were penned and fattened prior to their being herded to the coast for sale and slaughter. A rich English Tory named Saunders carried on a thriving business at Cowpens, and on that night he probably received the fright of his life, for David Vance said that the Rebels "came to a Tory's house, pulled him out of bed, treated him roughly, and asked him at what time Ferguson has passed."[22] Saunders swore that Ferguson had not passed and they could hang him if any track was found. Scouts were sent out to look but none was found and Saunders was spared. But not his cattle or his corn. Fresh beef, especially, was too good to pass up. Silas McBee, a local boy raised on Thicketty Creek, then a fifteen-year-old South Carolina militiaman, told Lyman Draper in 1842 that several head were slaughtered and in ten minutes fifty acres of corn harvested. Cooking fires brightened the broad, open land. But the men could not tarry. They had to catch Ferguson before he could be reinforced or reach the safety of Cornwallis's lines.

A Rebel spy, Joseph Kerr, who had been crippled from infancy, had made his own forced march and entered the Rebel camp at Cowpens that night. He reported that he had been in Ferguson's noon camp at Peter Quinn's place, some seven miles from King's Mountain, that Ferguson had no more than 1,500 men, and that he intended to be at King's Mountain that evening. The colonels sent out a scout to gain more intelligence, but Kerr's remained as up to date as they could get that night. At a council they decided to pare their "flying column," as William Hill called it, even more and set out almost immediately due east, toward Charlotte. General James Williams was not allowed to attend the council, but he and his men were permitted to join the little army.

The flying column consisted of 910 picked horsemen: the 700 chosen at Green River, and another 210 from the South Carolinians who joined them at Cowpens. By commands it broke down as follows: Campbell's Virginians, 200; Shelby, 120; Sevier, 120; Cleveland, 110; McDowell, 90; Winston, 60; Hill and Lacey, 100; Williams, 60; and 50 men under Colonel William Graham and Lieutenant Colonel Frederick Hambright, the latter a fifty-three-year-old veteran fighter of German birth. Major William Candler's thirty Georgians were apparently attached to Williams's command, and Major William Chronicle's twenty South Fork Boys to Graham's. About fifty footmen caught up with the riders and took part in the battle. The horsemen were almost evenly divided between Over Mountain Men (440) and Back Country militia (470). They began their march about 9 o'clock on the night of their arrival at Cowpens. It was very dark, and soon there began a rain that alternated between drizzle and downpour and persisted well into the next day. They were about thirty-three miles from the mountain called King's.[23]

In the meantime Major Patrick Ferguson had made his decision. Anthony Allaire's diary carries a succinct entry: "Friday, 6th. Got in motion at four o'clock in the morning, and marched sixteen miles to Little King's Mountain, where we took up our ground." Ferguson had sent a message that day to Cornwallis.

> My Lord: A doubt does not remain with regard to the intelligence I sent your Lordship. They are since joined by Clarke and Sumter—of course are becoming an object of some consequence. Happily their leaders are obliged to feed their followers with such hopes, and to flatter them with accounts of our weakness and fear, that, if necessary, I should hope for success against them myself; but numbers compared, that must be doubtful.
>
> I am on my march towards you by a road leading from Cherokee Ford, north of King's Mountain. Three or four hundred good soldiers, part dragoons, would finish the business. *Something must be done soon.* This is their last push in this quarter, etc.
>
> Patrick Ferguson[24]

A strange message. Contempt for the enemy on one hand, confession of their strength on the other. He hopes for reinforcements so he can give battle, and admits that success without them is doubtful. The prudent course would have been to retire within Cornwallis's lines at Charlotte, and to me that is clearly what his message implies. Yet he did exactly the opposite. He sent two copies of the message. One never got through, the other was much too late.

Patrick Ferguson decided to make a stand atop King's Mountain. Tradition has it that Ferguson declared "He was on King's Mountain, that he was king of that mountain, and God Almighty could not drive him from it."[25]

16

King's Mountain

"I will . . . follow Ferguson into Cornwallis' Lines"

The "flying column" did not get off to an auspicious start that very dark and rainy night. The men guiding Campbell's Virginians got confused, then lost. Silas McBee told Draper the road was "pretty good," but Colonel William Hill in his *Memoirs* claimed the "path being small & the woods very thick the troop got scattered and dispersed through the woods, thus wandering the whole night." By morning the tail of Campbell's column was only five miles from Cowpens. At dawn those who had kept to the path missed the Virginians and sent scouts in all directions. They found Campbell and his men and put them right, but their false start, according to William Hill, "caused them to march uncommonly hard which caused many horses to give out as but few of them were shod." But the long column pushed on, too close to the goal to be denied.[1]

The colonels had intended to ford the Broad River at Tate's Crossing, the most direct route, but on reflection decided that was unwise and angled a bit to the south, downriver about two and one-half miles toward Cherokee Ford. They remained cautious. The column stopped in the hills near the river. In the ranks of Major William Chronicle's South Fork Boys was an intrepid and talented scout by the name of Enoch Gilmer. Chronicle described him as a "stranger to fear." What made him even more valuable was his ability to act any part, "cry and laugh in the same breath," or convince those who knew him best that he had gone stark raving mad. Shrewd, cunning, talented, and brave, Enoch Gilmer was sent out alone while the others waited and gave their horses a much-needed rest. It was still raining and the officers reminded the men to keep their rifles dry, which was undoubtedly obvious to the riflemen, but officers will be officers. Gilmer was gone a long time, according to David Vance, "when his voice was heard in the hollow singing Barney-Linn, a favorite blackguard song. This was notice that all was right." The sun was just rising over the

225

hills as the column reached the ford and began crossing. It was deep at that point but there were no mishaps. The riders had come eighteen miles from Cowpens. They were about fifteen miles from King's Mountain.[2]

Enoch Gilmer was sent out again and went off at a gallop. The column rode slowly. The men grew restless. Curses ripped the air. They had come to fight Ferguson. Where was he? Let's have the battle and be done with it. Three miles from Cherokee Ford they made a brief stop for a meager snack, then pushed on, harvesting a cornfield on the way to sustain themselves and their horses on the raw kernels. The rain was now coming down heavily, and Campbell, Sevier, and Cleveland decided a halt was needed. They told Shelby and the real commander of the expedition gave them the rough side of his tongue. "I will not stop until night if I follow Ferguson into Cornwallis' lines."[3] Silently, the three colonels turned their horses away and took their places at the heads of their regiments, and the column rode slowly on. The men used any means to keep their rifles dry in the downpour, some even removing their hunting shirts and wrapping them around the locks. In the long run the rain was an ally, for the red earth of the Piedmont was too wet to raise tell-tale dust clouds over the horsemen. They came to the house of Solomon Beason, whom we described earlier as "half-Whig, Half-Loyalist, as occasion required." Ferguson, they learned, was eight miles ahead. At Beason's they captured two Tories who were given a simple choice: guide us to King's Mountain or die. One joined Shelby, the other Cleveland. About noon the rain stopped and a cool breeze rose. Five miles past Beason's house some men at the house of a Tory told them that Ferguson was not far away. A girl followed a few of Sevier's men out of the house. Alexander Greer recalled her asking:

"How many are there of you?

"Enough to whip Ferguson if we can find him."

The girl pointed to a ridge three miles away. "He is on that mountain," she said.[4]

Farther down the road Enoch Gilmer's horse was spotted tied to a gate before a house. The officers leading the column galloped to the place and rushed into the house. Enoch Gilmer sat at the table eating, served by two women. Wiliam Campbell, who carried a rope with a noose, shouted, "You damned rascal, we have got you!" Enoch Gilmer played his role to the hilt: "A true King's man, by God!" Whereupon Campbell threw the noose around Gilmer's neck. Gilmer cried and begged for mercy. Campbell swore he would hang him from the gate. The two Tory women began to cry. William Chronicle intervened. Not at the gate, he begged Campbell, for then the rascal's ghost would haunt the poor women. From the nearest overhanging limb on the road then, said Campbell, and Gilmer was pulled from the house, still crying and begging for his life. Down the road and out of sight of the terrified Tory women, Enoch Gilmer told what he had learned. He had arrived at the house and identified himself to the women as a King's Friend who wished to join Ferguson, and when they told him that they too were loyal to George III he gave each of them a kiss. That very morning, the younger woman told him, she had taken some chickens to Ferguson himself, who was camped on a ridge between two streams where deer hunters had camped in the autumn of the previous year. Major Chronicle and Captain John Mattocks immediately identified the camp as theirs and said that Ferguson was on a spur of King's Mountain.[5]

The officers rode off a ways, conferred, and agreed on a very simple plan. They would surround the hill and attack. Since the riflemen would be firing up-hill, there would be no danger of men being hit by friendly fire. The officers explained their proposal to the men and got their approval. Given their grousing earlier in the day, they probably would have approved any reasonable plan just to get the whole thing over. The column pushed forward, the officers deciding among themselves as they rode the positions that each regiment would take around the mountain.

In the midst of these preparations for battle, as the long column of travel-stained riders closed in on their prey, a very human drama was playing out. Colonel William Graham, who had served well in past actions, asked of Colonel Campbell permission to leave the column. He said he had just received word that his wife was "dying of colic about sixteen miles off near Armstrong's Ford on the South Fork." Campbell was not enthusiastic and urged Graham to stay, and if they won the battle he could carry the news to his wife, which would be "as good as a dose of medicine." But Graham persisted in his desire to leave. "Oh my dear, dear wife. Must I never see her again?" Campbell became angry. He asked William Chronicle, also from the South Fork, if he should grant Graham leave. Chronicle said, "It is woman's business, let him go." Then Colonel Graham said that he needed an escort and chose David Dickey. "Dickey said he would rather be shot than go. Chronicle said—'Dave, you must go.' Dickey said he would rather be shot on the spot." But he had second thoughts about that, and obeyed Chronicle: "'But if I must go, I must go, I must.' They immediately disappeared into the woods." But the tale of Colonel William Graham and his behavior that day was not finished.[6]

By seniority Lieutenant Colonel Frederick Hambright should have taken Graham's place, but he did not object to relinquishing command to Major William Chronicle because the latter knew the ground. Chronicle called out, "Come on, my South Fork boys," and led them on the trail to Ferguson.[7]

Colonel Sevier had men in advance, and a few miles from King's Mountain they captured some Tories on a scout. Under questioning they not only corroborated what Enoch Gilmer had learned of Ferguson's position but also revealed the locations of his pickets. Next they captured a fourteen-year-old boy, John Ponder, who was mounted and riding hard with a dispatch from Ferguson to Cornwallis asking for immediate reinforcement. Young John Ponder was asked how Ferguson was dressed and said that he wore a checked shirt, or duster, over his bright red uniform coat. The German-born Frederick Hambright then said to the men, "Well, poys, when you see dot man mit a pig shirt on over his clothes, you may know who him is, and mark him mit your rifles."[8]

Final verification that Ferguson had not left his position was made one mile from King's Mountain when the van of the column met a Rebel, George Watkins, who had been taken prisoner by Ferguson and then paroled. Ferguson and his men were still on the mountain, Watkins told them. Up to this point the riflemen had been marching as they pleased, but now the colonels decided that strict march discipline was in order. The horsemen were formed into two parallel columns, each being a column of twos; Campbell led the right column, Cleveland the left. From this point there would be absolutely no talking, and the order was obeyed. Often fractious militia they might be, but they were also veteran Indian or guerrilla fighters who knew what was at stake. They had set out to catch Ferguson, and at last, after twelve days on the trail, it seemed that they had caught him.

The silent columns wended their way over broken, rain-soaked country, across Ponder's Branch, past King's Creek, "up a branch and ravine between two rocky knobs, beyond which the top of the mountain and the enemy's camp upon it were in full view, about a hundred poles in front." At 3 o'clock on Saturday afternoon, 7 October 1780, behind trees on the east side of King's Creek, the long columns of horsemen halted. A few quiet orders were given: "dismount and tie your horses . . . take off and tie up great coats, blankets, etc., to your saddles." The horses of the rank and file were put in charge of a few guards, but in the manner of the time the officers led their men into battle on horseback.[9]

Young James Collins remembered that "we were paraded and harangued in a short manner on the prospect before us. The sky was overcast with clouds, and at times a light mist of rain was falling; our provisions were scanty, and hungry men are apt to be fractious; each one felt his situation; the last stake was up and the severity of the game must be played; everything was at stake—life, liberty, property, and even the fate of wife, children and friends seemed to depend on the issue: death or victory was the only way to escape suffering."[10]

All cowards were invited to leave. No one moved, although James Collins later admitted that he would "willingly have been excused . . . but could not well swallow the appelation of coward," thus putting his finger on the primary motivator of men about to go into battle. The final general order was issued: "Fresh prime your guns, and every man go into battle firmly resolving *to fight till he dies.*" Silently, swiftly, the wet leaves underfoot making no sounds, the grim host moved out to their assigned positions around King's Mountain. They had been given a countersign. The choice was ominous—Buford![11]

"We were a formidable flock of blue hen's chickens of the game blood"

On the mountain Captain Alexander Chesney (1755–1845) of Daniel Plummer's Fair Forest Regiment of Tories had mounted his horse and was out inspecting the pickets, making sure they were alert. He saw and heard nothing that gave him cause for concern. Chesney was one of the Scotch Irish who had remained loyal to the crown. He was a local man, his family's 400-acre farm about twenty-four miles to the southwest of King's Mountain as the crow flies. Chesney's tour of inspection should not have taken a great deal of time, for King's is not really a mountain. It is part of a range of hills about sixteen miles long extending from North Carolina into South Carolina. Some thirty miles to the east, a day's march, was Charlotte, where Ferguson had he chosen could have found refuge with Cornwallis and the British army. Ferguson and his men were on a ridge that rises about sixty feet above the countryside. The ridge, roughly shaped like a human foot, is about 600 yards long at its crest. The width at the crest ranges from about sixty yards at the southwest heel of the foot to about 200 yards at the northeast ball of the foot. The crest was then clear of trees and undergrowth. The sides of the ridge were then as now heavily wooded, steep, and rocky, terrain made to order for irregulars experienced in guerrilla and Indian fighting. There is a military principle that one should always take the high ground. There is another military principle that tactics for each occasion depend on the situation and the terrain. Whatever Patrick Ferguson thought about the situation, in choosing King's Mountain he obviously decided that the terrain was in his favor.

Ferguson's force had been camped at the ball of the foot since the previous day. The baggage wagons had been brought up and the men had pitched their tents. They were apparently resting or engaged in normal camp chores. Although British sources maintained then and since that Ferguson was heavily outnumbered by the Rebels, that was not the case. The truth is the British had an edge, with some 1,125 men, according to Ferguson's morning report. The Americans numbered between 900 and 1,000. Although we Americans habitually use the word British, there was only one British national at the Battle of King's Mountain—the Anglicized Scotsman Major Patrick Ferguson. This would be *Bruderkrieg* with a vengeance. Nor were there, as romantics claim, Highlanders or pipers at King's Mountain on either side.

Although Ferguson had been on the ridge long enough to build stout breastworks and redoubts from stones and logs had he wanted to, he had not taken that elementary precaution. Discipline and cold steel would carry the day if the "mongrels" chose to attack him.

They not only so chose, they caught him by surprise. Over 900 Rebels slipping through the woods almost reached the base of the ridge before Shelby's men were detected. Alexander Chesney wrote that "I was in the act of dismounting to report that all was quiet and the pickets on the alert when we heard their firing about half a mile off."[12]

The Rebel columns had split to carry out their intention of surrounding the foe. At the southern base of the ridge near the heel were Campbell's Virginians; next to them and stretching in order to the toe of the foot were the men of McDowell, Winston, and Hambright and Chronicle. Opposite Campbell's position on the northern side of the ridge were Sevier, then Shelby, followed by Williams, Lacey, and Cleveland, the latter linking with Hambright and Chronicle at the toe of the ridge. The regiments at the toe had the farthest to go to get into position, and some were about ten minutes short of their starting points when the fighting began.

The battle was notable in that once it commenced no one on the Rebel side was in overall command. The simplicity of the plan and its execution were described by Colonel William Hill. "There was very little military subordination as all that was required or expected was that every Officer & man should ascend the mountain so as to surround the enemy on all quarters which was promptly executed." Thomas Young recalled that "the orders were at the firing of the first gun for every man to raise a whoop, rush forward, and fight his way as best he could." Young's fellow teenager, James Collins, had "come to this conclusion: never to retreat alone, shoot without an object, or lay down my gun until the last extremity; for, I thought, a gun, though empty, might keep an enemy at bay." He continued, "We were soon in motion, every man throwing four or five balls in his mouth to prevent thirst, also to be in readiness to reload quick."[13]

The attack was begun by Shelby and Campbell. The shrill, drawn-out war cries of the Over Mountain Men resounded clearly on the crest. Ferguson's deputy, Captain Abraham DePeyster, had heard those blood-curdling cries from Shelby's men during the carnage at Musgrove's Mill. He said to his chief, "This is ominous. These are the damned yelling boys."[14] Up they went, weaving through the trees, leaping over boulders, firing when they had a target. All around King's Mountain there soon erupted an explosion of fire, smoke, and wild yells.

Patrick Ferguson fought the battle as if he were on an open field like Camden facing unsteady militia drawn up in formal ranks. The American Volunteers were on the ridge between Campbell and Shelby. They were ordered to form into line and charge Campbell's Virginians with fixed bayonets. They responded with elan. The Virginians turned and fled back down the slope. Lieutenant Anthony Allaire, "mounted on an elegant horse," caught up with a six-foot Rebel Captain and killed him "with one blow of my sword."[15] The Virginians ran to the bottom of the slope and up the one behind, but they were made of sterner stuff than the militia at Camden and Campbell and his officers were able to rally them. Having successfully driven back the Virginians, the American Volunteers were recalled by blasts on Ferguson's silver whistle to meet the threat from Shelby attacking up the opposite ridge. Campbell's men, now turned around, their rifles reloaded, returned to the fight. That was the pattern of the Battle of King's Mountain. Three times the Over Mountain Men at the heel of the ridge were chased down the mountain side. Three times they returned. And all the while their rifles took a deadly toll.

Captain Alexander Chesney led one of the bayonet charges against the Virginians and described the "mountaineers flying whenever there was danger of being charged by the bayonet, and returning again so soon as the British detachment had faced about to repel another of their parties." The same pattern began repeating itself around the mountain as the regiments of the Carolinas came into action. Colonel William Hill stated that "the ground was so rough ... that they were not able to overtake the americans to injure them ... and when they had went a certain distance they had orders to retreat to their camp."[16]

Not all Rebels got away unscathed from the bayonets. Sixteen-year-old Robert Henry was one of Billy Chronicle's South Fork Boys at the toe of the ridge: "Enoch Gilmer called on Hugh Erwin, Adam Barry and myself to follow him close to the foot of the hill." Major William Chronicle, who had taken Colonel William Graham's place so Graham could visit his sick wife, ten paces in front of his men raised his hat and cried, "Face to the hill." Whereupon twenty-five-year-old Billy Chronicle was shot dead. Frederick Hambright rode to the front and took command. About six feet away William Rabb was killed. The men followed Hambright up the hill. The British presented bayonets and charged. One Tory militiaman, bayonet leveled, came straight at Robert Henry, who "was in the act of cocking my gun when his bayonet was running along the barrel of my gun, and gave me a thrust through my hand and into my thigh; my antagonist and myself both fell. The Fork boys retreated and loaded their guns. I was then lying under the smoke and it appeared that some of them were not more than a guns length in front of the bayonets, and the farthest could not have been more than twenty feet in front when they discharged their rifles. It was said that everyone dropped a man. The British then retreated in great haste and were pursued by the Fork boys." Meanwhile, Robert Henry lay on the ground with a bayonet sticking through his hand and into his thigh with the Tory lying on top of him. "Wm. Caldwell saw my condition and pulled the bayonet out of my thigh, but it hung to my hand; he gave my hand a kick and went on. The thrust gave me much pain, but the pulling of it was much more severe." The Tory who had bayoneted him was dead. Robert Henry had fired when the Tory thrust his bayonet into him, and "the load must have passed through his bladder and cut a main artery, as he bled profusely."[17]

Thomas Young, fighting with James Williams's command between Shelby and Lacey, had obeyed his orders to follow his instincts. "I well remember how I behaved. Ben Hollingsworth and myself took right up the side of the mountain, and fought from tree to tree, our way to the summit. I recollect I stood behind one tree and fired until the bark was nearly knocked off, and my eyes pretty well filled with it. One fellow shaved me pretty close, for his bullet took a piece out of my gun stock. Before I was aware of it, I found myself apparently between my own regiment and the enemy, as I judged, from seeing the paper which the whigs wore in their hats and the pine knots the tories wore in theirs."[18]

The local Tory, Captain Alexander Chesney, remarked in his journal on the manner in which Thomas Young and his comrades fought. "Kings Mountain from its height would have enabled us to oppose a superior force with advantage had it not been covered with wood which sheltered the Americans and enabled them to fight in their favorite manner . . . from behind trees and other cover."[19] One may well ask why Patrick Ferguson, knowing how his enemy fought, given his soldier's eye for terrain, chose to make his stand on King's Mountain? There is no reasonable explanation. Was he then truly as contemptuous of his enemy as his public pronouncements and messages to Cornwallis make him appear?

There was another very important disadvantage in defending King's Mountain. Men firing downhill tend to overshoot, and two eyewitnesses, one Rebel and one Tory, testified that this happened on the mountain. James Collins wrote "that their great elevation above us proved their ruin: they overshot us altogether, scarce touching a man, except those on horseback, while every rifle from below seemd to have the desired effect." The Tory Drury Mathis said that "his Loyalist friends were very generally over-shooting the Americans." Mathis also offered a dramatic picture of what it was like to be on King's Mountain as the fighting raged up and down the bloody slopes. In the third charge against Campbell's Virginians he was badly wounded and fell to the ground halfway down the mountain. Mathis "used to relate that as the mountaineers passed over him he would play possum; but he could plainly observe their faces and eyes; and to him those bold, brave riflemen appeared like so many devils from the infernal regions, so full of excitement were they as they darted like enraged lions up the mountain. He said they were the most powerful looking men he ever beheld; not over-burdened with fat, but tall, raw-boned, and sinewy, with long matted hair—such men as were never before seen in the Carolinas." Or as David Vance put it fifteen years later in a backwoods brag: "We were a formidable flock of blue hen's chickens of the game blood . . . our equals were scarce, and our superiors hard to find."[20]

James Collins and his comrades had gone up the hill twice and each time "were fiercely charged upon and forced to fall back to our first position . . . the fight seemed to become more furious. Their leader, Ferguson, came in full view, within rifle shot as if to encourage his men, who by this time were falling very fast; he soon disappeared. We took the hill a third time; the enemy gave way; when we had gotten near the top, some of our leaders roared out, 'Hurrah, my brave fellows! Advance! They are crying for quarter.'"[21]

The end was near, but Patrick Ferguson refused to acknowledge it. The regiments of Shelby, Sevier, and Campbell had gained the crest of the ridge at the heel and were driving toward the British camp located at the ball and toe, where the Carolina regiments were nearing the lip of the crest. This phase of the battle lasted twenty minutes at close range—twenty to thirty yards. The Tory militia, on the brink of being beaten, retreated to the campsite where the supply wagons had been drawn up and in their growing fear began to huddle. White flags appeared, but Patrick Ferguson, spurring his white charger from one trouble spot to another, slashed at them with his sword and renewed the blasts on his silver whistle to rally his troops. The encircling Rebels were so close now that some were firing at pistol range. Resistance was crumbling. Even Ferguson finally saw the futility of his position, but surrender to "damned banditti" remained unacceptable. With a few officers he tried to cut his way through the Rebel lines. Near John Sevier's regiment several rifles leveled, fired, and Major Patrick Ferguson was shot from his horse. He was hit several times and may have been dead before he hit the ground. One foot was caught in the stirrup and he was dragged a bit before some of his officers got his horse under control and released his lifeless body. When the first reports of the battle reached General William Davidson in North Carolina his reaction expressed it for all: "Ferguson, the great partizan, has miscarried."[22]

To Captain Abraham DePeyster, more attuned to reality than Patrick Ferguson, fell the distasteful task of raising the white flag and asking quarter for the survivors. Lieutenant Anthony Allaire agreed with the decision, for "Capt. DePeyster, on whom the command devolved, saw it impossible to form six men together, thought it necessary to surrender to save the lives of the brave men who were left."[23]

What occurred following DePeyster's action has been argued ever since, but it is clear that unnecessary killing took place after the request for quarter. From here and there in the Rebel ranks the chilling cry, "Give them Buford's play!" was heard. According to Alexander Chesney, DePeyster "sent out a flag of truce, but as the Americans resumed their fire afterwards ours was also resumed under the supposition that they would give no quarter; and a dreadful havoc took place until the flag was sent out a second time, then the work of destruction ceased; the Americans surrounded us with double lines, and we grounded arms with the loss of one third of our numbers." Isaac Shelby gave the best account of what happened without whitewashing Rebel behavior. "It was some time before a complete cessation of the firing on our part could be effected. Our men who had been scattered in the battle were continually coming up and continued to fire, without comprehending in the heat of the moment what had happened; and some who had heard that at Buford's defeat, the British had refused quarters . . . were willing to follow that bad example.

"Owing to these causes, the ignorance of some, and the disposition of others to retaliate, it required some time and some exertion on the part of the officers to put an entire stop to the firing."[24]

Colonel Campbell was active in stopping the slaughter. Andrew Evins, one of his riflemen, still firing with others at helpless men, admitted that Campbell ran up and knocked his gun up and shouted, "Evins, for God's sake, don't shoot! It is murder to kill them now, for they have raised the flag!" Campbell continued his efforts, dashing about, shouting, "Cease firing! For God's sake, cease firing!" DePeyster, mounted on a grey horse, protested the killings to Campbell. "Colonel Campbell, it is damned unfair, damned unfair!" Campbell told DePeyster to get off his horse, the officers to form a separate group, and the other ranks to "take off your hats and sit down."[25]

Shelby, too, was in the thick of it. A Virginia rifleman, Benjamin Sharp, wrote, "At the close of the action, when the British were loudly calling for quarters, but uncertain whether they would be granted, I saw the intrepid Shelby rush his horse within fifteen paces of their lines, and commanded them to lay down their arms and they should have quarters. Some would call this an imprudent act, but it showed the daring bravery of the man."[26]

Order was finally restored, the men brought under control. James Collins thought that the "situation of the poor Tories appeared to be really pitiable; the dead lay in heaps on all sides, while the groans of the wounded were heard in every direction." It had taken the Rebels about one hour to vanquish Ferguson. As word of his death spread, men gathered to look upon the body of a man whose name had both frightened and enraged them. "On examining the dead body of their great chief," wrote James Collins, "it appeared that almost fifty rifles must have been leveled at him at the same time; seven rifle balls had passed though his body; both of his arms were broken, and his hat and clothing were literally shot to pieces." His personal belongings were looted. "Samuel Talbot turned him over and got his pocket pistol," Robert Henry stated. Elias Powell took his small silver whistle, Shelby the large one, and John Sevier a silk sash. Major Joseph McDowell got china dinner plates and a cup and saucer from Ferguson's table service. His white charger went to Colonel Benjamin Cleveland, whose horse had been killed during the battle. Pieces of his clothing probably ended in various hands, because he was stripped naked.[27]

The story that some Rebels gathered around Ferguson and urinated on his naked corpse is based on less than credible evidence. Of course there were men on the mountain capable of such an act, but no eyewitness, Tory or Rebel, even hinted at it, and in his written complaint to Nathanael Greene about the treatment of the prisoners Lord Cornwallis does not even allude to an indignity committed on Ferguson's corpse. The sole source is Banastre Tarleton, who was not there, but wrote in his postwar memoirs: "The mountaineers, it is reported, used every insult and indignity, after the action, towards the dead body of Major Ferguson."[28] But Tarleton, always suspect when commenting on British disasters, does not state who reported it. The corpse was wrapped in a raw beef hide and buried below the crest. A cairn now marks Ferguson's grave, and visitors to King's Mountain may follow the Scottish custom of leaving a stone on the cairn. Legend has it that he had two mistresses with him, Virginia Sal and Virginia Paul, and that Sal was killed during the fighting and buried beside him.

In a letter to his brother after the war Cornwallis blamed Tarleton for not riding to Ferguson's assistance, as Cornwallis urged. This was unfair, even if Tarleton was not as ill as he claimed. After all, it was Cornwallis who sent into the dangerous Back Country an officer in whom he lacked confidence on a mission His Lordship by his own admission did not believe could succeed. In the same letter Cornwallis stated that he had ordered Ferguson not to engage the enemy, but even if that is true, the claim of Cornwallis's biographers that he bore no fault in the affair cannot be sustained. He was the chief, he sent an officer he doubted into hostile country, the buck stopped with him. On the other hand, Tarleton's charge in his memoirs that Cornwallis's blame lay in not sending the British Legion to rescue Ferguson is ridiculous. With Tarleton himself too weak to ride, who was to command the Legion? George Hanger, who had displayed his incompetence at Charlotte in full view of Cornwallis? In the end, the postwar post mortems are tiresome to consider and quite irrelevant. One person bears the major share of the blame for the disaster at King's Mountain, and his name was Patrick Ferguson. The man who has been celebrated for two centuries as a brilliant partisan officer had defended with the bayonet a position unsuitable for that weapon but perfect for the tactics of the enemy. If he was brilliant, as many have claimed, he certainly gave no evidence of that gift at the supreme test of his career or during the days before the battle. Brilliance during those fateful days resided on the other side of the line, especially in Isaac

Shelby, who conceived the goal of catching Ferguson and with boundless energy and single-mindedness drove the rude backwoods army to victory. Patrick Ferguson displayed erratic, impulsive behavior and in the forest he used the kinds of unimaginative, indeed, disastrous tactics that we usually associate with the Colonel Blimps of the military world against seasoned, forest-wise foes. In the end, we are led to the inescapable conclusion that Major Patrick Ferguson did not live up to his historical clippings.

But he was not a fool. Ferguson was intelligent, if erratic, an experienced soldier, and gave some evidence of awareness that he faced a dangerous enemy. Why then did he not withdraw to the safety of Cornwallis's lines? If he was determined to fight, why choose King's Mountain to make a stand? It was the worst possible terrain given the enemy he presumably knew. The answers to both questions died with Ferguson, but reasonable speculation leads to an ever present factor when soldiers take the field. Patrick Ferguson was thirty-six years old and only a major. Deserved or not, he had a reputation for being difficult. He was a Clinton appointment serving under Clinton's enemy. He did not belong to Lord Cornwallis's club of young favorites: Balfour, Rawdon, Ross, Tarleton. But a smashing victory would set things right. His name would be up there with Tarleton's. Odd man out but proud, ambitious, an ardent warrior, he must have brooded on this, and in such temper judgment clouds, delusions gather, glory beckons. Banastre Tarleton spoke for the ages on the subject: "The more difficulty, the more glory."[29]

"Would to God every tree in the wilderness bore such fruit as that"

Infinitely more melancholy than Patrick Ferguson's death and unceremonious burial are the events that occurred after the battle that drive home the reality of civil war. A Tory named Branson was wounded. He saw his Rebel brother-in-law, Captain James Withrow, and begged for help. "Look to your friends for help," Withrow answered.[30] The bitterness of feeling revealed by this exchange should prepare us for the grim march of the prisoners that began the next day.

But first, even in war there are lighter moments, and one came after the shooting was over. Young Robert Henry, suffering intense pain from his bayonet wounds, and driven by equally intense thirst, walked down the side of the ridge to a stream, where he was astounded at the sight that met him: "When I got near to the branch met David Dickey and Col. Wm Graham riding his large black horse, wielding his sword around his head, crying at the top of his voice, 'Damn the Tories,' and ascended the hill. Having seen him get leave of absence . . . to see his wife, I was filled with excitement and a conflict of passion and extreme pain; but this brought on another set of feelings, that may be understood, but I am not possessed of language to describe."[31]

One hundred and fifty-seven dead Tories lay on the field, one hundred and sixty-three too badly wounded to be moved, all "weltering in their Gore," recalled Isaac Shelby. Six hundred and ninety-eight prisoners would endure a march of terror to the north. The gallant American Volunteers would never again "get in motion." Lieutenant Allaire reported that of the seventy who marched north with Ferguson all but twenty were killed or wounded. "Awful indeed," recalled Thomas Young, "was the scene of the wounded, the dying and the dead on the field after the carnage of that dreadful day." Colonel J. H. Witherspoon wrote to Lyman Draper that "my father, David Witherspoon, used to describe the scenes of the battle-ground the night after the contest as heart-rending in the extreme—the groans of the dying, and the constant cry of 'water! water!'" John Spelts, one of the footmen who caught up with the "fly-ing column" and took his place in the assault, recalled the dying and wounded "begging piteously for a little water; but in the hurry, confusion, and exhaus-tion of the Whigs these cries, when emanating from the Tories, were little heeded." While dying and wounded Tories begged in vain for water, plunder was distributed to the Rebels. The swords of Tory officers were given to poor militia officers who never thought they would own such fine weapons. "My fa-ther and myself," wrote James Collins, "drew two fine horses, two guns, and some articles of clothing, with a share of powder and lead; every man repaired to his tent, or home." This implies that the victors got the Tory tents too be-cause they had none of their own.[32]

With the dawn came a new horror. James Collins described it. "Next morn-ing, which was Sunday, the scene became really distressing; the wives and chil-dren of the poor Tories came in, in great numbers. Their husbands, fathers, and brothers lay dead in heaps, while others lay wounded or dying; a melancholy sight indeed." Young James and his father were dismissed, but before leaving for home they helped in a grisly job. "We proceeded to bury the dead, but it was badly done; they were thrown into convenient piles, and covered with old logs, the bark of old trees, and rocks; yet not so as to secure them from becoming a prey to the beasts of the forest, or the vultures of the air; and the wolves be-came so plenty, that it was dangerous for anyone to be out at night for several miles around; also, the hogs in the neighborhood gathered in to the place to de-vour the flesh of men, inasmuch as numbers chose to live on little meat rather than eat their hogs, though they were fat; half of the dogs in the country were said to be mad, and were put to death. I saw myself, in passing the place a few weeks after, all parts of the human frame lying scattered in every direction."[33]

Twenty-eight Rebels were killed. Among them was Colonel James Williams, Thomas Sumter's rival, who received a mortal wound at the head of his men. Thirteen officers of Campbell's Virginians died, including three of eight Edmondson's involved. Sixty-two Rebels were wounded. One, Private William Moore of Campbell's Virginians, had his leg amputated on the field, probably by the British surgeon Dr. Uzal Johnson of Newark, New Jersey. Moore was left in a friendly home nearby. When his wife in far-off Washing-ton County, Virginia, finally received the news, she saddled a horse and rode alone through the mountains in November to his sanctuary to nurse him. When Moore was able to travel, she took him home, and it may well be due to her faithfulness that William Moore lived to collect an invalid's pension until 1826.[34]

The morning after the battle was a scene of frenetic activity. While Tory women and children went from body to body searching for loved ones, the colonels prepared to march, for they were aware how close they were to Cornwallis and the British army. So were the men. During the battle a rumor suddenly arose that Tarleton and the Legion were upon them, and John Sevier had to quickly squelch it. A similar rumor, also untrue, circulated the morning after the battle. But the possibility that a British relief force was on the way had to be taken seriously. The British wagons used to carry tents and other baggage were set afire before they left. They would only slow the march. Colonel Campbell stayed behind to supervise the burial detail. The Rebel wounded who could travel were placed on litters of tent cloth suspended on poles between horses.

About 10 o'clock on Sunday morning "we marched at a rapid pace towards Gilbert's Town between double lines of mounted Americans," wrote Alexander Chesney. The Rebels had captured 1,500 stand of arms, and with the firing locks removed each Tory prisoner was forced to carry two muskets. The column stopped for the night at Fondren's plantation, where there was a good camping ground, enough dry fence rails for fires, and, wrote Benjamin Sharp, "a sweet potato patch sufficiently large to supply the whole army. This was most fortunate, for not one in fifty of us had tasted food for the last two days and nights, that is, since we left the Cowpens." But according to Alexander Chesney the prisoners were not fed until Monday night, when each was given an ear of raw Indian corn. There was, in fact, little food available for either the victors or the vanquished, and treatment of the latter was harsh. Chesney reported being "stripped of my shoes and silver buckles in an inclement season," and Draper repeats a secondhand story of Colonel William Brandon hacking to death with his sword a Tory who tried to escape by hiding in a hollow sycamore tree.[35]

Certainly the prisoners were being plundered of personal belongings and treated harshly, and evidence of helpless men being killed is provided in a General Order issued by Colonel Campbell on 11 October in camp south of Gilbert Town. "I must request the officers of all ranks in the army to endeavor to restrain the disorderly manner of slaughtering and disturbing the prisoners. If it cannot be prevented by moderate measures, such effectual punishment shall be executed upon delinquents as will put a stop to it."[36]

The hastily assembled little army was falling apart, and the situation would get much worse. Thomas Young claimed that by the time they reached Cane Creek "we all came near starving to death. The country was very thinly settled, and provisions could not be had for love or money. I thought green pumpkins, sliced and fried, about the sweetest eating I ever had in my life." The footman John Spelts told Draper that the prisoners were thrown raw corn on the cob and raw pumpkins, just as farmers throw feed to their hogs.[37]

On 14 October, at their camp at a place called Biggerstaff's about nine miles northeast of Gilbert Town, Colonel Campbell found it necessary to issue a General Order against militiamen deserting and imploring officers "not to discharge any of their troops until we can dispose of the prisoners to a proper guard." But he was especially concerned with troops ravaging the countryside. "It is with anxiety I hear the complaints of the inhabitants on account of the plundering parties who issue out from the camp and indiscriminately rob both Whig and Tory, leaving our friends, I believe in a worse situation than the enemy would have done. I hope the officers will exert themselves in suppressing this abominable practice, degrading to the name of soldier, by keeping their soldiers close in camp, and preventing their straggling off upon our marches."[38] Campbell was right, of course, but the reader must not think that this was occurring because the troops were militiamen. The British army and their Hessian allies were infamous everywhere they went throughout the war for plundering Tories and Rebels alike.

At Biggerstaff's Campbell was also concerned with a matter of far more consequence than plundering troops. Officers from South Carolina and North Carolina complained that among the prisoners were parole breakers, robbers, house burners, and assassins. They demanded that Campbell convene a court to try those prisoners for their crimes, but they were to be tried as well for a reason as old as the species. Isaac Shelby wrote that a paroled Rebel officer told them "he had seen eleven patriots hung at Ninety Six a few days before, for being Rebels. Similar cruel and unjustifiable acts had been committed before. In the opinion of the patriots, it required retaliatory measures to put a stop to these atrocities." They were in North Carolina, and several officers from that state, including to the Tories' misfortune Benjamin Cleveland, were magistrates, empowered under North Carolina law to summon a jury and try and execute the guilty. Twelve field officers served as the jury. Anthony Allaire called it an "infamous mock jury," and in truth the verdicts were in before the trial began. The extant records make no mention of a defense attorney.[39]

A British military surgeon witnessed the entire affair. At "ten o'clock in the morning," he wrote, "their guard paraded and formed a circle. Capt. DePeyster & the rest of our officers were ordered within the ring. They proceeded to trying the militiamen for treason."[40] DePeyster and his officers were kept in the rain all day. James Crawford and Samuel Chambers, the deserters from John Sevier's regiment who had warned Ferguson of the numbers and intent of the Over Mountain Men, were saved before the trial by Sevier. Crawford was a neighbor and old friend. Sevier could not bear to see him hang and had him pardoned. Crawford led a charmed life; Patrick Ferguson had condemned him to hang the evening of 7 October for bearing false information. Young Chambers was pardoned because of his youth and the belief that the older man had enticed him into desertion.

But thirty-six men were not so fortunate. The ranking officer was Colonel Ambrose Mills of North Carolina, a man of high character who was well regarded by most people. He was the brother-in-law of a man familiar to us, Colonel Thomas Fletchall, the South Carolina Tory from Fair Forest. The only charge made against him, that he had incited the Cherokee against the frontier, probably was not true. Ambrose Mills was undoubtedly convicted because of who he was and what he stood for, as an example to Tories everywhere. John McFall almost got off. All he had done was verbally abuse a Rebel's wife and whip their ten-year-old son with a switch cut from a tree for refusing to feed the horses of McFall's band and telling McFall, "If you want your horses fed, feed them yourself." Major Joseph McDowell recommended leniency. Colonel Benjamin Cleveland sternly disagreed. "That man, McFall, went to the house of Martin Davenport, one of my best soldiers, when he was away from home fighting for his country, insulted his wife, and whipped his child; and no such man ought to be allowed to live." McFall was found guilty. The McDowells were successful in saving John McFall's brother, Arthur, who after the war became a famous hunter in the mountains, never forgot the McDowell's for saving him, and lived to between the ages of ninety and 100.[41]

The thirty-six men tried were found guilty and sentenced to hang. There were, of course, no appeals to a higher court. As the trial was summary, so the executions were immediate, from the stout limb of a large old oak that became known as the Gallows Oak. They were hanged at night. The Rebels formed four deep around the tree. To illuminate the barbaric scene hundreds of pine knot torches were held aloft. The British surgeon tells us that "what increased this melancholy scene was the seeing Mrs. Mills take leave of her husband & two of Captain Chitwood's daughters take leave of their father. The latter were comforted with being told their father was pardoned. They then went to our fire where we had made a shed to keep out the rain. They had scarce set down when news was brought that their father was dead. Here words can scarce describe the melancholy scene, the two young ladies swoon'd away and continued in fits all night."[42]

The condemned were brought out three at a time, hanged, and left suspended. They were either mounted and the horses walked out from under them or stood on logs that were kicked away; in either case, the fall was not far enough to break their necks, so they would have kicked a while as they strangled to death before the upraised faces of the victors, as the pine knot torches cast dancing lights and shadows across their tortured features. Colonel Ambrose Mills ... Captain James Chitwood ... Captain Wilson ... Captain Walter Gilkey ... Captain Grimes ... Lieutenant Lafferty ... John McFall ... John Bibby ... Augustine Hobbs. ... Lieutenant Allaire wrote that all went to their deaths bravely, and "Mills, Wilson, and Chitwood died like Romans." Nine men swung on the limb of the large old oak when Isaac Shelby, according to his statement after the war, proposed that the hangings end. He said the other officers agreed. Whatever the particular circumstances, the next three to hang were untied, and Shelby said that one of them told him, "You have saved my life, and I will tell you a secret. Tarleton will be here in the morning. A woman has brought the news."[43]

It was 2 o'clock the morning of 15 October. The Rebels broke camp immediately. The wounded, said Shelby, were "sent into secret hiding places in mountains, and the line of march taken up." With their prisoners the Rebels set out on a twenty-four-hour forced march through a day of incessant rain, forded the Catawba with the waters at their breasts, and thirty-two miles from their starting point bivouacked on the other side at 2 o'clock the morning of the 16th. During the march 100 prisoners escaped. Later in the morning the river had risen too high to ford, which meant they were safe from pursuit. The information given Shelby had been half right. Tarleton, fully recovered from his fever, had been sent by Cornwallis to search for Ferguson. In the meantime, Cornwallis received news of Ferguson's defeat and death along with alarming reports that the victorious Rebel host, numbering at least 3,000, was now on the march toward him. Cornwallis decided to retreat and recalled Tarleton. Sixty-two years later, at his home in Pontotoc, Mississippi, Silas McBee recalled the situation for Lyman Draper: "It was amusing when we learned the facts, how Lord Cornwallis was running in fright in one direction, and we mountaineers as eagerly fleeing in the other."[44]

At Biggerstaff's the living bent to melancholy tasks after the departure of the Rebels and their prisoners. As soon as they had left, Mrs. Martha Biggerstaff and an old man who worked on the farm approached the hanging tree. Her Tory husband Aaron had received a mortal wound at King's Mountain. Martha Biggerstaff and the old man cut down the bodies. "Mrs. Mills with a young child in her arms set out all night in the rain with her husband's corpse and not even a blanket to cover her from the inclemency of the weather."[45] Seven bodies were buried nearby in a shallow trench. Captain Chitwood's body was laid on a plank and carried by friends, presumably accompanied by his daughters, to a nearby graveyard.

The travail of the hanged was over. The living marched north at the mercy of men like Captain Patrick Carr of Georgia, who had pointed at the nine Tories dangling from the Gallows Oak, and exclaimed with deep satisfaction, "Would to God every tree in the wilderness bore such fruit as that." Carr was reputed to have killed with his own hands over 100 Tories during the war. It is also said that his death in August 1802 in Jefferson County, Georgia, was murder at the hands of some Tory descendants. His reputation for evil was such that when he was finally buried in December and the Jefferson County Light Horse assembled at his grave to fire a volley, Lieutenant Robinson delivered a brief but remarkably candid eulogy: "Though a honey of a patriot," he left a name "mixed with few virtues, and a thousand crimes."[46]

The prisoners were marched another seven days to the Moravian settlements at Salem (modern Winston-Salem). Men kept escaping, but not always successfully. One man, wounded in his attempt, was executed. Throughout the march prisoners had been cut and stabbed. Lieutenant Allaire related, "Several of the militia that were worn out with fatigue, and not being able to keep up, were cut down and trodden to death in the mire." At Salem on 1 November the British surgeon, who had treated Rebels as well as Tories, was beaten by Benjamin Cleveland "for attempting to dress a man whom they had cut on the march." On 5 November Allaire and three other men escaped and began about a 200-mile flight, mostly on foot, to Ninety Six. Furtively, often spending nights "very snug in the bushes," they found Tories who relayed them from one friendly farm to the next, traveling mostly at night and holing up in the woods by day, on the 23rd they entered Ninety Six.[47]

Two days later Allaire "set out for Charleston, Where I arrived the 29th of November; nothing worth notice on the journey."[48] Thus passes from our story twenty-five-year-old Lieutenant Anthony Allaire, American and loyal King's man, who fought hard for his beliefs, lost, and, with many thousands of men and women who thought as he did, in the tradition of his Huguenot forebears left forever his ancestral home for sanctuary far north of King's Mountain. He died 9 June 1838, on his farm near Fredericton, New Brunswick.

Captain Alexander Chesney was also twenty-five when at King's Mountain he saw his first major action. During the march of the prisoners northward, Colonel Benjamin Cleveland offered Chesney his freedom if he would teach the Rebel militia Ferguson's exercises. He refused, and was fortunate that he was not cut down on the spot or strung up from the first stout branch. Cleveland "swore that I should suffer death for it at the Moravian town." Chesney was left with no alternative but escape. "I reached home on the 31st of October. I found the Americans had left me little. My wife had a son on the 20th whom I named William which was all the christening he had." Until late in the year Chesney was forced to hide in a cave dug under a hollow poplar, with his cousins Hugh Cook and Charles Brandon. It was so small they could only lie flat. Cook's wife brought "food and news every night." When he finally left the cave he joined a Tory militia regiment but was again captured by Rebels whose commander, Major Benjamin Roebuck, had led a company at King's Mountain. Roebuck and Chesney were acquaintances, and Roebuck paroled him to Ninety Six, where Chesney was subsequently exchanged for Captain John Clarke, the son of Elijah Clarke. We will meet Alexander Chesney again, for he became a scout for Banastre Tarleton and witness to yet another critical action in the South Carolina Back Country.[49]

Some 200 years ago Sir Henry Clinton admitted that the American victory at King's Mountain "unhappily proved the first link in a chain of evils that followed each other in regular succession until they at last ended in the total loss of America."[50] No one since has summed it up better. After the twin disasters of Charleston and Camden, Rebel morale desperately needed a boost; King's Mountain made it soar. On the other hand, it was a terrible blow to the Tories of the Back Country, and they never recovered from it. Their activities did not entirely cease, but their enthusiasm was considerably dampened. Thereafter the Rebels maintained the initiative. Most important of all, the great militia victory forced Lord Cornwallis to retreat to South Carolina and delayed his re-entry into North Carolina by four months, and by then he faced an American general who had much to teach him about the art of war.

17

Retreat and Turmoil

Cornwallis Retreats

The dramatic victory of the Over Mountain Men and their Back Country allies
at King's Mountain forced Lord Cornwallis to set aside for the time being his
plan to invade North Carolina. On his western flank the King's Friends had
been smashed. From the swamps and woods on his eastern flank Marion and his
men emerged at will for sudden, terrorizing strikes on the Tories. Cornwallis had
hoped to hold the Cheraw region with Tory militia but the militiamen refused
to turn out, so apprehensive were they of Marion, who had cowed them according to James Wemyss by "burning houses and distressing the well effected
in a most severe manner," although Marion hotly denied burning houses.[1] Nor
could the army remain where it was, for the countryside surrounding Charlotte,
indeed all Mecklenburg County, harbored inveterate partisan foes brilliantly led
by Major William Richardson Davie under the overall command of General
William Lee Davidson. Even before Ferguson's disaster, and with Cornwallis's
victorious army poised at Charlotte to strike north, the Tories of North Carolina
were conspicuous only by their failure to take the field. Cornwallis may have
owned Charlotte, but the Rebels owned the countryside. Outside their lines
British foraging parties could move only in strength. Lone couriers were dead
men. And the army was sick. Fever swept the ranks. A relatively friendly place
was needed for the troops to rest and recover from illness, and for Cornwallis
to take stock of his situation. The commandant of Ninety Six, John Harris
Cruger, recommended Winnsboro, in South Carolina. Some seventy miles south
and slightly west of Charlotte, Winnsboro in 1780 was a Back Country village
of about twenty houses. There were no bridges across the Catawba and its trib-
utaries, and the roads through the red hills were miserable under the best of
conditions. On Cornwallis's march, wrote his commissary Charles Stedman, who
experienced it, rain fell for "several days without intermission," the river and

streams were swollen, and the red clay roads turned into quagmires. The retreat from Charlotte began on 14 October. It ended at Winnsboro on 29 October.[2]

The long column set out in the late afternoon and almost immediately ran into trouble. The army's guide was, in the words of Lieutenant Roderick McKenzie, a "Presbyterean fanatick" from Charlotte, William McCafferty, who led the troops by design onto the wrong road and then left them and rode to William Richardson Davie's camp.[3] The British wandered amid hills and ravines the rest of the night and left behind at least twenty wagons with supplies including the baggage of the British Legion. They found the right road but the discovery did not improve the conditions of the march. The Carolina mud remained deep, the streams high and swift, the rain incessant. The troops had no tents. Food was in short supply and for five days there was nothing to eat but Indian corn harvested on the way and cooked by parching it over campfires. Always hovering on their rear and flanks were Davie's mounted Rebel militia, unable to do serious damage but ever ready to cut off stragglers, take advantage of sniping opportunities, and engage in running fights with Tory militia scouring the countryside for food for the army.

Cornwallis had caught a bad cold, and shortly after the retreat began he too was stricken with fever and had to be transported in a wagon. Lord Rawdon took command. Another occupant of a wagon was Major George Hanger, desperately ill with what he called yellow fever, so weak he could hardly move. Lying with him in the wagon on a common bed of straw were five fellow British officers down with fever. The streams that had to be crossed were so high that water rose over the axles and wet their straw bed. Only Hanger survived. His five comrades were dead inside a week and buried far from home in lonely and long-forgotten graves dug hastily on the side of the road in the wet red clay of the South Carolina Back Country. Hanger lost so much weight that his bones split his skin, and he felt that he survived only by taking opium and port wine.[4]

If not a nightmare, Cornwallis's retreat to Winnsboro was a bad dream. It also reveals in stunning detail the festering relations between the British Army and the rude Tory militia of the interior. It was a problem of attitude that eventually descended to cruel treatment. This attitude was summed up two years later in the *Observations* of a Tory militia colonel, Robert Gray, who wrote that "almost every British officer regarded with contempt and indifference the establishment of a militia among a people differing so much in customs and manners from themselves." Lord Cornwallis was aware of the problem. At Charlotte, about two weeks before setting out for Winnsboro, he issued an order urging troop officers and soldiers to "treat with kindness all those who have Sought protection in the British Army, & to believe that Altho their Ignorance and want of Skill in Military Affairs may at present render their appearance Awkward in a Veteran and Experienced Army; When they are properly Arm'd, Appointed, & Instructed they Will shew the same Ardour, & Courage in the Cause of Great Britain As their Countrymen who repair'd to the Royal Standard in the Northern Colonies."[5] His effort had little and perhaps no effect. Five months later in North Carolina he felt the need to officially repeat the order, and his commissary Charles Stedman in his *History* clearly described the incredible behavior of some British officers and the alienation of many Tory militiamen during the retreat to Winnsboro.

The British troops, wrote Stedman, "with all their resolution and patience . . . could not have proceeded but for the personal exertions of the militia, who, with a zeal that did them infinite honour, rendered the most important services." At every night's bivouac, Stedman continued, "the duty of the militia began. They were assembled by the author, who always attended them in person, and went in quest of provisions, which were collected daily from the country through which the army marched. Nor were their difficulties in this service trifling; they were obliged to ride through rivers, creeks, woods, and swamps, to hunt out the cattle. This service was their constant and daily duty; they were frequently opposed, sometimes worsted, and with no inconsiderable loss." Stedman maintained that the army could not have been maintained "in the field without them. Cattle-driving was of itself a perfect business; it required great art and experience to get the cattle out of the woods. The commissary was under the greatest obligations to those people, without whose assistance he could not possibly have found provisions for the army." On at least one occasion Tory militiamen acted as beasts of burden to further the army's progress, and for their sacrifice were awarded with abuse. "The continual rains had swelled the rivers and creeks prodigously, and rendered the roads almost impassable. The waggon and artillery horses were quite exhausted by the time the army had reached Sugar Creek. The creek was very rapid, its banks nearly perpendicular, and the soil, being clay, as slippery as ice. The horses were taken out of some of the waggons, and the militia, harnessed in their stead, drew the waggons through the creek. We are sorry to say that, in return for these exertions, the militia were maltreated by abusive language and even beaten by some officers in the quarter-master-general's department. In consequence of this ill treatment, several of them left the army the next morning for ever, chusing to run the risque of meeting the resentments of their enemies rather than submit to the derision and abuse of those to whom they looked up as friends."[6]

The officers of the quartermaster's department did not merely alienate British friends. All that winter at Winnsboro Cornwallis struggled with little effect against the venality of these men, for enriching themselves took precedence over supplying the army, and given a system that fostered corruption they got away with it. Adding to Cornwallis's troubles was the necessity of supplying strong escorts for supplies from London and New York coming upcountry through Charleston. The much-needed supplies got through, but not without wear and tear on men and horses that the little army could ill afford.

Thus passed the winter of 1780–1781 for His Lordship and his army of reconquest. He was not in dire straits, his men were not going hungry, their quarters were crude but snug, and there could be no doubt that when called on the other ranks would exhibit the unwavering stoicism that has been the hallmark of the British soldier and led Napoleon to describe them as "that grim, silent infantry." But their position was not enviable. They were few in numbers. Sickness had not abated. They were a long way from the sea and their lifeline, the British Navy. Their Tory allies were nearly useless as a fighting force, while their Rebel foes were relentless, implacable, often merciless. During the months of October and November 1780, following King's Mountain and Cornwallis's retreat, couriers rode into Winnsboro with news that would have weakened the resolve of many generals.

Bloody Ban Meets the Swamp Fox

About seventy miles north of Charleston, in a broad field on the edge of Tearcoat Swamp, in flat farm country that has apparently changed little in appearance since the Revolution, Colonel Samuel Tynes and a newly raised Tory militia unit bivouacked in late October. Nisbet Balfour had ordered Tynes to the area to replace the force commanded by James Wemyss, who had been ordered to return to Camden.

Francis Marion was at Port's Ferry on the Pee Dee River, over fifty miles east of Tearcoat Swamp. He had gone through one of his black moods because of the failure of the militia to answer his summons to gather. He had told his officers that he was going to North Carolina to take service under General Gates, but his close friend and comrade Hugh Horry convinced him to delay a while. When men began to straggle into camp, the little partisan chief took heart and began planning a foray. Small patrols rode out every night seeking intelligence of the enemy. News of Tynes's presence came on 24 October, and that same day Marion crossed the Pee Dee with 150 riders and marched some thirty miles southwest to Kingstree. He told no one of his plans but allowed the impression to form that they were going to attack a group of Tories at McCallum's Ferry. The riders left Kingstree the following morning and headed west. They forded the Black River that night and kept going until they neared Tearcoat Swamp. They had come about twenty miles. Stopping the column, Marion sent out two boys to scout the position of Colonel Tynes and his Tory band. The Tories were camped in the field with the swamp at their backs. Some were sleeping. Two men played fiddles and others were talking or playing cards. Three large campfires burned. Satisfied with the situation, Marion told his men to rest.

He roused them at midnight and divided them into three groups. They would attack in the early hours of 26 October 1780. Barring ill luck, the Tories' surprise would be complete as the riders bore in from three directions: both flanks and the front. Francis Marion would lead the frontal assault and give the signal to attack by firing his pistol. Slowly and silently the riders peeled off to take their respective positions. Marion's pistol cracked and instantly 150 Rebel horsemen spurred their mounts and galloped from three directions out of the darkness into the dancing firelight, whooping and hollering, shooting and slashing. Tories who could fled in what they wore into Tearcoat Swamp with their leader, Colonel Tynes. The forty-three who did not make it offered hardly any resistance, so overwhelming and terrorizing was the surprise attack. Marion lost two horses. Six Tories lay dead on the field, fourteen wounded, twenty-three prisoners. A cardplayer, wounded and dying, still held his last hand—ace, jack, deuce of clubs.

Another small fight with large results. Once more a Tory band was broken and scattered before it had a chance to do anything effective, and the stories carried by survivors increased fear and gloom in Tory ranks. Almost all the horses and equipment issued to the Tories at Camden a short time before were captured by the Rebels. And according to William Dobein James, the fifteen-year-old who rode with Marion and in 1821 published a *Sketch* of his hero's life and the exploits of his partisan brigade, "most of Tyne's men soon after joined Gen. Marion and fought bravely."[7]

But Marion was not satisfied. He wanted Colonel Samuel Tynes. He thought, as William Henry Drayton did in 1775, that with their leaders out of action the rank and file would give little trouble. Captain William Clay Snipes was sent to Tyne's home territory, the High Hills of Santee, to bring in Tynes and any other Tory officers he could catch. Shortly after Marion had withdrawn to Kingstree Snipes returned with Colonel Tynes and several other Tory officers and Justices of the Peace in tow.

This was not to be endured. The northern Tory officer, Lieutenant Colonel George Turnbull, asked for Banastre Tarleton and the British Legion to march against Marion. Tarleton agreed and Cornwallis approved. The operation began on 5 November. Tarleton confiscated horses in order to mount his infantry for fast movements. Marion soon learned of Tarleton's mission, and during the ensuing days he maneuvered in an attempt to surprise the Englishman. But the little man with the gimpy leg had to be extra cautious. Bloody Ban knew the tricks of the trade, and behind him rode the veteran Legion, some 400 strong and all mounted now. Learning of Marion's general location, Tarleton arrived on 7 November at the plantation of General Richard Richardson. Richardson had died not long before and was buried on his plantation, which was located on the left bank of the Santee. The terrain bordering both sides of the Santee was wide, flat, and wet. Here Marion and his men rode in their deadly game of ambush and surprise attacks, and over the broad sweep of country north of the river where the brigade was equally at home.

Tarleton had brought with him two small artillery pieces. They were called grasshoppers because they were mounted on legs instead of wheels and hopped on their carriages when fired. Weighing 500 pounds each, they were transported by teams of four or six horses, but in emergencies two horses could manage or the gun could be removed from the carriage and carried by eight men while others lugged the carriage and wheels. It was an excellent gun for fast-moving mounted troops. With the grasshoppers covering his position, Tarleton showed that on occasion he could devise tactics other than a headlong frontal assault. His men were deployed in concealed places. He then spread the word through the countryside that most of the Legion had returned to Camden. Patrols were sent out, but they were not aggressive. Tarleton instructed them to show "Tokens of fear."[8] He left his campfires burning. His aim, of course, was to draw Marion into a trap.

Francis Marion's antennae for danger signals were keen, and he was the most cautious of the partisan leaders. But he saw the flames of Tarleton's campfires reflected in the night sky and drew closer. If he was saved from falling into Tarleton's trap, it was by a woman, Mary Richardson, widow of Richard Richardson. Her son, also Richard Richardson, a paroled captain of Continentals, was hiding on the plantation. Under Tarleton's nose she sent him to warn Marion. Two miles from the British camp Captain Richardson came on Marion, who was moving ever closer. He told Marion that ahead of him was Banastre Tarleton with two artillery pieces and 400 horse and foot, alert and awaiting his attack. Marion did not hesitate. He immediately galloped away with his brigade and did not stop for six miles.

That night, however, a Tory prisoner escaped from Marion's band. He reached Tarleton in the morning darkness and reported that a "treacherous Woman"[9] had foiled his plan. Tarleton's reaction was as immediate as Marion's. The Legion mounted and the chase was on. Ahead of them, having learned of the escape of the prisoner, Marion expected Tarleton would be on his trail. With local men as guides, the Brigade rode off before first light. Heading in a northeasterly direction, away from the Santee, all that day they led the British Legion through swamps and woods. Having traveled for many miles along Pocotaligo Swamp, at about the present site of Manning, South Carolina, Marion turned east into Ox Swamp, then bore a little north some eight miles to the Black River and Benbow's Ferry. Marion and his men had ridden thirty-five miles that day, and at Benbow's Ferry they stopped, for it was a good place to fight. Marion ordered the men to fell trees across the narrow way to the ferry. Pickets were stationed far enough in front to give timely warning. In case they had to retreat and scatter, Marion gave the men instructions on where to rendezvous. Then they settled in and waited for Tarleton.

But he never came. Seven hours and twenty-seven miles after he had begun Tarleton reined in, looked into one more forbidding Carolina swamp, and said, "Come my Boys! Let us go back, and we will find the Gamecock. But as for this damned old fox, the Devil himself could not catch him." Throughout the land the story was told, and thus Francis Marion became the Swamp Fox.[10]

But Tarleton was not through with the people who succored Marion and his partisan brigade, and his subsequent actions illustrate the awful position of civilian populations caught in guerrilla wars. Between Jack's Creek and the High Hills of Santee Tarleton taught the populace the "Error of Insurrection," as he put it, with the application of terror—the traditional and usually ineffective tactic of regulars trying to defeat guerrillas. He burned thirty plantation homes, their outbuildings, and the harvest. The women, the children, and the old literally were allowed only the clothes on their backs and were seen gathered under the sky around campfires. Wrote Marion of Tarleton, "he spares neither Whig nor Tory." Tarleton even went so far as to have General Richard Richardson dug out of his six-week-old grave in order, he claimed, to "look upon the face of a brave man," but no one believed that then or since. It was the family plate he was after, believing it had been hidden in the General's grave. He did not stop there, for a "treacherous Woman" must be especially convinced of the "Error of Insurrection." He ordered the cattle, hogs, and fowl driven into the barn where the corn was stored, the doors closed, and the barn put to the torch. Francis Marion claimed that in a vain effort to discover where the Swamp Fox was hiding Tarleton had Mrs. Mary Richardson flogged.[11]

If America could have been conquered by proclamations, the Rebels would have laid down their arms long before Tarleton tried to catch Marion. But British officers persisted, and Tarleton was no exception. He issued his on 11 November. It promised pardons to all who came in and assured the populace that "It is not the wish of Britons to be cruel or destroy, but it is now obvious to all Carolina that Treachery Perfidy & Perjury will be punished with instant fire and sword." Marion's flight apparently convinced Tarleton that he no longer represented a serious threat, and Tarleton convinced Cornwallis, who wrote that Marion was now "cautious and vigilant." But Marion had always been cautious and vigilant. Cornwallis reported to Clinton that Tarleton had "pursued Marion for several days, obliged his Corps to take to the Swamps, and by convincing the Inhabitants that there was a power superior to Marion who could likewise reward and Punish, so far checked the Insurrection, that the greatest part of them have not dared openly to appear in Arms against us since his expedition."[12]

Three days after Tarleton issued his proclamation Cornwallis recalled him. As the British Legion rode west another armed force trailed at a respectful distance. It was, of course, Marion and his brigade. As soon as he was sure that Tarleton was on his way west, Marion turned and rode many miles to the east and in a few days was engaging Tories around Georgetown. And on 25 November Lord Cornwallis, who believed that Thomas Sumter and Elijah Clarke had been killed, wrote to Nisbet Balfour, "We have lost two great plagues in Sumpter and Clarke. I wish your friend Marion was as quiet."[13]

Fishdam Ford: The Reappearance of the Gamecock

I believe I have made quite clear up to this point my dislike of Thomas Sumter and my dismissal of him as either tactician or strategist. I hope I have also, however, made equally clear my recognition of his unwavering opposition to the British and the power of what was obviously a remarkable personality, for how else can we explain the devotion to his leadership shown by his followers despite failures of judgment and elementary military security? It is a theme to which we now return. We observed him, following his well-deserved, devastating defeat at Fishing Creek, as he rode bareback and alone into William Richardson Davie's camp at Charlotte. Many men would have been finished after such self-inflicted humiliation. But Sumter possessed a resiliency and an ability to inspire men when all seemed lost that defies explanation and begs admiration. It was his ability to command allegiance and his relentless fighting spirit that led Cornwallis to write to Tarleton that Sumter "certainly has been our greatest plague in this country." Consider that Sumter's debacle at Fishing Creek had occurred on 18 August, yet Cornwallis wrote to Sir Henry Clinton on 29 August that "the indefatigable Sumter is again in the field, and is beating up for recruits with the greatest assiduity," and Horatio Gates informed George Washington that Sumter "has reinstated and increased his corps to upwards of a 1,000 men."[14]

When Major James Wemyss, hanger of men and burner of Presbyterian churches, came to Lord Cornwallis on 7 November with information that Sumter with some 300 men was camped at Moore's Mill, only thirty miles northwest of Winnsboro, Cornwallis immediately seized the opportunity. Wemyss, Cornwallis later reported to Clinton, said "that he had accurate accounts of his position and good guides, and that he made no doubt of being able to surprize and rout him. As the defeating of so daring and troublesome a man as Sumpter, and dispersing such a banditti, was a great object, I consented to his making the trial on the 9th at daybreak, and gave him forty of the dragoons which Tarleton had left with me, desiring, however, neither to put them in front nor to make any use of them during the night." He undoubtedly would have preferred to send the Rebels' greatest nemesis, Banastre Tarleton, after the Gamecock but Bloody Ban was then chasing in vain through "swamps and defiles" the ever elusive Francis Marion. And the temptation to clip the Gamecock's spurs was overpowering.[15]

Sumter's presence so close to the British main army was part of Horatio Gates's strategy to squeeze the British at Camden. Although waiting to be relieved by his successor, the Hero of Saratoga was trying to retrieve his shattered reputation. Sumter told one of his colonels, Richard Winn, "it has been agreed that I shall march as near to Winnsboro as can be done with safety; this will draw Tarleton and a large body of infantry after us; this will weaken Lord Cornwallis so much that General Smallwood, with the Continental troops and what North Carolinians can be collected, is to fall on Cornwallis."[16] The first part of the plan was reasonable, provided Sumter was alert and prudent. The planned denouement, however, was sheer folly. The thought of William Smallwood falling on Cornwallis makes one shudder. All concerned on the Rebel side should have fallen on their knees to thank their Maker that it never came to pass.

Wemyss left Winnsboro on the night of November 8 with Tarleton's forty dragoons and 100 mounted infantry of his own 63rd Foot. They were going up against 300 to 400 partisans, but they were, after all, British and Tory regulars and supremely self-confident. Wemyss had with him Lieutenant John Stark, a very young officer but nevertheless second in command, leading the mounted infantry of the 63rd Foot. He was also accompanied by a Tory named Sealy, who had been in Sumter's camp at Moore's Mill. Sealy had been captured by the Rebels but had convinced Sumter of his conversion to the cause and was released. He had then joined Wemyss and offered to guide the British to Sumter.

Wemyss gave Sealy an additional mission: with five dragoons he was to pene-trate the Rebel camp once the attack began, find Sumter, and either kill or cap-ture him. Wemyss neglected to inform his deputy, Lieutenant Stark, of his plan of attack once he caught up with Sumter, or of Cornwallis's instructions not to attack with cavalry at night.

Marching fast, Wemyss reached Moore's Mill shortly after midnight to find that Sumter had moved. Local Tories placed him five miles down the Broad River at Fish Dam Ford, where there was an old stone weir probably constructed by the Cherokee. The Rebels were camped on the east bank of the Broad. Sumter's tent was near the road by the ford, and apparently Wemyss had intel-ligence from local Tories about its precise location. The units of Colonels Winn, Taylor, Bratton, Hill, and Lacey, were spread around and behind, with the lat-ter three on a ridge some 200 yards from the ford. That 200 yards was open ground. Sumter, as usual, had partially undressed and went to sleep in his tent. His colonels, however, uneasy at being so close to the enemy's main army, re-mained alert. Campfires were built, but the men were ordered to lay on their arms beyond the firelight. Pickets were thrown out to warn of danger.

Wemyss pushed on, too fast it seemed to follow Cornwallis's orders to at-tack at daybreak. About 1 A.M. 9 November, Wemyss bumped into Sumter's pickets, who got off five rounds that, as it turned out, decided the outcome of the fight. Wemyss was shot off his horse. With a shattered knee and bro-ken arm he was out of the fight. Lieutenant John Stark took over. He was ig-norant not only of Cornwallis's express orders to Wemyss but also of the ground before him and the strength of the enemy. He gave the order to charge and the British horsemen galloped in the darkness against an invisible enemy. But the British were quite visible, for they rode into the light cast by Rebel campfires. Colonel William Hill, who was at the fight, claimed that the British "collected in great numbers around their fires and began to plunder, not sup-posing they would meet with any interruption, and while they were in this po-sition around the fires the Americans, taking advantage of the light, poured on them such a fire that they killed & wounded a great many."[17] Lieutenant Stark withdrew a short distance and did what he ought to have done in the first place, ordering his men to dismount and fight on foot. The men of the 63rd Foot formed, fixed bayonets, and went forward again. Colonel Thomas Taylor's men received the assault like regulars and delivered a volley at close range. Some of Taylor's men were bayoneted. The action was decided in the Rebels' favor when Colonel Edward Lacey's command on the British flank began firing at the 63rd from the woods.

While all this confused action was going on in the dark, with shadowy fig-ures dashing back and forth in the light of the campfires, the assassination team made its way to Thomas Sumter's tent pitched at the ford. According to Colonel Winn, Sumter was almost caught in his tent "owing to the orderly sergeant not giving notice of the alarm in time. Before he could put on his clothes, they were up with him. By jumping a fence and running through a briar patch he saved himself."[18] Sumter hid from the killers under a cut in the bank along the Broad River while the fighting raged. Given the firing by the pickets, how he got caught napping remains unexplained, despite Colonel Winn's criticism of the orderly sergeant.

Meanwhile, Lieutenant Stark wisely decided to withdraw from the field. Whether he should have withdrawn thirty miles to Winnsboro, which he did, would be second guessing. He left under a flag of truce, and under the care of a sergeant major four dead and twenty wounded, including James Wemyss. As the first grey light began to filter through the treetops, the British sergeant major and the wounded looked out onto an empty battlefield. The Rebels had also withdrawn. But they had not gone far, and about two hours after dawn they reappeared and took possession of the field. Sumter appeared about noon. The wounded were treated very well, and Sumter probably saved James Wemyss's life. Wemyss's pocket held a list of the men he had hanged and the buildings he had burned during his march through Marion's country. Sumter read it, showed it to no one, and dropped it into a campfire. This act invites speculation, for Thomas Sumter was a hard man. Did he fear that he would not be able to control the wrath of his men, who would leave Wemyss hanging from the nearest tree and thus force Cornwallis into terrible retribution? If that was his reason, and I can think of no other that rings true, it speaks well of his judgment on that occasion. James Wemyss was exchanged, recovered from his wounds, after the war was promoted to Lieutenant Colonel of the 63rd Foot, and two years later disappeared from the *Army Lists* and history.

The Rebels suffered four dead and ten wounded. Sumter spread the word of a victory not over Tory militia but over regulars, and most of them from a British line infantry regiment. Recruits flocked to his standard. Cornwallis was furious. He referred to Wemyss as a "Mad Trooper." There was obviously only one answer to the problem of Thomas Sumter, and his name was Banastre Tarleton. Cornwallis recalled him immediately.

Blackstocks: Bloody Ban and the Gamecock Meet Again

Cornwallis's urgent order reached his cavalry commander on 14 November 1780 and Tarleton of course wasted no time. The troopers of the British Legion turned their horses west that day and rode away from smoking ruins and bitter enemies along the upper Santee. Cornwallis was fearful for the safety of Ninety Six and sent more couriers, one after another, to hasten Tarleton's progress and keep him informed of the latest news of Sumter. To Brierly's Ferry on the Broad River Cornwallis dispatched the veteran Major Archibald McArthur and the 250-man 1st Battalion of Fraser's Highlanders (71st Foot) and eighty survivors of the 63rd Foot. Commanding the 63rd was young Lieutenant John Money, Cornwallis's aide-de-camp, whom His Lordship treated more as a son than a subordinate. Brierly's Ferry was about twenty-two miles southwest of Cornwallis's position with the main army at Winnsboro. Tarleton was ordered to join McArthur at Brierly's and take command for the pursuit of Sumter.

The Gamecock in the meantime was planning and acting. He was not aware that Tarleton was rapidly approaching by a series of forced marches. Sumter had with him the same officers and their units who had been at Fish Dam Ford, but news of that action had swelled his ranks as he marched until he could boast of a 1,000 or more riders. They included 100 Georgians, among them that rough warhorse, Colonel Elijah Clarke, recovered from his wounds as well as his defeat at Augusta. Other senior officers from Georgia were Colonel John Twiggs, who would assume a critical role in the ensuing action, and two veterans of King's Mountain, Major William Candler and Major James Jackson. Sumter camped at Hawkins Mill on the Tyger River, a tributary of the Broad, and sent out reconnaissance and raiding parties.

Major Samuel Hammond, who in the spring of the year had hidden from Tories in swamps and canebreaks, rode south like an avenging angel to convince by fear the pro-British but largely inactive German settlers of the Dutch Fork between the Broad and Saluda Rivers that it would be in their best interests to remain inactive. Colonel Thomas Taylor was sent to raid the British depot at Summer's Mills. The infamous Captain Patrick Carr of Georgia was sent to Brierly's Ferry to keep a watchful eye on Major McArthur and his regulars. Sumter still did not know that Tarleton was heading in his direction and coming on fast.

Tarleton and 190 dragoons of the Legion, hot, dusty, and sweaty, rode into McArthur's camp early on 18 November. The dragoons and mounted infantry of the Legion and their horses were travel weary after their three-day forced march, but their commander as usual was solicitous of neither man nor beast. The combined force crossed the river that day, but to hide the presence of his green-jacketed British Legion, Tarelton sent the redcoats of McArthur's Highlanders and the 63rd Foot across the Broad by ferry. He and his Legion, their green jackets covered, crossed three miles below by a ford, joined Major McArthur, and continued until 10 P.M. when they bivouacked well inside the Dutch Fork. On 19 November Tarleton's scouts ranged widely in quest of information about Sumter's whereabouts. One party pinpointed Sumter's location and intention. He was north of Tarleton's bivouac, gathering to attack a British post held by Tory militia at Williams Plantation, some fifteen miles north of Ninety Six. Tarleton immediately broke camp, marched that night to the Enoree, and made a late camp at the mouth of Indian Creek. Still Sumter remained unaware of Tarleton's proximity.

Then fortune smiled on Sumter. Sometime in the early morning hours of 20 November a British soldier deserted from the 63rd Foot, stole a horse, rode to Sumter's camp, and revealed Tarleton's location, strength, and mission. Historians have reasonably speculated that Tarleton was trying to cut Sumter's access to the river fords and drive him far enough south to where that tough New York Tory John Harris Cruger could sally with his garrison at Ninety Six and together with Tarleton and his regulars put a finish to the career of Brigadier General Thomas Sumter. Whether the plan was quite that detailed or even correct is irrelevant, for Bloody Ban would take the Gamecock any way he could get him, and his opportunity would soon be at hand.

Sumter and his officers were faced with a difficult decision. They had upwards of 1,000 mostly seasoned Back Country militia. Tarleton had only 520 men. But they were all regulars, over 300 of them British Army regulars, and they were led by a commander who was all fighter, as feared as hated, and never defeated. Yet given Tarleton's reputation for rapid pursuit, to run was to invite being caught either strung out on the road or in the middle of a river crossing. Either could be disastrous. And even if they successfully evaded Tarleton, continual retreat would end their mission, embolden Tories, and discourage the Patriot militia. At a council of war the colonels were unanimous: find a strong defensive position, wait for Tarleton, and fight him when he arrived. It was a recommendation that suited Sumter's temperament, for like his adversary he was a born fighter. Colonel Thomas Brandon, who had followed Sumter's rival James Williams until Williams's death at King's Mountain, was on home ground and suggested that the place to fight was Captain William Blackstock's farm on the Tyger River. Leaving Captain Patrick Carr with a small detachment at the Enoree to give early warning of Tarleton's approach, Sumter rode north with the militia regiments to Blackstocks and one of the most important engagements of the Carolina campaign.

The old battlefield is about ten miles west of Union, South Carolina. The fighting took place on Blackstock's Farm, where the land had been to a great extent cleared, providing fields of fire and room for maneuver. The road leading to the farm descended from a hill to a shallow stream, then ascended a gentle slope through a field of some fifty acres to the house and outbuildings, which were solid log structures on a hill. Behind the house the road descended steeply about 200 yards to the Tyger River. To the right of the house was a thickly wooded ridge with steep slopes. To the left of the house, wrote Colonel William Hill, for "about a quarter of a mile there was a very large and strong fence not made with common rails but with small trees notched one on the other."[19] It was late afternoon when the Rebels arrived. Sumter and his officers examined their surroundings while the men built fires and cooked a meal of meat and bread. Then he made his dispositions.

Sumter set up his command post on the wooded ridge to the right of the house and the road leading to the river; he kept the regiments of McCall, Bratton, and Taylor with him. The outbuildings around the house were not chinked between the logs, thus providing narrow but convenient openings for men firing from behind cover. Here Sumter placed Colonel Henry Hampton and his South Carolina riflemen. Below the ridge on which he had his command post were the regiments of Colonel Lacey and Colonel Hill. Sumter stationed Colonel Twiggs and his 100 Georgia riflemen opposite them on the left side of the road, along the stout fence described by Colonel Hill and in the upper part of the field in front of the house and outbuildings. Colonel Winn commanded the reserve stationed between Sumter's position and the house. They now had nothing to do but wait, and if the fight was to be on that day it had to come soon, for the shadows were beginning to lengthen. Captain William Blackstock was off serving with Colonel Benjamin Roebuck's Rebel militia regiment, but his wife Mary was at home with their family, and she took a dim view of armed men deploying on the homestead. It is reported that she marched up to Thomas Sumter and said, "General, I won't have any fighting around my house."[20] Sumter's reply was not preserved, but it was late in the day for Mary Blackstock to object, and all she could do was retreat to the house and hope for the best.

Tarleton was pushing hard. In the late morning his scouts had found Sumter's trail leading to a ford at the Enoree, where Captain Carr waited with his detachment on the other side. Carr had with him some five Tory prisoners. The van of Tarleton's column appeared and immediately charged across the ford. Carr and his force galloped off, leaving the prisoners behind, and before these unfortunates could identify themselves to the Legion dragoons they were cut down by slashing sabers. In his postwar *History* Tarleton misrepresented the incident, identified the Tories as Rebels and described their defeat "with considerable slaughter."[21] It would not be the last time that his horsemen in their impetuosity took the lives of helpless friends of the King.

About mid-afternoon it was apparent that the infantry and the artillery could not keep up, whereupon Tarleton did what we would expect: instructing the veteran Major McArthur to come on with his Highlanders and the artillery as fast as possible, Bloody Ban set his usual torrid pace with the Legion horse and the mounted infantry of the 63rd Foot. Not very far ahead of him Major William Candler of Georgia was returning from a foraging expedition and had just entered Sumter's lines when Tarleton's van came into view and was fired on by Rebel pickets. Colonel Thomas Taylor and his party, returning from his raid on the British supply depot at Summer's Mills, was not far behind Candler and came at the gallop with wagons loaded with flour and Tarleton's van at his heels. Taylor slipped into Sumter's lines with little to spare.

The sun was fading. With only one hour of light left, Tarleton was desperate not to allow Sumter to get across the Tyger. Even he, however, hesitated. This was not Fishing Creek. The Rebels were neither asleep nor relaxing unguarded. He knew that he was greatly outnumbered, 270 to 1,000, with the artillery and the bulk of his infantry hours behind him. His soldier's eye for terrain must have told him that the ground also was not to his advantage. Sumter, on the other hand, was confident. He knew that Tarleton's infantry and artillery was well behind, for a woman, Mrs. Mary Dillard, who lived on a farm six miles from Blackstocks, had seen Tarleton's advance column and had saddled a horse and galloped to Sumter's camp and told him the strength and composition of Tarleton's force.

Authorities differ on who initiated the action. Tarleton did not follow his usual style and charge pell mell at the Rebels on reaching Blackstock's, but he wanted to keep Sumter on his side of the river while awaiting the arrival of artillery and McArthur's Highlanders, and the manner in which he deployed invited Sumter's reaction. Tarleton formed on top of the hill that descended to the shallow stream, where the ground began to rise again to the Blackstock farmhouse and outbuildings on the opposite hill. He ordered Lieutenant John Money to dismount the eighty men of the 63rd Foot, cross to the right side of the road, and advance downhill until he reached Blackstock's field. Lieutenant Money formed his men, ordered bayonets fixed, and swept toward Colonel Twiggs's 100 Georgia riflemen stationed in Blackstock's field. Watching from his own high ground, Sumter countered by ordering Colonel William Few and Major Joseph McJunkin to take 400 men and go to the support of Twiggs by marching down the field, across the shallow stream, and attacking uphill against the 63rd Foot. They carried out the first part of their assignment, but they were out in the open and ahead of them disciplined British regulars with fixed bayonets were advancing steadily. Whether that sight unnerved them or not, we do know that about halfway down the field they halted and delivered a volley at too great a distance. Unharmed, Lieutenant Money and his eighty men swept forward with bayonets presented in a counterattack that the Rebel militia would not meet. Twiggs's Georgians and the militia of Few and McJunkin retreated, we suspect not in an orderly manner, and could not be rallied until they passed Blackstock's house.

It was a sterling performance by Money and his little force. But in the euphoria of the moment Lieutenant John Money led his infantryman too far up Blackstock's field and came well within killing range of Henry Hampton's riflemen sheltered in the log outbuildings and firing through the spaces between the logs. At 200 yards Hampton's sharpshooters took the 63rd under fire. They followed the familiar Rebel tactic of aiming first at epaulets and crossbelts. Lieutenant Cope was shot dead. Lieutenant Gibson was also shot dead. Lieutenant John Money, as dear as a son to Lord Cornwallis, sword in hand at the head of his charging line, was shot, knocked off of his feet, and put out of action with a very bad wound. Death rained down on the 63rd Foot. According to an officer of Fraser's Highlanders who arrived on the scene after the battle, one-third of the privates fell. But those stoic Englishmen would not back off and continued to contest the field.

Meanwhile, Sumter had galloped to Colonel Lacey's position on the American right and ordered Lacey to slip through the woods to Tarleton's flank and take the British Legion under fire. Tarleton and his troopers were still astride their horses on top of the hill watching the infantry fight on the opposite slope. Tarleton had made no effort to stop Money's impetuous advance. Intent on the action in front of them, neither Tarleton nor his men observed Lacey's stealthy movement through the woods. At a point fifty to seventy-five yards from the British cavalry Lacey's men opened up with buckshot. Twenty troopers were shot out of their saddles. But the situation was brought immediately under control, Tarleton wrote, when "Lieutenant Skinner bravely repulsed the detachment that threatened the flank" by charging with the saber.

There remained, however, a worsening situation on the opposite slope. The 63rd needed help, and Tarleton gave it to them in his customary manner. The Legion bugle echoed over the little valley and the horsemen in column thundered down the hill behind Tarleton, galloped across the stream, and with sabers raised charged up the far hill. Tarleton told his version in the third person after the war. "Though the undertaking appeared hazardous . . . Tarleton determined to charge the enemy's center with a column of Dragoons, in order to cover the 63rd, whose position was now become dangerous. The attack was conducted with great celerity and was attended with immediate success. The cavalry soon reached the houses and broke the Americans, who from that instant began to disperse. The 63rd immediately rallied, and darkness put an end to the engagement." Tarleton claimed that three American colonels "fell in the action, and . . . upwards of one hundred Americans were killed and wounded, and fifty were made prisoners." He admitted to fifty-one British killed and wounded.[22]

Tarleton lied. He lied in his battle report to Cornwallis, and he lied in his *History*. He did indeed extricate the 63rd Foot, and he performed an act of personal heroism when he dismounted under fire and picked up the badly wounded Lieutenant John Money; throwing him over his horse, he remounted and carried Money off the field. But he did not reach the buildings, he did not break the American center or any part of its line, he did not cause the Rebels to immediately disperse, he inflicted minimum casualties on them, and he lost far more men than he admitted. He was stopped cold by decisive fire from his front and right flank. Hampton's South Carolina riflemen in the outbuildings and the riflemen behind the stout log fence and in the thick woods nearby met the charge of the Legion dragoons with the same volume of accurate fire that crippled the 63rd. In his own postwar memoirs, which are supported by other sources, Colonel William Hill remembered "The Americans having the advantage of the before mentioned fence, together with the thick wood just by the fence, that before they got through the Lane their front both men and horses fell so fast that the way was nearly stopt up—a retreat was then ordered which was a pleasing sight for the Americans to behold—so many falling either by wounds or stumbling over the dead horses or men."[23]

Lieutenant Roderick McKenzie of Fraser's Highlanders, who admittedly bore considerable personal animosity against Tarleton for reasons we will discuss in another chapter, nevertheless in his published criticism of Tarleton's memoirs presented a more accurate account of what really happened at Blackstocks. He claimed that his version was "collected from the concurrent testimony of several officers of veracity, who were in action in that engagement." McKenzie admitted that "British valour was conspicuous in this action; but no valour could surmount the obstacles and disadvantages that here flood in its way. The 63rd was roughly handled; the commanding officer, two others, with one-third of their privates, fell. Lieutenant Colonel Tarleton, observing their situation, charged with his cavalry; unable to dislodge the enemy, either from the log barn or the height upon his left, he was obliged to fall back. Lieutenant Skinner, attached to the cavalry, with a presence of mind ever useful in such emergencies, covered the retreat of the 63d. In this manner did the whole party continue to retire, till they formed a junction with their infantry, who were advancing to sustain them, leaving Sumter in quiet possession of the field." As for American casualties, McKenzie wrote, "The real truth is that the Americans being well sheltered, sustained very inconsiderable loss in the attack; and as for the three Colonels, they must certainly have been imaginary beings, 'men in buckram'."[24] The best estimate of Rebel casualties is three killed and four wounded. Tarleton lost ninety-two killed and seventy-six wounded, or sixty-two percent of his command that engaged the enemy.

Of the Rebel wounded, however, one was Thomas Sumter, and it was serious. It happened after the shambles of Tarleton's cavalry charge, when the survivors of the Legion and the 63rd were stumbling back down the road, with the cries of the wounded and the shrieks of dying horses adding to the horror and confusion. Sumter, followed by his officers, rode down for a close look, probably to within fifty to eighty yards of the retreating British. A platoon of the 63rd, perhaps under the command of the Lieutenant Skinner praised by McKenzie, was covering the retreat. They saw Sumter and his party, raised their muskets, and fired a volley. Captain David Hopkins wrote to his sons that "Captain Gabriel Brown was killed on my left hand and General Sumter was on my right. It happened from one platoon of the enemy on their retreat."[25]

It is said that Sumter, seeing his danger at the last minute, twisted sideways, giving the Redcoats his right profile instead of his heart. He was hit by six buckshot. Five went into the side of his chest. The sixth hit him under his right shoulder, kept going and chipped his spine, and finally came to rest under his left shoulder. Sumter made neither a sound nor a movement to indicate that he had been shot. His sword was still gripped in his right hand. He and his surviving officers rode back to the command post on the hill. He dismounted, and still his officers were unaware that he had been wounded. Then Captain Robert McKelvey heard liquid spattering on fallen leaves, looked at Sumter and in the dim light left of the day saw blood running down the General's back and onto the ground. He exclaimed that the General had been wounded. Sumter told him to be quiet. He asked Colonel Henry Hampton, whose sharpshooters in the outbuildings had done such deadly work that day, to please take his sword from him and sheath it, as he could not move his right arm. Sumter then attempted to continue to direct the action, but he soon saw that he could not and asked Colonel Hampton to inform the senior colonel, John Twiggs of Georgia, to take command of the troops.

Sumter was carried into the Blackstock farmhouse and laid on a bed. By now he could hardly speak. His manservant Soldier Tom was there, and it was to him that Sumter admitted that he was very badly hurt and to fetch the doctor. Dr. Robert Brownfield, who was on the battlefield tending the wounded, came immediately. The shot under Sumter's left shoulder presented the most danger, and there was nothing to do in the total absence of anesthetics but for the general to grit his teeth while Dr. Brownfield probed for the shot and then dug it out. Sumter was semiconscious when he was laid gently on a raw bull's hide that was attached to poles and slung between two horses. The faithful Colonel Edward Lacey and a bodyguard of 100 riders escorted their fallen general by torchlight down the steep incline behind Blackstock's house to the Tyger, across the ford, then cross-country over two more rivers, the Pacolet and the Broad, to safety in the partisan camp at Steel Creek in present-day York County, South Carolina.

In the meantime Colonel John Twiggs had taken charge in a convincing manner. Horsemen were sent to harass the retreating British, and during this foray Major James Jackson and his Georgians captured thirty riderless horses. The wounded of both sides were brought in. The fallen British were treated well, Roderick McKenzie recorded, with the "strictest humanity" and "supplied with every comfort."[26] Twiggs ordered Colonel Winn to light decoy campfires. Then, in a cold late November drizzle, the partisans rode slowly from the field, and once across the Tyger dispersed to their homes to await yet another battle.

Tarleton had withdrawn to another hill two miles from Blackstocks and camped for the night. There he waited for McArthur's Highlanders and the artillery. In the morning he intended to take another crack at Sumter, and arrived of course to find only the dead and the wounded, whom he buried or cared for. It has been maintained that even though it was a tactical defeat for Tarleton, he had successfully carried out Cornwallis's overall purpose of protecting the post at Williams Plantation as well as Ninety Six, and furthermore had dispersed the partisans. But partisans almost always dispersed after a fight, victorious or otherwise, only to spring up again when the need arose. Sumter had been diverted from Williams Plantation, but it is most unlikely that he intended to attack Ninety Six. It has also been claimed that the partisans dispersed because they were disheartened after Sumter was struck down, but that view is not based on evidence. As for the real consequence of Sumter's wounds, that is quite another matter.

On 22 November Tarleton wrote to Cornwallis claiming victory and his intention not to attack Sumter, "only to harass and lie close to him till I could bring up the rest of the Corps, as he could never pass the Tyger if I had attacked. The 63rd were attacked by the Enemy which brought on the affair." He also reported that Sumter had been badly wounded, and that "three young men of Ferguson's Corps have promised to fix Sumter immediately. I have promised them for the deed 50 guineas each in case he falls into our hands." Cornwallis replied, "I shall be very glad to hear that Sumter is in a position to give us no further trouble." He also congratulated Tarleton on his success, "but wish it had not cost you so much." He discovered that it had cost more than he realized when Major Archibald McArthur wrote His Lordship on 1 December to inform him that Lieutenant John Money had that night died of his wounds.[27]

The fiction of Tarleton's victory carried over to Cornwallis's official report to Sir Henry Clinton. "It is not easy for Lieutenant-Colonel Tarleton to add to the reputation he has acquired in this province; but the defeating one thousand men, posted on very strong ground, and occupying log houses, with one hundred and ninety cavalry and eighty infantry, is a proof of that spirit and those talents which must render the most essential services to his country."[28]

The overwhelming importance of Blackstocks was not that Banastre Tarleton had been defeated for the first time, although the puncturing of his balloon was a not inconsiderable by-product. Nor was it the severe losses suffered by Tarleton, even though Cornwallis's little army would sorely miss the hard-to-replace regulars. The defeat of those regulars by militia was heartening but not unique, for it had been done by accurate firepower delivered from behind cover; militia had yet to prove that it could face and overcome regulars on an open field.

The crucial significance of Blackstocks was the wounding of Thomas Sumter, but not for the reasons ascribed by the British. The platoon of the 63rd that laid Sumter low never realized it but their deed was of the greatest benefit to the Rebel cause. Sumter would be out of action for the next two months. During those months highly significant changes took place in the command and strategy of the Southern Department, and a battle that was critical to the campaign was fought. Had the prickly Sumter remained in active command, he almost certainly would have seriously compromised if not wrecked the plans of the new commander of the Southern Department through his lack of strategic sense and his stubborn refusal to cooperate with Continental commanders. The Gamecock had rendered valiant service in dark and perilous times and would survive his terrible wound and again take the field. But at this particular time it was a boon for the cause that he was forced to the sidelines.

18

A General from Rhode Island

"I lament the want of a liberal Education"

Nathanael Greene has long been regarded by students of the War of the Revolution as second only to Washington, and the great Virginian considered him his successor if he should be struck down. Yet the names of other men are more familiar. He was one of the great generals of American history, and could have held his own on any stage, but even Horatio Gates has greater name recognition. For Nathanael Greene lacked traits that add color to a personality and thus strike an immediate chord for contemporaries or appeal to distant posterity. I would wager that a minor player like Ethan Allen is better known than Nathanael Greene. How ironic that Greene, who dared more than most generals, comes across as bland. Although he was a superb field commander, saw much action, and often risked his life in battle, he was not a legendary battle captain. He made his mark as a brilliant strategist. Unfortunately, cerebral superiority, and Greene was a very cerebral man, does not always make one a popular hero for the ages. He was also a military craftsman whose mastery of geography, supply, and transport was unmatched by his contemporaries, but these essential virtues of a great commander lack the glamor of battlefield feats.[1] Finally, despite its critical importance to the cause and the attention paid to it by generations of students and writers, the war in the South remains an historical terra incognita. And it was in the South that Nathanael Greene displayed his brilliance as an independent theatre commander.

In the British army it would have been difficult for Greene to become an officer, much less a general. He was a Quaker, anchorsmith, forgemaster, and small merchant, lame for life because of a stiff knee, and he suffered so severely from asthma that in 1772 he wrote to a kinsman, "I have not slept six hours in four nights, being obliged to sit up the last two nights."[2] Of the fifth generation of his family in America, Nathanael Greene was born 27 July 1742 in Po-

Nathanael Greene, by Charles Willson Peale.
(Independence National Historical Park Collection.)

towomut, Rhode Island, in a farmhouse, still standing today, that was built by
his great-grandfather in 1684. His father, also Nathanael, was prosperous; the
elder Greene and his brothers inherited the farm, a flour and grist mill, a
sawmill, ironworks, a wharf and warehouse, a dam, and a sluiceway from their
father. Later they established a forge, anchorworks, and mills on the Pawtuxet
River in Coventry. The family owned a small vessel and engaged in coastal
trade, and this aspect of the family business would later play a role in Nathanael
Greene's progression from an obscure provincial forgemaster and small merchant without apparent strong political feelings to one of England's most dangerous military foes. Despite his father's prosperity the boy was expected to pull
his weight; he knew hard labor on the farm from an early age and spent long
years at the forge learning his craft.[3]

His father did not believe in book learning, and thus Nathanael had limited formal education, which he deplored in a letter of 1772: "Early, very early,
when I should have been in pursuit of knowledge, I was diging into the Bowels
of the Earth after Wealth." But the boy had a keen intellect, an inquiring mind,

and from his late teens a voracious appetite for books. Encouraged by others, including the future president of Yale, Ezra Stiles, and the grammarian Lindley Murray, he read widely. Although Quakers then objected to higher education, Nathanael's passion for knowledge was so intense that he persuaded his father to hire a local schoolmaster to tutor him in Latin and mathematics. He devoted himself to the study of Euclid. His brother Christopher told Nathanael's grandson that he would go to a little room over the kitchen to study his book uninterrupted, and "in my boyhood," wrote the grandson George Washington Greene, "his brothers still loved to point out the seat by the forge where he would study it while the iron was heating and . . . how when his turn called him to the grist-mill he would often forget himself in his book long after the last kernel had been shaken from the hopper."[4]

Although he gave up Latin, over the years he accumulated a library of translations of the best-known works in Latin that he obviously studied closely. George Washington Greene related that in 1835 he and Longfellow were told by Pierre Etienne Duponceau, who had been an aide to Baron von Steuben, "that in a long evening which he passed with General Greene and Baron Steuben, on their journey southward in 1780, 'Greene turned the conversation upon the Latin poets, with whom he seemed perfectly familiar.'"[5] In addition to his collection of Latin translations, Greene put together an eclectic library of over 200 books on various subjects, and as war threatened he added books on military affairs, especially the writings of the two famous French marshals, Saxe and Turenne. Despite his intellectual endeavors, however, he remained a forge-master and small merchant.

Greene's persistence from an early age in pursuing knowledge reveals a man with a mind of his own and an aversion to the religion of his ancestors. His father died in 1770, and thereafter his attendance at Quaker Meetings was spotty. And on 5 July 1773 Nathanael and his cousin Griffin Greene were suspended from the East Greenwich Meeting of the Society of Friends. The editors of Greene's papers make it clear that the reason was not, as repeated by several writers since 1822, for attending a military parade but for being at "a Place in Coneticut of *Publick Resort* where they had No Proper Business." A public resort in the eighteenth century was a place of pleasure, which could have been in Nathanael's case at least a tavern and at most a whorehouse or "other place of questionable repute." It is reasonable to speculate that the suspension had little effect on him, although the pious members of the family were undoubtedly scandalized. He had made his feelings quite clear in a letter of 9 October 1772 to his friend Samuel Ward, Jr. "I lament the want of a liberal Education. I feel the mist [of] Ignorance to surround me, for my own part I was Educated a Quaker, and amongst the most Supersticious sort, and that of its self is a sufficient Obstacle to cramp the best of Geniuses; much more mine. This constrained manner of Educating their Youth has prov'd a fine Nursery of Ignorance and Supersticon instead of piety; and has laid a foundation for Form instead of Worship." His alienation from the Quakers extended to their pacifism. Writing to his brother Jacob five years later from camp in New Jersey he described Penn-sylvania as being "in great confusion. The Quakers are poisoning everybody; foolish people." He had already withdrawn from the Society. On 5 April 1777 he requested of the East Greenwich Meeting to be "put from under the care of Friends . . . for the Futur."[6]

Prior to 1772 surviving records reveal no interest on the part of Nathanael Greene in the momentous political and constitutional issues that were building to a boiling point between mother country and the colonies. Then, on the night of 17 February 1772, Lieutenant William Dudingston, a particularly tough British naval officer and skipper of HMS *Gaspee*, sailed into Narragansett Bay to stop the favorite avocation of New Englanders in general and Rhode Islanders in par-ticular—smuggling. Off North Kingstown he seized the sloop *Fortune*. It carried rum, Jamaica spirits, and brown sugar and was commanded by Rufus Greene, Nathanael Greene's twenty-three-year-old cousin. *Fortune* was the Greene fam-ily's coastal trading vessel. Rufus Greene was insulted, pushed around, hit on the head, knocked down, and threatened by a British officer with a sword. The Greenes were incensed and Rhode Islanders took up the family's cause as theirs, for what happened to one merchant could happen to others, who were, after all, only engaged in their God-given right to smuggle rum, sugar, and molasses rather than pay duties that everyone knew Parliament had no right to levy. On the night of 9 June 1772, after *Gaspee* ran aground seven miles south of Providence, a mob that included respectable merchants rowed silently from the city in eight longboats to *Gaspee*, shot Lieutenant Dudingston in the arm and groin, evacu-ated the vessel, and burned it. It was the most celebrated incident of defiance in Rhode Island before the climate was changed by the event in Lexington, Mas-sachusetts. The evidence points strongly to Rufus Greene being one of the mob. And thereafter Nathanael Greene feared that the "Priviledges and Liberties of the People will be trampled to Death by the Prerogatives of the Crown," as he wrote on 25 January 1773 to his friend Samuel Ward, Jr.[7]

About a year before first blood was spilled at Lexington, Nathanael Greene's personal life took a sharp turn. He fell totally and forever in love. Catherine Littlefield, known always as Caty, was born on wind-blown Block Is-land to a well-connected Rhode Island family. She was nineteen years old in the summer of 1774, thirteen years his junior. She had looks and wit, and accord-ing to tradition "her power of fascination was absolutely irresistible." A con-temporary described her as a "small brunette with high color, a vivacious expression, and a snapping pair of dark eyes." Following a swift courtship, they were married on 20 July 1774. Nathanael Greene was enchanted with her for the rest of his life. They lived in a house he had built in Coventry for less than a year before he went to war for the greater part of their married life, and for most of that period she was plagued by gossips who accused her of infidelity. That other men fell in love with her is true, that she probably encouraged them is a reasonable assumption, that she was unfaithful to her husband some have accepted without offering solid evidence. Isaac Briggs, a Georgia politician who on his own investigated the story that Nathanael Greene was suing for divorce for infidelity, "found 'twas all a lie," and in a letter of 1785 left a delightful description of Caty's character as well as her own charming summing up of her predicament and how she met it: "She confesses she has passions and propensities & that if she has any virtue 'tis in resisting and keeping them within due bounds." Briggs had a high regard for her, and Nathanael Greene staunchly defended her against slander in New England and Georgia.[8]

The year of their marriage, perhaps in August, East Greenwich formed a militia unit called The Military Independent Company, soon renamed, more stylishly, the Kentish Guards. Nathanael Greene was one of the principal men involved in its formation, and he expected to be elected one of its lieutenants. Given his role establishing the Guards and his family's solid middle-class status it seemed a reasonable expectation. His rejection on 25 October 1774 by his fellow militia members came as a shock. Six days later he wrote to the captain of the Guards, James Varnum, "I was informd the Gentlemen of East Greenwich said that I was a blemish to the company. I confess it is the first stroke of mortification that I ever felt from being considered either in private or publick Life a blemish to those with whom I associated." Further on in the letter he referred for the only known time in writing to a subject that pained him deeply. "I confess it is my misfortune to limp a little but I did not conceive it to be so great: but we are not apt to discover our own defects. I feel the less mortified at it as its natural and not a stain or defection that resulted from my Actions." The penultimate sentence reveals how much the Gentlemen of East Greenwich had hurt him. "I feel more mortification than resentment, but I think it would have manifested a more generous temper to have given me their Oppinions in private than to make a proclamation of it in publick as a capital objection, for nobody loves to be the subject of ridicule however true the cause." He considered resigning but stayed and served as a private in the ranks.[9]

Then something mysterious occurred. After the clash in April 1775 between the Minutemen and the Redcoats at Lexington, Rhode Island increased its military establishment. When Boston came under siege by the Rebels, the Assembly sent it what was officially called the Rhode Island Army of Observation. Such a force required a brigadier general to lead it. On 8 May 1775, a little over six months after his public rejection by the "Gentlemen of East Greenwich," Nathanael Greene was elevated to Brigadier General of the Army of Observation. Private to brigadier general in one fell swoop, probably the fastest promotion in American military history. How had this happened? There were officers already available, including his own commander James Varnum, and some were veterans of the French and Indian War. It was true that he was deeply read in military affairs, undoubtedly better versed than anyone in Rhode Island and most in the Colonies. But it was all book knowledge. Outside of some eight months on the militia drill field, Nathanael Greene had no military experience. Perhaps he had impressed key Assembly members with his knowledge of the subject. He had good family connections, but they did not belong to the dominant faction in Rhode Island politics, and no colonial institution was more political than the militia. It is an intriguing historical question to which the answer may never be found. What matters is that the Rhode Island Assembly, for whatever reasons, had chosen most wisely.[10]

Learning His Trade:
"I feel mad, vext, sick, and sorry"

George Washington and Nathanael Greene met for the first time exactly one year before independence, 4 July 1775, outside Boston. Washington saw before him a man ten years younger than himself, standing five feet ten inches, with the broad shoulders and powerful arms of his craft, inclining to portliness, with bright blue eyes and a countenance marked by a candor, serenity, and well-being that lent confidence to almost all who knew him. If he spoke as well as he wrote, Washington had further reason to be impressed. They immediately liked each other. It was the beginning of a relationship that never came asunder. Alexander Hamilton wrote that Washington "marked him as the object of his confidence," and that Greene "preserved it amidst all the checkered varities of military vicissitude." The relationship was strengthened when their wives came to camp. Martha Washington and Caty Greene became good friends, and Washington, who always appreciated a pretty woman, liked her, too. Washington also quickly gained evidence of Greene's abilities; still an amateur soldier the anchorsmith turned brigadier general might be, but Washington observed that Greene's troops, "though raw, irregular, and undisciplined are under much better government than any around Boston." His readings in military history, his intuitive grasp of military affairs, his high intelligence, and his natural ability had already put him well on the way to the mastery of military administration. And as time went on he revealed a keen analytical mind that we will watch come to full fruition in the Carolina maelstrom.[11]

Congress soon appointed Greene a Brigadier General of Continentals, and he was a regular member of councils of war called by Washington during the siege of Boston, at which he learned that councils of war usually advise against aggressive action. The British evacuated Boston in March 1780, and a few months later Sir William Howe undertook the invasion of New York City. Greene was given command of the American forces on Long Island, but he along with several hundred of his troops was felled by sickness, probably malaria, and missed the overwhelming American defeat in Brooklyn. He wrote to his brother Jacob on 30 August, "Gracious God! to be confined at such a time. And the misfortune is doubly great as there was no general officer who had made himself acquainted with the ground as perfectly as I had. I have not the vanity to think the event would have been otherwise had I been there, yet I think I could have given the commanding general a good deal of necessary information." If behind his necessary modesty was the belief that he could have avoided defeat, Greene was deluding himself, for no American general and army were going to stop Howe's 20,000 British and Hessian regulars. Let John Adams and others think that "Greene's sickness I conjecture, has been the cause" of the British "stealing a march on us."[12]

Following his success in spiriting his defeated army across the East River to Manhattan, Washington called a council of war and asked his generals whether any further attempt should be made to defend New York City. Greene, who had returned to duty on 5 September, then advised Washington to "burn the city and Subburbs." He felt strongly that given the panic in the country over the debacle on Long Island the army could not risk another major defeat and that "A General and speedy retreat from this Island is necessary." But why turn over to the enemy a ready-made stronghold complete with comfortable shelter for his army? "Not one benefit can arise to us from its preservation that I can conceive off," Greene observed. In an excellent letter of advice one sentence especially stands out, for it highlights very early in Greene's career his understanding of the nature of the war and in very few words summarizes his strategy in the South. "Tis our business to study to avoid any considerable misfortune, and to take post where the Enemy wll be obligd to fight us and not we them." The council disagreed and urged that the city be defended. But the army was spread the length of Manhattan, from the Battery to King's Bridge across the Harlem River. As Greene had pointed out, "Our Troops are now so scatterd that one part may be cut off before the others can come to their support." He was so upset by the decision that he, along with other officers, prevailed on Washington to call another council, which he did on 12 September 1776. At that meeting the council reversed itself by a ten to three vote. The decision to evacuate was taken, but it was too late. Before Manhattan could be cleared of men and supplies the British were upon them.[13]

Greene's troops, all militia, were stationed in the Kip's Bay area. Greene was in his quarters in northern Manhattan, on Harlem Heights. On the morning of 15 September the troops at Kip's Bay looked onto the East River and saw the water covered with boats, eighty-four flatboats to be exact, so packed with Redcoats that an American militiaman described them as "a large clover field in full bloom" The fire of seventy cannon from five warships increased their anxiety to and beyond the breaking point. Like the Virginia and North Carolina militia at Camden, a brigade of Connecticut militia fled "with the utmost precipitation." The hysteria became contagious. Americans ran from Redcoats and Hessians as fast as their feet and energy could carry them. It was not a retreat, it was a rout: wild, disorderly, confused, and, in Washington's words, "disgraceful and dastardly." But it was partly his fault for deploying his troops so badly. He was lucky to escape with most of them, which was due to their speed afoot.[14]

The impact of this rout of militia upon Nathanael Greene was recorded less than two weeks later in a letter of 28 September to his brother Jacob. "The policy of Congress has been the most absurd and ridiculous imaginable, pouring in militia men who come and go every month. A military force established upon such principles defeat itself. People coming from home with all the tender feelings of domestic life are not sufficiently fortified with natural courage to stand the shocking scenes of war. To march over dead men, to hear without concern the groans of the wounded, I say few men can stand such scenes unless steeled by habit or fortified by military pride.

"There must be a good army established: men engaged for the war, a proper corps of officers, and then, after a proper time to discipline the men everything is to be expected."[15] Greene wrote for professional soldiers of all ages, and from a strictly military point of view there is no question that he was right. But four years later in the South he would express similar views to the wrong people. They would not forget, and they would take their revenge.

The day following the disgraceful rout at Kip's Bay the Americans took a stand on Harlem Heights, the neck at the northwestern end of Manhattan, where they began digging in on the high ground. The importance of this action should not be exaggerated. It was a two-hour skirmish, not a battle, and the Americans fought the British van, not the main army. But the spirited behavior of the Americans, including the Connecticut militia that had fled Kip's Bay, was in direct contrast to their pusillanimity only the day before. The British van was forced to withdraw. Americans stood against regulars in an open field and traded volleys. Greene's only comment on his role was, "I had the Honor to Command." But Colonel Joseph Reed describes Greene, himself, and other officers riding to the front in order to "animate the Troops," admitting that it was perhaps "rash and imprudent for Officers of our Rank to go into such a action."[16] On the contrary. The army badly needed a victory, however minor, needed to see the backs of Redcoats, needed to be so spirited that Washington had to stop them from pursuing too far. In his first experience in battle, Nathanael Greene had done what a general should do in such a situation.

True to his leisurely style, Lord Howe waited a month before making his next move, whether from natural torpor, political reasons, or a preference for the company of Mrs. Loring still a matter of historical debate. The Americans meanwhile strengthened their defenses, including Fort Washington on the cliffs overlooking the Hudson. The fort was made of earth, pentagonal in shape, with an abatis but no ditch, and it lacked a well. The nearest water was 230 feet below in the Hudson River. Captain Alexander Graydon of Pennsylvania described it as not "in any degree capable of withstanding a siege."[17] Worse, its only important function, to help prevent British ships from ascending the Hudson, had been proven useless. Yet Nathanael Greene, whose earlier advice on abandoning Manhattan had been correct, now committed the worst mistake of his military career. He insisted that Fort Washington could and should be held.

Following his failure to either trap Washington or crush him at White Plains, Howe decided to deal with Fort Washington. The commander in chief was deeply concerned, and wrote to Greene on 8 November, following the passage of three British ships up the Hudson River, "If we cannot prevent Vessells passing up, and the Enemy are possessed of the surrounding Country what valuable purpose can it answer to attempt to hold a post from which the expected Benefit cannot be had. I am therefore inclined to think it will not be prudent to hazard the Men and Stores at Mount Washington, but as you are on the

Spot, leave it to you to give such Orders as to evacuating Mount Washington as you judge best, and so far revoking the Order given Colo Magaw to defend it to the last." Washington had correctly identified why Fort Washington should not be defended and without making it an order had invited Greene to evacuate the post. But Greene supported the commander, Colonel Robert Magaw, who told him that he could hold the fort until the end of the year. Greene replied to Washington on 9 November, "Upon the whole, I cannot help thinking the Garrison is of advantage, and I cannot conceive the Garrison to be in any great danger. The men can be brought off at any time, but the stores may not be so easily removd. Yet I think they can be got off in spight of them if matters grow desperate."[18]

Washington's concern was so strong, however, that on 12 November he went to Fort Lee on the New Jersey side of the river and discussed the matter with Greene, but no conclusion was reached. On the 14th he returned, and early the next morning was rowed across the river with Greene to Fort Washington in time for a surprise—"a severe cannonade" that marked the beginning of Howe's attack. Having failed to overrule his self-confident young subordinate, Washington had left it too late. There was nothing to do but recross the river a half hour before the British surrounded Fort Washington and observe helplessly from Fort Lee while 8,000 British and Hessian regulars made a mockery of Magaw's brave words and Greene's inexplicable optimism. The attack began at 7:00 A.M. Magaw surrendered at 3:00 P.M. Taken prisoner were 230 officers and about 2,800 men. Over the next eighteen months two-thirds of them would die in appalling conditions of captivity. Also lost to the British here and elsewhere were 146 cannon, 12,000 rounds of artillery ammunition, 2,800 muskets, 400,000 cartridges, and all of the command's equipment. It was the worst defeat suffered by the Rebels until Benjamin Lincoln surrendered Charleston to Sir Henry Clinton.

Brigadier General Nathanael Greene was crushed. He wrote the next day to his friend Henry Knox, "I feel mad, vext, sick, and sorry. Never did I need the consoling voice of a friend more than now. Happy should I be to see you. This is a most terrible Event. Its consequences are justly to be dreaded. Pray what is said upon the Occasion. A line from you will be very acceptable."[19] To speculate on Greene's stubborn refusal to face reality in this particular situation would be fruitless. We know that he was a very self-confident man. We know that in November 1776 he was still a very inexperienced soldier. We also know that never again did he even come close to making such a serious error of judgment, although Lord Cornwallis almost caught him napping at Fort Lee four days later.

It was raining on the night of 19 November when Cornwallis, under orders from an unusually energetic Sir William Howe, mustered between 4,000 and 6,000 men on the New York side of the Hudson, and early the following morning landed undetected on the Jersey side. With his troops he scaled the Palisades by a perilous path and immediately marched toward Fort Lee, about six miles south on the banks of the Hudson River. It was a situation ripe for a disaster that might well have occurred but for the attention to duty of an American sentry on the Palisades. According to Greene's volunteer aide, the great political journalist and polemicist Tom Paine, the sentry spotted the British column and spread the alarm before Cornwallis could get his force to the top of the cliffs. Green got word to Washington at Hackensack, who ordered Fort Lee evacuated, a dignified term for a race to get away.

The Americans left in such a hurry the soldiers' breakfasts were still cooking in great cast-iron camp kettles over open fires, as Greene got them under arms and on the road to Hackensack. A "want of Waggons" meant another staggering loss of supplies and equipment. It was another lesson in the hard-earned education of Nathanael Greene. Luck, the handmaiden of every successful general, had been with him, however, and despite his blunder at Fort Washington his commander in chief did not lose faith in him. He and his men joined Washington and the rest of the army in the terrible retreat through New Jersey with Cornwallis at their heels.

With the Americans driven across the Delaware into Pennsylvania, their force decreased to some 5,000 ragged and poorly equipped men, and, as Howe proclaimed, "the Approach of Winter putting a Stop to any further Progress," Sir William officially closed the campaign of 1776.[20] Washington, desperate to keep the cause alive in "times that try men's souls," decided otherwise, and Nathanael Greene was with him in his brilliant winter campaign in New Jersey. He led one of the two principal columns at Trenton in the great victory over the Hessians, the same troops who had stormed Fort Washington. At Princeton he and General John Cadwalader assisted Washington in rallying Mercer's broken brigade. From despair to exhilaration in a few short months. Nathanael Greene was earning his spurs and storing in that incisive mind a rich vein of experience that he could draw on in the hard years of campaigning that lay before him. He would more than prove himself as a fighting general in the next major battle between the main Rebel army and Sir William Howe, but before that he became involved in that constant of the War of the Revolution, a fight with Congress.

It began when the American agent in Paris, Silas Deane of Connecticut, exceeded his authority and signed a contract making Philippe Charles Jean Baptiste Tronson de Coudray a Major General in the Continental Army with the title of General of Artillery and Ordnance. Coudray was a smart, energetic, well-connected, and highly professional artillerist—and an arrogant troublemaker. His commission was backdated to 1 August 1776, which made him senior to Greene and many other officers. When Coudray got to Philadelphia with Lafayette's party he demanded that Congress honor the contract. Congress was most reluctant, but at the same time, given Coudray's connections, felt it could not just brush him off without jeapordizing badly needed French aid. A compromise was required, but before that occurred Generals Greene, Knox, and Sullivan wrote prematurely to Congress threatening to resign. In one sense members of Congress were still good 18th-century Englishmen, having imbibed a deep distrust of the military with their mothers' milk, and they deeply resented "dictation" from soldiers.[21] The congressmen were deeply offended. Some wanted the generals dismissed. John Adams and Nathanael Greene were friends, and Adams suggested to Greene that he apologize. Greene refused. Adams was offended. The friendship ended, never to be repaired. Congress came up with a compromise that did not backdate Coudray's commission and made him a major general of staff instead of line, which simply meant that he had no command authority over generals of the line. The distinction is important. Line officers command troops and serve with the combat branches, whereas staff officers serve in various capacities at the headquarters of whatever command to which they are attached.

Whether the compromise would have ended the immediate problem was rendered academic when Coudray's arrogance extended to riding instead of leading a very nervous mare onto the Schuylkill River Ferry outside Philadelphia. The mare kept going, she and her rider ended in the river, and Tronson de Coudray drowned. His death, however, did not end the ill feeling over the affair between the army and Congress, and Greene's role was certainly filed in congressional minds into the compartment labeled old grievances.

Nathanael Greene had no time to worry about political fences when he next went into battle. As we know from Chapter 3, while Burgoyne in northern New York was getting himself into a fix that would end his military career, Sir William Howe had taken his army by sea to the head of the Elk River in Maryland from where he marched north, with Philadelphia as his goal. Washington waited to give battle in Pennsylvania at Chad's Ford on Brandywine Creek. Neither Washington nor his generals, including Nathanael Greene, distinguished themselves on this occasion, either in fathoming Howe's intentions or acquiring knowledge of the geography of the area. The latter failure was a rare lapse on Greene's part. In the South a precise knowledge of the country in which he was campaigning was one of his great strengths. At the Battle of Brandywine, 11 September 1777, Washington and his generals were confident that Howe would attack straight ahead, all but dismissing the possibility that he might do exactly what he had done on Long Island. Which, of course, is what he did.

Leaving the Hessian General Baron Wilhelm von Knyphausen to feint at Chadd's Ford and pin the American army there, Howe and Cornwallis led formidable units on a flanking movement north and then east that ended up in the American rear and threatened to destroy Washington's entire force. Leading the van was the famous partisan captain, Johann Ewald. General John Sullivan's wing was broken by the British assault. But Greene led one of his Virginia brigades, commanded by Brigadier General George Weedon, at a pace that one historian likened to A. P. Hill's dash in 1862 from Harper's Ferry to save Lee's right wing at Antietam. The brigade arrived in time to open its ranks to let through Sullivan's survivors; then it closed up and waged a stubborn and orderly withdrawal. Another defeat, but the main army was saved to fight again. The occupation of Philadelphia would avail the British nothing, and Nathanael

Greene had shown his ability to move a large force quickly. That talent would be absolutely critical in his southern campaign.

Early the next month at Germantown Greene again conducted a fighting retreat. On the fog-shrouded morning of 4 October, in a movement too complicated by far, Washington sent four columns on four parallel roads spread over seven miles to launch a simultaneous frontal assault against British lines outside Philadelphia. It ended in a race by the Americans to get away, but once again Greene exhibited the coolness under pressure that was his hallmark. Pursued by Lord Cornwallis, he saved most of his men and all his guns.

The main army then went into winter quarters. Some members of Congress and government officials expressed their unhappiness with the state of affairs. They looked toward the ragged little army whose winter sojourn at Valley Forge would become an American legend, at its aloof commander, and at the generals who surrounded him. They looked northward too, where Horatio Gates had humbled the proud Burgoyne, and some wondered whether the wrong man was commander in chief. There were those who truly believed that George Washington was incompetent and had to be replaced. Others thought that he was getting bad advice from some of his generals. This subject is highly complicated and just as confused and deserves far more space than we can give it. Our interest is that some voices talked about the "Beardless Youth"[22] whom they claimed dominated Washington. The Gates faction was especially critical. James Lovell, a Massachusetts congressman and ardent supporter of the Hero of Saratoga, described Greene and his 27-year-old friend Henry Knox as Washington's "privy counsellors," and Greene, Knox, and Lafayette as the "reigning Cabal."[23] That Greene opposed Gates's dream of another Canadian expedition no doubt increased the antipathy of this faction. But Congress as a whole should not be viewed as anti-Washington or anti-Greene, and in fact it was a congressional committee that urged Greene to take on the most difficult, and thankless, administrative job in the army. Thus began the most controversial phase of his career.

"I am taken out of the Line of splendor"

Nathanael Greene did not want to be Quartermaster General. He strongly resisted the appointment. He wrote Henry Knox on 26 February 1778, "The Committee of Congress have been urging me for several days to accept the Q M Generals appointment; His Excellency also presses it upon me exceedingly. I hate the place, but hardly know what to do." But something had to be done. The winter of 1777–1778 at Valley Forge was terrible for the troops not so much because of the weather, for it was a mild winter, but because of the wretched supply situation. Greene's success on an expedition earlier in the month, when Washington ordered him to "take, carry off and secure all such Horses as are suitable for Cavalry or for Draft and all Cattle and Sheep fit for slaughter together with every kind of Forage," revealed that he had the ability and moral toughness to do the job. "You must forage the country naked," he ordered one of his officers, and to Washington reported, "The Inhabitants cry out and beset me from all quarters, but like Pharoh I harden my heart." That sealed it. All concerned knew they had found the right man for the job. The Committee was "at me Night and Day," his friends entreated him, Washington, to whom he was devoted, "urged it upon me contrary to my wishes." Finally, he agreed, and on 2 March 1778 Congress approved his appointment with two of the conditions that he had set: the appointment as assistant quartermasters of two men of proven knowledge and ability, John Cox and Charles Pettit; and power given to him to appoint all officers, including the key jobs of forage masters and wagonmasters.[24]

What he wanted most of all, however, was denied him: to remain an officer of the line. Washington, the man he was alleged to dominate, made the decision. Greene continued to hold his rank of major general, but as a staff officer. It darkened his thoughts throughout his tenure. To his friend Joseph Reed he wrote, "I am taken out of the Line of splendor." And to Major General Alexander McDougall, "All of you will be immortallizing your selves in the golden pages of History, while I am confind to a series of druggery to pave the way for it." But it was to George Washington over a year later, in a letter complaining of the difficulties of the job, that he made his most telling comment: "No body ever heard of a quarter Master in History."[25]

Those who would make light of such sentiments misunderstand not only 18th-century soldiers, as the editors of Greene's papers wisely observe, but soldiers of all ages, including our own. But once he took on the job he pursued it with the vigor of an aggressive line officer. His methods worked. He improved the transportation system, established a system of field depots, and by the end of November 1778 the army for the first time was adequately clothed. And it was far better off in its camp at Morristown, New Jersey, during the bitter cold winter of 1778–1779 than it had been at Valley Forge the previous year. There can be no doubt that Greene did an outstanding job as Quartermaster General under horrendous conditions. Unfortunately, the story also has a shadowy side.

Nathanael Greene's 20th-century biographer Theodore Thayer suspected that despite Greene's stated reluctance to taking the job his reasons for finally accepting the appointment were mixed. Devotion to Washington, yes. Deep concern for the condition of the army, of course. Another reason, Thayer believed, was avarice. The system then was for the Quartermaster General to receive a commission of one percent on all expenditures, although Greene and his two deputies agreed to share the commissions equally, one-third to each. Greene himself lent credence to Thayer's view when he wrote in February 1778 with remarkable candor as well as deep insight into his countrymen—now as then: "Money becomes more and more the Americans' object. You must get rich, or you will be of no consequence."[26]

He did not get rich, and in fact at his death left his widow in straitened circumstances; however, there is no doubt that he tried. Keep in mind that there were no blind trusts in those days, nor, as the editors of Greene's papers observe, were there banks, stocks, or bonds. Shipping, real estate, and business were his only outlets for investment. He made his brother Jacob contractor for the Army in Rhode Island. Nathanael was a partner in the company that owned and operated the Coventry Iron Works, which was the family business and engaged in trade, privateering, and in a limited way supplied the army. Nathanael Greene hid his partnership from the public. He never borrowed from public funds, but he earned about $170,000 in specie from his commissions, and he gave his brother and his cousin Griffin Greene large sums of money from that to invest, largely in shipping and privateering. Almost all the privateering investments were lost. In 1779 he entered into a shipping and privateering enterprise with Jeremiah Wadsworth, his friend and the army's commissary, and Barnabas Deane, but all that netted him by 1784 was 960 pounds. Because he was receiving criticism for his dealings, all of their correspondence was encoded. Greene invested in other New England business houses, and also in the Batsto Furnace in New Jersey, which made ammunition and iron goods for the army. Some, including members of Congress, thought he was "too grasping and was making an immense fortune." Greene's reaction to that charge is in a letter of 24 April 1779 to Washington. "I believe it has been a received opinion that I was so very fond of the emoluments of the quarter Masters office, that nothing but absolute necessity would induce me to quit it. I will not deny but that the profits is flattering to my fortune but not less humiliating to my Military pride; and he who has entertained such Sentiments is a stranger to my feelings."[27]

In the end he lost most of the commissions earned, and although that is hardly the point it is still true that 18th-century quartermasters were expected to earn commissions. Standards of public probity were different then. Under our present purist standards, Nathanael Greene would be hounded by the media, crucified by Congress, investigated ad infinitum by a special prosecutor, and the nation thereby deprived of the services of a "great and good man."[28] That Greene wanted to get rich is irrefutable. That he was doing a thankless job superbly under a defective system is beyond challenge. That he wanted to secure his family's financial future while engaged in fighting a war that he might not survive is understandable. That what he did amounted to peccadilloes instead of serious corruption is not subject to serious question. Let us, therefore, after admitting that Nathanael Greene was less than financially pure, liked money very much, and used his office to try and get some, keep our eyes directly on what is really important about the man.

He served the cause for eight long, hard years. He became a truly brilliant soldier and a key player in winning the War of the Revolution. He shared with his troops hunger, heat, cold, fatigue, and danger. In battle he stayed close to the action and when necessary rode into the thick of it. Next to that record a little financial chicanery, if that is truly what it was, pales considerably. But it is also with a considerable sense of relief that we leave this uncomfortable subject for the "Line of splendor."

On two occasions during his tenure as Quartermaster General, Washington placed Greene on what we might call today special assignment and allowed him to command troops. At the Battle of Monmouth on 28 June 1778, when the temperatures reached 100° Fahrenheit and soldiers on both sides died of heat-stroke, Greene commanded the right wing. At one point Lord Cornwallis led a massive attack against Greene, using several elite units that came on in splendid, seemingly invincible, fashion. But Cornwallis now faced a new American army, and Greene's six guns and massed musketry fired in disciplined volleys and shattered the assault.

Later that summer Greene was sent to Rhode Island and commanded a division under General John Sullivan, who managed, as usual, to botch the campaign and in his maladroit way seriously offend America's French allies. But at the Battle of Rhode Island on 29 August, Greene distinguished himself leading his troops against the Hessian and Anspacher battalions, and with musketry and bayonets, he reported to Washington, "We soon put the Enemy to the rout and I had the pleasure to see them run in worse disorder than they did at the battle of Monmouth." This letter, finished on 31 August, also offers further evidence of a terrible burden that he bore during the war. "I would write your Excellency a more particular acount of the battle and retreat but I immagin General Sullivan and Col Laurens had done it already and I am myself very much unwell, have had no sleep for three Nights and Days, being severely afflicted with the asthma."[29] Greene's affliction was apparently quite severe, yet he retained the capacity not only to carry out the ordinary duties of campaigning but also to suffer the tension and terrors of battle.

From Rhode Island he returned to the job he hated and for which he was traduced without respite. His comrade in arms, the able and tough brigade commander from Virginia, General George Weedon, wrote to him in October to hail his performance in Rhode Island, but added information about the vilification by some that would not cease. "My own private opinion wanted nothing to establish your fame and worth with me but I've not been a little Supprized at hearing some people say, since the Rhode Island affair, that Green had retrieved his Character! I have Asked when he had lost it, or what rascal had ever defamed it, and have been answered that they had heard so and so."[30] In the summer of 1780, after more than two years on the job and facing a congressional reorganization of the quartermaster's office, Greene demanded from Congress a vote of confidence. Congress refused, and on 15 July adopted the new plan. Greene resigned as Quartermaster General. Congress, recalling his threat to resign in 1777 over the issue of foreign officers, was incensed. His resignation was accepted on 3 August, two weeks before Horatio Gates met the end of the road at Camden. Some congressmen wanted Greene sacked, expelled from the army, but the majority prevailed and the attempt fizzled. Washington gave him command of the Hudson Highlands, a vital strategic area. Congress was soon faced with another matter of deep concern. Who would replace Gates as commander of the Southern Department? Congress had first chosen Robert Howe, who was unsuited for theatre command and its political minefields; then Benjamin Lincoln, a good man badly placed; then Horatio Gates, a military bureaucrat self-deceived into fancying himself a warrior. Howe lost Savannah, Lincoln Charleston, Gates South Carolina. One army had gone into captivity, another had been shattered. Congress decided it was time for another to make the critical choice and turned the matter over to Washington.

"An elegant lesson of propriety"

On 14 October, the day after he received congressional authorization to appoint whom he wished, the great Virginian chose the man he had wanted instead of Gates, and because the situation in the South was so critical Nathanael Greene did not go home first to see his family and settle his affairs. He arrived in Philadelphia on 27 October to seek cavalry reinforcements and supplies from Congress. He received little of what he asked, and of clothing to cover half-naked troops there was none, from either Congress or comfortable Philadelphia merchants. Before he continued his ride on 2 November word had come of the victory at King's Mountain, which gave him breathing room. Baron von Steuben rode with him as far as Virginia, where the Baron stayed to forward reinforcements and supplies to Greene.

On the way south they stopped in Annapolis, where Greene begged for clothing. He repeated his pleas in Virginia to Governor Thomas Jefferson. What he received from Delaware, Maryland, and Virginia were protestations of poverty. Nathanael Greene and the army in the South could look to themselves for succor. He did, however, pick up in Virginia one of the unsung heroes of the Revolution. Lieutenant Colonel Edward Carrington (1749–1810) was an artilleryman who became Greene's Quartermaster General, and it was this job and his anonymity that prompted Mark Boatner to suggest that Greene had written Carrington's epitaph: "No body ever heard of a quarter Master in History." Carrington would turn in a sterling performance in that and other roles.

For now, Greene ordered Carrington to continue the assignment Gates had given him. He was to survey the Roanoke River for safe passages and to expand the survey to include the Dan River, a tributary of the Roanoke just north of the Virginia–North Carolina line. When Greene reached Hillsborough on 27 November he dispatched two other officers on similar missions: the Polish volunteer Colonel Thaddeus Kosciuszko to the Catawba River and Brigadier General Edward Stevens of Virginia to the Yadkin. Greene wanted to know if these rivers as well as the Dan could be used for bringing supplies, but other information was also gathered that would be of crucial importance.

Gates was in Charlotte with what passed for an army. Greene arrived on 2 December 1780. To describe the two men as not close would be a gross understatement. It could have been an awkward moment, but both carried it off with aplomb. Greene behaved toward the beaten general with respect and kindness. Gates retained his dignity. Otho Holland Williams was there, and described their conduct as "an elegant lesson of propriety exhibited on a most delicate and interesting occasion."[31] The following day Major General Horatio Gates issued his final order, handing over his command to Major General Nathanael Greene, and five days later the Hero of Saratoga turned his horse northward and began his long ride home.

19

The Stage Is Set

A Hero of the Revolution

On 3 December 1780 a living legend rode into Nathanael Greene's camp at Charlotte to report to his new commander. Rarely have two men of such uncommon martial gifts had the opportunity to complement one another. Renowned from Quebec to the Carolinas, celebrated in one army and feared by another, his life a succession of dramas one of which would be enough for most men, Brigadier General Daniel Morgan of the Virginia Line was by far the Continental Army's finest battle captain. If one were to judge him by all who have led Americans into battle, he would have no superiors and few peers. Daniel Morgan was the quintessential American, precisely the type Crèvecoeur had in mind in *Letters from an American Farmer*, a "new man" who had left behind in the Old World the designation and status of peasant.[1]

His boyhood and adolescence are shrouded in mystery and he chose to leave them that way. By his own reckoning he was born in the winter of 1735 in Hunterdon County, New Jersey. His parents were poor Welsh immigrants, his father a farm laborer. More than one writer has claimed that Daniel Morgan and Daniel Boone were related, no doubt because Boone's mother was a Sarah Morgan who had a brother named Daniel. But neither of Morgan's biographers even mentions it, nor does John Mack Faragher in his recent biography of Boone. It seems to be one of those tales that once committed to the printed page takes on a life of its own.[2]

Sometime during the winter of 1752–1753, following a dispute with his father, Daniel Morgan literally walked away from home forever. What it concerned, no one knows. He never discussed it. When he turned his back on home and family, to our knowledge he never publicly mentioned them, and in private revealed little. There is no evidence that he ever again saw his parents, and if he had brothers and sisters there is no record that he spoke of them. He

Daniel Morgan, by Charles Willson Peale.
(Independence National Historical Park Collection.)

spent a few weeks in Carlisle, Pennsylvania, taking day jobs to support himself. From Carlisle he turned south onto the northern branch of the Great Wagon Road, which followed the Cumberland Valley and joined the main road at Williamsport. There a ferry crossed the Potomac, and some thirty miles south of the river in the spring of 1753, while the future Lord Cornwallis trained at Eton for imperial duties, and Banastre Tarleton was a year shy of being born into affluence, Daniel Morgan walked alone and friendless into the frontier settlement of Charles Town, Virginia, near the head of the Valley called Shenandoah. He had neither money nor belongings. He was semi-literate at best. He had no patron to pave his way. But he was blessed with a strong body, six feet of it with powerful shoulders and arms, and rocklike fists that would earn him respect and followers. He was at the beginning of a long and remarkable journey. A commanding presence combined with valor, a high natural intelligence, and a stirring capacity to lead men would take him from the bottom of the heap to the very uppermost rank in the pantheon of heroes of the Revolution.

Morgan began as a farm laborer and soon became foreman of his employer's sawmill, but he was lured away by higher pay to become a wagoner. He saved most of his pay and within a year of his arrival bought his own team and wagon and became an independent wagoner. That same year, 1754, Major General Edward Braddock began his ill-fated march against the French and Indians at Fort Duquesne in the Pennsylvania wilderness, and Morgan was one of several wagoners pressed by the general for the lucrative duty of hauling supplies. As a wagoner he did not see action, and there is no reason why he would have met Colonel George Washington, whose good advice Braddock spurned and who behaved so well in this British debacle, or Captain Horatio Gates, about to go into battle for the first time. He saw the awful aftermath, however, and instead of hauling supplies evacuated wounded in his wagon.

It was either before or during Braddock's march that Morgan suffered an ordeal that would have broken many men and killed others, but his remarkable physique and indomitable will saw him through, terribly damaged in flesh but never in spirit. His trial enhanced the young wagoner in the eyes of his fellows and became part of the Morgan legend. Many years later, by the light of campfires on a frosty Carolina night, on the eve of one of the war's critical battles, he would once more tell the tale, once again show the evidence. And if he embellished the story, it is of little moment. For we do know that it happened; of that there is no doubt. Morgan carried to his grave the terrible scars to prove it.

British officers were accustomed to the lower orders keeping their distance and tugging the forelock, but American wagoners were a different breed, and there was constant trouble between the two groups. Morgan got into an altercation with a British lieutenant, who finally struck him with the flat of his sword, whereupon Morgan, a practiced brawler, did what came naturally, hit the officer with his fist, and knocked him senseless to the ground. Conviction, sentencing, and punishment followed immediately. Five hundred lashes. Young Morgan was stripped to the waist and tied to the whipping post in front of the assembled troops, wagoners, and assorted civilians. When it was over his bloody flesh hung in strips. When he healed, his back carried forever "scars and ridges from the shoulder to the waist." Ever after Morgan insisted that he not only never lost consciousness, but kept count with the drummer, and "I heard him miscount one," but "did not think it worth while to tell him of his mistake, and let it go so." He had only received 499 lashes, he always claimed, and George III "has been owing me one lash ever since."[3]

The area of Virginia where Morgan lived and worked was frontier country, and during the French and Indian War Indian raids reached within a few miles of Winchester. Morgan joined a company of rangers organized by a friend, and in April 1756 saw his first action, and almost his last. He had guided militiamen to Fort Edwards, twenty miles north of Winchester, and was riding back with dispatches accompanied by another ranger when seven Indians ambushed them. The other man was killed by the opening volley. A musket ball entered Morgan's neck, passed through his mouth, knocked out all his teeth on the left side, and exited through his left cheek. But he was able to keep his saddle, and the fine mare he rode headed back for the fort. Six of the Indians went for the dead man's scalp while the seventh dashed after Morgan. Many years later his grandson Morgan Neville wrote, "I well remember, when a boy, to have heard General Morgan describe, in his own powerful and graphic style, the expression on the Indian's face as he ran with open mouth and tomahawk in hand by the side of the horse, expecting every moment to see his victim fall. But when the panting savage found the horse was fast leaving him behind, he threw the tomahawk without effect, and abandoned the pursuit with a yell of disappointment."[4]

By 1758 the frontier had grown safer. Morgan resumed wagoning and also continued what he had probably been engaged in since his arrival in Virginia: brawling, boozing, gambling—and probably considerable wenching, if the gossips are to be believed. His favorite haunt was the tavern at Battletown, nine miles from Winchester. Immensely strong, excellent at riding, foot racing, and wrestling, Morgan was the leader of the young men who gathered there, and the enemy of anyone who challenged his status. His most dangerous foe was a noted fist fighter named Bill Davis. Morgan had two terrible fights with him. Morgan won the first, which led to a return match in which the followers of each man engaged in a wild, no-holds-barred frontier brawl. Morgan and his men won. In Morgan's final year his close friend and pastor, Reverend Dr. William Hill, was helping the old General out of bed: "I discovered one of his toes lying upon the top of his foot. 'General, what is the matter with this toe of yours?' I inquired. 'I got that many years ago,' he replied, 'in a fight I had with Bill Davis, and in kicking him at Battletown. I broke that toe then, and I could never get it to lie in its right place since.'"[5]

The Daniel Morgan of those days was well known to sheriffs and magistrates, being charged among other things with horse stealing, arson, assault and battery, and arming himself and refusing the lawful order of a deputy sheriff. Had he not possessed driving ambition and a strong character he might well have ended just another frontier ruffian one step ahead of the hangman's noose. But all the while he saved money and followed his occupation, hauling the agricultural produce of the Valley eastward over the Blue Ridge to the towns of eastern Virginia, trading with the merchants there, and returning with manufactured goods and such necessaries as sugar, salt, and rum. And he also went courting. Her name was Abigail Curry, the daughter of a local farmer, and we know less about her entire life than we do of Morgan's pre-Virginia youth. Morgan was about twenty-eight and she was in her late teens in 1763 when, without benefit of wedlock, they set up housekeeping. It was a sound, lasting relationship that produced two daughters, Nancy and Betsy. Abigail never tamed him. No one ever tamed Daniel Morgan. But his transgressions became fewer and a regularity was added to his life that served him well. By 1774 he had bought a home and 255 acres, leased his wagon, married Abigail, and become a farmer, a captain of militia, and the owner of ten slaves, and was well thought of by some of the leading men of Frederick County.

The year 1774 also marked a turning point in his life, for he went to war, first as a loyal subject of George III in Lord Dunmore's War against the

Shawnee, and almost immediately thereafter in rebellion against King and mother country. The company Morgan led was among the troops that penetrated deep into hostile territory in the Ohio country, where they had one of those short but sharp skirmishes common to the Indian wars, and then proceeded to burn and plunder Indian crops and villages. He was in the field about five months, and described his service as "very active and hard."[6]

Following Lexington and the beginning of the Patriot siege of Boston, in June 1775 the Continental Congress authorized the raising of ten companies of riflemen from Pennsylvania, Maryland, and Virginia. Of the two companies authorized from Virginia, one was to be supplied by Frederick County, and Daniel Morgan was the unanimous choice of a committee of six leading citizens to raise and lead the men of that county. On 15 July 1775, Captain Daniel Morgan and ninety-six riflemen he had personally chosen began a 600-mile march from Winchester, Virginia, to Cambridge, Massachusetts. His ensign was Charles Porterfield, whom we remember as the gallant officer who fell mortally wounded at the head of Virginia troops on the eve of the Battle of Camden. The farther north and east they marched the greater the sensation they created in the towns and villages they passed through. They were the frontier fighters of reality and romance, tall, lean men weathered by sun and wind, dressed as their Indian foes in long hunting shirts, leggings, breech clouts, and moccasins, armed with tomahawk, scalping knife, and the American rifle. In the middle states and New England they seemed to be from another planet; their displays of marksmanship among the wonders of the world in a region where the rifle was practically unknown. They arrived in the American camp outside Boston on 6 August: 600 miles in twenty-three days through fair weather and foul and not a man lost on the way. It was at the siege of Boston that the riflemen first made their fearsome reputation as makers of widows and orphans. British sentries and officers soon dared not show themselves within range of their rifles. Some rifle commands also built reputations as ill-disciplined brawlers in camp, but Morgan apparently had his men under control, probably because he could whip any man in his command.

We have referred on occasion to luck in war, and it is just as true that luck, or whatever one wishes to call it, often plays a role in determining the course a life takes. Congress, with George Washington concurring, decided to invade Canada and bring it into the Patriot fold. Only three of the ten rifle companies were assigned to the expedition to be led by twenty-four-year old Benedict Arnold, but all of them wanted to go. The captains drew lots, and the winners were two Pennsylvania captains and Daniel Morgan. He was then thirty-nine, a famous man in Frederick County, known to important men in Virginia, but his mark on a wider stage yet to be made, his capacity to engage in grand enterprises unknown. His physical appearance lent confidence, but a commanding presence is no guarantee of ability. Benedict Arnold, however, liked what he saw and heard, and before the expedition left Cambridge he made Morgan commander of the three rifle companies.

At their jumping off place in Maine Arnold announced that one of the rifle companies would be detached to the advance party under Lieutenant Colonel Christopher Greene of Rhode Island, a distant kinsman of Nathanael Greene. Morgan and the the other rifle captains would have none of that. They would not, they told Arnold, serve under any New England militia officer, and Morgan, throughout his career sensitive to a fault, made it clear that the plan challenged his authority as commander of the riflemen. Arnold wisely chose to retreat, and just as wisely selected Morgan to lead the advance with the three rifle companies. Christopher Greene was a good officer who would prove himself on many occasions until his ghastly death by sword and bayonet in 1781 at Croton River, New York—but he was no Daniel Morgan.

Arnold's expedition would engage in one of the epic marches of American military history. Starting on 25 September at Fort Western, near the modern Augusta, Maine, Morgan and his riflemen, followed at staggered intervals by the rest of Arnold's force, plunged into a nightmarish, rain-soaked wilderness of swollen waters, treacherous rapids, thundering waterfalls, punishing portages, bogs, and blow-downs. On 10 November, 350 miles from their starting point, 675 men of the original 1,050, gaunt and ragged, gazed across the St. Lawrence River from Point Levis. It was an incredible feat, and the man most responsible was the indomitable Benedict Arnold. But Morgan's performance was second only to Arnold's. John Joseph Henry, a Pennsylvania rifleman who made the march and for whom Morgan was forever a hero, left a brief but incisive description of the frontiersman. "By-and-by Morgan came—large, a commanding presence, and stentorian voice. He wore leggins and a cloth, in the Indian style. His thighs, which were exposed to view, appeared to have been lacerated by the thorns and bushes."[7] As was his style, Morgan pitched in and peformed manual labor with his men, hauling bateaux upriver and clearing a road for the main force.

Like his men he was constantly wet from rain and immersion in icy Maine waters, for which he would later pay a terrible price. He also showed himself a commander who would strive for perfection and not allow adversity to prevent him from doing what would be expected under normal conditions, a virtue not always understood or appreciated by those who must toe the mark. The Height of Land, which marked the watershed between the east-flowing Kennebec and the west-flowing Chaudiere, was a four-mile carry. John Joseph Henry told what happened. The two Pennsylvania captains, Hendricks and Smith, "to save their men, concluded to carry over the hill but one boat for each of their companies. This resolution was easily accomplished. Morgan, on the other hand, determined to carry over all his boats. It would have made your heart ache to view the intolerable labors of his fine fellows. Some of them, it was said, had the flesh worn from their shoulders, even to the bone. By this time an antipathy had arisen against Morgan, as too strict a disciplinarian." But the men did it, and Morgan's way, strict discipline and stern demands supported by great personal courage and leavened by an engaging personality, combined to produce one of the nation's outstanding leaders of men at war. Again, John Joseph Henry put it well. "His manners were of the severest cast; but where he became attached he was kind and truly affectionate. This is said from experience of the most sensitive and pleasing nature. Activity, spirit, and courage in a soldier procured his good will and esteem."[8]

On the night of 13 November Benedict Arnold took his little force across the river to the same cove where James Wolfe had landed his troops in 1759 and gone on to take Quebec. Morgan sent a reconaissance party close to the city's walls; Lieutenant William Heth reported to Morgan that they had encountered no sentries. All was quiet. Morgan's instinct was to immediately assault the city, a course that he recommended to Arnold, who agreed. But the Americans were discovered by a British patrol boat when some soldiers thoughtlessly lit a fire to warm themselves. Arnold assembled his commanders and asked their advice. The majority, along with Arnold himself, opposed an immediate attack because they feared the British commander had been alerted, and the moment was lost. Morgan's instinct may have been right, although whether the city would have fallen that night had the Americans attacked must remain in the realm of speculation.

The interesting thing about this affair is that at the council of war Morgan did not speak up and defend his proposal. We have seen that he was no shrinking violet, but there is, I believe, reason to wonder if his origins, background, and lack of education constrained him. In a century in which the status of gentleman counted for much and gentlemen expected deference, in which officers were either gentlemen or pretended to be, no one ever mistook Daniel Morgan for a gentleman. Throughout his life, despite his rise to fame and high rank in the army and his community, easily recognizable beneath a veneer so thin as to be practically nonexistent was the rough and ready wagoner, the Battletown brawler. In the council of war called by Arnold he was surrounded by men who if not gentlemen by English standards of the day certainly exceeded Morgan in family and position. Arnold was the great-grandson of a Rhode Island governor, the young Aaron Burr the son of a president of Princeton and the grandson of the great Jonathan Edwards, Christopher Greene a successful businessman, Henry Dearborn had studied and practiced medicine, Matthias Ogden was of a prominent and influential New Jersey family. My thoughts are pure speculation, but why else did the usually outspoken Morgan sulk in silence?

Was that also the reason why he almost came to blows with Arnold? On the 15th Morgan and the two other rifle captains, Hendricks and Smith, told Arnold that one pint of flour per man per day was not enough. Arnold had a temper to match Morgan's, and John Joseph Henry reported that "altercation and warm language took place. Smith, with his usual loquacity, told us that Morgan seemed at one time on the point of striking Arnold. We fared the better for this interview." Yet the two men respected each other and two years later would work in splendid harmony at the glorious victory at Saratoga, and even after Arnold's treason Morgan, in a letter to Thomas Jefferson, would refer to his former comrade as "my old friend."[9]

While all this was going on General Richard Montgomery, a former British officer who had espoused the Patriot cause and married a New York Livingston, had
taken Montreal with an American column that had followed the old invasion
route out of northern New York. In December Montgomery arrived outside Quebec with 300 men and took command. He and Arnold devised a plan to take Quebec by assaulting it at night from two directions during a snowstorm, Montgomery
from the south, Arnold from the north, with the two columns uniting at a predetermined point to carry all before them. It sounded simple but it was not, for it depended on the success of both columns penetrating enemy defenses and meeting
in the dark while a storm raged. They would number in all about 900 men. Inside
the city a good soldier, Major General Sir Guy Carleton, waited with 1,800 men.

The storm the Americans were waiting for rose on the afternoon of 30 December. By 2:00 A.M. on New Year's Day it was raging. Arnold advanced to the
assault. Because the field officers were to a man inexperienced, Arnold decided
that he and Morgan would lead, although he did not make Morgan second in
command. Arnold led the van of thirty infantry and forty New York artillerymen hauling a six-pounder on a sled. Morgan was right behind with the riflemen and New England troops, all in single file. Arnold and the van got into
the town and pressed foward through the heavy, swirling snow. All they could
see was the flash of muskets as the British on the walls fired down on them.
Morgan led his rifle companies on Arnold's trail and encountered the fiery Yankee commander a few hundred yards past the walls, in a narrow street blocked
with a tall barricade defended by two cannon and a squad of infantry. Arnold
called for his own cannon, but it had been abandoned in a snow drift. Arnold
did not hesitate. He ran forward shouting for all to follow him in a mad charge
to carry the barricade. They were met by the thunder of artillery and the roar of
musketry. Arnold was hit in the left leg by a musket ball and could not continue.
"I sent him off in the care of two of my men," Morgan later wrote, "and took his
place in command. For although there were three field officers, they would not
take the command, alleging that I had seen service and they had not."

A scaling ladder was placed in front of the barricade and Morgan climbed
it. He was met at the top by concentrated artillery and musket fire and literally
blown off the ladder and down into the snow on the street. His hat had been
pierced by a ball and his cheek scored by another. His face was black with powder burns. There were no volunteers among field officers or rank and file willing to try their luck. Morgan, however, was not to be denied. He rose from the
snow, a terrible wild and blackened figure, and went up the ladder a second
time. He wrote to a friend that "for fear the business might not be executed
with spirit, I mounted myself and was the first man who leaped into the town."
His luck continued to be incredible. "I lighted on the end of a heavy piece of
artillery which hurt me exceedingly and perhaps saved my life, as I fell from the
gun upon the platform where the bayonets were not directed."[10]

Ensign Charles Porterfield followed Morgan up the ladder and the rest
made haste to follow. Morgan bluffed thirty British soldiers into surrendering,

then led his column farther through the narrow streets to Sault au Matelot, where they were to rendezvous with Montgomery's column. Here they found scores of French Canadian militia who eagerly surrendered, but there was no sign of Montgomery. Neither, however, was there opposition, and Morgan went with an interpreter through the open gate of another barrier to the upper town. On his return he reported his findings to the assembled field officers. Morgan's instinct was that of the battle captain born. He wanted to push on, through the open gate of the undefended barrier, on to the upper town, and we know that he was almost certainly right.

But the field officers who had urged him to lead after Arnold went down, who had not volunteered to take his place when he was blown off the ladder at the first barrier, now asserted their higher ranks and overruled Morgan in favor of the caution often so fatal in times of battlefield crisis. The hour belonged to the bold and the swift, but their orders were to wait at that point for Montgomery, and they had prisoners to tend, and some of their own men were scattered. It was their belief, Morgan related, that "General Montgomery was certainly coming down the river St. Lawrence and would join us in a few minutes, so that we were sure of conquest if we acted with caution. To these arguments I sacrificed my own opinion and lost the town."[11] None of the officers huddled in conference knew that Montgomery would never come. He was dead, killed while leading the assault, and his deputy, Lieutenant Colonel Donald Campbell, had immediately turned tail and run away with his command.

The British rallied under the cool leadership of Sir Guy Carleton and soon Morgan and his men were surrounded in the narrow street. The firing became intense. Morgan raged like a cornered bear. Wrote the Pennsylvania rifleman George Morison, "Betwixt every peal the awful voice of Morgan is heard, whose gigantic stature and terrible appearance carries dismay among the foe wherever he comes." Morgan wanted to make a last desperate attempt to break out of the city the way they had come, but his superior officers refused and surrendered the entire force. Still he refused to give up. He was so incensed he wept. Backed against a wall, British bayonets at his breast, he dared them to take his sword, invited them to shoot him, and refused the entreaties of his riflemen to surrender. Finally, spotting a French Canadian priest in the crowd, he handed his sword to him, for he would not give it to an Englishman. That his instinct to press the attack was in all probability correct was supported by the post-battle assessment of Major Henry Caldwell, a British officer who fought that night. "Had they acted with more spirit, they might have pushed in at first and possessed themselves of the whole of Lower Town, and let their friends in at the other side, before our people had time to have recovered from a certain degree of panic, which seized them on the first news of the post being surprised."[12]

Morgan remained a prisoner in Quebec City until released on parole the following September. As with the other officers, he was well treated. His magnificent performance had gained the respect of the British, and many of their officers visited him, and finally one told him that he was authorized to offer him a Colonel's commission in the British army. Morgan's reply, undoubtedly revised into polite language, was unambiguous: "I hope, sir, you will never again insult me in my present distressed and unfortunate situation, by making me offers which plainly imply that you think me a scoundrel."[13]

Reports of Morgan's exploits in the wilderness and during the assault on Quebec City preceded his return. George Washington recommended him to Congress for promotion to colonel and command of a rifle regiment, but he was not exchanged for a British prisoner in American hands until January 1777. In June of that year Washington gave him command of a special light infantry corps of some 500 specially chosen Continentals, including Virginians Morgan had recruited for his rifle regiment. They were armed with rifles, as befitted men from the western reaches of Virginia, Maryland, and Pennsylvania. The purpose of the corps was much like Johann Ewald's Jägers: scouting, harrying the enemy's flanks, delaying their advance, falling on their rear guard. The new corps soon had occasion to test its mettle against Sir William Howe's forces in New Jersey. Morgan's corps, along with General Anthony's Wayne's brigade, severely mauled Howe's rear guard. Washington wrote to the President of Congress, "General Greene desires me to make mention of the conduct and bravery of General Wayne and Colonel Morgan and of their officers and men upon this occasion, as they constantly advanced upon an enemy far superior to them in numbers, and well secured behind strong redoubts."[14]

But a far more severe test of the rifle corps, and Morgan as a combat commander, was just over the horizon. We have touched on Burgoyne's invasion of northern New York and the Battles of Saratoga, but we need to take a closer look at it, for it was here that Daniel Morgan—for the first but not the last time—played a key role in the struggle for independence from Great Britain. Members of Congress as well as New Yorkers in peril asked for Morgan and his riflemen. Washington was reluctant but eventually agreed that the danger to the cause merited the temporary absence from the main army of Morgan's corps. He wrote to Morgan on 16 August 1777, "I know of no Corps so likely to check their progress in proportion to their number as the one you Command. I have great dependence on you, your Officers and Men."[15] On or about the 30th of August, near where the Mohawk River empties into the Hudson, Morgan and his corps joined the Northern Army under the command of Major General Horatio Gates.

The clash between Gates and the tempestuous Benedict Arnold, and the neverending debate on whether it was Arnold who really won the Battles of Saratoga, have to some degree overshadowed Morgan's performance at his first major battle. Again, he was superb, a battle captain for the ages. Daniel Morgan was as much responsible for the great victory as Gates and Arnold. His command was the army's elite corps, and he led it with imagination and the extraordinary coolness under fire that always marked his battlefield performances.

The first service rendered by the riflemen came before the main forces were engaged. Burgoyne's Indian allies were not just neutralized, they were driven out of the woods and inside Burgoyne's lines, where "not a man of them was to be brought within the sound of a rifle shot," Burgoyne wrote.[16] The British thereafter operated blindly, while Morgan's scouts kept Gates informed of Burgoyne's progress. At the first action between the two armies, the Battle of Freeman's Farm, Morgan's riflemen, supported by Major Henry Dearborn's 300 New Hampshire light infantrymen armed with muskets and bayonets, began the action, and throughout a long day inflicted severe punishment on the British with sustained rifle fire that British veterans of the Seven Years War claimed was longer and hotter than they had ever experienced. In the earliest stage the riflemen advanced too far too fast and had to scatter when the British counterattacked with bayonets; but Morgan rallied them with his turkey call, and thereafter they maintained discipline, relied on their fabled marksmanship, and forsook close engagements. The riflemen silenced the British artillery by shooting most of the gunners and every British officer except one. They reduced the 62nd Regiment from about 350 to less than sixty effective fighting men. In a battle fought largely in the forest, Morgan and his riflemen proved the efficiency of the weapon on the right terrain while supported by regulars with bayoneted muskets who could keep the enemy at bay while the riflemen reloaded.[17]

The tactics for the second Battle of Saratoga, called Bemis Heights, have been credited to Morgan. He suggested that he take the riflemen and Dearborn's infantry stealthily on a wide course through the forest and fall on Burgoyne's right flank, while another brigade attacked Burgoyne's left. Gates accepted the proposal. At both points of attack the British were surprised, overwhelmed, and driven back into their lines. What occurred following the initially successful American assault involves the still running Horatio Gates–Benedict Arnold controversy, and to get into it would unnecessarily detain us. We need only know that in the fighting that raged the rest of the afternoon the British were soundly defeated and their fate sealed, and the key figures in the American victory that day were Daniel Morgan and Benedict Arnold. It should also be made clear that at Saratoga Morgan did not lead militia or engage in the classic guerrilla tactic of hit and run. He commanded Continentals—the riflemen and Dearborn's Light Infantry—and the riflemen used concealment and cover, open skirmishing formations, and long-range rifle fire that anticipated modern infantry tactics. Saratoga was the prime example during the American Revolution of the effectiveness of experienced American riflemen against European line infantry when the riflemen could fight on terrain that offered ample cover and they were supported by their own line infantry trained to fight by volley fire and bayonet. But to extend the experience of this particular battle, vitally important as it was, to the war as a whole would be to accept the myth of keen-eyed American sharpshooters winning the War of the Revolution. Saratoga was an exception to the rule.

Morgan and his men left soon after Burgoyne's surrender to rejoin Washington, who sorely missed them—but not before Horatio Gates praised Morgan and his corps to his face and in writing to Congress. By that and other means the news of their exploits preceded them. Alexander Hamilton told Morgan that his services were regarded as "essential."[18]

Between his return to the main army in the late fall of 1777 and the Monmouth campaign of June–July 1778, Morgan and his riflemen skirmished and scouted in Pennsylvania and New Jersey, invariably giving good accounts of themselves. They missed the major action, the Battle of Monmouth, because Charles Lee failed to keep Morgan specifically informed of what was going on. Morgan then took temporary command of the Virginia brigade of General William Woodford, who was ill. Although inexperienced in administrative matters, he quickly mastered them, showing that in that respect too he was ready for higher command. His desire to lead more than a regiment quickened when he learned that a light infantry brigade composed of young veterans was to be formed. He wanted that brigade: he set his heart on getting it. But it called for a brigadier general, he was a colonel, and Brigadier General Anthony Wayne, who was without a command, wanted the new brigade, too.

Wayne had not yet established his reputation as a very good combat commander and Morgan believed that by experience and accomplishments the command should be his. He was well aware that men junior and inferior to him had been promoted to general. But custom had it that a state could have only as many brigadier generals as there were units to command, and Virginia already had too many. Anthony Wayne got the light infantry brigade, did a first-rate job with it, and led it to glory in the famous night bayonet assault at Stony Point, New York. Congress refused to promote Morgan, and Washington declined to intercede, being especially careful not to seem to favor fellow Virginians. Morgan, offended and deeply disappointed, offered his resignation from the service to Congress, but that body instead convinced him to accept an "honorable furlough"[19] and held out the hope, however tenuous, that an opening might occur. George Washington believed that Morgan's action was without justification. I believe that Washington's failure to intercede and thus allow one of the few officers in the army who can truly be called brilliant to leave active service was an error in judgment.

Morgan went home in the late summer of 1779 and did not return to the field until a year later. It was just as well, for his magnificent body had finally rebelled. A lifetime of exposure to the elements, capped by his almost constant immersion in icy waters during the terrible march through the Maine wilderness, had brought on attacks of sciatica so severe he had to take to his bed. He was still in terrible pain in the summer of 1780 when his old commander from Saratoga, Horatio Gates, was appointed commander of the Southern Department. Gates immediately wrote to Morgan and apprised him of Congress's intention to call him for service in the Southern army. Gates wanted Morgan to lead the light troops. The two men met at Battletown. Morgan asked Gates to ask Congress to promote him to Brigadier General, and Gates sent a sincere plea to Congress to act.

Morgan's physical condition prevented him from joining Gates until late September 1780, and by then Gates had suffered the debacle of Camden. When Morgan heard the terrible news he was still suffering from wracking pains, and

Congress had not yet acted on his promotion. Nevertheless, in this time of peril to the cause he departed almost immediately on the long ride to Hillsborough, North Carolina. He took along a spare horse to sell in order to meet his travel expenses. Congress also finally did the right and wise thing and promoted him to Brigadier General on 13 October 1780, although the members spent three months in study and debate before acting. He had been campaigning with the light troops between Charlotte and Camden when Nathanael Greene arrived. The new commander of the Southern Department would retain Morgan in the role assigned to him by Gates. But Greene would use the Old Waggoner, as Morgan liked to call himself, with a skill and imagination that Gates did not possess.

General Greene Prepares for General Cornwallis

The new commander of the Southern Department was cut of different cloth than the old. In his first night in camp he studied the resources of the countryside with Colonel Thomas Polk, chief of Gates's commissariat. Polk later told Elkanah Watson that by the "following morning he better understood them than Gates had done in the whole period of his command."[20] Nathanael Greene was superior to Horatio Gates in all respects. His planning for the southern campaign was masterly. He also excelled as an organizer and administrator, making men forget Gates. And he was a genuine not an ersatz fighter, exhibiting a judicious mixture of caution and daring. Nathanael Greene took risks for which lesser men and pedagogues have criticized him, which only convinces us how fortunate that Greene and none of his critics commanded the Southern Department during the final years of the war.

The command to which Greene succeeded was in a pitiful state. On his arrival it numbered 2,307 men, of whom 1,482 were present and fit for duty. Absent were 547; of those 128 were on detached duty. Continentals from the crack Maryland and Delaware Lines numbered 949. They were the backbone of the army. But of the overall total, only 800 men were properly clothed and equipped. As small as his army was, there were not adequate provisions and forage for them in the immediate countryside and Greene therefore ordered General von Steuben in Virginia not to send him unarmed and unclothed men.

To prepare for the coming campaign required tedious hours of attention to detail, and almost immediately following his long night's session with Colonel Polk, Nathanael Greene began laying the groundwork. In fact, on 1 December, two days before he arrived at the camp in Charlotte, he wrote a letter to General Edward Stevens that is worth quoting at some length.

"Lt Co Carrington is exploring the Dan River, in order to perform transportation up the Roanoke as high as the upper Saura Town, and I want you to appoint a good and intelligent officer with 3 privates to go up the Yadkin as high as Hughes Creek to explore carefully the River, the Depth of Water, the Current, and the Rocks, and every other obstruction that will impede the Business of Transportation. All which I wish him to report to me. Let the officer be very intelligible, and have a Charge to be particular in his observations. It is immaterial of what rank he is; the object is so important and interesting to the Public that I hope no one will refuse the Service who has the Abilities for the appointment.

"When the officer gets to Hughes' Creek, I wish him to take a Horse and ride across the Country from that place thro' the town of Bethania to the upper Saura Town, and report the Distance and Condition of the roads. At upper Saura I expect the officer will meet the party exploring the Dan River. I wish him to get the report of that party also, and forward with his, as that is the Foundation of the whole. I also wish the officer to make inquiry respecting the transportation that may be had from the Yadkin to the Catawba River, and whether the transportation cannot be performed with batteaus down that river.

"It is my Intention to construct Boats of a peculiar kind for this Service, that will carry Forty or Fifty barrels, and yet draw little more Water than a common Canoe half loaded. The officer who goes upon this service should have that in Idea when making his observations and Remarks. I am sensible the Business of Transportation will be attended with difficulty down these rivers if it can be done at all. But water transportation is such an immense saving of expenses that small difficulties should not discourage the attempt. And besides the expense that will be saved, there is also another consideration, which is, that Waggons and Forage cannot be had to transport across the Country all by land."[21]

This letter reveals that Greene had closely questioned all the people he met who had knowledge of the Carolinas, a part of the country in which he had never set foot until late November 1780. The information that was gathered would be of critical importance in several respects during the ensuing campaign. But gathering intelligence was only part of the job, and the easiest. It is all very well to acquire useful information, but without the wherewithal to put it to good use the data might as well be retired to archives. On 4 December Greene instructed Edward Carrington to procure tools and supplies vital to the campaign: "I . . . wish you to have forwarded . . . 500 felling Axes, 5888 Pair Horse Shoes, and if you found the Dan River navigable agreeable to your Expectations, half a Ton of Boat nails for constructing the batteaus. Let those come forward as soon as possible. One Third of the nails to be deposited on the Roanoke at the most convenient Place for building the batteaus, and the rest come on to Salisbury. . . . It will be well for you to consult with a good Shipwright the tools that will be necessary for Building about 100 large batteaus, and to take measures for having them forwarded without Loss of Time. Without Tools we can do nothing, and none are to be got in this Country, not even a common felling Axe.

"You will inquire of the Govr [Thomas Jefferson of Virginia] what steps have been taken by the Assembly to furnish the Artificers and Waggons required by me of the State, and press their immediate Compliance. For without Artificers we can not aid the Transportation."[22]

Two days later Greene wrote to Colonel Nicholas Long, Deputy Quartermaster of North Carolina, "We are much in want of every kind of smith and carpenter tools. I wish you would procure us a number, which I am told may be had out of a Prize on the sea Board. Files and cross-cut saws are very much wanted; and if you could forward us a quantity of both, it would relieve us from great distress."[23]

Also on 4 December he paid close attention to the human element of his design for the South. First assuring Francis Marion that "I have not the Honor of your Acquaintance but am no Stranger to your Character and merit," he continued in detail about what he required of the Swamp Fox. "Untill a more permanent Army can be collected than is in the field at present, we must endeavor to keep up a partizan war and preserve the tide of sentiment among the People as much as possible in our Favour. Spies are the Eyes of any army. . . . At present I am badly off for Intelligence. It is of the highest Importance that I get the earliest Information of any Reinforcements which may arrive at Charlestown or leave the Town to join Lord Cornwallis. I wish you therefore to fix some Plan for procuring such Information and for conveying it to me with all possible Dispatch. The Spy should be taught to be particular in his Enquiries, and to get the names of the Corps Strength and Commanding Officer's name, Place from whence they came and where they are going. It will be best to fix upon some Body in Town to do this, and have a Runner between you and him, to give you the Intelligence as a Person cannot make these Enquiries without being suspected who lives out of Town. The utmost Secrecy will be necessary in this Business."[24]

In this as in other letters to subordinates we have evidence of Greene's tendency to give detailed instructions on not only what to do but how to do it to very able and experienced officers who presumably could be trusted to do their jobs the right way, and one wonders if his stress on, "particulars," to use his language, exasperated the recipients. Yet so much was at stake in a region in which two American disasters had occurred that we can excuse his manner of telling men how to do jobs that they already well knew how to do. Whatever Francis Marion may have felt, he usually cooperated with Nathanael Greene throughout the campaign.

By at least 8 December and probably before Greene had decided to move the army from the barren camp at Charlotte. The men needed a steady supply of food, the horses forage, and a secure place had to be found to refit and reorganize an army that, Greene wrote to Alexander Hamilton, "is in such wretched condition that I hardly know what to do with it. The Officers have got such a habit of neglegence, and the soldiers so loose and disorderly, that it is next to impossible to give it a military complexion."[25] The soldiers were in the habit of going absent without leave and returning as if they had done nothing wrong. This had to be quickly stopped, and Greene showed his steel by choosing drastic action. A soldier returning to camp after an unauthorized absence was tried, convicted, sentenced to death, and hanged in front of the entire army. The message was clear and effective, the reaction of the troops stoic: "New lords new laws,"[26] they observed, acknowledging the first step taken in returning the army to the discipline that the regulars had shown when abandoned at Camden by Gates and the militia.

On 8 December Greene ordered his chief engineer, the Polish volunteer Colonel Thaddeus Kosciuszko, to seek a new encampment, and made clear that he wanted "particulars": "You will go with Major Polke and examine the Country from the Mouth of Little River twenty or thirty Miles down the Peedee and search for a good position for the army. You will report the make of the Country, the nature of the soil, the quality of the water, the quantity of Produce, number of Mills and the water transportation that may be had up and down the River. You will also Enquire respecting the creeks in the Rear of the fords and the difficulty of passing them, all of which you will report as soon as possible."[27]

And on the day that he instructed Kosciuszko, Greene turned to deal with a man who would be a source of trouble throughout the campaign. Thomas Sumter was still recuperating from the terrible wounds he had suffered at Blackstocks. Governor John Rutledge of South Carolina, who was in Greene's camp at Charlotte, wrote to Sumter on 3 December informing him of Greene's arrival and urging that he "come to or near this place as fast as your Health and the Weather permit."[28] Rutledge even sent his carriage and driver for him. Given Sumter's personality, his failure to accept the invitation is suspect, but let us allow him the benefit of the doubt because we do know that he could not yet mount a horse or wield a sword. He controlled too many men to be ignored, and on 8 December Greene and Governor Rutledge mounted and rode west to Tuckasegee Ford on the Catawba, where Sumter was recuperating in the fortress-like stone house of his armorer, John Price.

The three men had a long discussion on strategy. Sumter's recommendation, which he urgently pressed on Greene, was to attack Cornwallis. This is not surprising. Sumter was not a strategist, although he was unaware of it. His strategy, if it can be called that, was always to attack, and his favorite tactic was the frontal assault, although it is ironic that his greatest victory, at Blackstocks, was scored by deploying into a strong defensive position and allowing Banastre Tarleton, another devotee of headlong frontal assaults, to charge into defeat. But that lesson was lost on Sumter. Given the state of Greene's army, it would have been suicidal of him to attack Cornwallis. His Lordship had at hand about twice as many men as Greene, most of them were regulars, and although their supply situation could have been better they were by the standards of the wretched American army well fed, fit, and snug in warm winter quarters.

Nevertheless, on Greene's return to Charlotte he told Generals Morgan and Smallwood of Sumter's proposal. Daniel Morgan could never be accused of not being a fighter, but he joined Smallwood in arguing against it, pointing out that the army in its present condition was in no state to take on Cornwallis's regulars. Greene had to have known this as he listened to Sumter, yet when he wrote to the Gamecock of the reaction of Morgan and Smallwood, he added, "I am not altogether of this opinion, and therefore wish you to keep up a communication of intelligence, and of any changes of their disposition that may take place." The only explanation for Greene's words can be his desire to keep Sumter as contented as possible, for he never had any intention of attacking Cornwallis or even accepting battle until his army was fit and he could choose the ground. This brings us to another of Greene's plans for which one of Sumter's biographers has claimed credit for his hero.[29]

Greene decided to divide his army, "partly from choice and partly from necessity." This has bothered some military historians, who live by the hoary maxim that one never divides one's force when confronted by a superior enemy. Although Cornwallis was in camp at Winnsboro and not on the march, there was the danger that he might strike swiftly, catch one of the two forces by itself, and destroy it. But Greene had carefully weighed that possibility and judged it unlikely. Besides, what choice did he have? In addition to his desire to maintain a presence west of the Catawba, thereby stiffening the resolve of the Rebels there to continue their resistance, the army had to live off the land, and provisions and forage were too scarce wherever it went for the entire force to survive together. As Mark Boatner pointed out, Greene never heard of Napoleon but used the Napoleonic principle that an army divides to live and unites to fight.[30]

One of Sumter's biographers maintained that this plan was Sumter's, and quotes Greene's letter of 15 December to the Gamecock as proof: "Governor Rutledge shew me a couple of notes which you sent him, wherein you express a desire to have a detachment made from the army on the other side of the Catawba. The measure you wish I have been preparing for ever since I was with you." It was also suggested on 27 November by the North Carolina militia general, William Lee Davidson. An otherwise estimable man, Davidson like Sumter had in mind offensive operations against Cornwallis by sending Morgan deep into western South Carolina to Ninety Six, "at the same time the main Army to move down to the Waxhaws."[31]

But Greene had no intention of prematurely risking his little army. Before even arriving in the South he had outlined his thoughts in a letter of 2 November to Samuel Huntington: "As it must be some time before the Southern Army can be collected and equipped in sufficient force to contend with the Enemy in that quarter upon equal ground, it will be my first object to endeavour to form a flying army to consist of infantry and horse. It appears to me that cavalry and Partizan Corps are best adapted to the make of the Country and the state of the war in that quarter, both for heading and encouraging the Militia as well as protecting the persons and property of the inhabitants." In this letter and a subsequent one, in which he longed for a "superiority of horse" with which "we could soon render it difficult for Lord Cornwallis to maintain his position in this Country," Greene also revealed that he, quite unlike Gates, had a keen appreciation of the importance of cavalry in the South.[32]

Whoever was the father of the scheme to divide the army, or whether all three men arrived at it independently, Greene had to make the decision to risk it, and he was the only one with the strategic vision to carry out all that followed. Greene and Sumter also had vastly different plans for both the status and the mission of the detached force. In a letter of 14 December to Governor Rutledge, Sumter wrote that if Greene "thought proper to send over a party of horse or foot or both, they might well be supplied at my Camp and would be of very great service in supporting the foragers."[33] This makes it clear, I think, that Sumter expected the detachment to operate if not under his command at the very least with his forbearance, out of his camp, under his observation, for the purpose of providing escort for parties seeking food and forage. Nathanael Greene, however, had something far more ambitious in mind.

Greene sent the cream of his army west of the Catawba. In command was Daniel Morgan. Greene's orders of 16 December to Morgan were unambiguous. "With these troops you will proceed to the west side of the Catawba river, where you will be joined by a body of volunteer militia under the command of Brig. Gen. Davidson of this state, and by the militia lately under the command of General Sumter." Then came the key sentence. "For the present, I give you the entire command in that quarter, and do hereby require all officers and soldiers engaged in the American cause to be subject to your command."[34] Although not deliberately designed to incur Sumter's wrath, it did.

Another serious problem facing Greene was the appointment of a Commissary General, for Colonel Thomas Polk, who had filled that post under Gates, resigned because of age and the needs of his family. It was a critical appointment. Without food and forage the army could not survive to fight, and we have seen that there was precious little of either commodity. A man of high competence and ruthless will was required, a man who could, as Greene had described his own actions in the North, "forage the country naked" and like Pharaoh harden his heart. But the man he chose argued vigorously against his appointment. To paraphrase Nathanael Greene when he had earlier contemplated his own fate, Colonel William Richardson Davie was well aware that no one had ever heard of a commissary general in history. He was a warrior born and had proven himself a superb small-unit combat commander, and he certainly had the potential for higher command. He was about to raise a regiment of militia cavalry for service under Daniel Morgan, and, in his own words, "fired with the prospect of serving under this celebrated commander was entirely absorbed with this favorite project when General Greene applied to him to accept the appointment of Commissary General."[35]

Davie wriggled and squirmed and pleaded. Greene was adamant and persuasive. He wrote to Davie on 11 December that "Your character and standing in this Country lead me to believe you are the most suitable person. . . . It is a place of great consequence to the Army; and all our future operations depend upon it. As you are a single man, and have health, education, and activity to manage the business, it is my wish you should accept the appointment; especially as you have an extensive influence among the Inhabitants, and are upon a good footing and much respected in the Army." But, said Davie, Greene himself had approved his present mission. Yes, said Greene, but after studying the "exhausted situation of the Country, and the distressed condition of the army, concluded that if the army was not supplied it must retire to the interior towards Virginia or disperse, and the Enemy must be left in peaceable possession of the two Southern States." Whereupon Davie observed that "although he knew something about the management of troops, he knew nothing about *money or accounts*, that he must therefore be unfit for such an appointment." Greene easily countered: "The General replied that as to *Money* and *accounts* the Colonel would be troubled with neither, that there was not a single dollar in the military chest nor any prospect of obtaining any, that he must accept the appointment, and supply the army in the same manner that he had subsisted his own troops for the last six months; that he would render his country more essential service in this way than any other."

Poor Davie. Had he any choice but to abandon the field of splendor? "The General's eloquence prevailed," he wrote, "and the Colonel accepted under an express promise that it should be for as short a time as possible," which turned out to be for the duration. He was, as Greene knew, the right man for the job and performed admirably under the most difficult conditions.[36]

A man of considerable eloquence himself and possessed of captivating diction, Davie became one of North Carolina's leading lawyers after the war. He served in the state legislature for twelve years and was also elected governor. A staunch Federalist all his life, he was a delegate to the Constitutional Convention and led the ratification fight in North Carolina. Tall and elegant, noble in bearing, and quite handsome, Davie was always a presence in a crowd, and while serving with a diplomatic mission to France he graced many a sophisticated Parisian salon. He was anti-democratic to his core, and the ascendancy of Thomas Jefferson to the presidency and his own rejection by the voters led to his disillusion with politics. He retired to Tivoli, his plantation near Lancaster, South Carolina, surrounded by the countryside where as a young man he had proven his exceptional military ability, and by the Scotch Irish fighters who had followed him into battle. Ironically, his greatest service to his country and state paralleled that for which Thomas Jefferson, whom Davie referred to as "that man," wished to be remembered. As Jefferson was the father of the University of Virginia, William Richardson Davie is best known today as the father of the University of North Carolina.[37]

Having done as much as he could for the time being to see to the welfare of the army and having set in motion the machinery that would sustain the coming campaign, Greene chose 16 December as the day when he would lead the main army east to the site chosen by Kosciuszko. But heavy rains delayed departure until the 20th. It had rained for eleven consecutive days. Much of the land was under water. It took his 1,100 men, of whom 650 were Continentals, six days to march approximately seventy-five miles to their new camp across the Pee Dee from Cheraw, South Carolina. Getting to it, Greene wrote to Morgan, was a "very tedious and disagreeable march owing to the badness of the roads and the poor and weak state of our teams. Our prospects with regard to provisions is mended, but this is no Egypt."[38]

But it was a very strategic location, blocking the British from the Cross Creek Country of North Carolina, where Tory Highlanders awaited deliverance, and denying them, as Greene noted, "command of all the provisions of the lower Country, which is much less exhausted by the enemy and Militia than the upper Country."[39] He had placed Cornwallis in a quandry. In a letter to an unidentified person written after the army's move to the Pee Dee, Nathanael Greene made quite clear how vital to his strategy were his new location and the geography of the South.

"It makes the most of my inferior force," Greene wrote, "for it compels my adversary to divide his, and holds him in doubt as to his own line of conduct. He cannot leave Morgan behind him to come at me, or his posts of Ninety-six and Augusta would be exposed. And he cannot chase Morgan far, or prosecute his views on Virginia, while I am here with the whole country open before me. I am as near to Charleston as he is, and as near to Hillsborough as I was at Charlotte; so that I am in no danger of being cut off from my reinforcements; while an uncertainty as to my future designs has made it necessary to leave a large detachment of the enemy's late reinforcements in Charleston, and move the rest up on this side of the Wateree. But although there is nothing to obstruct my march to Charleston, I am far from having such a design in contemplation in the present relative positions and strength of the two armies. It would be putting it in the power of my enemy to compel me to fight him. At present, my operations must be in the country where the rivers are fordable, and to guard against the chance of not being able to choose my ground. Kosciusko is employed in building flat-bottomed boats to be transported with the army, if ever I shall be able to command the means of transporting them. I am now at the falls of the Pedee, and the region of my future operations must be above the falls of the rivers, until I can control the movements of my adversary. Below the falls, all through this country, from the Alleghany to the seacoast, and from the Chesapeake to Georgia, the country is Champaign, and presenting no passes that can be held by an inferior force. Below the falls, the rivers are deep, and their banks are covered with impassable swamps, across which, at long intervals, roads have been constructed which afford the only avenues of retreat. I cannot afford to get entangled among the difficulties they present until I can turn on my adversary and fight him when I please."[40]

In that relatively brief passage Greene laid out clearly what he in general intended to do and why geography was so important. Of course, planning a course of action in any endeavor is one thing, carrying it out successfully quite another, and in war fortune is often fickle. For the time being, while he rested, refitted, and retrained the main army, Nathanael Greene would await developments, relatively safe from attack. But over 150 miles to the west Daniel Morgan was maneuvering in an area close to a dangerous enemy. And not only the British gave him cause for concern. It was Morgan's turn to bear a cross named Sumter.

20

Tarleton Pursues Morgan

*"Washington and his dragoons . . . charged down
the hill like madmen"*

Morgan left Charlotte with the light troops on the 21st of December and
headed west. Once over the Catawba he was authorized to call out the South
Carolina militia under General Thomas Sumter and the North Carolina militia
under General William Davidson. The faithful Davidson would give Morgan no
problems, but Sumter was always difficult. Then Morgan was to establish himself in the fork between the Broad and Pacelot Rivers. Greene had been wise
enough to give Morgan general orders to act "either offensively or defensively
as your own prudence and discretion may direct, acting with caution and avoiding surprizes by every possible precaution." His purpose, Greene wrote, was "to
give protection to that part of the country and spirit up the people, to annoy
the enemy in the quarter." But "should the enemy move in force towards the
Pedee, where this Army will take a position, you will move in such direction as
to enable you to join me if necessary, or to fall back upon the flank or into the
rear of the enemy as occasion may require."[1]

Morgan's command consisted of approximately 600 foot and horse: 320
Maryland and Delaware Continentals; 200 Virginia militia who were discharged
Continental veterans and so could be counted on to behave as regulars; and 80
Continental dragoons. Three of Morgan's subordinate officers were among the
finest the Continental Army had produced. In command of the infantry, Lieutenant Colonel John Eager Howard (1752–1827) of Maryland, well born and
well educated, is fittingly memorialized in his state's lovely anthem, *Maryland,
My Maryland*. He was the grandson of Joshua Howard, who immigrated from
Manchester, and Joanna O'Carroll, who with her family had come to America
from Ireland. His father, Clarence, married Ruth Eager, who brought with her a
large estate. Described by Lighthorse Harry Lee as "placid in temper and re-

John Eager Howard, by Charles Willson Peale.
(Independence National Historical Park Collection.)

served in deportment," John Eager Howard in battle was always found where bayonets decided the issue. He fought with distinction at White Plains, Germantown, Monmouth, and Camden, and would continue to exhibit skill and gallantry in his next five actions. Late in the war on the bloody field of Eutaw Springs he suffered a wound that severely plagued him the rest of his years. After the war he became a lawyer and politician and served as a delegate to the Continental Congress, Governor of Maryland, and U.S. Senator. He and his wife married well; she was Elizabeth Shippen Chew of Pennsylvania. He was very rich. Much of the land now occupied by Baltimore was owned by John Eager Howard. Nathanael Greene's appreciation of him was sincere and accurate. "This will be handed to you by Colonel Howard, as good an officer as the world affords. He has great ability and the best disposition to promote the service. My own obligations to him are great—the public's still more. He deserves a statue of gold no less than the Roman and Grecian heroes."[2]

Serving under Howard was the incomparable Robert Kirkwood (1730–1791). Of English descent, he was a farmer in his native Delaware when war began. With his comrades of the Delaware Line Robert Kirkwood enlisted for the duration, was commissioned a lieutenant in January 1776, and promoted to captain in December of that year. Because Delaware's contingent was small, and after Camden reduced to two ninety-six-man companies, there was no room for advancement in rank, and he ended the war still Captain Kirkwood. Beginning with the Battle of Long Island, Kirkwood fought in every major action in the Northern states except Saratoga, and in the South starting at Camden did not miss a major action. One of Nathanael Greene's early biographers described him as the American Diomed. He moved to the Ohio Country after the war and settled on land granted to him as a veteran. At the age of sixty-one Kirkwood did what he did not have to do. During the wars with the Indians for control of the Old Northwest, he rejoined the service as the oldest captain of the oldest regiment, the 2nd U.S. Infantry, and had the bad luck to serve under the incompetent Major General Arthur St. Clair (pronounced Sinclair) against the Miami Indians under Little Turtle. In the disaster of 4 November 1791 he was killed while "bravely sustaining his point of the action." Lighthorse Harry Lee paid him a haunting tribute: "It was the thirty-third time he had risked his life for his country, and he died as he had lived, the brave, meritorious, unrewarded Kirkwood."[3]

Morgan's cavalry commander was William Washington (1752–1810) of Virginia, a distant kinsman of George Washington, described by Lee as "six feet in height, broad, strong, and corpulent." Washington was badly wounded at the Battle of Long Island, less seriously at Trenton. We covered earlier his two humiliating engagements with Bloody Ban, at Monck's Corner and Lenud's Ferry, where he was badly beaten in large part due to lack of basic security. Lighthorse Harry Lee gave the best measure of the man: "His military exploits announce his grade and character in arms. Bold, collected, and persevering, he preferred the heat of action to the collection and sifting of intelligence, to the calculations and combinations of means and measures, and was better fitted for the field of battle than for the drudgery of camp and watchfulness of preparation. Kind to his soldiers, his system of discipline was rather lax, and sometimes subjected him to injurious consequences when close to a sagacious and vigilant adversary." But in battle Washington fit Morgan's description of him: "Washington is a Great Officer." He served with distinction in the southern campaign until the Battle of Eutaw Springs, where he suffered his third wound for the cause and was captured. He did well for himself after the war, marrying a South Carolina woman and settling on the estate that was her dowry. Although a member of the South Carolina legislature, he had little interest in politics or public affairs. War was his game, and he was good at it.[4]

A difficult four-day march across country soaked by incessant rains, fording the Catawba and the Broad, brought Morgan to Grindal's Shoals on the north bank of the Pacelot River, a tributary of the Broad. On Christmas Day 1780, Morgan established his camp there about sixty miles southeast of Charlotte. Late on the day of his arrival a band of South Carolina volunteers rode into camp. There were only sixty of them, but the militia colonel who led them—

William Washington, by Charles Willson Peale.
(Independence National Historical Park Collection.)

Andrew Pickens—was a godsend for Morgan. He now had to recruit and lead militia a man who lacked Thomas Sumter's charisma but commanded allegiance and deep respect. A very able tactician and brave in battle, and far superior to Sumter in temperament, he would cooperate fully with Daniel Morgan and later with Nathanael Greene.

Andrew Pickens (1739–1817) was the third man in the triumvirate of South Carolina partisan leaders, but he has never commanded the historical press devoted to Thomas Sumter and Francis Marion. He was a stereotype of the lean, dour, long-faced Scotch Irishman. It was said that he rarely smiled. If anyone ever heard him laugh, it was not recorded. His speech was so guarded, an informant told Lyman Draper, that "he would first take the words out of his mouth, between his fingers, and examine them before he uttered them."[5]

As an eighteenth-century elected militia commander Andrew Pickens was a lieutenant Daniel Morgan could count on to the last extremity. He was born near Paxtang, Pennsylvania, of immigrant parents from Ulster, and they joined

Andrew Pickens, by an unidentified artist.
(Courtesy of Andrew Pickens Miller. Photograph and copyright
by Lowell Anson Kenyon.)

the hordes that poured south on the Great Wagon Road and eventually ended
with other Scotch Irish in the Waxhaws. After the Cherokee War of 1760–1761,
in which he served, Pickens and his brother sold the 800-acre farm in the Waxhaws that was their patrimony and bought land on Long Cane Creek in the
southwestern corner of South Carolina. It was in the Long Cane settlements
that Pickens met and married Rebecca Calhoun, the aunt of John C. Calhoun.
They had six children. Pickens was a farmer and justice of the peace when war
began, and a captain of patriot militia at Ninety Six during the troubles in 1775.
There he helped negotiate the treaty with the Tories that was later repudiated
by William Henry Drayton. In 1778, while maneuvering with his 300 men
against a 700-man Tory force, he showed tactical ability by circling the enemy
and following them without their knowledge until 14 February, when he surprised the Tories at Kettle Creek, Georgia. The Tories were defeated with considerable slaughter, and the fight at Kettle Creek ended serious British efforts in
the Back Country until the fall of Charleston.

General Lincoln's surrender of Charleston persuaded Pickens to accept parole, which he honored until late in 1780, when he came under considerable pressure from Major James McCall, one of his favorite officers, to renounce his parole and rejoin the struggle. The British made equally strenuous efforts to dissuade him, for the allegiance, or absence of it, of a highly respected man like Andrew Pickens was worth more than an ineffective Tory militia regiment. The story commonly accepted is that a Tory raid that frightened his family and destroyed much of his property prompted Pickens to officially inform the British that they had violated the terms of his parole and he was therefore joining the Rebels. The British considered his act treachery, which meant that Pickens not only exposed himself to the perils of the battlefield but also to the gallows if he were captured. Late in the war he again revealed his tactical ability by using mounted troops to crush a rising of the Cherokee in three weeks. After the war he served in the South Carolina and federal legislatures. The reader will not be surprised to learn that Andrew Pickens was a very strict Presbyterian and an elder of his church.

Pickens's arrival was fortuitous. Even if Thomas Sumter had been fit to fight and willing to take the field under Morgan, his ego combined with his faulty concepts of tactics and strategy at least would have hampered Morgan and in all probability ruined his mission. There were, however, other partisans who welcomed instead of resented Daniel Morgan's presence. That ferocious fighter Elijah Clarke was still recovering from wounds, but there were scattered parties of his Georgians throughout the Back Country, and Morgan appealed to their gallantry and patriotism to convince them to subject themselves to his direction in order to present a united front against the enemy:

"Gentlemen, Having heard of your sufferings, your attachment to the cause of freedom, and your gallantry and address in action, I had formed to myself the pleasing idea of receiving in you, a great and valuable acquisition to my force. Judge then of my disappointment, when I find you scattered about in parties subject to no orders, not joining in any general plan to promote the public service. The recollections of your past achievements, and the prospect of future laurels should prevent your acting in such a manner for a moment. You have gained a character and why should you risk the loss of it for the most trifling gratifications. You must know, that in your present situation, you can neither provide for your safety nor assist me in annoying the enemy. Let me then entreat you by the regard you have for your fame, and by your love to your country, to repair to my camp, and subject yourselves to order and discipline. I will ask you to encounter no dangers or difficulties, but what I shall participate in. Should it be thought advisable to form detachments, you may rely on being employed in that business, if it is more agreeable to your wishes: but it is absolutely necessary that your situation and movements should be known to me, so that I may be enabled to direct them in such a manner, that they may tend to the advantage of the whole."[6]

Many of the wandering Georgians answered Morgan's call, most conspicuous among them two of Elijah Clarke's best officers, Major John Cunningham and twenty-three-year-old Major James Jackson, the latter Devonshire born but a "fervid patriot in speech and a violent partisan in action."[7] In the critical weeks ahead the Georgians would more than justify Morgan's faith in them.

Two or three days after Pickens rode into Morgan's camp, General William Davidson arrived with 120 North Carolina militia, and then left immediately to gather another 500. Davidson, who had claimed to be able to raise 1,000 men in twenty days, was a fine officer, but he would find that his commitment was overly optimistic. At about the same time one of the scouts Morgan had sent to gather intelligence returned with news that there were Georgians other than Patriots abroad in the red clay hills. Some 250 Georgia Tories under Colonel Francis Waters were raiding Patriot settlements only twenty miles south of Grindal's Shoals, in the area of Fair Forest Creek below modern Spartanburg. Morgan did not hesitate. If he was to "spirit up the people" he had to defend them. He added 200 mounted militiamen under Major James McCall to William Washington's dragoons and ordered the hard-riding cavalryman to advance against the raiders.

Washington left with his 280 horsemen two days after Christmas. The Tories got wind of their approach and began to withdraw. On his second day out Washington covered another twenty-odd miles and caught up with the Tories at a lost site called Hammond's Store, about three miles south of the modern Clinton, South Carolina, on the road to Ninety Six. Thomas Young, our sixteen-year-old veteran of King's Mountain, was one of the mounted riflemen and he described what happened. "When we came in sight we perceived that the Tories had formed in a line on the brow of the hill opposite us. We had a long hill to descend, and another to rise. Washington and his dragoons drew their swords, gave a shout, and charged down the hill like madmen. The Tories fled in every direction without firing a gun."[8] But not quickly enough. In one of the war's more brutal actions the Rebels rode into the fleeing ranks of their fellow Americans and hacked at them without mercy. Washington and his men killed and wounded 150 Tories and captured forty without suffering one casualty. The Tories who were not killed were horribly slashed and mangled by the big cavalry sabers. What it must have been like was vividly revealed by Thomas Young in a macabre tale of men and boys at war:

"Here I must relate an incident which occurred on this occasion. In Washington's corps there was a boy of fourteen or fifteen, a mere lad, who in crossing the Tiger River was ducked by a blunder of his horse. The men laughed and jeered at him very much at which he got mad and swore that, boy or no boy, he would kill a man that day or die. He accomplished the former. I remember very well being highly amused at the little fellow chasing around a crib after a Tory, cutting and slashing away with his puny arm, until he brought him down."[9]

William Washington had not finished with the enemy. Not far away and only fifteen miles northeast of Ninety Six was a small stockade fort on Williams' Plantation that was part of the line of communication between Ninety Six and Lord Cornwallis at Winnsboro. It was garrisoned by 150 Tory militiamen under

Robert Cunningham, whom William Henry Drayton had driven out of the Back Country in 1775. He had returned to South Carolina with other King's Friends after Sir Henry Clinton's capture of Charleston. Following an aborted plan to raise a regiment of provincial regulars, Robert Cunningham was sent by Nisbet Balfour, then commandant at Charleston, to Winnsboro to discuss with Cornwallis command of the Tory militia in the Ninety Six District. The British were anxious for Cunningham's services. He was an influential man in the district, especially in the Saluda River country where he lived. On 23 November Cornwallis wrote to Nisbet Balfour, "Cunningham was here today full of zeal. I made him a brigadr. genl. of militia with Colonel's full pay from the 24th of last June."[10]

But Robert Cunningham's zeal within the safety of Cornwallis's camp at Winnsboro did not extend to a lonely Back Country stockade. Washington sent against Fort William forty mounted partisans and ten dragoons under Colonel Joseph Hayes. On hearing of the Rebel approach, Brigadier General Robert Cunningham and his men fled. Lord Cornwallis learned of it on the first day of January 1781, in a dispatch sent by Major Archibald McArthur, commanding the 1st Battalion of Fraser's Highlanders at Brierly's Ferry on the Broad: "General Cunningham & his people quitted the fort on Saturday night & mounted for 96 & the Rebels took possession of it ye Sunday morning at eight o'clock."[11]

Consternation reigned at Cornwallis's headquarters; but, given the many disappointments he had suffered in his hopes for effective militia activity, one has to wonder if His Lordship was really taken by surprise. His tough and skilled commandant at Ninety Six, the New Yorker John Harris Cruger, considered the militia of the Ninety Six District worthless, guilty of "pusilanimous behavior,"[12] and was convinced that he could not rely on them for the defense of Ninety Six. For the British definitely thought that this key strongpoint was in dire peril. By now Cornwallis knew that Morgan was west of the Broad, and wild rumors placed him with more men than he had advancing on Ninety Six. He could not strike into North Carolina and deal with Nathanael Greene until the uproar to his rear and on his left flank was dealt with. Even before the news of Cunningham's flight from Fort Williams ended his hopes of reliance on Tory militia, Cornwallis knew what he had to do. Decisive action was required, and His Lordship had at hand the perfect instrument.

In the meantime, one of his adversaries was also showing concern. Morgan wrote to Greene on New Year's Eve 1780 that he had ordered 100 swords for issue to "expert Riflemen, to be mounted and incorporated" with Washington's dragoons. He had also ordered 100 packsaddles in order to rid himself of wagons, for "It is incompatible with the Nature of Light Troops to be encumbered with Baggage." Greene would have agreed with these measures, for both he and Morgan were ardent proponents of mobile warfare. He would not be keen, however, on Morgan's proposal to mount an expedition into Georgia as soon as his forces were reunited. Morgan requested an early answer to his proposal, for "This Country has been so exhausted that the supplies for my Detachment have been precarious and scant ever since my Arival, and in a few day will be unattainable, so that a Movement is unavoidable."[13]

While he awaited Greene's reply Morgan got no help from Thomas Sumter, either with troops or provisions, and it is certainly a most reasonable assumption that neither Daniel Morgan nor Nathanael Greene could have done anything to bring the Gamecock around. Cold, imperious, self-centered, Thomas Sumter nursed wounds both physical and psychological. He brooded over Morgan's presence in his backyard. A letter of 8 January 1781 from Nathanael Greene did nothing to assuage him. Quite the contrary. Sumter never forgave Greene for these and later observations on the nature of militia, and long after the war, long after Nathanael Greene moldered in an early grave, Thomas Sumter waged an ignoble vendetta against Greene's nearly destitute widow.

After praising Sumter and wishing for his early reappearance at the head of his troops, Greene gave him the same message Morgan had addressed to the Georgians, but his words were like a shot across Sumter's bow: "The salvation of this Country don't depend upon little strokes; nor should this great business of establishing a permanent army be neglected to pursue them. Partizan strokes in war are like the garnish of a table, they give splendor to the Army and reputation to the Officers, but they afford no substantial national security. They are matters which should not be neglected, & yet they should not be pursued to the prejudice of more important concerns. You may strike a hundred strokes, and reap little benefit from them unless you have a good Army to take advantage of your success. The enemy will never relinquish their plan, nor the people be firm in our favour until they behold a better barrier in the field than a Volunteer Militia who are one day out and the next at home." Greene assured Sumter "That there is no mortal more fond of enterprise than myself, but this is not the basis on which the fate of this country depends. It is not a war of posts but a contest for States."[14]

If this were not enough for the Gamecock to swallow at one sitting, General Greene then proceeded to lecture General Sumter on the evils of civil war. "Plunder and depredation prevail so in every quarter I am not a little apprehensive all this Country will be laid waste. Most people appear to be in pursuit of private gain or personal glory. I persuade myself that though you may set a just value upon reputation your soul is filled with a more noble ambition."[15] Nathanael Greene, of course, was right, although the three sentences on civil war could have best been left unwritten. But it would have meant no difference whether he had written that letter or another far more carefully worded. Sumter was unbending then and later in his determination to act independently. He was also a fading meteor. When all had seemed lost he blazed brightly and contributed greatly to the cause. Now time and men had passed him by and the dim glow around him would grow dimmer until in the latter stages of the war he would initiate a bloody debacle that sickened and infuriated other men. The war had changed. The participation of the militia remained vital but under control and acting in close concert with the regular army.

To varying degrees neither Sumter nor Greene could see beyond their prejudices, but Sumter was far more limited in this sense than Greene. In a letter to Alexander Hamilton, Greene admitted that "There is a great spirit of enterprize among the back people; and those that come out as Volunteers are not a little formidable to the enemy. There are also some particular Corps under Sumpter, Marion and Clarke that are bold and daring; the rest of the Militia are better calculated to destroy provisions than the Enimy."[16] Nathanael Greene had seen the latter run too far too often to overcome his strong, sometimes unfair, feeling against these part-time soldiers. And for all militia there remained the problem of sending them against regulars on an open field.

In the meantime Morgan and his men needed food, and this led to trouble with Sumter. Morgan sent Captain C. K. Chitty to Colonel William Hill of Sumter's brigade to obtain men to assist him in gathering forage and provisions. Hill flatly rejected the order. Sumter had instructed his colonels that no order from Morgan should be obeyed unless it came through him.[17] Given Morgan's temper, here was the potential for a dramatic display of human fireworks had Morgan mounted and ridden to Sumter's place of refuge. What a glorious scene it would have been, how posterity would have relished a faithful recorder of the confrontation. But Morgan had the good sense not to seek out Sumter. He had been in the southern theatre long enough to learn from others about the ego-ridden personality of Thomas Sumter, and it takes no stretch of the imagination to see him listening to such sound men as William Davidson, William Richardson Davie, Andrew Pickens on the peculiar nature of the Gamecock. Morgan handed over the problem to Greene. He was discouraged and requested permission to withdraw from his present position and rejoin the main army. But that did not fit into Greene's strategy. Nor did Morgan's proposal that he raid into Georgia.

Morgan was the master battle captain and tactician, but Nathanael Greene had by far the surer grasp of strategy. He could allow neither too much distance between his main army and Morgan's essential light troops nor a plundering raid that placed the cream of his infantry in needless peril. He rejected, although tactfully, the Georgia expedition in a letter of 8 January. He had previously informed Morgan that Major General Alexander Leslie had arrived in Charleston with upwards of 2,000 British regulars and was on the march upcountry for an eventual linkup with Cornwallis. Leslie's reinforcements were formidable, among them an elite Brigade of Guards under Brigadier General Charles O'Hara, the Hessian Bose Regiment, and 103 Jägers. In both letters Greene expressed his concern that he would be the target of any British move and Morgan must be positioned to come to his aid. One of Greene's subordinates, Otho Holland Williams, a close friend of Morgan's, thought differently, and wrote to his friend on 30 December, "most probably that blow will be delivered at you, as our position in the centre of a wilderness is less accessible than your camp. I know your discretion renders all caution from me unnecessary; but my friendship will plead an excuse for the impertinence of wishing you to run no risk of defeat. May your laurels flourish when your locks fade, and an age of peace reward your toils in war."[18]

Williams was right. Three days earlier Cornwallis's aide, Lieutenant Henry Haldane, had written from Winnsboro to Banastre Tarleton, who had moved his

Legion to a drier upland camp twenty miles from Cornwallis. "If it would not be inconvenient, His Lordship would wish to see you tomorrow."[19]

"I should wish you to push him to the utmost"

The next day Tarleton rode into Cornwallis's camp at Winnsboro. Determined to launch an offensive into North Carolina and bring Greene to battle, Cornwallis once again had to assure the security of his left flank. Ferguson had failed disastrously. Now it was Tarleton's turn. His failure to catch Marion and that elusive warrior's immediate return to familiar raiding ways, and his defeat by Sumter at Blackstock—a defeat not officially recognized—had not lowered Cornwallis's confidence in his young cavalry commander. Tarleton was the *beau sabreur* of his time, still the brave, ruthless, fast-moving commander of light troops whose reputation among his enemies also remained undiminished. Cornwallis explained to Tarleton his plans for the coming campaign, and the necessity that Morgan be contained if not destroyed. But there was on that date, 28 December, no sense of emergency. Cornwallis knew that Morgan was west of the Broad, but of the twin defeats of Hammond's Store and Fort Williams, the former would happen that day and the latter was yet to come. Cornwallis had the leisure to consider and discuss strategy.

To Sir Henry Clinton he had written as early as 6 August, "It may be doubted by some whether the invasion of North Carolina may be a prudent measure; but I am convinced it is a necessary one, and that if we do not attack that province, we must give up both South Carolina and Georgia, and retire within the walls of Charles-town."[20] Despite setbacks and disappointments, despite the death of Ferguson and the destruction of his command, which ended the first invasion of North Carolina, despite his disillusion with repeated assurances that the King's men were ready and waiting, Lord Cornwallis never deviated from the strategy outlined in this letter. But he could have had no doubt of the perils involved, for he left a clear record of his view of the Tory militia and the seriousness of the situation in South Carolina.

Writing on 12 November to General Alexander Leslie about the possibility of Leslie's reaching the Cross Creek region of North Carolina, Cornwallis promised to "instantly march with everything that can be safely spared from this Province [South Carolina], which I am sorry to say is most exceedingly disaffected, to join you at Cross Creek. We will then give our friends in North Carolina a fair trial. If they behave like men it may be of greatest advantage to the affairs of Britain. If they are as dastardly and pusilanimous as our friends to the southward, we must leave them to their fate, and secure what they have got." Thus in a few brief sentences Lord Cornwallis revealed extreme pessimism, even disgust, with regard to the courage and abilities of the Tories of the Carolinas, a group that was the linchpin of British strategy in the South. And as late as 6 January 1781 he would describe to Sir Henry Clinton in the gloomiest terms the true situation in South Carolina. "But the constant incursions of Refugees, North Carolinians, and Back-Mountain men, and the perpetual risings in the different parts of this province; the invariable successes of all these parties against our militia, keep the whole country in a continual alarm, and renders the assistance of regular troops every where necessary."[21]

Yet he would not desist from his plan. His instructions from Sir Henry Clinton were quite clear: his primary responsibility was the security of Charleston and South Carolina. Only if such security could be maintained was he authorized to invade North Carolina. Cornwallis would maintain that rebellion in South Carolina was kept alive only by the presence in North Carolina of an American army and its potential threat to the British army and Tories across the line. Even his sympathetic biographers admit that he was wrong on this score. Charleston fell and an American army was lost but the flame of rebellion grew, fanned mainly by the great partisan chiefs, but also by patriots known and unknown, who decided in the same spirit as James Collins's father after Captain Christian Huck burned William Hill's ironworks that nothing short of their liberty was at stake. Under Horatio Gates a second American army was crushed and scattered, Sumter was soundly defeated and sent fleeing for his life. But the flame did not die. It burned brighter. Sumter was soon back in the field, and men like William Richardson Davie and Isaac Shelby and Elijah Clarke led their riders in a far-ranging, hard-hitting partisan war that the British could not put down. The hard men killed Patrick Ferguson, they cowed the Tory militia, they even mauled British regulars at Fishdam Ford and defeated them at Blackstocks.

Cornwallis himself admitted that the spirit of rebellion was alive and well in South Carolina. But he convinced himself that were it not first for the presence of Gates and his army to the north and now Greene that Rebel resistance would fade and finally disappear. Misjudgment of insurgencies is a common malady of officialdom. In striking northward, was Cornwallis also gripped by a human predilection, especially common among high public servants when faced by an intractable problem, to ignore it, go on to something else, and hope that somehow everything will work out?

Cornwallis also had the support of Lord Germain in London, with whom he was in direct contact. Germain, who never understood the American situation, had encouraged Cornwallis to take the offensive. The smashing victory at Camden had only whetted his appetite for more. He wrote to Cornwallis enthusiastically on 9 November 1780, "I impatiently expect to hear of your further Progress, and that Sir Henry Clinton and Vice Admiral Arbuthnot have found Means of sending a Force into the Chesapeak to cooperate with you: for if that be done, I have not the least doubt, from Your Lordship's vigorous and alert Movements, the whole Country South of Delaware will be restored to the King's Obedience in the Course of the Campaign."[22]

Germain wanted action, and in Cornwallis he had his man. Although the earl's public personality was reserved, his temper even and almost always under control, we also know that beneath the stolid exterior were banked deep fires of passion and resolve. We saw the shattering effect of the death of his wife on him. We watched too as he never hesitated to take his little army into battle and share with his troops all its dangers. Battle, I am convinced, was his second passion. He never revealed in America a gift for tactics; his battles were straightahead stuff, or, to paraphrase Wellington on Napoleon, exercises on who could take more pounding. He does not deserve the label of strategist. He ignored difficult problems that begged for close attention and sought solutions in farther places where armies clashed in grand battles that decided great issues. Lord Cornwallis's talent lay on the battlefield. He was a battle captain of the first rank: brave, cool, decisive, with the instinct that recognized the critical moment and the stomach to intervene and resolve the matter in his favor. Those are not common traits, and we recognize and honor his superior abilities in that most fundamental phase of warfare. We know that it also made him a very dangerous foe.

Tarleton returned to his bivouac. On the afternoon of New Year's Day 1781 a rider arrived in Winnsboro with two letters for Cornwallis from David George, a Tory spy who operated west of the Broad. George reported that his wife's sister had learned from Rebel officers' wives that as soon as Morgan appeared "with five or six Hundred Light horse" and "Washington with their artilliry and foot men . . . they intend to march against Ninety Six and agusta; they say they will have three thousand men to go against Them places." In the second letter George wrote that "I don't believe they have as many men as it is reported to my Wifes Sister," but he obviously believed that Morgan and Washington had joined up with the militia, "and I am well Informed that they Intend to March as fast as they can to Ninty Six."[23] George was for the most part wrong, especially about Daniel Morgan's intentions. But Cornwallis could not know that. He did know that Morgan was west of the Broad, and thus had to take seriously any report of danger to Ninety Six. And George's reports took on the imprint of hard intelligence when at almost the same time the courier from Major McArthur arrived with the startling news that Robert Cunningham had abandoned Fort Williams and Morgan's men were within fifteen miles of Ninety Six. Cornwallis acted with alacrity. Lieutenant Haldane was immediately dispatched to Tarleton with orders to move out immediately for Ninety Six. Haldane rode all night and arrived at 5:00 A.M. on 2 January. Tarleton responded as we would expect. Haldane dashed off a dispatch to Major McArthur of the 71st. "Lt. Col. Tarleton proposes moving immediately and will join your battalion at the ferry. Lord Cornwallis desired you would leave your heavy baggage at the encampment of the Legion." Cornwallis's anxiety was such that at 7:00 A.M. another rider pounded out of Winnsboro with a letter to Tarleton.

Dear Tarleton,
    I sent Haldane to you last night, to desire you would pass the Broad river, with the legion and the first battalion of the 71st, as soon as possible. If Morgan is still at Williams', or anywhere within your reach, I should wish you to push him to the utmost: I have not heard, except from M'Arthur, of his having cannon; nor would I believe it, unless he has it from good authority: It is,

however, possible, and Ninety Six is of so much consequence, that no time is to be lost.

Yours sincerely,
Cornwallis

Let me know if you think that the moving the whole, or any part of my corps, can be of use.

Thus began a swirl of foot and horse, of frantic maneuvers and desperate encounters, of terror and death, victory and defeat, in the harsh and unforgiving Back Country of the two Carolinas during the watersoaked winter of 1781.

"My Lord. I have been most cruelly retarded by the waters"

Tarleton, moving with his customary swiftness, crossed the Broad River the same day that Haldane rode into his camp. He struck into the Dutch Fork, between the Broad and the Saluda. His force consisted of 250 foot and 200 horse of the British Legion; the 249-man 1st Battalion of Fraser's Highlanders (71st Foot) commanded by Major Archibald McArthur; and fifty Royal Artillerymen with two of the light fieldpieces called grasshoppers. By the end of the next day, 3 January, he had searched the country westward for twenty miles and ascertained that the reports of Morgan marching on Ninety Six were false. He did believe, however, that Morgan's presence west of the Broad represented a threat to Ninety Six, and he wrote in a letter of 4 January to Cornwallis, "I beg leave to offer my opinion how his design may be prevented." First he asked to be reinforced with the 17th Light Dragoons and the Jägers, and temporarily by the Royal Fusiliers (7th Regiment of Foot). The Fusiliers were regulars but green, never in battle, recruits slated for garrison duty at Ninety Six before Tarleton asked for them. Cornwallis gave him the Dragoons and the Fusiliers but not the Jägers; later, when Tarleton asked to keep the Fusiliers for his sweep north, Cornwallis assented. Tarleton assured Cornwallis that he was camped "in a plentiful forage country, and I can lay in four days flour for a move." Then he got to the heart of the matter. "When I advance, I must either destroy Morgan's corps, or push it before me over the Broad river, towards King's Mountain. The advance of the army should commence (when your Lordship orders this corps to move) onward for King's Mountain. Frequent communication by letter can pass the Broad river. I feel myself bold in offering my opinion, as it flows from zeal for the public service, and well grounded enquiry concerning the enemy's designs and operations." Emphasizing his seriousness of purpose and desire to move fast, he noted that he had sent orders "to bring up my baggage, but no women." Finally, if Cornwallis approved his plan, the bearer of the letter "Captain M'Pherson may give my order to Lieutenant Munroe to escort me three puncheons of rum, and some salt; and upon their arrival, I will move." Cornwallis replied on 5 January. "You have exactly done what I wished you to do, and understood my intentions perfectly."[24] These two letters would lead to a bitter postwar controversy between Cornwallis and Tarleton.

In war in our time, with its sophisticated communications, units still move faster or slower than expected, orders are still misinterpreted, rendezvous still missed. In the eighteenth century the transmission of intelligence and orders on land depended on horses and men, often riding through hostile country, and even in the best of weather, many days could pass with parts of armies not knowing where the others were and what they were doing. In the Carolinas in 1781 fording places to cross rivers and streams were as important as bridges are to us. There were few bridges in the Low Country and none in the Back Country. Fords, therefore, were always critical locations in war, and they were never more vital than from this point until the end of our story. In fact, they became key factors in the campaign's outcome. As our tale progresses, readers with more than a passing knowledge of World War II will appreciate that for our antagonists getting to a ford before the enemy or preventing him from crossing was as important as the American capture in 1945 of the Remagen Bridge across the Rhine. We must also appreciate that fording places, normally shallow, could in time of high water become either very dangerous or impassable.

In January 1781 conditions for both armies in the Carolinas could hardly have been worse. A deluge fell on the land. What were bad roads in dry weather became muck and mire under the incessant heavy rains that not only flooded rivers and creeks and branches but the land itself for miles beyond. On one occasion, Greene informed Morgan, the Pee Dee rose twenty-five feet in thirty hours.[25] Faithful dispatch riders on both sides urged their jaded horses through a nightmare of water and mud. It was under these conditions that Cornwallis and Tarleton had to stay in close contact if they were to attain their goal of trapping Morgan between them.

For their maneuvers picture a rough inverted triangle in Back Country South Carolina. The apex rests on modern Columbia, the capital; the eastern line runs northward past Winnsboro to Charlotte; the western line runs northwest about twenty miles past modern Spartanburg; the line connecting the two corners runs just north of King's Mountain. Tarleton rode west into the triangle in search of Morgan. As we know, the intelligence reports were in error—Morgan was still at his camp at Grindall's Shoals on the Pacelot River well to the north. Knowing Morgan was somewhere west of the Broad, when Cornwallis approved his plan Tarleton turned his search northward. In the meantime Cornwallis marched north from Winnsboro, staying on the eastern side of the Broad, in theory roughly parallel with Tarleton and his light troops. Tarleton's goal was to catch and destroy Morgan. Failing that, he planned to drive Morgan across the Broad to the vicinity of King's Mountain, where he thought Cornwallis would be waiting

But Cornwallis also had to worry about General Leslie with vital reinforcements slogging slowly through the flooded Low Country and into the water-ravaged Back Country. Conditions on the lower Santee were so bad that Leslie's column was almost stopped in its tracks. Cornwallis slowed his progress northward from Winnsboro to wait for Leslie. By 9 January the "frequent communication" with Cornwallis that Tarleton had assumed had broken down. His courier of that day got through but a day late. Cornwallis wrote to Lord Rawdon on 9 January, "I think it prudent to remain here a day or two longer, otherwise by the corps on my flanks being so far behind, I should be in danger of losing my communication. I have not heard from Tarleton this day, nor am I sure whether he has passed the Enoree." On Friday, 12 January he wrote to General Leslie, "I have not heard from Tarleton since Tuesday. I believe he is as much embarrassed by the waters as you are." The same day he wrote to Lord Rawdon and announced a change in plans. "The Rains have impeded all operations on both sides. Morgan is still at Scull's Shoals on Pacelot, & Tarleton I believe still on the south of Enoree unable to pass either that River or the Tyger. The Broad River is so high that it is with difficulty a canoe can pass. If Leslie had not been likewise detained, I might have tried to stop Morgan's retreat, but the Corps I have with me altho' very good, will not afford a strong detachment to take care of Baggage and Provisions."[26]

But he did not tell Tarleton, who very early the morning of the 12th learned that his scouts had located Morgan's camp at Grindal's Shoals. He got off a report (misdated the 11th) to Cornwallis, who would receive it the morning of the 13th and reply mid-morning on the 14th. By then, however, Tarleton had moved well in advance of Cornwallis. On Friday the 12th, the day he learned of Morgan's location, Tarleton's camp was bustling with activity at 5:00 A.M. He was soon on the march. Scouts and Tory guides ranged forward to find fords on the Enoree and Tyger rivers where the waters had fallen enough to cross. It took him two days but Tarleton was not to be denied. He built rafts for his infantry and swam his horses across both rivers. He did not send another report to Cornwallis until Tuesday, 16 January, from his new position on the Pacelot River. "My Lord. I have been most cruelly retarded by the waters. *Morgan is in force and gone for Cherokee Ford.* I wish he could be stopped." Cornwallis was then camped on Turkey Creek, only forty miles north of Winnsboro, and from there he wrote to Tarleton, also on the 16th of January, "I have not heard from you since the 11. I fear Morgan has too much the start of you. I have ordered meal to be ground & propose marching in three or four days to Beatty's Ford. Leslie will join me tomorrow or Thursday."[27] Neither Tarleton nor Cornwallis knew it, but both letters were written on the eve of one of the most critical battles of the war, and both were en route while it was being waged.

"Boys, get up, Benny's coming!"

We have seen how the lack of speedy communications crippled coordination between Cornwallis and Tarleton, who were never more than approximately fifty miles from each other. It had the same effect on Rebel operations, for Greene and Morgan were about 140 miles apart. The reader should keep this in mind as our story develops.

Cornwallis did not know Tarleton's location, but Morgan did and thought it "more than probable we are his object." He was also keeping an eye on Cornwallis. Under the direction of Andrew Pickens, whom Morgan described as a "valuable, discreet and attentive officer" in whom the militia had confidence, patrols ranged far and wide and alerted Morgan that on Sunday, 14 January, Tarleton had crossed the Enoree at Musgrove's Mill.[28] He crossed the Tyger the same day, ever moving northward. On Monday, 15 January, he approached the Pacelot, where Morgan had men covering all the fords to inform him of a crossing. Acutely aware that he must not allow himself to be caught between Tarleton and Cornwallis, Morgan abandoned his bivouac at Grindal's Shoals on the Pacelot and retreated to Burr's Mills on Thicketty Creek, which put him approximately between the modern communities of Spartanburg and Gaffney, South Carolina.

In a letter of 15 January written from his new location, Morgan reported Sumter's refusal to cooperate to Greene. This, coupled with Davidson's failure to raise large numbers of North Carolina militia and the militia's habit of coming and going at will, had put Morgan in a pessimistic mood. That he was again in terrible pain from sciatica, unable to ride a trotting horse, had to have affected his outlook. "Upon a full and mature deliberation," he wrote, "I am confirmed in the opinion that nothing can be effected by my detachment in this country which will balance the risks I will be subjected to by remaining here. The enemy's great superiority in numbers and our distance from the main army, will enable Lord Cornwallis to detach so superior a force against me, as to render it essential to our safety to avoid coming to action; nor will this be always in my power. No attempt to surprise me will be left untried by them, and situated as we must be, every possible precaution may not be sufficient to secure us. The scarcity of forage renders it impossible for us always to be in a compact body; and were this not the case, it is beyond the art of man to keep the militia from straggling. These reasons induce me to request that I may be recalled with my detachment, and that General Davidson and Colonel Pickens may be left with the militia of North and South Carolina and Georgia. They will not be so much the object of the enemy's attention, and will be capable of being a check on the disaffected, which is all I can effect." Without the large numbers of militia he counted on, Morgan felt strongly that if at all possible he should avoid battle. At the time he wrote the letter he had only 200 South Carolina and Georgia and 140 North Carolina militiamen. Added to his regulars and the steady Virginians, that gave him 940 men. But he did not expect even two-thirds of the militia "to assist me, should I be attacked, for it is impossible to keep them collected." In this judgment he was overly pessimistic and too dismissive of his own powers over the riders of the Back Country. As he was finishing the letter scouts galloped into camp with the latest intelligence, which became his final sentence: "We have just learned that Tarleton's force is from eleven to twelve hundred British." The report was very close to the mark.[29]

Greene did not receive Morgan's letter until about midnight on the 18th, and he answered it the next day. By then the issue had been decided, but Greene's letter is of interest because of his recognition that Morgan is indeed the object and his apparent concern that the Old Waggoner might not show enough caution. "It is not my wish you should come to action unless you have a manifest superiority and a moral certainty of succeeding. Put nothing to the hazard,—a retreat may be disagreeable, but not disgraceful. Regard not the opinion of the day. It is not our business to risque too much, our affairs are in too critical a situation, and require time and nursing to give them a better tone." Greene must have suffered agonies of speculation, for he was aware that "before this can possibly reach you, I imagine, the movements of Lord Cornwallis and Col. Tarleton will be sufficiently explained, and you be obliged to take some dicisive measure. I shall be perfectly satisfied if you keep clear of a misfortune; for tho' I wish you laurels, I am unwilling to expose the common cause to give you an opportunity to acquire them."[30]

Yet despite his constant reminders of the need for great caution, to be ever vigilant against surprises, Greene had to know when he sent Morgan some 140 miles west that the possibility of battle would also be a constant. But he knew his man, and it was a mark of his trust in Morgan that he sent him with the cream of the army on detached command, for he would not have placed such a trust in the hands of commander he considered rash. We should not mistake an instinct for battle with rashness. Gates in the South was rash. Morgan was not. Morgan was always aware of the heavy responsibility he carried, but he also knew that there comes a time in war when one must fight. Despite his nervousness, Greene knew it too. Recall in the very cautionary letter just quoted Greene also wrote that Morgan might "be obliged to take some dicisive measure." And five days earlier he had written of "my wish also that you should hold your ground if possible, for I forsee the disagreeable consequences that will result for a retreat." That was on 13 January, and even then Greene had intelligence of Tarleton's sweep west of the Broad, for in the same letter he advised that "Col. Tarlton is said to be on his way to pay you a visit. I doubt not that he will have a decent reception and a proper dismission."[31] Given Tarleton's aggressive nature, Morgan could hardly hold his ground and not fight. Reading their correspondence, one gets the sense that both men knew an unavoidable conflict was fast approaching.

On the night of the 15th, with Pickens's men watching every ford, Tarleton marched his troops northward along the right bank of the Pacelot. For three hours they followed the river toward its source. The Rebel militia on the north bank kept pace. In the dark of night the resourceful Tarleton, aware of the watchers, stopped and pretended to bivouac, then silently turned his column around without alerting his shadows across the river and retraced his line of march to Easterwood Shoals, six miles below the Rebels and unguarded.

Morgan's camp on Thicketty Creek was some six miles north of Easterwood Shoals. His men were gathered around their campfires cooking and eating breakfast when a patrol arrived at a gallop with news that Tarleton was across the Pacelot. No time was wasted. Camp was broken immediately. Morgan's voice, far reaching and immediately recognizable, bellowed orders. The column quickly formed and moved out. Washington's dragoons formed a protective screen that enveloped the marching men. It was the 16th of January 1781.

Tarleton, meanwhile, was on the left bank of the Pacelot, taking advantage of some log buildings erected the previous year by another British invader of the Back Country, Major Patrick Ferguson. He sent out his own patrols to look for Morgan, writing after the war that he "intended to take post, with his whole corps, behind the log houses, and wait the motions of the enemy." But when word came back that Morgan had abandoned his camp on Thicketty Creek, that his breakfast fires were still hot, Tarleton immediately marched there, and his troops enjoyed the Americans' breakfast, "which they had left behind them, half cooked, in every part of their encampment."[32] At 8:00 A.M. Tarleton dashed off the note to Cornwallis that we quoted earlier, his first communication in four days, stating that Morgan meant to cross the Broad River at Cherokee Ford. The reader will remember Cherokee Ford as the crossing place of the King's Mountain men on their final march to catch Ferguson. Tarleton was telling Cornwallis that His Lordship and he could trap Morgan there. He did not know that Cornwallis was south of him, still camped on Turkey Creek, waiting for General Leslie and his reinforcements. Dragoon patrols were dispatched to follow Morgan until dark and ascertain his direction and purpose. Tory scouts were to continue the search until dawn for the same purpose.

Morgan was marching northwest, his goal not Cherokee Ford but Island Ford higher up on the Broad. His intention was to cross the Broad, get into the rough, hilly country near Thicketty Mountain, and await Tarleton and battle.[33] The distance from the camp where Tarleton's troops were eating Rebel breakfasts and Island Ford was about twenty miles. The road Morgan followed was a road in name only, rough and crooked and swampy; he turned off it onto an even worse one. Tarleton's scouts described it as a byway. It was a miserable track, largely a quagmire due to the rains, and led through several swamps. Among the riders who had left his breakfast behind was Thomas Young, one of our boy partisans turned seasoned veteran. "We were very anxious for battle," he later wrote, "and many a hearty curse had been vented against General Morgan during that day's march for retreating, as we thought, to avoid battle."[34]

It was slow going. By late afternoon the column was still six miles from the Broad. Scouts reported the river running high. Morgan could not risk a crossing that night. If Tarleton came on him during a river crossing the result could be disastrous. He still hoped to get to Thicketty Mountain, but he also had to be prepared to fight, for he knew the reputation of his swift-moving adversary. Although Morgan was a fighter by nature, and a soldier of supreme and well-earned self-confidence, the judgment of Lighthorse Harry Lee that he fought out of "irritation of temper, which seems to have overruled the suggestions of his sound and discriminating judgement" simply lacks credibility. Morgan's well-earned reputation for coolness in crises and his actions in the ensuing days offer all we need to reject Lee's conclusion. That well-tested veteran William Washington described Morgan as the coolest man in the face of danger he had ever seen.[35] Morgan was keenly aware of his awesome responsibility to keep his little force intact for an eventual reunion with the main army. But how was that best to be done? By risking a perilous river crossing just ahead of a rapidly closing enemy, or by choosing a position, resting and feeding his troops, and taking his time preparing for battle?

How fortunate for the cause that it was Daniel Morgan who faced that choice, not Lighthorse Harry Lee and other second guessers who persist to this day. He was on his own. There would be no telephone or radio conversations with an increasingly nervous Nathanael Greene. There would be no superior hovering overhead in a helicopter to micromanage him. This was all to the good. When it came to battle, Morgan was better left alone to make his own decisions.

With the long shadows of day's end falling over the column, he decided to stop at a landmark familiar to all Back Country people, to where Andrew Pickens and other leaders could bring the militia that were wandering the countryside scouting and foraging, the place where the men of King's Mountain had their final rendezvous. At Cowpens the little army settled down and lighted cooking fires. Lieutenant Colonel John Eager Howard recalled the arrival of large numbers of militia. "Some militia joined us in the march, but Pickens, with its principal force, did not join us until the evening before the battle of the Cowpens." Howard stated that Morgan decided to fight when Pickens arrived with the main militia force. Thomas Young wrote, "We arrived at the field of Cowpens about sunset, and were then told we would meet the enemy." The partisans were spoiling for a fight with Bloody Ban. "I well remember," John Eager Howard said, "that parties were coming in most of the night, and calling on Morgan for ammunition, and to know the state of affairs. They were all in good spirits, related circumstances of Tarleton's cruelty, and expressed the strongest desire to check his progress." One of the night riders was another of our boy soldiers, another King's Mountain veteran, James Collins, who rode into camp with James Moffitt's band. Sumter still sulked, and he did not send his men. "None of them were with us," recalled Andrew Pickens.[36]

Tarleton's hard-riding dragoons and Tory scouts swept the country behind the Americans. The evening of the 16th, after Morgan had stopped, Tories brought in an important captive, a straggling American militia colonel who had good information and was persuaded to share it. The tale he told, supported by other intelligence reports arriving soon after, convinced Tarleton of the "propriety of hanging upon General Morgan's rear, to impede the junction of reinforcements, said to be approaching, and likewise to prevent his passing the Broad River without the knowledge of the light troops, who could perplex his design, and call in the assistance of the main army if necessity required."[37] Tarleton's blood was up. The prey was near, and he was running. How familiar it all was. At 2:00 A.M., 17 January, the night air was pierced by the sharp notes of reveille from British bugles. At 3:00 A.M. Tarleton marched. The light infantry company of Fraser's Highlanders and the thee light companies of the 16th Regiment supported by the British Legion infantry composed the van. It was follwed by the Royal Fusiliers commanded by a veteran officer, Major Timothy Newmarsh. Behind them came the 1st Battalion of Fraser's Highlanders under the command of that grizzled veteran of the splendid Scottish Brigade of the

Dutch Army, Major Archibald McArthur. Banastre Tarleton and his cavalry brought up the rear. The British column followed the same terrible road that the Americans had taken.

Morgan in the meantime was making his preparations. He had been campaigning in the southern theatre since September of the previous year. Can we doubt that he began early to pick the brains of other men about Banastre Tarleton and his way of war? What better authority than William Washington, twice bested by Tarleton, who had ridden with Morgan for over three months? One of the statements Morgan made many years later in defending his choice of ground was true: "I knew my adversary, and was perfectly sure I should have nothing but downright fighting."[38] There can also be little doubt that he had pondered even before he came south the problem of using militia in formal battle.

The profession of arms does not often attract innovative minds. Good generals do what has been done before them better than run-of-the-mill generals, and great generals do it far better. On rare occasions, however, the uncommon man appears who solves a serious problem with a method untried yet on the face of it so simple that afterward others wonder why it took so long to discover. Daniel Morgan was one of those rare individuals. This untutored son of the frontier was the only general in the American Revolution, on either side, to produce a significant original tactical thought. As I have written before, he had no illusions about the behavior of militia in formal battle. But the use of militia in battle was vital to the cause because there were rarely enough Continentals to face the British alone. The unanswered question until Cowpens was how best to use them when their presence was required in orthodox eighteenth-century combat. Morgan answered the question. He would not try to get militia to do what they were not meant to do. For he knew them. He came from them, those country people and backwoodsmen, knew their faults and virtues, their capabilities and failings, knew as did William Moultrie that "the militia are brave men, and will fight if you let them come to action in their own way."[39]

Put the militia in the front ranks, said Morgan. But don't expect them to stand fast as generals before him had insisted. Instead, use their propensity to flee when faced by massed bayonets advancing on them to work for you. He called his officers to him: Howard, Pickens, Kirkwood, Washington, McCall, McDowell, Cunningham, Triplett, Jackson, Buchanan, Tate, and the others, strong leaders seasoned by long years of war. But the gathering was not a council of war. There would be no repeat of Horatio Gates's plaintive query before Camden: "Gentlemen, what is best to be done?" He was no longer Captain Daniel Morgan standing on a snow-swept Quebec lane frustrated by superior officers who lacked his instinct in battle. The officers were gathered to listen to Brigadier General Daniel Morgan explain how the troops would be deployed and how they would be brought into action. They were gathered to receive their orders.

The field of Cowpens, some 500 yards long and about the same width, was an open meadow, sparsely wooded and free of undergrowth, then kept clear by thousands of cattle gathered every spring by drovers for grazing on the rich grass and the peavine before being lined out and driven to Camden and the coast. Oaks and hickories and chestnuts and maples dotted the meadow. Nearby springs provided water for men and beasts. From the point where the road that both forces took emerged from thick woods onto the meadow, the ground rose so gently it appeared flat. But some 400 yards from the tree line there was an eminence so slight that it was hardly perceptible. Beyond that point was a shallow swale. Then the ground once more rose gently to another eminence that in no way can be dignified as a hill. On the first rise, Morgan told his officers, he would form his main line of resistance. Astride the road he would place John Eager Howard's 280 Maryland and Delaware Continentals. With them he would station the 200 former Virginia Continentals now serving as militia under Major Francis Triplett. John Eager Howard would command that line. In the swale behind the first rise, where a man on horseback could see the forward slope while remaining somewhat protected, William Washington and his eighty dragoons would deploy as the reserve. To augment Washington's horse, Morgan asked for volunteers to be mounted and armed with sabers, and forty-five men stepped forward, among them Thomas Young. They were commanded by Major James McCall, who had served under Washington on the Hammond's Store raid. "We drew swords that night," Thomas Young recalled, "and were informed we had authority to press any horse not belonging to a dragoon or an officer into our service for the day."[40]

So far there was nothing remarkable about Morgan's disposition of troops. It was what he did with the bulk of his militia that was quite unorthodox. Many of these men were expert riflemen, and the man who had once been a rifleman himself, who had commanded the Virginia riflemen who had done such terrible damage to the British at Saratoga, wanted to get the best that he could out of them without asking the impossible. About 150 yards in front of Howard's main line he would place 300 North and South Carolina and Georgia militia under Andrew Pickens. To support Pickens's right he would position 100 riflemen from Augusta County, Virginia, commanded by Captain Tate and Captain William Buchanan. From Pickens's command he would deploy 120 picked Georgia and North Carolina riflemen another 150 yards forward to act as a skirmishing line, to engage and then fall back and rejoin Pickens as the British advanced. He neither expected nor wanted the militia in the first two lines to stand their ground before a British bayonet charge. Their job was to soften up the British before they hit the main line of resistance—Howard's regulars and the veteran Virginians. All he would ask for were two volleys at fifty yards, with special attention paid to officers and sergeants. Then Pickens's militia would fall back across the left front of Howard's regulars and form on Howard's left to be held as a reserve. If necessary during their withdrawal, Washington's cavalry would come to their assistance. Morgan drew a rough map to illustrate the plan to his officers. Then he dragged his rheumatic-ravaged body from campfire to campfire to explain personally to the militia what he expected of them. One story has it that an aid helped him raise his shirt so the men could gaze on the ridges of scars that covered his back while Morgan told the tale of the terrible lashing he had received from the British over twenty-five years before. Whatever the details of that night before battle, his was a brilliant performance. Thomas Young described it:

"It was upon this occasion that I was more perfectly convinced of General Morgan's qualifications to command militia than I had ever before been. He went among the volunteers, helped them fix their swords, joked with them about their sweethearts, told them to keep in good spirits, and the day would be ours. And long after I laid down, he was going about among the soldiers encouraging them and telling them that the old wagoner would crack his whip over Ben in the morning, as sure as they lived.

"Just hold up your heads, boys, three fires," he would say, "and you are free, and when you return to your homes, how the old folks will bless you, and the girls kiss you for your gallant conduct.

"I don't believe he slept a wink that night."[41]

When he was not moving among the troops Morgan monitored patrols and scouts, who were kept moving all night, and sent messages by couriers to various militia units reported to be in the countryside. He ordered the militia to prepare twenty-four rounds of ammunition per man. And it was to Morgan about two hours before daybreak that a scout galloped with news he probably expected. Tarleton was five miles away and "marching very Rapidly."[42] Morgan mounted and with Andrew Pickens rode through the camp, past the huddled forms rolled in their blankets on the ground. That stentorian voice the Pennsylvania rifleman John Joseph Henry had first described in the Maine wilderness now echoed far and wide over a frosty Carolina field.

"Boys, get up, Benny's coming!"[43]

21

Cowpens

"It was the most beautiful line I ever saw"

In the gray time between dawn and sunrise a green-jacketed horseman followed by others emerged from the gloom of trees and brush flanking Thicketty Creek onto the edge of the meadow called Cowpens. Captain David Ogilvie of the British Legion horse had been sent by Tarleton to reinforce the van, and it was he who first saw the American lines in the dim light. Ogilvie immediately sent a rider galloping back to Tarleton, who was still a few miles away with his main force. Morgan, Ogilvie reported, was forming for battle.

Daniel Morgan had not changed the plans he had laid out for his officers and explained to his troops the night before. One hundred and fifty yards ahead of John Eager Howard's regulars, strung out some 300 yards across the field, Colonel Andrew Pickens arranged the militia of South Carolina, North Carolina, and Georgia, about 300 strong. Their horses were picketed and guarded in a pine grove at the very rear of the field, behind Washington's cavalry. From Pickens's force Major Joseph McDowell of North Carolina picked sixty of his best men and advanced some 150 yards to form a loose skirmish line on the right of the road. Major Charles Cunningham of Georgia did the same on the left side of the road. Morgan's full strength differs with every writer. Tarleton wrote after the war that the Americans numbered 1,900, which is nonsense. Morgan stated in his battle report, "We fought only 800 men," but later writers have ranged up to slightly over 1,000.[1] Let us leave it that he had between 800 and 1,000, for a true count will never be known. They had had a night of rest and, what is most important, breakfast. Morale was high among both regulars and militia. Sergeant Major William Seymour of the Delaware Line confided to his journal that the men were "seeming to be all in good spirits and very willing to fight."[2]

Tarleton, too, was very willing to fight. When Captain Ogilvie's rider reached him with the news that Morgan was forming his lines he called to him his local Tory guides, perhaps among them Alexander Chesney, and asked them for a description "relative to the ground which General Morgan then occupied, and the country in his rear. These people," Tarleton later wrote, "described both with great perspecuity. They said that the woods were open and free from swamps; that the part of the Broad river, just above the place where King's Creek joined the stream, was about six miles distant from the enemy's left flank, and that the river, by making a curve to the westward, ran parallel to their rear." Tarleton liked what he heard. He would later write that it was "certainly as proper a place for action as Colonel Tarleton could desire. America does not produce many more suitable to the nature of the troops under his command."[3] Tarleton drove his tired, hungry men forward, anxious to come to grips with the enemy.

At Cowpens, recalled Thomas Young, "The morning of the 17th . . . was bitterly cold. We were formed in order of battle, and the men were slapping their hands together to keep warm—an exertion not long necessary." Morgan rode his lines. To the 120 Georgia and North Carolina skirmishers he asked for courage and marksmanship when the enemy was within firing distance. They should then withdraw slowly, reloading and firing as they went, until they rejoined their comrades in the militia line 150 yards behind them. "Let me see," he called out just before leaving them, "which are most entitled to the credit of brave men, the boys of Carolina or those of Georgia." Then he rode back to Andrew Pickens's main line of militia and exhorted them to hold their fire until the British were within fifty yards, to deliver two volleys, then follow the plan by crossing to the left in front of Howard's Continentals and gathering just behind that main line of resistance. He complimented them for past actions and implored them to add to their gallant reputation. On this occasion, he said, they would not have to stand alone against regulars, for supporting them were American regulars superior to the enemy's. To flee, Morgan told them, would invite destruction. He briefly described to them his own exploits with riflemen against more formidable forces than Tarleton's, repeated his specific tactical instructions, and then rode back to Howard's Continentals of the Maryland and Delaware Lines and the former Continentals serving as Virginia militiamen. His voice laced with passion, booming across the field, he addressed the hardbitten regulars: "My friends in arms, my dear boys, I request you to remember Saratoga, Monmouth, Paoli and Brandywine, and this day play well your parts for your honor and liberty."[4] Twentieth-century cynics cocking skeptical eyes at this passage should keep in mind that we are writing about the eighteenth century, when such exhortations prior to battle were common. Morgan then took his station just behind the Continentals, where he could see everything and intervene when and where necessary.

Sunrise on 17 January 1781 was at 7:00 o'clock. At about 6:45 A.M. the Americans saw the head of the British column emerge from the woods, four companies of redcoated light infantry supported by the Legion Foot in green. As the British column penetrated deeper into the field of Cowpens, the Georgia and North Carolina skirmishers began an annoying fire that hindered Tarleton's effort to study Morgan's deployment. He ordered fifty of the Legion horse to charge and disperse the riflemen. The horsemen trotted forward, formed and drew sabers, and charged. The sound of pounding hooves echoed across the field, clods of damp earth flew up behind the galloping horses. Then the long rifles began to crack, and fifteen dragoons tumbled from their saddles. Chastened, reminded perhaps of the toll taken by Sumter's riflemen at Blackstocks, their comrades did not push home the charge but turned their mounts and fled for the protection of their lines, whereupon Tarleton ordered the infantry to drop their packs and form into line of battle. He did not finish his inspection of Morgan's dispositions. He did not wait until the Highlanders and his main body of cavalry, which he would hold in reserve, had gotten completely clear of the thick underbrush along Thicketty Creek. Nor did he consult with his two veteran infantry commanders, Major Archibald McArthur of the Highlanders and Major Timothy Newmarsh of the Fusiliers. Instead, he formed his main line for an immediate general advance. His force numbered 1,076.

Moving with their customary measured precision, the well-drilled British infantry wheeled into line as the Americans watched and waited. For most of the militia in the first two lines it was a sight they had never seen before, and one they would never forget: brilliantly uniformed British regulars, bayonets shining at sunrise, forming into line of battle in the backwoods of America. Tarleton described the deployment in his *History*. The light infantry of the 16th Foot and Fraser's Highlanders, in all 110 men, "were then ordered to file to the right until they became equal to the flank of the American front line." To their left he placed the 250 provincial regulars of the British Legion infantry. With one of the grasshoppers spewing grapeshot at the American skirmish line, "this part of the British troops was instructed to advance within three hundred yards of the enemy." They were then halted while the Royal Fusiliers, 167 strong, about to experience their first battle, marched into line to the left of the Legion foot. On each flank was a captain with fifty dragoons, "to protect their own and threaten the flanks of the enemy." The 249-man 1st Battalion of Fraser's Highlanders was ordered "to extend a little to the left of the 7th regiment and to remain one hundred and fifty yards in the rear. This body of infantry, and near two hundred cavalry composed the reserve." Tarleton was confident that he would prevail, for as he recalled, "During the execution of these arrangements, the animation of the officers and the alacrity of the soldiers afforded the most promising assurances of success."[5]

So impatient was Tarleton that he ordered his main line forward before Major Newmarsh had finished posting his officers. There began the noise of an eighteenth-century battle. The drums beat and the fifes shrilled. Artillery boomed. Officers and sergeants bawled orders. The British line, Morgan wrote in his battle report, "moved on with the greatest Impetuosity shouting as they advanced." He reported that the Georgia and North Carolina skirmishers who had turned back the Legion horse "gave them a heavy and galling fire" as they withdrew to Pickens's main militia line. Sixteen-year-old Thomas Young, astride his "tackey" with Washington's cavalry, had a clear view of the event. "About sunrise the British advanced at a sort of trot, with a loud halloo! It was the most beautiful line I ever saw. When they shouted, I heard Morgan say, 'They give us the British halloo, boys—give *them* the Indian halloo, by God!' And he galloped along the lines, cheering the men, and telling them not to fire until we could see the whites of their eyes. Every officer was crying, 'Don't fire!' for it was a hard matter to keep us from it." And all the while the two British grasshoppers had elevated their range and were firing shot "so fiercely upon the center that Colonel Washington moved his cavalry from the center towards the right wing."[6]

The American militia line stood steady "under the command of the brave and valuable Col. Pickens" and held their fire as the shouting British line trotted forward. From his vantage point Thomas Young was entranced by the sight: "The militia fired first. It was for a time, pop—pop—pop, and then a whole volley; but when the regulars fired, it seemed like one sheet of flame from right to left. Oh! it was beautiful."[7] But it hardly touched the American militia, whereas the Rebel volley had wrought considerable damage on the British infantry, especially officers and sergeants, who were favorite targets. One grievous loss was Major Timothy Newmarsh, who fell wounded and was unable to continue. But disciplined British infantry, even the Fusilier recruits, would not be stopped by a single volley. The British were rallied. They fired their volley but as usual it did little if any damage, for most of the balls flew high over the Americans' heads, to be found many years later imbedded in trees as high as thirty feet off the ground. The bayonet was their weapon. It had never failed them when confronting rabble. And to their eyes what now happened was an old story writ yet again. As the red and green line advanced, the light infantry and the Legion foot and the Fusiliers, bayonets presented, the militia regiments withdrew. But a keen observer would have noted that it was not a stampede as at Camden or Kip's Bay. Instead, the militia began filing off to the left, across the front of the Continentals, as Morgan had instructed.

Watching from the steady ranks of the Delaware Line was Lieutenant Thomas Anderson, who noted in his journal that the militia "Fought Well Disputing the ground that was between them and us, Flying from One tree to another." He is supported by Sergeant Major Seymour: the militia "retreated in very good order, not seeming to be in least confused." But some felt confusion, fear, and an overpowering desire to get as far away as possible. In the militia on the far right was young James Collins, who told what he did and in all candor what he intended to do. These men had the farthest to go to gain the protection of the Continentals: "We gave the enemy one fire, when they charged us with their bayonets. We gave way and retreated for our horses." To Tarleton the militia withdrawal had all the beginnings of a rout. He ordered the captain commanding the fifty 17th Light Dragoons on his right flank to charge the retreating militia, and it was James Collins and his comrades who took the brunt of a cavalry charge "executed . . . with great gallantry,"[8] wrote Tarleton. But Morgan was watching, and he had not forgotten his promise to the militiamen. He ordered William Washington to counterattack the British dragoons. Washington's reaction was swift and dramatic. James Collins and Thomas Young participated in this action and described their respective roles.

James found himself in the middle of a whirlwind of action that took only minutes to complete: "Tarleton's cavalry pursued us; now, thought I, my hide is in the loft. Just as we got to our horses they overtook us and began to take a few hacks at some, however, without doing much injury. They, in their haste, had pretty much scattered, perhaps thinking they would have another Fishing Creek frolic, but in a few moments Col. Washington's cavalry was among them, like a whirlwind, and the poor fellows began to keel from their horses, without being able to remount. The shock was so sudden and violent they could not stand it and immediately betook themselves to flight; there was no time to rally, and they appeared to be as hard to stop as a drove of wild Choctaw steers going to a Pennsylvania market. In a few moments the clashing of swords was out of hearing and quickly out of sight." Thomas Young was one of the riders who came to the rescue of Collins and his comrades: "In a moment the order to charge was given. We made a most furious charge, and cutting through the British cavalry we wheeled and charged them in the rear. In this charge I exchanged my tackey for the finest horse I ever rode; it was the quickest swap I ever made in my life."[9]

It was 7:15 A.M. Fifteen minutes had elapsed since the British advance had begun. Tarleton ordered his infantry lines redressed, and then the British advanced on Howard's Continentals, who stood fast in disciplined ranks and traded volleys with the steady ranks facing them. "The fire on both sides," wrote Tarleton, "was well supported and produced much slaughter." Sergeant Major Seymour described how John Eager Howard "all the time of the action rode from right to left of the line encouraging the men."[10]

At 7:30 A.M. Tarleton rode back where Major Archibald McArthur and his 249 Highlanders waited in reserve. He ordered McArthur to march to his left along the outer edge of Cowpens and outflank the American's main line of resistance. McArthur ordered the pipers forward, and another sound was added to the din of battle—the wild wail of the war pipes as the Scots began their advance.

While all this was going on Daniel Morgan had galloped to the rear to help Andrew Pickens and his officers rally the militia, many of whom if left to their own devices would have mounted their horses and scattered. It is said that some did slip away and swim their mounts across the Broad. But if Tarleton thought that the despised irregulars had abandoned their regular comrades as the Virginians and North Carolinians had done at Camden, he was about to get a very rude surprise. After Washington's horse had driven off the British dragoons, James Collins wrote that "we being relieved from the pursuit of the enemy began to rally and prepare to redeem our credit, when Morgan rode up in front, and waving his sword, cried out, "Form, form, my brave fellows! Give them one more fire and the day is ours. Old Morgan was never beaten."[11] The bulk of the militia, led by Pickens assisted by Jackson, Cunningham, McDowell, and others, gathered and followed their gallant leaders in a wide circuit behind the steadfast Continentals toward the right flank of Howard's main line of resistance.

Morgan left the militia in the capable hands of their commanders and galloped back to his main line where he met a situation that astounded and alarmed him. John Eager Howard had observed the flanking movement of the Scots, and to meet it he ordered Captain Wallace's company of Virginia militia on his right to turn toward the advancing Highlanders. But amid the roar of musketry, the shouting men, the cries of the wounded and the dying, and the thick smoke that always engulfed eighteenth-century battlefields, the order was misunderstood. The Virginians thought he had ordered them to face about and withdraw. Let John Eager Howard describe what happened:

"Seeing my right flank was exposed to the enemy, I attempted to change the front of Wallace's company (Virginia regulars); in doing it, some confusion ensued, and first a part, and then the whole of the company commenced a retreat. The officers along the line seeing this, and supposing that orders had been given for a retreat, faced their men about, and moved off." Recognizing that the rearward movement, although done by mistake, removed his right flank from the danger presented by McArthur's advance, the unflappable Howard allowed it to proceed.

This was the sight confronting Morgan on his return: the Virginians, the men of Maryland and Delaware, marching to the rear. Howard continued: "Morgan, who had mostly been with the militia, quickly rode up to me and expressed apprehensions . . . but I soon removed his fears by pointing to the line, and observing that men were not beaten who retreated in that order. He then ordered me to keep with the men until we came to the rising ground near Washington's horse, and he rode forward to fix on the most proper place for us to halt and face about."[12]

The British infantry, many of their officers and sergeants dead or wounded, misinterpreted an American withdrawal being performed with drill field precision. Howard was right. The Americans were far from being beaten men. But the British regulars thought the enemy beaten, believed the moment had come to charge on the retreating Rebels and seal their victory. They "set up a great shout," wrote Lieutenant Anderson, and came on, but in disorder, breaking their ranks, surging like a tumultuous crowd. Tarleton had lost control of his infantry. But the American command structure functioned with the same precision exhibited by the rank and file.[13]

It was 7:45 A.M. Morgan had chosen the spot where the Continentals and the Virginians would halt and turn on the British. The officers rode up and down the line and gave the order. As it was executed Morgan galloped along their front. His great voice boomed in the din. "Face about, boys! Give them one good fire, and the victory is ours!" The British regulars continued to rush on in great disorder, quickly closing the gap. Howard wrote, "In a minute we had a perfect line." "The enemy were now very near us." How near has been estimated by participants at ten to thirty yards, close enough in any case that when Howard gave the order to fire a sheet of flame burst from the American line that the British "little expected" and their surge came to a sudden, shocking halt. They were thrown into confusion. Above the tumult rose John Eager Howard's command: "Charge bayonets!"[14]

The Maryland and Delaware Lines ran at the British with glistening steel extended. "We were in amongst them with the bayonets," wrote Lieutenant Anderson. Hysteria consumed the British ranks. The unthinkable occurred. British regulars dropped their muskets and either fell to the ground and begged for mercy or, as Daniel Morgan described it, took to their "heels for security—helter skelter." Up and down the American line an ominous cry arose: "Tarleton's Quarters . . . Tarleton's Quarters!" But Morgan was not Tarleton. He was a man of honor and his officers were made of the same stuff. The men were quickly brought under control: "Not a man was killed wounded or even insulted after he surrendered," reported Morgan to Greene. Howard observed the British artillerymen still firing the grasshoppers and ordered them taken, which was done in short order, but the gunners, true to their rigid code of honor, refused to surrender their guns until death or serious wounds stopped further resistance. Howard personally saved a gunner who held the match from being bayoneted.[15]

Thomas Young recalled hearing the bugles sound the cavalry charge, and astride his fine new horse "we made a sort of half circuit at full speed came upon the rear of the British line, shouting and charging like madmen." But John Eager Howard claimed that Washington was engaged with Tarleton's cavalry during the bayonet charge, and Morgan's official account only nine days after the battle supports Howard's recollection.[16]

There was only one British unit on the field that fought on, but they were beleaguered. Andrew Pickens's militia, after being rallied behind Washington's horse, had come almost full circle and on the right charged the Scottish Highlanders. While Washington's horsemen pursued and rounded up the fleeing infantry from Tarleton's main line, John Eager Howard wheeled his Continentals to the right and came at the Scots from the other direction. The Americans had wrought that always-dreamed-of but ever-elusive goal of soldiers—a double envelopment. The Highlanders fought on alone, stubbornly, hand to hand against numbers rapidly becoming overpowering.

Tarleton attempted in vain to rally his fleeing infantry, but "neither promises nor threats could gain their attention," He sent word to the 200 dragoons of the British Legion, still in reserve, to go to the aid of the Scots. Tarleton described their reaction: "The cavalry did not comply with the order." He then galloped across the field to personally order them to charge, American riflemen marked the racing rider, and though he came through unscathed, his horse was killed beneath him. Dr. Robert Jackson, assistant surgeon of the Highlanders, rode up and dismounted and gave his horse to Tarleton, who at first demurred, but Jackson said, "Your safety is of the highest importance to the army." Jackson, a brave man, then tied his handkerchief to the end of his cane and walked toward the victorious Americans. When challenged he identified himself and offered his services to the wounded, which was accepted. Tarleton completed his ride on Jackson's horse, but to no avail. He harangued the Legion horse, but admitted that "all attempts to restore order, recollection, or courage proved fruitless. Above two hundred dragoons forsook their leader, and left the field of battle." Lieutenant Roderick McKenzie of the Highlanders put it more colorfully: they "fled through the woods with the utmost precipitation, bearing down such officers as opposed their flight."[17]

Major McArthur and his men were now truly alone. Twenty-three-year-old Major James Jackson with some of his Georgia boys rushed into the midst of the Highlanders and attempted to seize their colors. He got them in his grasp, lost them, then pushed on farther and seized Major McArthur, whom he made prisoner. Forsaken by their comrades, surrounded and hemmed in closely, further resistance meant useless slaughter. They had gone into battle with sixteen officers; nine were dead or wounded. John Eager Howard called out for surrender. The Scots grounded their arms. Major Archibald McArthur, proud veteran of a fighting people, handed his sword to Colonel Andrew Pickens of the Long Cane Creek Regiment of Militia. Joseph McJunkin said of the Scots: "They looked like a set of Nabobs, in their flaming regimentals," in contrast to the partisans, "in our tattered hunting shirts, black, smoked, and greasy."[18]

Banastre Tarleton to his credit gave it one more try. The British regulars of the 17th Light Dragoons, now numbering forty horsemen, had not fled the field. With them and fourteen officers, most from the Legion horse, Tarleton charged in an attempt to recover the artillery. He never got close, colliding instead with Washington's cavalry, which repulsed him. Washington spotted Tarleton and ordered a charge, but few of his men heard him and those who followed were left well behind as Washington spurred his mount toward the man who had twice humiliated him. The fearless Virginian was well in advance of his troopers when Tarleton and a few of his officers, riding in the rear of their small party, wheeled their horses and engaged Washington in a wild, swirling clash of horses and men that can probably be timed in seconds. A British officer and Washington swung their sabers at each other and Washington's broke at the hilt. His foe raised his saber to finish the job, but Washington's young black body servant rode up, leveled his pistol, and shot the officer through the shoulder of his sword arm. An officer to the left swung his saber at Washington, but Washington was saved by Sergeant Major Perry, who rode up just in time to parry it. Tarleton charged Washington and slashed with his saber but Washington managed to deflect the blade with the hilt of his broken sword. Tarleton pulled his pistol and fired, missing Washington but wounding his horse. Banastre Tarleton then wheeled and galloped after his fleeing men. He had probably fired the final shot of Cowpens. It was 8:00 A.M. The battle had lasted about one hour.

"We . . . swore you were the finest fellows on earth"

Cornwallis did not yet know it but he had lost his light troops. On the field at Cowpens Tarleton left eighty-six percent of his force dead, wounded, or captured: 110 killed in action, including ten officers; 712 prisoners, of whom 200 were wounded. Tarleton also left on the field the two grasshoppers, two regimental standards, thirty-five wagons, 100 horses, 800 muskets, a traveling forge, the officers' black servants, and "all their music," Morgan reported to Greene.[19]

Tarleton either never understood or was unwilling to admit that in Daniel

Morgan he met a master tactician who outgeneraled him. He never blamed himself. In his postwar memoirs he claimed that "the disposition was planned with coolness, and executed without embarrassment. The defeat of the British must be ascribed either to the bravery or good conduct of the Americans; to the loose manner of forming which had always been practiced by the King's troops in America; or to some unforseen event, which may throw terror into the most disciplined soldiers, or counteract the best-concerted designs." He decided for the record that the British manner of forming their lines in America was mainly responsible for his defeat. When infantry who are formed "very open and only two deep meet opposition they can have no stability. But when they experience an unexpected shock, confusion will ensue, and flight, without immediate support, must be the inevitable consequence." He also referred to the "total misbehaviour" of the troops.[20]

But on the ground at Cowpens lay a wounded officer of Fraser's Highlanders who never forgave Tarleton for that day, and regarded his remark on the "total misbehaviour" of the troops as insulting. In his book, *Strictures on Lt. Col. Tarleton's History* (1788), published the year after Tarleton's history of the southern campaign, Lieutenant Roderick McKenzie flayed the man he detested: "I leave to Lieutenant Colonel Tarleton all the satisfaction which he can enjoy, from relating that he led a number of brave men to destruction, and then used every effort in his power to damn their fame with posterity." Military post mortems can make for dreary and self-serving reading, and McKenzie's must be used as carefully as Tarleton's, but of Tarleton's blaming the manner of forming McKenzie offers a neat riposte: "if his files were too extended, why did he not contract them? For he says ... that 'the disposition was planned with coolness, and executed without embarrassment.' Any other mode of attack, or dispostion, therefore, which he might have planned, would doubtless have been executed with equal promptitude." And McKenzie is correct in charging that without proper reconaissance Tarleton rushed very tired and hungry men into battle before they were fully formed and before the reserve had been properly placed. This is not to say that if Tarleton had done all the proper things that he would have won, for he was up against a seasoned force led by some of the finest officers America had produced and commanded by a man who was a far better soldier than he. Another British officer, Cornwallis's commissary Charles Stedman, who was pro-Cornwallis and anti-Tarleton, nevertheless in his history of the war published in 1794 came the closest to describing Tarleton's abilities as a soldier: "That he possesses personal bravery inferior to no man is beyond a doubt; but his talents at the period of which we are speaking of never exceeded that of a partizan captain of light dragoons, daring in skirmishes. He could defeat an enemy in detail, by continually harassing and cutting off detached parties." Of all the comments on Tarleton's performance, however, no one summed it up better than the anguished commander of the Highlanders, Major Archibald McArthur. John Eager Howard wrote: "Major M'Arthur very freely entered into conversation, and said that he was an officer before Tarleton was born; that the best troops in the service were put under 'that boy' to be sacrificed."[21]

John Eager Howard also had another personal encounter that revealed what would have happened had "that boy" won the day and presents to posterity forever the true nature of Banastre Tarleton. "In the pursuit," Howard wrote, "I was led toward the right, in among the 71st, who were broken into squads, and as I called them to surrender, they laid down their arms, and the officers delivered up their swords. Captain Duncanson of the seventy-first . . . gave me his sword and stood by me. Upon getting on my horse, I found him pulling at my saddle, and he nearly unhorsed me. I expressed my displeasure and asked him what he was about. The explanation was, that they had orders to give no quarter, and they did not expect any; and as my men were coming up, he was afraid they would use him ill. I admitted his excuse and put him into the care of a sergeant. I had messages from him some years afterwards, expressing his obligation for my having saved his life."[22]

Despite having planned and executed the tactical masterpiece of the war, Morgan has not escaped criticism, for in dissecting battles and campaigns pedagogues and apologists for losers dote on the what-ifs of history. In Morgan's case, most of the criticism centers on his choice of ground on which to fight. It began then and persists today. It is quite true that his flanks were "in the air," that is, unprotected by natural barriers, such as swamps, and that in the event of defeat the Broad River to his rear was a trap. That Morgan felt the heat of such criticism is revealed by his explanation made several years after the battle:

"I would not have had a swamp in the view of my militia on any consideration; they would have made for it, and nothing could have detained them from it. And as to covering my wings, I knew my adversary, and was perfectly sure I should have nothing but downright fighting. As to retreat, it was the very thing I wished to cut off all hope of. I would have thanked Tarleton had he surrounded me with his cavalry. It would have been better than placing my own men in the rear to shoot down those who broke from the ranks. When men are forced to fight, they will sell their lives dearly. . . . Had I crossed the river, one half of the militia would immediately have abandoned me."[23]

His statement is often interpreted as self-serving because, it is charged, he chose the wrong ground on which to fight. But arguments can be made for all of Morgan's points, and he was certainly right about Tarleton's propensity for the "downright fighting" of frontal assaults. Many militiamen probably would have ridden away had he crossed the Broad. As we have seen by the testimony of Thomas Young, John Eager Howard, and Sergeant Major Seymour, the militia on 16 and 17 January were ready to fight, but their mercurial nature and habits of discipline did not lend them to prolonged retreats.

What Morgan failed to relate in his statement, written years later, is that although he wanted a "stroke" at Tarleton Cowpens was his second choice for a battle site and was forced on him. Morgan wrote to his friend Captain William Snickers nine days after the battle that he intended to cross the river "to a strong piece of Ground, & there decide the Matter but, as matters were Circumstanced, no time was to be Lost, I prepared for Battle." He knew that he must not allow Tarleton to catch up while he was either on the march or engaged in crossing the river. Either would have given Tarleton the tactical situation at which he was best. He had to accept battle on the right bank of the Broad. Cowpens was a well-known landmark where the militia bands he so desperately needed could rendezvous. And for the tactics Morgan had in mind to meet the man he had gauged correctly, Cowpens was not the wrong ground, it was exactly the right ground. As for those who maintain that an error, the mistaken rearward movement of the Virginians and the Continentals, of which Howard and Morgan had taken immediate advantage, determined the outcome of the battle, we can only offer the opinion of that hardbitten Jäger Captain Johann Hinrichs: "Luck is the main thing in war."[24]

Morgan's elation was such that he lifted his nine-year-old drummer boy and kissed his cheeks. His official battle report to Greene, written two days later on the other side of the Broad, was formal. It began, "The troops I had the Honor to command have been so fortunate as to obtain a compleat Victory over a Detachment from the British army, commanded by Lt. Col. Tarlton," and continued in similar vein, detailed but restrained. But to William Snickers he wrote: "When you Left me you remember that I was desirous to have a Stroke at Tarlton—my wishes are Gratified, & I have Given him a devil of a whiping, a more compleat victory never was obtained." It was, he added, "a Great thing Indeed."[25]

Precisely the opinion of his comrades 125 miles to the east encamped on the Great Pee Dee. On 23 January Morgan's aide, Major Edward Giles, rode his mud-spattered horse into Nathanael Greene's camp carrying the news of the great victory. The camp went wild. The rum was broken out. They had a *feu de joie*, or musket fire, one man after another firing a round into the air in a continual roar. Otho Holland Williams wrote to Morgan on the 25th. "Next to the happiness a man feels at his own good fortune is that which attends his friend. I am much better pleased that you have plucked the laurels from the brow of the hitherto fortunate Tarleton, than if he had fallen by the hands of Lucifer. Vengeance is not sweet if it is not taken as we would have it. I am delighted that the accumulated honors of a young partisan should be plundered by my old friend.

"We have had a *feu de joie*, drunk all your healths, swore you were the finest fellows on earth, and love you, if possible, more than ever. The General has, I think, made his compliments in very handsome terms. Enclosed is a copy of his orders. It was written immediately after we received the news, and during the operation of some cherry bounce."[26]

The victory was a "Great thing Indeed." Its primary consequence was the loss to Cornwallis of his light troops, which would have a crucial effect on the balance of the campaign. Its secondary consequence was psychological. Morale soared. Excitement coursed through the land from South to North. Major Edward Giles, after carrying the electrifying news to Nathanael Greene, pushed hard to inform Congress at Philadelphia, some 550 miles away. Along the way he disseminated the news to the famous and the obscure, but later admitted that he was so excited he forgot to stop at Williamsburg and inform Governor

Thomas Jefferson. Congress voted Morgan a gold medal, Washington and Howard silver medals, Pickens and Triplett each a sword. The Virginia House of Delegates voted Morgan "a horse with furniture, and a sword."[27] Governor John Rutledge of South Carolina made Andrew Pickens a Brigadier General. Letters overflowing with joy and congratulations poured in from all quarters. One, written eleven days after Cowpens, came from a man who had missed the battle; it underestimated Cornwallis's strength, and offered a restrained felicitation that has the appearance of an afterthought:

> Dear Sir: I have every reason to believe that the enemy are not more than 1,600 strong. I have had them repeatedly counted, and could ascertain their number to a man, if I knew what had escaped the defeat of Col. Tarleton— upon which happy event I most heartily congratulate you.
>
> I am, etc.,
> Thomas Sumter[28]

"Proud Gineral Tarleton run doon the road helter-skelter"

At Cowpens on the 17th of January all was not quite over. The mopping up and the always grisly cleaning up after men have at each other were seen to. William Washington had only one matter on his mind. Tarleton. He wanted him. He wanted him very badly indeed, and the brief, dramatic encounter at the end of the battle only enhanced his passion. Washington gathered his Continental Dragoons and they pursued Tarleton as fast as their horses could carry them.

Tarleton in the meantime had come upon his baggage train, which had been left under the protection of 100 men commanded by Lieutenant Fraser of the Highlanders. Tory guides had informed Fraser of the disaster, whereupon he destroyed the baggage he could not transport, put his men on some wagons and draught horses, and beat a hasty retreat, leaving most of the wagons and the officers' black servants. Fraser's were the only infantrymen who escaped Cowpens. After their departure, civilians came along and started helping themselves to what was left—a fatal error for some of them. Tarleton and his small party of Legion horse officers and 17th Light Dragoons galloped up, and Tarleton later claimed that he had "cut to pieces" and "dispersed" some Americans who had seized the baggage train. The Americans were some of his Tory guides, dressed in the clothing of the country. Following this glorious feat of arms, Tarleton then says he "heard with infinite grief and astonishment that the main army had not advanced beyond Turkey Creek," which was about thirty-five miles away.[29] Thus began his public campaign to attach some of the blame for his debacle on his patron, Lord Cornwallis. This discovery meant a change in route, and the party stopped at the house of a Rebel named Goudelock and left him with no choice but to guide them to Hamilton's Ford on the Broad River. Thirty minutes later Washington and his dragoons galloped up and asked a terrified Mrs. Goudelock if Tarleton had passed and which way he had gone. Fearful for her husband's safety in the middle of a fight, she pointed down the wrong road. Twenty-four miles later Washington decided he had been hoodwinked: by then it was too late to catch Tarleton.

One Rebel saw and talked to Tarleton during his flight, but not before a fierce saber fight with the British and the loss of his horse. Thomas Young, mounted on the fine horse he had taken from a fallen British dragoon, rode out with some of his comrades to loot British baggage, and during his plundering took two prisoners. He was on his way back to Cowpens when he was intercepted by British horsemen, probably troopers of the 17th Light Dragoons. He attempted to flee, but his horse was "stiff from the severe exercise I had given him that morning" and they overtook him. "My pistol was empty, so I drew my sword and made battle. I never fought so hard in my life. . . . In a few minutes one finger on my left hand was split open; then I received a cut on my sword arm . . . which disabled it. In the next instant a cut from a sabre across my forehead (the scar of which I shall carry to my grave) the skin slipped down over my eyes, and the blood blinded me. Then came a thrust in my right shoulder blade, then a cut upon the left shoulder, and a last cut (which you can feel for yourself) on the back of my head—and I fell upon my horse's neck. They took me down, bound up my wounds, and placed me again on my horse, a prisoner of war.

"When they joined the party in the main road, there were two tories who knew me very well—Littlefield and Kelly. Littlefield cocked his gun and swore he would kill me. In a moment nearly twenty British soldiers drew their swords, and cursing him for a damned coward, for wanting to kill a boy without arms and a prisoner, ran him off.

"Col. Tarleton sent for me, and I rode by his side for several miles. He was a very fine-looking man, with rather a proud bearing, but very gentlemanly in his manners. He asked me a great many questions, and I told him one lie, which I have often thought of since. In reply to his query, whether Morgan was reinforced before the battle? I told him, 'he was not, but that he expected a reinforcement every minute.' He asked me how many dragoons Washington had? I replied that 'he had seventy, and two volunteer companies of mounted militia; but you know they won't fight!' 'By God!' he quickly replied, 'they did today though!'

"We got to Hamilton Ford on the Broad river about dark. Just before we came to the river, a British dragoon came up at full speed and told Col. Tarlton that Washington was close behind in pursuit."

During the confusion of the crossing, Thomas escaped. He got home where he fell ill with a "violent fever eight or ten days; but thanks to the kind nursing and attention of old Mrs. Brandon, I recovered." Thomas Young was proud of his status as a mounted soldier, and very upset over the loss of the "finest horse I ever rode." Before he leaves us, hear him on how he managed to set that to rights. "One day I met old Molly Willard riding a very fine sorrel horse, and told her we must swap. She wouldn't listen to it—but I replied that there was no use in talking, the horse I would have and the exchange was made not much to the old woman's satisfaction, for she did not love the Whigs; and I don't believe the Willards have forgiven me for that horse-swap to this day."[30]

James Collins, after being rallied along with his comrades behind the lines, had followed the militia horde under Andrew Pickens in its full circuit of the field and participated in the assault on Fraser's Highlanders. He carried the rifle that the leader of his band, James Moffitt, had given him at Fishing Creek. "I fired my little rifle five times, whether with any effect or not I do not know. Next day, after receiving some small share of plunder, and taking care to get as much powder as we could, we (the militia) were disbanded and returned to our old haunts, where we obtained a few days rest."[31]

There would be no rest for the local Tory, Alexander Chesney. He had known total defeat and captivity at King's Mountain, and now he had watched the disaster at Cowpens, "where we suffered a total defeat by some dreadful bad management." This time he avoided capture. "I proceeded towards home to bring off my wife and child on the 17 Janry and found there was nothing left not even a blanket to keep off the inclement weather; or a change of garments; then leaving a pleasant situation without a shilling in my pocket ... we went to the Edisto River in order to settle, there being nothing but two horses and our clothes left, everything else being in the hands of the Americans and by them confiscated. I have not been at Pacolet since nor am I likely to be."[32]

Daniel Morgan's mission was far from over. The battle was won, Tarleton's detachment destroyed, but he and his men could not tarry at Cowpens and take their ease. He had to assume that as soon as Cornwallis heard the news he would strike north to catch him, take revenge, and free the prisoners. Morgan paroled the British officers and assigned some of Pickens's militia to tend the wounded and bury the dead. By noon or shortly thereafter he began a skillful and rapid retreat. He left Cowpens and marched his little army and prisoners some five miles to Island Ford, where he got safely across the Broad about 1,200 people, horses, and baggage. That night he camped on the left bank. On the morning of the 18th, before dawn, Morgan had troops and prisoners on the road north, marching fast. Cornwallis was still at Turkey Creek, where some of Tarleton's troopers who had fled the field had arrived the previous evening. His Lordship awaited definitive news, aware that something very bad may have happened, but probably hoping that his young commander of cavalry would be able to assure him that the early intelligence was exaggerated and the situation not so calamitous as reported.

The same morning that Morgan was hastening northward toward the Catawba, well on the road to Gilbert Town, Banastre Tarleton arrived at the Turkey Creek bivouac. Imagine the scene as he trotted—or did he walk his horse—to where Cornwallis stood. Certainly, all eyes had to be on him, including those of an American prisoner, Samuel McJunkin, who later related that as Tarleton reported Cornwallis placed the tip of his sword against the ground and leaned into the hilt, and leaned harder and harder, until the blade snapped. In his fury and sense of loss, Cornwallis swore that he would recover the prisoners. That episode and the letter he wrote four days later to Lord Rawdon reveal his extreme agitation over a defeat so unexpected as to be almost incomprehensible. "The late affair has almost broke my heart," he confessed to Rawdon. The feelings of other officers were torn between grief for their fallen comrades and a sense that Tarleton, never popular, resented for his rapid promotions over the heads of older officers, had gotten his just reward. "This defeat," wrote William Moultrie, "chagrined and disappointed British officers and Tories in Charlestown exceedingly. I happened to be in Charlestown at the time when the news arrived. I saw them standing in the streets in small circles, talking over the affair with very grave faces." When the older British officers who had been captured arrived in Charleston on parole, they were, added Moultrie, "exceedingly angry indeed at their defeat, and were heard to say, 'that was the consequence of trusting such a command to a boy like Tarleton.' "[33]

For ten days Tarleton endured the whispers, the looks, possibly even barely hidden gloating. He then wrote to Cornwallis asking permission to retire and a court martial to determine responsibility. Horatio Gates had asked for the same after Camden and never received it. Nor would Tarleton. On 30 January Cornwallis wrote to him: "You have forfeited no part of my esteem as an officer by the unfortunate event of the action of the 17th. The means you used to bring the enemy to action were able and masterly, and must ever do you honour. Your disposition was unexceptionable; the total misbehaviour of the troops could alone have deprived you of the Glory which was so justly your due."[34] None of this was true, and Cornwallis must have known it. His biographers believe he had no other choice because he knew that he needed Tarleton for the rest of the campaign. But bureaucracies—and the military is the epitome of bureaucracy—invariably protect their own regardless of the truth, and in this case the other ranks offered a convenient scapegoat. And after months of writing official reports to Clinton and Germain in which he praised Tarleton as the officer without whom they could do nothing, could Cornwallis possibly admit that he might have been wrong? Whatever the case, the words assuaged Tarleton's wounded feelings and he withdrew his request. Another, homelier, man provided a pithier description of both Tarleton at Cowpens and the entire British effort in the Back Country. His name was John Miller, and somewhere in western Carolina he was asked to give a prayer at a meeting.

"Good Lord, our God that art in heaven, we have great reason to thank thee for the many favors we have received at thy hands, the many battles we have won.

"There is the great and glorious battle of King's Mountain, where we kilt the great Gineral Ferguson and took his whole army. And the great battles of Ramsours's and at Williamson's. And the ever-memorable and glorious battle of the Coopens, where we made the proud Gineral Tarleton run doon the road helter-skelter, and, Good Lord, if ye had na suffered the cruel Tories to burn Billy Hill's Iron Works, we would na have asked any mair favors at thy hands. Amen."[35]

22

Bayonets and Zeal

*"It was resolved to follow Green's Army
to the end of the World"*

Tarleton's disaster did not deter Cornwallis from his strategy of striking into North Carolina and pursuing Greene to either catch and destroy him or to drive him permanently out of the Carolinas. He had written to his commander in chief, Sir Henry Clinton, on 6 January from Winnsboro that he was about to depart on his march northward. That letter would take a long time to reach New York. On 18 January, the day he learned that he had lost one-quarter of his army, Cornwallis once more wrote to Sir Henry, informing him that "nothing but the most absolute necessity shall induce me to give up the important object of the Winter's Campaign." Having discovered no such inducement, His Lordship disobeyed Clinton's order to protect Charleston and South Carolina at all costs, and he did not write to Sir Henry again for three months.[1]

On 15 January 1781, two days before Morgan destroyed Tarleton's command at Cowpens, the rank and file present and fit for duty of the army of Lieutenant General Charles, Earl Cornwallis numbered between 3,200 and 3,300. This included the British regulars with Cornwallis at Turkey Creek, Leslie's reinforcements slogging upcountry from Charleston, and Tarleton's doomed command. An hour after sunrise on 17 January at Cowpens, Cornwallis's army was suddenly slashed to some 2,550 men. This was not a large army with which to go adventuring in the American hinterland, and Tarleton had lost almost all His Lordship's fast-moving light troops. But it was still a formidable force for that part of America, approximately equal in number to Greene's army. And its some 2,000 high-quality British and German regulars outnumbered Greene's by two to one in that critical category.

Cornwallis had kept with him three first-rate units: his own 33rd Foot, commanded in the field by the intrepid Lieutenant Colonel James Webster; the

334

Royal Welch Fusiliers (23rd Foot); and, smoldering with resentment at Banastre Tarleton for the loss of their sister battalion at Cowpens, the 2nd Battalion
of the Fraser's Highlanders (71st Foot). Surviving Tarleton's debacle were the
100 infantrymen of the baggage guard brought in by Lieutenant Fraser, the forty
men of the 17th Light Dragoons who had stayed with Tarleton to the end, and
the 200 British Legion horse, who now could only be regarded as of dubious
quality.

On the same day and at about the same time that Tarleton arrived at
Turkey Creek, Cornwallis's reinforcements finally marched in under the
command of Major General Alexander Leslie. A descendant of the famous
seventeenth-century Scottish soldier, Alexander Leslie, 1st Earl of Leven, the
namesake inherited none of his ancestor's military skills. But Leslie had brought
with him three units of regulars and one regiment of 256 North Carolina Volunteers. The latter would be of marginal help to Cornwallis, but the regulars
were first-rate reinforcements. The Germans included the 347-man Hessian von
Bose Regiment and 103 Jägers. His British brigade comprised 690 crack Household guardsmen; it had been raised by taking fifteen men from each company
of the 1st Regiment of Foot Guards (today the Grenadier Guards). In command
of the Guards was one of the most colorful characters of the old British army,
the Anglo-Irishman Brigadier General Charles O'Hara (1740?–1802), whose letters to the Duke of Grafton present a graphic picture of Cornwallis's march
through the Back Country.[2]

O'Hara was the illegitimate son of James O'Hara, second Baron of Tryaw-
ley, who served under the great Marlborough and for thirteen years was envoy
extraordinary to the court of Portugal, from which he returned, according to
Horace Walpole, "with three wives and fourteen children." James O'Hara also
served as envoy extraordinary to Russia, and Walpole described him as "singu-
larly licentious, even for the courts of Portugal and Russia." He married the
daughter of the second Viscount Mountjoy but left no legitimate issue. James
O'Hara kept his bastard son Charles with him for much of his youth. Charles
O'Hara attended Westminster School, where so many South Carolina boys of
rich families went. In 1752, he became a cornet in the 3rd Dragoons, and four
years later a lieutenant in the 2nd Regiment of Foot Guards (Coldstream), of
which his father was colonel. He served under his father in Portugal in 1762, in
the same campaign in which Charles Lee had made his name while serving
under Burgoyne. In 1766, at about the age of twenty-two, O'Hara was appointed Lieutenant Colonel-Commandant in Senegal of the African Corps,
made up of British soldiers pardoned for crimes by accepting service for life in
Africa. Presumably the African sun darkened a complexion already ruddy, for
his close friend Horace Walpole once described "his face as ruddy and black and
his teeth as white as ever." He returned to service in America in October 1780,
and almost immediately entered a campaign as severe as any the British experienced in North America.

Although they were personal friends, Cornwallis's judgment of O'Hara
seems justified. "His zealous services under my command, the pains he took,

and the success he met in reconciling the guards to every kind of hardship, give him just claim, independent of old friendship, on my very strongest recommendations in his favor." O'Hara was an inveterate gambler, and in 1784 Cornwallis wrote that "poor O'Hara is once more driven abroad by his relentless creditors." He fled to Italy, where he met the author Mary Berry (1763–1852), who began in Florence in 1783 the *Journals and Correspondence* that she completed seventy years later. She was the actual editor of the collected works of Horace Walpole, who described her "as an angel inside and out." Her friendship with O'Hara was interrupted by the wars of the French Revolution. O'Hara was wounded and captured at Toulon in 1793 and spent two years as a prisoner in Paris during the Reign of Terror, living in relative comfort at the Luxembourg Palace. On his return to England, O'Hara and Mary Berry were engaged, but he was appointed Governor of Gibraltar and she would not leave England. He went, and at the end of 1796 the engagement was broken off. She never married, and to the end of her long life spoke of Charles O'Hara "as the most perfect specimen of a soldier and a courtier of the past age." In Gibraltar O'Hara was a popular and good governor at a critical time, and consoled himself with the favors of two ladies with whom he had families. The old "Cock of the Rock," as his troops called him, on more than one occasion chased out of England by creditors, on his death left his ladies and their children 70,000 pounds and his black servant plate valued at 7,000 pounds. He died from complications of old wounds, from which he suffered much.

O'Hara along with many of his countrymen was wrong in believing that England would fall from the ranks of great nations if it lost the rebellious colonies, but he was nevertheless an intelligent man who read correctly much of the American military and political landscape. His remarks to the Duke of Grafton in a letter of 1 November 1780, written from New York prior to his going to the South, reveal especially the reality of the American situation as opposed to the dream world of the King and his ministers: "every day confirms me more, in my old Opinions, that England has not only lost this Country for ever, but must for ever consider the People of this Continent as the most inveterate of her enemies. I am sensible that this Doctrine will appear very extraordinary, at a time when England is exulting over her Triumphs, in the reduction of Charlestown, and the defeat of . . . Gates . . . . the old and fatal delusion must now act with redoubled force, that our successes will enable our numerous Friends to exert themselves in the cause of Great Britain—that the Carolinas are permanently ours, and the Rebellion receiv'd such severe, decisive checks, that this Continent will very shortly be ours again—in this Country we do not see these Events through such flattering Mediums, on the contrary, we hold our situation much more precarious, and much more critical, as we are more materially vulnerable at this moment than we have been at any Period during the war." As for the Rebels, in the same letter he pointed out that "it is a fact beyond a doubt that their own Numbers are not materially reduced, for in all our Victories, where we are said to have cut them to pieces, they very wisely never staid long enough to expose themselves to those desperate extemities." And "how impossible must it prove to conquer a Country, where repeated successes cannot ensure permanent advantages, and the most trifling Check to our Arms acts like Electric Fire, by rouzing at the same moment every Man upon the vast Continent to persevere upon the least and most distant dawn of Hope."[3]

To this doleful state of affairs was added the extreme difficulties for a European army waging war in the American Back Country. Burgoyne had tried it, and in discussing Cornwallis's march into North Carolina O'Hara referred to the "unfortunate Affair of Saratoga."[4] It fell to Brigadier General Henri Bouquet, that splendid Swiss soldier in British service in the French and Indian War, to describe the difference between war in Europe and war in America. In the following passages he was referring to fighting Indians in the wilderness, but his words apply almost equally to the Back Country. "Those who have only experienced the severities and dangers of a campaign in Europe, can scarcely form an idea of what is to be done and endure in an American war. To act in a country cultivated and inhabited, where roads are made, magazines are established, and hospitals provided; where there are good towns to retreat to in case of misfortune; or at the worst, a generous enemy to yield to, from whom no consolation but the honour of victory, can be wanting; this may be considered as the exercise of a spirited and adventurous mind."

But in "an American campaign everything is terrible; the face of the country, the climate, the enemy. There is no refreshment for the healthy, nor relief for the sick. A vast inhospitable desart, unsafe and treacherous . . . where victories are not decisive, but defeats are ruinous; and simple death is the least misfortune which can happen to them."[5]

This was the environment into which Lord Cornwallis led his little army on the morning of 19 January 1781. And he began by heading in the wrong direction and for two days followed the wrong road. This was only the first instance in which the loss of his wide-ranging light troops would deprive Cornwallis of timely intelligence as well as a force to harry his fleeing foe. Cornwallis, and presumably Tarleton and the senior officers, believed that Morgan would attempt to hold the country in the vicinity of the Broad River. Morgan, however, knew that he had to get out of Cornwallis's range or risk being caught by a force that greatly outnumbered his own. He was also determined not to repeat the fiasco involving the King's Mountain prisoners, all of whom except for about 130 had escaped during the increasingly chaotic Rebel withdrawal. And he wanted breathing space in order to reestablish contact with Greene. By dusk on the 18th, about twelve hours before Cornwallis got his army in motion, Morgan had left the Broad River country well behind and was some twenty miles north of Cowpens at Gilbert Town. By that time Lieutenant Colonel Washington had rejoined him with the 3rd Light Dragoons. Aware that he would be pursued, anxious that whatever happened the British not recover the prisoners, Morgan sent them north in Washington's custody to cross the Catawba well upriver and rejoin him on the east bank downstream at Sherrald's Ford. Then he turned due east and struck out for Ramsour's Mill, site of that ferocious contest between

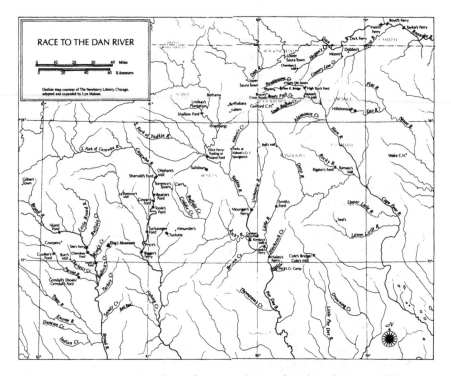

The Race to the Dan River. (From The Papers of General Nathanael Greene, Volume VII,
edited by Richard K. Showman. Maps updated by Lyn Malone. Copyright © 1994 by the
University of North Carolina Press. Used by permission of the publisher.)

Rebels and Tories, and beyond that Sherrald's Ford. The distance was some sixty
to seventy miles as the crow flies.

Two days after he started Cornwallis finally picked up Morgan's trail. Tarleton, ranging west of the Broad with the Legion horse and Jägers, had discovered that Morgan was nowhere near Cowpens, and Cornwallis, who camped on
the 21st at Buffalo Creek, just north of Cherokee Ford and a few miles south
of the North Carolina line, learned that Morgan had set out for Gilbert Town.
Cornwallis wrote that day to Lord Rawdon, "I shall march tomorrow with 1200
Infantry & the Cavalry to attack or follow him to the banks of the Catawba."
That night the Legion horse, the Guards, and the 33rd Foot were ordered to be
ready to march at 6:30 A.M. The rest of the army would follow. On 22 January
1781, Lord Cornwallis and the British army of reconquest marched into North
Carolina in pursuit of Morgan. To be able to move faster, they left behind camp
followers and part of the baggage train. It was the second time that Cornwallis
had struck north but this time there would be no turning back, and neither His
Lordship nor his soldiers would ever again see South Carolina.[6]

Three days later Cornwallis arrived at Ramsour's Mill on the Little
Catawba. Morgan had passed through two days before and was about twenty

miles east, camped on the other side of the Catawba River. The Old Waggoner had come about 100 miles or more in five days over terrible roads with a victorious but tired army that was not properly shod. Men who shared the march reported that Morgan had set his usual example, not sparing himself and continually encouraging them. Now, with the rains unceasing and the Catawba rising, he could rest his weary troops as well as himself, for his sciatica was flaring once again.

He reported to Greene on 23 January from Sherrald's Ford. "I arrived here this morning. The prisoners crossed at the Island ford, seventeen miles higher up the river. I expect them to join me this evening. Shall send them on to Salsbury in the morning Guarded by Major Tripletts Militia whose time expird this day." His intelligence had obviously been better than Cornwallis's. "Lord Cornwallis, whether from bad intelligence or to make a show, moved up towards Gilbert Town to intercept me, the day after I had passed him." The next day he wrote Greene to report that the prisoners were on their way to Salisbury, and that he was faring poorly. "I grow worse every hour. I cant ride out of a walk. I am exceedingly sorry to leave the field at such a time as this, but it must be the case. Pickens is an enterprising man and a very judicious one: perhaps he might answer the purpose. With regard to Gen. Sumter, I think I know the man so well that I shall take no notis of what he has done, but follow your advice in every particular." In a plaintive postscript he added a piece of information about rum rations that must have distressed his troops beyond measure: "We have nothing to drink." On 25 January, he wrote Greene two letters to keep him updated on intelligence that kept coming in on Cornwallis's movements. He sent off his wagons to Salisbury and was prepared to move his troops in that direction too, for William Lee Davidson had not yet come in with militia and Morgan considered his forces too weak to oppose a crossing. "I am convinced Cornwallis will push on til he is stopd by a force able to check him. I will do everything in my power but you may not put too much dependence on me, for I cant ride or walk. A pain in my hip prevent me."[7]

By 28 January, however, he knew that Cornwallis was still at Ramsour's Mill, and with the arrival of militia he felt he had a chance of stopping the British at the river: "I am Trying to Collect the Militia, to Make a stand at this place. Genl Davidson, with five hundred militia two hundred and fifty of which are without flints, I have ordered to Beaties Ford. We are filling all the Private fords to Make them impasseable. The one that I Lie at I intend to Leave Open. On Lord Cornwallis' approach, I thought it advisable to Order all the Prisoners and Stores from Salisbury towards the Moravian town [modern Winston-Salem]. I am told they are gone under a Weak guard; I wish some of them dont get away.

"If the enemy pursued I ordered them towards Augusta in Virga." Morgan was a "Little Apprehensive, that Lord Cornwallis Intends to Surprise me, lying so Still this day or two, but if the Militia dont Deceive me who I am Obliged to Trust as guards up and down the River I Think I will put it out of his Power." By then his physical condition was so bad that he had moved from a camp bed in his tent. "If I were Able to ride and see to every thing my Self Should think myself perfectly safe, but I am Obliged to lie in a house out of Camp, not being able to engage the Badness of the Weather." But the next day, feverish, brushing aside the protests of his aides, he endured the torment of dragging himself from bed and house to ride out and see things for himself. He wrote Greene from Beattie's Ford. "I have just arrived at this place to view the situation. Gen Davidson is here with Eight hundred men. The enemy is within ten miles of this place in force, their advance is in sight. It is uncertain whether they intend to cross here or not. I have detached two hundred men to the Tuckaseega Ford to fill it up & Defend it." Morgan was interrupted by a courier. "An express Just arrived who inform that they have burnd their waggons and loaded their men very heavy." This was the first indication in the Rebel camp of the drastic measure Lord Cornwallis had taken.[8]

It was when he arrived at Ramsour's Mill only to find that Morgan was two days ahead of him and across the Catawba that Cornwallis probably felt most deeply the primary consequence of the Battle of Cowpens. "The loss of my light troops could only be remedied by the activity of the whole corps," he later wrote to Lord Germain, in explanation of his solution to his problem. Almost all of Cornwallis's remaining units were regiments of the line, accustomed to a traditional way of war, to tents at night and all the other impedimenta of an eighteenth-century European army, transported by a long, cumbersome, slow-moving baggage train of wagons pulled by teams of horses that had to be cared for and fed. In the Carolina Back Country that winter, under pelting rains on wretched red clay roads that were quagmires by day and frozen moonscapes by night, Cornwallis faced a logistical nightmare. Benson Lossing traveled those roads in the winter of 1849. They had not changed, and he wrote, "No one can form an idea of the character of the roads in winter, at the South, where the red clay abounds, without passing over them. Until I had done so, I could not appreciate the difficulties experienced by the two armies in the race toward Virginia, particularly in the transportation of baggage wagons or of artillery." Rain, roads, rivers, and fords were the critical factors in that winter campaign, and to deal with them Cornwallis chose a solution even more unorthodox than Greene's division of his army.[9]

Cornwallis burned his baggage train. He kept only enough wagons for medical supplies, salt, and ammunition, and four empty wagons for the sick and wounded. Otherwise everything went. At the Catawba a few days later Cornwallis told the troops that "The Supply of Rum for a time will be Absolutely impossible." This was the cruelest cut of all, for rum was very important to eighteenth-century soldiers. Recall Morgan's plaintive sentence: "We have nothing to drink." A huge bonfire was built, and into it went wagons, tents, excess clothing, anything deemed not vital to the army's functioning. What the troops needed they would carry on their backs. The officers did not escape the sacrifice, for Charles O'Hara reported to the Duke of Grafton, "Lord Cornwallis sett the example by burning all his Wagons, and destroying the greatest part of his Bagage, which was followed by every Officer of the Army without a mur-

mur." All the fine china and plate and silver and wine and other luxuries that officers then considered their due when they took the field—all were thrown into the vast conflagration. To further increase his army's mobility, Cornwallis ordered that the large supply of leather found at Ramsour's Mill be used to repair and resole the soldiers' shoes, with every company commander directed to see to it. Each soldier would also carry an extra pair of soles.[10]

Cornwallis's action was unprecedented, and probably no other British general who served in America would have even considered it. His decision was one of those that bring on soldiers either post-mortem praise or ridicule—all depending on whether it works. Dramatically, with a good eighteenth-century mixture of truth and hyperbole, Charles O'Hara described the situation for the Duke of Grafton.

"In this situation, without Baggage, necessaries, or Provisions of any sort for Officer or Soldier, in the most barren inhospitable unhealthy part of North America, opposed to the most savage, inveterate perfidious cruel Enemy, with zeal and with Bayonets only, it was resolved to follow Green's Army to the end of the World."[11]

"The river was full of 'em a snortin, a hollerin' and a drownin' "

The fords Daniel Morgan referred to, Sherrald's and Beattie's, no longer exist, for in the area where Britons and Americans faced each other across swollen waters the wild Catawba has disappeared. Sherrald's Ford was about thirty-five miles northwest of Charlotte and Beattie's Ford was south of it. Today both fords lie under Lake Norman, created in the early 1960s when the Catawba was dammed downstream. Beneath its waters, hidden away forever, are the places Daniel Morgan and Robert Henry and Sergeant Roger Lamb and others told us about, where General William Lee Davidson fought his last fight.

Cornwallis marched from Ramsour's Mill on 28 January. The following day his advance was in sight of Beattie's Ford. But for two days the heavens had opened and on the night of the 29th the Catawba began to rise swiftly and by the next morning it was impassable. The morning after that Nathanael Greene arrived and took charge of the retreat.

In his camp at Cheraw Greene had been pondering what to do since learning of Morgan's dramatic victory. At first he considered marching on Ninety Six to lure Cornwallis away from Morgan. But the enlistments of Brigadier General Edward Stevens's Virginia militia were up and they were bent on going home. Poor Stevens, who still lived with the shame of his men's wild flight at Camden, appealed to their sense of duty and patriotism. Once more he had reason to be mortified at the behavior of his fellow Virginians. A few listened to him, the overwhelming number turned their faces north. Their time was up. Greene abandoned all thoughts of striking south. On the 27th, according to General Stevens, Greene learned that Cornwallis had burned his baggage train, and "he expected what would follow and imedeatly" sprang to action. His strategy of dividing the army had worked. It was now time to reunite it and get in Cornwallis's way. In case further retreat was necessary, he ordered the tireless Colonel Edward Carrington to begin gathering boats on the Dan River in Virginia just over the North Carolina line. General Isaac Huger was left in charge of the main army and ordered to march immediately for Salisbury to link up with Morgan. A courier galloped south with a message for Lieutenant Colonel Henry Lee, then campaigning in South Carolina with Francis Marion. Light Horse Harry was directed to immediately head north with his 280-man Legion of horse and foot and catch up with Huger. Then, on 28 January, the day Cornwallis left Ramsour's Mill, Greene rode out of camp with a guide, an aide, and three dragoons on a dangerous 100-odd mile journey across country where Tories and bandits lurked to join Morgan on the Catawba. Three days later the mud-stained riders trotted into the clearing at Beattie's Ford. Greene wrote that day to General Isaac Huger: "It is necessary we should take every possible precaution. But I am not without hopes of ruining Lord Cornwallis, if he persists in his mad scheme of pushing through the Country and it is my earnest desire to form a junction as soon as possible for this purpose. Desire Lt Col Lee to force a March to join us. Here is a fine field and great glory ahead."[12]

Daniel Morgan is said by some to have disagreed with his chief's strategy of retreating before Cornwallis and strongly recommended the army seek refuge, according to the contemporary historian William Gordon, "over the mountains." Morgan had in a letter to Greene of 24 January suggested a move into Georgia, although he made no specific mention of the mountains, his stated purpose to draw Cornwallis from marching through North Carolina and linking with British forces in Virginia. Yet the next day he informed Greene that he intended to move north, "toward Salsbury in order to get Near the main army," for he assumed that Greene would "move somewhere on the Yadkin, to oppose their crossing," and he thought it advisable to join our forces and fight them." In this he does not appear to be a man bent on taking his command out of play. If Greene and Morgan disagreed, whether their difference was as serious as claimed rests on whether Gordon can be trusted to have related accurately what he may have been told by Greene and gleaned from the general's papers, for Gordon was not always a faithful interpreter. Whatever may have passed between the generals, Greene's strategy was followed and relations between the two were undamaged. If indeed Morgan argued for retreating "over the mountains," it only confirms that Daniel Morgan's sure grasp of combat command did not extend to strategy.[13]

Nathanael Greene had written to Alexander Hamilton, "I call no councils of war; and I communicate my intentions to very few." But on the 31st, the day after his arrival, he set aside his habit of reaching solitary decisions and keeping his own counsel and met at Beattie's Ford with Morgan, General William Lee Davidson, and Colonel William Washington. John Eager Howard did not attend because he had been ordered north with the Continentals toward Salisbury. Captain Joseph Graham, who was there, reported that the four officers retired a little distance from camp, sat down on a log, and held a council of war.[14]

While they conferred, a sizeable party of British horsemen appeared on the right bank of the Catawba, and an officer they assumed to be Cornwallis raised a spyglass and studied the American defenses. Greene and his officers saw the situation as critical. It had at least temporarily stopped raining. The Catawba had started falling that day. In a few days, they thought, it could be forded, and they did not view with equanimity the possibility of stopping the British from crossing. There were several fords up and down the river, and to guard them they had only Davidson's 800 militiamen. Davidson had hoped for many more, but it had taken him almost a month to persuade the 800 to turn out, and only by promising them that six weeks' service would count for three months. Morgan would complain bitterly the next day in a letter to Thomas Jefferson of the failure of the militia to turn out in large numbers. "The inhabitents seem to make a stir, what they will do is unceartain, but I fear not much" He exploded with indignation. "Great God what is the reason we cant Have more men in the field—so many men in the country Nearby idle for want of employment. How distressing it must be to any anxious mind to see the country Run over and destroyed for want of assistance which I am realy afraid will be the case if proper exertions are not made." The answer to his question lay in the approach of Cornwallis's army and the decision by the great majority of men to see to the safety of their families and property by getting them out of the way.[15]

In his *Autobiography* James Collins was probably describing the situation in South Carolina, where he lived and to which he returned after Cowpens, but his words also hold true for those who lived north of the state line. As Cornwallis chased Morgan, "There was much excitement throughout the whole country—scarce a man staid at home. Those that were not collected in parties lay out in the woods, every article of furniture, clothing, provisions—that was worth anything was hid out; some in hollow trees, and often hardware that would stand it was buried in the ground. A horse that was worth anything was not to be seen, unless tied in some thicket, or perhaps on some high open hill where no one would go to look for property—and if a woman had but one quart of salt to salt mush for her children, or spoon to sup it with, she must keep it hid, or if she had any decent apparel she would scarce dare to wear it. Scouting parties, of both sides, were scouring the country in every direction." There were also sights with which we in the twentieth century have become all too familiar: civilian refugees with every possible conveyance piled high with belongings fleeing before an advancing army. Although Morgan obstructed some fords, he kept Beattie's open to accommodate these terrified people, who had every reason for their fears. The tenacity of British and Hessian regulars extended from the battlefield to tireless plundering and mistreatment of the civilian population. On several occasions during his march north Cornwallis fulminated in orders of the day against the burning of houses along the way, "Plundering . . . Marauding . . . Scandalous Crimes," and ordered officers "to put a stop to this Licentiousness which must inevitably bring disgrace and Ruin on his Majesty's Service." His need to repeat those orders and his threats to severely punish those responsible, if he could find them, also tell us that the troops generally ignored their general in this regard. Love him deeply they might, follow him blindly into maelstroms of smoke and blood they definitely would, but to be denied the pleasures of the march was intolerable.[16]

It took Greene and his officers only twenty minutes to come to the obvious conclusion and a plan of action. Wiliam Lee Davidson would later tell his militia cavalry commander "that though General Greene had never seen the Catawba before, he appeared to know more about it than those who were raised on it."[17] Davidson and his militia would contest Cornwallis's crossing, with no expectation of stopping him permanently but to delay him long enough to give the regulars a good start on the way to Salisbury and their rendezvous with Huger's column coming from the Great Pee Dee. Then Davidson would execute a quick getaway. It was well that Morgan had decided to move that afternoon to evacuate the Continentals, for Lord Cornwallis had also come to a decision. He would move out the next morning and force the Catawba.

Nathanael Greene and his party took the main road to Salisbury, to the farm of David Carr, from where Greene planned to direct Davidson's retreat after Cornwallis crossed the river. It was sixteen miles from Beattie's Ford. Morgan and Washington went another way that would take them to Howard and the Continentals. Behind them General William Lee Davidson of North Carolina, who had served in the North as a Continental officer in George Washington's army, prepared to defend the Catawba with his 800 militiamen against Cornwallis's 2,500 stripped-down regulars.

Four miles south of Beattie's Ford was a private ford called Cowan's. It too no longer exists. A British sergeant who crossed the river wrote later that it was half a mile wide, but he made the crossing in a fog at dawn, under fire as well as at risk of drowning, and it must have seemed forever. A width of 400 to 500 yards is closer to the mark. The banks on both sides were well wooded and quite steep. The Americans were not unmindful that Cowan's Ford might be tempting for the British, since it was not one of the major fords and therefore might not be guarded in strength. Captain Joseph Graham described Davidson's deployment.

"In about an hour after General Greene's departure, General Davidson gave orders to the cavalry and about two hundred and fifty infantry to march down the river to Cowan's Ford, four miles below Beattie's, leaving nearly the same number at that place." Greene had "thought it probable" that Cornwallis might throw cavalry across the river at night in order to attack the rear of Americans resisting an infantry assault elsewhere; he therefore had ordered Davidson that cavalry "patrols who were best acquainted with the country should keep passing up and down all night."

At the ford Davidson divided his force, for while there was one entrance into the water on the right bank, there were two exits on the left. From the entrance on the right bank the ford led straight ahead about halfway across the river. There it split. The wagon ford continued ahead into the deeper part of the stream. The shallower horse ford turned right at a forty-five degree angle, headed downriver over the end of a little island, and emerged on the left bank about one-quarter of a mile below the wagon ford exit. The bottom was rocky, the water two to four feet deep, the current powerful. Davidson posted a small picket guard where the wagon ford emerged from the river. At the exit point for the horse ford, where he obviously expected any force to attempt to cross, he placed his 250 infantrymen on a hill half a mile above and overlooking the exit. His horsemen were posted several hundred yards in the rear on a small rise; with their homemade swords and draught horses they were cavalry in name only.[18]

With the picket guard was young Robert Henry, our King's Mountain veteran, who had recovered from being bayoneted through his hand and thigh. He was ten days shy of his sixteenth birthday. Born in 1765 in Tryon County, North Carolina, "in a rail pen," according to his son, he lived in the vicinity of Tuckasegee Ford, ten miles below Cowan's Ford. His father was an Ulster-born Protestant. After the war Robert Henry became a surveyor and was on the team that surveyed the North Carolina–Tennessee line in the late 1790s. That occupation led him to the law, and a man who knew him called him "a great land lawyer."[19] His narrative of his new adventure in war reveals a mixture of boyish bravado, courage, and terror.

Henry was attending school near his home, taught by a lame schoolmaster named Robert Beatty, when word came to the classroom that Cornwallis was camped about seven miles away, and "that Tarleton was ranging through the country catching Whig boys to make musicians of them in the British army." Robert Beatty immediately dismissed school and told the boys to spread the news. That night Robert Henry and five of his schoolmates hid outdoors to escape Tarleton's dragnet, for the tale, true or not, was fervently believed. The next day they went upriver to John Nighten, "who treated us well by giving us potatoes to roast and some whisky to drink. We became noisy and mischievous. Nighten said we should not have any more whisky." Emboldened by the whiskey, Robert Henry said he would go to Cowan's Ford if he had a gun and ammunition, whereupon his brother Joseph, who had joined them, gave him his gun. Robert's schoolmate Charles Rutledge said he would go too if he had a gun, and another schoolmate, Moses Starrett, handed Charles his gun. "When about to start I gave Nighten a hundred dollar Continental bill for a half a pint of whiskey. My brother gave another bill of the same size for half a bushel of potatoes. We dispatched the whiskey."[20]

Being thus fortified, Robert and his friend Charles Rutledge made their way to Cowan's Ford, which was about a mile and a half off. The picket guard at the exit of the wagon ford, numbering thirty men, "made us welcome. The officer of the guard told us . . . that each one of the guard had picked their stands . . . so . . . they would not be crowded, or be in each other's way—and said we must choose our stands." Robert chose the lowest, where the wagon ford left the river. He recalled quite matter-of-factly that he would man his post as long as "I could stand it, until the British would come to a place where the water was riffling over a rock; then it would be time to run away." Besides his friend Charles Rutledge, the only members of the guard he knew were Joel Jetton and his lame schoolmaster, Robert Beatty. "Shortly after dark," said Robert Henry, "a man across the river hooted like an owl and was answered; a man went to a canoe some distance off, and brought word from him that all was silent in the British camp. The guard all lay down with their guns in their arms, and all were sound asleep at day-break except Joel Jetton, who discovered the noise of horses in deep water."[21]

Silent the British camp may have been the evening of 31 January, but the Rebel spies should have maintained their watch. Cornwallis and his troops rolled out of their blankets at 1:00 A.M. on 1 February. It was very dark but the rain had stopped. Sending Webster with half the army and most of the artillery to Beattie's Ford to create a diversion, Cornwallis marched downriver with the Brigade of Guards, the Royal Welsh Fusiliers, the German Von Bose Regiment, and the British Legion Horse, the latter led by Tarleton. Their guide was a local Tory, either Dick Beal or Frederick Hager, depending on whose recollection you accept, Robert Henry's or Captain Joseph Graham's. Both were there, but Robert Henry was closer to the action at riverside, and said he saw Dick Beal taking aim at him.

About daybreak, through the thick mist, some 1,200 British and German soldiers approached Cowans's Ford quietly enough so that the Americans on the other side had not an inkling of their arrival. The soldiers carried heavy knapsacks and unloaded muskets with bayonets fixed. Their cartouche boxes containing ammunition were tied around their necks. Cornwallis could see Rebel campfires flickering on the other side and was surprised that there were so many, for the King's Friends had led him to believe that Cowan's would be lightly guarded. But the sight did not stop him. Nor did the swift, treacherous waters of the Catawba that might have given pause to a timid general. And in time of peril for his troops the man always knew where he belonged. Sergeant Roger Lamb of the Royal Welsh Fusiliers watched as "Lord Cornwallis, according to his usual manner, dashed first into the river, mounted on a very fine, spirited horse, the brigade of guards followed, two three pounders next, the Royal Welch Fuzileers after them." The water became breast high, reported Sergeant Lamb. The current wrapped around them and tugged. Following their general on his "very fine, spirited horse" the British troops struggled forward to about midstream, past where the horse ford forked off, before Joel Jetton heard the splashing of horses in the river.[22]

Robert Henry stated that the Tory guide "Dick Beal, being deceived by our fires" had not turned downstream onto the horse ford but had continued straight ahead on the wagon ford, or, as young Robert put it, "had led them into swimming water." That was the noise Joel Jetton heard. "Jetton ran to the ford. The sentry being sound asleep, Jetton kicked him into the river. He endeavored to fire his gun, but it was wet." He ran back to the campfires. "'The British! The British!'" Joel Jetton cried.[23]

Robert Henry and his comrades jumped to their feet and ran to their posts. At riverside Robert thought he was seeing red from lack of sleep and threw water in his face and then knew his eyes were not deceiving him: "I then heard the British splashing and making a noise as of drowning." For the current was sweeping men and horses off their feet. General Leslie's horse was swept downstream but recovered. General "O'Hara's horse," wrote Sergeant Lamb, "rolled with him down the current near forty yards." A bombadier tumbled away head over heels but was saved by Sergeant Lamb. But what happened to some did not deter the rest. Hundreds of Redcoats and Hessians led by their general successfully fought the current and bore straight ahead. Cornwallis's horse was hit but did not fall until he carried his rider to the far bank. At his stand Robert Henry "fired and continued firing until I saw that one on horse-back had passed my rock in the river, and saw that it was Dick Beal, moving his gun from his shoulder, I expect, to shoot me. I ran with all speed up the bank, and when at the top of it William Polk's horse breasted me, and Gen. Davidson's horse, about twenty or thirty feet before Polk's horse, and near to the water's edge." Robert heard Colonel Polk shout, "Fire away, boys! Help is at hand!" But Robert's flight was only stopped when, "I saw my lame schoolmaster, Beatty, loading his gun by a tree. I thought I could stand it as long as he could and commenced loading. Beatty fired, and then I fired, the heads and shoulders of the British being just above the bank. They made no return fire. Silence still prevailed. I observed Beatty loading again. I ran down another load. When he fired, he cried, 'It's time to run, Bob.'" During this action Robert recalled that Beatty, "an excellent marksman, fired twice at a distance of not more than twenty five yards . . . and I fired twice about the same distance. I . . . think Beatty . . . killed two, and I killed one."[24]

Sergeant Lamb described the action from the British side. Their position in breast-high water with unloaded muskets "urged us on with greater rapidity, till we gained the opposite shore, where we were obliged to scramble up a very high hill under a heavy fire: several of our men were killed and wounded before we reached the summit. The American soldiers that night did all that brave men could do . . . and I believe that not one of them moved from his post till we mounted the hill, and used our bayonets."[25]

Robert Henry "looked past my tree and saw their guns lowered and then straightened myself behind my tree. They fired and knocked some bark from my tree.

"In the meantime, Beatty had turned from his tree, and a bullet hit him in the hip, and broke the upper end of his thigh bone. He fell, still hallowing for me to run. I then ran at the top of my speed about one hundred yards, when a thought struck me that the British had no horsemen to follow me, and that Davidson's army would be down at the river and battle would take place. Whereupon I loaded my gun and went opposite the Ford, and chose a large tree, and sat down behind it and fired about fifty yards at the British."[26] But there was no battle, and Robert Henry could not have lingered too long after that or he would have found himself alone. Almost immediately after he saw General William Lee Davidson ride to the water's edge, Davidson was shot off his horse by a single rifle ball that struck him in the breast. He is said to have died instantly. Word spread quickly and was transmitted to the main force by

Colonel Polk. Davidson's death and British and German discipline and bayonets took the edge off of the militia's will to continue the action, and soon the road to Salisbury was clogged with confused militiamen and civilian refugees, the latter fleeing the great booms of diversionary cannonading by Colonel Webster at Beattie's Ford. The action at Cowan's Ford was summed up colorfully and quite accurately by a local Tory, whose narration was recorded by Robert Henry.

"I will begin with the report of Nicholas Gosnell, one of our neighbors, a Tory who was in Cornwallis' army when they crossed the Catawba at Cowan's Ford. It was repeated from the extraordinary language he used, and from his manner of expression—it is therefore better imprinted on my memory. I will endeavour to give it in his own language: 'His Lordship chose Dick Beal for his pilot, as he well know'd the Ford, and a durned pretty pilot he was, for he suffered himself to be led astray by the rebel fires, and then he had to go down to the Ford afterwards; but if he did bad one way, he did good another, for he killed their damn Rebel General. The Rebels were posted at the water's edge—there wasn't many of 'em, but I'll be durned if they didn't slap the wad to his Majesty's men suicidally! for a while; for I saw 'em hollerin' and a snortin and a drownin—the river was full of 'em a snortin, a hollerin' and a drownin' until his Lordship reached the off Bank; the Rebels made straight shirt tails, and all was silent—then I tell you his Lordship . . . when he rose the bank he was the best dog in the hunt, and not a Rebel to be seen."[27]

Cowan's Ford was a daring and gallant action by the British, but the cost was dear. Cornwallis did not admit that his losses were heavy. He reported four dead and thirty-six wounded, but that certainly cannot be true. The Tory Nicholas Gosnell saw soldiers drowning, and Robert Henry and his neighbors were also witnesses to the heavy toll taken by the Catawba. The day after the action Robert and his friends went to the river to see if James Cunningham's fish trap contained any fish and found in it fourteen dead men, "several of whom appeared to have no wound, but had drowned. We pushed them into the water, they floated off, and each went to his home." Then he gave the reports of "every person who lived at or near the river between Cowan's Ford and Tuckaseage Ford: That a great number of British dead were found on Thompson's fish-dam, and in his trap, and numbers lodged on brush, and drifted to the banks; that the river stunk with dead carcases; that the British could not have lost less than one hundred men on that occasion."[28]

"We may precipitate him into some capital misfortune"

Hysteria ran like wildfire in the path of Cornwallis's army. An entire countryside had, to use Lieutenant Anthony Allaire's phrase, got in motion. People had one thought, to save themselves and their worldly goods. Wagons were piled high. Refugee columns grew and clogged the roads. Men, women, children, cats, dogs, chickens, pigs, cows—Cornwallis scattered them all. To add to their misery heavy rains came down again. Into this human flotsam rode a man seeking revenge for his humiliation at Cowpens.

About ten miles from Beattie's Ford on the road to Salisbury was a place called Torrence's Tavern (often identified as Tarrant's Tavern), which no longer exists. At the tavern on the day Cornwallis crossed Cowan's Ford confusion gripped several hundred people. Fleeing militiamen and refugees with their wagons thronged around the tavern. Pails of whiskey were passed around, and we can be assured without direct evidence that the rumor mill was working overtime. It was a situation made to order for Tarleton. He did not take the multitude by surprise. Someone rode in with the news that "Tarleton is coming!" That would have caused consternation, but apparently some militiamen were not too far gone with whiskey to take positions behind a fence and await his arrival. But given the large numbers of refugees and the jumble of wagons around Torrence's Tavern pandemonium must have ensued when, on the afternoon of 1 February, some 200 green-jacketed British Legion cavalrymen burst into view and charged with flashing sabers and Tarleton's cry ringing in their ears: "Remember the Cowpens."[29]

Tarleton claimed that the Legion killed "near 50 on the spot, wounded many in pursuit, and dispersed near 500 of the enemy," and "diffused such terror among the inhabitants that the King's troops passed through the most hostile part of North Carolina without a shot from the militia." But Charles Stedman reported that a "British officer who rode over the ground not long after the action, relates that he did not see ten dead bodies." It would be foolish to deny that the skirmish at Torrence's Tavern was a factor in the failure of the North Carolina militia to turn out in great numbers, but we know that they had already failed to do that prior to this action. Had Tarleton not lived to write his history of the campaign Torrence's Tavern probably would have merited at most a footnote.[30]

If Tarleton had captured Nathanael Greene at David Carr's farm six miles away, that would have been another story indeed. But Greene was warned of Cornwallis's successful crossing of the Catawba and the skirmish at Torrence's Tavern. In the early morning hours of 2 February he left for Salisbury. He spent the day there seeing that supplies were moved to keep them from the British, and what he found strengthened his opinion of militia. Almost 1,700 militia muskets were nearly useless because of poor storage conditions. The usually temperate Greene exploded: "These are the happy effects of defending the Country with Militia from which the good Lord deliver us!"[31]

The goal of both armies was Trading Ford on the Yadkin. There Greene joined Morgan and the Continentals on 3 February. The rain had been incessant and torrential, "every step being up to our Knees in Mud it raining On us all the Way," wrote Lieutenant Thomas Anderson. Brigadier General Edward Stevens of Virginia had arrived at Trading Ford on 2 February and found it impassable for men. Six days later he wrote to Thomas Jefferson, "The Great Quantitiy of Rain that fell the night before raised the River in such a manner as made it difficult to Cross even in Boats." As perilous as such a crossing would be, the expected juncture with General Isaac Huger's column had not occurred, and Greene had with him less than half the army. To fight Cornwallis, especially with a raging river at his back, was out of the question. He had to cross.[32]

All day the boats went back and forth, carrying the troops and their supplies and the refugees and most of their wagons, all without loss or mishap. O'Hara's van, pushing hard through Salisbury on the road to Trading Ford, came up that evening to find only a few civilian wagons left with some 150 militia as rear guard. Shots were exchanged, O'Hara got the wagons and contents. The rear guard, O'Hara wrote, "in the language of this country, split and squandered, that is run away." But General Stevens wrote that the rear guard had been ordered "to give them a fire or Two and then Disperse down the River and Cross in Canoes which they executed very well." O'Hara saw the boats that the King's Friends had not told Cornwallis about secured under a high bluff on the American side of a river that showed no signs of falling. Once more the British could stand on one side of a river and look at the Americans on the other side.[33]

It had been a long, wet day in the field for Daniel Morgan. The man must have been in agony. That night Dr. William Read found him in his tent, lying on a bed of leaves, a blanket over him, "rhuematic from head to foot." But later Read saw him down at the river checking on the whereabouts of a scouting party. The next morning Morgan and the Continentals left for Guilford Courthouse, forty-seven miles away. They were short on food. It rained all the way. Pushing himself as hard as he pushed the troops, Morgan made the march in forty-eight hours. On arrival Morgan immediately sent out parties to collect forage and provisions for his own troops and the other columns. To his debilitating sciatica was added another painful ailment that can only be described as an indignity. He wrote to Greene on 6 February. "I am much indisposed with pains, and to add to my misfortunes, am violently attacked with the piles, so that I can scarcely sit upon my horse. This is the first time that I ever experienced this disorder, and from the idea I had of it, sincerely prayed that I might never know what it was. When I set everything in as good a train as I can respecting provisions, etc., I shall move slowly to some safe retreat, and try to recover."[34]

On 4 February, the same day Morgan left the Yadkin behind and led the Continentals toward Guilford Courthouse, Cornwallis reached the banks of the river with the main army. Whether he thought he could do some real damage or acted out of sheer frustration at once again finding a river running high between him and his prey, Cornwallis ordered the artillery forward, and soon the guns were booming and iron balls sailed over the Yadkin. Cool, collected, his mind always at work, Greene wrote his dispatches, watched Cornwallis, and waited for His Lordship's next move. He sent word to General Isaac Huger, who had obviously missed the Salisbury rendezvous, to halt and await orders. When he learned that Cornwallis was marching upstream to find a place to ford, he ordered Huger to join Morgan at Guilford Courthouse. By the 5th of February, convinced that Cornwallis would not back off, Nathanael Greene thought it possible that "from Lord Cornwallises pushing disposition, and the contempt he has for our Army, we may precipitate him into some capital misfortune."[35]

By either 7 or 8 February the little American army rendezvoused. Light Horse Harry Lee and his Legion had caught up with Huger's troops and marched with them into the camp at Guilford Courthouse, where Morgan had gathered provisions and forage for men and horses badly in need of them. Lee's Legion was the only unit in Huger's force that could be described as adequately clothed and shod. Although they had not the worry of a pursuing foe, Isaac Huger's men had performed admirably under conditions of roads and weather and short rations as adverse as any faced by Morgan's Continentals. To call their clothing and shoes inadequate does not really describe their woeful condition. They were in rags, and many men were literally barefoot. The old stories of Continentals leaving bloody footprints are not myths, and Valley Forge was not the only place they were seen. Yet there were no stragglers on the road from Cheraw to Guilford Courthouse. Huger lost not a man on the march.

In the meantime, Trading Ford remaining impassable, Cornwallis sent Tarleton upriver in search of a crossing place. While he waited two days in Salisbury, he learned from spies another reason why he should make haste to the upper fords, and that reason will fall into place as we follow the fortunes of our two worthy opponents. After a "long patrole with the cavalry," Tarleton found a passable, unguarded ford, in the beautiful, rolling Carolina Piedmont at a place still remote, Shallow Ford by name, and there, with his newfound intelligence, Cornwallis marched. Shallow Ford was twenty-five miles upstream from Trading Ford—as the crow flies—but the British had forty miles of wet red clay to slog through. The troops were ordered to maintain the "Strictest Silence in getting off their Ground & during the March."[36]

Greene, his spies watching Cornwallis's progress, reorganized his army and contended with disappointments. For at Guilford Courthouse we must, as reluctantly as Nathanael Greene, take our leave of Daniel Morgan. Morgan simply could no longer continue in active service in the field. Greene offered him command of an elite force of light troops that would act as rear guard for the army. Morgan declined, and according to one of his biographers he recommended that the command go to his friend Otho Holland Williams. Greene agreed, and granted Morgan a leave of absence until he was able once again to take the field. About the same time Rebel leaders in the Charlotte area asked Greene to allow Morgan take charge of their militia. Greene's reply reveals his awareness of Morgan's condition: "The general is so unwell that he could not discharge the duties of his appointment if he had it." On 10 February Daniel Morgan heaved his pain-wracked body into a carriage and headed for Virginia and home. Nathanael Greene fixed his place in history better than anyone: "Great generals are scarce—there are few Morgans to be found."[37]

The loss of Morgan was not Greene's only problem. We have emphasized his gifts as a strategist and his mastery of the less glamorous but vital skills of his trade, but we must not ignore another facet of Greene's character. He was a fighting general. Despite his repeated and earnest admonitions to subordinates to be cautious, not to risk all for martial laurels, Nathanael Greene himself yearned for military glory, and there is only one place to acquire that—on the field of honor, of which he wrote with passion. But there was also within him a well-developed sense of his higher responsibility to the cause. Greene was apparently tempted to fight, for he feared the effect of continued retreat on the morale of the people of North Carolina and Virginia as well as the criticism it might bring on him. Yet his pleas to the North Carolina militia "to fly to arms" had gone largely unheeded, and of the few who answered, news that Cornwallis was approaching Guilford Courthouse "struck such terror on them that some of that number deserted," as the commander of the Guilford Militia testified. On 9 February Greene had 2,036 men, of whom 1,426 were regular infantry, and Huger's men, who constituted the majority, were in bad condition. The 600 militiamen were "badly armed." Cornwallis, on the other hand, even with desertions and his losses at Cowan's Ford, had about 2,440 men, and at least 2,000 were regulars. Although they too had experienced the same foul weather, miserable roads, and grueling marches, they were better equipped and in better condition. Greene knew that under these circumstances he could not fight. But he wanted cover, and on 9 February, calling another rare council of war, he put the issue to his senior officers: should they stand and fight or continue the retreat? It was the last council attended by Morgan, and the Old Waggoner, a fighter all his life, added his voice to Isaac Huger's and Otho Holland Williams's in a unanimous recommendation not to fight at that time. The retreat must continue.[38]

The march from Cowpens to the army's rendezvous 150 miles away at Guilford Courthouse was a skillful, orderly retreat accomplished in stages. Now, however, a race began to the Dan River. It also was conducted with skill and precision and the added fillip of heart-pounding tension. The key players on the American side were Morgan's light troops, now commanded by the intelligent, highly competent Otho Holland Williams. They were reinforced by a small but very professional unit of horse and foot led by a brave and dashing cavalryman from Virginia.

Lieutenant Colonel Henry Lee, Jr. (1756–1818) was the father of a far more famous American, General Robert E. Lee. But at the time of which we write the father's was a household name in America.[39] Known in his lifetime and since as Light Horse Harry, he ranks as one of the nation's finest cavalry commanders. The Lees arrived in Virginia about 1641. Henry Lee graduated from Princeton (then the College of New Jersey) when he was seventeen, and would have gone to London to study law at Middle Temple had not the war intervened. He was commissioned a captain of Virginia cavalry in 1776; the following year his company joined the 1st Continental Dragoons with Washington's army. Despite his youth he became an intimate of George Washington, and they were friends to the great man's death. It was Lee who wrote Washington's funeral oration, with its immortal words, "First in war, first in peace, first in the hearts of his countrymen." Lee was promoted to major in 1778, and on 19 July 1779, he overcame his own youthful errors to score one of the brilliant coups of the war by surprising the British at Paulus Hook, New Jersey. It was a small victory but important as a morale builder and for establishing Lee's reputation. He received from Congress one of the eight gold medals awarded during the

Henry "Light Horse Harry" Lee, by Charles Willson Peale.
(Independence National Historical Park Collection.)

war. On 30 November 1780 Light Horse Harry Lee was promoted to Lieutenant Colonel and given command of Lee's Legion, consisting of his original three troops of cavalry to which was added three companies of infantry: their original strength was 100 horse and 180 foot. They wore short green jackets similar to Tarleton's British Legion—an important detail to remember. A passionate admirer of good horseflesh, Lee saw to it that his cavalry troops were always mounted on well-bred, powerful stock. It was Nathanael Greene, ever seeking good cavalry, who arranged Lee's transfer to the Southern Department, and on 13 January 1781, Light Horse Harry and his Legion reported to Greene at his camp on the Pee Dee.

Light Horse Harry would distinguish himself throughout the southern campaign, beyond our tale, and return home a hero of the Revolution, a young man of twenty-six possibly suffering from combat fatigue. He recovered and in 1782 married his cousin Martha Lee, the heiress of the family seat of Stratford, and fathered several children with her. His wife died in 1790, and he considered going to France to offer his services as a soldier. Instead, he married Anne Hill Carter. They had five children. One was Robert E. Lee.

Lee became Governor of Virginia from 1792 to 1795, and in 1794 he was chosen by Washington to command the expedition against the Whiskey Rebellion in western Pennsylvania. Daniel Morgan served under him on that occasion. The rebellion was put down without casualties on either side, and this enhanced his reputation. War hero, renowned orator, distinguished public servant—he was in the prime of life and seemed to have it all. But from then his life was all downhill. He speculated heavily in land and lost just as heavily. He had no head for business but lived well beyond his means. In 1808–1809, Light Horse Harry Lee suffered the indignity of imprisonment for debt. The only good thing that came out of it was his valuable *Memoirs of the War in the Southern Department*, published in 1812. During the War of 1812 he was scheduled to accept a Major General's commission, but during a period of political turmoil in Baltimore Lee received injuries in a riot that prevented him from entering the army and hastened his death.

Poor and in bad health, with government assistance Lee went to the West Indies to recover. In 1818, told that he was about to die, he sailed for home. His condition worsened on board and he was put ashore on Cumberland Island, Georgia, where he was nursed by the daughter of his old commander, Nathanael Greene, until his death on 25 March 1818. He was buried on the island. In 1913, his remains were reinterred in the Lee Chapel of Washington and Lee University at Lexington, Virginia. But now let us watch as the dashing twenty-four-year-old Light Horse Harry Lee, before time and the gods dealt their blows, led his Legion in perilous maneuvers as the rear guard of Nathanael Greene's retreating army.

"I am ready to receive you and give you a hearty welcome"

To understand the race from Guilford Courthouse to the Dan River, we must briefly consider Cornwallis's position and the geography of the area. Cornwallis, having to detour to cross the Yadkin, had accomplished that on 9 February and the next day entered Salem (now Winston-Salem). He was twenty-five miles west of Guilford Courthouse. Based on the information he had received earlier from Tory spies, Cornwallis expected Greene to enter Virginia and attempt a crossing of the Dan River at one of the shallow fords on the upper part of the river. Greene, the spies had reported, could not possibly cross at the ferry crossings on the lower part of the river because during the winter rains the Dan was too deep there to ford, and not enough boats were available to ferry even a small part of his army. Greene would be forced to use the shallow upper fords, which lay roughly due north of Guilford Courthouse. By crossing the Yadkin at Shallow Ford and marching to Salem, Cornwallis was as close as Greene to the upper fords of the Dan, well positioned to intercept and force his elusive opponent to battle."[40]

But at Guilford Courthouse Greene and his officers laid different plans. All of Nathanael Greene's study and planning, his attention to detail and to broad strategy, the advance work he had ordered, and the intelligence, energy, and devotion to duty of Lieutenant Colonel Edward Carrington came into play. Cornwallis's Tory spies were wrong. As they had failed to inform him that the Rebels had boats to cross the Yadkin, they had misinformed him about boats on the Dan. The lower ferry crossings were northeast of Guilford Courthouse: Dix's Ferry in the vicinity of modern Danville, Virginia, just over the North Carolina line; Irwin's Ferry, twenty miles downriver from Dix's; and Boyd's Ferry, four miles downriver from Irwin's. Boyd's and Irwin's were in the vicinity of modern South Boston, Virginia, about ten miles above the North Carolina line. Carrington had six boats between Dix's Ferry and Boyd's Ferry to transport the army across the river, and he recommended using the two lower crossings. Greene instructed him to begin assembling the boats immediately. Carrington, recalled Light Horse Harry Lee, "his subordinate officers habituated to expedients and strangers to system, his implements of every sort in wretched condition, and without a single dollar in the military chest," went to work.[41]

Cornwallis was to the west, or left, of the Americans. The light troops of Otho Holland Williams, 700 strong, would act as a screen between Cornwallis's column and Greene with the main force. Williams's mission was to keep Cornwallis far enough away to mask Greene's true destination. As the columns marched north, Greene would angle eastward and then head directly toward the lower ferries, putting as much distance as possible between himself and Cornwallis, while Williams led Cornwallis toward the shallow upper fords. At some point, of course, Williams would have to make a dash for the lower ferries and get there far enough ahead of Cornwallis to cross unscathed.

Greene moved out with the main force early on 10 February. Williams marched with the elite light troops after breakfast. Lee's Legion was Williams's rear guard. According to Lee, Williams led his screening force slightly to the left in order to get in front of Cornwallis. The British van commanded by General Charles O'Hara soon came into contact with Lee's Legion. Unaware of the strength of the American force, Cornwallis slowed his march and tightened his columns. Williams continued to incline to the left and eventually took a road that put him between the opposing armies: "The British army," wrote Lee, "being on his left and in his rear, the American in front and on his right. This was exactly the proper position . . . and Williams judiciously retained it." While Cornwallis followed Williams, Greene was marching northeast as fast as he could, making for the lower ferries, seventy miles from Guilford Courthouse.[42]

Alert to the danger that Cornwallis might get between him and the main army or launch a night assault, Williams maintained a "respectable distance" when the opposing armies camped at night, and Lee described "numerous patrols and strong pickets" that guarded the camp and swept the surrounding countryside. Williams used "country men" from the local population as well as dragoons to scout for intelligence. The soldiers' "shoes were generally worn out, the body clothes much tattered." The nights were cold, blankets scarce, and they did not use their tents in order to save time in the mornings. One man always stayed awake by a campfire to keep it roaring. They marched every morn-

Edward Carrington.
Engraving. (Library of Congress.)

ing at 3:00, and when they had put enough distance between the rear guard and O'Hara's van, Williams allowed them to stop for a quick breakfast, their only meal of the day, Lee claimed. "The single meal allowed us was always scanty, though good in quality and very nutritious, being bacon and corn meal." Fatigue was a constant, yet Lee described the troops as being "in fine spirits and good health; delighted with their task, and determined to prove themselves worthy [of] the distinction with which they had been honored."[43]

On 11 February Williams reported to Greene that an "accident informed me the enemy were within six or Eight miles of my Quarters." He was probably referring to one of his "country men" who rode in to report that the British were closer than Williams had thought. It led to a skirmish that Lee described at length many years later, claiming that Tarleton's men butchered his bugler, a boy named Gillies, and that he and his men charged and sabered to death eighteen of Tarleton's dragoons. Tarleton stated that Lee's attack was "repulsed with some Loss; but an officer of the advanced guard continuing the pursuit too far, was made prisoner with three of his followers." The prisoners told Williams that "Cornwallis & the whole British Army preceded by Col Tarltons Legion is close in our rear." If Lee's memory was correct and he did not embellish, Cornwallis had ordered O'Hara to slow the British van's rate of march while His Lordship and his column moved to the right and got immediately behind Williams. Whatever occurred, Cornwallis continued to press hard on Williams's rear. Skirmishing throughout these tense days and nights was constant, and Lee described one occasion in which carelessness almost led to disaster.[44]

Williams turned northeast and made his break for the lower fords. Lee decided to take a shortcut to the road being followed by Williams, and believing that Cornwallis would not choose an obscure byway he stopped at a farm, in front of which was a bridge spanning a creek swollen by rain, and got bacon and meal from the farmer. It takes little imagination to see expectant troops circling the cooking fires, sniffing the aroma of frying bacon. Lee felt so safe that the horses were unbridled, "with an abundance of provender before them." In this situation Cornwallis's van encountered the advanced American vedettes and was fired on. Both sides were surprised. The British van "halted, to report and be directed." The Americans went into a whirlwind of action. The cavalry bridled and saddled and galloped off to support the vedettes, "while the infantry were ordered, in full run, to seize and hold the bridge." Soon the entire Legion was streaming along the byway, from which the "British army was in full view of the troops of Lee as the latter ascended the eminence, on whose summit they entered the great road to Irwin's Ferry." I find the story believable because in his *Memoirs* Lee did not try to avoid responsibility for his error in judgment. "Thus escaped a corps which had hitherto been guarded with unvarying vigilance, whose loss would have been severely felt by the American general, and which had been just exposed to imminent peril from the presumption of certain security. Criminal improvidence! A soldier is always in danger when his conviction of security leads him to dispense with the most vigilant precautions." Light Horse Harry does not mention stopping again that day for breakfast.[45]

By now, of course, Cornwallis knew that the American army was headed for the lower fords. The chase reached its most critical phase. Cornwallis pressed his troops forward with the utmost vigor. Lee stated that the British were so close that "more than once were the Legion of Lee and the van of O'Hara within musket shot." Ahead of them Greene had two days before sent baggage and supplies ahead "with orders to cross as fast as they got to the river." On the long day of 13 February Cornwallis and Williams were at forced march. The Americans greeted nightfall with enthusiasm. Surely the British would now bivouac. But Lee wrote, "illusory was the expectation; for the British general was so eager to fall on Greene whom he believed within his grasp, that the pursuit was not intermitted. The night was dark, the roads deep, the weather cold, and the air humid. Williams, throwing his horse in front, and the infantry of the Legion in the rear, continued his retreat."[46]

At 7:00 P.M. Williams wrote a gloomy letter to Greene, for what he knew of Greene's progress made him fear that he must turn on Cornwallis and "risque

the Troops I've the Honor to command and in doing that I risque everything."
At just about that time American hearts sank. Ahead, through the trees, campfires burned. Was it the main army? Williams and his men prepared to sacrifice
themselves. But it was an old campsite, Greene had long departed, and the fires
had either been kept going by friends for the relief of the light troops or were
sputtering remnants. The retreat continued until Lee sent word ahead to
Williams that Cornwallis had finally stopped. The American column halted,
built fires, and, as Daniel Morgan would have said, eased their joints. They were
forty miles from the Dan.[47]

They rested only a few hours. Lee reports that by midnight O'Hara's van
was advancing on the American pickets. "The light troops resumed their march
with alacrity. The roads continued deep and broken, and were rendered worse
by being encrusted with frost." About mid-morning on the 14th both armies
stopped for an hour to feed the troops. Then, relentlessly, the contestants
pushed on. Later in the day a mud-splashed courier came at full gallop with a
letter from Greene to Williams. It had been written at 2:00 P.M. "The greater
part of our wagons are over and the troops are crossing." That evening another
courier rode in with a message from Greene at Irwin's Ferry: "1/2 past 5 o'clock.
All our troops are over and the stage is clear . . . I am ready to receive you and
give you a hearty welcome." According to William Gordon the light corps raised
a great cheer heard by O'Hara, who realized what it meant. Otho Holland
Williams had brilliantly executed one of warfare's most difficult maneuvers.
Now their task was to save themselves. As Greene had unnecessarily reminded
Williams in one letter, he had under him the flower of the army. To lose it would
be disastrous.[48]

Fourteen miles from the Dan, Otho Holland Williams headed for the crossing with the Continentals and the Virginia riflemen. Lee's Legion continued as
the rear guard. Gordon reports that Greene was on the bank to greet Williams
and cross with him. Following the schedule given him by Williams, Lee sent on
his infantry. "Between the hours of eight and nine, the cavalry reached the river,
just as the boats had returned from landing the Legion infantry." Lee recalled.
Waiting on the bank for Light Horse Harry and his dragoons was the faithful
Edward Carrington, whose planning and execution had been faultless. He directed the dragoons with their equipment into the boats; the horses would
swim. Some of the horses panicked and swam back to the right bank and disappeared into the woods. But they were recovered and forced back into the
river and on the second try followed the other horses. The last boat across
brought Carrington, Light Horse Harry Lee, and the last troop to the "friendly
shore."[49]

O'Hara and the British van arrived at the river after daybreak the next
morning. Cornwallis had driven his army forty miles in thirty-one hours, but the
Americans had done it in twenty.[50]

23

Patience and Finesse

His Lordship "in all things partook of our sufferings"

Cornwallis had been outgeneraled, once again faced by a river he could not cross. Although Banastre Tarleton had broken with Cornwallis by the time he wrote and took every opportunity to criticize the man who had been his patron, he correctly described the American retreat as "judiciously designed and vigorously executed."[1] Greene had gained refuge in a friendly countryside close to reinforcements and supplies. Cornwallis was ignorant of the temper of the immediate country surrounding him, had not a hope of receiving reinforcements, and had burned his supplies. He had no supply depots, no hospitals for his sick and wounded, no strong towns to retreat to should misfortune strike. His commander in chief, Sir Henry Clinton, did not even know his whereabouts.

Greene had drawn Cornwallis 240 miles from his nearest base of communications and supply, Camden, South Carolina, and there were no supplies moving in his direction and precious few communications. It is true that his was the only army in North Carolina, but now that he was there what was he going to do with it? Had he by marching the length of the state conquered it? The English admiral Samuel Graves answered that question when he compared the British army in America to "the passage of a ship through the sea whose track is soon lost." The perils of war in the American Back Country were now visited on Lord Cornwallis, and in a subsequent letter to Lord Germain, after the end of the Carolina campaign, he admitted as much: "The immense extent of this country, cut with numberless rivers and creeks, and the total want of internal navigation, which makes it impossible for our army to remain long in the heart of the country, will make it very difficult to reduce this province to obedience by a direct attack upon it."[2]

Logistics had taken over the conduct of the campaign. To Lord Rawdon Cornwallis described the army's condition on reaching the Dan: "the fatigue of our troops and the hardships which they suffered were excessive." The British needed food, and although Cornwallis no longer had any illusions about the steadfastness of the King's Friends, the effort had to be made. If he could rally the Tories to him so much the better. He explained his next move to Lord Germain: "My force being ill-suited to enter . . . so powerful a province as Virginia, and North Carolina being in the utmost confusion, after giving the troops a halt of one day I proceeded by easy marches to Hillsboro, where I erected the King's Standard and invited by proclamation all loyal subjects to repair to it and to . . . take an active part in assisting me to restore order and constitutional government."[3]

Hillsborough, North Carolina, was about fifty miles south of Cornwallis's position on the wrong side of the Dan River. According to local historians in 1780 it had an "aura of sophistication and elegance," but Otho Holland Williams, who spent considerable time there following Gates's defeat at Camden, described Hillsborough as a "dirty, disagreeable hole."[4] It was here on 22 February that Cornwallis planted the King's standard, issued his proclamation, and waited for the Tories. And they came. They came as country people used to gather from miles around for sights rarely seen—a circus, a traveling medicine show, voting day . . . or an army. Charles O'Hara described it.

"The novelty of a camp in the backwoods of America more than any other cause brought several people to stare at us. Their curiosity once satisfied, they returned to their homes. I am certain that in our march of near a thousand miles, almost in as many directions, thro' every part of North Carolina, tho' every means possible was taken to persuade our friends as they are called and indeed as they called themselves to join us, we never had with us at any one time one hundred men in arms. Without the experiment had been made, it would have been impossible to conceive that government could in so important a matter have been so grossly deceived. Fatal infatuation! When will government see these people thro' the proper medium? I am persuaded never."[5]

Food was as scarce as King's Friends. Cornwallis's commissary Charles Stedman had to undertake stern measures, recording that "such was the situation of the British army, that the author with a file of men, was obliged to go from house to house, throughout the town, to take provisions from the inhabitants, many of whom were greatly distressed by this measure, which could be justified only by extreme necessity." But the food supply situation remained critical, and Cornwallis was forced to go against his word and order the slaughter of farmers' oxen. It did not stop with other people's animals. Sergeant Roger Lamb reports that "such was the scarcity of provisions at Hillsborough, that it was found impossible to support the army in that place. They were even obliged to kill some of their best draft horses." His Lordship had indeed gotten himself and his army into a fix.[6]

While the British searched desperately for food, the Rebel army was enjoying "wholesome and abundant supplies of food in the rich and friendly county of Halifax," Virginia, whose people "received us with the affection of brethren" wrote Lee. But Greene's thoughts were on reentering North Carolina. Corn-

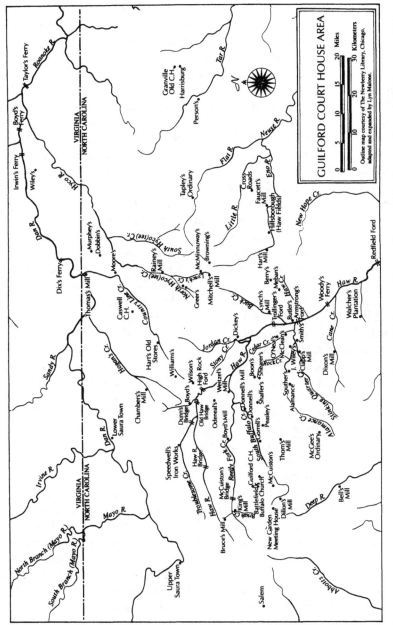

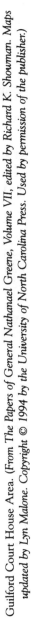

Guilford Court House Area. (*From The Papers of General Nathanael Greene, Volume VII, edited by Richard K. Showman. Maps updated by Lyn Malone. Copyright © 1994 by the University of North Carolina Press. Used by permission of the publisher.*)

wallis's predicament should not blind us to Greene's situation. He personally was "fatigued to death," he wrote Thomas Jefferson, but his job was only half done. He could not leave Cornwallis unmolested in North Carolina, to recover, establish contact with the British navy, inflame Tory passions, dash Rebel hopes, and deliver the wrong message to fence-sitters. Greene had avoided battle on Cornwallis's terms, but now, in his own time but relatively soon, and on ground of his own choosing, he had either to offer battle or, at the very least, "I shall attempt to gall his rear."[7]

During the retreat most of the North Carolina militia, officers as well as men, had left the army. On the day before he crossed the Dan, Greene wrote to General John Butler that all but eighty of the North Carolina militia had deserted the army. Virginia militia began to come in, but not in numbers to justify seeking battle. Yet he could not await necessary reinforcements before making a show of force south of the Dan.[8]

Andrew Pickens was already there. On 3 February Greene had instructed Pickens to raise militia "in the rear of the enemy" and harass them. Pickens probably had about thirty Georgians and South Carolinians with him. On 9 February Greene had written to Colonel Francis Locke and other North Carolina Militia officers that because of the death of William Lee Davidson he had sent Pickens "into the rear to take command." Captain Joseph Graham, who would serve under Pickens, recalled that about 11 February "it was mutually agreed to by the field officers to invest Pickens with the command of Davidson's troops." Pickens had led them in Cornwallis's footsteps over the Yadkin and through Salem to Guilford Courthouse. There on 19 February he wrote Greene that he had about 700 men, but those from south of the Catawba had come reluctantly and were interested in an "expedition into South Carolina where their thoughts seem universally bent." In his reply the following day Greene begged Pickens to "continue to pursue the Enemy and harrass them as much as possible." Pickens faithfully followed his orders, even though the Salisbury miltia, he told Greene, "are continually deserting, and no persuasion can prevail with them." He considered them "among the worst Men," he had ever commanded.[9]

The movement of the army south began on 19 February when Greene sent Light Horse Harry Lee with his Legion and two companies of the Maryland Line back across the Dan to collect intelligence and join Pickens. Lee sought Pickens for several days, and when the two forces linked up on the 23rd Pickens's rear guard mistook Lee's Legion, with its short green jackets, for Tarleton's British Legion. "Too late to retreat, so prepared to fight," recalled Captain Joseph Graham, but fortunately recognition came before friendly fire. On the same day, Lord Cornwallis put into motion an operation that led to a dramatic and bloody event that was important to the campaign and still remains controversial.[10]

Anxious that Tory militia assembling to join his army not be hindered, Cornwallis ordered Tarleton, with 200 horse, 150 men of the 33rd foot, and 100 Jägers to proceed west of the Haw River to protect the militia while they assembled and then escorted them to camp. Rebel scouts picked up the movement and reported to Pickens and Lee. Cautiously, with patrols before and behind them, the combined force followed what they first thought was a foraging party but learned was Tarleton himself with his sizeable force. Lee recalled in his *Memoirs* that Tarleton's path was marked by devastation, all the houses plundered, and not a man to be seen. The women told them that the Tories were gathering between the Haw and Deep Rivers, and they heard the British soldiers say that they would be back in a few days.[11]

The Americans shadowed the British until the 25th, with every intention of surprising Tarleton in his camp. Even dour Andrew Pickens's blood quickened: "Never was there a more glorious opportunity of cutting off a detachment than this." Tarleton later wrote that reports of Lee's being in the vicinity had prompted him to send warnings to the Tories, urging them to hasten to him, but "inspired by whiskey and the novelty of their situation, they unfortunately prolonged their excursions" by visiting relatives and friends.[12]

The most extensive record by a participant of what happened on the afternoon of 25 February 1781 was written thirty-one years later by Light Horse Harry Lee, and he had a large stake in the opinion of posterity. It began when two young riders from the 400-man Tory band of Colonel John Pyle, while searching for Tarleton, met Lee's van. Seeing the green-jacketed Rebel dragoons, "they were rejoiced in meeting us" and were so deceived that they thought Lee was Tarleton. Lee and Pickens had been carrying out this deception since crossing the Haw. They both reported to Greene that they hoped to pass Pyle's column and attack Tarleton. In his *Memoirs* Lee claimed that he asked Pickens to move the Rebel militia, "distingished by the green twigs in their hats, off the road into thick woods on the columns left flank" so they would not be seen by Pyle's men. But there is no mention of this in either Lee's or Pickens's battle reports or in the recollections of Captain Joseph Graham, who was in the militia column. Subsequent events argue that Lee's message to Pickens was either never sent or was misunderstood, because the Rebel militia stayed on the road. One of the Tory scouts was sent to Colonel Pyle "with Lieutenant Colonel Tarleton's gratulations," and a request that Pyle's column move to the side of the road to allow the "much fatigued troops to pass without delay to their night position." Lee claimed that he planned to confront Pyle, reveal his identity, and promise no harm if the Tories either went home or united with their countrymen. Word came back from Pyle that he would be pleased to make way for Tarleton and his men. For all the differences in the minor details of this action, there is little doubt of its main course.[13]

Probably at a walk, at the most a slow trot, Lee's Legion proceeded along the road. Drawn up on the side, Colonel John Pyle's Tory militia stared at the man they thought to be the legendary Banastre Tarleton leading his hard-bitten British Legion. Light Horse Harry recalled that he rode the length of the Tory column "with a smiling countenance, dropping occasionally expressions complimentary to the good looks and commendable conduct of his loyal friends," and he probably did. A North Carolina militiaman in his pension application stated that the Tories "frequently uttered salutations of a friendly kind, believing us to be British." Lee reached Pyle at the head of the column and grasped the Colonel's hand, with the intention of unmasking himself and offering Pyle his two choices. Then fighting began in the rear and quickly escalated. Lee said that the Tories recognized the Rebel militia and started it. Captain Graham said that it started when he recognized Pyle's men as Tories and told Captain Joseph Eggleston of Lee's Legion, who asked a Tory, "'To whom do you belong?' The man promptly answered, 'A friend of his Majesty.' Thereupon Captain Eggleston struck him over his head."[14]

What followed was quick and bloody. Lee's dragoon wheeled their mounts and charged at completely surprised men who were at the most two horse-lengths from them and began hacking away. They sabered to death at least ninety Tories and wounded most of the survivors, who dispersed in all directions. As they were being sabered some Tories, still deceived, cried out that they were the King's Friends. Some of the wounded who managed to flee to Tarleton's camp complained to him "of the cruelty of his dragoons." Tradition has it that Colonel John Pyle, severely wounded, got to a nearby pond and hid by lying underwater with only his nose showing. Charles Stedman labeled it a "foul massacre" and claimed that "between two and three hundred men were inhumanly butchered while in the act of begging for mercy," but ninety dead Tories remains the accepted figure. Lee lost one horse.[15]

There was unnecessary killing. That night a twenty-one-year-old North Carolina militiaman, Moses Hall, was taken to see a considerable number of prisoners. "We went to where six were standing together. Some discussion taking place, I heard some of our men cry out, 'Remember Buford,' and the prisoners were immediately hewed to death with broadswords." Thus continued the neverending cycle of retaliation.[16]

Pyle's Massacre, as it came to be called, has been compared to Tarleton's massacre of Buford's men. But Nathanael Greene's reaction was hard: "It has had a very happy effect on those disaffected Persons, of which there are too many in this Country." Lee, however, became sensitive to the charge and in his *Memoirs* defended himself on the ground of military necessity. The two actions did have at least one thing in common: their significance lay not with the controversies surrounding them, but in their effect on other men. Buford's Massacre inflamed Rebel passions. Pyle's Massacre devastated Tory morale. Under Tarleton's nose a large Tory band had been bloodied and dispersed. After that, there was little hope of Tory recruits flocking to the King's standard. As Andrew Pickens expressed it to Greene, "It has knocked up Toryism altogether in this part."[17]

But they still wanted Tarleton. He was camped a few miles away, but night had fallen and Pickens and Lee assumed that he must have been alerted. They decided to retire and attack at dawn. During this movement they were joined by Colonel William Preston and 300 Virginia riflemen. Tarleton wrote that having been alerted by some of Pyle's men he dispatched scouts who found the Rebel camp, and "when the British troops were under arms at midnight, to proceed towards their encampment, an express arrived with an order" from Cornwallis for Tarleton to return immediately to Hillsborough. He marched at once, and though Pickens and Lee pursued, his rear passed the Haw shortly after the arrival of their van. Had it not been for the timely arrival of Cornwallis's order, it could have proven a very interesting night for both sides, although Light Horse Harry liked to believe that "the capricious goddess gave us Pyle and saved Tarleton."[18]

On 22 February Greene had recrossed the Dan with the main army, and this news had prompted Cornwallis to recall Tarleton. Greene had been reinforced. That doughty fighter General Edward Stevens of Virginia had brought "several hundred militia," and Greene waited expectantly for the arrival of Colonel William Campbell of King's Mountain fame with 1,000 Virginia riflemen. But over the next three weeks his militia rosters would go up and down as the part-time soldiers came and went as their fancy took them, and from day to day Greene was never quite sure of his true strength. Moving westward, he operated in a relatively constricted area roughly east and north of the modern city of Greensboro. It was a dangerous game he was playing, yet he saw it as necessary, for Cornwallis could not be allowed to gain in strength and encourage the Tories, nor could the Rebels of North Carolina, regardless of their failure to join him in the great retreat, be left with the feeling that they had been abandoned by the regular army.[19]

In the meantime Cornwallis was forced out of Hillsborough because the town and surrounding area became barren of supplies, and he felt himself, as he wrote to Lord Germain, "amongst timid friends and adjoining inveterate rebels." He was also losing troops to temptation of a very basic sort. On 22 February he informed the army, "It is with great concern that Lord Cornwallis hears every day reports of Soldiers being taken by the Enemy, in consequence of their Straggling out of Camp in search of whiskey." Three days after warning his thirsty troops, Cornwallis moved the army westward, to a camp on the south side of Alamance Creek between the Haw River and the Deep River to the south, an area known to harbor many friends of the King. Charles O'Hara wrote, "From that time to the 15th of March the two armys were never above twenty miles asunder, they constantly avoiding a general action and we as industriously seeking it. These operations obliged the two armys to make numberless moves which it is impossible to detail."[20]

When Greene was notified that Cornwallis was south of him, he again detached Otho Holland Williams and his light troops to screen the main army. Williams ordered Pickens and Lee to join him with the Virginia riflemen they had met after Pyle's Massacre, and situated himself on the north side of Alamance Creek, just a few miles from Cornwallis's camp. Greene moved his camp to within fifteen miles of Cornwallis. American patroling was constant, aggressive, and led to sharp skirmishes. It was a tense time. Sentries were nervous. Early on the morning of 4 March a Tory band intent on joining Cornwallis approached Tarleton's lines and were mistaken for Rebels. Dragoons of the British Legion charged, sabered some, and dispersed the others in wild flight. When the Legion realized its error riders were sent to round up the terror-stricken men, but they would not hear apologies or assurances of protection. The following night an American dragoon patrol found Tories driving cattle to Cornwallis's camp. They killed twenty-three drovers. Word of these incidents was spread far and wide, and if after Pyle's Massacre there had been any glimmer of hope among the King's Friends that their day of deliverance might arrive, it vanished amid the shrieks of men being hacked to death by hard-charging dragoons of both sides.[21]

Greene did not remain long at his new camp. Constant movement and unceasing vigilance were the hallmarks of the game of hound and hare. Greene was tireless, after a day on horseback spending the better part of the night writing dispatches, sleeping little, rising before dawn. During this time, he later said, he received the greatest compliment of his life. One night not long before daybreak, he heard snoring inside the tent of Colonel John Green (no relation) of Virginia. He went inside, laid his hand on the colonel's shoulder, and said, "Good heavens, Colonel, how can you sleep with the enemy so near, and this the very hour for a surprise?" The Virginian replied, "Why, General, I knew that you were awake."[22]

Problems with the militia added to his burdens. Not only were they not appearing in large enough numbers, they were either going home or making other difficulties. The riflemen with Otho Williams refused to serve under the officer sent to command them and demanded their own choice, for "they say they are Volunteers, and shod be treated with distinction." Almost all the militia from western parts arrived with their horses, and lack of forage and their disposition to wander in search of it became a serious problem. The key to their effectiveness as guerrilla warriors was their mobility, but now they were engaged in joint operations with regulars, and when dismounted for action and required to move to another position their first thought was to retrieve their horses and vanish. Greene and his officers also needed to build auxiliary infantry units to support the Continentals in a major action with Cornwallis. But when Otho Williams and Lee proposed to the officers under Pickens and Preston that "half of their number organized as infantry would be of more service to the cause than all of them as they were," they met a stone wall of opposition: "Their men would not consent to their horses being sent home." A few days later Andrew Pickens was "sorry to acquaint" Greene "of the fast desertion that prevails," and laid most of it to "the plan to dismount them." On 4 March Lee informed Greene that "The militia company now with me have furnished twelve riflemen to act with me for three months, on condition that the remainder be discharged. I have bargained with them on these terms." But the worst blow came when William Campbell, expected to march in with 1,000 riflemen from the western mountains, wrote Greene from the Moravian town of Bethabara that he was "vex'd, asham'd and affronted," but he had arrived with "only about sixty men." Otho Holland Williams was "astonish'd." Greene asked Jefferson to investigate. Meanwhile, the war went on.[23]

The sparring continued until 6 March, when Cornwallis decided to go after Otho Holland Williams with a vengeance and push him so hard that Greene would be forced into a general action. For Cornwallis was in trouble. On occasion during the campaign his troops had been hungry, but now for the first time they were hungry not just now and then but consistently, day after day. Cornwallis and his officers shared their privation, for His Lordship would allow "no distinction." Sergeant Roger Lamb recorded that "sometimes we had turnips served out for food, when we came to a turnip field; or arriving at a field of corn we converted our canteens into rasps and ground our Indian corn for bread; when we would get no Indian corn, we were compelled to eat liver as a substitute for bread, with our lean beef. In this his lordship participated, nor did he indulge himself even in the distinction of a tent; but in all things partook of our sufferings, and seemed much more to feel for us than for himself." Yet desertions were mounting at a rate that forced increased roll calls, and British and Hessian plundering of both Tory and Rebel inhabitants reached levels striking for even those accomplished looters. Harangues against such behavior were ignored. The camp followers were worse than the soldiers. Charles O'Hara in his anger ordered that women not present at roll calls would be whipped and drummed out of the brigade, and so they would know what faced them he required their presence at all whippings. Hence Cornwallis's pressing need to seek a final grand battle against Nathanael Greene and his ragtag army.[24]

At 5:30 on the morning of 6 March Cornwallis marched north toward the Haw River. The van was led by Lieutenant Colonel James Webster's brigade and Tarleton's British Legion. They set a torrid pace. On that very morning Otho Williams had determined to storm a small British force holding a mill about one mile from his camp, so the Americans, too, were about in the thick early morning fog. When Williams's patrols reported that Cornwallis had marched, Webster and Tarleton were already within two miles of him on his left. Williams immediately turned his corps around and headed for Weitzel's Mill on Reedy Fork Creek, which he intended to put between him and the British. He had about ten miles to go. Williams detached patrols to slow the British march, but they failed.

It became a chase, and there must have been times when it seemed that the Americans would lose the race for the ford on Reedy Fork Creek. Occasionally Williams's rear guard, instead of being in front of the British van, was on its flanks. Although he got to the ford just ahead of the British, they began appearing on the rise behind him as the Continentals were crossing. Williams quickly deployed a covering party composed of Pickens's South Carolina and Georgia militia and the Virginia riflemen of Colonel James Preston and Colonel William Campbell. The cavalry of Lee and Washington were posted on the flanks. Blazing fire from the covering party sent British advance troops reeling. The American troops who had crossed now provided covering fire for the militia and cavalry who had laid down fire for them. The "aire was calm and dense," wrote Captain Joseph Graham, who fought at Weitzel's Mill. The antagonists were enveloped in smoke. Then the "militia were seen running down the hill from under the smoke. The ford was crowded, many crossing the watercourse at other places. Some, it was said, were drowned."

Most of the Americans crossed safely, but it had been close, very close, and it was not over, for Cornwallis was determined to force battle. Lieutenant Colonel James Webster galloped to the front and under his inspirational leadership the British stormed across Reedy Fork Creek. But Williams carried out a successful withdrawal covered by the superior cavalry of Washington and Lee. Once again frustration was Cornwallis's lot.[25]

"We marched yesterday to look for Lord Cornwallis"

A consequence of Weitzel's Mill was the loss to the army of Andrew Pickens. The South Carolina and Georgia militia had so deeply resented their deployment to provide covering fire for the regulars that they decided to go home. They felt that they had been improperly used and unnecessarily exposed to British fire. There were probably other reasons too. Militia rarely ventured as far from home as they had, and they had been away from their families for almost two months in uncertain and perilous times. They were adamant, Pickens reported to Greene and Governor John Rutledge of South Carolina. Both men agreed to their departure—what choice had they?—but insisted that Pickens go with them to keep the regiments in a body and maintain discipline on the march home. He was encouraged to continue raiding British posts, and Greene promised Pickens that once he had dealt with Cornwallis the army would return to South Carolina. Of the great South Carolina partisan chiefs, Andrew Pickens was the most faithful to Greene in following orders and cooperating to the fullest. His prestige among militiamen and his proven ability on a battlefield would very soon be missed.[26]

Lack of numbers kept Greene maneuvering and refusing to offer battle. As he moved along the north bank of the Haw River, Cornwallis, some dozen miles away, followed on the south bank. Greene finally took a position at a place called High Rock Ford, and Cornwallis camped in the forks of the Deep River at the Quaker meetinghouse at New Garden and waited for Greene's next move. On 10 March Greene wrote to Thomas Jefferson that "the Militia indeed have flocked in from various quarters . . . and go and come in such irregular Bodies that I can make no calculations on the strength of my Army, or direct any future operations than can ensure me the means of Success. . . . Hitherto I have been obliged to practice that by finesse which I dare not attempt by force. I know the People have been in anxious suspence, waiting the event of an Action, but be the consequence of Censure what it may, nothing shall hurry me into a Measure that is not Suggested by prudence or connects not with it the interest of the southern department."[27]

That said it all. Greene would fight in his own time. But he had already received reinforcements, and even as he wrote to Jefferson he must have known that the time was drawing near. On either 10 or 11 March two brigades of North Carolina militia numbering some 1,000 men arrived under the command of Brigadier General John Butler and Brigadier General Thomas Eaton. Several hundred Virginia militia came in under Brigadier General Robert Lawson. General von Steuben sent Greene 400 unblooded Continentals from Maryland. On the 10th Greene reincorporated Otho Williams's indomitable light corps into the main army. On the 12th he marched south for Guilford Courthouse. Morale was high; soldiers of all ranks expected battle soon. To his wife, his "dearest Fanny," Major St. George Tucker, who had progressed from private in the Virginia militia, wrote with bravado on the 13th: "We marched yesterday to look for Lord Cornwallis, who probably marched a different route because he did not choose to fight us. We are now strong enough, I hope, to cope with him to advantage. Our army . . . in strength is rather better than I expected. . . . I should conclude that we had about six thousand men, of which, I believe, fifteen hundred are regulars. But this is all conjecture, for we little folks walk about with a bandage over our eyes and with wool in our ears."[28]

On the 14th Cornwallis received intelligence that Greene had taken up position at Guilford Courthouse, and that night the first reports were confirmed. The British camp was twelve miles away. Cornwallis could not be sure that Greene was ready to fight, but he was certain that he must fight soon or retire. Shortage of food was critical, his men were on their second pair of the leather soles made at Ramsour's Mill, and many of those had worn out. And though he had not fought a major action since leaving Winnsboro, he had lost some 400 men through death, wounds, illness, and desertion. His strength was now about 2,000. His obsession to fight and destroy Greene had become dire necessity. At daybreak on 15 March Lord Cornwallis marched with the intention of fighting that day. Waiting at Guilford Courthouse, Nathanael Greene had the same intention.

Greene, we recall, had studied the ground carefully on at least one occasion, and it had obviously remained the place where he would offer Cornwallis the trial of arms the Englishman so strongly desired. Lord Cornwallis had given the area little notice. The battlefield was about a mile and a half long and ranged from about a mile to a mile and a half wide. It began where the road from New Garden on which Cornwallis marched emerged from a narrow defile flanked by densely wooded hillsides and crossed a brook onto a clearing that was roughly one-quarter of a mile square. The road ran through the field into thick woods. Only slightly curving, first right, then left, then right again, the road climbed a very gradual slope through the woods to a larger clearing roughly shaped like a low boot. Near the top of the boot, on the crest of the hill and to the left of the road, was Guilford Courthouse, a hamlet of about 100 people. Nothing remains of either the buildings or the community. Shrubs and underbrush covered the forest floor, making progress off the road difficult, and the ground was broken by small hills and gullies. We can see why Greene chose to fight there. After crossing the field at the bottom of the slope, the British regiments would be unable to maintain their lines in the woods and thick underbrush. Scattered and broken into individual soldiers and small parties, it was hoped that British inability to present their fearsome bayonets in linear formation would encourage the Rebel militia to stand firmly, and that the cover provided by the trees and heavy growth would lend them confidence.

Daniel Morgan, making his painful way home, had written to Greene on 20 February from the home of Carter Harrison, where he was forced by the rigors of travel to stop for several days. Of the militia, he said, "If they fight, you will beat Cornwallis; if not, he will beat you, and perhaps cut your regulars to pieces." His advice was to "put the militia in the centre, with some picked troops in their rear, with orders to shoot down the first man that runs." Greene did not do that, but he did borrow from Morgan's deployment at Cowpens.[29]

The fighting began that day in the wee hours along the New Garden Road four miles west of Guilford Courthouse.[30] Greene had sent Lee down the road with his Legion and William Campbell and a detachment of Virginia riflemen to maintain contact with the enemy. The evening of the 14th Lee sent forward Lieutenant Heard of the Legion horse with a patrol of dragoons to hang on the outskirts of Cornwallis's camp. About 2:00 A.M. the next morning Heard sent word that a "large body of horse" was on the move. Lee passed the information by dispatch rider back to Greene at Guilford Courthouse, and he ordered Heard to leave some dragoons on the road, lead the others in an attempt to pass the British flank, "discover whether the British army was in motion," and report every half hour. Heard learned that the British continued to approach, but slowly. They were as security conscious as Lee. Heard reported that he could not pass the British flanks, "having been uniformly interrupted by patrols ranging far from the line of march; yet that he was persuaded that he heard the rumbling of wheels, which indicated a general movement." This convinced Lee that battle was in the offing.

He sent Heard's latest report to Greene, then called his troops to arms and bade them prepare a hasty breakfast. It was 4:00 A.M. They had just finished breakfast when a dispatch rider arrived from Greene's headquarters with orders for Lee to advance with the Legion horse and "ascertain the truth." Lee mounted and "took the road to the enemy at the head of the horse, having directed the infantry and the rifle militia to follow, the first on his right, and the second on his left." Two miles down the road he met Lieutenant Heard and his dragoon patrol, "who were retiring, followed leisurely by the enemy's horse."

It was the British van, Banastre Tarleton commanding. Light Horse Harry decided on an ambush. He ordered his cavalry to withdraw by troops, with the rear troop under Captain Rudolph at full gallop and the center troop under Captain Eggleston at the same speed. The front troop under Captain Armstrong would retire at a walk. Lee stayed with Armstrong. Hearing the Americans galloping off ahead of him, Tarleton ordered his lead section of horse to press harder. Under Lee's direction Armstrong continued at a walk, whereupon the British horsemen fired their pistols, shouted, and charged the Americans.

"At this moment, Lee ordered a charge, the dragoons came instantly to the right about, and, in close column, rushed upon the foe. This meeting happened in a long lane, with very high curved fences on each side of the road, which admitted but one section in front." The Americans, riding "stout, active horses . . . kept in the highest condition" literally rode down the first section of the British, who "were mounted upon small weak horses." The entire lead section "was dismounted, and many of the horses prostrated; some of the dragoons killed, the rest made prisoners; not a single American soldier or horse injured." Tarleton ordered an immediate retreat and "retired with celerity." Light Horse Harry admitted that given the difference in horseflesh an American defeat would have been a disgrace. He was equally candid about the next encounter.

Tarleton retreated toward Cornwallis's main force by leaving the road and following an "obscure way." Lee led his cavalry down the road in full gallop in an attempt to cut off Tarleton. Instead, as the bright rays of the morning sun cleared the treetops, he ran directly into the light infantry of the Guards, who raised their muskets. The sunlight suddenly reflecting off the barrels so frightened Lee's horse that he had to "throw himself off" and mount another. It was Light Horse Harry's turn to order an immediate retreat. His Legion horse retired "with great precipitation," wrote Tarleton. The Legion infantry and Campbell's riflemen came up at double time and began exchanging fire with the Guards. "The action became very sharp, and was bravely maintained on both sides" for about thirty minutes.

The appearance of the Guards convinced Lee that Cornwallis was not far behind with the main army, and also that nothing further was to be gained by remaining where he was. Tarleton was equally convinced "that General Greene was at hand." Lee claimed his casualties were lighter than those of the British. Tarleton claimed victory and said the riflemen "were dispersed with considerable loss," and he did take prisoners. Tarleton himself took a musket ball in his right hand and rode the rest of the day with his arm in a sling. In truth, honors seemed about even. Light Horse Harry drew off his infantry. Protecting them against the British Legion cavalry with his own horse, he retired down New Garden Road. "General Greene," Lee wrote, "being immediately advised of what had passed, prepared for battle; not doubting that the long avoided, now wished-for, hour was at hand."

24

Guilford Courthouse:
"Long, Obstinate, and Bloody"

"Come on, my brave Fuzileers"

On the day of Guilford Courthouse Nathanael Greene had about 4,440 troops.[1] Of these some 1,762 were Continentals. Although the terrain was radically different from the field at Cowpens, Greene's deployment and tactics were largely based on Morgan's, and he also followed subsequent advice given by the Old Waggoner. He deployed in three lines. In the first line were his least reliable troops, about 1,000 North Carolina militia: two regiments commanded by Brigadier General John Butler and Brigadier General Thomas Eaton.

These were not the formidable Back Country militia from the western parts described by Light Horse Harry Lee as "never alarmed at meeting with equal numbers of British infantry." They resembled the militia gathered at Camden instead of Cowpens. Nor were their commanders the North Carolina Continental generals Greene had recommended to state authorities. North Carolina politics saw to that. Greene put the militia at the edge of the woods behind a split-rail fence, where they could look directly across a plowed field at the point where the New Garden road emerged from the woods.

William Richardson Davie, who was at the battle, recalled many years later that about half of the militia were behind the fence, a "cover too insignificant to inspire confidence." The militia were on either side of the road, just before it disappeared into the tangled forest behind them. Greene had four six-pounders and about 100 artillerymen under Captain Anthony Singleton. He posted Singleton and two of the guns on the road between the militia regiments. In his letter of 20 February Morgan had advised Greene to post riflemen "on the flanks under enterprising officers who is acquainted with that kind of fighting." Greene did this but reinforced the riflemen with regular cavalry and in-

372

fantry. On the right, next to Butler's regiment, were Colonel Charles Lynch's 200 Virginia riflemen supported by William Washington's ninety dragoons and Captain Robert Kirkwood's eighty-man company of the Delaware Line. On the left, next to Eaton's regiment, were Colonel William Campbell and 200 riflemen, augmented by Lee's Legion of seventy-five horse and eighty-two foot; Lee's men would take position following their return from the morning's action on New Garden Road.[2]

Nathanael Greene, who was no Morgan when it came to inspiring troops, nevertheless tried. It was past noon when he followed Morgan's example and rode down the split-rail fence to talk to the militiamen and rouse them into a fighting mood. Some men who were there said he took off his hat and mopped his forehead. He spoke of liberty and the cause and their honor, and all he asked of them was to volley twice. Then, he told them, they could retire.

Three hundred to 350 yards behind the first line, also astride the road but out of sight in the thick woods, was the Virginia militia brigade, one regiment of about 600 men commanded by Brigadier General Robert Lawson, the other also numbering about 600 under Brigadier General Edward Stevens. There were many discharged Continentals in the ranks. Still mortified by the behavior of his Virginians at Camden, Stevens stationed forty picked riflemen twenty paces behind the brigade. Their orders were to shoot any man who ran.

The main line of resistance was about 550 yards to the right and rear of the second line, in the clearing where the courthouse commanded the large boot-shaped field. Here waited slightly over 1,400 Continentals from Virginia, Maryland, and Delaware. The Virginia Brigade commanded by Brigadier General Isaac Huger included the 4th and 5th Regiments under, respectively, Lieutenant Colonel John Green and Lieutenant Colonel Samuel Hawes. The Maryland Brigade was commanded by Colonel Otho Holland Williams. Colonel John Gunby led the 1st Maryland, which also included Captain Peter Jacquett's Delaware Company, and Lieutenant Colonel Benjamin Ford commanded the 2nd Maryland. Colonel Gunby was wounded during the fighting and replaced by his deputy, the cool, intrepid Lieutenant Colonel John Eager Howard. The other two six-pounders, under Captain Samuel Finley, were placed between the Virginia and Maryland fronts. Of these units, only the 1st Maryland and the Delaware companies were hardened veterans, equal to any regiment Cornwallis could throw at them. Recruits composed most of the 2nd Maryland, and the two Virginia regiments had been raised to replace those lost at Charleston the previous year and had seen little if any action.

There were two main differences between Morgan's deployment at Cowpens and Greene's at Guilford Courthouse. The field of battle at Guilford Courthouse was a much larger area, and because of the thickly wooded terrain Greene's three lines could neither see nor support one another. Nor did Greene, unlike Morgan, have the entire battlefield in view, and thus he did not have the ability to react immediately to events. Greene also did not establish a reserve to throw in at the critical moment, should it come. We can be certain that the North Carolina militia manning the first line felt very lonely and exposed.

When Light Horse Harry Lee returned from the fighting on New Garden Road to take up his position on their left, he like Greene rode their line and harangued them in fiery tones. They had no reason to be afraid of the British regulars. Hadn't he whipped them three times that morning? He promised to do it again, and urged them to stand firm. The North Carolina militia listened, stared at the spot where the British regulars would appear on the New Garden road, and waited. A little before 1:00 P.M. Major Richard Harrison of Granville County began writing a letter to his wife, who was scheduled that day to give birth. "It is scarcely possible to paint the agitations of my mind . . . struggling with two of the greatest events that are in nature at the same time: the fate of my Nancy and my country. Oh, my God, I trust them with thee; do with them for the best!"[3]

About 1:30 P.M. on 15 March 1781, the head of the British column appeared on the New Garden road and with measured tread and to the beat of drums and sounds of fifes and Highland pipes marched across the brook and spread in both directions on the edge of the cleared area. Captain Anthony Singleton of the Continental artillery started the battle with his two six-pounders, and Lieutenant John McLeod of the Royal Artillery rushed three six-pounders forward and answered.[4] While the gunners dueled, apparently without doing much damage, Cornwallis deployed. He had on the field about 1,950 men to oppose Greene's 4,440, but he did not know how many men Greene had. He thought 10,000 Americans faced him, but that did not deter him. He was ignorant of the terrain too, for he had not paid attention to it when last there, and his Tory guides were unable to provide an adequate description. That too did not deter him. Except for what he could see in the distance across the old corn field, he also lacked intelligence on Greene's dispositions. Nor did that deter him. What he had been seeking since January, had marched hundreds of miles for, had driven his army to rags and hunger to effect, was finally at hand. The reason Lord Cornwallis was a soldier lay before him, and he did not hesitate.

To the left of the road he placed the Royal Welsh Fusiliers and to their left the 33rd Foot. This wing was led by Lieutenant Colonel James Webster. Behind them in support were the 2nd Guards Battalion, the Grenadier and light infantry companies of the Guards, and the Jägers, all commanded by Brigadier General Charles O'Hara. To the right of the road were the 2nd Battalion of Fraser's Highlanders under Lieutenant Colonel Duncan McPherson. To its right was the blue-coated Hessian Regiment von Bose commanded by Lieutenant Colonel Johann Christian du Puy. In support was Lieutenant Colonel Norton's 1st Guards Battalion. Major General Alexander Leslie was in overall command of the right wing. Lieutenant McLeod's artillery was on the road between the two wings. In reserve in column on the road was Banastre Tarleton and the British Legion Horse. There were no Tory auxiliaries. Officers and men had been on short rations since late January. They had not been given breakfast and they had marched twelve miles that day while the Americans ate their breakfast and rested. They were outnumbered over two to one. If they lost they had nowhere to retreat, no one to come to their aid. But every unit was regular, every man a veteran, every soldier a product of iron discipline. It being the dying time, their officers from cornets to generals were all with them. When Lord Cornwallis gave the order to advance they too did not hesitate.

To the beat of drums and the wail of pipes and the sucking sounds of feet tramping through the muddy corn field, the tattered regiments under faded colors went forward. Four hundred yards away behind the split-rail fence William Montgomery watched them come and waited with his militia comrades for the order to fire.

The response of the North Carolinians remains and will continue a subject of debate. Nathanael Greene, harshly critical of their behavior, said at about 140 yards "part of them began a fire, but a considerable part left the ground without firing at all; some fired once, and some twice." But Greene was over 1,000 yards away when it happened. Captain Anthony Singleton of the Continental artillery was on the spot and said "the militia, *contrary to custom*, behaved well for militia." And British officers who courted death on that rain-soaked field had no doubt as to the damage wrought by the militia volleys, ragged, spotty, or otherwise. Captain Dugald Stuart said that "one half of the Highlanders dropt on the spot." Sir Thomas Saumarez of the Fusiliers remembered a "most galling and destructive fire." On the Rebel side of the fence, William Montgomery thought the British lines resembled "the scattering stalks of a wheat field, when the harvest man passed over it with his cradle."[5]

But the sergeants bawled their orders and dressed ranks and the officers shouted words of encouragement and the British and Germans stepped over their dead, dying, and wounded and kept coming. On the left James Webster, wrote Sergeant Roger Lamb, led his wing "in excellent order in a smart run . . . when arrived within forty yards of the enemy's line it was perceived that their whole line had their arms presented, and resting on a rail fence. . . . They were taking aim with the nicest precision." This shook even the disciplined redcoated line. "At this awful moment," Lamb continued, "a general pause took place; both parties surveyed each other with a most anxious suspence." Then "colonel Webster rode forward in front of the 23rd regiment and said, with more than even his usual commanding voice . . . 'Come on, my brave Fuzileers.' This operated like an inspiring voice, they rushed forward amidst the enemy's fire; dreadful was the havoc on both sides."[6]

This was the end of the line for the North Carolina militia. It was bayonet time and that was not their way of fighting. They had more or less delivered their volleys and General Greene himself had said they could then retire and they were for home. Retire meant one thing to Greene but quite another to those part-time soldiers. Orderly retirement to perhaps reform elsewhere on the field as the militia at Cowpens had done was not in their plans that day, and although it lies in the realm of speculation I would wager that Daniel Morgan and Andrew Pickens were sorely missed. One company stayed and fought; they were stationed next to Campbell's riflemen and were perhaps inspired by those veteran mountaineers. Their Captain, Arthur Forbes of Guilford County, was killed in action. But almost 1,000 terror-stricken men stampeded for the rear. They dropped weapons, ammunition boxes, knapsacks, canteens, anything that would impede their progress through the dense woods behind them.

Their officers may have run with them. William Richardson Davie recalled that "it is justice to the men to observe that they never were so wretchedly officered as they were that day," although Nathanael Greene in his official report claimed "the General and field Officers did all they could to induce the Men to stand their Ground."[7] Davie, taking temporary leave of his hated duties as Commissary General, tried to stop them but they were listening to no one. Light Horse Harry Lee galloped from his post on the left flank and threatened to turn his cavalry on them, but that was an empty threat given the dense woods into which the militia had fled. Fortunately, Brigadier General Edward Stevens had warned the Virginians some 350 yards behind in the second line that the North Carolinians would be "retiring" in their direction and they should merely open their lines and let them through. They did and remained steady, although the panic of the fleeing mob must have set them to wondering. On the breaking of the first line, Captain Anthony Singleton harnessed his horses to his two six-pounders and galloped back up the road all the way to the third line.

The British, however, could not take immediate advantage of their rout of the North Carolinians. The riflemen and Continental infantry on their flanks stood firm and delivered galling enfilading fire that had to be dealt with. On the left Webster wheeled the 33rd and the Jägers and went after Lynch's Virginians and Kirkwood's company of the Delaware Line, and on the right Regiment von Bose dealt with Lee's Legion and Campbell's Virginians. Cornwallis extended his lines by ordering forward the support units. Tarleton, however, was ordered to maintain his position. The Jägers and the light infantry of the Guards and the 33rd Foot were now on the extreme left of the British line facing Lynch, Kirkwood, and Washington's dragoons. To the right of the 33rd were the Fusiliers, the Grenadier company of the Guards, and the 2nd Guards Battalion. Lieutenant McLeod's Royal Artillery kept pace on the road. Immediately to the right of the road was the now decimated 2nd Battalion of Fraser's Highlanders, then Regiment von Bose, and on the far right the 1st Guards Battalion.

Cornwallis's sole reserve was Tarleton's cavalry, which would only be used if the Americans were about to overrun a British unit. Kirkwood's flanking force slowly withdrew through the woods to its next assigned position, on the right flank of the second line. Lee, however, failed to move his flanking party to the second line. He blamed this failure on the flight of the North Carolinians, and some writers maintain that Regiment von Bose got between him and the second line. Whatever the reason, Lee's Legion, Campbell's Virginians, and the North Carolina militia company, engaged by Regiment von Bose and the 1st Guards Battalion, curved to the left instead of falling straight back. Retiring in a northeasterly direction, they eventually ended about a mile from the main fighting. The contest was fierce, degenerating into a backwoods fight in woods and hills in which the British and Germans sometimes found themselves assaulted from behind after clearing their front. But it quickly became a sideshow, and only affected the main battle by depriving both generals of badly needed units.

When the British moved into the woods the fighting became confused. Stevens's Virginia brigade on the second line behaved very well, but William Richardson Davie recalled that "Lawson's Brigade fought as illy as the No Carolinians. The only difference was they did not run entirely home." Nevertheless, amid the trees and tangled forest floor the British could not maintain their well-ordered lines or use the bayonet with maximum effectiveness. In many places the action became firefights between small parties. Edward Stevens, who deeply wanted his men to erase the shame of Camden, had his thigh smashed by a musket ball and was carried from the field. Cornwallis was also in the thick of it. At one point his horse was shot from under him and he mounted another but found himself quite alone. Sergeant Roger Lamb of the Fusiliers discovered him not far from the Americans. "His Lordship was mounted on a dragoon's horse; the saddlebags were under the creature's belly, which much retarded his progress, owing to the vast quantity of underwood that was spread over the ground; his lordship was evidently unconscious of his danger." Sergeant Lamb grasped the bridle of the horse and led Cornwallis to the Fusiliers.[8]

The firefights at the second line should have ended forever the myth that British regulars could not adapt to woods fighting. The dogged Britons kept slugging away and gradually forced the Virginians to the right of the road to swing back to the road like a door, and many took this opportunity to use the New Garden road to escape. Three days later, with the action fresh in his mind, Major St. George Tucker of Lawson's Brigade wrote to his Fanny that when the men discovered British troops in their rear "this threw the militia into such confusion that, without attending in the least to their officers who endeavored to halt them and make them face about and face the enemy, Holcombe's regiment and ours instantly broke off without firing a single gun and dispersed like a flock of sheep frightened by dogs." Tucker managed to rally sixty or seventy men, continued skirmishing, and drove back one group of British soldiers. But the stubborn redcoats never let up and their final assault, led by Cornwallis himself, cleared the woods. They had paid dearly for it. The forest floor was littered with their comrades, some still forever, others moving feebly. Despite St. George Tucker's disgust with those who ran, many Virginians had fought very well and done their jobs. General Edward Stevens, lying at the third line with his thigh smashed, praised his men, and put the ghost of Camden behind him.[9]

When the tired and bloodied British battalions began to emerge from the woods they were on the lip of a natural amphitheater that farmers had cleared of trees and undergrowth. Opposite them, a few hundred yards across the intervening space, they could see the buff and blue of the Continentals, including Kirkwood's Delaware Company, which had withdrawn in good order to the third line. The first on the scene were the Jägers, the light infantry of the Guards, and the 33rd Foot. The other battalions had not cleared the woods, where fighting was still going on. The intrepid James Webster then made a mistake. Perhaps caught up in the madness of battle, he led these units down into the bowl of the amphitheater, across it, and charged up the other side at the waiting Continentals. He drove his men at the cream of Greene's army: 1st Maryland and the Delaware companies of Kirkwood and Jacquett. Grim, silent, those tested veterans held their fire until Webster and his men were within 100 feet, and then shattered them with a thunderous volley. Webster was severely wounded by a musket ball that struck him directly in the knee. The British were repulsed in disorder.

Many writers have described this as the critical point of the battle, and it has been speculated that if Greene had then thrown in the rest of his Continentals and attacked the British he might have routed Cornwallis's army. Tarleton later wrote, "at this period the event of the action was doubtful, and victory alternately presided over each army." But the operative words here are "might have," and it was not in the plans of Nathanel Greene the bold strategist to risk his entire force with a roll of the tactical dice.[10]

If the fighting had been fierce up to then, it was about to get worse. As Webster, badly wounded but unwilling to leave the field, regrouped his men, the 2nd Guards Battalion cleared the woods. Charles O'Hara had been wounded twice, in the thigh and chest, and had turned over his command to Lieutenant Colonel James Stuart, who like Webster never hesitated. Seeing 2nd Maryland on the other side of the amphitheater he formed the Guards and headed straight at them. He did not even stop to order a volley. Sunlight glittered on their bayonets. The sight was too much for the raw recruits of 2nd Maryland. They turned and ran as fast as the North Carolina militia before them. The Guards pursued and took Captain Finley's two six-pounders.

The 1st Maryland, its view blocked by a grove, was unaware of this event until its deputy commander John Eager Howard was told by a staff officer. "I rode to Colonel Gunby," Howard wrote, "and gave him the information. He did not hesitate to order the regiment to face about and we were immediately engaged with the guards. Our men gave them some well directed fire, and we then advanced and continued firing." A North Carolina militiaman, Nathaniel Slade, watched from the courthouse. "This conflict between the brigade of guards and the first regiment of Marylanders was most terrific, for they fired at the same instant, and they appeared so near that the blazes from the muzzles of their guns seemed to meet." In this exchange Colonel Gunby's horse was killed and he was pinned under it, and John Eager Howard took over the regiment he had led so brilliantly at Cowpens.[11]

Suddenly a bugle call echoed over the amphitheater. William Washington, as vigilant as he had been at Cowpens, had swung his dragoons to the rear of the Guards. Washington led a thundering charge that hit 2nd Guards from behind and swept through them, riding them down, sabering them. Stunned by the unexpected, the Guards were not ready for Washington's encore. He and his dragoons had their splendid Virginia chargers under control, got them turned, and with sabers swinging charged back through the broken British ranks.

The Guards were in disorder. Many, although not badly hurt, had been knocked down by the big chargers. John Eager Howard took immediate advantage and drove 1st Maryland with bayonets extended in a fierce charge that ended in a desperate hand-to-hand encounter between two elite units. Amid the fury of men shouting, stabbing, clubbing, the Guards commander Lieutenant Colonel James Stuart rushed at Captain John Smith of Maryland and lunged at him with his sword. Smith twisted his body to the left and raised his right arm, his own sword now high over his head. Stuart's blade passed under his right arm, so close the hilt struck him in the chest. But in his haste Stuart stepped on a dead man, slipped, and went to one knee. Guardsmen rushed to help their commander but before they could reach him Captain Smith brought his sword down in a back-handed slice across Stuart's head that killed him. Stuart's orderly sergeant immediately attacked Smith, but Smith's sergeant killed him. Another Guardsman attacked. Smith killed him with his sword. Then a guardsman from behind shot Smith in the back of the head and he fell among the dead. Carried from the field, it was found that he had only been stunned by a single buckshot. John Smith survived the war to tell his tale. A monument to James Stuart marks the spot where he died. Such was the nature of the fighting between 1st Maryland and 2nd Guards.[12]

Under the onslaught of Howard's Continentals the Guards wavered, bent, seemed to be on the verge of breaking. Incredibly, the flower of Cornwallis's army was in grave danger of being driven from the field, perhaps destroyed. John Eager Howard recalled that "the whole were in our power." Was Guilford Courthouse another Cowpens in the making? It might have been had another general commanded the British that day. Cornwallis emerged from the woods and surveyed what was happening before him. Then he did what he had to do. What he did was terrible but what choice had he?

Lieutenant John McLeod was at hand with his six-pounders. Young McLeod spent the better part his life at war, became a general himself, commanded the artillery at Waterloo. But surely what he was commanded to do at Guilford Courthouse was one of the searing experiences of his life. Cornwallis ordered McLeod to fire grapeshot into the mass of struggling men, into friend and foe alike. Charles O'Hara lying painfully wounded on the ground beside the cannon begged him not to do it. Lieutenant McLeod hesitated. Cornwallis sternly repeated the order. The cannons roared, spewing grape into the flesh of Britons and Americans. The melee dissolved as soldiers of both sides scattered. Cornwallis had done what he had to do. The crisis passed.[13]

From the woods the Highlanders and the Fusiliers and the Grenadier company of the Guards now appeared, finished with mopping up against scattered parties of Virginians. Webster had reformed his units and was attacking. Cornwallis pressed forward toward the gap from which 2nd Maryland had fled. Cornwallis had to win. But Greene had only to avoid serious defeat while making Cornwallis pay too dearly for victory. He decided that he had accomplished both and at 3:30 P.M. ordered a withdrawal from the battlefield. John Green's 4th Virginia, which had not been committed, was brought up to cover the withdrawal, which was "conducted with order and regularity," wrote Charles Stedman. It bothered Greene that he had to abandon his artillery, but all the draught horses had been killed. What was important, the army was unbowed. Their morale unbroken, the Continentals tramped off, ready to fight another day. Greene's army had suffered seventy-nine killed and 184 wounded, about a mere six percent casualty rate. Of the 1,046 missing, 885 were militia—gone home.[14]

There was still some fighting to the east where Light Horse Harry Lee was conducting his private war, but that petered out and ended when Lee took his Legion to look for Greene and left Campbell and his Virginians to shift for themselves. This embittered Campbell, for Tarleton suddenly appeared and, with no cavalry to oppose him, charged the riflemen and routed them, he wrote, "with confusion and loss." The commander of Regiment von Bose, Colonel du Puy, told Howard in Philadelphia after hostilities ceased that he "lost a number of men . . . and that his regiment would have been cut up if Tarleton had not so seasonably come to his relief."[15]

At the main line the fighting ended with Greene's orderly withdrawal from the battlefield. Cornwallis at first ordered a pursuit by the Fusiliers and the Highlanders but quickly recalled them. His army was in no condition to pursue. Behind him, around him, lay hundreds of dead and wounded British soldiers. It was a notable victory he and they had won, as fine it has been said as any in the long British annals of war. The performance of the rank and file had been magnificent, their officers had conducted themselves with their usual contempt for death. But for what purpose? They had taken over twenty-seven percent casualties: ninety-three killed in action, 413 wounded of whom fifty died during the night, twenty-six missing. The casualty rate of the Guards alone was fifty percent. Cornwallis had set out in January with between 3,200 and 3,300 men. Despite Tarleton's disaster at Cowpens he had pushed on with some 2,550 men. Now his force was reduced to slightly over 1,400 effectives, and they were no longer fit to campaign. Charles, 2nd Earl Cornwallis, had ruined his army.[16]

Had His Lordship managed after Guilford Courthouse to extricate himself from the mess he had made of the campaign, had the British eventually forced George Washington to abandon the field, had the Revolution simply petered out, Nathanael Greene would have been forever damned as the hesitant, timid commander who had Cornwallis reeling and failed to destroy him. Benedict Arnold would have gone for the jugular. Daniel Morgan, not reckless as was Arnold, probably would have maintained better control of the action and seized the main chance. Given the inspirational qualities each brought to a battlefield, their power over the minds and emotions of men, it is not unreasonable to speculate that Morgan or Arnold would have succeeded. Greene's courage was unquestioned, and at Guilford Courthouse he was nearly captured when he "rode into the heat of the action full tilt directly in the Midst of the enemy."

But Nathanael Greene was neither a first-rate tactician nor a charismatic battle commander.[17] He was a cool strategist of the first order and always had uppermost in mind that he could not, he must not, lose the army. Another American army lost inside a year? The thought itself was unacceptable. It could have meant losing all. There is more than one example in history of certain victory turning into sudden, inexplicable defeat. A misunderstood order, the death of a commander, a superhuman effort by the enemy . . . any one of a number of things can lead to the unexpected. As one follows the course of the battle and comes to the climax, one must admit a yearning for Greene to roll the dice, to crush Cornwallis once and for all. But as Greene's cool head prevailed, so must ours.

Tactically, by a narrow margin, Lord Cornwallis had won the Battle of Guilford Courthouse. Strategically, by a wide margin, Nathanael Greene had set up Cornwallis for an even worse disaster, and laid the firm foundation on which he would proceed to win the campaign for the Carolinas.

"I never saw such fighting since God made me"

The day had been bright and crisp. As night fell the weather turned. The "rain fell in torrents," wrote Charles Stedman. "Near fifty of the wounded . . . sinking under their aggravated miseries, expired before the morning. The cries of the wounded and dying, who remained on the field of action during the night, exceed all description." They had no tents—all had gone onto the great bonfire at Ramsour's Mill—and there were too few "houses near the field of battle to receive the wounded." The British troops had last eaten about 4:00 P.M. the day before the battle, and Stedman reported that they did not eat again until about the same time the day after the battle, "and then but a scanty allowance, not exceeding one quarter of a pound of flower, and the same quantity of very lean beef." Another participant, Light Horse Harry Lee, wrote, "The night succeeding this day of blood was rainy, dark, and cold; the dead unburied, the wounded unsheltered, the groans of the dying and the shrieks of the living cast a deeper shade over the gloom of nature."[18]

Charles O'Hara writing about one month later to the Duke of Grafton was equally gloomy: "I never did, and hope I never shall, experience two such days and Nights as those immediately after the Battle, we remained on the very ground on which it had been fought cover'd with Dead, with Dying and with hundreds of wounded, Rebels as well as our own—a violent and constant Rain that lasted above Forty hours made it equally impracticable to remove or administer the smallest comfort to many of the Wounded." But a surgeon did find time to amputate the index and middle fingers of Banastre Tarleton's right hand.[19]

There was little doubt among the participants on the British side of what the battle had meant. A young British officer, Francis Dundas, wrote home on 3 April that they had held the field, but, "I must own, without any brilliant advantage arising from it." It remained for Charles O'Hara, however, to paint the bleakest picture of the result of Cornwallis's failure. "I wish it had produced one substantial benefit to Great Britain, on the contrary, we feel at the moment the sad and fatal effects our loss on that Day, nearly one half of our best Officers and Soldiers were either killed or wounded, and what remains are so completely worn out by the excessive Fatigues of the campaign, in a march of above a thousand miles, most of them barefoot, naked and for days together living upon Carrion which they had often not time to dress, and three or four ounces of ground Indian corn has totally destroyed this Army—entre nous, the Spirit of our little army has evaporated a good deal. No zeal or courage is equal to the constant exertions we are making. Tho you will not find it in the Gazette, every part of our Army was beat repeatedly, on the 15th March, and were obliged to fall back twice." Never publicly, but privately in a letter of 10 April to General Phillips, Cornwallis also admitted that "we had not a regiment or corps that did not at some time give way." And he is reported to have said, "I never saw such fighting since God made me. The Americans fought like demons."[20]

Three days after the battle the commander of the men who had "fought like demons" knew that although he had narrowly lost the battle he had accomplished his purpose. "The battle was long, obstinate, and bloody," Nathanael Greene wrote to Joseph Reed of Pennsylvania. "We were obligd to give up the ground and lost our Artillery. But the enemy have been so soundly beaten, that they dare not move towards us since the action; notwithstanding we lay within ten miles of him for two days. Except the ground and the Artillery, they have gained no advantage, on the contrary they are little short of being ruined." He admitted that "I have never felt an easy moment since the enemy crossed the Catawba until . . . the defeat of the 15th, but now I am perfectly easy, being perswaded it is out of the enemies power to do us any great injury."[21]

As he had been right so often, Greene was right once again. The British army stayed two days at Guilford Courthouse. On the second day seventeen wagons loaded with wounded were sent back the way they had come to the Quaker settlement at New Garden. Later that day the camp followers left. The more serious cases were given an extra day of rest. The next morning, Sunday, 18 March, Lord Cornwallis issued a proclamation declaring a "compleat victory" and invited the King's Friends to rise and join the victorious British army in sealing the King's rule. At noon the column marched for New Garden, which they reached the next day. His troops were so tired Cornwallis gave them a two-day rest. Seventy of the wounded could travel no farther and it was decided to leave them in the care of the Quaker community. This was Tory country, and Cornwallis described in a letter to Clinton the reaction of the King's Friends who came and observed an army that did not give the appearance of having won a "compleat victory." "Many of the inhabitants rode into camp, shook me by the hand, said they were glad to see us, and to hear that we had beat Greene, and then rode home again; for I could not get one hundred men in all the regulator's country to stay with us, even as militia."[22]

Leaving the kindly Quaker community, the army made a slow, painful march to the hamlet of Cross Creek (modern Fayetteville), at the head of navigation of the Cape Fear River. Cornwallis reported to Clinton: "With a third of my army sick and wounded . . . the remainder without shoes and worn down with fatigue, I thought it was time to look for some place of rest and refitment." Many of the wounded officers, including O'Hara, were unable to ride and endured swaying horse litters, but they must have been better than the jolting wagons in which the other ranks suffered. At Cross Creek, home of Scottish

Highlanders, who were loyal but had suffered overwhelming defeat early in the war at Moore's Creek Bridge, Cornwallis expected food and assistance. But he found, "to my great mortification, and contrary to all former acounts, that it was impossible to procure any considerable quantity of provisions, and that there was not four days forage within twenty miles." His Lordship also discovered that hopes are no substitute for proper reconnaissance carried out by trusted lieutenants, the kind of ground-laying for campaigning at which Nathanael Greene excelled. "The navigation of Cape Fear, with the hopes of which I had been flattered, was totally impracticable, the distance from Wilmington by water being one hundred and fifty miles, the breadth of the river seldom exceeding one hundred yards, the banks generally high, and the inhabitants on each side most universally hostile." For Rebel militia in an area thought to be controlled by the King's Friends occupied the high banks and peppered supply boats with such hot fire they all turned back to Wilmington. "Under these circumstances," Cornwallis continued, "I determined to move immediately to Wilmington."[23]

Five officers died of their wounds on this leg of the journey. One was irreplaceable. In Elizabethtown, North Carolina, the army buried Lieutenant Colonel James Webster. Cornwallis mourned him deeply. "I have lost my scabbard," he said.[24]

On 7 April the exhausted survivors of Lord Cornwallis's "mad scheme" arrived at Wilmington. The day before Nathanael Greene, who had shadowed Cornwallis on his march to a safe haven, wheeled his army south and marched for South Carolina, which he would liberate after more conflicts "long, obstinate, and bloody." Cornwallis, however, had all he wanted of the Carolinas. He wrote to General Phillips, "I assure you that I am quite tired of marching about the country in quest of adventures." As he had once thought the key to holding South Carolina was the suppression of rebellion in North Carolina, he now decided that the key to the entire rebellion was to abandon the Carolinas, abandon New York, and "bring our whole force into Virginia; we then have a stake to fight for, and a successful battle may give us America."[25]

On 25 April 1781 Lord Cornwallis, relinquishing his responsibility to secure Charleston and South Carolina, pursuing his delusion of a grand, climactic battle, turned his worn and decimated army northward where he found more adventures and fulfilled his American destiny in a village in Virginia called Yorktown.

The Major Characters
(in Order of Appearance)
and What Happened to Them

SIR HENRY CLINTON (1730–1795)

Sir Henry became the scapegoat for the loss of America. Recalled to England in 1782, he had thirteen years to live and spent them defending himself to whoever would listen to his monologues or read endless pages of self-justification. It is easy to imagine people attempting to avoid him on the street. He once met his friend Sir John Jervis and went on so long that later he felt constrained to write a letter in defense of his outburst. "What possessed me I know not, to do so on a public street. The fact is this: I have found few friends who are willing to give due attention to me, still fewer to whom I wish to communicate . . . and not one among them all whose good opinion I am more anxious of preserving than that of S J Jervis. Thus circumstanced—having much to say to you, seldom seeing you—it was natural to suppose I should not miss so fair an opportunity as you gave me. . . . Nor can you now be quit without giving me one full hour's patient hearing at such time as you shall please to name." Sir John declined, and Sir Henry did not take it amiss, for his saving grace was a firm grasp on reality. He chewed the subject to death but he did not allow his obsession, which he well knew to be an obsession, to ruin the years left to him or the lives of his households. He accepted Sir John's rebuff with good humor and candor: "I know I am a horrid *bore*, and therefore do not in the least take it ill, my good friend, that you do not wish to hear me."[1]

Sir Henry divided his time between two households: his legitimate family, overseen by his sister-in-law, Elizabeth Carter, in a house in Portland Place; and in Paddington where his mistress, Mary O'Callaghan Baddeley, whom he had met in Boston in 1775, presided with the several children they had together. In his will Clinton provided handsomely for Mary and the children. When his sons by Harriet were not away at Eton he spent much time with them in London and a leased country house. There were also frequent dinner invitations as well as his own dinner parties in Portland Place. He strongly opposed his daughter Augusta's choice for a husband, but after she eloped he soon accepted the couple's plea for forgiveness and received them into the family.

Had Clinton shown similar wisdom in handling his obsession his life would have gone much more smoothly and perhaps rewards would have been his. But that is an easy position for an outsider who has not experienced being made a scapegoat for disaster to take. From his arrival in England, despite his busy family and social life nothing deterred him from the campaign to regain his reputation. He spent the years remaining to him writing an apologia that was not ready for the printer when he died and remained unpublished until 1954. But he also wrote letter after letter, memorandum after memorandum, arguing ad infinitum that others, not he, were responsible for the loss of the Thirteen Colonies. He bore a good share of the blame, of course, but there was plenty to go around. Yet all the others except General Gage, who was dying, received positions and honors. Even the Howe brothers were honored—Sir William became the Lieutenant General of Ordnance, his brother First Lord of the Admiralty. Lord Cornwallis's American career contributed to Sir Henry's daydreams of an abject Cornwallis confessing to him that "All, all gave way to my ambition." Contemplating his fate, he wrote in 1789 to his nephew, " I have been disgraced for trying to save what others have been rewarded for losing."

In the beginning Sir Henry thought all would be well, for he claimed that in his audience with the King, George III burst out, "Come, come, you acknowledge Lord Cornwallis rambled about, lost himself, and did not know what he was doing. He advised me to be quiet, and truth would at last come out." But when he witnessed the king on the very next day greet Lord Cornwallis with the same warmth, the same friendliness, his faith in the monarch disappeared. He engaged in a war of pamphlets with Cornwallis that he lost. He sought a peerage but it came to nothing. Deeply hurt, haunted by his fate, year after year he churned out countless writings to himself that were not even part of his official apologia. But he much preferred an audience and cornered friends and anyone who would listen to his interminable monologues.

Slowly, through a few friends and acquaintances of eminent rank, he was drawn back into political and military affairs. Through Lord Percy, who succeeded his father as 2nd Duke of Northumberland, Sir Henry entered the House of Commons and gained access to the company of the Prince of Wales, who was once heard calling out loudly to a mutual friend, "I have a *very great regard indeed for Sir Henry!*" He gave a confidential report to the king on the war of Austria and Prussia against revolutionary France and submitted it in writing to the prince. But it was not until July 1794, with the help of the king's younger brother, the Duke of Clarence, who thought Clinton "an able and an honourable man" who "has been very ill-used," that Sir Henry finally received an offer "worthy of acceptance," the governorship of Gibraltar, where twenty-five years before he had served as a colonel.

But he never returned to the Rock. A month later Clinton became ill. He lingered for a year and a half and died three days before Christmas 1795. Of America and its loss Sir Henry once wrote, "I confess it haunts me," and he spent the years after his return to England repeating that theme in one way or another: "I confess it haunts me."

BANASTRE TARLETON (1754–1833)

Tarleton had one last hurrah. In Virginia Cornwallis loosed Tarleton and the Legion on sweeping raids into the interior. At Monticello he came within a whisker of capturing Governor Thomas Jefferson, who was warned in time and fled. The mission also revealed what the army thought of Tarleton. Cornwallis ordered the 2nd Battalion of Fraser's Highlanders to march with the Legion under Tarleton's command. Charles Stedman reported that the officers, still embittered by the fate of their sister battalion at Cowpens, "drew up a remonstrance and presented it to Cornwallis, stating their unwillingness to serve under Tarleton, from a recollection of his conduct at the Cowpens." Cornwallis did not press the issue and sent another unit in place of the Highlanders.[2]

After that it was all downhill. In his final combat action in America his horse went down, pinning him, and only quick action by his men saved him from being run through by a French lancer. He would reward them many years later by libeling them as "bad materials." After Cornwallis surrendered at Yorktown, Tarleton was subjected to indignities by the Americans, and his life was probably in danger. One story has it that he was riding down Yorktown's main street on his magnificent black charger when an American countryman stopped him, claimed the horse was his, made the former terror of the Carolinas dismount, and rode off, leaving Tarleton in the dust. As was customary in the eighteenth century, the officers of the victorious American and French armies invited the officers of Cornwallis's defeated army to a series of dinner parties. Every British officer received a dinner invitation. Except one. Tarleton. He was outraged and complained about his treatment to the French. He feared enough for his life that he sought French protection, which was granted by the comte de Rochambeau, but not without a stinging remark: "Colonel Tarleton has no merit as an officer—only that bravery that every grenadier has—but is a butcher and a barbarian."[3]

Incredibly, this man, despised by friend and foe alike, who had led British regulars to their only clear-cut defeat of the war in a formal, open-field battle, returned to adulation in England. Had he behaved wisely, he might well have overcome his reputation and gone on to other fields of glory and a place of honor among British soldiers. But in the end character told, although for some years his star, if not shining brightly, flickered intermittently and kept him in the public eye.

He arrived home early in 1782. Everywhere he went he was the center of attention. On 2 February Edward Jerningham wrote to his brother, "The famous Tarleton looks as young as when you knew him at Norwich. He is much in vogue. He is invited, known or unknown, to all the assemblies; and wherever he stands a circle is formed." Sir Joshua Reynolds painted his portrait. It was in the Royal Academy exhibition (Cat. # 139) that year, along with another by Gainsborough. What a pity the Gainsborough portrait is lost, for Gainsborough was not as flattering to his subjects as Reynolds. In late May 1782 the American Tory Samuel Curwen, "Returning through St. James Park and seeing many people collected around the rails of Buckingham stopt to see the Prince of Wales who soon appeared in a phaeton with Colonel Tarleton who I was told is frequently to be seen with him." Curwen's information was correct. Tarleton had been drawn into the dissolute circle surrounding the heir to the throne, and the two men remained on intimate terms until the Prince, by then George IV, died. Tarleton's mistress, the well-known actress and author Mary Robinson, popularly known as Perdita, had been intended for the royal bed, but the Prince had a change of heart and passed her on to Tarleton. They had a long and eventually stormy relationship.[4]

Opinion on Tarleton was not unanimous. A cartoon attributed to the caricaturist James Gillray appeared in August; it satirized the Reynolds portrait and insulted Tarleton, his mistress, and his new patron with broad sexual and other innuendo. Horace Walpole remarked: "Tarleton boasts of having slaughtered more men and lain with more women than anybody else in the army," to which Sheridan, who had known Tarleton before the war at Middle Temple, replied: "Lain with! What a weak expression! He should have said ravished. Rapes are the relaxation of murderers!"[5]

Gambling, drinking, and wenching, normal pastimes of the Prince's circle, occupied Tarleton for some years, but he also hoped to continue his military career. Cornwallis went to India in 1786, and Tarleton wanted to go as His Lordship's cavalry commander. But he had become an ardent Whig, and the British East India Company would have no part of such a political animal. That avenue closed, the following year Tarleton published his apologia, which was, in addition to everything else, a disgraceful assault on his former chief and patron, Lord Cornwallis. Roderick McKenzie, the Scottish officer wounded and taken prisoner at Cowpens, immediately published a scathing criticism. In one sentence, McKenzie neatly summarized Tarleton's version of the war: "From too great attention to his own exploits, Lieutenant Colonel Tarleton pays not that decent regard to those of others, which historical truth indispensably requires." He was never able to rid himself of the ghost of Cowpens, for though he always denied being at fault, how interesting that in the second edition of his *History*, in a preface summarizing the campaigns from 1776 through 1781, Cowpens is not mentioned.[6]

From 1790 until 1812, with the exception of one year, he represented Liverpool in the House of Commons, where he was noted for posing as a military expert and for his steadfast defense of the slave trade. At rallies he was famous for raising his right hand to reveal the stump where once were fingers lost at Guilford Courthouse, and crying out, "For King and country!"[7] His bête noir was Sir Arthur Wellesley, who became the Duke of Wellington and Britain's greatest soldier since Marlborough. Tarleton continually attacked Wellesley in the House, and on at least one occasion made a fool of himself. He was also ridiculed for stating during a debate that one day he hoped to have the pleasure of discussing battles with Napoleon.

While he watched men of his generation with whom he had served in America make names for themselves in the wars against the French, his own military career languished. He was promoted to Major General in 1794 and General in 1812, but he served in domestic backwaters and never again saw action. He hungered for the rewards being handed out to his contemporaries. But he had made too many enemies with his attacks on Cornwallis, who had done very well in India, and Wellesley, who was on his way to enshrinement in the British pantheon, and he jumped parties twice. Said Lord Grey, leader of the Whigs, "He has not behaved well in politics." Neither party endorsed him in 1812. He received five votes.[8]

In 1815 Tarleton did not appear on the long list of new Knights of the Bath, rewards for victory over Napoleon, and his appeals were rejected. He then asked the Duke of York for a baronetcy, and on 23 January 1816 he became Sir Banastre Tarleton, Baronet. Perhaps that made up some for the gout from which he had suffered since his forties, and the beginning of arthritis. His final reward came in 1820, when his old friend the Prince Regent became George IV. In the honors handed out for the coronation, Sir Banastre finally became a Knight Grand Cross of the Order of Bath, and with the other knights marched in the coronation procession.

He lingered for another thirteen years, too infirm to attend the coronation of William IV in 1830, and toward the end "confined by gout to his chair." Death came at his home in Shropshire on 16 January 1833. The London papers took little notice.[9]

LORD CORNWALLIS (1738–1805)

The Yorktown campaign is not part of our story, but it was very much part of His Lordship's career.[10] After continuing the plundering of Tidewater and Piedmont, Virginia, that had been going on before his arrival, Cornwallis almost caught a vulnerable American army under Lafayette at Green River. The preliminaries were very neatly done, showing once again that Cornwallis in America should have stuck to the battlefield and left strategy to others. But nightfall and spirited resistance by the American van saved the Rebel army.

Cornwallis then moved on to Yorktown. On the afternoon of 5 September the French and British fleets off the Chesapeake Capes inflicted approximately equal damage on each other. But in one of history's decisive naval battles, the French scored a strategic victory by forcing the British navy to abandon its Chesapeake station. When that happened, Lord Cornwallis, his army, and the first British empire were as good as finished. The Franco-American army under Washington, on the march from New York, arrived in late September and opened siege operations on 6 October. With any chance of seaborne relief blocked by de Grasse's fleet, and the flimsy defenses he had erected unable to withstand the battering of heavy siege guns, Cornwallis made a weak defense, giving up his outer works without even a fight. On 17 October 1781 a British drummer climbed onto the parapet of the hornwork and beat for a parley. It was the fourth anniversary of Burgoyne's surrender at Saratoga.

Cornwallis had first ruined his army, then lost it, and with it America. One would think his career finished. One could picture him slinking home in disgrace. Quite the contrary, for history is not about justice. Like Tarleton, Cornwallis went home a hero, at Exeter actually carried on the shoulders of an adoring public. But Tarleton's status was ephemeral, His Lordship's permanent. Cornwallis had powerful friends, more powerful than Clinton's, and with the fall of Lord North and his ministry they came to power. The right place to be at a time of shifting alliances and the passage of power was London. Cornwallis arrived home on 22 January 1782. Clinton did not return until five months later. While Sir Henry sat in New York waiting for his successor, scribbling away, thinking dark thoughts, Cornwallis cemented his position. Clinton's friend Sir John Jervis wrote him an ominous letter about Cornwallis's reception. "No officer was ever so popular under misfortune as he. The officers who served with him sound his praises beyond example, the Court flatters him, and John Bull is delighted with the blood spilt under his Lordship's auspices."[11] Cornwallis's ability to survive a disaster largely of his own making is a wonder to behold. It went beyond his powerful friends, as important as they were. It also went beyond the very different personalities of Cornwallis and Clinton. Unlike Clinton, Cornwallis was not a querulous man. After his initial ripostes in the pamphlet war, he remained dignified and silent while Clinton quickly became a bore. But the key factor in Cornwallis's retention of favor was the king. George III had always liked Cornwallis, and His Lordship's disastrous Carolina campaign followed by the debacle of Yorktown had not diminished his regard. Lord Cornwallis, the king decided, was not at fault.

In 1786, Cornwallis was given a plum. He went to India as Governor General and Commander in Chief of Bengal. It was a second chance, and he made the most of it. In America he had the reputation of being an indifferent administrator who, according to General Alexander Leslie, "never had time to settle anything."[12] In India, however, in addition to the normal responsibility of protecting British interests, he had arrived with instructions to reform the system of land taxation, and he did not ignore his new master, the British East India Company, as he had Sir Henry. He established a rational system, and he also reformed the criminal justice system. These were responsibilities that would have bored him to distraction in America. They probably bored him in India too. But in India he did not neglect them.

He remained, however, a soldier burning with ambition, but with a critical difference in approach. His American education had been dearly bought, but adversity had tempered the steel within him, and he emerged from that maelstrom a wiser, more cautious man. He never again faced a general of Nathanael Greene's caliber. But in India he also encountered vast distances, enervating heat, a harsh if different terrain, a warrior people, and a fierce, then famous enemy, Tippoo Sahib, Sultan of Mysore. In 1791 Tippoo invaded and ravaged the lands of the Raja of Travancore, who was under British protection. Properly provoked, Cornwallis took personal command of the army in the field. Unlike America, he had strong local allies and the able assistance of English residents at Indian courts. Conspicuous also during the long, hot march to Mysore was His Lordship's close attention to logistics. Never again did Cornwallis burn his entire baggage train. He invaded Mysore and stormed and took Bangalore deep in the south of India, advanced on Tippoo's great fortress-capital, Seringapatam, defeated Tippoo's hordes, and drove the Sultan inside his fortress. Tippoo Sahib capitulated and by treaty ceded half of his lands.

The 2nd Earl Cornwallis returned to England in 1793 in triumph and was rewarded with a marquessate and the position of Master General of Ordnance. In 1798 the 1st Marquess Cornwallis became Lord Lieutenant of Ireland. During his tenure in that turbulent and unhappy land the Act of Union was passed by Parliament. It was largely the work of his lieutenant, Castlereagh, but Cornwallis strongly supported him, and he was especially firm in supporting Castlereagh's efforts to push through the necessary twin to Union: Catholic emancipation. But George III was as stubborn and wrong-headed about Ireland as he had been about America. Pitt resigned and Cornwallis followed, explaining his action in a letter of 15 February 1801: "No consideration could induce me to take a responsible part with any administration who can be so blind to the interest, and indeed to the immediate security of their country, as to persevere in the old system of proscription and exclusion in Ireland."[13]

In 1802, Cornwallis was sent to the Continent to serve as ambassador plenipotentiary in negotiating the Treaty of Amiens with France. As unfit for a diplomatic role as he had been for independent command in America, he was no match as a negotiator for Joseph Bonaparte and Talleyrand. But England wanted peace and Cornwallis was but a servant of his government. Besides, everyone knew that it was only a truce.

The Marquess Cornwallis returned to India for a second tenure as Governor General in 1805, aged sixty-seven. He was not well, and on his way up-country took ill and died 5 October 1805 in Ghazipore. Perhaps fitting for a man who spent so much of his life serving in foreign places, he lies there. A mausoleum was built over his remains, and there is a statue of him in St. Paul's. The estimate of Cornwallis in the *Dictionary of National Biography* has alway appealed to me, not because it is true for his entire career, but because there is enough truth in it and gets closer to the mark in fewer words than longer summaries: "If not a man of startling genius, he was a clear-sighted statesman and an able general, as well as an upright English gentleman."

THOMAS SUMTER (1734–1832)

"In war he was a politician, and in politics he was an old soldier," wrote Sumter's biographer Anne King Gregorie over sixty years ago, and if the truth of that statement has not yet been made apparent, Sumter's subsequent behavior leaves no room for doubt.[14] Following the disappearance of Cornwallis into North Carolina in pursuit of Morgan and Greene, Sumter once more took the field. He was the senior South Carolina general, and Governor John Rutledge, knowing his men, wrote very diplomatic letters to Marion and Pickens requesting that they cooperate with Sumter. It was now Sumter's turn to experience treatment similar to that to which he had subjected Morgan. Three times he wrote to Marion requesting cooperation, but from the dark swamps of the Santee and the Pee Dee there was only silence.

While trying to bring Marion under his wing, Sumter engaged in a futile expedition against British posts on the Santee. Between 19 and 28 February he attacked in succession Fort Granby near modern Columbia; Belleville, thirty-five miles downriver; and Fort Watson, which was perched on an Indian mound that now overlooks the flooded lands of the old Santee on the shore of Lake Marion. Each attempt failed, and at Fort Watson his repulse was bloody. Retreating upriver, Sumter stopped at his plantation at Great Savannah to collect his crippled wife and only child. On 6 March his column was attacked by Major Thomas Fraser commanding South Carolina Tories. Who won or whether it was a draw depends on the source. Whatever the case, Sumter kept retreating until he reached the relative safety of the High Hills of Santee, and it was not a happy column that he led there. Marion had been wise to stay clear of the Gamecock's grandiose plan.

Sumter now came up with a scheme to raise troops for a much longer period than militia usually stayed in the field. He set out to raise regiments of state troops to serve for a period of ten months. It was to plague him for decades after the war because of his method of paying the men. Each man was to receive one or more black slaves, depending on his rank, as well as other loot. It was known as Sumter's law, and has been almost universally condemned since he established it—not because it encouraged traffic in blacks, for they were then property, but because it encouraged plunder, either organized or freelance. Even his ardent champion, the South Carolina historian Edward McCrady, admitted that it was not a success and that Sumter raised few men under the scheme.

After Guilford Courthouse and the return of the Continental Army to South Carolina, Nathanael Greene was assiduous in his courtship of Sumter, hoping that he would cooperate and join forces against Lord Rawdon. But at the first opportunity, despite Greene's urgent requests, Sumter ignored him in favor of freebooting. Not long afterward Greene said to William Richardson Davie, "Sumter refuses to obey my orders, and carries off with him all the active force of this unhappy State on rambling predatory expeditions unconnected with the operations of the army."[15] Following further difficulties between these two strong personalities, Sumter resigned, but Greene courted him and the Gamecock withdrew his resignation. This turned out to be unfortunate, for a little over two months later Sumter sent many a good man to his death in the debacle at Quinby Bridge.

On 17 July 1781 a British force took up a strong position protected by an artillery piece and buildings and fencing at Quinby Bridge on the Shubrick Plantation, some thirty miles from Charleston. Marion and Lee had reconnoitered before Sumter came up with his partisans late in the afternoon. They advised that the British position was too strong to attack. Sumter disagreed and formed a battle line for his favorite tactic: frontal assault. Marion and Lee begged him to at least wait until their own artillery piece, a six-pounder, arrived, but he refused. In the fighting that followed the Americans were defeated with costly losses, especially to Marion's Brigade and the regiment of Colonel Thomas Taylor, a Sumter lieutenant. The rest of Sumter's forces fired from the protection of buildings and did not take part in the assault.

Quinby Bridge was the end of the line for Sumter as a commander. Light Horse Harry Lee, in disgust and without a farewell or by your leave, marched off with his Legion to Greene's camp in the High Hills of Santee, where he told the commanding general precisely what he thought of Thomas Sumter. Francis Marion gathered his dead and wounded and left for familiar haunts. It remained, however, for a man who had faithfully followed Sumter since the early desperate days to deliver a scathing rebuke that echoes down the centuries. Colonel Thomas Taylor's son told Lyman Draper that his father walked up to Sumter, who was sitting under a shade tree, and said, "Sir, I don't know why you sent me forward on a forlorn hope, promising to sustain me, & failed to do so, unless you designed to sacrifice me. I will never more serve under you."[16]

Following Quinby Bridge Sumter disbanded his force and retired to North Carolina for the summer. This infuriated Greene, who eventually dismounted Sumter's men. Governor Rutledge returned to South Carolina in August, and one of his first acts was to put an end to Sumter's Law. After the war Sumter faced lawsuits for the plundering that had occurred under his scheme, but the legislatures of South and North Carolina enacted legislation forbidding courts to accept suits for losses under Sumter's Law.

Sumter served in the House and the Senate. A Jeffersonian who opposed Jefferson, he was nevertheless able to obtain for his son Thomas appointments as Secretary of the Legation to France and Minister to first Portugal and then Brazil. But in the first Congress he also used his influence in a dishonorable way. Toward the end of the war Nathanael Greene had incurred large personal debts to supply the army in South Carolina, and his widow petitioned Congress for indemnification. In January 1792 Sumter rose in the House to deny that she had a valid claim, and made it clear in his concluding remarks that his reason was revenge for Greene's unfavorable writings about the Carolina militia. Otho Holland Williams thought the speech shameful and was so indignant that he resolved to publish a reply. Apparently whatever he wrote was not published, but despite the efforts of Sumter and congressional allies Caty Greene rightfully received indemnification for debts that the general had incurred for the cause.

Thomas Sumter died in 1832, aged ninety-eight, vigorous to the end, having taken his customary horseback ride that day. He was the oldest surviving general of the War of the Revolution. He and his wife Mary are buried in a lovely spot in the High Hills of Santee, surrounded by family. Their only child married a French woman, Nathalie de Delage de Volude, and she and Thomas, Jr. lie with them. On Sumter's tomb is a memorial to two of his descendants, Charles and Etienne de Fontenay, both of whom in 1916 died for France.

If he was one of the Revolution's more unlikable characters, as a soldier a poor tactician and strategist, as a subordinate guilty of insubordination that imperiled operations, let it also not be forgotten that at the very darkest time in South Carolina he, unlike so many others, scorned parole, took the field in what appeared a hopeless cause, and raised a standard that inspired men to sacrifice and others to emulate him. Cornwallis paid him his finest tribute when he described the Gamecock as his greatest plague.

HORATIO GATES (1728–1806)

It should come as no surprise to the reader to learn that after Camden Gates never again commanded in the field. On being relieved at Charlotte, Gates requested that General Greene convene a court of inquiry into his conduct at Camden to clear his name of imputations of mismanagement and misconduct. But Greene, who had no time for military niceties, was able to decline on the ground that he did not have enough general officers on hand to serve on the court. Gates then went home to Traveller's Rest. He could not be employed in the army until the matter was settled, because Congress had passed a resolution calling for an inquiry, and for the next two years he pressed for it.

Home could not have been a happy place. His only child Bob had died on 4 October 1780, while he was in the South. Relations with his old friend Charles Lee became strained and finally broke when Gates's wife unwisely challenged the articulate, rapier-tongued soldier. In her cups at dinner, she demanded that Lee support her in an argument. Lee got up from the table and said, "I think, madam, that you're a tragedy in private life and a farce to all the world." He then put on his hat and walked out of Traveller's Rest for the last time.[17]

In 1782 Congress repealed its resolution calling for a court of inquiry and allowed Gates to take service in the army at Washington's direction. Washington ordered him to report for duty at Army Headquarters at Newburgh, New York, where he was the ranking general after the great Virginian. There he became involved, to an extent that remains uncertain, in a dangerous affair that required Washington's personal intervention.

The Newburgh Conspiracy remains so shadowy that the word conspiracy may be an exaggeration. It had its roots in the perilous condition of public finances and its effect on the army, which had not been paid since 1781, and the concern of its officers that Congress abide by its promise of half pay for life following discharge. Failure to reach agreement and deep suspicion between the army and Congress resulted in the appearance in camp in the spring of 1783 of two anonymous Newburgh Addresses, one of which was inflammatory, threatening Congress with dire consequences should the officers' demands not be met. Deeply involved in the affair were Gates's aide-de-camp, his former aide-de-camp, and a close friend of the Hero of Saratoga. But at a general meeting of officers held on 15 March, the crisis passed when the greatest American of his age, George Washington, dramatically proclaimed the primacy of civil authority.

Gates's role? We do not know for certain. His deserved reputation for intrigue begs his inclusion in the conspiracy, if indeed there was a conspiracy for military action against Congress, but the matter rests with the old Scottish verdict of not proven.

In the summer of 1783 Gates's wife died. His offer of marriage the following year to Janet Livingston Montgomery, widow of the gallant General Richard Montgomery, killed in action while leading his troops in the 1776 assault on Quebec, was firmly, if politely, rejected. In July 1786, aged fifty-nine, he married forty-six-year-old Mary Vallance, who had a fortune of 500,000 dollars. They lived happily ever after in a style to which Horatio Gates had long wished to become accustomed. In 1790 he sold Traveller's Rest and moved north. They bought an estate in northern Manhattan and entered New York society. The Gates's spent the rest of their lives living the sweet life and spending or giving away, largely to indigent veterans, most of her fortune, one-fifth of which remained at her death in 1810. Gates served one term in the New York State legislature. His support of Jefferson for president over his old friend and supporter John Adams ended that friendship. Adams confided to his diary, "Gates's resentment against Jay, Schuyler, and Hamilton made him turn against me, who had been the best friend ... he ever had in America." In a 1794 letter to Jefferson, Gates indulged in hypocrisy when he condemned those former friends and supporters who had done so much for him, the New Englanders, for their greed. He had "long known the Character of the Sordid individuals that inhabit their Trading Towns," further stating that "gain is their God, and present gain their Polar Starr, to which they forever Steer." All very well to say for a man who made his fortune by way of the marriage bed.[18]

Gates died on 10 April 1806. He lies in the graveyard of Trinity Church at the head of Wall Street, but his gravesite and remains are lost. He does not have a monument.

FRANCIS MARION (c.1732–1795)

As a classic guerrilla leader Marion's only peers in American history were such great native warriors as Osceola or Cochise. Unlike Sumter, who had grandiose ideas and fancied himself a grand strategist, Marion for the most part engaged in the stock-in-trade of guerrillas throughout the ages: ambushes and hit-and-run raids. He dispersed and disappeared when the odds were against him, and reappeared after his enemies announced that he had been driven from the field. When Cornwallis disappeared into North Carolina in pursuit of the Continental army, Marion, now a brigadier general, immediately engaged the forces under Lord Rawdon. But unlike Sumter's disastrous raid down the Santee, Marion again revealed his mastery of irregular warfare. Also unlike Sumter, his attitude and actions were largely governed by the principle of cooperation. Overall the dark-visaged little genius, as proud a man as Sumter but lacking the Gamecock's overweening ego-ridden personality, put the common cause ahead of himself.

Beginning in the first week of March 1781 and lasting until the 28th, a savage series of fights took place between Marion and Colonel John Watson Tadwell Watson, a British officer of the 3rd Foot Guards (Scots Guards), who was dispatched by Lord Rawdon along the Santee with a 500-man column largely composed of Harrison's Regiment of South Carolina Tory militia, "for the purpose of dispersing the plunderers that infested the eastern frontier." The Watson expedition revealed Marion at his most brilliant as a partisan leader.[19]

Although Watson outnumbered him and he was very short on ammunition, instead of retreating on 6 March he met Watson's column at Wiboo Swamp. He put Colonel Peter Horry with some men on a causeway, while he waited behind with the rest of the brigade in reserve, part of which under Captain Daniel Conyers was concealed in order to take an anticipated British charge in the flank. Horry was finally driven off by Watson's artillery. British cavalry then charged but as planned was attacked by Conyers, who himself killed the officer leading the charge. Captain James McCauley with his command also charged and the British were driven back. Marion and his men then disappeared into the swamp.

A few days later about fifteen miles away at Mount Hope Swamp a similar scenario was enacted. With Peter Horry again commanding Marion's rear guard, Watson was engaged and delayed while Marion's Brigade once more faded away into the gloomy fastness of yet another swamp. But John Watson was a tough professional who would not give up. Trying to give the impression that he would continue down the Santee, Watson headed northeast toward Kingstree, meaning to cross the Lower Bridge of the Black River about five miles below the town. Marion was not fooled. Watson arrived to find that Marion's advance of seventy men under Major John James had beaten him there and partially destroyed the bridge, while the Swamp Fox himself had come up with the rest of the Brigade and deployed to support Major James. With James were thirty riflemen under Captain William McCottry. When Watson found his artillery ineffective from a distance, he moved the guns closer to the river. But McCottry's men picked off the artillerymen. When he then decided to charge across the ford, McCottry aimed at the lead officer, who was waving his sword in the air, and dropped him. His men poured forth a deadly fire that sent Watson's van running. Four men who tried to retrieve the officer's body were also shot down. It was another display of what accurate, long-range rifle fire could do in the right situation and on the right terrain.

Blocked from Kingstree, for about the next ten days Watson bivouacked and rested, but he was continually harassed by Captain Daniel Conyers's cavalry and Captain William McCottry's riflemen; one of the latter, a man named McDonald, is said to have dropped one British officer at 300 yards. Tradition also states that Watson had so many dead he weighted the bodies and sank them in the Black River to hide his true losses. He was certainly in trouble because of casualties and lack of supplies. And all around him, like the terrible mosquitoes of the Low Country, emerging from and then disappearing into the swamps, were Marion's men. The hound had become the hare.

Watson and his command fled for Georgetown. Marion followed and harried him. One party of guerrillas riding ahead of Watson partially destroyed the bridge across the Sampit River, ten miles from Georgetown. There on 28 March Marion caught Watson fording the river, and there the riflemen again took their toll. Watson's horse was shot out from under him, his rear guard was badly cut up, he had twenty men killed, and he rolled into Georgetown with two wagons full of wounded. "I have never seen such shooting before in my life," he said, but thought it quite objectionable that Francis Marion "would not fight like a gentleman or a Christian."[20]

With the return of the Continentals to South Carolina Marion largely acted in concert with Greene's intentions. He once again teamed with Light Horse Harry Lee, and on one of those occasions an incident occurred that revealed that Marion, too, guarded his prerogatives and when necessary forcefully asserted himself. It is also a macabre tale that again reveals the awful consequences of civil war. In mid-May 1781 Marion and Lee besieged and took Fort Motte, a British post on the Congaree River. After the surrender the Rebels began hanging Tories they accused of atrocities. A Tory justice of the peace and militiaman, Levi Smith, was seconds from the hangman's noose. "I had nearly taken farewel of this world," he later wrote, "when . . . I perceived Gen. Marion on horseback with his sword drawn. He asked in a passion what they were doing there. The soldiers answered, 'We are hanging them people, Sir.' He then asked them who ordered them to hang any person. They replied, 'Col. Lee.' " Whereupon the little Swamp Fox took over. " 'I will let you know, damn you, that I command here and not Col. Lee. Do you know if you hang this man Lord Rawdon will hang a good man in his place, that he will hang Sam Cooper who is to be exchanged for him?' " Marion ordered Levi Smith returned to the quarter guard.[21]

Marion's most serious quarrel with Nathanael Greene was over horses, of which Greene was in urgent need. Greene reprimanded Marion quite sharply and criticized the militia taking Tory horses for their own. Marion's reply denied that the horses were taken for private use, then shocked Greene by announcing his intention to resign and seeking permission to go to Philadelphia. Greene scrambled backwards. He could not imagine, he wrote, that Marion could be serious. Yes, Marion replied, "I am very serious." But he sent Greene "a horse for yourself" and promised to send more if possible, and of course he stayed. Not even the price he paid for Sumter's debacle at Quinby Bridge discouraged him to the point of retiring from the fight, and at the fierce Battle of Eutaw Springs, commanding the militia, he and his men showed that they could fight the British in an open field. Greene praised their "firmness" to Congress, and wrote to von Steuben that their "conduct would have graced the veterans of the Great King of Prussia."[22]

Marion's postwar years were uneventful. He served in the State Senate and the South Carolina Constitutional Convention, but he was not politically ambitious. He did not fear retribution from his actions during the war. When the legislature offered him the same protection against lawsuits given Sumter and Pickens, he declined. To his further credit, no one more vigorously opposed confiscation of Tory property. The old partisan's policy was to forget and forgive. His personal fortunes suffered greatly during the war, and he found himself land poor. The legislature came to his assistance and made him commandant of Fort Johnson in Charleston Harbor at 500 pounds a year. In 1786 he married his cousin, Mary Esther Videau. He was fifty-four, she was forty-nine, and it was a first marriage for both of them. She was a large woman with a shrewish temper. According to tradition, whenever he rode up to his home he would take off his hat and sail it through an open window. If it came sailing out again he rode on. But his wife was wealthy and he was never again in want.

In death they lie quietly together with family in a lovely place on a site once part of his brother Gabriel's Belle Isle Plantation, about five miles north of where the Santee once ran free. Befitting the Swamp Fox, the land around is wet. Dogwoods bloom in the spring, and the only sounds are of birds singing.

NATHANAEL GREENE (1742–1786)

Leaving an impotent Cornwallis to lick his wounds in Wilmington, Nathanael Greene fastened on his ultimate objective—the reconquest of South Carolina. It would take about twenty months, but some of the bloodiest fighting of the war was crammed into the period between 25 April and 8 September 1781.

At Hobkirk's Hill, now within the city limits of Camden, Greene met the young but very able Lord Rawdon in battle for the first time. Rawdon had slightly over 8,000 British and Hessian regulars and Tory regulars and militia in South Carolina but they were scattered in the great arc from Charleston to Ninety Six, and at Augusta and Savannah in Georgia. Directly under him at Camden Rawdon had about 800 men fit to serve to face Greene's approximate 1,400, of whom 1,174 were Continentals. In a daring move Lord Rawdon marched out and surprised Greene. But the indomitable Captain Robert Kirkwood and his Delaware company fought a delaying action that gave Greene and the rest of the army precious minutes to dash from their breakfasts and prepare for battle. The American line was advancing toward apparent victory when the probable mishandling followed by misbehavior of the crack 1st Maryland spread to other units and forced Greene to abandon the field.

Both Greene and Rawdon exposed themselves to enemy fire, Greene, recalled the American officer Guilford Dudley, "with his cool intrepidity risking his invaluable person in the thickest of the battle." To save his artillery, Greene dismounted and held his bridle with one hand and helped pull on the ropes with the other. Greene was deeply disappointed but also philosophical over the defeat. "We fight, get beat, rise and fight again," he wrote in an oft-quoted statement. But Lord Rawdon, who won, was still compelled to abandon Camden and pull back to Charleston because of his losses, which he could ill afford, and the operations of Marion and Lee in his rear and Sumter wherever his fancy took him. The "whole interior country had revolted" Rawdon later wrote. As at Guilford Courthouse, Greene had lost the battle and won the prize.[23]

With the major British base at Camden having fallen and by mid-May the line of forts along the Santee in American hands, Greene on 22 May opened the siege of Ninety Six. He had about 1,600 men, mostly Continentals. The British garrison numbered only 550, but 350 were seasoned Tory regulars from the North commanded by the very able Lieutenant Colonel John Harris Cruger of New York. The siege was botched from the beginning, with both Greene and his engineering officer, Thaddeus Kosciuszko revealing their total inexperience with siege operations. By mid-June, with Lord Rawdon approaching with a relief column of 2,000 troops, including three fresh regiments of foot, Greene decided to gamble and storm Ninety Six. But in some of the fiercest bayonet fighting of the war the Rebel forlorn hope was cut to pieces by fellow Americans and forced to retreat.

The next day Greene raised the siege and marched off, defeated once again, while Lord Rawdon marched in to cries of joy and promptly marched out again. Ninety Six could not be held permanently. John Harris Cruger was given the job of destroying what he could and then escorting a long, sad column of Tory refugees to a miserable collection of huts outside Charleston, derisively called Rawdontown. Lord Rawdon himself, ill, physically worn down, gave up his command and sailed for home. The British kept winning battles but losing the campaign.

After resting his army in the High Hills of Santee and collecting reinforcements, Greene and his tireless Continentals marched again. At Eutaw Springs on 8 September 1781, one of the fiercest battles of the war took place, between Greene and the new British field commander, Lieutenant Colonel Alexander Stuart. In three to four hours of bloody seesawing, often hand to hand and with each side suffering heavy casualties, on the verge of victory Continentals and militia found themselves amid untold riches in the British camp and went wild in an orgy of drunken looting. Only John Eager Howard was able to restrain his troops.

Greene had again failed to win a battle, but once again in the long run the British lost, for after Eutaw Springs their army in South Carolina was no longer fit for operations in the field. Eutaw Springs was the last major battle in the Carolinas. It was now truly only a matter of time and attrition.

Nathanael Greene had fought four times, had yet to win his first battle and never would, but he had effectively reconquered the Carolinas, and Georgia would fall into place. He was, wrote Abner Nash, Governor of North Carolina, master of the "peculiar Art of making your Enemies run away from their Victories leaving you master of their Wounded and of all the fertile part of the Country." A British officer wrote, "The more he is beaten the farther he advances in the end."[24] In battle he was brave and decisive but neither a gifted tactician nor an inspirational battle captain. He had first what is absolutely necessary for commanders under intense and ceaseless pressure: mental toughness and physical endurance. High intelligence and exceptional ability are of no avail without them, for the absence of one or both leads to collapse and inability to proceed. His brilliance lay in foresight, precise knowledge of geography, careful planning and preparation with special attention to supply and transport, and the strategic vision of a master soldier. In the end, on the morning of 14 December 1782 the British evacuated Charleston, and that afternoon at 3 o'clock Nathanael Greene entered the city in triumph.

Sadly, it was his final triumph. In order to clothe his soldiers during the winter campaign he had dealt through a merchant named John Banks to buy uniforms on credit from Charleston merchants even while the British still occupied the city. The merchants had a poor opinion of Banks and would not deliver unless Greene signed the promissory notes. He did, and the debts he personally incurred when Banks & Co. failed haunted him to his grave and as we know pursued his widow until the federal government finally indemnified her. After the war Nathanael Greene never knew financial peace. Georgia rewarded him with a splendid plantation, Mulberry Grove, where he and Caty made their home. But he remained land poor. He wrote to Caty on 8 September 1784, "I am not anxious to be rich, but wish to be independent. (For I agree perfectly with Lord Littleton that he that cannot pay his Taylor bill is a dependent character tho even a Lord.) To have a decent income is much to be wished; but to be free from debt more so. I never owned so much property as now, yet never felt so poor."[25]

On the 12th of June 1786, on their way from Savannah to Mulberry Grove, he and Caty stopped at the neighboring plantation of William Gibbons. Under a glaring sun, with neither hat nor umbrella, Greene spent much of the day inspecting Gibbons's rice fields. On his way home later in the day he complained of a headache. On the 13th his head ached all day. It became more intense the following day, right over his eyes, and his forehead swelled. He became depressed and did not want to converse. A doctor bled him but it did no good. His head became very swollen. Another doctor diagnosed sunstroke, applied blisters, and bled him again. Caty sent the children to a neighbor and Greene's old comrade General Anthony Wayne came. Greene sank into a coma. Anthony Wayne, who was mad about Caty and would one day become her lover, maintained a vigil. At 6:00 A.M. 19 June 1786 Nathanael Greene died. He was forty-four. Caty and Wayne were at his bedside.

Anthony Wayne wrote that day to Colonel James Jackson with regard to funeral arrangements and ended with an apology. "Pardon this scrawl; my feelings are but too much affected because I have seen a great and good man die."[26]

DANIEL MORGAN (1735–1802)

Cowpens was Morgan's last fight. But when Cornwallis's army was ravaging parts of Virginia, Morgan took the field once more at the behest of Lafayette, who asked him to raise a force of riflemen and come to his aid. Morgan, who liked the young Frenchman, never hesitated and joined Lafayette's command on 7 July 1781. Morgan and General Anthony Wayne tried to corner Tarleton during one of his raids, but Benny had had quite enough of Morgan and went far out of his way to avoid him. The excessive activity brought on a severe attack of sciatica, and Morgan soon was forced to return home, where he apparently came close to dying.

Morgan's great will to live served him well, however, and he survived and the years were good to him. His daughters Nancy and Betsy gave him nineteen grandchildren, upon whom he doted and to whom he told war stories in language one of them remembered as "powerful and graphic."[27] A non-martial adventure sometime in the mid-1780s resulted in the birth of a son, Willoughby Morgan. The boy's mother is unknown, and Morgan never wrote to him or to our knowledge spoke of him and left him out of his will. The boy resembled his father physically and took after him in compiling a distinguished combat record in the War of 1812. He became a career soldier, attained the rank of Lieutenant Colonel, and died in 1832. In 1782 Morgan completed a personal monument that still stands eleven miles from Winchester. The handsome two-story stone house, today privately owned, he called "Saratoga." Tradition has it that it was built by Hessian prisoners of war.

He engaged in business activities locally and with Eastern merchants. And of course he speculated in land. By 1795 he owned 250,000 acres in various states and territories. At the same time he saw to the good education of his daughters and entertained old army friends who visited him at Saratoga—such familiar names as John Eager Howard, Horatio Gates, and, above all, his closest "old sword," Otho Holland Williams. They were opposites, Williams a frail man, well educated, cultivated, but they truly enjoyed each other's company.

Like most who claw their way from the bottom of the heap, Daniel Morgan craved respectability, and he attained it, along with honors and distinctions enough to please any man. But there was always something of the Old Waggoner in him, and he remained pugnacious to the end. In 1794, during the Whiskey Rebellion in western Pennsylvania, Major General Daniel Morgan led part of the Virginia militia against the rebels. The distinguished Hero of the Revolution wrote to Light Horse Harry Lee, then Governor of Virginia, that at Parkinson's Ferry on the Monongahela River he "was obliged to give the tavern keeper where we lodged a knock on the mouth, for selling whiskey to the soldiers for a dollar a gallon—these sales he kept up nearly all night, and when I told him his fault, he began to treat me with indignity, and I broke his mouth, which closed the business."[28]

Morgan was not cut out to be a congressman. He was elected to the House in 1797 and was a staunch, even rigid Federalist. His most memorable statement during his short political career was his description of the party of Jefferson as a "parsell of Egg sucking dogs." He was too ill to run for reelection in 1799.[29]

It is as a soldier that he must be judged, and only one conclusion can be reached: he was an exceptional field commander, and as a battle captain he would have had few superiors in any age. All the necessary attributes were his: command presence, coolness under fire, uncommon inspirational qualities, and the ability in critical situations to "think on his feet." Contemplation of his military career gives fresh meaning to that tired old word charisma. Add his tactical brilliance and you have a commander of rare gifts.

By the turn of the new century the illnesses that had plagued him in the waning years of the Revolution wracked him once again and persisted. In the final months of his life he became feeble, but the spirit and the will that marked this uncommon man of the common people never died. According to the son of the attending physician, the following conversation took place between Morgan and Doctor Conrad.

"General Morgan, if you have any worldly matters to be settled, I think it is my duty to inform you of the importance of attending to them. I know you have faced death in battle and I presume it will not be a cause of alarm or surprise to you."

Doctor Conrad presumed too much. "Doctor, do you mean that I am about to die?"

"I do."

"Why, won't I live some time, a month or so?"

"I think not, sir."

"Well, a week?"

"I don't think you can possibly last a week."

There was a long silence.

"Doctor, if I could be the man I was when I was twenty-one years of age, I would be willing to be stripped stark naked on the top of the Alleghany Mountains, to run for my life with the hounds of death at my heels."[30]

Daniel Morgan died on 6 July 1802, aged sixty-seven, surrounded by family and friends. The epitaph on his long-lost gravestone expressed the honors due him but was commonplace. His unofficial epitaph, by his old friend and comrade in arms, Light Horse Harry Lee, best described the Hero.

"No man better loved this world, and no man more reluctantly quitted it."[31]

Notes

1. The Battle of Sullivan's Island

1. William B. Willcox, *Portrait of a General: Sir Henry Clinton in the War of Independence* (New York: Knopf, 1964), pp. 66–68, has a brief outline of the plan; a fuller discussion, very good on the political and administrative difficulties, is in Eric Robson, "The Expedition to the Southern Colonies, 1775–1776," *English Historical Review* 66 (October 1951), pp. 535–60.

2. Henry Clinton, *The American Rebellion: Sir Henry Clinton's Narrative of His Campaigns, 1775–1782*, William B. Willcox, ed. (New Haven: Yale University Press, 1954), p. 23.

3. *Ibid.*

4. My brief description of the Moore's Creek Bridge campaign is based on Hugh F. Rankin, *The North Carolina Continentals* (Chapel Hill: University of North Carolina Press, 1971), Ch. 2.

5. Willcox, *Portrait of a General*, pp. 77–84; Franklin and Mary Wickwire, *Cornwallis: The American Adventure* (Boston: Houghton Mifflin, 1970), pp. 81–82; Christopher Ward, *The War of the Revolution*, 2 vols. (New York: Macmillan, 1952), 2: pp. 669–70; Mark M. Boatner, III, *Encyclopedia of the American Revolution*, 3rd Ed. (Mechanicsburg, PA: Stackpole Books, 1994), p. 199.

6. Willcox, *Portrait of a General*, p. 84.

7. *Ibid.*, pp. 85–86; for the battle, William Moultrie, *Memoirs of the American Revolution, So Far as it Related to the States of North and South Carolina, and Georgia*, 2 vols. (Charleston, SC 1821), 1, and John Drayton, *Memoirs of the American Revolution as Relating to the State of South Carolina*, 2 vols. (Charleston, 1821), 2; are indispensable; also important is William B. Willcox, "The Clinton Parker Controversy Over British Failure at Charleston and Rhode Island," in Howard H. Peckham, *Sources of American Independence: Selected Manuscripts from the Collections of the William L. Clements Library*, 2 vols. (Chicago: University of Chicago Press, 1978), 1: pp. 188–210; good secondary accounts are Boatner, *Encyclopedia*, pp. 197–205; Terry W. Lipscomb, *South Carolina Revolutionary War Battles: 1. The Carolina Low Country, April 1775–June 1776* (Columbia: South Carolina Department of Archives & History, 1991), pp. 20–43; and Ward, *War of the Revolution*, 2: pp. 665–78.

8. Drayton, *Memoirs*, 2: p. 311.

9. For the introduction and cultivation of Carolina Gold rice, which got its name from the color of its outer hull, see Duncan Clinch Heyward, *Seed from Madagascar* (Spartanburg, SC: The Reprint Company, 1972; reprint of University of North Carolina Press 1937 edition); William M. Dabney and Marion Dargan, *William Henry Drayton and the American Revolution* (Albuquerque: The University of New Mexico Press, 1962), p. 8.

10. Jeremy Belknap, "Journal of my Tour to the Camp and the Observations I Made There," *Proceedings of the Massachusetts Historical Society, 1858–1860*, 1st Series, 4 (1860), p. 83.

11. John R. Alden, *General Charles Lee: Traitor or Patriot* (Baton Rouge: Louisiana State Press, 1951), p. 104; Charles Francis Adams, ed., *Familiar Letters of John Adams and His Wife Abigail Adams during the Revolution* (Freeport, NY: Books for Libraries Press, 1970; reprint of 1875 edition), p. 79; Thomas Girdlestone, *Facts Tending to Prove that General Lee . . . was the Author of Junius* (London, 1813), pp. iii–iv; John C. Dann, *The Revolution Remembered: Eyewitness Accounts of the War for Independence* (Chicago: The University of Chicago Press, 1980), p. 105.

12. Moultrie, *Memoirs*, 1: p. 141; Dabney and Dargan, *William Henry Drayton*, p. 134.

13. Drayton, *Memoirs*, 2: p. 280; Lipscomb, *Carolina Low Country*, p. 24; Moultrie, *Memoirs*, 1: pp. 141–42.

14. Moultrie, *Memoirs*, 1: p. 143.

15. *Ibid.*, pp. 143–44.

16. *Ibid.*, pp. 144, 158–62.

17. *Ibid.*, p. 173, for Moultrie's gout; Drayton, *Memoirs*, 2: p. 312, on replacing Moultrie.

18. Hinrichs, *Diary*, in Bernard A. Uhlendorf, ed., *The Siege of Charleston . . . Diaries and Letters of Hessian Officers from the Von Jungken Papers in the William L. Clements Library* (Ann Arbor: University of Michigan Press, 1938), p. 325. Clinton, *American Rebellion*, p. 30.

19. A. T. Mahan, *The Major Operations of the Navies in the War of American Independence* (Boston: Little, Brown, 1913), p. 32.

20. Alden, *General Charles Lee*, p. 125; Mahan, *Major Operations*, p. 33; Moultrie, *Memoirs*, 1: p. 312; Drayton, *Memoirs*, 2: p. 282, for the weather.

21. Mahan, *Major Operations*, p. 34; Drayton, *Memoirs*, 2: pp. 282, 291, 296.

22. Moultrie, *Memoirs*, 1: p. 174; Lipscomb, *Carolina Low Country*, p. 28.

23. Lipscomb, *Carolina Low Country*, p. 25, for a modern nautical chart of the Breach; Clinton, *American Rebellion*, p. 31; James Murray, *Letters from America, 1773–1780*, Eric Robson, ed. (Manchester, England: Manchester University Press, 1951), pp. 25–26; Drayton, *Memoirs*, 2: pp. 289, 295–96; Jim Stokeley, *Fort Moultrie: Constant Defender*, National Park Service Handbook 136 (Washington, DC: U.S. Department of the Interior, 1985), p. 23.

24. Moultrie, *Memoirs*, 1: p. 178; see Lipscomb, *Carolina Low Country*, pp. 26–27, for bad Admiralty planning.

25. Lipscomb, *Carolina Low Country*, pp. 28–29; Murray, *Letters from America*, p. 26; Stokeley, *Fort Moultrie*, p. 22; Moultrie, *Memoirs*, 1: p. 166.

26. For a description of the fort and expenditure of powder see Drayton, *Memoirs*, 2: pp. 290–91, 296–97. On the nature of palmetto wood see Edward McCrady, *The History of South Carolina in the Revolution, 1775–1780* (New York: Russell & Russell, 1969; reissue of 1901 edition), p. 141n.2; Moultrie, *Memoirs*, 1: pp. 167, 178.

27. Henry Steele Commager and Richard B. Morris, *The Spirit of 'Seventy-Six: The Story of the American Revolution as Told by Participants*, 2 vols. (Indianapolis: Bobbs-Merrill, 1958), 2: p. 1067; Moultrie, *Memoirs*, 1: pp. 176, 178–79.

28. Moultrie, *Memoirs*, 1: pp. 175, 180; on Parker's breeches and wounds see Drayton, *Memoirs*, 2: p. 2: 327; for British casualties and the possible burial site of Captain Morris see Lipscomb, *Carolina Low Country*, p. 33.

29. Ward, *War of the Revolution*, 2: p. 676; Commager and Morris, *Spirit of 'Seventy-Six*, p. 1067; Lipscomb, *Carolina Low Country*, p. 35.

30. Frank Moore, *Songs and Ballads of the American Revolution* (New York: Appleton & Co., 1856), pp. 135–37.

2. The Rice Kings

1. Archibald Rutledge, "Plantation Lights and Shadows," and Alfred Huger, "The Story of the Low-Country," in Augustine T. Smythe, et al., *The Carolina Low-Country* (New York: Macmillan, 1931), pp. 122, 149–50. In fairness to Rutledge, despite his rose-colored view of the Old South, he was a fine writer and naturalist, and his many books on a bygone life on Hampton Plantation deserve the attention of new generations of readers.

2. David Duncan Wallace, *South Carolina: A Short History, 1520–1948* (Columbia: University of South Carolina Press, 1961), pp. 25–31; for the Barbadian influence see Richard S. Dunn, *Sugar and Slaves: The Rise of the Planter Class in the English West Indies, 1624–1713* (Chapel Hill: University of North Carolina Press, 1972), pp. 111–16 and *passim*.

3. Wallace, *Short History*, pp. 93–98.

4. Peter A. Coclanis, *The Shadow of a Dream: Economic Life and Death in the South Carolina Low Country, 1670–1920* (New York: Oxford University Press, 1989), pp. 82–83; Peter H. Wood, *Black Majority: Negroes in Colonial South Carolina from 1670 Through the Stono Rebellion* (New York: Knopf, 1974), pp. 124–30; Wallace, *Short History*, pp. 86-92.

5. Coclanis, *Shadow of a Dream*, pp. 31–47, and Wood, *Black Majority*, pp. 63–91, contain excellent discussions of the fascinating but complicated and treacherous subject of disease.

6. Wallace, *Short History*, pp. 149–56, 195; Jeanne A. Calhoun, *The Scourging Wrath of God: Early Hurricanes in Charleston, 1700–1804*, The Charleston Museum Leaflet No. 29 (Charleston: The Charleston Museum, April 1983), p. 2 and *passim*.

7. Wallace, *Short History*, p. 225.

8. Roger Lamb, *An Original and Authentic Journal of Occurrences during the Late American War, from its Commencement to the Year 1783* (Dublin, 1809), p. 294; Hinrichs, *Diary*, pp. 327, 329.

9. Josiah Quincy, *Memoir of the Life of Josiah Quincy Jun. of Massachusetts: By His Son . . .* (Boston: Cummings, Hilliard & Co., 1825), pp. 74, 94–96; "Journal of Josiah Quincy," Massachusetts Historical Society *Proceedings*, October 1915–June 1916 (Boston, 1916), 49: p. 441.

10. Josiah Quincy, *Memoir of the Life of Josiah Quincy*, p. 101; "Journal of Josiah Quincy," p. 453. Charles Fraser, *A Charleston Sketchbook, 1796–1806* (Rutland, VT: Charles E. Tuttle Co., 1959).

11. Wallace, *Short History*, pp. 146, 183, 219; Charles Woodmason, *The Carolina Backcountry on the Eve of the Revolution: The Journal and Other Writings of . . .*, Richard J. Hooker, ed. (Chapel Hill: University of North Carolina Press, 1953; paperback reprint edition), p. xxii; I have used the population statistics in the table and text in Coclanis, *Shadow of a Dream*, pp. 64, 66.

12. Richard J. Lathers, *Reminiscences of . . . Sixty Years of a Busy Life in South Carolina, Massachusetts, and New York* (New York: The Grafton Press, 1907), pp. 4–5.

13. For contrary views see Frederick P. Bowes, *The Culture of Early Charleston* (Chapel Hill: University of North Carolina Press, 1942), p. 115; and George C. Rogers, Jr., *Charleston in the Age of the Pinckneys* (Columbia: University of South Carolina Press, 1980; reprint of 1969 edition), pp. 23–25, 40.

14. For Arthur Middleton see his entry in the *Dictionary of American Biography*, references to his role with Drayton as a revolutionary in Drayton, *Memoirs*, *passim*, and a brief but interesting sketch in Barbara Doyle, ed., *Middleton Place Compendium* 1 (1979–1983), p. 9; for Drayton see Drayton, *Memoirs*, 1: pp. xiii–xxvii, and Dabney and Dargan, *William Henry Drayton*, pp. 25–26.

15. Dabney and Dargan, *William Henry Drayton*, pp. 26, 39; J. Russell Snapp, "William Henry Drayton: The Making of a Conservative Revolutionary," *Journal of Southern History* 57: 4 (November 1991), 637–58.

16. Quincy, *Memoir*, pp. 115–16.

17. Stewart L. Mims, *Colbert's West India Policy* (New Haven: Yale University Press, 1912), p. 222.

18. Bowes, *Culture of Early Charleston*, pp. 129–30.

3. Southern Strategy

1. For an excellent, concise discussion see Willcox, *Portrait of a General*, p. 293–99; see also Piers Mackesey, *The War for America, 1775–1783* (Lincoln: University of Nebraska Press, 1993; reprint of 1964 edition), pp. 249–78, 338–42.

2. Hinrichs, *Diary*, p. 119; Clinton, *American Rebellion*, pp. 159–60.

3. Johann Ewald, *Diary of the American War: A Hessian Journal*, Joseph P. Trustin, tr. and ed. (New Haven: Yale University Press, 1979), p. 193.

4. *Ibid.*

5. *Ibid.*, p. 194.

6. Clinton, *American Rebellion*, p. 159 and n.1.

7. Ewald, *Diary*, p. 194.

8. *Ibid.*, pp. 194–95.

9. Clinton, *American Rebellion*, p. 160.

10. Ewald, *Diary*, p. 195.

11. Clinton, *American Rebellion*, 11; Ewald, *Diary*, p. 195.

12. My sketch of Clinton is based on Willcox, *Portrait of a General*, pp. 3–114: only quotations are cited.

13. For my description of the purchase system I relied on the excellent Cecil Woodham-Smith, *The Reason Why* (New York: McGraw-Hill, 1953), pp. 21–25.

14. Willcox, *Portrait of a General*, pp. 30–34, for this quotation and all other Clinton quotations.

15. *Ibid.*, pp. 31–32.

4. The Approach March

1. Hinrichs, *Diary*, pp. 151, 183; "The Siege of Charleston: Journal of Captain Peter Russell, December 25, 1779, to May 2, 1780," *American Historical Review*, 4 (1899), 3: p. 484; Ewald, *Diary*, pp. 196–97.

2. For the sketch of his life and quotations, see Ewald, *Diary*, pp. xxi–xxxi.

3. Ewald, *Diary*, pp. 197–202 describes the march to the Stono, its crossing, and the reconnaissance mission. The description of Webster is on p. 195. Lincoln to Moultrie, 2/19/1780, Moultrie, *Memoirs*, 2: pp. 45–46.

4. Moultrie, *Memoirs*, 2: pp. 47, 52.

5. Ewald, *Diary*, pp. 202–3 for the fight described in this and the two previous paragraphs.

6. *Ibid.*, pp. 203–5.

7. *Ibid.*, p. 208; Drayton, *Memoirs*, 2: p. 330.

8. Elkanah Watson, *Men and Times of the Revolution; or, Memoirs of Elkanah Watson, Including His Journals of Travels in Europe and America from the Year 1777 to 1842*, 2nd Ed., Winslow C. Watson, ed. (New York: Dana and Company, 1857), p. 56.

9. Ewald, *Diary*, p. 211.

10. *Ibid.*, p. 214.

11. *Middleton Place* (Charleston: Middleton Place National Historical Landmark, Inc., and the Middleton Place Foundation, 1976). Peter Coats, *Great Gardens of the Western World* (London: Spring Books, 1968), pp. 182–88.

12. Jane Brown Gillette, "American Classic," *Historic Preservation* 43:2 (March–April 1991), pp. 22–29; Robert Tavernor, *Palladio and Palladianism* (London: Thames and Hudson, 1991), p. 185.

5. Charleston Besieged

1. For the weather see Russell, "The Siege of Charleston," p. 493; for the boats see Clinton, *American Rebellion*, p. 163, and John A. Tilley, *The British Navy and the American Revolution* (Columbia: University of South Carolina Press, 1987), pp. 179–80; for the troop units see Ewald, *Diary*, pp. 215–16.

2. Ewald, *Diary*, pp. 215–16; Russell, "The Siege of Charleston," p. 493.

3. Ewald, *Diary*, pp. 216–18 for all quotations from the landing on the left bank to the arrival at Quarter House.

4. Clinton, *American Rebellion*, p. 163.

5. Ewald, *Diary*, pp. 218–20 for all quotations and the army's activities to the end of "The Noose Tightens."

6. All quotations are from and my sketch of Lincoln is based on Clifford K. Shipton, "Benjamin Lincoln: Old Reliable," in George Athan Billias, *George Washington's Generals and Opponents: Their Exploits and Leadership* (New York: Da Capo Press, 1994), pp. 195, 209, 199, 206, 197 (one volume reprint of 1964 and 1969 editions); helpful in understanding Lincoln's motivation in defending Charleston was the new biography, David B. Mattern, *Benjamin Lincoln and the American Revolution* (Columbia: University of South Carolina Press, 1995), although it did not change my overall judgment of Lincoln and his generalship.

7. Gardner W. Allen, *A Naval History of the Revolution*, 2 vols. (Boston: Houghton Mifflin, 1913), 2: pp. 491, 493–94; McCrady, *History, 1775–1780*, pp. 438–440.

8. On preparations for and crossing the bar see Tilley, *The British Navy and the American Revolution*, pp. 178–79; Willcox, *Portrait of a General*, p. 304, for the Clinton quotation, and for whom it was meant.

9. Allen, *A Naval History of the Revolution*, 2: p. 495; McCrady, *History, 1775–1780*, pp. 439–40.

10. George Washington to Lieutenant Colonel John Laurens, 26 April, 1780, in George Washington, *The Writings of George Washington, from the Original Manuscript Sources, 1745–1799*, John C. Fitzpatrick, ed., 39 vols. (Washington, DC: U.S. Government Printing Office, 1931–1944), 18: p. 299.

11. Ewald, *Diary*, p. 226; Tilley, *The British Navy and the American Revolution*, pp. 180–81.

12. For the following discussion of Vauban and his method see Sebastien LePrestre de Vauban, *A Manual of Siegecraft and Fortification*, George A. Rothrock, tr. (Ann Arbor: University of Michigan Press, 1968); Henry Guerlac, "Vauban: The Impact of Science on War," in Edward Meade Earle, et al., *Makers of Modern Strategy: Military Thought from Machiavelli to Hitler* (Princeton: Princeton University Press, 1943), pp. 26–48; and Russell F. Weigley, *The Age of Battles: The Quest for Decisive Warfare from Breitenfeld to Waterloo* (Bloomington: Indiana University Press, 1991), pp. 53–58, especially for his brief but clear description of Vauban's publications.

13. Ewald, *Diary*, pp. 240–41.

14. *Ibid.*, pp. 221–26 for this paragraph and the rest of the chapter.

6. The Rise of Banastre Tarleton

1. For the portrait, see Nicholas Penny, ed., *Reynolds* (New York: Abrams, 1986), pp. 300–1; for the quotation, see Robert D. Bass, *The Green Dragoon: The Lives of Banastre Tarleton and Mary Robinson* (New York: Henry Holt, 1957), p. 294.

2. Bass, *Green Dragoon*, pp. 11–22, 38; the Simcoe quotation is on p. 49.

3. *Ibid.*, p. 48.

4. Banastre Tarleton, *A History of the Campaigns of 1780 and 1781 in the Southern Provinces of North America* (London, 1787), p. 16; *Diary of Lieut. Anthony Allaire, of Ferguson's Corps*, in Lyman C. Draper, *King's Mountain and its Heroes* (Cincinnati, 1881; 1992 reprint), pp. 484–515.

5. Tarleton, *History*, p. 16; Allaire, *Diary*, p. 490.

6. Tarleton, *History*, pp. 16–17.

7. Tarleton, *History*, pp. 16–17; Allaire, *Diary*, p. 490; George F. Scheer and Hugh F. Rankin, *Rebels and Redcoats* (New York: Da Capo Press, 1987; paperback reprint of 1957 edition), p. 398.

8. Charles Stedman, *The History of the Origin, Progress, and Termination of the American War*, 2 vols. (London, 1794), 2: p. 183

9. Stedman, *Ibid.*; Allaire, *Diary*, p. 491.

10. Tarleton, *History*, p. 18.

11. Ewald, *Diary*, p. 228; Willcox, *Portrait of a General*, p. 306.

12. Willcox, *Portrait of a General*, p. 306.

13. Ewald, *Diary*, p. 229; Willcox, *Portrait of a General*, pp. 306, 108n.5; "Journals of Lieut.-Col. Stephen Kemble," *Collections* of the New-York Historical Society for the Year 1883 (New York, 1884), 16: p. 154.

14. Ewald, *Diary*, p. 231; Moultrie, *Memoirs*, 2: p. 64.

15. Moultrie, *Memoirs*, 2: pp. 69, 105, for Clinton's 10 April summons and Rutledge's departure; Ewald, *Diary*, p. 232; Clinton, *American Rebellion*, p. 167; Boatner, *Encyclopedia*, p. 210.

16. Mattern, *Benjamin Lincoln and the American Revolution*, pp. 93–94, for Lincoln's decision to defend the city; Moultrie, *Memoirs*, 2: p. 80.

17. Ewald, *Diary*, p. 234.

18. *Ibid.*, pp. 234–35.

19. Cornwallis to Tarleton, 4/25/1780 in Bass, *Green Dragoon*, pp. 75–76.

20. Tarleton, *History*, p. 20.

21. Moultrie, *Memoirs*, 2: pp. 96–97.

22. David Ramsay, *The History of the Revolution of South-Carolina*, 2 vols. (Trenton, NJ: Isaac Collins, 1785), 2: p. 58; Ewald, *Diary*, p. 237.

23. Ewald, *Diary*, p. 237.

24. Scheer and Rankin, *Rebels and Redcoats*, p. 399.

25. See Willcox, *Portrait of a General*, p. 309, for a good description of Clinton's triumph.

26. *Ibid.*, pp. 504, 28.

27. *Ibid.*, p. 511n.7.

28. *Ibid.*, p. 321, has a brief but excellent discussion of Clinton's mistake with regard to parole.

7. Into the Back Country

1. My sketch of Cornwallis's life prior to his service in America is based on the excellent biography by the Wickwires, *Cornwallis*, pp. 1–78.

2. Ward, *War of the Revolution*, 1: pp. 225–26, 306–18; Wickwire, *Cornwallis*, pp. 86–90, 95–99.

3. Ward, *War of the Revolution*, 1: pp. 347–53 and 2: pp. 584–85; Wickwire, *Cornwallis*, pp. 100–4, 109–13.

4. Clinton, *American Rebellion*, pp. 53–54n.31, 65n.15; Willcox, *Portrait of a General*, pp. 114, 160n.3; and for a more sympathetic view of Cornwallis's conduct, Wickwire, *Cornwallis*, pp. 161–62.

5. Willcox, *Portrait of a General*, pp. 203–9; the North quotation is on p. 207.

6. Wickwire, *Cornwallis*, p. 114.

7. *Ibid.*, pp. 115–16.

8. Willcox, *Portrait of a General*, p. 316; Clinton, *American Rebellion*, p. 184.

9. Clinton, *American Rebellion*, p. 184; Willcox, *Portrait of a General*, pp. 318–19; Wickwire, *Cornwallis*, pp. 128–29.

10. Willcox, *Portrait of a General*, pp. 320–21.

11. Tarleton, *History*, pp. 27–28; Bass, *Green Dragoon*, p. 80.

12. Tarleton, *History*, p. 28; Robert Brownfield to William Dobein James, in William Dobein James, *A Sketch of the Life of Brig. Gen. Francis Marion and a History of His Brigade* (Charleston: Gould and Milet, 1821), Appendix, 1–7; to compare Tarleton's march rate with some in antiquity and modern times, see Peter Green, *Alexander of Macedon, 356–323 B.C.: A Historical Biography* (Berkeley: University of California Press, 1992; reprint of 1974 rev. ed.), p. 325 and n.

13. Tarleton, *History*, pp. 28–30.

14. *Ibid.*, p. 30.

15. *Ibid.*; Stedman, *History*, 2: p. 193.

16. Bass, *Green Dragoon*, pp. 80–83, for the texts.

17. Brownfield to James, 1821 (see n.12, above, for complete citation).

18. Stedman, *History*, 2: p. 193; Tarleton, *History*, pp. 30–31.

19. Woodmason, *Carolina Backcountry*, pp. 60–61; James G. Leyburn, *The Scotch-Irish: A Social History* (Chapel Hill: University of North Carolina Press, 1962), pp. 192–93; and David Hackett Fischer, *Albion's Seed: Four British Folkways in America* (New York: Oxford University Press, 1989), p. 613. Ned C. Landsman, "Border Cultures, the Backcountry, and 'North British' Emigration to America," *The William and Mary Quarterly*, 3rd series, 47:2 (April 1991), pp. 253–59, is a critique of Fischer's *Albion's Seed*, with Fischer's reply on pp. 294–302.

20. For this and the preceding paragraph, see the authoritative T. C. Smout, *A History of the Scottish People, 1560–1830* (Glasgow: Fontana/Collins, 1972), pp. 17–46; Linda Colley, *Britons: Forging the Nation, 1707–1837* (New Haven: Yale University Press, 1992), pp. 14–16, 387n.12, is also helpful in understanding the profound differences between Lowlanders and Highlanders; for a brief but authoritative discussion of the language of the Lowlands and its history, see the "Introduction" to Mairi Robinson, ed., *The Concise Scots Dictionary* (Aberdeen: Aberdeen University Press, 1985), pp. iv–xvi.

21. Smout, *History of the Scottish People*, pp. 104–5.

22. *Ibid.*, pp. 32–34, for the importance of the Borders; an excellent history of the Border fighting and raiding is George MacDonald Fraser, *The Steel Bonnets: The Story of the Anglo-Scottish Border Reivers* (London: Harvill, 1989; reprint of 1971 edition); Colley, *Britons*, p. 16, for cultural and even physical similarities.

23. For a sensible and up-to-date summary of seventeenth- and eighteenth-century relations between Ulster Scots and Irish Catholics, see Maldwyn A. Jones, "The Scotch-Irish in British America," in Bernard Bailyn and Philip D. Morgan, eds., *Strangers Within the Realm: Cultural Margins of the First British Empire* (Chapel Hill: The University of North Carolina Press, 1991), p. 287.

24. See, for example, Alan C. Davies, " 'As Good a Country as Any Man Needs to Dwell in,': Letters from a Scotch Irish Immigrant in Pennsylvania, 1766, 1767, and 1784," *Pennsylvania History* 50:4 (October 1983): p. 319.

25. Fischer, *Albion's Seed*, pp. 642–50.

26. Leyburn, *The Scotch-Irish*, p. 193.

27. For the settling of the Waxhaws, see Robert L. Meriwether, *The Expansion of South Carolina, 1729–1765* (Kingsport, TN: Southern Publishers, Inc., 1940), pp. 136–46.

8. Hearts and Minds

1. Robert Weir, "A Most Important Epocha": The Coming of the Revolution in South Carolina (Columbia: University of South Carolina Press, 1970), for a full account.

2. Moultrie, *Memoirs*, 1: p. 64.

3. Drayton, *Memoirs*, 1: pp. 263, 285–86, 301–2; Lewis Pinckney Jones, *The South Carolina Civil War of 1775* (Lexington, SC: The Sandlapper Store, Inc., 1975), p. 41, is a clear and succinct account of events in the Back Country in 1775.

4. Allaire, *Diary*, pp. 498–99.

5. Richard Walsh, *Charleston's Sons of Liberty: A Study of the Artisans, 1763–1789* (Columbia: University of South Carolina Press, 1959), p. 53.

6. Drayton, *Memoirs*, 1: pp. 324, 351–52.

7. Woodmason, *Carolina Backcountry*, pp. xxv, 13.

8. *Ibid.*, 12; R. W. Gibbes, ed., *Documentary History of the American Revolution . . . Chiefly in South Carolina . . . 1776–1782*, 3 vols. (New York: D. Appleton, 1853–1857), 1: pp. 128–29, 226, 228.

9. Andrew Pickens to Henry Lee, 28 August 1811, Pickens Papers, South Caroliniana Library.

10. Edward J. Cashin, *The King's Ranger: Thomas Brown and the American Revolution on the Southern Frontier* (Athens: University of Georgia Press, 1989), pp. 27–28.

11. Drayton, *Memoirs*, 1: p. 367; Jones, *Civil War*, p. 48.

12. Drayton, *Memoirs*, 1: p. 368, 370; Gibbes, *Doc. Hist.*, 1: pp. 150–51. For the Tory point of view see Cashin, *The King's Ranger*, especially Ch. 2, James H. O'Donnell, "A Loyalist View of the Drayton-Tennent-Hart Mission to the Upcountry," *South Carolina Historical Magazine* 67, no. 1 (January 1966), pp. 15–28, and Gary D. Olson, "Loyalists and the American Revolution: Thomas Brown and the South Carolina Backcountry, 1775–1776," *South Carolina Historical Magazine* 68 (1967), pp. 201–19; 69 (1968), pp. 44–58.

13. Jones, *Civil War*, p. 52.

14. Drayton, *Memoirs*, 1: pp. 378–79; Gibbes, *Doc. Hist.*, 1: pp. 157, 230.

15. Drayton, *Memoirs*, 1: p. 375.

16. *Ibid.*, pp. 396–98.

17. *Ibid.*, pp. 398–404.

18. O'Donnell, "A Loyalist View," p. 22; Drayton, *Memoirs*, 1: pp. 417–18.

19. Drayton, *Memoirs*, 1: pp. 417–18.

20. O'Donnell, "A Loyalist View," pp. 22–23; Drayton, *Memoirs*, 1: pp. 419–27, for this and the preceding paragraph.

21. Drayton, *Memoirs*, 2: p. 61.

22. Drayton, *Memoirs*, 2: pp. 64–68, 107–13; Gibbes, *Doc. Hist.*, 1: p. 129.

23. For the Tory insurrection and its failure see Drayton, *Memoirs*, 2: pp. 115–55, for the quotations, pp. 127, 131–33, 135; the secondary accounts are cited in n.12, above.

24. O'Donnell, "A Loyalist View," p. 24; Cashin, *The King's Ranger*, p. 33.

9. Trouble in the Back Country

1. "Memoir of Major Thomas Young, a Revolutionary Patriot of South Carolina," *Orion* 3 (October 1843), pp. 85–86, for all quotations from the beginning of the chapter.

2. Terry W. Lipscomb, *Battle, Skirmishes, and Actions of the American Revolution in South Carolina* (Columbia: South Carolina Department of Archives & History, 1991), pp. 3–24.

3. Harold A. Larrabee, *Decision at the Chesapeake* (New York: Clarkson N. Potter, 1964), pp. 32–33.

4. Benjamin Franklin Stevens, *The Campaign in Virginia, 1781: An Exact Reprint of Six Rare Pamphlets on the Clinton-Cornwallis Controversy*, 2 vols. (London, 1882), 1: p. 223.

5. David Schenck, *North Carolina, 1780–1781: Being a History of the Invasion of the Carolinas by the British Army under Lord Cornwallis in 1780–81* (Raleigh, NC: Edwards & Broughton, 1890), p. 53.

6. *Ibid.*, pp. 53–54.

7. William Richardson Davie, *The Revolutionary War Sketches of William R. Davie*, Blackwell P. Robinson, ed. (Raleigh: North Carolina Division of Archives & History, 1976), p. 7.

8. Schenck, *North Carolina*, pp. 56–57.

9. *Ibid.*, p. 57.

10. *Ibid.*, p. 62.

11. Commager and Morris, *Spirit of 'Seventy-Six*, 2: p. 1119.

12. *Ibid.*; Davie, *Sketches*, p. 8.

13. Charles Ross, ed., *Correspondence of Charles, First Marquis Cornwallis*, 3 vols., 2nd. Ed. (London: John Murray, 1859), 1: p. 49.

14. Davie, *Sketches*, p. 8.

15. See Lipscomb, *Battles, Skirmishes, and Actions*, p. 7, for dates.

16. A. S. Salley, Jr., ed., *Colonel William Hill's Memoirs of the Revolution* (Columbia: The Historical Commission of South Carolina, 1921), pp. 6–7, for all quotations in this paragraph.

17. Lyman C. Draper, *King's Mountain and its Heroes: History of the Battle of King's Mountain, October 7th, 1780, and the Events which led to it* (Cincinnati, 1881; 1992 reprint), pp. 73–75, for the account.

18. McCrady, *History, 1780–1783*, pp. 594–99, for Huck's raid on the McClure House and subsequent events; Robert D. Bass, *Ninety Six: The Struggle for the South Carolina Back Country* (Lexington, SC: The Sandlapper Store, Inc., 1978), p. 203, for Turnbull to Cornwallis; Cornwallis to Clinton, 6/30/1780, Stevens, *Campaign in Virginia*, 1: p. 223.

19. McCrady, *History, 1780–1783*, pp. 594–99.

20. For the two versions of who rode for help, see McCrady, *ibid.*, p. 594, and Wade Buice Fairey, *Historic Brattonsville: A Wedge of County History* (McConnells, SC: Historic Brattonsville, 1993), p. 14.

21. McCrady, *History, 1780–1783*, pp. 597–98; Allaire, *Diary*, p. 500.

22. James Collins, *Autobiography of a Revolutionary Soldier*, in *Sixty Years in the Nueces Valley: 1870–1930* (San Antonio: Naylor Printing Company, 1930; reprint of 1859 edition), p. 239; Tarleton, *History*, p. 219; McCrady, *History, 1780–1783*, p. 599; Hill's *Memoirs*, p. 10.

23. Bass, *Ninety Six*, p. 219.

24. This sketch of Sumter is largely based on the works of his two biographers: Anne King Gregorie, *Thomas Sumter* (Columbia, SC: The R. L. Bryan Co., 1931), and Robert D. Bass, *Gamecock: The Life and Campaigns of General Thomas Sumter* (New York: Holt, Rinehart and Winston, 1961). Quotations, and a few specific events are noted separately.

25. Bass, *Gamecock*, pp. 61–62.

26. Gregorie, *Sumter*, p. 4.

27. Bass, *Gamecock*, p. 32.

28. *Ibid.*, p. 52.

29. *Ibid.*, p. 56.

30. Hill's *Memoirs*, p. 8.

31. Henry Lee, *Memoirs of the War in the Southern Department of the United States*, New Edition, with revisions (New York: University Publishing Company, 1869), p. 175.

10. More Trouble in the Back Country

1. Collins, *Autobiography*, p. 227.
2. *Ibid.*, p. 228.
3. *Ibid.*, p. 232.
4. *Ibid.*, p. 235.
5. *Ibid.*, p. 236
6. *Ibid.*, pp. 237–38.
7. "Colonel Robert Gray's Observations on the War in Carolina," *South Carolina Historical and Genealogical Magazine* 11, no. 3 (July 1910), 153.
8. Rachel N. Klein, *Unification of a Slave State*, esp. pp. 106–8.
9. Collins, *Autobiography*, pp. 235–36.
10. *Ibid.*, p. 238.
11. *Ibid.*, pp. 245–47.
12. Fitzpatrick, *Writings of George Washington*, 18: pp. 197–98.
13. My sketch of von Steuben is based largely on Ward, *War of the Revolution*, 2: pp. 550–54, with only minor disagreements on his background.
14. Von Steuben to Baron von der Goltz, n.d., in Scheer and Rankin, *Rebels & Redcoats*, p. 307.
15. My sketch of de Kalb is based on the biography by Friedrich Kapp, *The Life of John Kalb* (New York: Henry Holt, 1884).
16. Frank Moore, *Diary of the American Revolution*, 2 vols. (New York: Charles Scribner, 1860), 2: p. 310.
17. See Wickwire, *Cornwallis*, pp. 137–48, for Cornwallis's activities and administrative problems at this time.
18. Tarleton, *History*, pp. 87–88.
19. Cornwallis to Clinton, 9/3/1780, in Wickwire, *Cornwallis*, p. 47.
20. Ross, *Cornwallis Correspondence*, 1: pp. 514–15.
21. Sir John Fortescue, *History of the British Army*, 13 vols. (London, 1899–1930), 3: p. 404; see *Dictionary of National Biography* for Rawdon's later career.
22. For the action at Rocky Mount see Graham, *Graham*, p. 236, who was there; Davie, *Sketches*, p. 11, who was not there but close by and talked to participants the next day; Bass, *Gamecock*, pp. 63–67.
23. Allaire, *Diary*, p. 502.
24. Davie, *Sketches*, pp. 11–12.
25. *Ibid.*, 13; Marquis James, *Andrew Jackson: Border Captain*, 20 (New York: Garden City Publishing Co., 1940), p. 22; Robert V. Remini, *Andrew Jackson and the Course of American Empire, 1767–1821* (New York: Harper & Row, 1977), p. 17.
26. My account of Hanging Rock is based largely on Davie, *Sketches*, pp. 13–16, who participated, and all quotations are from Davie; see also Graham, *Graham*, pp. 238–40, another participant; a good secondary account is Ward, *War of the Revolution*, 2: pp. 709–11.
27. Winn insisted that he commanded the right. See Samuel C. Williams, ed., "General Richard Winn's Notes—1780," *South Carolina Historical and Genealogical Magazine*, 43, no. 4 (October 1942): 209ff. and n.18; but see also Bibliography.
28. Allaire, *Diary*, pp. 499–500.
29. *Ibid.*, p. 500.
30. Moultrie, *Memoirs*, 2: p. 252.
31. Allaire, *Diary*, p. 501.
32. *Ibid.*, p. 502.
33. *Ibid.*, pp. 502–3.
34. Draper, *King's Mountain*, p. 89.

35. Allaire, *Diary*, p. 503; J. G. de Roulhac Hamilton, ed., "Kings Mountain: Letters of Colonel Isaac Shelby," *Journal of Southern History* 4, no. 3 (August 1938), 371; Draper, *King's Mountain*, p. 94.

36. George Hanger, An *Address to the Army in Reply to Strictures by Roderick McKenzie . . . on Tarleton's History of the Campaigns of 1780 and 1781* (London, 1789), p. 82.

37. Greene to Hamilton, 1/10/1781, Richard K. Showman, Dennis M. Conrad, et al., eds., *The Papers of General Nathanael Greene*, 8 vols. to date (Chapel Hill: The University of North Carolina Press, 1976–), 7, p. 88.

38. For sketches of Clarke, see *Dictionary of American Biography*, and Boatner, *Encyclopedia*, pp. 233–34.

11. A Hero Takes Charge

1. Hoffman Nickerson, *The Turning Point of the Revolution, or Burgoyne in America* (Boston: Houghton Mifflin, 1928), pp. 277–78, 282; Lynn Montross, *Ragtag and Bobtail: The Story of the Continental Army, 1775–1783* (New York, 1952), p. 222; Paul David Nelson, *General Horatio Gates: A Biography* (Baton Rouge: Louisiana State Press, 1976).

2. My sketch of Gates's life until his emigration to America is based on Max Mintz, *The Generals of Saratoga: John Burgoyne and Horatio Gates* (New Haven: Yale University Press, 1990), pp. 15–18, 29–48; Charles Lee's description of Gates's wife is on p. 33; Monckton's recommendation is on p. 43. The opinions expressed on Gates's motivations and character are mine.

3. *Ibid.*, p. 75.

4. *Ibid.*, p. 77.

5. *Ibid.*, pp. 76–82.

6. Jeremy Belknap, "Journal of My Tour to the Camp and the Observations I Made There," *Proceedings of the Massachusetts Historical Society, 1858–1860*, 1st Series, 4 (1860), 83; Mintz, *The Generals*, p. 87. For the value of Gates's service during those early months, see Douglas Southall Freeman, *George Washington: A Biography*, 7 vols. (New York: Scribner's, 1948–1957), 3: pp. 474, 528.

7. Nelson, *Gates*, p. 75.

8. Nickerson, *The Turning Point of the Revolution*, p. 282.

9. Nelson, *Gates*, pp. 207, 209.

10. "A Narrative of the Campaign of 1780, by Colonel Otho Holland Williams, Adjutant General," in William Johnson, *Sketches of the Life and Correspondence of Nathanael Greene*, 2 vols. (Charleston, 1822), 1: p. 486.

11. My sketch of Marion, aside from the quotations, is based on Hugh Rankin, *Francis Marion: The Swamp Fox* (New York: Thomas Y. Crowell, 1973), pp. 1–58.

12. Moultrie, *Memoirs*, 2: p. 223n.

13. *Ibid.*, p. 222.

14. Williams, "Narrative," 1: p. 486.

15. *Ibid.*, p. 487.

16. *Ibid.*

17. Scheer and Rankin, *Rebels & Redcoats*, p. 405.

18. Williams, "Narrative," 1: pp. 487–88.

19. *Ibid.*, p. 488; William Seymour, A *Journal of the Southern Expedition, 1780–1783*, in *Historical and Biographical Papers*, 2: p. 15 (Wilmington: The Historical Society of Delaware, 1896), p. 4.

20. Williams, "Narrative," 1: p. 488.

21. Nelson, *Gates*, pp. 224–25.

22. Williams, "Narrative," 1: pp. 489–90.

23. See Nelson, *Gates*, pp. 229–30, for a defense of this decision, a defense I obviously disagree with.

24. Williams, "Narrative," 1: p. 488.

25. Nelson, *Gates*, pp. 228; 230; Robert Scott Davis, Jr., ed., "Thomas Pinckney and the Last Campaign of Horatio Gates," *South Carolina Historical Magazine* 86, no. 2 (April 1985), pp. 86–87;

H. L. Landers, *The Battle of Camden, South Carolina, August 16, 1780* (Washington, DC: U.S. Government Printing Office, 1929), p. 23.

12. The Battle of Camden

1. Ross, *Cornwallis Correspondence*, 1: p. 506.

2. Edward E. Curtis, *The Organization of the British Army in the American Revolution* (New Haven: Yale University Press, 1926), p. 30n.74.

3. Henry Lumpkin, *From Savannah to Yorktown: The American Revolution in the South* (New York: Paragon House, 1981; reprint edition), pp. 135–42, is a convenient work with a good discussion of the flintlock musket and battle tactics; another first-rate discussion is in John Womack Wright, *Some Notes on the Continental Army*, New Windsor Cantonment Publication No. 2 (Cornwallville, NY: Hope Farm Press, 1975), pp. 66–69.

4. George Hanger, *To All Sportsmen and Particularly to Farmers and Gamekeepers* (London, 1814), p. 205.

5. For the history and a technical discussion of the bayonet, see Charles Ffoulkes and E. C. Hopkinson, *Sword, Lance & Bayonet: A Record of the Arms of the British Army and Navy* (Cambridge: Cambridge University Press, 1938), p. 108ff.

6. E. B. O'Callaghan, ed., *Orderly Book of Lieut. Gen. John Burgoyne* (Albany, 1860), p. 3.

7. Williams, "Narrative," 1: p. 493.

8. *Ibid.*; Seymour, *Journal*, p. 5.

9. Williams, "Narrative," 1: p. 494.

10. *Ibid.*, pp. 494–95.

11. *Ibid.*, p. 495, for the line of battle; Seymour, *Journal*, p. 8.

12. Williams, "Narrative," 1: p. 495; Davis, "Thomas Pinckney and the Last Campaign of Horatio Gates," pp. 86, 92–94; for a brief but illuminating explanation, with examples, of the crucial matter of "posts of honor," see Wright, *Some Notes on the Continental Army*, pp. 9–10; for its roots in antiquity and development into early modern times, see Oliver Lyman Spaulding, et al., *War: A Study of Military Methods from the Earliest Times* (New York: Harcourt, Brace, 1925), pp. 57–58, 66, 294–95, 499; further to the concept of "posts of honor," John S. Pancake, *This Destructive War: The British Campaign in the Carolinas, 1780–82* (Tuscaloosa: The University of Alabama Press, 1992), p. 104, is the only historian I know of who mentions that the British usually fought "right-handed," as he put it, but he also refers to Gates's blunder as "inadvertent."

13. Clinton, *American Rebellion*, pp. 95, 131; Tarleton, *History*, p. 289.

14. The words on a general's place in battle are General James Gavin's, the famous commander of the U.S. 82nd Airborne Division, in James M. Gavin, *On to Berlin: Battles of an Airborne Commander, 1943–1946* (New York: Viking, 1978), p. 252. Ward, *War of the Revolution*, 1: p. 348.

15. Williams, "Narrative," 1: p. 495; Davis, "Thomas Pinckney and the Last Campaign of Horatio Gates," p. 93; for Gates's clothes and horse, Blackwell P. Robinson, *William R. Davie* (Chapel Hill: University of North Carolina Press, 1957), p. 57.

16. Williams, "Narrative," 1: p. 495.

17. Davis, "Thomas Pinckney and the Last Campaign of Horatio Gates," p. 93.

18. Williams, "Narrative," 1: p. 495.

19. Tarleton, *History*, pp. 132–33.

20. Williams, "Narrative," 1: p. 495–96.

21. *Ibid.*, p. 497.

22. Julian P. Boyd, ed. *The Papers of Thomas Jefferson* (Princeton: Princeton University Press, 1950–), 3: p. 558.

23. Dann, *The Revolution Remembered*, pp. 194–95.

24. Williams, "Narrative," 1: p. 496; Tarleton, *History*, pp. 132–33; Wickwire, *Cornwallis*, p. 162.

25. Lamb, *Occurrences*, p. 304.

26. Williams, "Narrative," 1: p. 496.

27. Tarleton, *History*, pp. 107–8.

28. Williams, "Narrative," 1: p. 496; Wickwire, *Cornwallis*, p. 163.

29. Tarleton, *History*, pp. 107–8; Williams, "Narrative," pp. 497–98.

30. Stedman, *History*, 2: p. 210.

31. Davis, "Thomas Pinckney and the Last Campaign of Horatio Gates," p. 94.

32. Tarleton, *History*, pp. 146–47.

33. Williams, "Narrative," 1: pp. 499, 502.

34. Schenk, *North Carolina*, p. 74.

13. The Partisans Fight On

1. Davie, *Sketches*, p. 18.

2. Lossing, *Pictorial Field-Book of the Revolution*, 2: p. 451.

3. Tarleton, *History*, p. 113.

4. Davie, *Sketches*, p. 19.

5. Collins, *Autobiography*, p. 250.

6. Tarleton, *History*, pp. 114–15.

7. *Ibid.*, p. 114; Collins, *Autobiography*, pp. 252–53.

8. Tarleton, *History*, p. 115; Davie, *Sketches*, p. 20.

9. Collins, *Autobiogaphy*, pp. 253–54.

10. *Ibid.*

11. Shelby, *Letters*, pp. 371–72; Draper, *King's Mountain*, p. 105.

12. Draper, *King's Mountain*, p. 106.

13. *Ibid.*, p. 108.

14. *Ibid.*

15. Shelby, *Letters*, p. 372; Schenk, *North Carolina*, p. 78; Draper, *King's Mountain*, p. 109.

16. Shelby, *Letters*, p. 372; Draper, *King's Mountain*, pp. 109–10.

17. Shelby, *Letters*, pp. 372–73.

18. Robert Henry, *Narrative of the Battle of Cowan's Ford . . . and Narrative of the Battle of King's Mountain by Captain David Vance* (Greensboro, NC: D. Schenck, 1891, p. 18; hereinafter cited, respectively, as Henry, *Narrative*, or *Vance's Narrative*.

19. Tarleton, *History*, p. 135; Wallace, *Short History*, p. 306.

20. Moultrie, *Memoirs*, 2: pp. 166–71, for the exchange of letters between Lord Charles Montague and Moultrie.

21. Archibald Rutledge, *My Colonel and His Lady* (Indianapolis: Bobbs-Merrill, 1937), pp. 49–50.

22. Rankin, *Swamp Fox*, p. 26; for Marion, Rankin's biography has been my guide.

23. *Ibid.*, p. 15; Rawdon to Clinton, 3/23/1781, Clinton, *American Rebellion*, p. 501.

24. Graham, *Graham*, p. 235.

25. Moultrie, *Memoirs*, 2: p. 223.

26. William Gordon, *The History of the Rise, Progress, and Establishment, of the Independence of the United States of America: including an Account of the Late War; and of the Thirteen Colonies, from their Origin to That Period*, 4 vols. (London, 1788), 3: p. 455.

27. Rankin, *Swamp Fox*, p. 65.

28. *Ibid.*, p. 70.

29. *Ibid.*, p. 71.

30. *Ibid.*, p. 73.

31. *Ibid.*, pp. 79–80.

32. Davie, *Sketches*, pp. 21–25, for all quotations in this paragraph and until otherwise indicated.

33. Stedman, *History*, 2: p. 239.

34. Davie, *Sketches*, p. 25; Graham, *Graham*, pp. 256–57.

35. Hanger, *An Address to the Army*, pp. 55–60, for his account of the affair; Tarleton, *History*, p. 159; Mackenzie, *Strictures*, pp. 47–48.

36. Davie, *Sketches*, p. 25.

37. Rankin, *Swamp Fox*, pp. 83–87, for the action at Black Mingo.

38. "Gray's Observations," p. 144.

14. The Rise of Patrick Ferguson

1. Allaire, *Diary*, 504–6.

2. Hugh Rankin, "Charles Lord Cornwallis: Study in Frustration," in George Athan Billias, ed., *George Washington's Generals and Opponents: Their Exploits and Leadership* (New York: Da Capo Press, 1994; reprint of separate 1964 and 1969 editions), 2: p. 205; Ross, *Cornwallis Correspondence*, 1: p. 59.

3. There is no biography, and information on Ferguson is scattered; my sketch of his early years is based largely on James Ferguson, *Two Scottish Soldiers, A Soldier of 1688 and Blenheim, A Soldier of the American Revolution, and a Jacobite Laird and His Forebears* (Aberdeen: D. Wyllie & Sons, 1888).

4. David Patten, "Ferguson and His Rifle," *History Today* 28, no. 7 (July 1978), 447–48, for the quotation, but the author's excessive enthusiasm for the rifle should be disregarded.

5. For a description of Chaumette's invention and Ferguson's modification, see especially J. F. Hayward, *The Art of the Gunmaker, V. II, England and America, 1660–1830* (London: Barie and Rockliff, 1963), pp. 47–48, 205–6; also, Leonid Tarassuk and Claude Blair, *The Complete Encyclopaedia of Arms and Weapons* (New York: Simon & Schuster, 1982), p. 222ff; and Harold L. Peterson, *Arms and Armor in Colonial America, 1520–1783* (New York, Bramhall House, 1956), p. 220.

6. Hugh Rankin, "An Officer Out of His Time: Correspondence of Major Patrick Ferguson, 1779–1780," in Howard H. Peckham, ed., *Sources of American Independence: Selected Manuscripts of the William L. Clements Library* (Chicago: University of Chicago Press, 1978), 2: p. 288.

7. Ferguson to Adam Ferguson(?), 1/31/1778, in *ibid.*, p. 300; for support of his view see Higginbotham, *Morgan*, pp. 78–79.

8. Ferguson, *Two Scottish Soldiers*, p. 68.

9. James Fenimore Cooper to the Editor, 1/28/1831, New-York *Mirror* 8, no. 41 (April 16, 1831), p. 327.

10. J. N. George, *English Guns and Rifles* (Plantersville, SC: Small-Arms Technical Publishing Company, 1947), pp. 150, 159; Howard L. Blackmore, *British Military Firearms, 1650–1850* (London: Herbert Jenkins, 1961), pp. 86–87.

11. Ward, *War of the Revolution*, 2: pp. 617–18; Rankin, "Officer Out of His Time," p. 290; Clinton, *American Rebellion*, p. 123.

12. Ferguson to Clinton, 8/1/1778, in Rankin, "Officer Out of His Time," pp. 306–7, 310; Wickwire, *Cornwallis*, p. 204.

13. Ferguson to Clinton, 8/1/1778, in Rankin, "Officer Out of His Time," pp. 308–9.

14. George C. Rogers, Jr., ed., "Letters of Charles O'Hara to the Duke of Grafton," *South Carolina Historical Magazine*, 65, no. 3 (July 1964), 160; Ferguson to Clinton, 8/1/1778, in Rankin, "Officer Out of His Time," p. 311; Mackesey, *War for America*," p. 33.

15. Rankin, *"Officer Out of His Time,"* p. 291.

16. Clinton, *American Rebellion*, pp. 175–76, 411, for Ferguson's appointment and instructions; Rankin, "Officer Out of His Time, p. 293, for Balfour's opinion of Ferguson.

17. Bass, *Ninety Six*, pp. 224, 245.

18. Robert Stansbury Lambert, *South Carolina Loyalists in the American Revolution* (Columbia: University of South Carolina Press, 1987), pp. 133–34.

19. *Ibid.*, p. 134.

20. Allaire, *Diary*, p. 506.

21. *Ibid.*, p. 508.

22. *Ibid.*, p. 507.

23. *Ibid.*; Draper, *King's Mountain*, pp. 150, 197–98 for the story of the cattle herds.

24. Allaire, *Diary*, pp. 507–8.

25. L. P. Hartley, *The Go-Between* (New York, 1954), p. 3.

26. Boatner, *Encyclopedia*, p. 523.

15. To Catch Ferguson

1. Draper, *King's Mountain*, p. 169. This indispensable work has been a steady guide for this and the following chapter.
2. Their sketches are largely based on *ibid.*, pp. 411–16 for Shelby, and pp. 418–22 for Sevier.
3. *Ibid.*, pp. 378–402 for the sketch of Campbell.
4. *Vance's Narrative*, p. 18.
5. Draper, *King's Mountain*, p. 176.
6. John W. Wright, "The Rifle in the American Revolution," *American Historical Review* 39, no. 2 (January 1924), pp. 297–98, for the opinions of Wayne and Muhlenberg; Graham, *Graham*, p. 135, has the Morgan quotation.
7. Draper, *King's Mountain*, p. 535.
8. *Ibid.*, pp. 425–54, for Cleveland, and pp. 454–56 for Winston.
9. *Hill's Memoirs*, pp. 17–18; Bass, *Gamecock*, pp. 87–88.
10. Draper, *King's Mountain*, p. 564.
11. *Ibid.*, for Campbell's appointment and the Shelby quotations in this and the next two paragraphs.
12. Allaire, *Diary*, p. 509.
13. Lambert, *South Carolina Loyalists*, p. 139.
14. Allaire, *Diary*, p. 509.
15. *Virginia Gazette*, 11/11/1780.
16. *Ibid.*, p. 230; Allaire, *Diary*, p. 509.
17. Draper, *King's Mountain*, p. 477; Collins, *Autobiography*, p. 258.
18. Draper, *King's Mountain*, pp. 217–21, for the confrontation between Hill and Williams and the Hill quotation.
19. *Vance's Narrative*, p. 21; Draper, *King's Mountain*, p. 221.
20. Draper, *King's Mountain*, p. 220; Bass, *Gamecock*, p. 90.
21. Collins, *Autobiography*, pp. 258–59.
22. *Vance's Narrative*, p. 22.
23. Draper, *King's Mountain*, p. 227.
24. Allaire, *Diary*, p. 510; Ferguson, *Two Scottish Soldiers*, pp. 90–91.
25. Draper, *King's Mountain*, p. 511.

16. King's Mountain

1. Draper, *King's Mountain*, p. 228; *Hill's Memoirs*, p. 22.
2. *Vance's Narrative*, pp. 22–23; Draper, *King's Mountain*, p. 225.
3. Draper, *King's Mountain*, p. 229.
4. *Ibid.*, p. 230.
5. *Vance's Narrative*, pp. 23–24.
6. *Ibid.*, p. 25.
7. Draper, *King's Mountain*, p. 232.
8. *Ibid.*, p. 233.
9. *Ibid.*, pp. 234–35.
10. Collins, *Autobiography*, p. 259.
11. *Ibid.*, pp. 259–60; Draper, *King's Mountain*, p. 235.
12. *The Journal of Alexander Chesney, a South Carolina Loyalist in the Revolution and After*, Alfred E. Jones, ed. The Ohio State University Bulletin 26, no. 4 (October 30, 1921), p. 17.
13. *Hill's Memoirs*, p. 23; Young, "Memoir," p. 86; Collins, *Autobiography*, pp. 260–61.
14. Henry Lumpkin, *From Savannah to Yorktown: The American Revolution in the South* (New York: Paragon House, 1981), p. 100.
15. Allaire, *Diary*, p. 517.
16. Chesney, *Journal*, p. 18; *Hill's Memoirs*, p. 23.

17. Henry's Account, in *Vance's Narrative*, p. 35; Draper, *King's Mountain*, p. 257.

18. Young, "Memoir," p. 86.

19. Chesney, *Journal*, p. 17.

20. Collins, *Autobiography*, p. 26; Draper, *King's Mountain*, p. 313; *Vance's Narrative*, p. 28.

21. Collins, *Autobiography*, pp. 260–61.

22. Wiliam Lee Davidson to Jethro Sumner, 10/10/1780, in Draper, *King's Mountain*, p. 520.

23. Allaire, *Diary*, p. 510.

24. Chesney, *Journal*, p. 18; Scheer and Rankin, *Rebels & Redcoats*, p. 419.

25. Draper, *King's Mountain*, p. 283.

26. *Ibid.*, p. 558.

27. Collins, *Autobiography*, p. 26; Scheer and Rankin, *Rebels & Redcoats*, p. 419.

28. Tarleton, *History*, p. 165.

29. Other writers have reached the same conclusion, for example, Lumpkin, *From Savannah to Yorktown*, pp. 93–96; Tarleton to Henry Haldane, 12/24/1780, in Wickwire, *Cornwallis*, p. 258.

30. Draper, *King's Mountain*, pp. 265–66.

31. Henry's Account, in *Vance's Narrative*, pp. 35–36.

32. Shelby, *Letters*, p. 375; Allaire, *Diary*, p. 510, for American Volunteer casualties; Draper, *King's Mountain*, p. 308 for Young, Witherspoon, and Spelts quotations; Collins, *Autobiography*, p. 262.

33. Collins, *Autobiography*, p. 261.

34. Draper, *King's Mountain*, pp. 304–5.

35. Chesney, *Journal*, p. 18; Draper, *King's Mountain*, pp. 326, 557.

36. Draper, *King's Mountain*, p. 531.

37. Young, "Memoir," p. 87; Draper, *King's Mountain*, p. 328.

38. Draper, *King's Mountain*, pp. 329–30.

39. *Ibid.*, p. 544; Allaire, *Diary*, p. 511.

40. Wiliam P. Cumming and Hugh Rankin, *The Fate of a Nation: The American Revolution Through Contemporary Eyes* (London: Phaidon, 1975), p. 288.

41. Draper, *King's Mountain*, p. 334.

42. Cumming and Rankin, *Fate of a Nation*, p. 289.

43. Draper, *King's Mountain*, pp. 339–40, 544; Allaire, *Diary*, p. 511.

44. *Ibid.*, pp. 346, 511.

45. Cumming and Rankin, *Fate of a Nation*, p. 289.

46. Draper, *King's Mountain*, p. 341.

47. *Ibid.*, p. 518; Allaire, *Diary*, pp. 512–13.

48. Allaire, *Diary*, p. 515.

49. Chesney, *Journal*, pp. 19–21.

50. Clinton, *American Rebellion*, p. 226.

17. Retreat and Turmoil

1. Wickwire, *Cornwallis*, p. 220; Marion to Gates, in Gordon, *History*, 3: p. 456.

2. Stedman, *History*, 2: p. 224.

3. McKenzie, *Strictures*, p. 48.

4. George Hanger, *The Life, Adventures, and Opinions of Colonel George Hanger, Written by Himself*, 2 vols. (London, 1801), 2: p. 179: this is a work that unfortunately is rarely as informative as in this instance.

5. *Grays's Observations*, p. 144; A. R. Newsome, "A British Orderly Book, 1780–1781," *North Carolina Historical Review*, 9, no. 4 (October 1932), p. 381.

6. Stedman, *History*, 2: pp. 225–26.

7. Rankin, *Swamp Fox*, pp. 103–5, for the action at Tearcoat Swamp.

8. Rankin, *Swamp Fox*, p. 112.

9. *Ibid.*

10. *Ibid.*, p. 113.

11. *Ibid.*, p. 114.

12. *Ibid.*, pp. 114–15; Cornwallis to Clinton, 12/3/80, in Clinton, *American Rebellion*, p. 477.

13. Rankin, *Swamp Fox*, p. 121.

14. Tarleton, *History*, p. 203; Bass, *Gamecock*, p. 85.

15. Clinton to Cornwallis, 12/3/1780, in Clinton, *American Rebellion*, p. 477; Rankin, *Swamp Fox*, p. 113.

16. "Winn's Notes" 46, no. 1 (January 1943), p. 2.

17. *Hill's Memoirs*, p. 15.

18. Bass, *Gamecock*, p. 98.

19. *Hill's Memoirs*, p. 14.

20. Bass, *Gamecock*, p. 105.

21. Tarleton, *History*, pp. 176–77.

22. *Ibid.*, p. 178.

23. *Hill's Memoirs*, p. 15.

24. McKenzie, *Strictures*, pp. 75–77.

25. Bass, *Gamecock*, p. 197.

26. McKenzie, *Strictures*, p. 77.

27. Bass, *Gamecock*, p. 110; Tarleton, *History*, p. 202.

28. Tarleton, *History*, p. 205.

18. A General from Rhode Island

1. Greene's mastery of what we today call logistics is stressed in the fine study by Dennis M. Conrad, "Nathanael Greene and the Southern Campaigns, 1780–1783" (Ph.D. dissertation, Duke University, 1979), pp. iii–iv, 334–35, *passim*. The vital nature of logistics is perhaps best gauged by its importance to the campaigns of history's greatest field commander, as described in the brilliant biography by Peter Green, *Alexander of Macedon, 356–323 B.C.: A Historical Biography* (Berkeley: University of California Press, 1991; reprint of revised 1974 edition), p. 394: "One of the crucial factors behind Alexander's continuous and unbroken success was the unparalleled efficiency of his supply and transport commands."

2. *Papers of General Nathanael Greene*, 1: p. 37.

3. I have generally based my sketch of Greene's early years on the *Papers of General Nathanael Greene* and the learned editorial notes that accompany them; also very helpful was George Washington Greene, *The Life of General Nathanael Greene*, 3 vols. (Freeport, NY: Books for Libraries Press, 1972; reprint of 1867–1871 edition); see also Theodore Thayer, *Nathanael Greene: Strategist of the Revolution* (New York: Twayne Publishers, 1960).

4. *Papers of Nathanael Greene*, 1: p. 48; Greene, *Life of Greene*, 1: p. 14.

5. Greene, *Life of Greene*, 1: p. 13.

6. *Papers of Nathanael Greene*, 1: pp. 69–70n.2 for suspension; p. 47 on his education; 2: p. 104 and n.4 on the situation in Pennsylvania and his withdrawal from the Society.

7. *Ibid.*, 1: p. 53.

8. John F. Stegeman and Janet A. Stegeman, *Caty: A Biography of Catherine Littlefield Greene* (Athens: University of Georgia Press, 1985; reprint of 1977 ed.), pp. 10, 121.

9. *Papers of Nathanael Greene*, 1: pp. 75–76.

10. *Ibid.*, pp. xviii–xix, 78–79.

11. Thayer, *Strategist of the Revolution*, pp. 65, 67.

12. *Papers of Nathanael Greene*, 1: pp. 291, 292n.2, 293n.3.

13. *Ibid.*, pp. 294–95.

14. Ward, *War of the Revolution*, pp. 1: 242, 244.

15. *Papers of Nathanael Greene*, 1: p. 303.

16. *Ibid.*, pp. 302, 307.

17. Ward, *War of the Revolution*, 1: p. 269.

18. *Papers of Nathanael Greene,* 1: pp. 342–44.

19. *Ibid.,* p. 352.

20. Ward, *War of the Revolution* 1: p. 291.

21. Boatner, *Encyclopedia,* p. 454.

22. Don Higginbotham, *The War of American Independence: Military Attitudes, Policies, and Practice, 1763–1789* (New York: Macmillan, 1971), p. 211.

23. Thayer, *Strategist of the Revolution,* p. 213, for both quotations.

24. *Papers of Nathanael Greene,* 2: p. 294, for congressional urgings; p. 281 for Washington's orders; pp. 283, 285; for Greene's orders to his officers and civilian reaction; pp. 326, 547; for the pressures exerted on him to accept.

25. *Ibid.,* pp. 307, 326; 3: p. 427; for a full explanation of why Washington denied Greene a line appointment, see GW to NG, 9/3/1779, 4: p. 358–60.

26. *Ibid.,* 2: p. 277; see Thayer, *Strategist of the Revolution,* p. 226ff for a good discussion of this matter.

27. *Papers of Nathanael Greene,* 3: p. 388; p. 427 for NG to GW, 4/24/1779.

28. Anthony Wayne to James Jackson, 6/19/1786, in Greene, *Life of Greene,* 3: p. 534.

29. *Papers of Nathanael Greene,* 2: p. 502.

30. *Ibid.,* p. 544.

31. Williams, "Narrative," p. 510.

19. The Stage Is Set

1. My sketch of Morgan is based on the authoritative biography by Don Higginbotham, *Daniel Morgan: Revolutionary Rifleman* (Chapel Hill: University of North Carolina Press, 1961); also helpful was James Graham, *The Life of General Daniel Morgan, of the Virginia Line of the Army of the United States* (New York: Derby & Jackson, 1856).

2. In addition to this strong indirect evidence, correspondence between the author and Professors John Mack Faragher and Don Higginbotham verified the absence of any kinship.

3. The "scars and ridges" were seen and described by Morgan's pastor, Reverend William Hill, who is quoted in Graham, *Morgan,* p. 30; there also can be found Morgan's claim of keeping count of the lashes.

4. *Ibid.,* p. 34.

5. *Ibid.,* p. 38.

6. Higginbotham, *Morgan,* p. 18.

7. Henry, "Journal," in Kenneth Roberts, *March to Quebec* (New York: Doubleday, Doran, 1938), p. 327.

8. *Ibid.,* pp. 335–36 for the portage; p. 302 for Morgan's manner.

9. *Ibid.,* p. 356; Morgan to Jefferson, 3/23/1781, in Boyd, *Jefferson Papers,* 5: pp. 218–19.

10. Graham, *Morgan,* p. 465, for taking command; Scheer and Rankin, *Rebels & Redcoats,* pp. 125–26, for other quotations.

11. Scheer and Rankin, *Rebels & Redcoats,* p. 126.

12. Morison, "Journal," in Roberts, *March to Quebec,* pp. 537–38; Henry Caldwell(?) to James Murray, 6/15/1776, in Commager and Morris, *Spirit of 'Seventy-Six* 1: p. 206.

13. Graham, *Morgan,* p. 112.

14. Greene, *Life of Greene,* 1: p. 395.

15. Fitzpatrick, *Writings of George Washington,* 9: p. 71.

16. Higginbotham, *Morgan,* p. 65.

17. This subject, including Morgan's opinion, is discussed in Chapter 15, with citations in n.6.

18. Higginbotham, *Morgan,* p. 78.

19. *Ibid.,* p. 97.

20. Elkanah Watson, *Men and Times of the Revolution: or, Memoirs of Elkanah Watson, Including His Journals of Travel in Europe and America from the Year 1772 to 1842,* 2nd Ed., Winslow C.

Watson, ed. (New York: Dana and Company, 1857), p. 297.

21. *Papers of Nathanael Greene*, 6: pp. 512–13.

22. *Ibid.*, pp. 516–17.

23. *Ibid.*, p. 532.

24. *Ibid.*, pp. 519–20.

25. NG to Hamilton, 1/10/1781, *ibid.*, 7: p. 90.

26. Gordon, *History*, 4: p. 28.

27. *Papers of Nathanael Greene*, 6: p. 554.

28. Bass, *Gamecock*, p. 115.

29. *Papers of Nathanael Greene*, 6: p. 564; Bass, *Gamecock*, p. 116, claiming credit for Sumter.

30. NG to von Steuben, 12/28/1780, *Papers of Nathanael Greene*, 7: p. 11; Boatner, *Encyclopedia*, pp. 1018–19.

31. *Papers of Nathanael Greene*, 6: p. 581; Chalmers Gaston Davidson, *Piedmont Partisan: The Life and Times of Brigadier-General William Lee Davidson* (Davidson, NC: Davidson College, 1951), p. 98.

32. *Papers of Nathanael Greene*, 6: p. 459; NG to Hamilton, 1/10/1781, 7: p. 89.

33. Bass, *Gamecock*, p. 116.

34. *Papers of Nathanael Greene*, 6: pp. 589–90.

35. Davie, *Sketches*, p. 39.

36. The exchange can be followed in *Papers of Nathanael Greene*, 6: pp. 561–62; and Davie, *Sketches*, p. 39.

37. For Davie's life see Blackwell P. Robinson, *William R. Davie* (Chapel Hill: University of North Carolina Press, 1957).

38. 1/29/1780, *Papers of Nathanael Greene*, 7: p. 22.

39. NG to Samuel Huntington, 1/28/1781, *ibid.*, 7: p. 8.

40. William Johnson, *Sketches of the Life and Correspondence of Nathanael Greene*, 2 vols. (Charleston, 1822), 1: pp. 350–52.

20. Tarleton Pursues Morgan

1. *Papers of Nathanael Greene*, 6: p. 589.

2. Lee, *Memoirs*, p. 592, for both quotations on Howard; reference to his wound is in draft letter, W. Howard to B. Walsh, Jr., 3/20/1830, MS. 469, Maryland Historical Society.

3. Lee, *Memoirs*, p. 185n.

4. *Ibid.*, p. 588; Morgan to William Snickers, 1/26/1781, Gates Papers, New-York Historical Society.

5. *Dictionary of American Biography* for quotation. The best and most thorough biography of Pickens remains unpublished: Clyde R. Ferguson, "General Andrew Pickens" (Ph.D. dissertation, Duke University, 1960).

6. Higginbotham, *Morgan*, pp. 125–26.

7. *Dictionary of American Biography*.

8. Young, "Memoir," p. 87.

9. *Ibid.*, pp. 87–88.

10. Lambert, *South Carolina Loyalists*, p. 153.

11. Bass, *Green Dragoon*, p. 142.

12. Lambert, *South Carolina Loyalists*, p. 161.

13. *Papers of Nathanael Greene*, 7: p. 31.

14. *Ibid.*, pp. 74–75.

15. *Ibid.*, p. 75.

16. 1/10/1781, *ibid.*, p. 88.

17. For this incident, see Morgan to NG, 1/15/1781, *ibid.*, p. 127–28.

18. Graham, *Morgan*, p. 272.

19. Bass, *Green Dragoon*, p. 141.

20. Stevens, *Campaign in Virginia*, 1: pp. 237–38.

21. *Ibid.*, pp. 295–96, 315.

22. Pancake, *This Destructive War*, pp. 146–47.

23. Bass, *Green Dragoon*, pp. 142–43, for George's messages, Haldane's dispatch, and Cornwallis's note to Tarleton.

24. *Ibid.*, pp. 144–46.

25. NG to Morgan, 1/19/1781, *Papers of Nathanael Greene*, 7: p. 147.

26. Bass, *Green Dragoon*, pp. 148–49.

27. *Ibid.*, pp. 150–51.

28. Morgan to NG, 1/15/1780, *Papers of Nathanael Greene*, 7: p. 128.

29. *Ibid.*

30. NG to Morgan, 1/19/1781, *ibid.*, pp. 146–47.

31. NG to Morgan, 1/13/1781, *ibid.*, p. 106.

32. Tarleton, *History*, p. 214.

33. On the critical point of where Morgan meant to fight, see Morgan to William Snickers, 1/26/1781, and for his early awareness that Tarleton had eventually to be dealt with, Morgan to Horatio Gates, 11/23/1780, both in the Gates Papers, New-York Historical Society (the importance of these letters was first recognized several years ago by Professor Don Higginbotham); see also Higginbotham, *Morgan*, pp. 131–32.

34. Young, "Memoir," p. 88.

35. Lee, *Memoirs*, p. 226; Higginbotham, *Morgan*, p. 132, for Morgan's coolness in a crisis.

36. Lee, *Memoirs*, pp. 222n, 226n, for Howard's recollections; Young, "Memoir," p. 88; *Papers of Nathanael Greene*, 7: p. 129n.4, for Pickens's recollection.

37. Tarleton, *History*, p. 214.

38. Higginbotham, *Morgan*, p. 132.

39. Moultrie, *Memoirs*, 2: p. 245.

40. Young, "Memoir," p. 88.

41. *Ibid.*

42. Morgan to William Snickers, 1/26/1781, Gates Papers, New-York Historical Society.

43. Joseph McJunkin, "Memoir of Joseph McJunkin," *The Magnolia; or, Southern Appalachian*, 2 (January 1843), p. 38.

21. Cowpens

1. Morgan to NG, 1/19/1781, *Papers of Nathanael Greene*, 7: p. 155. This, Morgan's official report, with the very useful editorial notes (pp. 152–61), along with Tarleton's *History*, are the basic sources for the battle; important supplements are cited below.

2. Seymour, *Journal*, p. 13.

3. Tarleton, *History*, pp. 215, 221.

4. Young, "Memoir," p. 100; Graham, *Morgan*, p. 297; McJunkin, "Memoir," p. 38.

5. Tarleton, *History*, p. 216.

6. *Papers of Nathanael Greene*, 7: p. 154; Young, "Memoir," p. 100.

7. Young, "Memoir," p. 100.

8. Thomas Anderson, "Journal of Lieutenant Thomas Anderson of the Delaware Regiment, 1780–1782," *The Historical Magazine*, 1, no. 4 (April 1867), p. 209; Seymour, *Journal*, p. 13; Collins, *Autobiography*, p. 264; Tarleton, *History*, p. 216.

9. Collins, *Autobiography*, p. 264; Young, "Memoir," p. 100.

10. Seymour, *Journal*, pp. 14–15.

11. Collins, *Autobiography*, p. 264.

12. Howard in Henry Lee, *The Campaign of 1781 in the Carolinas* (Philadelphia, 1824), p. 97n (the author was Light Horse Harry Lee's son); see also John Eager Howard to [Bayard?], n.d., Bayard Papers, Ms. 109, Maryland Historical Society.

13. Anderson, "Journal," p. 209.

14. Graham, *Morgan*, p. 304; Lee, *The Campaign of 1781 in the Carolinas*, p. 97n; Howard to [Bayard?], n.d.

15. Anderson, "Journal," p. 209; Higginbotham, *Morgan*, p. 140; *Papers of Nathanael Greene*, 7: p. 153; Howard to [Bayard?], n.d.

16. Young, "Memoir," p. 100; Howard to [Bayard?], n.d.; *Papers of Nathanael Greene*, 7: p. 154.

17. Tarleton, *History*, pp. 217–18; McKenzie, *Strictures*, p. 100; Bass, *Green Dragoon*, for Tarleton's exchange with Dr. Jackson.

18. McJunkin, "Memoir," p. 39.

19. *Papers of Nathanael Greene*, 7: p. 155.

20. Tarleton, *History*, p. 221.

21. McKenzie, *Strictures*, pp. 115, 118; Stedman, *History*, 2: p. 324; Lee, *The Campaign of 1781 in the Carolinas*, p. 98n.

22. Lee, *The Campaign of 1781 in the Carolinas*, p. 98n.

23. Johnson, *Sketches of the life . . . of Nathanael Greene*, 1: p. 376.

24. Morgan to Snickers, 1/26/1781, Gates Papers, New-York Historical Society; Hinrichs, *Diary*, p. 213.

25. *Papers of Nathanael Greene*, 7: p. 152; Morgan to Snickers, 1/26/1781.

26. Graham, *Morgan*, p. 323.

27. *Ibid.*, p. 320.

28. *Ibid.*, pp. 323–24.

29. Tarleton, *History*, p. 218.

30. Young, "Memoir," pp. 101–2, from his fight with the dragoons and meeting Tarleton through his appropriation of Molly Willard's horse.

31. Collins, *Autobiography*, p. 265.

32. Chesney, *Journal*, p. 22.

33. McJunkin, "Memoir," p. 39; Wickwire, *Cornwallis*, p. 269; Moultrie, *Memoirs*, pp. 256–57.

34. Bass, *Green Dragoon*, p. 161.

35. Scheer and Rankin, *Rebels & Redcoats*, p. 433.

22. Bayonets and Zeal

1. Pancake, *Destructive War*, p. 150.

2. My sketch of O'Hara, with quotations, is based on his entry in the *Dictionary of National Biography*.

3. "O'Hara Letters," pp. 159–60.

4. *Ibid.*, p. 161.

5. William Smith, *Historical Account of Bouquet's Expedition Against the Ohio Indians in 1764*, Ohio Valley Historical Series, no. 1 (Cincinnati: Robert Clarke & Co., 1868; reprint, with additions, of 1765 edition), p. 19.

6. Wickwire, *Cornwallis*, p. 275; "British Orderly Book," p. 285.

7. *Papers of Nathanael Greene*, 7: pp. 178, 192, 200.

8. Morgan to NG, 1/28/1780 and 1/29/1780, *ibid.*, pp. 211, 215.

9. Ross, *Cornwallis Correspondence*, 1: p. 517; Lossing, *Pictorial Field-Book of the Revolution*, 2: p. 395n.1.

10. "British Orderly Book," p. 288; "O'Hara Letters," p. 174.

11. "O'Hara Letters," p. 174.

12. Stevens to Jefferson, 2/8/1781, Boyd, *Jefferson Papers*, 4: p. 562; Johnson, *Sketches of the life . . . of Nathanael Greene*, 1: p. 394, for Greene's dangerous ride; NG to Huger, 1/30/1781, *Papers of Nathanael Greene*, 7: p. 220.

13. Gordon, *History*, 4: p. 38; Morgan to NG, 1/24/1781 and 1/25/1781, *Papers of Nathanael Greene*, 7: pp. 192, 201.

14. NG to Hamilton, 1/10/1781, *Papers of Nathanael Greene*, 7: p. 90; Graham, *Graham*, p. 289.

15. Morgan to Jefferson, 2/1/1781, Boyd, ed., *Jefferson Papers*, 4: pp. 495–96.

16. Collins, *Autobiography*, p. 270; "British Orderly Book," pp. 296–97.

17. Graham, *Graham*, pp. 289–90.

18. *Ibid.*; Davidson, *Piedmont Partisan*, pp. 114ff and *passim*, contains an excellent, detailed account of the battle as well as judicious assessments of the sources.

19. Henry, *Narrative*, pp. 4–5.

20. *Ibid.*, pp. 8–9.

21. *Ibid.*, pp. 9–10.

22. Lamb, *Occurrences*, p. 343.

23. Henry, *Narrative*, p. 11.

24. *Ibid.*, pp. 11–12; Lamb, *Occurrences*, p. 345.

25. Lamb, *Occurrences*, p. 344.

26. Henry, *Narrative*, pp. 11–12.

27. *Ibid.*, pp. 13–14.

28. *Ibid.*

29. Wickwire, *Cornwallis*, p. 282; Tarleton, *History*, p. 226.

30. Tarleton, *History*, p. 226; Stedman, *History*, p. 329n.

31. Rankin, *North Carolina Continentals*, p. 278.

32. Anderson, "Journal," p. 209; Boyd, ed., *Jefferson Papers*, 4: p. 561.

33. Wickwire, *Cornwallis*, p. 283; Stevens to Jefferson, 2/8/1781, Boyd, ed., *Jefferson Papers*, 4: p. 262.

34. Higginbotham, *Morgan*, p. 152; Graham, *Morgan*, p. 355.

35. NG to Isaac Huger, 2/5/1781, *Papers of Nathanael Greene*, 7: p. 251.

36. Tarleton, *History*, pp. 227–28; "British Orderly Book," p. 295.

37. Graham, *Morgan*, pp. 358–59. Although Graham's claim that Morgan recommended Williams cannot be documented, Graham married into the Morgan family and was perhaps passing on family tradition; that and the close friendship between Morgan and Williams argue for the truth of the story.

38. NG "To the Officers Commanding the Militia in the Salisbury District of North Carolina," 1/31/1781; NG "To the Commanding Officer of the Guilford Militia," 2/5/1781; "Proceedings of a Council of War," 2/9/1781, *Papers of Nathanael Greene*, 7: pp. 227–28, 253 and n.4, 261–62.

39. My sketch of Lee is based on his entry in the *Dictionary of American Biography*; Robert E. Lee's "Life of General Henry Lee," in Lee, *Memoirs*, pp. 11–79; but especially on that splendid work by Charles Royster, *Light-Horse Harry Lee and the Legacy of the American Revolution* (Baton Rouge: Louisiana State University Press, 1994; paperback reprint of 1981 edition).

40. Cornwallis to Germain, 3/17/1781, in Ross, *Cornwallis Correspondence*, 1: Appendix 7, pp. 516–20, clearly explains Cornwallis's plan, especially pp. 518–19.

41. *Papers of Nathanael Greene*, 7: p. 271n3; Lee, *Memoirs*, pp. 236, 250.

42. Lee, *Memoirs*, pp. 237–38.

43. *Ibid.*, pp. 238–39; Williams to NG, 2/11/1781, *Papers of Nathanael Greene*, 7: p. 283.

44. *Papers of Nathanael Greene*, 7: p. 283; Lee, *Memoirs*, pp. 239–43; Tarleton, *History*, p. 228.

45. Lee, *Memoirs*, pp. 243–44.

46. Lee, *Memoirs*, p. 245; NG to Williams, 2/13/1781, *Papers of Nathanael Greene*, 7: p. 285.

47. Williams to NG, 2/13/1781, *Papers of Nathanael Greene*, 7: p. 286; Lee, *Memoirs*, pp. 245–46.

48. Lee, *Memoirs*, p. 246; *Papers of Nathanael Greene*, 7: p. 287, for both of Greene's letters; NG to Williams, 2/13/1781, p. 285, for the "flower of the army" quotation; Gordon, *History*, 4: p. 45.

49. Gordon, *History*, 4: p. 45; Lee, *Memoirs*, pp. 246–47.

50. "O'Hara Letters," p. 176.

23. Patience and Finesse

1. Tarleton, *History*, p. 229.

2. Mackesy, *War for America*, p. 252, for the Graves's quotation; Ross, *Cornwallis, Correspondence*, 1: p. 88.

3. Ross, *Cornwallis Correspondence*, 1: 85; Stevens, *Campaign in Virginia*, 1: p. 360.

4. Scheer and Rankin, *Rebels & Redcoats*, p. 426.

5. "O'Hara Letters," pp. 176–77.

6. Stedman, *History*, 2: p. 335; Lamb, *Occurrences*, p. 348.

7. Lee, *Memoirs*, pp. 249, 251; NG to Jefferson, 2/15/1781, NG to Richard Caswell, 2/18/1781, *Papers of Nathanael Greene*, 7: pp. 289, 309.

8. 2/13/1781, *Papers of Nathanael Greene*, 7: p. 284.

9. NG to Pickens, 2/3/1781, NG to Colonel Francis Lock and Others, 2/9/1781, Pickens to NG, 2/19/1781, NG to Pickens, 2/20/1781, Pickens to NG, 2/20/1781, *Papers of Nathanael Greene*, 7: pp. 241, 262, 320, 322, 325; Ferguson, "General Andrew Pickens," p. 156, for the thirty men; Graham, *Graham*, p. 203.

10. For the date of Lee's recrossing of the Dan, see Lee to NG, 2/18/1781, Otho Williams to NG, 2/18/1781, Lee to NG, 2/20/1781, *Papers of Nathanael Greene*, 7: pp. 313 and n.1, 315, 324; Graham, *Graham*, p. 205.

11. Cornwallis to Germain, 3/17/1781, Ross, *Cornwallis Correspondence*, 1: p. 519; Tarleton, *History*, p. 231; Lee, *Memoirs*, p. 254.

12. Pickens to NG, 1/26/1781, *Papers of Nathanael Greene*, 7: p. 355; Tarleton, *History*, p. 232.

13. Lee, *Memoirs*, pp. 256–58, gives his version of the affair; the quotations are cited separately.

14. Dann, *Revolution Remembered*, pp. 201–2; Graham, *Graham*, p. 319.

15. Dann, *Revolution Remembered*, p. 202; Tarleton, *History*, p. 232; Stedman, *History*, 2: p. 334.

16. Dann, *Revolution Remembered*, p. 202.

17. NG to Jefferson, 1/29/1781, Pickens to NG, 2/26/1781, *Papers of Nathanael Greene*, 7: p. 358.

18. Tarleton, *History*, p. 233; Lee, *Memoirs*, p. 233.

19. NG to John Butler, 2/21/1781, NG to Jefferson, 3/10/1781, *Papers of Nathanael Greene*, 7: pp. 327, 420; in addition to the specific examples cited below, NG's militia problems can be studied in his correspondence for the period.

20. Cornwallis to Germain, 3/17/1781, Ross, *Cornwallis Correspondence*, 1: p. 519; "British Orderly Book," p. 373; Wickwire, *Cornwallis*, p. 289.

21. Otho Williams to NG, 3/4/1781, *Papers of Nathanael Greene*, 7: pp. 393–94, for the British Legion attack on Tories; Rankin, *North Carolina Continentals*, p. 292, for the American attack on Tory drovers.

22. Greene, *Life of Greene*, 3: pp. 186–87.

23. Otho Williams to NG, 2/26/1781, Pickens to NG, 3/5/1781, Lee to NG, 3/4/1781, William Campbell to NG, 3/2/1781, Otho Williams to NG, 3/4/1781, NG to Jefferson, 3/10/1781, *Papers of Nathanael Greene*, 7: pp. 360, 399, 393, 380, 391, 420; Graham, *Graham*, 334, for half the militia to be organized as infantry and the opposition to it.

24. Lamb, *Occurrences*, p. 381; "British Orderly Book," pp. 378–81.

25. For Weitzel's Mill see Otho Williams to NG, 3/7/1781, *Papers of Nathanael Greene*, 7: pp. 407–8; Graham, *Graham*, pp. 342–46; Lee, *Memoirs*, pp. 265–67; Tarleton, *History*, p. 238; Rankin, *North Carolina Continentals*, pp. 295–97.

26. For Pickens's departure, see Pickens to NG, 3/5/1781and n.6, NG to Pickens, 3/8/1781, *Papers of Nathanael Greene*, 7: pp. 399, 410.

27. NG to Jefferson, 3/10/1781, *ibid.*, p. 420.

28. St. George Tucker to Francis Bland Tucker, 3/23/1781, "The Southern Campaign, 1781, from Guilford Court House to the Siege of York, as Narrated in the Letters of St. George Tucker to his Wife," *The Magazine of American History*, 7, no. 1 (July 1881), p. 39.

29. *Papers of Nathanael Greene*, 7: p. 324.

30. For the action on the New Garden Road, and all quotations to the end of the chapter, see Lee, *Memoirs*, pp. 272–75; and Tarleton, *History*, p. 271.

24. Guilford Courthouse: "Long, Obstinate, and Bloody"

1. NG to Samuel Huntington, 3/16/1781, *Papers of Nathanael Greene*, 7: pp. 433–35, is Greene's official battle report, and is accompanied by extensive editorial notes, pp. 436–41.

2. Lee, *Memoirs*, p. 260; the political situation concerning command of the militia can be followed in NG to North Carolina Legislature, 2/15/1781, NG to Thomas Polk, 2/16/1781, NG to Abner Nash, 2/17/1781, NG to Richard Caswell, 2/18/1781, NG to Jethro Sumner, 2/18/1781 and n.4, Alexander Martin to NG, 2/19/1781, and Jethro Sumner to NG, 2/25/1781 and n., *Papers of Nathanael Greene*, 7: pp. 290–91, 298, 302–3, 309–10, 312, 348–49; Davie, *Sketches*, p. 32; Morgan to NG, 2/20/1781, *Papers of Nathanael Greene*, 7: p. 324.

3. Scheer and Rankin, *Rebels & Redcoats*, p. 447.

4. Previous accounts, based on Schenck, North Carolina, p. 330, assert the British had three-pounders, but see *Papers of Nathanael Greene*, 7: p. 437n.8, based on studies of Thomas Baker, Historian/Ranger at the Guilford Courthouse National Military Park.

5. NG to Samuel Huntington, 3/16/1781, *Papers of Nathanael Greene*, 7: p. 434; Rankin, *North Carolina Continentals*, p. 311; Schenck, *North Carolina*, pp. 349–50, 352, for Stuart and Montgomery quotations.

6. Lamb, *Occurrences*, p. 361.

7. Davie, *Sketches*, p. 31; NG to Samuel Huntington, 3/16/1781, *Papers of Nathanael Greene*, 7: p. 434.

8. Davie, *Sketches*, p. 31; Lamb, *Occurrences*, p. 362.

9. St. George Tucker to Francis Bland Tucker, 3/18/1781, *Magazine of American History*, p. 39.

10. Tarleton, *History*, p. 273

11. John Eager Howard to [Bayard?], n.d., Bayard Papers, Ms. 109, Maryland Historical Society; Thomas Baker, *Another Such Victory* (Eastern Acorn Press, 1981), p. 65.

12. The British claimed Smith killed Stewart after he had surrendered. John Eager Howard wrote, "The fact was not so; Steuart refused to surrender; I saw the transaction." John Eager Howard to [Bayard?] n.d.

13. John Eager Howard to [Bayard?], n.d.; Tarleton, *History*, p. 275; Lee, *Memoirs*, pp. 280, 283n.; Wickwire, *Cornwallis*, pp. 307–8.

14. Stedman, *History*, 2: p. 341; for American casualty figures see *Papers of Nathanael Greene*, 7: pp. 440–44n.16.

15. John Eager Howard to [Bayard?], n.d.

16. For a good discussion of British casualty figures see Wickwire, *Cornwallis*, pp. 454–55n.25.

17. NG to Catherine Greene, 3/18/1781, *Papers of Nathanael Greene*, 7: p. 446; Lee, *Memoirs*, p. 283n.

18. Stedman, *History*, 2: p. 346; Lee, *Memoirs*, p. 286.

19. "O'Hara Letters," pp. 177–78.

20. Hugh Rankin, "Charles Cornwallis: Study in Frustration," 2: p. 213; "O'Hara, Letters," p. 177; Ross, *Cornwallis Correspondence*, 1: p. 88; Rankin, *North Carolina Continentals*, p. 310.

21. NG to Joseph Reed, 3/18/1781, *Papers of Nathanael Greene*, 7: pp. 450–51.

22. Cornwallis to Clinton, 4/10/1781, Clinton, *American Rebellion*, p. 508.

23. *Ibid.*, pp. 508–9.

24. Lamb, *Occurrences*, p. 360.

25. Cornwallis to Phillips, 4/10/1781, Ross, *Cornwallis Correspondence*, 1: p. 88.

The Major Characters (in Order of Appearance) and What Happened to Them

1. My sketch of Clinton's post-American years is based on the penultimate chapter in Willcox, *Portrait of a General*, pp. 445–91, where the quotations can be found, in order, on the following pages: 481–82, 469, 480, 471, 472, 484, 484n.9, 481.

2. Stedman, *History*, 2: p. 432n.

3. Bass, *Green Dragoon*, p. 407, 4.

4. *Ibid.*, p. 8; Andrew Oliver, ed., *The Journal of Samuel Curwen Loyalist*, 2 vols. (Cambridge: Harvard University Press, 1972), 2: p. 832.

5. Nicholas Penny, ed., *Reynolds* (New York: Abrams, 1986), pp. 377–78, for an image of the caricature and the quotation.

6. McKenzie, *Strictures*, pp. 26–27.

7. Bass, *Green Dragoon*, p. 235.

8. *Ibid.*, p. 439.

9. *Ibid.*, pp. 452–53.

10. My sketch of Cornwallis's post-American career is based largely on his entry in the *Dictionary of National Biography*, but I have also benefited from reading Franklin and Mary Wickwire, *Cornwallis: The Imperial Years* (Chapel Hill: University of North Carolina Press, 1980).

11. Willcox, *Portrait*, p. 459.

12. Rankin, "Charles Cornwallis: Study in Frustration," 2: p. 222.

13. Ross, *Cornwallis Correspondence*, 3: p. 337.

14. *Dictionary of American Biography*.

15. Robinson, *William R. Davie*, p. 112.

16. Gregorie, *Sumter*, p. 79n.83.

17. Nelson, *Gates*, p. 257.

18. *Ibid.*, pp. 293, 291.

19. Boatner, *Encyclopedia*, p. 677; see also Rankin, *Swamp Fox*, pp. 164–75.

20. Boatner, *Encyclopedia*, p. 677.

21. Catherine S. Crary, *The Price of Loyalty: Tory Writings from the Revolutionary Era* (New York: McGraw-Hill, 1973), pp. 288–90.

22. Pancake, *Destructive War*, p. 205; Boatner, *Encyclopedia*, p. 205.

23. Dann, *Revolution Remembered*, p. 220; Scheer and Rankin, *Rebels & Redcoats*, p. 458.

24. Rankin, *North Carolina Continentals*, p. 361; Hugh Rankin, *The American Revolution* (New York, 1964), p. 313.

25. Stegeman, *Caty*, p. 112.

26. Greene, *Life of Greene*, 3: p. 534,

27. Higginbotham, *Morgan*, p. 183; although much condensed, my sketch is based on this work, pp. 156–215.

28. North Callahan, *Daniel Morgan: Ranger of the Revolution* (New York: Holt, Rinehart and Winston, 1961), p. 279.

29. Higginbotham, *Morgan*, p. 207.

30. Callahan, *Ranger of the Revolution*, pp. 294–95

31. Lee, *Memoirs*, p. 584.

A Select and Annotated Bibliography

PRINTED PRIMARY SOURCES: BRITISH AND GERMAN

Sir Henry Clinton, *The American Rebellion: Sir Henry Clinton's Narrative of His Campaigns, 1775–1782, with an Appendix of Original Documents*, William B. Willcox, ed., New Haven: Yale University Press, 1954, is the only complete memoir by a general on either side, and though an apologia by an embittered man, if used with that knowledge in mind it is a most valuable document.

Most of Cornwallis's papers are in manuscript, but *Correspondence of Charles, First Marquis Cornwallis*, Charles Ross, ed., 2nd Ed., 3 vols., London: John Murray, 1859, contains many valuable letters for his American period in Vol. 1. The postwar Clinton/Cornwallis imbroglio is very conveniently brought together in Benjamin Franklin Stevens, *The Campaign in Virginia, 1781. An Exact Reprint of Six Rare Pamphlets on the Clinton-Cornwallis Controversy*, 2 vols., London, 1882, which also contains much valuable correspondence that describes the campaign in the Carolinas.

As with all memoirs, Banastre Tarleton, *A History of the Campaigns of 1780 and 1781 in the Southern Provinces of North America*, London, 1787, must be used with care, but I believe my judgment in the text is valid: when he clearly won he can be trusted, when he lost he either did not admit it or blamed it on others. But he cited his sources and included complete copies of many important documents. It should be used in conjunction with Roderick McKenzie, *Strictures on Lieut. Col. Tarleton's History*, London, 1787, who although often mistaken on details is sound in his overall criticism.

R. Kent Newmyer in the *American Historical Review* (July 1958) pointed out that Charles Stedman, *History of the Origin, Progress, and Termination of the American War*, 2 vols., London, 1794, extensively plagiarizes from the *Annual Register* and Tarleton's *History*; but as Cornwallis's commissary general Stedman's account remains valuable when he was either an eyewitness to events or close to the action.

Roger Lamb, *An Original and Authentic Journal of Occurrences during the late American War, from its Commencement to the Year 1783*, Dublin, 1809; and *Memoirs of His Own Life*, Dublin, 1811, are classics by the intrepid sergeant of the Royal Welsh Fusiliers, with the former the most useful. For a special treat the reader should try *Sergeant Lamb's America*, a first-rate historical novel by Robert Graves, which is based on Lamb's accounts of his adventures.

Hugh F. Rankin, ed., "An Officer Out of His Time: Correspondence of

Major Patrick Ferguson, 1779–1780," in Howard H. Peckham, ed., *Sources of American Independence: Selected Manuscripts from the Collections of the William L. Clements Library*, Chicago: The University of Chicago Press, 1978, Vol. II, 287–360, is very revealing of Ferguson. In his introduction Professor Rankin comes to a conclusion about Ferguson opposite to mine.

George C. Rogers, Jr., ed., "Letters of Charles O'Hara to the Duke of Grafton," *The South Carolina Historical Magazine*, 65:3 (July 1964), 158–80, is valuable for the condition of Cornwallis's army during and after the campaign as well as the views of soldiers in the field faced with reality and the myopia of their masters 3,000 miles away.

The Journal of Alexander Chesney, a South Carolina Loyalist in the Revolution and After, Alfred E. Jones, ed., in The Ohio State University *Bulletin*, XXVI: 4 (Oct. 30, 1921), 1–149 (the original is in the British Museum, Additional MSS. 32627), contains a rare eyewitness Tory account of King's Mountain and its aftermath, and also presents a clear picture of the consequences of defeat in civil war. Action at King's Mountain and the plight of the prisoners is also found in the *Diary of Anthony Allaire, of Ferguson's Corps*, which is printed in Lyman C. Draper, *King's Mountain and its Heroes*, Cincinnati, 1881, and all subsequent editions; but Allaire is most valuable for his picture of the daily drudgery of campaigning.

A. R. Newsome, ed., "A British Orderly Book, 1780–1781," *The North Carolina Historical Review*, IX: 3 (July 1932) pp. 273–298, and IX: 4 (October 1932) pp. 366–392 is helpful on the chronology of Cornwallis's campaign as well as a good picture of the concerns of a field commander, especially with regard to the maddening but age-old and neverending transgressions of the other ranks.

A candid Tory account of the problems of the Tory militia and the inferiority of its leadership relative to Rebel militia leaders is in "Colonel Robert Gray's Observations on the War in Carolina," *The South Carolina Historical and Geneological Magazine*, XI: 3 (July 1910), 1–159.

Bernhard A. Uhlendorf, tr. and ed., *The Siege of Charleston, with an Account of the Province of South Carolina: Diaries and Letters of Hessian Officers from the von Jungken Papers in the William L. Clements Library*, Ann Arbor: University of Michigan Press, 1938, contains much important material, including the diary of Captain Johann Hinrichs.

For completeness, candor, reliablity, and good reading, Captain Johann Ewald, *Diary of the American War: A Hessian Journal*, Joseph P. Tustin tr. and ed., New Haven: Yale University Press, 1979, is hard to match.

PRINTED PRIMARY SOURCES: AMERICAN

A perusal of the notes to this book will reveal the heavy use I have made of *The Papers of General Nathanael Greene, 1766–29 March 1781*, vols. 1–7,

Richard K. Showman, et al., ed., Chapel Hill: University of North Carolina Press, 1976–1994. These volumes meet the rigorous standards of modern historical editing and also contain very informative and learned editorial footnotes. There will be thirteen volumes.

John Drayton, *Memoirs of the American Revolution as Relating to the State of South Carolina*, 2 vols., Charleston, 1821, are the papers of William Henry Drayton that were salvaged by his son, John Drayton, and arranged by him and published. They are indispensable.

William Moultrie, *Memoirs of the American Revolution, So Far as it Related to the States of North and South Carolina, and Georgia*, 2 vols., New York: David Longworth, 1802, is a key source for the Battle of Sullivan's Island and of interest on other aspects of the war in the South.

Charles Woodmason, *The Carolina Back Country on the Eve of the Revolution: The Journal and other Writings of Charles Woodmason Anglican Itinerant*, Richard J. Hooker, ed., Chapel Hill: University of North Carolina Press, 1953, is vastly entertaining as well as very informative. Woodmason's savage descriptions of Back Country folk have led some to dismiss his account as highly exaggerated, but I believe the preacher knew of what he wrote. Hooker provides a judicious introduction.

Henry Lee, *Memoirs of the War in the Southern Department of the United States*, 2 vols. Philadelphia, 1812, is Light Horse Harry Lee's partisan view of the war. His ever-present sense of the dramatic gives understandable pause to students of the war, but if used with care it remains one of the most valuable sources by a participant. I used the 1869 edition edited by his son, Robert E. Lee.

The Revolutionary War Sketches of William R. Davie, Blackwell P. Robinson, ed., Raleigh: North Carolina Department of Cultural Resources, Division of Archives and History, 1976, are the recollections of a very active participant that strike me as straightforward; it includes extensive and most helpful editorial notes.

James Potter Collins, *Autobiography of a Revolutionary Soldier*, John M. Roberts, ed., Clinton, LA: Feliciana Democrat, 1859, and reprinted in Susan Francis Miller, *Sixty Years in the Nueces Valley: 1870–1930*, San Antonio: Naylor Printing Company, 1930, which I used, is a splendid view of a countryside at war as well as the emotions of a boy who became a soldier before his time.

The best eyewitness account of Gates's Camden campaign is "A Narrative of the Campaign of 1780, by Colonel Otho Holland Williams, Adjutant General," in William Johnson, *Sketches of the Life and Correspondence of General Nathanael Greene*, 2 vols., Charleston, 1822, V. I, Appendix B, 485–510. What a pity that Williams, intelligent and honest, did not continue his narrative through the next two years.

William A. Graham, *General Joseph Graham and His Papers on North Carolina Revolutionary History*, Raleigh, 1904, written some forty years after the events, are nevertheless one of the most valuable recollections of a participant, often giving different perspectives from the views of his contemporaries.

Robert Henry, *Narrative of the Battle of Cowan's Ford, February 1, 1781*, and *Narrative of the Battle of King's Mountain by Captain David Vance*, Greensboro, NC: D. Schenck, 1891, strike one as on the whole trustworthy accounts that add a sense of immediacy to events as seen by front-line militiamen. Henry wrote seventy years after the event, but on the basis of comparison with independent accounts was credited by the closest student of the action at Cowan's Ford (see Chalmers Davidson, below) with a phenomenal memory.

Thomas Young, "Memoir of Thomas Young, a Revolutionary Patriot of South Carolina" *Orion* 3 (October 1843), 84–88 (November 1843), 100–105, adds valuable details to events well known and little known.

Joseph McJunkin, "Memoir of Joseph McJunkin of Union," *The Magnolia, or Southern Appalachian* 2 (January 1843), 30–40, supplements the other militia acounts.

William Hill, *Colonel William Hill's Memoirs of the Revolution*, A. S. Salley, Jr., ed., Columbia, SC: The Historical Commission of South Carolina, 1921, by an important follower of Thomas Sumter, used in conjunction with other sources provides minor additions to relatively well-known events, but is of special interest for its description of the organization of resistance in the Back Country after the fall of Charleston.

On the other hand, Richard Winn, "General Richard Winn's Notes—1780," Samuel C. Williams, ed., *The South Carolina Historical and Genealogical Magazine*, 43: 4 (October 1942), 201–212, and 44: 1 (January 1943), 1–10, by another important Sumter lieutenant, might be subtitled, How I Won the War in the Carolinas. Among other things he manages to leave the erroneous impression that without his advice Morgan would not have known how to fight the Battle of Cowpens. It is of interest as an example of self-serving accounts.

Isaac Shelby, "King's Mountain Letters of Colonel Isaac Shelby," J. G. de Roulhac Hamilton, ed., *The Journal of Southern History*, IV: 3 (August 1938) 367–377, is of more interest for its account of the fight at Musgrove's Mill.

There are several collections of eyewitness accounts edited with commentary by authorities in the field. Perhaps the best known is Henry Steele Commager and Richard B. Morris, *The Spirit of 'Seventy-Six: The Story of the American Revolution as Told by Participants*, 2 vols., Indianapolis: Bobbs-Merrill, 1958. Another excellent work is George F. Scheer and Hugh Rankin, *Rebels & Redcoats: The American Revolution Through the Eyes of Those Who Fought and Lived It*, Cleveland: World, 1957. Pension applications by veterans provide the accounts in the fascinating work edited with assessments by John C. Dann, *The Revolution Remembered: Eyewitness Accounts of the War for Independence*, Chicago: University of Chicago Press, 1980.

SECONDARY WORKS

Under the heading of reference works pride of place must go to the indispensable Mark M. Boatner, III, *Encyclopedia of the American Revolution*, Mechanicsburg, PA: Stackpole Books, 1994, first published in 1966 and now happily back in print after becoming quite scarce on the used book market. Boatner's detailed analysis of actions and campaigns make this more than a reference work. His *Landmarks of the Revolution: People and Places Vital to the Quest for Independence*, Rev. Ed., Stackpole, 1992, is valuable to travelers as well as writers and historians. Another useful book for travelers is Sol Stember, *The Bicentennial Guide to the American Revolution: The War in the South*, Vol. III, New York: Saturday Review Press, 1974. Volume 2 of Benson J. Lossing, *The Pictorial Field-Book of the Revolution*, 2 vols., New York: Harper Brothers, 1850, covers the South. In addition to its importance as a reference, reading Lossing is like taking a trip through mid-nineteenth-century America with a friend. Patricia L. Hudson and Sandra L. Ballard, *The Smithsonian Guide to Historic America: The Carolinas and the Appalachian States*, New York: Stewart, Tabori & Chang, 1989, is excellent for its description of historic buildings and sites, but the historical introduction to the region is misleading, and spreads the Celtic myth of the American South.

In addition to maps in many of the works listed, three books are basic. Kenneth Nebenzahl and Don Higginbotham, *Atlas of the American Revolution*, Chicago: Rand McNally, 1974; Douglas W. Marshall and Howard Peckham, *Campaigns of the American Revolution: An Atlas of Manuscript Maps*, Ann Arbor: University of Michigan Press, c. 1975; Lester J. Cappon, et al., ed., *Atlas of Early American History: The Revolutionary Era, 1760–1790*, Princeton: Princeton University Press, 1976. I also used Cappon as a guide for spellings of places. Map lovers will also find handy good modern road maps of the Carolinas.

A contemporary source that can be occasionally useful is William Gordon, *The History of the Rise, Progress, and Establishment of the United States of America: including an Account of the Late War; and of the Thirteen Colonies, from their Origin to that Period*, 4 vols., London, 1788. Gordon interviewed generals and had access to their papers, but whenever one reads him on any subject it would be well to keep in mind William Richardson Davie's observation about Gordon's account of the Battle of Guilford Courthouse: "Mr Gordon appears to have garbled as his fancy or prejudices directed the relation made by Genl Greene of this action" (Davie, *Sketches*, 31).

Leading the pack of biographers is William B. Willcox, *Portrait of a General: Sir Henry Clinton in the War of Independence*, New York: Knopf, 1964, a model of scholarship and the biographer's art and one of the best books ever written on the war. It was very helpful. I also relied heavily on Franklin and Mary Wickwire, *Cornwallis: The American Adventure*, Boston: Houghton Mifflin, 1970, which is the product of prodigous research and is especially good on Cornwallis's personality; but I believe it overestimates his generalship and underestimates the fighting qualities of the Back Country Rebel militia. For those who are interested, their *Cornwallis: The Imperial Years*, Chapel Hill: University of North Carolina Press, 1980, tells how Cornwallis progressed from humiliating defeat to become one of the builders of the second British Empire. Robert D. Bass, *The Green Dragoon: The Lives of Banastre Tarleton and Mary Robinson*, New York: Holt, 1957, is important, as it is based on the Tarleton papers discovered by the author; much of the book is on Tarleton's postwar career as well as the life of his mistress. There is no biography of Patrick Ferguson, and information is scattered, but James Ferguson, *Two Scottish Soldiers*, Aberdeen: D. Wylie & Son, 1888 is useful, and Rankin, "An Officer Out of His Time" (above) is important.

On the American side Theodore Thayer, *Nathanael Greene: Strategist of the Revolution*, New York: Twayne Publishers, 1960, is good on particular aspects of Greene's career but disappointing overall. Still helpful is George Washington Greene, *The Life of General Nathanael Greene: Major-General in the Army of the Revolution*, 3 vols., Freeport, NY: Books for Libraries Press, 1972, which is a reprint of the 1867–1871 edition. Not to be ignored is William Johnson, *Sketches of the Life and Correspondence of General Nathanael Greene*, 2 vols., Charleston, 1822. The General impatiently awaits his biographer. John F. Stegeman and Janet A. Stegeman, *Caty: A Biography of Catherine Littlefield Greene*, Providence: Rhode Island Bicentennial Foundation, 1977, is a very sympathetic but well-done portrayal of a woman who fascinated contemporaries and posterity.

Daniel Morgan has two important biographers. James Graham, *The Life of General Daniel Morgan of the Virginia Line of the Army of the United States*, New York: Derby & Jackson, 1856, by a man who married one of Morgan's great granddaughters, should by no means be neglected because of its age; it also contains many important documents. Very sound, as one would expect, is Don Higginbotham, *Daniel Morgan: Revolutionary Rifleman*, Chapel Hill: University of North Carolina Press, 1961; it has a very good essay on sources. Gates finally got his biographer in Paul David Nelson, *General Horatio Gates: A Biography*, Baton Rouge: Louisiana State University Press, 1976, a very scholarly and useful work packed with information, but even-handed to a fault and too often gives Gates the benefit of the doubt on speculative grounds. Nelson's subsequent article, "Major General Horatio Gates as a Military Leader: The Southern Experience," in W. Robert Higgins, ed., *The Revolutionary War in the South: Power, Conflict, and Leadership*, Durham: Duke University Press, 1979, 132–158, has similar merits and flaws, and I disagree with his analysis of the Battle of Camden. The reader is warned against Samuel White Patterson, *Horatio Gates: Defender of American Liberties*, New York: Columbia University Press, 1941, which purports to be scholarly but best resembles a political campaign biography. Max Mintz, *The Generals of Saratoga: John Burgoyne and Horatio Gates*, New Haven: Yale University Press, 1990, contains much useful information about Gates's early life and career; and it may therefore seem churlish of me to observe that the author, while admitting that the man had flaws, is a Gates champion, and against overwhelming evidence takes the position that Gates was the only American general who knew how to combine militia with regulars, when the truth of it is he had not a clue.

Thomas Sumter has two biographers. Anne King Gregorie, *Thomas Sumter*, Columbia, SC: R. L. Bryan Company, 1931, is helpful and readable. Robert D. Bass, *Gamecock: The Life and Campaigns of General Thomas Sumter*, New York: Holt, Rinehart & Winston, 1961, is useful if read quite critically, especially when the author maintains that Sumter was a master tactician and grand strategist. Marion is well served by Hugh Rankin, *Frances Marion: the Swamp Fox*, New York: Crowell, 1973. The best biography of Andrew Pickens is the very thorough doctoral dissertation by Clyde R. Ferguson, "General Andrew Pickens," Duke University, 1960. Although not a full-scale biography, my personal choice for Lee is Charles Royster, *Light-Horse Harry Lee and the Legacy of the American Revolution*, New York: Knopf, 1981, a well-written and perceptive study by one of our finest historians. (I used the LSU Press paperback edition.) Wiliam M. Dabney and Marion Dargan, *William Henry Drayton and the American Revolution*, Albuquerque: The University of New Mexico Press, 1962, fills in gaps on Drayton's life, but its judgment on his famous mission to the Back Country is a near total misinterpretation of his effectiveness. J. Russell Snapp, "William Henry Drayton: The Making of a Conservative Revolutionary," *The Journal of Southern History*, LVII: 4 (November 1991), 637–658, argues convincingly that his main political principle never changed: rule by an establishment comprised of the rich and well born and fierce opposition to whoever threatened it.

William Richardson Davie is well served by Blackwell P. Robinson, *William R. Davie*, Chapel Hill: University of North Carolina Press, 1957. Although William Lee Davidson made few appearances in our narrative and met an early death, his biography by Chalmers Gaston Davidson, *Piedmont Partisan: The Life and Times of Brigadier-General William Lee Davidson*, Davidson, NC: Davidson College, 1951, is useful overall and very important on the action at Cowan's Ford. Helpful essays by specialists on American and British generals and admirals are in two works by George Athan Billias, ed., *George Washington's Generals*, New York: William Morrow, 1964, and *George Washington's Opponents*, by the same publisher, 1969 (I used the one-volume paperback 1994 edition).

For South Carolina in general I depended on the excellent David Duncan Wallace, *South Carolina: A Short History*, 1520–1948, Columbia: University of South Carolina Press, 1961. If I were limited to two books on Charleston and the Rice Kings I would choose George C. Rogers, Jr., *Charleston in the Age of the Pinckneys*, Norman: University of Oklahoma Press, 1969; and Frederick P. Bowes, *The Culture of Early Charleston*, Chapel Hill: University of North Carolina Press, 1942: two slim, well-written volumes that have much to say in few words. Another, and indispensable, view of the Low Country is well presented in Peter H. Wood, *Black Majority: Negroes in Colonial South Carolina from 1670 Through the Stono Rebellion*, New York: Knopf, 1974. By no means to be neglected is the fine view of the Low Country in Charles Fraser, *A Charleston Sketchbook, 1796–1806: Forty Watercolor Drawings of the City and the Surrounding Country, Including Plantations and Parish Churches*, Rutland, VT: Charles E. Tuttle, 1959.

The Back Country is not as well served, although Charles Woodmason's first-hand account, discussed above under *Primary Printed Sources: American*, is a minor classic. Many of the works discussed here contain information on the Back Country, but those interested in pursuing the subject further might start with Robert Lee Meriwether, *The Expansion of South Carolina, 1729–1765*,

Kingsport, TN, Southern Publishers, Inc., 1940; and Robert M. Weir, *Colonial South Carolina*, Millwood, NY, 1983, which is excellent.

The best military history of the war by far remains Christopher Ward's first-rate *The War of the Revolution*, John Richard Alden, ed., 2 vols., New York: Macmillan, 1952; it was always at hand during the writing of this book. Volume 2 covers the war in the South. Brief but also very good is Willard M. Wallace, *Appeal to Arms*, New York, 1951. Two excellent and well-written little books by Lieutenant Colonel Joseph B. Mitchell that one does not often see in bibliographies are *Decisive Battles of the American Revolution*, New York: Putnam's, 1962; and *Discipline and Bayonets: The Armies and Leaders in the War of the American Revolution*, New York: Putnam's, 1967. Broader in scope, authoritative, and containing copious citations and a long bibliographical essay is Don Higginbotham, *The War of American Independence: Military Attitudes, Policies, and Practice, 1763–1789*, New York: Macmillan, 1971. From the British point of view Piers Mackesy, *The War for America, 1775–1783*, Cambridge, Harvard University Press, 1964, has, if I may be allowed, no peer in its discussion of British strategy; unlike most American writers Mackesy places the war in the context of world politics and, germane to our study, clearly reveals the importance the British placed on the West Indies. John A. Tilley, *The British Navy and the American Revolution*, Columbia: University of South Carolina Press, 1987, is the first major study of the subject in sixty years, and was useful for ship movements and amphibious warfare during the siege of Charleston. On battle casualties I have usually followed the standard source, Howard H. Peckham, ed., *The Toll of Independence: Engagements and Battle Casualties of the American Revolution*, Chicago: University of Chicago Press, 1974.

Several books have been written on the southern campaign by specialists over the past thirty-odd years—John Pancake and Henry Lumpkin are cited in the Notes—but I found especially helpful Hugh F. Rankin, *The North Carolina Continentals*, Chapel Hill: University of North Carolina Press, 1971; by a fine historian, it ranges far wider than the title indicates. Harold A. Larrabee, *Decision at the Chesapeake*, New York: Clarkson N. Potter, 1964, is well written and sound. M. F. Treacy, *Prelude to Yorktown: The Southern Campaign of Nathanael Greene, 1780–1781*, Chapel Hill: University of North Carolina Press, 1963, is good as well as readable. Very good, of course, is Russell F. Weigley, *The Partisan War: The South Carolina Campaign of 1780–1782*, Tricentennial Booklet No. 2, Columbia: University of South Carolina Press, 1970; but it can be hard to obtain, and Chapter Two of his *American Way of War: A History of United States Military Strategy and Policy*, New York: Macmillan, 1973, contains an excellent summary of the campaign as well as a judicious assessment of Nathanael Greene.

Turning to narrower scopes, Terry W. Lipscomb, *The Carolina Low Country: April 1775–June 1776*, Columbia: South Carolina Department of Archives and History, 1991, largely covers the Battle of Sullivan's Island, and is well researched and packed with details. A National Park Service publication by Edwin C. Bearss, *The Battle of Cowpens: A Documented Narrative & Troop Movement Maps*, Office of Archaeology and Historic Preservation, 1957, is very useful.

Helpful for the Battle of Guilford Courthouse, by a National Park Service historian, is Thomas E. Baker, *Another Such Victory*, Eastern Acorn Press, 1981. A lifetime of teaching and research went into Robert Stansbury Lambert, *South Carolina Loyalists in the American Revolution*, Columbia: University of South Carolina Press, 1987. This book also ranges wider than the title leads one to believe, and offers much information on the war in the Back Country. The first 100-odd pages of Rachel N. Klein, *Unification of a Slave State: The Rise of the Planter Class in the South Carolina Backcountry, 1760–1808*, Chapel Hill: University of North Carolina Press, 1990, contains much useful information, is largely cautious in its conclusions, but errs, I believe, in overemphasizing greed for slaves as a motivation for joining the Rebels. Lewis Pinckney Jones, *The South Carolina Civil War of 1775*, Lexington, SC: The Sandlapper Store, Inc., 1975, is quite useful.

Lyman C. Draper, *King's Mountain and Its Heroes: History of the Battle of King's Mountain, October 7th, 1780, and the Events Which Led to It*, Cincinnati, 1881, is first-rate; it is the product of exhaustive research judiciously if not elegantly presented. It also contains a wealth of information on the war in the Back Country. Generation of historians and writers are in Draper's debt, and happily, the book is kept in print.

Two other older publications, products of diligent research, should not be ignored because of the extreme patriotic bias of the authors. Edward McCrady, *The History of South Carolina in the Revolution, 1775–1783*, 2 vols., New York: Macmillan, 1901–1902, in addition to being a staunch South Carolina patriot was pro-Sumter at the expense of Greene and Morgan, but with this knowledge firmly in mind McCrady can be very rewarding. The same holds for the North Carolina patriot, David Schenck, *North Carolina, 1780–81: Being a History of the Invasion of the Carolinas by the British Army under Lord Cornwallis in 1780–81*, Raleigh: Edwards & Broughton, 1890, who in one marvelous passage accuses the British of "committing acts of vindictiveness that would have made the Duke of Alba blush with shame." On the other hand, a more recent work that can be safely ignored is Kenneth Roberts, *The Battle of Cowpens: The Great Morale-Builder*, Garden City: Doubleday, 1958, which purports to be work of history but invents dialogue, includes too many errors, is an apologia for Banastre Tarleton, and misinterpets the real significance of the battle. Roberts was a fine historical novelist, but of this book one can only wonder why it is kept in print.

The Scotch Irish have had numerous publications devoted to them since early in the century, but the best place to start is James G. Leyburn, *The Scotch-Irish: A Social History*, Chapel Hill: University of North Carolina Press, 1962. Next I would turn to a fine recent book, David Hackett Fischer, *Albion's Seed: Four British Folkways in America*, New York: Oxford University Press, 1989, which is the first volume in a planned cultural history of America. See also the notes for Chapter 7. The leading proponents of the Celtic myth of the American South are Forrest McDonald and Grady McWhinney, "The Antebellum Southern Herdsmen: A Reinterpretation," *The Journal of Southern History*, 41

(1975), pp. 147–166, and other writings. For readers who wish to delve into that prickly scholarly labyrinth, the best critique I know of is Rowland Berthoff, "Celtic Mist Over the South," *The Journal of Southern History*, 52: 4 (November 1986), 523–546. For the Scottish background and the distinct ethnic and cultural differences between Lowlanders and Highlanders, see the splendid study by T. C. Smout, *A History of the Scottish People, 1560–1830*, Glasgow: William Collins, 1969.

For readers interested in the technical side of warfare, there are some excellent publications. Sebastien LePreste de Vauban, *A Manual of Siegecraft and Fortification*, George A. Rothrock, tr., Ann Arbor: University of Michigan Press, 1968. Henry Guerlac, "Vauban: The Impact of Science on War," in Edward Mead Earle, *Makers of Modern Strategy: Military Thought from Machiavelli to Hitler*, Princeton: Princeton University Press, 1943. Leonid Tarassuk and Claude Blair, *The Complete Encyclopedia of Arms and Weapons*, New York: Simon and Schuster, 1979, was produced by editors and contributors who are museum specialists. The fine points of muskets and rifles can be explored in J. N. George, *English Guns and Rifles*, Plantersville, SC: Small-Arms Technical Publishing Company, 1947, by a man who loaded a Chaumette/Ferguson rifle. Howard L. Blackmore, *British Military Firearms, 1650–1850*, London: Herbert Jenkins, 1961, who along with the two foregoing sources and Hayward, below, is very good on the Chaumette/Ferguson rifle. J. F. Hayward, *The Art of the Gunmaker, V. II, England and America, 1660–1830*, London: Barrie and Rockliff, 1963. All you ever really wanted to know about the smoothbore flintlock musket is in Torsten Lenk, *The Flintlock: Its Origin and Development*, G. A. Urquart, tr., J. F. Hayward, ed., New York: Bramhall House, 1965. For the history of the bayonet see Tarassuk and Blair, above; A. N. Harden, Jr., *The American Bayonet, 1776–1964*, Philadelphia: Riling and Lentz, 1964; and especially Charles Ffoulkes and Captain E. C. Hopkinson, *Sword, Lance & Bayonet: A Record of the Arms of the British Army and Navy*, Cambridge: Cambridge University Press, 1938. Harold L. Peterson, *The Book of the Continental Soldier: Being a Compleat Account of the Uniforms, Weapons, and Equipment with Which He Lived and Fought*, Harrisburg: Stackpole Books, 1968, is, of course, standard on the subject.

Edward E. Curtis, *The Organization of the British Army in the American Revolution*, New Haven: Yale University Press, 1926, remains standard and very good. An up-to-date supplement is Sylvia R. Frey, *The British Soldier in America*, Austin: University of Texas Press, 1981, who is good on origins of the rank and file. J. F .C. Fuller, *British Light Infantry in the Eighteenth Century*, London: Hutchinson & Co. [c. 1925], also remains valuable. Sound and succinct, although he overrates Patrick Ferguson, is Eric Robson, "British Light Infantry in the Mid-Eighteenth Century: The Effect of American Conditions," *The Army Quarterly*, 63: 2 (January 1952), pp. 209–222.

Index

A

Adamson, Captain John, 113, 115
Alexander, Captain William, 109
Alexander Old Field, 111
Allaire, Lieutenant Anthony, 61–62,
    137–139, 204–206
    King's Mountain, battle of, 233,
        236, 238–241
American Rebellion, 4
American Volunteers (Tories), 61,
    137–139, 230, 236
*A Narrative of the Southern Campaign
    of 1780*, 151
Anderson, Lieutenant Thomas, 322,
    324–325, 349
Anderson, Major Archibald, 169
A New War Song, 16
Arbuthnot, Admiral Marriott, 25, 27,
    28, 51–52, 64–66
    See also Carolina campaign
        (1780); Charleston, siege of
        (1780)
Armand, Colonel Charles, 155,
    161–163, 169
Armstrong, Captain, 109
Arnold, General Benedict,
    280–286
The Association, 91–92, 94
*Autobiography of a Revolutionary
    Soldier*, 114, 122

B

Back Country, 80–103, 104–141,
    190–1919
    attempt by Rice Kings to forge
        alliance, 90–103
    farmers and frontiersmen, 90–103
    militia. *See* militia

Tory resistance, high point at
    Ninety Six, 101, 105
Tory strength overestimated, 102
backwater men
    See Shelby, Colonel Isaac, subhead:
        Over Mountain men
Balfour, Lieutenant Colonel Nisbet,
    80, 115, 202
    Charleston commandant, 303
    chasing rebels, 138
Ball, Colonel John Coming, 191
Barefield, Captain Jesse, 183–184
Barry, Adam, 231
Beatty, Robert, 345–347
Bibby, John, 239
Black Mingo, 291–292
Blackstock's Farm, battle of, 251–259
Blue Savannah, 184
Bouquet, Brigadier General Henri,
    337
Bowman, Captain, 109
Brandon, Colonel Thomas, 104–105,
    107–108
    Blackstock's Farm, battle of, 253
    Ferguson, pursuit of, 220, 222
Brandon, Colonel William, 176,
    237
Bratton, Colonel William, 113–115,
    121
    Fish Dam Ford, 250, 253
British army
    description, 158–161
    food and supplies, shortage of in
        Back Country, 130, 359–360,
        365, 367
    manpower after Cowpens, 334
    plunder by, 343–344
    treatment of Tory militia, 243–245

British army (*Continued*)
   weaponry and tactics, 158–161,
      196–198
   See also weaponry
British Legion, 114–115, 130, 157
   Blackstock's Farm, battle of, 251
   Camden, battle of, 163, 165, 169
   Cornwallis's retreat, 243
   Cowpens, battle of, 315, 320–321,
      326
   Hanging Rock, 134–136
   Lenud's Ferry, 68
   Monck's Corner, 62, 85
   Torrence's Tavern, 349
   The Waxhaws, 80, 83–85
Brown, Captain Gabriel, 257
Brown, Thomas "Burnfoot," 95–100,
   103, 192
Brownfield, Dr. Robert, 84–85
Bryan, Colonel Morgan, 133–135,
   164
Buchanan, Captain William, 316–317
Buffalo Ford on Deep River, 129
Buford, Colonel Abraham, 68, 80–85,
   107, 120
   errors at The Waxhaws, 83
Buford's Massacre, 82–85, 364
Burgoyne, General John, 149,
   285–286, 286
Butler, Brigadier General John, 368,
   372

C
Camden, 80, 81, 153, 155–156
Camden, battle of (1780), 157–172
   American rout, 165–170
   Gates, as commander, 161
   Saunders creek, 163
   Campbell, Captain Charles, 120
   Campbell, Captain Peter, 178
   Campbell, Colonel Arthur, 212–213
   Campbell, Colonel William,
      211–212
   Dan River to Guilford Courthouse,
      365–367, 371

Guilford Courthouse, battle of, 373,
   375–376, 380
King's Mountain, battle of, 223,
   225–230, 232–233, 237–238
Campbell, Governor William, 99–101,
   103
Campbell, John, 5
Campbell, Lieutenant Colonel
   Donald, 284
Candler, Major William, 223, 252,
   254
Cane Creek, 205
Cape Fear, Royalist rendezvous, 4
Carden, Major John, 134
Carey, Colonel Matthew, 136
Carleton, Major General Sir Guy,
   283–284
Carolina campaign (1780)
   approach march, 34–43
      Ashley River, 39, 41
      Clarke Brigade attacked,
         39–40
      Drayton Hall, 41–43
      James Island, 36, 39–40
      Johns Island, 36
      Magnolia Gardens, 42
      Middleton Place, 41–43
      Stono River, 36, 38–40
      Wappoo Cut, 40
   British tactics, 32–33
   Charleston, siege of. *See*
      Charleston, siege of (1780)
   events leading up to, 25–26
   Simmons Island, 25, 28, 34
Carr, Captain Patrick, 240,
   252–254
Carrington, Lieutenant Colonel Edward,
   356
Carrington, Lieutenant Colonel
   Edward, 275, 288–289
   Dan River crossing, 355, 358
Carson, Colonel John, 205
Carter, Captain, 82
Caswell, General Richard, 154, 162,
   165, 170–171

Catawba River, 131–132, 141,
216–217, 292–293, 296, 298,
341–344
See also Cowan's Ford
Cedar Springs, 111–112, 139
Chad's Ford, 270
Chambers, Samuel, 214, 219, 238
Charleston, 1–2
British evacuate, 399
The Culture of Early Charleston, 24
objective of Sir Henry Clinton's
expedition (1776), 4
pre-revolutionary history, 17–24
siege. *See* Charleston, siege of
(1780)
Charleston, siege of (1780), 55–57,
60–71
American council of war, 66
American flotilla
outnumbered and outgunned, 51
unable to anchor inside bar, 51
withdrawn to inner harbor, 52
American fortifications, 55
trenches, draining water from,
67–68
American reinforcements arrive,
56–57
Americans trapped, 64
American Volunteers (Tories), 61
Ashley River, British cross
unobserved, 44
Biggins Bridge, 60
Blonde (ship), 52
Boston (ship), 50, 56
British bombardment, 64–66, 70
British flotilla
harbor entered, unchallenged, 53
sandbanks successfully
negotiated, 51–52
British reinforcements arrive, 63–64
British siege line, 55
casualties, 65, 70
channel incorrectly declared
defensible, 51–52
Charleston Neck, 45

Clarke's Brigade, 44
defend or surrender, 66
Fort Moultrie, Sullivan's Island, 45
surrender, 69
Fuller, British landing at plantation
of, 44
greatest British victory of war, 71
harbor as key to defense, 50
Lenud's Ferry, 68–69
Americans taken by surprise,
68–69
Monck's Corner, 60–63
American errors, 62
American goal, 60
Americans taken by surprise,
61–62
British goal, 60
post-battle incidents, 63
The Operations Against Charleston
(1780), 50
post-siege pacification of rest of
state, 81
Providence (ship), 50, 56
Queen of France (ship), 50
Raleigh (ship), 52
Ranger (ship), 50
Renown (ship), 52
Richmond (ship), 52
Roebuck (ship), 51
Romulus (ship), 52
Sandwich (ship), 52
Santee River, 68
sieges, handbook of, 53–55
South Carolina neutrality
possibility, 48
surrender
negotiations, 65–66
parole for some, 70, 72
terms, 70
urged by citizens, 69–70
Virginia (ship), 52
Webster's 33rd Foot, 44
Charlotte, 80, 290
Charlotte Court House, battle of,
188–190

Cheraw, 80
Cherokee War (1760–1761), 100,
    116, 151, 300
Cherokee War (1776–1777), 25
Chesney, Captain Alexander,
    228–231, 233, 241, 332
Chitty, Captain C.K., 305
Chitwood, Captain, 239
Chronicle, Major William, 220, 222
    King's Mountain, battle of, 223,
    225–227, 229–231, 237
Clarke, Colonel Elijah, 192, 301
    Blackstock's Farm, battle of, 253
    Cedar Springs, 139–141
    Ferguson, pursuit of, 218–220
    Musgroves's Mill, 176–179
    partisan raids, 307
Clary, Colonel Daniel, 178
Cleveland, Colonel Benjamin, 206,
    212, 215–216, 219
    King's Mountain, battle of, 223,
    226, 227, 229, 238, 238–241
Clinton, Sir Henry, 30
Clinton, Sir Henry
    approach march to South Carolina,
    38–40
    Back Country campaign, 81
    character, 71–72
    Charleston, voyage to New York,
    27–29
    Cornwallis, Lord Charles, personal
    animosity between, 76–80
    early life (pre-1780), 29–33
    later life (post-1782), 384–386
    self-justification, obsession with,
    384–385, 384–386
    siege of Charleston, 45, 52, 56,
    64–65, 67–68
    Sullivan's Island, battle of, 3, 12–13
    Tarleton, promotion of, 60
    See also Carolina campaign (1780);
    Sullivan's Island, battle of
    (1776); Charleston, siege of
    (1780)
Cochrane, Major Charles, 61

Colleton, Sir John, 63
Collins, James Potter, 114–115,
    122–125, 343
    Autobiography of a Revolutionary
    Soldier, 114, 122
    Cowpens, battle of, 315, 322–323,
    332
    Ferguson, pursuit of, 220, 222
    Fishing Creek, 174–176
    King's Mountain, battle of, 228,
    232–234, 236–234
communications, 310–311
Continental Army, 126–129, 147
    foraging for food, 129
    march south, 129
    training, 126–127
Conyers, Captain Daniel, 395
Cope, Lieutenant, 255
Corbet, Captain, 83
Cornwallis, Lord Charles, 74
Cornwallis, Lord Charles, 129–130,
    290, 294
    Back Country, 105–106, 110,
    185–186, 190–191
    battle tactics, 307–308
    Camden, battle of, 157, 161–162,
    164–170, 173
    Chad's Ford, 270
    Charleston, approach to, 25, 28,
    36, 38–40
    Charleston, siege of, 44, 65–66, 68
    Charlotte, battle of, 188–190
    Clinton, Sir Henry, personal
    animosity between, 76–80
    consequences of Cowpens defeat,
    329, 333
    Dan River to Guilford Courthouse,
    359–371
    early life (pre-1780), 73–79
    Fort William, reaction to defeat at,
    303
    Guilford Courthouse, battle of,
    372–383
    Guilford Courthouse to Dan River,
    353–358

King's Mountain, battle of, 240
later life (post-1782), 389–390
North Carolina, invasion of,
306–307, 334–358
retreat after King's Mountain,
240–259
Sullivan's Island, battle of, 3–4
Yorktown, 388–389
See also Carolina campaign (1780)
Council of Safety, 91, 97–99, 101
Cowan's Ford, 344–348
Cowpens, battle of, 315–333
casualties, 326
pre-battle
communications, 310–311
floods, 310–311
maneuvering, 309–320
Sumter's refusal to cooperate,
312
Crawford, James, 214, 219, 238
Cruger, Lieutenant Colonel John
Harris, 218, 242, 252
Musgrove's Mill, 179
Ninety Six, siege of, 398
Culbertson, Josiah, 178
Cunningham, Brigadier General
Robert, 95–101, 103, 303,
308
Cunningham, Major Charles, 316,
319, 323
Cunningham, Major John, 301
Cunningham, Patrick, 101–103

D
Dan River crossing, 352–358
Davidson, General William Lee, 232,
242, 292–293
called on for help by Morgan, 296
Cowan's Ford, 347–348
joins Morgan's forces, 302
retreat north after Cowpens,
339–345
Davidson, Major George, 186,
188–190
Davie, Major William Richardson, 187

Davie, Major William Richardson,
186–191, 242–243
Back Country, 141
Camden, battle of, 171, 173
Charlotte, battle of, 188–190
Commissary General, appointment
by Greene, 293–294
Guilford Courthouse, battle of, 372,
376–377
Hanging Rock, 132–136
partisan raids, 307
Ramsour's Mill, 106–107, 109–110
De Kalb, 128–129
Back Country, 136
Camden, battle of, 151–153,
162–163, 166–170, 172
De Lancey, 132, 177, 198
DePeyster, Captain Abraham, 137,
178, 233, 238
desertion, 131, 238, 362
de Vauban, Sebastien le Prestre,
53–55
Dixon, Lieutenant Colonel Henry,
168, 170
Doak, Reverend Samuel, 213
Dobson, Captain, 109
Drayton, Dorothy, 42
Drayton, William Henry, 93
Drayton, William Henry, 10, 23–24,
42–43, 90–103
Duncanson, Captain, 328
Dunlap, Captain James, 139
du Puy, Lieutenant Colonel Johann
Christian, 374, 380

E
Eaton, Brigadier General Thomas,
368, 372
Eggleston, Captain Joseph, 364, 370
Elphinstone, Captain George, 28–29
Charleston, siege of, 44, 52, 56, 60,
64
See also Charleston, siege of (1780)
Erwin, Hugh, 231
Eutaw Springs, battle of, 396, 398

Ewald, Captain Johann, 37
Ewald, Captain Johann
   approach march to Charleston,
      35–48
   Chad's Ford, 270
   Charleston, siege of, 52–53, 55–56,
      64–67, 70–71

F
Falls, Captain, 108–109
Fanning, David, 192
Ferguson, Lieutenant John, 14
Ferguson, Major Patrick, 28, 61, 69,
      137–141
   Back Country, 80, 194, 203–205
   Cedar Springs, 112
   early life (pre-1780), 195–202
   Ferguson Rifle, 196–199
   General Washington or Count
      Pulaski saved from death?,
      198–199
   Inspector of Militia, 202
   King's Mountain, battle of,
      226–232, 234–235
   Little Egg Harbor, 200
   Moncke's Corner, 63
   Musgrove's Mill, 176–177,
      179–180
   Over Mountain men, threat to
      destroy, 208
   pursuit of, by Rebels, 208–224
   recommendations to Clinton on
      winning war, 200–202
Few, Colonel William, 255
Finley, Captain Samuel, 373
Fish Dam Ford, 248–251
Fishing Creek, 173–176
Flenniken, Captain David, 133
Fletchall, Colonel Thomas, 96–100,
      102, 124
food supply
   See British army
Forbes, Captain Arthur, 375
Ford, Lieutenant Colonel Benjamin,
      168, 373

Fort Moultrie, Sullivan's Island
   See Charleston, siege of (1780)
Fort Sullivan, 3, 5, 7, 11, 14
Franklin, Benjamin, 127
Fraser, Lieutenant, 330, 335
Fraser, Major Thomas, 178, 391

G
Gadsen, Lieutenant Governor
      Christopher, 66, 69
Ganey, Major Micajah, 183–184
Gates, Major General Horatio, 143
Gates, Major General Horatio, 129,
      137, 141, 153–157, 218, 249
   Camden, battle of, 161–163,
      169–172
   early life (pre-1780), 142–151
   hands over command to Nathaniel
      Greene, 275
   Hero of Saratoga, 149, 285–286
   later life (post-1780), 392–394
   Newburgh Conspiracy, 393–394
George, David, 308
Germain, Lord George, 105, 110, 307
Germantown, 271
Gibson, Lieutenant, 255
Gilkey, Captain Walter, 239
Gilmer, Enoch, 225–226, 231
Gist, Brigadier General Mordecai,
      128, 162, 169
governing conquered territory,
      129–131
   food and other supplies, 130,
      359–360, 365, 367
   rebel activity, 130–131
Graham, Captain Joseph, 188, 342
   Cowan's Ford, 344
   Pyle's Massacre, 363–364
   Ramsour's Mill, 106–108
   Weitzel's Mill, 367
Graham, Colonel William, 223
   King's Mountain, behavior at battle
      of, 227, 231, 235
Great Cane Break on Reedy River,
      102

Great Savannah, 183–184
Green, Lieutenant Colonel John, 373, 379
Greene, Major General Nathaniel, 261
Greene, Major General Nathaniel, 129, 296
   Chad's Ford, 270
   Dan River to Guilford Courthouse, 359–371
   early life (pre-1780), 260–275
   Eutaw Springs, battle of, 398
   General George Washington, relationship with, 265–275
   Germantown, 271
   Guilford Courthouse, battle of, 372–383
   Guilford Courthouse to Dan River crossing, 353–358
   Hobkirk's Hill, 397
   later life (post-1780), 397–399
   Long Island command, 265
   New York City campaign, 266–269
   Ninety Six, siege of, 398
   planning attack on Cornwallis, 291–305
   retreat north after Cowpens, 334–358
   retreat through New Jersey, 269
   South Carolina, reconquest of, 397–399
   Southern Department
      appointment as commander, 275
      army in pitiful state, 288
      consolidation of command, 288–291
   Sumter, antagonism with, 304
Gregory, General, 168
Grimes, Captain, 239
Guilford Courthouse, battle of, 372–383
   American forces, deployment of, 372–374
   battlefield, description of, 369
   British forces, deployment of, 374–375
   Dan River to Guilford Courthouse, 359–371
   Morgan's march from Trading Ford, 350
   New Garden Road, 373–374
   post-battle analysis, 380–382
   post-battle misery, 380–383
Gunby, Colonel John, 373, 378

H
Haldane, Lieutenant, 308
Hambright, Colonel Frederick, 223, 227, 229, 231
Hamilton, Alexander, 290, 304
Hamilton, Colonel John, 134–135, 164
Hammond, Captain Sir Andrew Snape, 64
Hammond, Major Samuel, 252
Hampton, Colonel Henry, 219, 253, 255–257
Hanger, Major George, 186, 190, 243
Hanging Rock, 80, 132–134
Harrison, Major Richard, 374
Hart, Reverend Oliver, 94
Hawes, Lieutenant Colonel Samuel, 373
Hawsey, Captain William, 178
Hayes, Colonel Joseph, 303
Heard, Lieutenant, 370
Henry, Robert, 222, 231, 235, 345–348
Hill, Colonel William, 121, 132, 305
   Ferguson, pursuit of, 217, 220–223
   Fish Dam Ford, 250, 253, 256
   Iron Works, 111–113, 124
   King's Mountain, battle of, 225
Hillsborough, 81
   Cornwallis's attempt to rally Tory citizenry, 360
   government-in-exile set up by Rutledge, 217
Hinrichs, Captain John, 11, 20, 329
Hobbs, Augustine, 239
Hobkirk's Hill, 397

Horry, Colonel Peter, 181, 192, 245, 395

Horry, Hugh, 182–183, 191

Houston, Captain, 109

Howard, Lieutenant Colonel John Eager, 297

Howard, Lieutenant Colonel John Eager, 128

Camden, battle of, 162, 169

Cowpens, battle of, 315–317, 319–320, 323–326, 328–329

early life, 296–297

Eutaw Springs, battle of, 398

Guilford Courthouse, battle of, 373, 378–379

honored by Congress after Cowpens, 330

retreat north after Cowpens, 342, 344

Howe, Robert, 129

Howe, Sir William, 4, 265, 267–270

Huck, Captain Christian, 112–115, 124, 131, 307

Huger, Daniel, 180

Huger, General Isaac, 60–62, 81, 171

Guilford Courthouse, battle of, 373

retreat north after Cowpens, 342, 344, 350, 350–352

Hunt, Lieutenant, 114

I

Inman, Captain Shadrach, 177, 179

Innes, Colonel Alexander, 177–178

Iron Works, 111–113, 124, 307

Irwin, Colonel, 134

J

Jackson, Andrew, 134

Jackson, Major James, 252, 302

Blackstock's Farm, 258

Cowpens, battle of, 316, 323, 326

Jacquett, Captain Peter, 373, 378

Jägers, 35

James, Major John, 183–185, 191–192, 395

Jamieson, Colonel, 62, 68–69

Jefferson, Thomas, 167, 289, 294

Jetton, Joel, 345–346

Johnson, Sergeant James, 132, 134

K

Kershaw, Joseph, 94, 97–98

Kettle Creek, 300

King's Creek, 95

King's Friends, ix, 111, 124, 191, 303, 346, 350

King's Mountain, battle of, 223–241

Buford's defeat at the Waxhaws, remembered, 233

post-battle

analysis, 234–235

Cornwallis's decision to retreat, 240–242

militia desertions, 237–238

prisoners, treatment of, 237–240

reclaiming bodies, 236–237

slaughter and mayhem, 233–241

Tories surrender, 233

Kinlock, Captain David, 82–83

Kirkland, Moses, 97–99

Kirkwood, Captain Robert, 128, 297–298

Camden, battle of, 162, 169

Cowpens, battle of, 316

Guilford Courthouse, battle of, 373, 376–378

Hobkirk's Hill, 397

Knox, Henry, 271

Kosciuszko, Colonel Thaddeus, 275, 291, 398

L

Lacey, Captain Edward Jr., 114, 121

Lacey, Colonel Edward, 217, 220–221

Fish Dam Ford, 250, 253, 255, 257

King's Mountain, battle of, 223, 229, 231

Lafferty, Lieutenant, 239

Land's Ford, 132–133

Laurens, Henry, 91, 94, 98

Lawson, Brigadier General Robert, 368, 373

Lee, Lieutenant Colonel Henry (Light Horse Harry), 354

Lee, Lieutenant Colonel Henry (Light Horse Harry), 342, 352–353
  Dan River crossing, 355–358
  Dan River to Guilford Courthouse, 362–368
  Fort Motte, 396
  Guilford Courthouse, battle of, 351, 373–374, 376, 380–381
  Legion's green uniform causes confusion, 362–364
  Quinby Bridge, 391–392

Lee, Major General Charles, 9

Lee, Major General Charles, 8–16, 60, 126
  commander of state troops and militia, 10
  court martial conviction, 9
  failings and strengths, 8–10
  micromanagement of battle, 10–11
  Monmouth, battle of, 8
  reprimanded by George Washington, 8–9
  See also Sullivan's Island, battle of (1776)

Lenud's Ferry, 68–69

Leslie, General Alexander, 42, 305, 310–311, 314
  Cowans's Ford, 347
  Guilford Courthouse, battle of, 374
  pursuit north after Cowpens, 334–335
  See also Carolina campaign (1780)

Lincoln, General Benjamin, 33, 39–40
  Charleston, siege of, 65, 71
  early life, 48–49
  replaced by Gates, 129
  See also Carolina campaign (1780); Charleston, siege of (1780)

Little Egg Harbor, 200

Lock, Colonel Francis, 106–109

Logan, Captain George, 192

Long, Colonel Nicholas, 289

Low Country, 90–103
  Rice Kings, 90–103
  Scotch Irish, 94–95

The Lower South, 81

Lynch, Colonel Charles, 373, 376

M

MacDonald, Donald, 4

Mackenzie, Lieutenant Roderick, 190

Manigault, Gabriel, 180

Marion, Francis ("Swamp Fox"), 152

Marion, Francis ("Swamp Fox"), 8, 151–152, 155–156, 242, 290, 342
  Black Mingo, 291–292
  Blue Savannah, 184–185
  early life (pre-1780), 151–152
  Eutaw Springs, battle of, 396
  Great Savannah, 181–184
  later life (post-1780), 394–397
  Mount Hope Swamp, 395
  Quinby Bridge, 391–392, 396
  Richardson's plantation, 246–248
  Sumter, relationship with, 391
  Tearcoat Swamp, 245–246
  Wiboo Swamp, 395

Martin, Edward, 112–113, 115

Martin, Josiah, 4

Mattocks, Captain John, 227

McArthur, Major Archibald, 251–252, 308
  Blackstock's Farm, 254, 258
  Cowpens, battle of, 316, 321, 323, 326–327

McCafferty, William, 243

McCall, Major James, 316–317

McCauley, Captain James, 395

McClure, Captain John, 111–114

McClure, James, 112–113, 115

McCottry, Captain William, 395

McDowell, Charles, 141, 179
  Cane Creek, 205
  Cowpens, battle of, 316, 319, 323

McDowell, Charles (*Continued*)
  Ferguson, pursuit of, 210–212, 215, 218–219
  King's Mountain, battle of, 223, 229
McDowell, Joseph, 215, 218, 239
  Cane Creek, 205
  Mudgrove's mill, 176
  Ramsour's Mill, 107–108
McFall, Arthur, 239
McFall, John, 239
McIntosh, General Lachlan, 66
McJunkin, Major Joseph, 255, 326
McKenzie, Lieutenant Roderick
  Blackstock's Farm, battle of, 256–257
  Cowpens, 325, 327, 387
McKissick, Captain, 109
McLeod, Donald, 4–5
McLeod, Lieutenant John, 374, 376, 379
McPherson, Lieutenant Colonel Duncan, 374
McQueen, Captain Alexander, 151
Middleton, Arthur, 43, 91, 99–100
Military tactics
  close-order formations, 126–127
militia
  abilities, 306, 316, 328
  Back Country, 190–192
  desertion, 238, 362
  discipline, 202–206, 366, 377
  manner of service, 181–182, 341, 368, 375
  outfitting, 125
  provisions, 213
  treatment by military, 243–245
Mills, Colonel Ambrose, 238–239
Moffitt, Captain, 123–125, 174, 176, 315
Monck's Corner
  See Charleston, siege of (1780)
Money, Lieutenant John, 251, 255–256, 258

Montgomery, General Richard, 283–284
Montgomery, William, 375
Moore, Lieutenant Colonel John, 106–107, 109–110
Moore, Private William, 236–237
Moore's Creek, 5, 110
Morgan, *Brigadier General Daniel*, 277
Morgan, Brigadier General Daniel, 218, 276–330
  Cowpens, battle of, 315–330
  crosses the Catawba, 296, 298
  early campaigns
    Bemis Heights, 286
    Quebec City, 280–285
    Saratoga, 285–286
  early life (pre-1780), 276–288
  Georgians, appeal to, 301
  Guilford Courthouse, battle of, advice to Greene, 370
  honored by Congress after Cowpens, 330
  honored by Virginia House of Delegates after Cowpens, 330
  later life (post-1780), 399–401
  post-Cowpens praise and criticism, 328–330
  pursued by Tarleton, 306–318
  replaced by Otho Holland Williams, 351
  retreat north after Cowpens, 337–351
  sick leave, 351
  Sumter, antagonism with, 296, 304–305, 312, 315, 339
  welcomed by partisans except Sumter, 296, 301
  Whiskey Rebellion, 400
Morris, Captain John, 14
Moultrie, *General William*, 6
Moultrie, General William, 6–16, 39, 48, 71
  failings and strengths, 6–7
  refusal to co-operate with British, 180–181

sacking of, considered by Lee, 11
See also Carolina campaign (1780);
   Sullivan's Island, battle of
   (1776); Charleston, siege of
   (1780)
Moultrie, Lieutenant Governor John,
   7
Mount Hope Swamp, 395
Mouzon, Captain Henry, 192
Muhlenberg, John Peter, 8
Murray, Captain James, 13
Musgrove's Mill, 141, 176–180

N
Neel, Colonel Andrew, 111, 132
Nelson's Ferry, 81
Newburgh Conspiracy, 393–394
New Garden, 382
New Garden Road, 373–374,
   377
Newmarsh, Major Timothy, 315,
   321–322
New York City campaign, 266–269
Ninety Six, 80, 92–93, 105, 308
   siege of, 398
   Treaty of, 99–102
North Carolina
   invasion of, by Cornwallis,
      306–307, 334–358
Norton, Lieutenant Colonel, 374

O
Ogilvie, Captain David, 319
O'Hara, Brigadier General Charles,
   305
   Cowan's Ford, 347
   Dan River crossing, 355–358,
      367–358
   Guilford Courthouse, battle of, 374,
      378–379, 381
   Hillsborough, 360
   pursuit north after Cowpens,
      335–337, 340–341, 350,
      355–358
outfitting of militia, 125

Over Mountain men, 141, 178–179,
   205–224
   Ferguson, pursuit of, 208–224
   threat to destroy, by Major Patrick
      Ferguson, 208

P
Parker, Commodore Sir Peter, 3–4, 13,
   15–16
parole system, 70
Paterson, Brigadier General James,
   28
Pearson, Lieutenant, 82
Perry, Sargeant Major, 326
Pickens, Andrew, 192
Pickens, Andrew, 192, 339, 391
   Carolina campaign, 25
   Cherokee War (1760–1761), 300
   Cowpens, battle of, 312–313,
      315–318, 319–323, 325–326,
      332
   Dan River to Guilford Courthouse,
      362–368
   early life (pre-1780), 299–301
   joins Morgan's forces, 302
   Kettle Creek, 300
   lawsuits, protection against, 397
   paroled by British, 80
   parole renounced, 301
Pinckney, Charles, 91
Pinckney, Colonel Francis, 180
Pinckney, Thomas, 156, 163, 166,
   170
Plummer, Daniel, 228
Polk, Colonel Thomas, 288, 293
Polk, Colonel William, 347–348
Porterfield, Lieutenant Colonel
   Charles, 156, 162
Preston, Colonel William, 364,
   366–367
Proclamation Line of 1763, 207
Provincial Congress, 91, 97–98,
   100–101, 119–120
Pyle, Captain Joseph, 363–364
Pyle's Massacre, 363–364, 366

Q

Quinby Bridge, 391–392

R

Ramsour's Mill, 106–110
Rawdon, Lieutenant Colonel Francis
    Lord, 106, 110–111, 129–131,
    136, 157
    Camden, battle of, 163–164
    Cornwallis' retreat after King's
        Mountain, 106
    Hobkirk's Hill, 397
    Monck's Corner, 63, 65
rebels, chasing of, 139–140
Reminiscences, 22
Rice Kings, 17–24, 124, 192
    alliance with Back Country,
        attempt to forge, 90–103
    paintings of, 21
    post-Camden, 180
    "rice and slave labor," 19
    Sullivan's Island, battle of, 8
    See also Low Country; South
        Carolina
Richardson, Colonel Richard, 94,
    97–98, 101–103
    Snow Campaign, 119–120
Richardson, General Richard,
    246–248
Richardson's plantation, battle of,
    246–248
Roberts, Captain Jonathan, 183
Robertson, James, 207
Robertson, John, 206
Rocky Mount, 80, 132–133
Roebuck, Major Benjamin, 241
Rudolph, Captain, 370
Rugeley's Mill, 82
Rutherford, Brigadier General Griffith,
    106–109
Rutherford, Major James, 110
Rutledge, Governor John
    Charleston, siege of, 65
    government-in-exile at
        Hillsborough, 217

    militia released after Weitzel's Mill,
        368
    requests Marion and Pickens
        cooperate with Sumter, 391
    Rugeley's Mill, 81–82
    Sumter's law repealed, 392
    Sumter summoned, 291–292

S

Saratoga, battle of, 149, 285–286
Scotch Irish, 85–89, 94–95, 111,
    206–207, 294
Scott, Lieutenant John, 192
Sealy, 249–250
Senf, Colonel John Christian, 156
Sevier, John, 207
    Ferguson, pursuit of, 210–212, 215
    King's Mountain, battle of, 223,
        229, 237–238
Seymour, Sergeant Major William,
    154, 319, 322–323, 328
Shelby, Colonel Isaac, 209
Shelby, Colonel Isaac, 139–141,
    176–180
    early life (pre-1780), 208–210
    Ferguson, pursuit of, 210–212, 215,
        219
    King's Mountain, battle of, 223,
        226, 229–235, 238–239
    Over Mountain men, 141,
        178–179, 205–224
    partisan raids, 307
    Shelby's riders. *See* subhead: Over
        Mountain men
Simmons Island
    See Carolina campaign (1780)
Simpson, Reverend John, 111, 113
Singleton, Captain Anthony, 372,
    374–376
Skinner, Lieutenant, 255–257
Smallwood, Brigadier General
    William, 128
    battle of Camden, 162, 165, 168,
        170
Smith, Captain, 109

Smith, Captain John, 379
Snickers, Captain William, 328–329
Snipes, Captain William Clay, 246
Snow Campaign, 119, 151
South Carolina
 pre-revolutionary history, 17–24
  resentment against Crown
   appointees, 22–24
  "rice and slave labor," 19
  settlement, 17–20
  settlers from Barbados, 18
  slavery, 19, 22
  yellow fever and malaria, 18–19
 reconquest of, 397–399
Southern strategy
 loyal subjects, dependence on, 26
Stark, Lieutenant John, 249–251
Stedman, Charles, 170, 327, 364
Stevens, Brigadier General Edward,
 155, 275, 288
 Camden, battle of, 162, 165–167
 Dan River to Guilford Courthouse,
  365
 Guilford Courthouse, battle of, 373,
  376–377
 retreat north after Cowpens, 341,
  349–350
Stokes, Captain John, 84–85
Stuart, Captain Dugald, 375
Stuart, Lieutenant Colonel Alexander,
 398
Stuart, Lieutenant Colonel James,
 378–379
Sullivan, General John, 270
Sullivan's Island, battle of (1776),
 3–16
 accuracy of American fire, 15
 Actaeon (ship), 13–14, 16
 Active (ship), 13
 American pleas for assistance
  answered
   Marion, Francis ("Swamp Fox"),
    8
   Muhlenberg, John Peter, 8
   Rice Kings, 8

Sumter, Brigadier General
 Thomas, ("Gamecock"), 8
Thompson, William, ("Old
 Danger"), 8
The Breach, fording of, 13
Bristol (ship), 12, 15
British routed at Moore's Creek, 5,
 110
Charleston as primary objective, 4
Cornwallis's delayed arrival at Cape
 Fear, 5
difficulties in crossing the bar into
 harbor, 11–12
Experiment (ship), 12, 14
failure to reconnoiter before
 landing, 13
Fort Sullivan, fortification of, 5, 7,
 11, 14
Friendship (ship), 13
inadequacy of defenses, 11
Solebay (ship), 13
Sphynx (ship), 13–14
Syren (ship), 13–14
Thunder (ship), 12–13
Sumter, Brigadier General Thomas,
 ("Gamecock"), 116
Sumter, Brigadier General Thomas,
 ("Gamecock"), 8, 101,
 112–113, 192, 291–293
 Back Country, 141
 Blackstock's Farm, battle of,
  251–259
 called on for help by Morgan, 296
 called on to help Greene by
  Rutledge, 291
 Camden, battle of, 153, 155–156,
  173
 early life (pre-1780), 115–121
 Ferguson, pursuit of, 220–221
 Fish Dam Ford, 250–251
 Fishing Creek, 173–176, 248–249
 Greene, antagonism with, 304, 391
 later life (post-1781), 390–393
 lawsuits, protection against, 392,
  397

Sumter, Brigadier General Thomas
(*Continued*)
Morgan, antagonism with, 296,
304–305, 312, 315, 339
Quinby Bridge, 391–392, 396
refusal to cooperate with Morgan
before Cowpens, 312, 315
Rocky Mount and Hanging Rock,
131–136
Sumter's law, 391–392
Sumter's law, 391–392

T

Tarleton, Banastre, 59
Tarleton, Banastre, 4, 28, 130, 134
apologia attacking Cornwallis,
387
Back country campaign, 80–84
Blackstock's Farm, battle of,
251–259
"Bloody Ban," 85
"Bloody Tarleton," 85
Britain's hero, America's villain,
84
Camden, battle of, 157, 161, 165,
169, 171
Cowpens, battle of, 315–333
Dan River to Guilford Courthouse,
362–365, 367, 370–371
early life (pre-1780), 59–60
Fishing Creek, 175
Guilford Courthouse, battle of, 374,
376, 380
King's Mountain, battle of, 234,
237, 240
later life (post-1782), 58,
386–388
Lenud's Ferry, 68–69
Monck's Corner, 60–64
Monticello, 386
post-Cowpens
attempt to blame Cornwallis,
326–328
criticism, 326–328

flight, 330–332
offer to resign rejected, 333
pursuit north after Cowpens,
306–318, 337–338, 346,
356–357
Richardson's plantation, battle of,
246–248
Torrence's Tavern, 349
The Waxhaws, 120
Yorktown, 386
Tate, Captain, 316–317
Taylor, Colonel Thomas, 136, 250,
252–254, 392
Tearcoat Swamp, 245–246
Tennent, Reverend William, 94,
97
Thomas, Colonel John Jr., 112
Thomas, Jane, 112
Thompson, William, ("Old Danger"),
8, 13, 98, 102–103
Torrence's Tavern, 349
Trading Ford, 349–351
Traille, Major Peter, 64
Triplett, Major Francis, 316–317, 330,
339
Turnbull, Colonel George, 112–113,
115
Richardson's Plantation, battle of,
246
Rocky Mount, 132
Twiggs, Colonel John, 252, 254–255,
257–258
Tynes, Colonel Samuel, 245–246

V

Valley Forge, 271
Vance, Colonel David, 205, 212
de Vauban, Sebastien le Prestre,
53–55
Vernier, Chevalier Pierre-François,
39–40, 45, 63
Volunteers of Ireland, 130, 157, 163,
168
Von Steuben, 126–127, 288, 369

W

Wahab, Captain James, 186–188

Waites, Captain Thomas, 191–192

Wallace, Captain, 324

Washington, Colonel William, 298

Washington, Colonel William, 45,
  155, 298
  Cowpens, battle of, 313, 316–317,
    319, 321–322, 324–325,
    330–331
  Dan River to Guilford Courthouse,
    367–368
  Fort William, 302–303
  Guilford Courthouse, battle of, 376,
    378
  Hammond's Store, 302
  honored by Congress after
    Cowpens, 330
  Lenud's Ferry, 68, 69
  Monck's Corner, 60, 62
  retreat north after Cowpens, 337,
    342, 344

Washington, General George, 8, 129
  Chad's Ford, 270
  Germantown, 271
  Greene, relationship with, 265–275
  New York City campaign,
    266–269
  retreat through New Jersey, 269
  Valley Forge, 271

Wateree Ferry, 136, 141

Waters, Colonel Francis, 302

Watson, Colonel John Watson
  Tadwell, 395, 395–396

Watt, Garret, 167

The Waxhaws, 80, 82–84, 120
  post-battle massacre, 84–85
  surrender by Buford, 84

weaponry
  American rifle, 213–214
  bayonet, 160–161, 200
  Chaumette's rifle, 196
  Deckhard rifle, 213
  Ferguson rifle, 196–199

  Kentucky rifle, 213
  musket, 158–160, 199

Webster, Lieutenant Colonel James,
  61, 63
  Camden, battle of, 164–166, 168
  Charleston, siege of, 66
  Chatlotee Courthouse, battle of,
    189
  Dan River to Guilford Courthouse,
    367–368
  Guilford Courthouse, battle of,
    374–379, 383
  pursuit north after Cowpens, 334,
    346
  See also Charleston, siege of (1780);
    Camden, battle of (1780);
    Charlotte, battle of

Weedon, Brigadier General George,
  270

Weitzel's Mill, 367–368

Welch, Major Nicholas, 107, 109

Wemyss, Major John, 245
  Fish Dam Ford, 249–251
  terror tactics, 185, 191

Whipple, Commodore Abraham,
  50–52

Whiskey Rebellion, 400

White, Colonel Anthony, 68, 69

Wiboo Swamp, 395

Williams, Colonel James, 176–179
  Ferguson, pursuit of, 217, 220–221
  King's Mountain, battle of, 223,
    229, 231, 236

Williams, Colonel Otho Holland, 164

Williams, Colonel Otho Holland, 151,
  153–154, 161–163, 275, 329
  Camden, battle of, 165–169
  Dan River crossing, 355–358
  Dan River to Guilford Courthouse,
    365–369
  Guilford Courthouse, battle of,
    373
  replaces Morgan, 351–352
  retreat north after Cowpens, 352

Williamson, James, 113–114
Williamson, Major Andrew, 98,
    101–102
Wilson, Captain, 239
Wilson, Major, 109
Winn, Major Richard, 111, 121, 134,
    253, 258
Winnsboro, 111, 243, 292
Winston, Major Joseph, 206, 215–216
  King's Mountain, battle of, 223,
    229

Woodford, Brigadier General William,
    57

Y
Yadkin River, 349–351
Young, Thomas, 104–105
  Cowpens, battle of, 314–315,
    320–323, 325, 328, 331–323
  Ferguson, pursuit of, 222
  Hammond's Store, 302
  King's Mountain, 231, 236–237

9 780471 327165